MODERN HUMANITIES RESEARCH ASSOCIATION
TUDOR AND STUART TRANSLATIONS
VOLUME 26 (1)

General Editors
ANDREW HADFIELD
NEIL RHODES

ERASMUS IN ENGLISH, 1523–1584

MODERN HUMANITIES RESEARCH ASSOCIATION
TUDOR AND STUART TRANSLATIONS

General Editors
Andrew Hadfield (University of Sussex)
Neil Rhodes (University of St Andrews)

Associate Editors
Guyda Armstrong (University of Manchester)
Fred Schurink (University of Manchester)
Louise Wilson (Liverpool Hope University)

Advisory Board
Warren Boutcher (Queen Mary, University of London)
Colin Burrow (All Souls College, Oxford)
A. E. B. Coldiron (Florida State University)
Patricia Demers (University of Alberta)
José María Pérez Fernández (University of Granada)
Robert S. Miola (Loyola College, Maryland)
Alessandra Petrina (University of Padua)
Anne Lake Prescott (Barnard College, Columbia University)
Quentin Skinner (Queen Mary, London)
Alan Stewart (Columbia University)

For details of published and forthcoming volumes please visit our website:

http://www.tudor.mhra.org.uk

ERASMUS IN ENGLISH, 1523–1584

VOLUME 1
THE MANUAL OF THE CHRISTIAN SOLDIER AND OTHER WRITINGS

EDITED BY
ALEX DAVIS, GORDON KENDAL, AND NEIL RHODES

Modern Humanities Research Association
Tudor and Stuart Translation 26 (1)
2022

Published by

*The Modern Humanities Research Association
Salisbury House
Station Road
Cambridge CB1 2LA
United Kingdom*

© *Modern Humanities Research Association 2022*

Alex Davis, Gordon Kendal, and Neil Rhodes have asserted their right under the Copyright, Designs and Patents Act 1988 to be identified as the author of this work. Parts of this work may be reproduced as permitted under legal provisions for fair dealing (or fair use) for the purposes of research, private study, criticism, or review, or when a relevant collective licensing agreement is in place. All other reproduction requires the written permission of the copyright holder who may be contacted at rights@mhra.org.uk.

First published 2022

*ISBN 978-1-78188-943-5 (PB)
ISBN 978-1-78188-942-8 (HB)*

CONTENTS

General Editors' Foreword	vi
Acknowledgements	vii
Abbreviations	viii
General Introduction	1
The Manual of the Christian Soldier	23
A Treatise upon the Pater Noster	195
An Exhortation to the Diligent Study of Scripture	221
The Dialogue Between Julius the Second, Genius, and Saint Peter	243
An Epistle in Praise of Matrimony	305
Proverbs, or Adages	333
Textual Notes	403
Neologisms	419
Glossary	424
Bibliography	446

GENERAL EDITORS' FOREWORD

The aim of the *MHRA Tudor & Stuart Translations* is to create a representative library of works translated into English during the early modern period for the use of scholars, students and the wider public. The series will include both substantial single works and selections of texts from major authors, with the emphasis being on the works that were most familiar to early modern readers. The texts themselves will be newly edited with substantial introductions, notes, and glossaries, and will be published both in print and online.

The series aims to restore to view a major part of English Renaissance literature which has become relatively inaccessible and to present these texts as literary works in their own right. For that reason it will follow the same principle of modernisation adopted by other scholarly editions of canonical literature from the period. The series will have a similar scope to that of the original *Tudor Translations* published early in the last century, and while the great majority of the works presented will be from the sixteenth century, like the original series it will not be rigidly bound by the end-date of 1603. There will, however, be a very different range of texts with new and substantial scholarly apparatus.

The *MHRA Tudor & Stuart Translations* will extend our understanding of the English Renaissance through its representation of the process of cultural transmission from the classical to the early modern world and the process of cultural exchange within the early modern world.

Andrew Hadfield
Neil Rhodes

ACKNOWLEDGEMENTS

The editors gratefully acknowledge the outstanding work of Erasmus's previous editors, and in particular those of the Toronto Collected Erasmus, which they have drawn upon in preparing these volumes. They would also like to give warm thanks to the anonymous reader provided by the MHRA for their meticulous attention to the typescript; to Elena Spinelli for research assistance in the final stages of this work; and to Simon Davies for bringing the edition to publication with his characteristically scrupulous care.

ABBREVIATIONS

Texts in this edition

Manual	*The Manual of the Christian Soldier*
Pater Noster	*A Treatise upon the Pater Noster*
Exh.	*An Exhortation to the Diligent Study of Scripture* [preface to the New Testament]
Jul.	*The Dialogue Between Julius the Second, Genius, and Saint Peter*
Matrimony	*An Epistle in Praise of Matrimony*
Proverbs	*Proverbs, or Adages*
Tav.	*Proverbs, or Adages* [individual proverb]
Folly	*The Praise of Folly*
Paraphrase	*Paraphrase on the New Testament* [extracts from Matthew and John]
Bellum	from *Bellum Erasmi* [Adage IV. i]
Sileni	*Sileni Alcibiadis* [Adage III. iii]
Peace	*The Complaint of Peace*
1523	London, British Library, Manuscript Additional 89149
1526	earliest existing English edition of *Pater Noster*
1531	second English edition of *Pater Noster*
1533	first printed edition of English *Enchiridion*

Cross-references between texts in this edition are to line number unless otherwise stated.

Biblical texts

Gen.	Genesis
Exod.	Exodus
Levit.	Leviticus
Numb.	Numbers
Deut.	Deuteronomy
Josh.	Joshua
Judg.	Judges
Sam.	Samuel
Chron.	Chronicles
Nehem.	Nehemiah
Esth.	Esther
Ps.	Psalms

Prov.	Proverbs
Eccles.	Ecclesiastes
Song	Song of Solomon
Jerem.	Jeremiah
Lam.	Lamentations
Ezek.	Ezekiel
Dan.	Daniel
Obad.	Obadiah
Habak.	Habakkuk
Zeph.	Zephaniah
Hag.	Haggai
Zech.	Zechariah
Mal.	Malachi
Wisd.	Wisdom of Solomon
Matt.	Matthew
Rom.	Romans
Corinth.	Corinthians
Galat.	Galatians
Ephes.	Ephesians
Philipp.	Philippians
Coloss.	Colossians
Thessal.	Thessalonians
Tim.	Timothy
Philem.	Philemon
Hebr.	Hebrews
Rev.	Revelation

Other

ASD	Erasmus, *Opera Omnia* (Amsterdam: North-Holland, 1969–)
BCP	Church of England *Book of Common Prayer*
CWE	*Collected Works of Erasmus* (Toronto: University of Toronto Press, 1974–)
CWM	*The Yale Edition of the Complete Works of St. Thomas More* (New Haven and London: Yale University Press, 1963–1997)
Devereux	E. J. Devereux, *Renaissance English Translations of Erasmus: A Bibliography to 1700* (Toronto: University of Toronto Press, 1983)
E.	Erasmus
EEBO	Early English Books Online
ELH	*English Literary History*
KJB	King James Bible (Authorised Version) 1611
LB	Erasmus, *Opera Omnia*, ed. by J. Leclerc (Leiden, 1703–06)

NRSV	New Revised Standard Version 1989[1]
NT	New Testament
ODCC	Oxford Dictionary of the Christian Church
ODNB	Oxford Dictionary of National Biography
OED	Oxford English Dictionary
OT	Old Testament
PE	Prefatory Epistle 1518 (in *1533*)
Perry	*Aesopica*, ed. by Ben Edwin Perry. Perry Index: https://fablesofaesop.com/perry-index
PMLA	*Proceedings of the Modern Language Association*
PQ	ProQuest
R.	Margaret More Roper
RES	*The Review of English Studies*
Sept.	Septuagint (Greek Bible)
ST	Thomas Aquinas, *Summa Theologica*
STC	Short Title Catalogue (2nd series)
T.	1523 translator, probably Tyndale
Tilley	Morris Palmer Tilley, *Dictionary of the Proverbs in England in the Sixteenth and Seventeenth Centuries* (Ann Arbor: University of Michigan Press, 1950)
Vulg.	Vulgate (Latin Bible)

Unless otherwise stated, the most recent translations in the Loeb Classical Library have been used for ancient Greek and Latin texts.

°	word in Glossary
[ ]	editorial addition or change
Marg.	marginal note
absol.	absolute
adj.	adjective
adv.	adverb
annot.	annotated
art.	Article (*ST*)
attrib.	attributive
c.	circa
ch.	chapter
conj.	conjunction
Eng.	English
f.	and following; folio
fig.	figuratively
Gk	Greek

[1] *NRSV* is used in this edition as the basis for biblical references and names.

L.	Latin
lit.	literally
mod.	modern
MS	manuscript
n.	note
pass.	passive
pl.	plural
q.	Question (*ST*)
r.	recto
sb.	substantive, noun
sc.	namely
sing.	singular
s.v.	under the word
tr.	transitive
v.	verb, verso, verse
viz.	namely

GENERAL INTRODUCTION

Alex Davis

Desiderius Erasmus (c. 1467–1536) was the greatest scholar of early sixteenth-century Europe: editor of a revolutionary edition of the New Testament; author of the *Enchiridion militis Christiani* and the *Praise of Folly*, the age's most famous work of lay piety and its most brilliant satire, respectively; the compiler of vast, astonishingly erudite collections such as the *Adages*, the *Parabolae*, and the *Apophthegmata*; the early modern period's most influential educational thinker and its most copious writer of familiar letters. *Erasmus in English* collects for the first time the most significant sixteenth-century translations into English of Erasmus's writings.[1]

These translations were made by various hands, over some sixty years, in the service of a range of interests. Collected here are satirical texts, educational ones, works of practical devotion, and works dealing with social questions such as marriage and war. The first translation, dated to 1523, is the previously unpublished manuscript of Erasmus's exploration of Christian religion, the *Enchiridion militis Christiani*, which we cautiously ascribe to William Tyndale; the last is a version of the colloquy *Alcumista*, printed in 1584 in Reginald Scott's treatise *The discouerie of witchcraft*. The translators include scholars, a rogue friar, a princess, a diplomat, and a woman whom Erasmus celebrated as the glory of Britain for her brilliant mind.[2] That variety is characteristic. As Gregory D. Dodds has rightly said, 'there is no simple story of Erasmus' influence in England'.[3] His impact was vast — but also quite hard to pin down.

---

[1] The presentation is broadly chronological, with texts arranged very roughly by date of translation, modified to allow for some generic grouping. The *Colloquies*, versions of which span the period covered by this edition and which form a coherent body of work in themselves, appear in a separate, third volume, currently in preparation. For a full catalogue of sixteenth- and seventeenth-century translations of Erasmus into English, see E. J. Devereux, *Renaissance English Translations of Erasmus: A Bibliography to 1700* (Toronto, Buffalo, and London: University of Toronto Press, 1983).

[2] Letter to Margaret Roper, 6 September 1529, *CWE* 16. 40.

[3] Gregory D. Dodds, *Exploiting Erasmus: The Erasmian Legacy and Religious Change in Early Modern England* (Toronto, Buffalo, and London: University of Toronto Press, 2009), p. xiii. Dodds offers the most up-to-date survey of Erasmus's English fortunes. See also C. R. Thompson, 'Erasmus in Tudor England', in *Extrait de Actes du Congres Erasme, Rotterdam 27–29 Octobre 1969* (Amsterdam: North Holland Publishing Company, 1971), pp. 29–68; and, for a general discussion, *The Reception of Erasmus in the Early Modern Period*, ed. by Karl A. E. Enenkel (Leiden: Brill, 2013).

In sixteenth-century England, Erasmus's was a name to conjure with. The prefaces to the translations collected in *Erasmus in English* refer to 'the most famous doctor Master Erasmus of Rotterdam'; 'that famous clerk Erasmus'; 'the incomparable learned man, Erasmus'; 'Erasmus Roterodamus, one of the excellentest clerks of our time'.[4] The most famous, the incomparably learned, the most excellent: adulation invites detractors, and Erasmus was also the object of criticism, even from those he influenced. The Elizabethan Gabriel Harvey complained that 'Erasmus [...] will teach a man to Temporise & Localise at occasion'.[5] By this Harvey meant that the rhetorical skills taught by humanists like Erasmus — skills that he had absorbed at Saffron Walden grammar school — equipped their students too well for the task of addressing themselves to contingent circumstances. (He also means to glance towards the places or 'loci' of verbal invention that helped them do this.) The charge is one of excessive facility, verging on a want of principle. It resonates with accusations made during Erasmus's lifetime of culpable amorphousness. Martin Luther, for instance — a man of radically opposed temperament — branded him 'king of the amphibians'.[6] It is a perception that we will return to, but in many ways it must seem quite unfair. Erasmus's was a powerful and distinctive voice. It spoke against pointless and frivolous scholarship, against corruption in the church, against the ubiquitous militarism of early modern elites. It spoke for certain kinds of social change. But Harvey's comment is useful in our present context because in contemporary communications theory 'localisation' refers to the activity of adapting a translation to a specific region or culture.[7] In sixteenth-century terms, it identifies the field of cultural *translatio*, lying beyond linguistic translation narrowly conceived. It opens out questions of transmission and appropriation, within which doubts such as Luther's can find purchase in a new set of issues. How does the activity of translation adapt a distinctive point of view, and to what ends? Does it reproduce it, or bend it out of shape? And what does that activity have to do with the skills taught in the humanist classroom? This introduction will pursue these questions within a narrative about how translation localised Erasmus's writings and about the influence that translations of Erasmus exerted on English culture and history at large. The simultaneous ubiquity and indefinition of Erasmus's presence in early modern English culture were the product of the specific ways he was received into it.

---

[4] See *Pater Noster* 1–2, *Sileni* 4, *Proverbs* 6, *Peace* 4.
[5] See Gabriel Harvey, *Gabriel Harvey's Marginalia*, ed. by G. C. Moore Smith (Stratford Upon Avon: Shakespeare Head Press, 1913), p. 138.
[6] See Neil Rhodes's introduction to the English *Adages* in this volume (p. 336).
[7] The term is widespread in discourse concerning video games, and implies a restricted conception of what translation itself entails. For a discussion, see Laura Gonzales and Rebecca Zantjer, 'Translation as a User-Localization Practice', *Technical Communication*, 62.4 (2015), 271–84.

1

In 1522 Erasmus declined an invitation to settle in Zurich, explaining that he wanted to be known as a 'citizen of the world' — 'to be a fellow citizen to all men'.[8] Although he appeared on early modern title pages as 'Erasmus Roterodamus' or 'Erasmus of Rotterdam', after his place of birth, Erasmus was tied to no one location. He was the very model of the European man of letters. Nonetheless, his association with England was both substantial and productive. Erasmus first visited England in 1499; his longest period of residence ran from August 1509 to August 1514. The first visit was made in the company of his pupil William Blount, Lord Mountjoy, later the first dedicatee of the *Adages*, and was decisive in turning Erasmus towards the serious study of theology; the five-year stay produced works as such as the *Praise of Folly* and the colloquy *A Pilgrimage for Religion's Sake*, inspired by trips to shrines at Walsingham and Canterbury. In all, Erasmus visited England six times, with three extended periods of residence. In 1512 he went so far as to describe himself as being 'almost entirely transformed into an Englishman'.[9]

Erasmus spoke little or no English himself. A letter survives from 1513 in which he asks Humphrey Walkden to translate a letter to the father of one of his pupils from Latin into English; another from an agent of Cardinal Wolsey begins by ruing Erasmus's inability to understand his mother tongue.[10] All the evidence suggests that communication in vernaculars unknown to Erasmus was a duty that devolved onto the members of Erasmus's *familia*, the young men of his household who received a humanistic training in exchange for domestic and secretarial service, or onto looser associates such as Walkden.[11] It would be wrong, however, to position Erasmus as simply uninterested in vernacular writing. Although he wrote in Latin for a European audience, Erasmus was prepared to specify which of his works he thought particularly suitable for translation into

---

[8] Letter to Huldrych Zwingli, [3?] September 1522, *CWE* 9. 185.

[9] Letter to Antoon van Bergen, 6 February [1512], *CWE* 2. 213. Erasmus could be disparaging about England too. Elsewhere he describes Londoners as 'Cyprian oxen and eaters of ordure, [who] still believe that they alone eat heavenly fare and feast on the brain of Zeus'. Letter to Andrea Ammonio, 26 November 1511, *CWE* 2. 205.

[10] See the letters to [William] G[onnell?] and H[umphrey Walkden], October 1513, *CWE* 2. 255–56, and from Richard Sampson to Erasmus, 2 March 1518, *CWE* 5. 317. Erasmus's letter is discussed alongside other evidence for his lack of knowledge of English in Neil Rhodes, *Common: The Development of Literary Culture in Sixteenth-Century England* (Oxford: Oxford University Press, 2018), p. 114. C. R. Thompson comments that he can remember only one moment of English in Erasmus's correspondence, a brief postscript by Thomas Boleyn. See the letter from Gerard of Friesland, 4 November 1529, *CWE* 16. 86, and Thompson, 'Erasmus in Tudor England', p. 35.

[11] See Lisa Jardine, *Erasmus, Man of Letters: The Construction of Charisma in Print*, rev. edn (Princeton: Princeton University Press, 2015), pp. ix–xi.

other tongues.[12] Furthermore, the impulse towards communication was fundamental to Erasmus's project. He was, if not exactly a populariser, then certainly a great collector and disseminator, and he was well aware of the role that translation could play in opening up hitherto closed bodies of knowledge and in spreading his own message. Perhaps most importantly, the *Paraclesis*, Erasmus's preface to his edition of the New Testament, contains a passionate argument for the necessity of biblical translation:

> Peradventure it were most expedient that the councils of kings should be kept secret, but Christ would that his councils and mysteries should be spread abroad as much as is possible. I would desire that all women should read the Gospel and Paul's epistles, and I would to God they were translated into the tongues of all men so that they might not only be read and known of the Scots and Irishmen but also of the Turks and Saracens. (*Exh.* 124–30)

There is a democratic edge to this passage that — it must be admitted — sits uncomfortably with many of Erasmus's other commitments. He remains Latinate, humanist, elitist, even cliquey; and incorrigibly male-oriented. Nonetheless, the texts collected in *Erasmus in English* are the product of the inspiration that Erasmus himself provided for a vernacular humanism that sought to draw on antique culture to expand the expressive resources of the sixteenth-century modern languages.

2

'Erasmus laid the egg that Luther hatched.'

The *Paraclesis* was published in 1516. By 1528, William Tyndale was citing it as offering a 'thousand reasons' in favour of Scripture in the vernacular.[13] Tyndale's own English New Testament had appeared in 1526. Before that, the first text in this volume was completed: a manuscript dated to 1523, translating Erasmus's handbook of Christian piety, the *Enchiridion militis Christiani*. The manuscript is anonymous, but *Erasmus in English* echoes recent scholarship by Brian Cummings in cautiously ascribing it to Tyndale.[14] The next significant translation of Erasmus into English, and the next to appear in this collection, was *A devout treatise upon the Pater Noster*, printed in 1526. It was written by Margaret Roper, the daughter of Thomas More. By 1529, the *Paraclesis* itself had appeared in English — but not, initially, attached to an edition of the Bible. Instead, it was scandalously re-purposed as the preface to a commentary by Martin Luther on Paul's first letter

---

[12] Letter to Emilio de' Migli, 17 May 1529, *CWE* 15. 264–65.
[13] *The Obedience of A Christian Man*, ed. by David Daniell (London: Penguin, 2000), p. 25.
[14] Brian Cummings, 'William Tyndale and Erasmus on How to Read the Bible: A Newly Discovered Manuscript of the English *Enchiridion*', *Reformation*, 23.1 (2018), 29–52.

to the Corinthians. This is the third text to appear in this volume, *An Exhortation to the Diligent Study of Scripture*, which was printed anonymously but which has been ascribed to an apostate friar, William Roy. Within six years of the 1520s the first three main translations of Erasmus into English had been produced. They were written by two men and one woman, in manuscript and in print, with Erasmus's writing taken up by (in turn) a future Protestant martyr, the daughter of a future Catholic one, and a reader of Luther. What are we to make of this seemingly scattershot pattern of appropriations?

In some measure at least it must track Erasmus's own ambiguous positioning in relation to the Reformation. *Erasmus posuit oua; Luther exclusit pullos*: it is ironic — or perhaps telling — that the first recorded instance of the claim that 'Erasmus laid the egg that Luther hatched' seems to appear in a letter from Erasmus himself. Writing to Johannes Caesarius in 1524, Erasmus reported that it was being circulated among Franciscans hostile to him, and rejected the idea that reformers were acting under his influence. 'Luther', he claimed, 'has hatched a chick of very, very different feather'.[15] It feels characteristic that Erasmus should in one gesture give currency to the accusation and rebut it. As the Reformation gathered pace throughout the 1520s and 30s, becoming ever more acrimonious and divisive, and as demands to choose a side in the conflict became ever more insistent, Erasmus first hedged and then ultimately elected to remain within the bounds of the Roman church. He ended up disputing bitterly with Martin Luther over the issue of free will. Yet Erasmus's elaboration of a theology grounded in the exemplary character of the life of Christ, his scorn for rote forms of worship, his biblical scholarship, and his religious satire all offered challenges to institutionalised authority and acted as inspirations to movements for both reform and radical change of the church.

The English Erasmus reflects the divided quality of this thinking. A representative, and hugely influential, document is John Foxe's great Protestant history, *Actes and Monuments*, also known as the *Book of Martyrs*. Foxe names Erasmus as one of those who had participated in 'the first pushe and assault to be geuen against the ignoraunt & barbarous faction of the popes pretensed Churche'. Foxe cannot quite disguise where Erasmus's ultimate allegiances lay, but he is identified as an important precursor to the project of Protestant reformation. 'Erasmus Roterodamus', Foxe writes, 'had somewhat broken the way before & hadd shaken the monkes houses, But Luther gaue the stroke, & pluckt downe the foundation.' When it comes to individual acts of reading, the *Book of Martyrs* is even more emphatic. In the martyrologies, reading Erasmus is associated with conversion. Foxe's narrative of Thomas Bilney begins with Bilney's reading of Erasmus's New Testament, while the corrosive influence of the colloquy on pilgrimage features in the recantation of Thomas Topley, which begins: 'All

---

[15] Letter to Johannes Caesarius, 16 December 1524, *CWE* 10. 464.

Christen men beware of consentyng to Erasmus fables'.[16] From a Catholic point of view, meanwhile, Erasmus was invoked against Tyndale by Thomas More. 'I fynde', More writes, 'in Erasmus my derlynge that he detesteth and abhorreth the errours and heresyes that Tyndale playnely techeth and abydeth by.' The descriptor 'my derlynge' picks up the phrase *Erasme charissime* from Erasmus's and More's correspondence, which Tyndale had mocked. And yet even here the ambivalent note is struck. More is obliged to concede that he would burn Erasmus's *Encomium Moriae*, and his own *Utopia*, were they to appear in the vernacular.[17]

Erasmus was a central presence as sixteenth-century Englishmen and women tried to make sense of the history they were living through, even as the nature of his influence on events was hotly contested. He also plays a key role in the historiography of early Tudor religion. In 1965, James McConica published *English Humanists and Reformation Politics Under Henry VIII and Edward VI*. This book argues that the English Reformation was, substantially, an Erasmian Reformation. McConica charts the circulation of Erasmus's writing and the spread of his influence in the first half of the sixteenth century. During this period, for McConica, 'the main current of English thought [was] continuously Erasmian'.[18] It is in many ways a very Erasmian reading of Erasmus's influence on the English Reformation, at once decisive and amorphous. McConica's critics have noted how *English Humanists* ties together figures who were in reality bitter enemies: Thomas More, Cuthbert Tunstall, John Fisher, Thomas Cromwell. But this is in some ways the strength of the thesis. McConica's Erasmus, who figures both as a general influence and specific inspiration, speaks to Erasmus's ability to be all things to all men.

Certainly McConica persuasively highlights the way in which the networks of affiliation and clientage around Thomas Cromwell during his period as Henry VIII's chief minister were particularly interested in Englishing Erasmus's writings. This marks a difference from the first phase of Erasmus in English. The texts translated in the 1520s were produced unsystematically. In the 1530s we encounter a focused programme of translation. *The Dialogue Between Julius the Second, Genius, and Saint Peter* is a scandalous anti-papal satire, printed in 1534 by John Byddell. The same printer was responsible for the first printed version of Erasmus's *Enchiridion*, for translations of Erasmus's colloquy *Funus* and of his paraphrase of the epistle to Titus — and for the English Bible produced by Richard Taverner in 1539. This was a project, driven by Cromwell, that aimed to advance an evangelical religious agenda.[19] Taverner played a central role in these activities.

---

[16] John Foxe, *Actes and Monuments* (London: John Day, 1583), sigs Ddd5^r, Ddd6^r, Sss3^r, Xxx6^r (pp. 841, 843, 1005, 1047).
[17] See *The Confutation of Tyndale's Answer*, CWM 8. 177.
[18] James McConica, *English Humanists and Reformation Politics Under Henry VIII and Edward VI* (Oxford: The Clarendon Press, 1965), p. 271.
[19] On 'Cromwell's grafting his own evangelical religious enthusiasm on to Henry VIII's break

He has been described as both 'Cromwell's principal propagandist for religious reform' and as 'the most prolific popularizer of Erasmus whom England produced'.[20] The two roles went together. In 1532, Taverner sent to Cromwell his translation of the oration *Encomium matrimoni*, printed as *The Praise of Matrimony* in 1532–33. The dedication to Cromwell frames the text as an attack on 'the blind superstition of men and women which cease not day by day to profess and vow perpetual chastity' (*Matrimony*, 15): that is, as an attack on the doctrine of clerical celibacy, which was certainly not how Erasmus would have put it.

Of translations produced during this moment, *Erasmus in English* reproduces Byddell's *Dialogue* and Taverner's *Praise of Matrimony*, alongside (in volume three) a version of Erasmus's colloquy *Perigrinatio Religionis ergo*, translated as *The Pilgrimage of Pure Devotion* in the wake of the Pilgrimage of Grace. These are publications that take pious explorations of Erasmus's 'philosophy of Christ', many of them produced before the Reformation, and redirect them to the task of agitating for evangelical reform. One should not neglect those translations that do not fully fit into this story. This period also sees English versions of Erasmus's *Exomologesis*, discussing confession, and of an epistle on the sacraments — both much closer to works of orthodox piety, even though the former was also printed by Byddell.[21] Nonetheless, there is a body of translations from the 1530s, emerging through the networks of clientage surrounding Thomas Cromwell, that aimed to produce a general climate of opinion favourable to reformed theology, and also to edge a reluctant monarch closer to these positions. They represent, in a sense, an arm of the Henrician administrative state attempting to radicalise its centre, and the effort of accommodating these different positions can lead to some uneasy results. *The Pilgrimage of Pure Devotion* attacks the 'superstitious worship' of traditional religion while also denouncing those who 'make insurrectyones contrary to the ordynaunce of gode, agaynst theyr kynge and liege lorde'.[22] The absorption of Erasmus's reformist satire into a combination of religious iconoclasm and counter-revolutionary fervour was a more-or-less coherent position, so long as the monarch was committed to a programme of religious reform. But of course he — or she — might not be. Later appearances of Erasmus in English from the 1540s and 50s would only extend this narrative of the vexed circuit linking together Erasmian originals, translation, and state power.

---

with Rome', see Diarmaid MacCulloch, *Thomas Cromwell: A Life* (London: Penguin Books, 2018), p. 260. On 'evangelical' as a term to describe early English Protestant thought, see Alex Ryrie, 'The Strange Death of Lutheran England', *Journal of Ecclesiastical History*, 53 (2002), 64–92.

[20] See Andrew W. Taylor's *ODNB* entry for Taverner, and McConica, *English Humanists*, p. 117.

[21] See Devereux, *Renaissance English Translation of Erasmus*, 20 and 19.3.1. Both confession and the Eucharist were subjects of debate among Protestants in the 1530s, and one should not retrospectively assume a settled consensus on either.

[22] *A dialoge or communication of two persons [...] intituled ye pylgremage of pure deuotyon* (London: n.p., 1537?), sig. *4^v.

3
'Without Erasmus, no Shakespeare.'[23]

Richard Taverner also serves to introduce the second theme that must dominate any account of Erasmus's presence in English culture, which is his influence on literary production and elite habits of expression more generally, exercised through school pedagogy and through a range of associated educational texts. In 1539, Taverner published his first translations from Erasmus's *Adages* under the title *The Second Booke of the Garden of Wysedom*. These were expanded and reprinted as *Proverbs* in the same year, and then again in 1545; *Erasmus in English* reproduces this version of the text. Erasmus's *Adages* were one of his major projects. They collected sayings from the ancient world and attached to them explanatory essays. Part of the significance of the *Adages* lay in their opening up of classical thought and history to a broad readership; James McConica describes them as 'a vade-mecum of ancient culture'.[24] They also offered Erasmus the opportunity to expand the format into essays on topics that particularly concerned him, and several of these longer entries were translated into English as independent publications, two of which appear in this edition. But in origin the *Adages* belong with texts such as Erasmus's *Parabolae* (a collection of comparisons) and his *Apophthegmata* (pithy sayings and anecdotes, also adapted by Taverner in *The Garden of Wysedom*). These were above all practical volumes that anthologised notable phrases as elements of elegant Latin style and as the grounds of effective argumentation. They aimed to expand the expressive resources of the reader.

Taverner's *Proverbs* can therefore also be aligned with texts such as the *De copia* and *De ratione studii* — explicitly educational works associated with St Paul's School in London, founded by Erasmus's friend John Colet. Even satirical works like the *Colloquies* have their roots in this educational context, as dialogues for teaching Latin. That the grammar school held the key to the significance of Erasmus for the literary culture of the English Renaissance was the argument of T. W. Baldwin's 1944 two-volume, 1500-page study of early modern school teaching, *William Shakspere's Small Latine & Lesse Greeke*. Baldwin's major insight was that the pedagogy of the period was, at root, Erasmian. Following on from the foundation of St Paul's School in 1509, Baldwin saw in England a conscious effort to reorganise school curricula along Erasmian lines. He identified the period 1530 to 1545 as that in which this programme began to be regularised across the country.[25] This was an education in the language arts that taught Latin and

---

[23] Emrys Jones, *The Origins of Shakespeare* (Oxford: The Clarendon Press, 1977), p. 13.
[24] James McConica, *Erasmus* (Oxford and New York: Oxford University Press, 1991), p. 28.
[25] T. W. Baldwin, *William Shakspere's Small Latine & Lesse Greeke*, 2 volumes (Urbana: Illinois University Press, 1944), I, 79–80, 164.

persuasive expression through a combination of classical texts and modern supplements, the latter often written by Erasmus himself or produced in his wake. Its flavour is caught by George Gascoigne, born in 1535, who has a character in one of his plays say that 'my Brother here, and I haue bene taught first the rules of the grammer, after that wee had read vnto vs the familiar communications called the *Colloquia* of *Erasmus*, and next to that the offices of *Cicero* [his *De officia*]'.[26]

Emrys Jones's judgment 'without Erasmus, no Shakespeare' thus refers not just to specific borrowings or allusions but to the creation of a whole cultural landscape. The Erasmian grammar school curricula of the sixteenth and seventeenth centuries decisively moulded almost every significant thinker of this period.[27] This instruction would have been carried out in Latin, but a range of translations such as Taverner's extended this project into the vernacular. Volumes such as his *Proverbs* offered practical resources for expanding and enriching the resources of cultivated expression in English, while essays and orations such as *The Praise of Matrimony*, the translations of Erasmus's *Ducli bellum inexpertis* and *Sileni Alcibiadis*, *The Praise of Folly*, and *The Complaint of Peace* — all of which are reproduced in this edition — represented models of polished, sophisticated literary discourse.

Even the more polemical texts collected in *Erasmus in English* have a rhetorical function. It takes nothing away from their pious or controversial intent to note that they also offered models of resourceful and decisive discourse in the Erasmian mode. In his *Apology For Poetry*, Philip Sidney — another late sixteenth-century product of the humanist school system — wrote that the true poet could 'bestow a Cyrus upon the world to make many Cyruses'. (The reference is to Xenophon's *Cyropaedia*.) Sidney's vision is that of an almost infinitely generative rhetorical efficacy, and it echoes a number of statements in Erasmus about the potency of copious language. But Sidney's comment has a revealing postscript: 'to make many Cyruses', he writes, 'if they will learn aright why and how that maker made him'.[28] The replicative function of eloquence is grounded in an understanding of the deep rhetorical structures of a text. To read knowingly is not just to take note of effectively deployed figures of speech, sayings, and allusions. It is also to

---

[26] George Gascoigne, *The glasse of government* (London: [Henry Middleton] for C. Barker, 1575), sig. B1^r.

[27] Those who would not have gone to grammar school were principally the poor, the very rich (who might be educated within aristocratic households), and women. But Elizabeth I received a good humanist education at the hands of tutors such as Roger Ascham.

[28] Sir Philip Sidney, *An Apology For Poetry (Or, The Defence of Poesy)*, ed. by Geoffrey Shepherd, rev. by R. W. Maslen (Manchester and New York: Manchester University Press, 2002), p. 85. The classic study of this aspect of the Erasmian educational programme is Terence Cave, *The Cornucopian Text: Problems of Writing in the French Renaissance* (Oxford: The Clarendon Press, 1979).

understand something about how discourse can be organised in relation to (for example) commonplace formulations such as those collected in Taverner's *Proverbs*.

Consider the deployment of the injunction 'know thyself' in Erasmus's *Enchiridion*. *Nosce teipsum*: it is one of Erasmus's adages, reproduced by Taverner, who comments that 'this divine sentence [...] is both true and godly and worthy of Christian men to be continually borne in mind' (Tav. 61, *Proverbs*, 403–05).[29] In its opening phases, the *Enchiridion* is dominated by a different commonplace formulation, drawn from the Vulgate Bible. This is Job 7. 1: *militia est vita hominis* — or, as Erasmus's English translator puts it, 'the life of mortal men is nothing but a certain perpetual exercise of war' (*Manual*, 21–22). This metaphor is fundamental to Erasmus's conception of the text, with its conflation of handbook and hand weapon, and it is carefully designed to speak to his ostensible addressee, a courtier attached to worldly ideals. In the opening phases of the text, *militia est vita hominis* generates a range of topics — faith to one's lord, the spoils of victory, the gravity of the conflict — that explore the idea of warfare against sin. At the same time, it is endowed with a belligerent edge that is in some measure at odds with Erasmus's purposes. *Nosce teipsum* redirects his argument onto more congenial ground. Erasmus's third chapter addresses the topic of true wisdom, arguing that pagan authority is confirmed by Christian precept:

> The chief part of this wisdom is that thou shouldst 'know thyself': which word to have descended from heaven believed antiquity, and so much that saying pleased great authors that they judged the ground of all wisdom utterly to be contained in that point only. (*Manual*, 733–36)

The *Enchiridion*'s initial metaphor is never completely left behind, but *nosce teipsum* serves to launch Erasmus's discussion in a new direction, as the text moves from this moment to develop an anthropology that can support his vision of true Christian piety, with sections on the outward and inward man, on the diversity of affections, on the parts of a man, spirit, soul, and flesh, and so on.

What Erasmus taught was to understand a text as a continuous, evolving discourse. To modern tastes, the results can feel unstructured; Johan Huizinga comments on the 'lack of depth and the prolixity' that characterise Erasmian *copia*.[30] In sixteenth-century terms, however, the effect was felt to be that of a coordinated discursive force. The *De copia* offers an admiring analysis of Cicero's prose, with its 'close packed convincing details [where] each individual word has more effect than the one before'.[31] And part of the point was to be able to catch

---

[29] In *CWE*, it is *Adages* I. vi. 95. Proverbs translated by Taverner are cross-referenced within this edition by the abbreviation 'Tav.' followed by the proverb number; other references to this text are by line number.

[30] Johan Huizinga, *Erasmus and the Age of Reformation*, trans. by F. Hopman (Princeton: Princeton University Press, 1984 [1924]), p. 106.

[31] *CWE* 24. 592.

hold of the motivating structures that generated these waves of argumentation. These were texts that aimed not just to persuade but also to teach, and all of Erasmus's works are marked by an interest in their own communicative potential. How best to ornament a discourse, or to convey the power of Scripture? What happens when the goddess Folly praises herself? How can the goddess Peace speak to a world marked by incessant conflict? These and other such questions are not narrowly self-referential for Erasmus. Rather, they reflect his consistent concern to reach out and to change the world through persuasive discourse.

4

This discursive energy was part of what made Erasmus worth laying claim to, just as his investment in what might be called an ethos of communication is one of the things that made him congenial to those engaged in the project of nation building in the newly reformed English Protestant state. The colloquy *Epicureus* exemplifies the ambitions for Erasmus in English as we pass into the 1540s and the reigns of Henry VIII's successors. Translated in 1545 by Phillip Gerrard, a groom of Prince Edward's chamber — the future king was at this point eight years old, and himself undergoing a humanistic education — and printed by Richard Grafton, who would hold the post of king's printer under Edward VI, *The Epicure* (edited in volume three of *Erasmus in English*) puts a Protestant spin on Erasmus's discussion of antique and Christian thinking on the nature of true human happiness. What had been in the original a virtuous Franciscan becomes in Gerrard's rendition a suffering poor man.[32] But the text's most substantial engagement with present circumstances comes in its dedicatory epistle, addressed to Edward. Here, Gerrard denounces 'popery, ypocrisie, and damnable ydolatrie' and sets out his programme for fashioning a godly Christian nation:

> Now truely the godlyest thynge that can bee deuysed, for any christian realme, is to haue emongst them one maner and fourme of doctryne, & too trace trueli the steppes of God and neuer to seeke any other by wayes. Who hath not redde in the scriptures? but that realme is endued with godly ornamentes & riches, where all men prospere, go forward and florishe in gods woord, delectyng day and night in the swete consolations of the holy testament.[33]

Gerrard is speaking from within the inner circle of the household of the future king. His is a publication with something approaching official status.[34] It offers an insight into the mindset of the evangelical thinkers surrounding the prince in the last years of Henry VIII's monarchy, highlighting the centrality of godly

---

[32] See *CWE* 40. 1082 and *A very pleasaunt and fruitful diologe called the Epicure*, trans. by Philip Gerrard (London: Richard Grafton, 1545), sig. D7^{r-v}.
[33] *The Epicure*, sigs A8^r, A6^{r-v}.
[34] On *The Epicure*, see Cathy Shrank, 'Mirroring the "Long Reformation": Translating Erasmus' Colloquies in Early Modern England', *Reformation*, 24.2 (2019), 59–75 (p. 65).

reading of Scripture to their vision of the nation. It also brings out something new: their desire to control that reading. If the central issue of the 1520s and 30s had been access to Scripture in the vernacular, that is now taken for granted. The focus switches to its regulation. One manner, one form: this was to be a key ambition of the monarchy of Edward VI, and Erasmus played a key role in its implementation.

Gerrard's *Epicure* provides context for the subsequent decades of religious policy in England, in which the English Erasmus first became required reading under the evangelical Protestant administration of Edward VI, and then survived largely intact through the reign of his Catholic successor Mary Tudor, who was also one of Erasmus's translators. The central text here is Erasmus's *Paraphrases* of the Bible, described by Gregory Dodds as 'one of the most interesting and unlikely books to emerge from the English Reformation'.[35] This was another of Erasmus's major projects. In English it comprises two huge folio volumes of exposition of the text of the New Testament. The *Paraphrases* had their distant origins in double translation exercises of the kind that Erasmus recommended for the pupils of St Paul's School.[36] Erasmus himself explained them as an extension of the activities of the school teacher, 'who, commenting on Virgil, first explains the subject of the poem in plain style and in plainer words'.[37] The *Paraphrases* engaged in a novel kind of textual ventriloquism that aimed to open out the affective dimensions of Scripture. As Jean-François Cottier explains, it was a format to which rhetorical skills were central; this quality of the *Paraphrases* was what set them apart from associated forms like commentary and exegesis. 'They were', Cottier writes, 'intended not only to instruct (*docere*) but equally to move and please (*movere* and *placere*)'; rather than breaking down the text in the manner of a scholastic exegete, Erasmus instead developed the biblical text into what he called 'an oratorical stream of speech'.[38] At the same time, he set out to explain Scripture as discourse directed to specific audiences with specific aims in mind: as a fundamentally persuasive document.

---

[35] See Dodds, *Exploiting Erasmus*, p. 3.
[36] See *CWE* 42. 11–12.
[37] See Jean-François Cottier, 'Erasmus's *Paraphrases*: A "New Kind of Commentary?"', trans. by Karen Mak and Nancy Senior, in *The Unfolding of Words: Commentary in the Age of Erasmus*, ed. by Judith Rice Henderson (Toronto, Buffalo, and London: University of Toronto Press, 2012), pp. 27–46 (p. 31), quoting from Erasmus's *Supputatio errorum in censuris Bedae*.
[38] See Cottier, 'Erasmus's *Paraphrases*', pp. 28, 30 — the latter again quoting from the *Supputatio* addressed to Noël Béda. More recently, Jennifer Richards has emphasised the oral and communal aspects of the rhetoric of the *Paraphrases*. Erasmus, she writes, 'aimed to clarify the books of the New Testament by translating them into a first-person, spoken idiom', and the *Paraphrases* should be understood as 'the most influential of the talking books in sixteenth-century England'. See *Voices and Books in the English Renaissance: A New History of Reading* (Oxford: Oxford University Press, 2019), pp. 209, 181.

The Englishing of the *Paraphrases* was initiated by Catherine Parr in the wake of the publication of the Great Bible in 1540, and undertaken by a range of translators. Of the extracts presented in *Erasmus in English*, the Gospel of Matthew was undertaken anonymously, while the Gospel of John was translated by Princess Mary, with the assistance of her chaplain Francis Mallet.[39] By the time the first volume was ready for publication, Edward VI was king, and the reforming administration that surrounded the new monarch added the *Paraphrases* to a set of official publications that aimed to standardise religious practice across the realm. On 31 July 1547, it was decreed that copies of the *Great Bible*, the *Book of Common Prayer*, the *Book of Homilies*, and Erasmus's *Paraphrases* should be placed in every church in the land.[40]

Erasmus was now officially mandated reading. The first volume of *Paraphrases* was superintended by Nicholas Udall, and Udall's prefatory dedication to Edward VI situates the text as a supplement to a wider project of vernacularisation. 'Untill the Bible and other good traitises for the explanacion of the same wer in Christian regions turned and set forth in the vulgare languages', he asks, 'what kind of idolatry, supersticion, poperie, errour, ignorance, or counterfaict religion did not reign?' (B3^v). 'Explanation' plays a central role in this project. Udall may celebrate 'the moste heauenly iewell and treasure of Goddes holy scripture, in the mother language', but it is to be promulgated alongside other 'good traitises' that guide its reception (A4^v)....

Udall's preface positions Erasmus's Latin writings as just the starting point for an outward movement in which translation is the natural prelude to official sanction:

> For Erasmus [...] did helpe onely such as are sene in latin: the Quenes goodnesse extendeth to the help of the vnlearned also which haue more nede of helping foreward: and your Maiesties benefit it is that maketh so precious a treasour common to as many as may take profit or fruict thereby. (B3^r)

The royal decree makes common what had been restricted; it is a step beyond even translation. And yet, the English *Paraphrases* are elusive and sometimes outright contradictory texts that struggle to assimilate the details of their author's theology. Udall himself negotiates the awkward fact of Erasmus's Catholicism by simply ignoring it. Instead, Erasmus is presented as a proto-reformer. 'Neither',

---

[39] See the dedicatory letter prefacing the *Paraphrase* of John, in *The first tome or volume of the Paraphrase of Erasmus vpon the Newe Testamente*, trans. by Nicholas Udall et al. (London: Edward Whitchurch, 1548), sigs Aaa2^{r-v}. Further references appear parenthetically. Mary's authorship is further discussed in Aysha Pollnitz, 'Religion and Translation at the Court of Henry VIII: Princess Mary, Katherine Parr and the *Paraphrases* of Erasmus', in *Mary Tudor: Old and New Perspectives*, ed. by Susan Doran and Thomas S. Freeman (Houndmills: Palgrave Macmillan, 2011), pp. 123–37.

[40] Dodds, *Exploiting Erasmus*, p. 10.

Udall writes, 'doth any writer more wittily, more earnestly, more aptly, more finely, more substauncially, more piththily, or more playnely describe and peyncte out the vsurped state, pre-eminence, and pompe of the bishop of Rome, then he doth' (B2^v) — a commendation that is itself (with its accumulation of comparatives) a demonstration of the principles of Erasmian *copia*, but one that also seriously equivocates over the distinction between a reformist stance within the Catholic church and a radical one committed to its rejection. The second volume of *Paraphrases* is less willing to smooth over these differences. Miles Coverdale's dedicatory preface to Edward compares the text to the jewels used to ornament the tabernacle in Exodus — 'if', he adds, 'they be distinctelye red, and practiced with suche discrecion, as your highnesse hathe commaunded'. Meanwhile, John Olde, translator of the epistles, is more forthright still in describing Erasmus as 'a manne subiecte to infirimitie and imperfeccion'.[41]

Uncomfortable though the fit may have been, however, the Erasmus of the 1548 *Paraphrases* was part of a government-sponsored push towards Protestant religious uniformity. When Edward died in 1553 and his sister Mary acceded to the throne, one might have expected the *Paraphrases* to have joined the *Book of Common Prayer* and the *Book of Homilies* as illicit literature, subject to confiscation and destruction. In fact, this seems not to have happened. There are records of nine parishes being ordered to remove copies by the Archdeacon of Canterbury Nicholas Harpsfield, but none of any sweeping ban.[42] Possibly the *Paraphrases* were saved by their author's orthodoxy; possibly too the fact that the queen had contributed to the text made its proscription unthinkable. At any rate, when Elizabeth I became queen, she reaffirmed the decree that a copy of the *Paraphrases* should appear in every parish church. Erasmus's text had outlasted three monarchs and two major shifts in religion.

The history of Erasmus's *Paraphrases* offers a resonant case study of the major political and historical forces that could be exerted on the activity of translation in this period. In many ways, the story of *Erasmus in English* is one of this gravitational pull from the centre of political life. Over the course of several decades we see the writings of a man born in the Low Countries, one who wrote only in Latin, dead by 1536, being drawn into the key dramas of monarchical rule and religious regime change in England during the first half of the sixteenth century. Even an ostensibly literary text such as *The Praise of Folly* cannot quite escape this field of force. The *Encomium Moriae* was translated in 1549 by Thomas

---

[41] *The seconde tome or volume of the Paraphrase of Erasmus vpon the Newe Testament*, trans. by various hands (London: Edward Whitchurch, 1549), sig. *2^v, and the dedication to the canonical epistles, sig. *1^v. My account here is indebted to the first two chapters of Dodds's *Exploiting Erasmus* (pp. 3–59), which discuss the *Paraphrases* in detail.

[42] See Pollnitz, 'Religion and Translation', p. 123, and more generally Dodds, *Exploiting Erasmus*, p. 11.

Chaloner, a diplomat and justice of the peace — that is, by a member of the early Tudor administrative classes. As Jennifer Richards has argued, Chaloner's invention of a vigorously colloquial voice for Folly has to be read alongside the projects of vernacularisation and religious reform being pursued by Edward VI's administration at this time.[43]

Still, one would not want to over-emphasise the regimenting effects of political and religious history on the English Erasmus. Erasmus's own educational writings strongly emphasised the qualities of volatility and mutability inherent in eloquent language; the *De copia* refers to 'someone who has it at his fingertips to turn one idea into more shapes than Proteus himself is supposed to have turned into'.[44] Two translations from the reign of Elizabeth I, the second of which completes this anthology, offer a suggestive pairing of case studies: an occasional Erasmus on the one hand, and a Protean one on the other. The English translation of Erasmus's oration *Querela pacis* was printed in 1559 as *The Complaint of Peace*. The date makes it contemporaneous with Elizabeth I's accession to the throne, a moment that threatened civil unrest and instability. The translation, by Thomas Paynell, was dedicated to Antony Browne, Viscount Montagu, a Catholic nobleman who had been dropped from the Privy Council following Elizabeth's accession.[45] In context, the *Complaint* can be understood as a plea for civil order addressed to Catholic subjects hostile to the new queen, and as a gesture of conformity on Montagu's part. It continues a narrative about Erasmus and high politics, although its interest is certainly not limited to that.

The final item in *Erasmus in English*, by contrast, comes out of left field. Published in 1584, Reginald Scott's *Discouerie of Witchcraft* aims to debunk popular beliefs about witches. It also contains a translation of Erasmus's colloquy *Alcumistica*, 'Alchemy'.[46] It is not that one can't see the point. 'Alchemy' presents the alchemist as an outrageous conman, his victim as a prodigy of credulity, and Scott translates the dialogue as part of an attack on a culture of (as Scott sees it) Catholic superstition. But we are a long way here from the regimenting force of high politics, and of texts that speak back directly to their occasions. Scott's deployment of Erasmus is unexpected, even a little wayward. It is a fitting end to a collection in which Erasmus's authority is always being appropriated, but never to any fully predictable or settled effect.

---

[43] See Richards, *Voices and Books*, pp. 121–29.
[44] *De copia*, CWE 24. 302.
[45] See Dodds, *Exploiting Erasmus*, pp. 61–63.
[46] *The discouerie of witchcraft* (London: [Henry Denham] for William Brome, 1584), sigs Ee5^r–8^v.

5

In her 1993 book *Erasmus, Man of Letters* Lisa Jardine offered a ground-breaking account of Erasmus's meticulous construction of his scholarly identity through editions, prefaces, dedications, and personal letters. Jardine's Erasmus is a virtuoso orchestrator of the new possibilities for self-fashioning opened up by the medium of print. The Erasmus of *Erasmus in English* exists in the aftermath of this success: a world of contradictory appropriations and uncertain remaking, of which the garbled and frequently incoherent text of the English *Sileni Alcibiadis* might stand as an emblem. The translations collected here are eager to lay claim to the name of Erasmus, and they do so in startlingly diverse ways. Over half a century, we encounter texts produced in manuscript and in print, written by women and men, by Catholics and by Protestants; we encounter both contraband texts and government-sponsored ones. *Erasmus in English* collects these texts for the first time. Within this whirl of diversity, what does the English Erasmus show us?

In the first place: the influence of Erasmus in England was principally textual. His shaping of the curriculum of St Paul's School certainly depended upon his friendship with John Colet, but the subsequent transformation of grammar school teaching across the country did not; while the promulgation of the *Paraphrases* as required reading occurred after his death. As James Kearney comments, despite his extended periods of residence in England, Erasmus's impact on English culture effect 'is almost certainly a product of Erasmus as text rather than a product of his charismatic presence in England'.[47] Or rather, to adapt Lisa Jardine's point — the subtitle of her book is 'The Construction of Charisma in Print' — Erasmus's charismatic presence *was* his writing, not his person.

Secondly, though: Erasmus's influence on English culture was not exerted solely through the medium of English translations. Erasmus in English did not replace Erasmus in Latin. On the contrary, they run side-by-side and can even be understood as parallel tracks of the same humanist project. In 1520, Erasmus was by far the most popular single author to feature in the account books of the Oxford bookseller John Dorne.[48] Well over a hundred years later, Erasmus in Latin still dominated the reading lists and commonplace books of students in seventeenth-century Cambridge. Richard Holdsworth, Master of Emanuel College from 1637 to 1649, specifically recommended the *Colloquies*, the *Adages*, *De lingua*, and the *Encomium Moriae* to his students.[49] Translations of Erasmus into English would certainly have made many of these texts available to non-scholarly readers, as Nicholas Udall's preface to the *Paraphrases* suggests, but they should not be

---

[47] James Kearney, *The Incarnate Text: Imagining the Book in Renaissance England* (Philadelphia: University of Pennsylvania Press, 2009), p. 71.

[48] See Thompson, 'Erasmus in Tudor England', p. 37.

[49] See Margo Todd, *Christian Humanism and the Puritan Social Order* (Cambridge: Cambridge University Press, 1987), pp. 83–86.

understood purely as replacements for them. The same humanistically-educated reader might own both Erasmus's *Encomium Moriae* in a Latin edition printed in Basel and the English translation by Thomas Chaloner. Chaloner's preface imagines a reader of both (*Folly*, 77–80). Comparison might be a motive to translation, then, just as much as popularisation was, while vernacularisation could figure as an aspect of a wider humanist project devoted to demonstrating the relevance of antique culture to present circumstances. Richard Taverner's English *Adages* aim to supply the resources to enable the vernacular to match the ancient languages in eloquence and sophistication. His volume was conceived, he wrote, 'for the love I bear to the furtherance and adornment of my native country' (*Proverbs*, 9–10).

Thirdly, there is the way in which vernacularisation may have shaped Erasmus's reputation into the present. It is suggestive to note how the translations of Erasmus into English from the sixteenth century in many ways fix a canon of his works that endures to this day. We can compare the texts collected in *Erasmus in English* with a modern anthology like Erika Rummell's *Erasmus Reader*.[50] This contains the *Enchiridion*, the *Praise of Folly*, *Complaint of Peace*, *Julius exclusus*, select colloquies, and the adage *Dulce bellum inexpertis*. Probably the most significant disparities are the presence in Rummell's collection of the *Institutio principis Christiani* (of which no English translation survives from this period), and the absence from it of the *Paraphrases*, alongside Erasmus's educational writings and correspondence. These last were texts that stayed in Latin, as did Erasmus's editorial work. In some ways therefore, the English Erasmus was a very authorial figure — a distinctive, individual voice that his translators aimed to lay claim to by reproducing — although our collection certainly aims to underline the importance of paraphrase and commentary to Erasmus's English reception.

Finally: Erasmus's influence on early modern English culture was at once huge and curiously diffuse. It is no coincidence that commentators have disagreed, at times radically, in their assessments of it. For James McConica and T. W. Baldwin, Erasmus stands at the heart of two foundational narratives for understanding the evolution of sixteenth- and seventeenth-century English culture: the Reformation on the one hand, and educational reform on the other. Yet at the same time, Cornelis Augustijn can say — at the conclusion of a book devoted to exploring Erasmus's 'Life, Works and Influence' — that 'there never was an Erasmian renaissance'.[51] Erasmus founded no church. To be an Erasmian implied no clear commitments in the way that being (say) a Lutheran did. His influence quickly becomes indistinct, or shows up in forms that seem at odds with much of what

---

[50] *The Erasmus Reader*, ed. by Erika Rummell (Toronto, Buffalo, and London: University of Toronto Press, 1990).
[51] Cornelis Augustijn, *Erasmus: His Life, Works, and Influence*, trans. by J. C. Grayson (Toronto, Buffalo, and London: University of Toronto Press, 1991), p. 200.

Erasmus believed in. Nobody would dispute Erasmus's centrality to educational reform, but even James McConica can see Erasmus's adoption by the radical Protestant regime of Edward VI as, however oddly, rather un-Erasmian.[52]

In order to gain some purchase on this elusive phenomenon, we need to take into account what is historically specific about the English Erasmus. We can identify the key institutional vectors for Erasmus's presence in early modern English culture. The printed book is one. The grammar school classroom and the Edwardian parish church are two others, and both of these are, in the sense explored by Michel Foucault, disciplinary spaces.[53] That is, they are spaces that aim to regulate the behaviour of individuals in society via an internalisation of norms. It is no coincidence that the need for self-reflection is an insistent motif in Erasmus's writing. His adage *Quo transgressus* endorses a recommendation of Pythagoras, that we always should ask ourselves: 'Where have I slipped? What have I done? Or what duty have I omitted?'[54] Another adage, translated by Taverner, praises the effects of continual work upon the self, or 'exercise':

> *Exercitatio potest omnia.* Exercise can bring to pass all things. Nothing, sayeth Seneca, is so hard but man's mind can overcome it, and continual practising bring it into an acquaintance. There be no affections so wild, so unruly, but discipline and awe may tame them. What thing soever the mind commandeth, she obtaineth. (Tav. 99, *Proverbs*, 642–45)

Erasmus can be understood as a central figure in the development of early modern disciplines of the self.[55]

Disciplinarity is elusive because it goes to work at the point of contact between the individual psyche and wider historical movements. It identifies the ground on which the Edwardian aspiration towards 'one maner and fourme of doctryne' can be pursued — seemingly paradoxically — through the official promotion of the intense personal piety advocated by Erasmus's *philosophia Christi*, grounded in the rejection of external forms, in self-scrutiny, and in a fervent inner life. The intersection between personal experience and attempts to define and control religious culture goes to the very heart of this period. Similarly, for Lisa Jardine and Anthony Grafton in their book *From Humanism to the Humanities*, humanist

---

[52] See the comments in *English Humanists*, pp. 236–37, although this judgement is nuanced in the succeeding pages of McConica's discussion.

[53] See Michel Foucault, *Discipline and Punish: The Birth of the Prison*, trans. by Alan Sheridan (London: Penguin, 1991 [1977]).

[54] *Adage* III. x. i, *Quo transgressus, etc.*, 'Where have I transgressed, etc.?'.

[55] To the examples given we can add Erasmus's interest in the disciplining of manners, evinced by his treatise *De civilitate morum puerilium*, and in correct pronunciation (*De recta latini graeciaque sermonis pronuntiatione*); the way in which the commonplace notebook method encouraged students to internalise their reading; the way the *Paraphrases* rework Scripture into a first-person format; and so on.

pedagogy serviced the needs of early modern states for a class of efficient, docile administrators: a bureaucratic elite.[56] Once again the claim for a momentous historical shift is grounded in the minutiae of what Erasmus's adage calls 'exercise': the 'continual practicing' of educational drills of memorisation, recitation, and composition, all of which take centre stage in Jardine and Grafton's account.

Certainly we should not assume the absolute efficacy of the impulse towards control and regulation. Nor should it be construed simply as a matter of submission to external authority. Erasmus himself was clear, as we have seen, about the unpredictable, Protean energies harnessed by copious rhetoric, and a certain creative freedom is absolutely part of the point of the humanist educational programme. Erasmus installed techniques of persuasion at the heart of the sixteenth-century educational curriculum; the object of this training was to deploy language creatively in ways that might change the world. The often wayward patterns of adaptation and customisation recorded in *Erasmus in English* speak to the success of that project, and to its ongoing capacity to produce change. But it is perhaps little wonder that Erasmus's influence should feel so elusive, and that the key debates in the scholarship should have been concerned with questions of how to map and delimit it. For Foucault, disciplinary regulation is to be contrasted with the forms of direct coercion available to sovereign power. It is subtle and evanescent. It is as much a matter of inner life as it is of institutional structures. And it is within this space that Erasmus's influence on the histories of education and of religion is exerted.

Patterns of modification must make themselves felt in the consideration of any author's afterlife. Some aspects of a text move into the foreground, while others are quietly dropped; meanings shift as they are transplanted from one set of circumstances into another. With Erasmus, however, these processes are particularly acutely felt, given his institutionalisation in England, and given his own focus on motifs of communication and influence. The most far-reaching claims for the centrality of Erasmus to English cultural history are made in Margo Todd's 1987 book *Christian Humanism and the Puritan Social Order*. Whereas James McConica's Erasmian period is confined to the early sixteenth century, Todd argues for a broad consensus of 'Christian humanism' shaped by Erasmus's writings that underpinned the mainstream of English thinking throughout the early modern period. This was a lay piety committed to social and religious reformation in the service of a godly commonweal:

> the generations of Englishmen brought up on the *Colloquies* and *Adages*, the *Praise of Folly* and the *Enchiridion*, were people whose assumptions about the social order and its prospects were subtly shaped by the presuppositions that

---

[56] See Anthony Grafton and Lisa Jardine, *From Humanism to the Humanities: Education and the Liberal Arts in Fifteenth- and Sixteenth-Century Europe* (Cambridge, MA: Harvard University Press, 1986), p. xiv.

underlay all of Erasmus' works — that all is not well with the world, and that change for the better is possible. The ideal of social reform germinating in the generation of Colet and Vives and More would not come to full fruition until the decades of Civil War and Interregnum.[57]

For Todd, the events of the mid-seventeenth century were the product of a conservative, Laudian reaction against this Christian humanist ideal. Civil war, the execution of Charles I, the interregnum, and the Cromwellian Protectorate: all are for Todd moments within an ongoing history, one that begins for this volume with the translation of the English *Enchiridion*. For Todd, therefore, Erasmianism is a reforming project, but we might wonder if the scope of the influence she maps is not more wide-reaching even than that. A late product of this moment might be a text like Margaret Cavendish's 1662 *Orations of Divers Sorts, Accommodated to Divers Places*: a compendium of some two hundred model orations on themes arranged *pro et contra*, in which we see Erasmus's belief in the centrality of eloquence to civil life filtered through the preoccupations of the Restoration political settlement. Cavendish offers orations for peace, against war, for war, against civil war, orations from discontented citizens addressed to their sovereign, and from a sovereign to his mutinous subjects. There are moments in this volume that touch on key Erasmian motifs, as with the claim in 'An Oration For Peace' that 'they are either fools or mad that will make war when they may live in peace'.[58] Cavendish makes no overt allusions, however, and indeed may never have read Erasmus; certainly she never attended grammar school or received a formal humanistic education. There is little here of Erasmus's own projects for social change. Yet in some sense it is almost impossible to imagine the *Orations* existing without the prehistory provided by over a hundred years of Erasmus in England, and in English.

Erasmus's writing fuses together the conviction that human societies should act differently with a characteristic localising evasiveness; there is also a tendency to collapse out from projects of critique into dualisms that separate worldly and godly values, eschewing the former as beyond hope.[59] His reception only intensifies these contradictions. In its very expansiveness, Margot Todd's reading goes to the heart of the matter. Here, above all, questions about the scope and definition of an English Erasmianism become unignorable.[60] But these

---

[57] Todd, *Christian Humanism*, p. 18.
[58] Margaret Cavendish, *Political Writings*, ed. by Susan James (Cambridge: Cambridge University Press, 2003), p. 132.
[59] An early devotional text, *De contemptu mundi*, was translated by Thomas Paynell in 1531 (see Devereux, *Renaissance English Translation of Erasmus*, p. 11). This is a discussion of monastic life that ultimately turns against it; but the impulse towards rejecting the world was a persistent one in Erasmus.
[60] Consider for example the objections to Todd's thesis advanced in Christopher Hill's review of *Christian Humanism and the Puritan Social Order* in *Albion*, 211 (1989), 102–04. Hill argues that the category of 'Christian humanist' is too fuzzy, and that the break with medieval ideals of reform is exaggerated.

uncertainties are grounded in concrete features of the way in which Erasmus's thought was taken up throughout the sixteenth and seventeenth centuries, and are not to be fully dispelled. The influence of Erasmus in English, and in England, was that of the most famous scholar of his day. It had something about it that was both all-pervasive and unlocatable. Erasmus in England was an author who became an environment.

The Manual Of The Christian Soldier

Translated by William Tyndale (1523)

Edited by Gordon Kendal

Introduction

Until recently the earliest known English translation of Erasmus's 'Manual' of Christian living, his *Enchiridion*, was the anonymous 1533 edition published in London by Wynkyn de Worde for John Byddell, suspected by many to be the work of William Tyndale: he was known to have produced a translation in the early 1520s before leaving England for Germany, but internal analysis and comparison — always tricky with a translation, particularly when it is done well and when years have gone by — proved indecisive.[1]

The acquisition by the British Library in 2015 of a manuscript from Alnwick Castle dated 1523 (though also anonymous) has altered the situation dramatically. Its existence confirms part of the rumour — there *was* a 1520s translation — and it at least enhances the credibility of the other part: that it was the work of Tyndale. It sets the task of internal analysis on a much firmer basis, expanding the provenance of *1533* and supplying fresh angles from which to assess its authorship: the later and earlier versions can be compared and appraised as siblings, lineally and developmentally. Despite many adjustments the printed edition is unmistakably a reworking of the manuscript. Some changes suggest the same translator, freshening his work proprietorially, even fussily, but keeping its essential tone and conformation. Others suggest a different hand, ironing wrinkles out (or in) — and taking responsibility for its publication. What was already a quite colourable scenario has now the benefit of an actual text at either end of the process. In 1523 the translating would have been for Tyndale an important exercise in clarification: a nascent theologian wrestling with a key text by an established contemporary, making clear what Erasmus was saying so that he and others could become clear about what it might mean for them. Ten years later Erasmus would seem at best a weak ally in the Reforming cause, and a re-issue of his 'Manual' would be low on a fugitive translator's agenda — though he might well have made earlier corrections of his own, with others supplying final touches.[2]

---

[1] William Tyndale, born late fifteenth century, executed in 1536, is best known as an early translator of the New Testament (1525). See John Foxe, *Acts and Monuments* (London: John Day, 1563), Bk 3, pp. 513-14; quoted in David Daniell, *William Tyndale: A Biography* (New Haven CT: Yale University Press, 1994), p. 63; also John Archer Gee, 'Tindale and the 1533 English *Enchiridion* of Erasmus', *PMLA*, 49.2 (1934), 460-71; and 'John Byddell and the First Publication of Erasmus' *Enchiridion* in English', *ELH*, 4.1 (1937), 43-59. For analysis of *1533* see J. F. Mozley, 'The English Enchiridion of Erasmus, 1533', *RES*, 20.78 (1944), 97-107; also *Enchiridion Militis Christiani, An English Version* [1534], Early English Text Society, ed. by Anne M. O'Donnell SND (Oxford: Oxford University Press, 1981), pp. xxxix f., and Elizabeth Bell Canon, *The Use of Modal Expression Preference as a Marker of Style and Attribution: The Case of William Tyndale and the 1533 English 'Enchiridion Militis Christiani'* (New York: Peter Lang, 2010).

[2] For some further remarks on the style of *1523* see pp. 31f. below.

The *Enchiridion* (written in 1501 and published in 1503)[3] is characteristically Erasmian: crisp and light but inherently serious. Nominally it is addressed to a worldly, semi-literate courtier-soldier[4] at the behest of his despairing wife, but the nature of the book — its length and complexity, its reference to other texts, extensive quotations, and the diversity of its implicit readers — suggests a collation of material already generated and waiting for an occasion. The topic — how to be a Christian in the modern world — lay near to Erasmus's heart, and required practical thought grounded in philosophy and Scripture. On his first visit to England in 1499 he met John Colet (whose lectures on St Paul were attracting attention) and Thomas More.[5] He found keen debate on the use of the Bible, and acquaintance with Platonism old and new. When he returned to Paris in 1500 he was studying Greek and was deep into Origen and Augustine.[6] All pointed to the possibility of a kind of spiritual guidance which — unlike what the common run of monks and academics had (in his view) to offer — might combine depth with usefulness. The blending of different tributaries and layers of experience has given the 'Manual' a lasting versatility, accessible but 'meaty': but also a certain inherent instability, as readers (including translators) appropriate its contours in different ways — from full-blown scriptural theism to moralistic agnosticism.

The book is crisper in its constituent parts than in its overall structure, and the chapter numbering added in 1533 promises more formal precision than it delivers. It is essentially a book to dip into. But despite its rambling and repetition it has a logical plan — Dominican rather than Franciscan in prioritising understanding as a precondition of genuine love[7] — with parallels in contemporary preaching and spiritual writings.[8] From its opening remarks urging vigilance in applying

---

[3] For the background see Introduction to *CWE* 66, ed. by John W. O'Malley (Toronto: Toronto University Press, 1988), and James McConica, *Erasmus* (Oxford: Oxford University Press, 1991), especially ch. 4.

[4] See O'Donnell, *An English Version*, p. xvi. For 'courtier-soldier' see pp. 56 and 102 below.

[5] John Colet (c. 1466–1519), dean of St Paul's, was a pioneer in the study of Greek in England. Thomas More (1478–1535), ultimately Lord Chancellor and a lay defender of Catholicism, was executed on the ground of high treason. He was the father of Margaret Roper, translator of E.'s *Pater Noster*.

[6] Origen (c. 185–c. 254) and Augustine (354–430), respectively Greek and Latin, were among the most influential of the Church Fathers.

[7] Cf. Dante, *Paradiso* 28. 109–11, trans. by C. H. Sisson (Oxford: Oxford University Press, 1993):
Here may be seen how being blessed
Has its foundation in the act of sight,
And not in love, which comes afterwards.

[8] On a late medieval theology that was both mystical and practical, see Oliver Davies, *God Within: The Mystical Tradition of Northern Europe* (London: Darton, Longman and Todd, 2006). A good example of the balance, admired by Reformers and Catholics, is the fourteenth-century Dominican John Tauler (died 1361), whose sermons show him to be a loyal but critical churchman. See *John Tauler: Spiritual Conferences*, trans. and ed. by Eric Colledge and Sister

ourselves to the Christian life (chapters 1–2) it moves on to outlining with the help of Plato and Paul what being human involves (3–7). This provides the background for learning the 'craft of blessed living' in the face of our three major defects: 'blindness', 'the flesh', and 'infirmity or weakness' (8) — each linked with one of the three aspects of human nature commonly identified in scholastic philosophy, namely reason (9), and will (10), and their application to particular circumstances, i.e. for Erasmus assessing whether particular decisions lead to or away from Christ (11–12). Right understanding of who we are is crucial, hence is re-emphasised (13–15). There follow miscellaneous rules (16–26), a further underlining of the Christian view of life (27–29), a reminder of the urgency of the task (30–31), and an appendix dealing specifically with some of the deadly sins (32–38).

The backdrop for Erasmus is a world that has repudiated peace,[9] in its broad sense of the pleasant harmony of a life held together inwardly and outwardly by orderly fulfilment of God's law. Radical disconnection was the enemy, most culpably among theologians — angry professionals disengaged from real Christian thinking, interested more in secondary material and peripheral agendas than in sharing Christian truth and goodness, men with a world view that broke up reality (socially and intellectually)[10] and bore little resemblance to the lively warmth of Scripture or the early Church Fathers — and among monks, purveying a system of good works and guilt which infantilised ordinary Christians through its focus on particular rules and images.[11] Erasmus detected symbiosis between a theory that general characteristics are real in name only and a religious practice that was Christian in name only: two kinds of 'nominalism', so to speak.[12]

Like St Paul (and Luther and Tyndale) he believed that human nature is

M. Jane, OP (Rockford: Tan Books, 1978), and *Johannes Tauler: Sermons*, trans. by Maria Shrady (Mahwah: Paulist Press, 1985), with introduction by Josef Schmidt.

[9] Treated extensively in his *The Complaint of Peace* (1517); see its 1559 English translation, ed. by Alex Davis, in volume two.

[10] For the philosophical background see Alister E. McGrath, *The Intellectual Origins of the European Reformation* (Oxford: Blackwell, 2004), and Anthony Kenny, *Medieval Philosophy* (Oxford: Oxford University Press, 2005). To pursue passing references in the text to personalities and ideas, see particularly *ODCC*.

[11] See J. Huizinga, *The Waning of the Middle Ages* (Harmondsworth: Penguin, 1955), ch. 12. The English reader had to wait until 1549 to experience the full force of E.'s denunciation of religious stupidity, in exploiter and exploited alike: see Chaloner's *The Praise of Folly* (ed. by Alex Davis) in volume two.

[12] But lumping together Duns Scotus (*c.* 1265–1308) with the nominalist Ockham (*c.* 1285–1347) — both were Franciscans — was polemical and unfair. Scotus was not a nominalist. Like Thomas Aquinas (Dominican, *c.* 1225–1274) he believed that general properties are as real as particular things, though he did believe (an idea taken up by later humanists) that each particular has its unique 'universal' or 'thisness'. The Franciscan spiritual tradition made good use of nominalism, emphasising particularised love and will, and God's freedom to reveal or not to reveal his truth. For a longer discussion of scholasticism and Erasmus, see *Exhortation* below (ed. by Alex Davis).

distorted and incompetent and needs to be set free, initially through understanding who we are, especially in the light of Plato and the Bible. His Platonism is the 'new' Platonism revived in Florence and significantly modified through the influence of Aristotle,[13] who (despite his dry logic and his vulnerability to deterministic interpretations) could be a firm ally to Christians, especially in moral matters. Without Aristotle and the Stoics, Platonism was liable to be too disjunctive ('spirit versus body') for a religion based on the Incarnation. His metaphysic of form and matter (developed by Aquinas, 'perhaps the first Christian philosopher to take the corporeal character of human existence calmly')[14] held the different layers together, and Erasmus regularly discusses ethical situations like a practical-minded Aristotelian. His 'philosophy of Christ' (PE 92)[15] is personal, not academic, the genitive being chiefly definitional ('which is'), and — in the *Enchiridion* at least — he skirts around the deeper philosophical or theological implications of taking Christ as the archetype of wisdom who came and lived and died 'for us'.[16] It suffices that he is real and that he authoritatively embodies goodness: the superlative but accessible epitome of our species.

For keeping our lifestyle in focus we need the Bible — the *Enchiridion* is steeped in biblical references and allusions — but read with an imaginative common sense (present in non-Christians too) that can detect significant undertones of meaning planted in Scripture and nature by their creator God.[17] The third-century Church Father Origen (trained in Platonism as well as Scripture) became the recognised master of this, and for a sixteenth-century humanist the liberation of language from literality was an important feature of the new project. The rationale had been set out by Aquinas:

> The author of Holy Writ is God, in whose power it is to signify His meaning, not by words only (as man can do), but also by things themselves. [...] Therefore that first signification whereby words signify things belongs to the first sense, the historical or literal. That signification whereby things signified

---

[13] An influence going back at least to the third century. See Paul Henry, SJ, 'The Place of Plotinus in the History of Thought', in *Plotinus: The Enneads*, abridged by John Dillon (Harmondsworth: Penguin, 1991), pp. xlii–lxxxiii. A Latin translation of Plotinus (c. 205-270) was produced in Florence by Marsilio Ficino in 1492.

[14] Kenneth E. Kirk, *The Vision of God* (London: Longmans, Green and Co., 1932), p. 384.

[15] For discussion of this important concept (though the phrase does not occur in the *Enchiridion* proper) see Introduction by John W. O'Malley in *CWE* 66. xxi–xxviii; also the 'Prefatory Epistle' below (i.e. E.'s letter 858 to Paul Volz, in *CWE* 6. 72–91).

[16] But 'personal' does not mean 'content-less'. Explicitly or latently, the live practical imprint of the mind of Christ in his followers carries definite ideas both *from* and *about* him. For E.'s summary see his letter to Jan Šlechta (1039, in *CWE* 7. 120–28), particularly lines 245–54 (reproduced in O'Malley, 66. xxiv); also PE below, e.g. p. 40, lines 169f.

[17] E. uses the *Vulg.* A modern English rendering of its post-Tridentine revision is helpful: *A Translation from the Latin Vulgate*, by Ronald Knox (London: Burnes and Oates, 1955).

by words have themselves also a signification is called the spiritual sense, which is based on the literal, and presupposes it.[18]

Tyndale was more wary:[19]

> Thou shalt understand therefore that the scripture hath but one sense which is the literal sense. [...] And if thou leave the literal sense thou canst not but go out of the way. Neverthelater° the scripture useth proverbs, similitudes, riddles or allegories as all other speeches do, but that which the proverb, similitude, riddle or allegory signifieth is ever the literal sense which thou must seek out diligently.[20]

He blames Origen for throwing open too widely the area where potential significance might be 'discovered',[21] but Origen had been alert to the danger. When Noah was told to use 'squared planks' (*Sept.*; *NRSV* 'cypress') in building the Ark, this meant that we should take our ideas

> not from the volumes of secular authors, but from the prophetic and apostolic volumes. For these authors, who have been hewn by diverse temptations, all vices having been curtailed and excised, contain life which has been squared and set free in every part. For the authors of secular books [...] speak indeed in a lofty manner and use flowery eloquence; they have not, however, acted as they have spoken.[22]

In Augustine's words, 'a good and a true Christian should realise that truth belongs to his Lord, wherever it is found':[23] but the temple of God is the place for setting these truths in a clear light.[24]

Erasmus suggests two scriptural resource-points to ensure fruitful study. One is spirit (or Spirit), what good philosophers mean by 'reason', the power to sense how things seem from God's point of view, appreciating particulars (words in a sentence, members of a species) with that all-at-once affection and interest with which God regards them, and accordingly perceiving everyday things and people in a more Christlike way. The second is membership of the body (or Body),

---

[18] Aquinas, *Summa Theologica*, trans. by Fathers of the English Dominican Province, 3 vols (London: Burnes and Oates, 1947), I, q. 1, art. 10.
[19] But see Brian Cummings, 'William Tyndale and Erasmus on How to Read the Bible: A Newly Discovered Manuscript of the English *Enchiridion*', *Reformation*, 23.1 (2018), 29–52 (esp. pp. 49–51).
[20] William Tyndale, *The Obedience of a Christian Man* [1528], ed. by David Daniell (Harmondsworth: Penguin, 2000), p. 156.
[21] *Obedience*, p. 160.
[22] Origen, *Homilies on Genesis and Exodus*, trans. by Ronald E. Heine (Washington: The Catholic University of America Press, 1982), p. 87.
[23] *On Christian Teaching*, trans. by R. P. H. Green (Oxford: Oxford University Press, 1999), II. 72.
[24] See below 388f. (p. 67), 1761f., and 4768f.

specifically the Christian Church as the 'body of Christ' but by implication all humanity. (For Erasmus, like Paul, 'member' has its organic sense of 'part of an integral' rather than 'one of a community'.)[25] An internalised understanding of humanity as 'spirit' and corporate 'body', applied to the 'craft of blessed living', provides an antidote to the externalism of much current Christianity, as well as to the opposite excesses of mystical withdrawal: rational solidarity in place of chronic dismemberment.

The 'Manual' has little to say about sacraments, reverence for the saints, techniques of prayer, modes of worship, and so forth, but two pieces of pragmatic advice are offered: 'remember your Baptism' and 'ponder the Cross'. In a religious world overflowing with vows, remember that the primary vow, the supreme act of Christian definition (and the great leveller of lay and cleric), is baptism — an event which also equips its recipients with strength to live well. As for visualising the crucifixion, this popular devotional practice led easily to emotional self-indulgence. Here is the fourteenth-century Dominican John Tauler:

> Now they say this to me: 'Sir, I meditate on the suffering of our Lord every day, how he stood before Pilate, before Herod, how he was flayed at the pillar, I see him in this place and in that.' Let me teach you something concerning this: you should not see your God only as a man but you should see him as the greatest, most powerful and eternal God who created Heaven and Earth with a single word and who can destroy them again; you should see him as beyond all being and knowledge. Now consider that God wished to be broken for his poor creatures and then blush for shame that you, a mere mortal, have ever thought of honour, advantage and vanity.[26]

Erasmus (without denying the value of interiorising, or that Christ had reconstituted the human species through sacrificial dying as well as living) proposes functional authenticity as the primary corrective: look at the Cross for lessons to fortify your moral conduct.[27]

A reader or translator with Reformed sympathies might welcome Erasmus's call for authenticity but wonder whether it merely left us with a different kind of externality and 'justification by works' — too much about freedom, not enough about grace, too much about thinking and doing, not enough about forgiveness and love received. Erasmus (like Aquinas, whose theology suffered similar reproaches) believes that God has devolved upon human beings a limited but real capacity to rethink and reshape themselves. For Luther and Tyndale freedom without divine grace was merely a 'running loose' in denial of our basic helplessness and disconnection from God:

---

[25] The definitions are Dr Johnson's.
[26] Quoted in Davies, *God Within*, p. 89.
[27] See ch. 26 (p. 169).

Now when a man has learned through the commandments to recognise his helplessness and is distressed about how he might satisfy the law [...] then, being truly humbled and reduced to nothing in his own eyes, he finds in himself nothing whereby he may be justified and saved. Here the second part of Scripture comes to our aid, namely, the promises of God which declare the glory of God, saying, 'If you wish to fulfil the law and not covet, as the law demands, come, believe in Christ in whom grace, righteousness, peace, liberty, and all things are promised you.'[28]

It is not enough merely to speak about the teachings and works of Christ

as if the knowledge of these would suffice for the conduct of life. [...] Rather ought Christ to be preached to the end that faith in him may be established that he may not only be Christ, but be Christ for you and me, and that what is said of him and is denoted in his name may be effectual in us.[29]

Faced with its swirling variety of implicit readers and its shifting doctrinal and philosophical tributaries, a translator of the *Enchiridion* has a delicate task: how, if at all, to singularise its meaning. By and large Tyndale (if it is he) opts, even in marginal notes, not to homogenise or qualify or judge what Erasmus has to say. He lets it be. Behind the many scribal imperfections — usually obvious enough to be harmless, and resolvable by reference to the Latin — is a translator sure-footed, learned, articulate, and confident enough to 'love, honour, and obey' his text. If he is not Tyndale he is someone else with the makings of a great Bible translator (and who conceivably might that be?). He knows not to tamper, has a pretty good understanding of when amplifications can be incorporated in the text and when they should be fenced off in the margin, and keeps the communicative impulse alive — in all these respects responding to major concerns of Reformers and humanists alike, weary of interpositions and remodulations official or unofficial in what they read, and yearning for a straight encounter with what was 'there'.

It is not certain which Latin version the translator was using (for 1533 the notion of a *single* source text is anyhow problematic), and the editors of two major Latin editions in modern times report that differences in the various printings are insignificant — from the first in 1503, through the important 1518 edition of Froben at Basel (by which time some eight editions had been published, and which included for the first time the Prefatory Epistle to Paul Volz),[30] to the spate of

---

[28] Martin Luther, *The Freedom of a Christian*, trans. by W. A. Lambert, rev. by Harold J. Grimm, in *Three Treatises* [1520], with *To the Christian Nobility of the German Nation* and *The Babylonian Captivity of the Church* (Philadelphia: Fortress Press, 1978), p. 283.

[29] Luther, *Freedom*, pp. 292–93.

[30] That 1523 does not translate PE (it is supplied in this edition from 1533) need not be significant. Readers and translators often skip prefaces.

editions which followed in the early 1520s.[31] Since many marginal notes in 1523 are original to it, tracking a source text through comparison of the margins of different Latin editions appears fruitless.[32] Reproduction of misprints offers a livelier hope, and there are at least two instances where an unexpected 1523 rendering is warranted by the Strasburg edition of Knobloch (August 1522), but not apparently (jointly) elsewhere: at line 1372 the usual 'fili' (thread) is translated as 'children' (as if it is 'filii'), and at 3147 the usual 'ferae' (wild beasts) is translated as 'which thing men do almost everywhere' (as if it is 'fere'). The argument is not conclusive[33] and a translator might use more than one version, but the date makes this edition a strong candidate, pending further analysis.

In place of the compact energy of the Latin, the translator offers his own euphony, balance, clarity, and lightness, with something of Erasmus's homespun or proverbial quality.[34] Some adjustments are purely navigational, keeping readers on track ('I mean', 'that is to say'), others define ('labyrinth' is 'a certain cumbrous maze under the ground') or expound ('to do a good thing and not well' is 'to do a thing and not with due circumstance and for an honest purpose'). An insertion or replacement may be very brief ('God' or 'Christ') or quite long: where Erasmus in eleven words urges his readers — if they have to honour the saints — at least to pick out relevant vices and virtues, 1523 has 'for the honour of every saint (saint by saint) look thou change and put away all thy vices (vice by vice singularly), or else study to embrace and counterfeit some one virtue singularly in every saint, such as thou perceivest to have reigned most chiefly in every saint singularly of them whom thou worshippest so specially'. Lengthy, but note the precision.[35]

He sometimes avoids loaded words, notably 'piety' or 'pious' (in 1523 'charitable things', 'good and obedient', 'good living, the love of God', 'perfect honouring of

---

[31] See *Erasmus: Ausgewählte Werke*, ed. by Hajo and Annemarie Holborn (Munich: Beck'sche Verlag, 1964), p. xiii, and *ASD* v-8, ed. by J. Domański (Leiden: Brill, 2016), p. 45. The latter has been used in the present edition when L. is quoted.

[32] Though composed (presumably by T.) after the translation proper, these rarely correct scribal errors, even when those directly confute what the note says — as if the 'fair copy' is to be left unspoiled for the time being (consistent with the story that the translation was given or loaned to his employers, Sir John and Lady Walsh; see Daniell, *William Tyndale*, p. 63). Most of the original ones explain classical or biblical allusions. Many were retained in 1533 and 1534: see O'Donnell, *An English Version*.

[33] The translator might have been using a standard text and misread its 'fili' and 'ferae' as 'filii' and 'fere', or assumed a misprint, even a slip by Erasmus — the 'thread' was not strictly Daedalus's at all, but Ariadne's (Daedalus escaped from Minos with wings, so 'children' would be 'followers'). The reading 'fere', though rare after 1515, was familiar enough before then.

[34] The Latin *Enchiridion* (excluding the Prefatory Letter) has about 40,000 words, 1523 approximately 66,000, and the faithful English version of Charles Fantazzi in *CWE* 66 about 50,000.

[35] 2207f.; 'singularly' is 'particularly' and 'counterfeit' is 'imitate'.

God', 'Christian', 'devout and holy', 'virtuous and holy', etc.); less frequently 'merit' (a 'bene merenti', one who merits good from me, becomes one 'who had showed kindness, or done me any good'); and for 'ecclesia' he happily uses 'Church', not the controversial 'congregation' of *NT* 1526.

For clarity he may leave out a phrase altogether, or substitute one not requiring background knowledge. 'Pythagorean' is dropped from a mention of modest 'herbs and fruits' and 'Greek symposium' becomes 'pastime together at the tavern or alehouse'. Metaphors are sometimes changed ('seaweed' becomes 'rush of straw') or added ('snails in winter').[36] An abstract phrase may be replaced by something more vivid or pictorial: 'grown old in their way of life' is 'waxed even crooked with long countenance in their own imaginations or inventions'.

A common technique is to translate a single Latin word with an English pairing (or longer — as many as five words),[37] sometimes to unpack a meaning (L. 'virtutem' is 'strength or virtue'), often retaining the Latin (L. 'iniquitas' is 'iniquity or churlishness'); but sometimes, it seems, simply to enjoy the fulness which English offers ('gloria' is 'glory, praise, or fame', 'colluvies' is 'a filthy puddle, a gout, or a sink'). The translator has a keen ear for alliteration ('purged, and made perfect', 'favoured, feigned, or fashioned', 'pleasant poison and a merry mischief'). The occasional expletive or apostrophe (e.g. 'Oh, good Lord') keeps up the emotional charge.[38] Formally, the multiples also help to rein in the 'headlong' quality of the English, giving it some resemblance to the compact centripetality of the Latin and providing the reader with time to pause and savour the meaning. All these techniques help in conveying information and the original persuasive intent. They rarely amount to modification of the meaning.

Reading *1533*[39] after *1523* is a little like coming to the *KJB* after acquaintance with Tyndale's Bible. Some changes involve mere reversal of word order, some the replacement of concrete by abstract (or vice versa). Some make *1533* less vivid or concise, but others more. In some places a gloss or internal expansion added in *1523* is removed, in other places fuller (and sometimes clearer) explanation is added. Sometimes (but not always) there is closer adherence to the Latin.[40] *1533* is less nervous about 'piety', but any change in the balance of theological sensitivities is slight. Navigational aids are sometimes removed, and usually when they are retained the Latin has them too. Multiples of words are sometimes

[36] This is in *1523* but not in *1533*.
[37] See 4519.
[38] On the three principal tasks of oratory — to instruct, delight, and move — see Augustine, *On Christian Teaching* IV. 74.
[39] O'Donnell, *An English Version* indicates *1533*'s differences from *1534*. For a part-modernised version of *1533* see *A Book Called in Latin Enchiridion Militis Christiani* (London: Methuen, 1905).
[40] No revising appears to have been done simply stylistically on the basis of the English alone: there is evidence of knowledge of the Latin (though less perhaps of Greek: see note on PE 205).

collapsed, sometimes expanded. Tenses are occasionally reconfigured, with apparently a reduction in the overt presence of the subjunctive. If some additions seem particularly Tyndale-like (and so evidence that T.'s involvement with the work did not end in 1523) — 1533's 'tumble and walter in our beds' for 1523's 'be locked up in our closets', or the catchier 'say many Lady psalters or Saint Catherine's knots' for 1523's 'to iterate, to repeat thy devotions and prayers appointed, which thou customably sayest day by day' — it is not difficult conversely to find instances that disappoint. And in general it is difficult to see a single policy behind the changes in 1533. The safest hypothesis, pending more research, is that it embodies successive stages of adjustment, including at least one that involved 1523's translator (probably Tyndale). It had a long life ahead of it.[41]

Further Reading

BIETENHOLZ, PETER G., *Encounters with a Radical Erasmus: Erasmus' Work as a Source of Radical Thought in Early Modern Europe* (Toronto: University of Toronto Press, 2008)

CHADWICK, OWEN, *The Reformation* (Harmondsworth: Penguin Books, 1968)

COPLESTON, FREDERICK, *A History of Philosophy, Vol. III* (Late Medieval and Renaissance Philosophy) (Westminster, MD: Newman Press, 1953)

CUMMINGS, BRIAN, 'William Tyndale and Erasmus on How to Read the Bible: A Newly Discovered Manuscript of the English Enchiridion', *Reformation*, 23.1 (2018), 29–52

DANIELL, DAVID, *William Tyndale: A Biography* (New Haven: Yale University Press, 1994)

DAVIES, OLIVER, *God Within: The Mystical Tradition of Northern Europe* (London: Darton, Longman and Todd, 2006)

DEMOLEN, R. L., ed., *Essays on the Works of Erasmus* (New Haven: Yale University Press, 1978)

ERASMUS, *Opera Omnia Desiderii Erasmi Roterdami [Amsterdam edition]*, v-8, ed. by J. Domański (Leiden: Brill, 2016) [in French]

—— *The Handbook of the Christian Soldier*, trans. by Charles Fantazzi, in Collected Works of Erasmus, vol. 66, ed. by John. W. O'Malley (Toronto: Toronto University Press, 1988)

—— *Enchiridion Militis Christiani, An English Version* [1534], Early English Text Society, ed. by Anne M. O'Donnell SND (Oxford: Oxford University Press, 1981)

---

[41] See Douglas H. Parker, 'Religious Polemics and Two Sixteenth Century English Editions of Erasmus's *Enchiridion Militis Christiani*, 1546–1561', *Renaissance and Reformation*, 9.3 (1973), 94–107, and 'The English "Enchiridion Militis Christiani" in the Seventeenth, Eighteenth, and Nineteenth Centuries', *Renaissance and Reformation*, 19.3 (1995), 5–21. Among early editions was an abridgement by the Bible translator Coverdale (1545). There were at least three twentieth-century English retranslations for the general reader, 'which can only be described as lacunar, inaccurate, and untrue to the Erasmian mode of expression', says Charles Fantazzi (*CWE* 66. 7) — but attesting the work's longevity.

Huizinga, J., *Erasmus of Rotterdam* (London: Phaidon Press, 1952)
—— *The Waning of the Middle Ages* (Harmondsworth: Penguin, 1955)
Kenny, Anthony, *Medieval Philosophy* (Oxford: Oxford University Press, 2005)
Livingstone, E. A., ed., *The Oxford Dictionary of the Christian Church*, 3rd edn (Oxford: Oxford University Press, 1997)
McConica, James, *Erasmus* (Oxford: Oxford University Press, 1991)
McGrath, Alister E., *The Intellectual Origins of the European Reformation* (Oxford: Blackwell, 2004)
Moynahan, Brian, *William Tyndale: If God Spare My Life* (London: Abacus, 2003)
Mozley, J. F., 'The English Enchiridion of Erasmus, 1533', *The Review of English Studies*, 20.78 (1944), 97–107
—— *William Tyndale* (London: SPCK, 1937)
Rhodes, Neil, Gordon Kendal, and Louise Wilson (eds), *English Renaissance Translation Theory* (London: MHRA, 2013)
Rummel, Erika, *Erasmus* (London: Continuum, 2004)
Tyndale, William, *New Testament 1526*, ed. by David Daniell (New Haven: Yale University Press, 1989)

PREFATORY EPISTLE

[*1533* a2ʳ]¹ Erasmus Rotterdam sendeth greeting to the reverend father in Christ (and lord), the lord Paul Volz,² the most religious abbot of the monastery the which is commonly called Hugh's Court.

Albeit, most virtuous father, that the little book to the which I have given this name or title *Enchiridion militis christiani* — which many a day ago I made for myself only and for a certain friend of mine (being utterly unlearned) — hath begun to mislike° and displease me the less, forasmuch as I do see that it is allowed° of you and other virtuous and learned men such as you be, of whom (as ye are indeed endued with godly learning and also with learned godliness) I know nothing to be approved but [a2ᵛ] that which is both holy and also clerkly:° yet it hath begun well nigh also to please and like° me now when I see it (after that it hath been so oftentimes printed) yet still to be desired and greatly called for, as if it were a new work made of late — if so be the printers do not lie to flatter me withal.°

But again° there is another thing which oftentimes grieveth me in my mind, that a certain well learned friend of mine long ago said, very properly and sharply checking° me: that there was more holiness seen in the little book than in the whole author and maker thereof. Indeed he spake these words in his jesting bourdingly,° but would to God he had not spoken so truly as he bourded bitterly! And that grieveth me so much the more, because the same thing hath chanced to come likewise to pass in him for the changing of whose manners principally I took upon me this labour and travail: for he also not only hath not withdrawn himself from the court, but is daily much deeper drowned therein than he was aforetime. For what good purpose I cannot tell, but (as he confesseth himself) with much great misery. And yet for all that I do not greatly pity my friend, because that peradventure [a3ʳ] adversity of fortune may teach him once° to repent himself and to amend, seeing that he would not follow and do after my counsel and admonitions.

And verily — though I, enforcing° me to the same thing and purpose, have been turned and tossed with so many chances and tempests that Ulysses (a man living ever in trouble, whom Homer speaketh of) might be counted in comparison

---

¹ *1533* 2b] The Prefatory Epistle does not appear in *1523* and is here supplied from the first printed edition (*1533*). The corresponding facing-page images (2020) on EEBO are 8–24.

² (and lord), the lord] L. suggests that both 'lord's apply to Volz, expressing his office (monastic superior) and his title, but *1533* may intend with the bracketing to apply the first to Christ. Paul Volz (1480–1544) became Abbot of the Benedictine community of Hügshofen in 1512; he exchanged correspondence with E. and was by 1526 a supporter of Reform.

to me even Polycrates (who ever lived in prosperity without any manner trouble) — I do not utterly repent me of my labour, seeing it hath moved and provoked so many unto the study° of godly virtue. Nor I myself am not utterly to be blamed and rebuked, although my living be not in all points agreeing to my own precepts and counsels. It is some part of godliness when one with all his heart desireth and is willing to be made good and virtuous; nor such a mind, so well intending, I suppose is not to be cast away although his purpose be not ever luckily° performed. To this we ought to endeavour ourselves all our life long, and no doubt but — by the reason that we so oftentimes shall attempt it — once at the last we shall attain it. Also, he hath dispatched a good piece of a doubtful journey who hath [a3ᵛ] learned well of the journey the way.

Therefore am I nothing moved with the mocks of certain persons, who despise this little book as nothing erudite and clerkly, saying that it might have been made of° a child that learneth his ABC, because it treateth nothing of Duns's questions[3] — as though nothing without those could be done with learning. I do not care if it be not so quick,° so° it be godly. Let it not make them instructed and ready to disputations in schools, so that it make them apt to keep Christ's peace. Let it not be profitable or helping for the disputation in divinity, so it make for a divine life.

For what good should it do to treat of that thing that every man intermeddleth° with? Who hath not in handling questions of divinity, or what else do all our swarms of schoolmen°? There be almost as many commentaries upon the Master of the *Sentences*[4] as be names of divines. There is neither measure nor number of summularies° who (after the manner of apothecaries) mingle oftentimes sundry things together and make of old things new, of new things old, of one thing many, of many things one.

How can it be that these great volumes instruct us to live well and after a Christian manner, which a man [a4ʳ] in all his life cannot have leisure once to look over? in like manner as if a physician should prescribe unto him that lieth sick in peril of death to read Jacques Desparts[5] or such other huge volumes, saying that there he should find remedy for his disease — but in the mean time the patient dieth, wanting° present remedy wherewith he might be helped. In such a fugitive life it is necessary to have a ready medicine at the hand. How many volumes have they made of 'restitution', of 'confession', of 'slander', and other things innumerable? And though they bolt° and search out by piecemeal everything by itself, and so define everything as if they mistrusted all other men's

---

[3] Duns's questions] The medieval question-and-answer mode of dealing with a particular issue was used with celebrated forensic skill by Duns Scotus.

[4] Master of the *Sentences*] Peter Lombard (*c.* 1100–1160), whose *Sentences* was a primary theological text and basis for commentaries by others.

[5] Jacques Desparts] A doctor and teacher at Paris (died 1458) whose commentary on the Arabian commentator on Aristotle, Avicenna, was published in 1498.

wits° — yea, as though they mistrusted the goodness and mercy of God while they do prescribe how he ought to punish and reward every fact,° either good or bad — yet they agree not amongst themselves, nor yet sometimes do open the thing plainly, if a man would look near upon it: so much diversity both of wits and circumstances is there.

Moreover, although it were so that they had determined all things well and truly, yet besides this (that they handle and treat of these things after a barbarous and unpleasant fashion) [a4ᵛ] there is not one amongst a thousand that can have any leisure to read over these volumes. Or who is able to bear about with him *Secundam secundae*, the work of Saint Thomas?[6] And yet there is no man but he ought to use° a good life: to the which Christ would that the way should be plain and open for every man — and that not by inexplicable crooks° of disputations not able to be resolved, but by a true and a sincere faith, and charity not feigned, whom hope doth follow which is never ashamed.[7] And finally let the great doctors — who must needs be but few in comparison to all other men — study and busy themselves in those great volumes: and yet nevertheless the unlearned and rude° multitude which Christ died for ought to be provided for.

And he hath taught a great portion of Christian virtue who hath inflamed men unto the love thereof. The wise king,[8] when he did teach his son true wisdom, took much more pain in exhorting him thereunto than in teaching him; as who should say that to love wisdom were in a manner to have attained it. It is a great shame and rebuke both for lawyers and physicians that they have, of a set purpose and for the nonce,° made their art [a5ʳ] and science full of difficulty and hard to be attained or come by, to the intent that both their gains and advantage might be the more plentiful, and their glory and praise among the unlearned people the greater. But it is a much more shameful thing to do the same in the philosophy of Christ, but rather contrariwise we ought to endeavour ourselves with all our strengths to make it so easy as can be and plain to every man. Nor let not this be our study, to appear learned ourselves, but to allure very many to a Christian man's life.

Preparation and ordinance° is made now for war to be made against the Turks;[9] which for whatsoever purpose it is begun, we ought to pray, not that it may turn to the profit° of a few certain persons, but that it may be to the common and

---

[6] Saint Thomas] The 'second part of the second part' of Aquinas's *Summa Theologica* deals with the major virtues: theological (faith, hope, charity) and moral (prudence, justice, courage, temperance).

[7] Cf. 1 Tim. 1. 5 and Rom. 5. 5.

[8] wise king] Solomon; probably alluding to the tenor of Proverbs in general. See also Wisd. 6. 11–20.

[9] Turks] For more on the Turkish wars of the early sixteenth century see *Bellum* (ed. by Neil Rhodes) in volume two.

general profit of all men. But what think you should come of it if, to such of them as shall be overcome (for I do not suppose that they shall all be killed with weapons), we shall lay the works of Ockham, Durandus, Duns, Gabriel, Alvarus, or any such schoolmen,[10] for the intent to bring them in mind to take Christ's profession upon them? What shall they imagine and think in their minds (for surely even they, though they be nought else, are men [a5ᵛ] and have wit and reason) when they shall hear those thorny and cumbrous, inextricable, subtle imaginations of 'instants', of 'formalities', of 'quiddities', of 'relation': namely° when they shall see these great doctors and teachers of religion and holiness so far disagreeing, and of so sundry opinions among themselves, that oftentimes they dispute and reason so long one with another until they change colour, and be pale, and revile one another, spitting each at other, and finally dealing buffets and blows each to other? when they shall see the Black friars fight and scold° for their Thomas, and then the Grey friars matched° with them, defending on the other party° their subtle and fervent hot doctors (whom they call 'seraphic'), some speaking as 'reals',° some as 'nominals'°? when they shall also see the thing to be of so great difficulty that they can never discuss° sufficiently with what words they may speak of Christ — as though one did deal or had to do with a wayward spirit which he had raised up unto his own destruction if he did fail never so little in the prescribed words of conjuring;° and not rather with our most merciful Saviour, who desireth nothing else of us but a pure life and a simple?[11]

I beseech thee, for the love of God, show me [a6ʳ] what shall we bring about with all these reckonings, especially if our manners and our life be like to the proud doctrine and learning? and if they shall see and well perceive our ambition and desirousness of honour by our gorgeousness (more than ever any tyrant did use); our avarice and covetousness by our bribing and polling;° our lecherousness by the defiling of maidens and wives; our cruelness by the oppressions done of us? With what face,° or how for shame, shall we offer to them the doctrine of Christ, which is far away contrary to all these things?

The best way and most effectual to overcome and win the Turks should be if they shall perceive that thing which Christ taught and expressed in his living to shine in us; if they shall perceive that we do not highly gape° for their empires, do not desire their gold and goods, do not covet their possessions, but that we

---

[10] schoolmen] A miscellany of (in E.'s estimation) darkeners and fracturers of Christian truth; cf. the roll-call in *Exhortation*, p. 238f., notes 50 and 51. Durandus of St-Pourçain (*c.* 1275–1334) was a bishop and early nominalist, Gabriel Biel (*c.* 1420–1495) a philosopher and member of the influential devotional movement 'Brethren of the Common Life'; Alvarus Pelagius (*c.* 1280–1352) taught canon and civil law at Bologna.

[11] Black friars were Dominicans, popularly distinguished for cool rationality, while Grey friars (to whom Scotus and Ockham belonged) were Franciscans, who in contrast emphasised a passionate love of God like that ascribed to the celestial order of 'seraphs': the Hebrew etymology of this term suggests 'burning heat', but E. claims they are 'heated' in the wrong way.

seek nothing else but only their souls' health and the glory of God. This is that right true and effectuous° divinity, the which in time past subdued unto Christ arrogant and proud philosophers, and also the mighty and invincible princes. And if we thus do, then shall Christ ever be present and help us. For truly it is not meet° nor convenient° to declare ourselves Christian men by this proof or token, if [a6ᵛ] we kill very many, but rather if we save very many; not if we send thousands of heathen people to hell, but if we make many infidels faithful; not if we cruelly curse and excommunicate them, but if we with devout prayers and with all our hearts desire their health,° and pray unto God to send them better minds. If this be not our intent, it shall sooner come to pass that we shall degenerate and turn into Turks ourselves than that we shall cause them to become Christian men. And although the chance of war, which is ever doubtful and uncertain, should fall so luckily to us that we had got the victory, so should it be brought to pass that the Pope's dominion and his cardinals' might be enlarged: but not the kingdom of Christ, which finally flourisheth and is in prosperity if faith, love, peace, and chastity be quick° and strong.

Which thing I trust shall be brought to pass by the good governance and provision of the Pope Leo the tenth, unless the great trouble and rage of worldly business pluck him from his very good purpose another way. Christ doth profess to be Primate and Head himself in the heavenly kingdom, which never doth flourish but when celestial things be advanced. Nor Christ did not die for this purpose, that goods of the [a7ʳ] world, that riches, that armour, and the rest of ruffling° fashion of the world, be now in the hands and rule of certain priests: which things were wont to be in the hands of the Gentiles,° or at the least amongst lay princes not much differing from Gentiles.

But in my mind it were the best, before we should try° with them in battle, to attempt them with epistles and some little books. But with what manner of epistles? Not with threatening epistles, or with books full of tyranny, but with those which might show fatherly charity and resemble the very heart and mind of Peter and Paul, and which should not only pretend° and show outwardly the title of the Apostles, but which also should savour° and taste of the efficacy and strength of the Apostles — not because I do not know that all the true fountain and vein of Christ's philosophy[12] is hid in the Gospel and the Epistles of the Apostles, but the strange manner of phrase, and oftentimes the troublous speaking of divers° crooked figures and tropes,° be of so great difficulty that oftentimes we ourselves also must labour right sore before we can perceive them.

Therefore, in my opinion, the best were that some both well learned men, and good of [a7ᵛ] living, should have this office° assigned and put unto them: to make a collection and to gather the sum of Christ's philosophy out of the pure fountain of the Gospel and the Epistles and most approved interpreters, and so plainly that

---

[12] Christ's philosophy] See Introduction, p. 28, and p. 47 (note 41).

yet it might be clerkly and erudite, and so briefly that it might also be plain. Those things which concern faith or belief, let them be contained in a few articles. Those also that appertain to the manner of living, let them be showed and taught in few words, and that after such fashion that they may perceive the yoke of Christ to be pleasant and easy,[13] and not grievous and painful; so that they may perceive that they have got fathers and not tyrants; feeders° and not robbers, pillers,° nor pollers; and that they be called to their souls' health and not compelled to servitude. Undoubted they also be men, neither their hearts be of so hard iron or adamant but that they may be mollified and won with benefits and kindness, wherewith even very wild beasts be waxed gentle and tame. And the most effectuous thing is the true verity of Christ. But let the Pope also command them whom he appointeth to this business that they [a8ʳ] never swerve nor go from the true pattern and example of Christ, nor in any place have any respect° to the carnal affects° and desires of men.

And such a thing my mind was about° to bring to pass, as well as I could, when I made this book of *Enchiridion*. I did see the common people of Christendom, not only in affects[14] but also in opinions, to be corrupted. I considered the most part of those who profess themselves to be pastors and doctors to abuse the titles of Christ to their proper° advantage. And yet will I make no mention of those men after° whose will and pleasure the world is ruled and turned up and down, [at] whose vices (though they be never so manifest) a man may scarcely once winch.° And in such great darkness, in such great troublous ruffling of the world, in so great diversity of men's opinions, whither should we rather fly for succour than to the very,° great and sure anchor of Christ's doctrine, which is the Gospel? Who, being a good man indeed, doth not see and lament this marvellous corrupt world? When was there ever more tyranny? When did avarice reign more largely° and less punished? When were ceremonies at any time more in estimation? [a8ᵛ] When did our iniquity so largely flow with more liberty? When was ever charity so cold?[15] What is brought,[16] what is read, what is decreed or determined, but it tasteth and savoureth of ambition and lucre? Oh, how unfortunate were we if Christ had not left some sparks of his doctrine unto us and (as it were) lively° and everlasting veins of his godly mind!

Hereto therefore we must enforce ourselves: to know these sparks,[17] leaving the coals of men's fantasies. Let us seek these veins until we find fresh water which

---

[13] Matt. 11. 30.
[14] affects] 1533 'effecte', but L. 'affectibus'.
[15] Matt. 24. 12.
[16] is brought] Translating non-committally the ambiguous 'affertur' (is conveyed, presented); perhaps just 'is done'.
[17] know these sparks] Gk 'anazōpurōmen' ('kindle') — a reference to Paul (II Tim. 1. 6), as L. makes clear in words omitted in Eng.

springeth into everlasting life. We delve and dig the ground marvellously deep for to pluck out riches, which nourish vice — and shall we not labour then the rich earth of Christ, to get out that thing which is our souls' health? There was never no storm of vices that did so overcome and quench the heat of charity but it might be restored again at this flintstone. Christ is a stone, but this stone hath sparks of celestial fire and veins of lively water. In time past Abraham in every land did dig pits and holes, searching in every place the veins of lively water; but those same being stopped up again by the Philistines with earth, Isaac and his servants [b1^r] did delve again and — not being only content to restore the old — did also make new.[18] But then the Philistines did scold and chide — yet he did not cease from digging. And in this our time we have Philistines, who do prefer the naughty° earth to the lively fountains:[19] even° those who be worldly-wise and have their respect to earthly things, and wring and wrest God's doctrine and his Gospel to their carnal affections,° making it serve to their ambition, bolstering up therewith their filthy lucre and tyranny. And if now any Isaac or any of his family should dig and find some true and pure vein, by and by° they brabble° and cry against him, perceiving right well that that vein should hurt their advantage, should hurt their ambition, although it make never so much for the glory of Christ. Straightway they cast in naughty earth, and with a corrupt interpretation they stop up the vein and drive away the digger; or at the least they make it so muddy with clay and filthiness that whosoever drinketh thereof shall draw unto him more slime and naughtiness than he shall good liquor. They will not that those that thirst and desire righteousness do drink of the pure liquor, but they bring them unto [b1^v] their old worn and all-to-trodden cisterns, which have broken stones and mortar, but water they have none.

But yet, for all this, the very true children of Isaac (that be the true worshippers of Christ) must not be wearied and driven away from this labour — for verily even they who thrust naughty earth into the fountain of the Gospel would be counted the very worshippers of Christ, so that indeed nothing nowadays is more perilous than to teach truly Christ's learning,° so greatly have the Philistines prevailed, fighting for their earth, preaching earthly things for celestial, and men's inventions for God's commandments: that is to say, not teaching those things which make for the glory of Christ, but those things which be for their own advantage (which be pardons, compositions° and suchlike pilfery). And these they do so much more perilously, because they cloak their covetousness with the

---

[18] Gen. 26. 12-22. See Lawrence Humphrey's application of this story to the translator's role as expositor, in his *Interpretatio Linguarum* (1559), pp. 217-18, translated by Gordon Kendal in *English Renaissance Translation Theory*, ed. by Neil Rhodes, Gordon Kendal, and Louise Wilson (London: MHRA, 2013), pp. 279-80, lines 539-60.

[19] naughty earth … lively fountains] L. 'terra gratior est vitalibus fontium scatebris' ('the earth is more pleasing than the living sources of the fountains'). Perhaps 1533 took 'scatebris' ('sources') to be 'scabris' ('filthy'); 'naughty' is also added at 225 and 234 below.

titles and names of great princes, of the Pope of Rome,[20] yea, of Christ also himself. But there is no man that doth more for the Pope's profit or business than he that teacheth Christ's learning purely and truly; whereof he is the chief teacher. There is no man that doth more good to princes, or deserveth more of them, [b2ʳ] than he who endeavoureth himself that the people may be wealthy and in prosperity.

But some of the flock of schoolmen will here speak against me, saying, 'It is easy to any man to give general precepts — what is to be desired and what is to be eschewed — but what shall be answered then to those that ask counsel for so many fortunes and chances?' First, I answer that there be more diverse kinds of such worldly business than that any living person can give direct and sure answer to each one of them. Secondly, there is such diversity of circumstances, which if a man do not know, it is not well° possible to make an answer. In conclusion, I doubt greatly whether they themselves have any sure answer that they may make, seeing they differ in so many things amongst themselves. And those also who amongst them be more wise than others do not thus answer, 'This ye shall do, this ye shall not do', but of this manner, 'This in my opinion were the better, this I suppose to be tolerable'. But if we have that simple and bright eye which the Gospel speaketh of,[21] if the house of our mind have in it the candle of pure faith set upon a candlestick,[22] all these trifles shall easily be put away and avoided,° as it were clouds or mists. [b2ᵛ] If we have the rule and pattern of Christ's charity, to it we may apply and make meet all other things right easily.

'But what will ye do when this rule doth not agree with those things which have been commonly used so many hundred years, and which be ordained and established by the laws of princes (for this thing chanceth very oft)? Ye must not condemn that thing which princes do in executing their office.' But again:° Do not corrupt and defile the heavenly philosophy with men's deeds.[23] Let Christ continue and abide (as he is indeed) a very centre or middle point, unmoved, having certain circles going round about him. Move not the mark° out of its own place.

Those who be in the first circle next to the centre (that is to say next to Christ) — as,° priests, bishops, cardinals, popes, and such to whom it belongeth to follow the Lamb whithersoever he shall go[24] — let them embrace and hold fast that most pure part and, so far forth as they may, let them communicate and plenteously give the same unto their next neighbours.

In the second circle all temporal and lay princes be, who, in keeping war and

---

[20] Pope of Rome] After 1534 'bishop' was substituted for 'Pope' in Eng. versions.
[21] Matt. 6. 22.
[22] Matt. 5. 15.
[23] deeds] Here legal: L. 'decretis'.
[24] Rev. 14. 4.

making laws, after a certain manner do service to Christ, either when with rightful battle they [b3ʳ] drive away their enemies and defend and maintain the public peace and tranquillity of the commonwealth, or else when with punishment according to the laws they punish malefactors and evil-doers. And yet, because they cannot choose but of necessity be occupied and busied in such things as be joined with the most vile dregs and filth of the earth, and with the business of the world, it is jeopardous lest they do fall further from the centre and mark — as, lest they should make sometimes war for their own pleasure and not for the commonwealth; lest under the pretext of justice they should use cruelty upon those whom they might reform with mercy; lest under the title of lordship they should pill and poll those people whose goods they ought to defend.

And moreover, as Christ — like the fountain of everlasting fire[25] — doth draw next unto him the order of priests, and maketh them of like nature (that is to say, pure and clean from all corruption of worldly dregs and filthiness): so in like case it is the office of priests, and especially of the highest, so much as they can, to call and draw unto them those that be princes and have power and authority. And if it fortune at any time that war do rise suddenly in [b3ᵛ] any place, let the bishops endeavour themselves, so much as in them is, either to end the strifes and variances without shedding of blood, or — if that cannot be brought to pass, by reason of the great storms of worldly business — yet let them so do that as little blood as may be be shed, and that the war may shortly be brought to an end. In times past the bishops' authority had place even in just punishments, and hath got divers times (as Saint Augustine plainly in his epistles[26] doth testify) the malefactor from the hands of temporal judges.

For some things there be, so necessary unto the order of the commonwealth, that partly yet Christ did dissemble° at them, and partly he put them from him, and partly (neither approving nor disallowing° them) did in a manner wink° and look beside° them. He would not know° the money of Caesar, nor the scripture° upon it.[27] The tribute he commanded to be paid if it were due and debt, as though it little pertained to him, so° that God had his duty. The woman taken and found in adultery he neither condemned nor openly absolved, but only did bid her that she should no more do so.[28] Of those who were condemned of Pilate, whose blood [b4ʳ] he intermingled amongst their sacrifices, he neither said it was well done nor evil, but only threatened every man that they should be punished with a like destruction if they did not amend.[29] Moreover, when he was desired to divide the

---

[25] everlasting fire] See below (359), also Aristotle, *On the Heavens* 1. 8, and Dante, *Paradiso* 1. 97f.
[26] epistles] *1533* 'epistle' but L. (pl.) 'epistolis'.
[27] Matt. 22. 15–22.
[28] John 8. 2–11.
[29] Luke 13. 1–5.

inheritance between the two brethren, he plainly refused it as an unworthy thing for him to give judgement of such gross° matters, who did teach things heavenly.³⁰

And also, of the other part, there be certain things which he openly abhorred: as, the covetous Pharisees, the hypocrites, the proud rich folks, saying unto them, 'Woe be unto you!'³¹ He never rebuked the Apostles more sharply than when they would have been avenged, or when they were ambitious. When they asked him whether they should command fire to be sent down from heaven, to have burned up the city from whence they were shut forth, he answered and said to them, 'Ye know not of what spirit ye are'.³² When Peter was about to have called him unto the world from his Passion-suffering, he called him an 'adversary'.³³ When they contended about pre-eminence, which of them should be the best, how often and how many ways doth he call them back to a contrary mind?³⁴

And other things there be which he teacheth and commandeth openly [b4ᵛ] to be observed: as, not to resist evil,³⁵ to do good to thine enemies,³⁶ to use meekness of mind,³⁷ and other like.

These must be departed° asunder, and every° of them set in order in its own place. Let us not therefore straightway make Christ an author of all things which be done by princes and temporal officers, nor defend it (as we call it) to be done 'by God's law'. They deal and meddle with many things which be low and gross, not altogether of the very pureness of a Christian man; yet they be not to be rebuked, inasmuch as they be necessary to the maintenance of order to be observed. Nor we be not, by the ministering of their office, made good; albeit that by them it is caused that we be less evil, and that they who be evil do less hurt and noyance° to the commonwealth. And therefore they also ought to have their honour, because they do somewhat serve the justice of God and the public and common tranquillity, without the which sometimes those things be troubled and vexed which belong to godly holiness. They must be honoured when they do their office, and — if sometimes they use their power for their own pleasure or profit — yet peradventure it were the best to suffer° them, lest more hurt [b5ʳ] should spring thereof; for there appeareth an image (or rather a shadow)° of the divine justice in them; which justice yet ought to shine more evidently and more purely in the living and laws of priests: an image doth of another manner show in a mirror of glass than it doth in iron.

---

³⁰ Luke 12. 13–15.
³¹ Matt. 23. 13–33.
³² Luke 9. 54–55.
³³ Matt. 16. 22–23; L. 'Satanam'.
³⁴ Mark 9. 33–37.
³⁵ Matt. 5. 39.
³⁶ Luke 6. 27.
³⁷ Matt. 5. 5.

And in the third circle must all the common people be, as the most gross part of all this world, but not yet so gross but that they pertain unto the mystical° Body of Christ: for the eyes be not only members of the body, but also the legs, the feet, and the privy° parts. And those who be in the third circle we ought so to suffer in their infirmity that, as much as is possible, we do call them unto those things which be more approved of Christ; for in the mystical Body he that but late was the foot may be the eye. And like as the princes, if° they be not all the best, must not with chiding be exasperated, lest (as Saint Augustine sayeth)[38] when they be moved they stir up more perilous tragedies: so the weak people — like as Christ suffered his Apostles and nourished them — must be suffered and after a fatherly manner cherished, until they wax more aged and strong in Christ. For godliness also hath its infancy, it hath mean° age, it hath full [b5ᵛ] strength and perfect° age: yet all men after their degree must endeavour themselves to attain and come unto Christ. The elements have every one its proper place, but the fire (which hath the highest place) by little and little draweth all the others unto it and, so much as it can, turneth them into its nature. The clear water it turneth into the air, and the air clarified it transformeth into its own nature. Saint Paul doth in many things suffer and pardon the Corinthians, but in the mean season° putting difference between those things which he did proffer (in the name of his Lord) unto them that were perfect, and those things which he did pardon° (that were written in his own name) to them that were yet weak and young in Christ — but ever on this trust, that they should profit and go forward to more strength and perfection. And also he travaileth again to bring forth the Galatians until Christ be fashioned in them.[39]

Now if any man will think this circle[40] to be more convenient for princes, I will not strive greatly with him. But whatsoever is without° the third circle is at all times and in all points to be hated and refused: as, ambition and [b6ʳ] desire of money, lechery, ire, vengeance, envy, backbiting, and such other pestilences; which then only be made incurable when they (disguised with the visor and cloak of holiness and virtue) do creep into the circles afore-spoken — that is when, under the pretext of executing the law and justice, we use our tyranny; when, by the occasion of religion, we provide for great lucre; when, under the title of defending the Church, we hunt for worldly power and authority; and whensoever those things be commanded as things pertaining unto Christ which be disagreeing° much from his learning.

Therefore the mark must be set before every man which they ought to shoot at

---

[38] Saint Augustine] Even wicked secular rulers may be God's means in regulating a society. See *The City of God against the Pagans*, ed. and trans. by R. W. Dyson (Cambridge: Cambridge University Press, 1998), v. 21; also Rom. 13. 3–4.
[39] Galat. 4. 19.
[40] this circle] The third.

— and there is but one mark, which is Christ and his most pure learning.[41] If thou set forth a worldly mark instead of a celestial mark, then shall there be nothing whereunto a man ought justly enforce himself, who laboureth to profit and go forward. Every man ought to enforce himself to that which is best and most perfect, that at the least we may attain and come to the mean things. And there is no cause why we should put away any kind or manner of living from this mark. [b6ᵛ] The perfection of Christ consisteth only in the affects, and not in the manner or kind of living. It consisteth in the minds, and not in the garments or in meats° and drinks. There be among the monks who be scarce able to be put in the third circle (and yet I speak of those who be good, but yet weak and not perfect). There be, amongst these that have had two wives,[42] whom Christ thinketh worthy for the first circle.

Nor yet in the mean time I do no wrong to any manner of living or profession, though I propound and set forth afore every man that thing which is best and most perfect — unless ye would think Plato to have done injury against all cities because, in his book[43] of the governing of a city or a commonwealth, he feigned° such example of a commonwealth as yet never any man could see; or except ye do think that Quintilian[44] hath hurt the whole order of orators because he feigned such an example of an orator as yet never was. And though thou be far from the principal and chief pattern Christ, thou art not yet therefore cast away, but stimulated and moved to go forward and profit. Art thou near the mark? Then art thou admonished and counselled to approach more near. For there was never yet [b7ʳ] any man that went so far forward but that he might have gone much more near the mark.

There is no kind of living but it hath some perilous points annexed unto it, to cause men to degenerate from the truth; and whosoever showeth those jeopardous and dangerous points doth not derogate or diminish the honour of the order, nor speak against it, but rather is for the profit thereof. As the felicity of princes is in danger to fall into tyranny, is in danger and jeopardy of foolishness and flattering, now whosoever showeth those dangers to be eschewed doth deserve thanks of the order of princes. Nor he doth not speak against their majesty (wherein they glory) who doth show in what things their very majesty doth consist, who also doth put them in remembrance whereto they were sworn when they took their

---

[41] most pure learning] With this and 'principal and chief pattern Christ' below (401) cf. Humphrey: 'in Christ Jesus, the author of the New Testament, there is a kind of pattern not only for living aright but also for expressing things aright' (Rhodes, *Translation Theory*, p. 279, lines 553–54).
[42] have had two wives] i.e. have remarried after being widowed.
[43] book] *Republic*. E. supports the right kind of idealising or utopias: not the kind which is 'dreaming' and 'unfruitful'; cf. 413 (p. 68) and 2070 below.
[44] Quintilian] First-century Spanish-Roman rhetorician and author of *Institutio Oratoria* ('The Education of an Orator').

authority, what is their duty unto their people, and what they ought to do unto their officers.

The heads and rulers of the Church have in a manner affinity with two pestilent vices: avarice and ambition. Which well perceiving, Saint Peter, the chief pastor next unto Christ, doth admonish the bishops to feed their flock and not to pill, poll, and flay them; nor that they [b7ᵛ] should not feed them because of any filthy advantage, but of their free and ready will; nor that they should use themselves as lords upon them, but that by the example of life they should provoke them to godliness, rather than by threatening and power.[45] Doth he then speak against the order of priests, who doth show by what means and how the bishops may truly be great, mighty, and rich?

Moreover, the kind° of religious° men[46] is accompanied most commonly (besides other enormities) with superstition, pride, hypocrisy, and backbiting. He doth not straight condemn their manner of living who doth show and admonish them in what things most true religion doth stand or rest; and how much the true godliness of a Christian man is away from pride; and how far true charity is from all feigning and deceit; how much backbiting and slandering and venomousness of tongue is contrary to pure and true holiness; and especially if he show what is to be eschewed after such sober and discreet manner that he do neither name any man, nor touch° any order. What thing is that in this mortal life [is] so fortunate and prosperous but hath some pestilent things annexed unto it? Therefore, like [b8ʳ] as he doth not noy° the health of the body, but helpeth it, whosoever showeth what things corrupt health, and what things preserve it: so he doth not dissuade men from religion, but exhorteth them rather unto it, who showeth the corruptious° infections thereof and also the remedies.

For I am informed that there be divers who so judge of this book as though the precepts thereof did withdraw and turn away men's minds from the life of religious men, because they do not so much praise and allow ceremonies, nor yet man's constitutions,° as some would — who indeed overmuch regard them. And there can be nothing so circumspectly spoken, but that thereof lewd° and evil persons do take occasion either of quarrelling, or else of sinning; so that it is dangerful nowadays to any man to teach anything well. If a man should dissuade from such war and battle which now of long time hath been used, worse than was ever any amongst the Gentiles, for things of no value, he should be noted° by and by of the pick-quarrels° to be one of those who think that no war is lawful for a Christian man. For these who were [b8ᵛ] the bringers-up and authors of this sentence° we have made heretics, because a pope — I wot not who[47] — doth seem

---

[45] 1 Peter 5. 1–3.
[46] kind of religious men] L. 'monachorum genus' ('stock of monks').
[47] I wot not who] Courteously dismissive ('some pope or other') while pointing to the supreme authority of 'Christ and his Apostles'.

to approve and allow war. And yet he is not suspected nor noted of heresy who doth provoke and stir up men to battle, and bloweth the trumpet thereunto for every trifling matter, against the doctrine both of Christ and of his Apostles. If a man admonish that this is a deed truly belonging to the successor of an Apostle, to bring the Turks unto religion with Christ's help rather than with war, anon° he is suspected as though he affirmed not to be lawful for Christian men to withstand the Turks when they invade° us. If a man show and praise the temperance that was in the Apostles, and speak anything against the great superfluity that is used nowadays, he should be noted as a favourer of the Ebionites.[48] And if a man did exhort diligently that these who be married should rather be joined together by the consents and agreeing of their minds than by the embracings of their bodies, and so purely to use matrimony that — as much as might be — it were made like to virginity, he should be anon suspected to think that every act of [c1ʳ] matrimony were sin and unlawful, as the Marcionites did. If a man do admonish that in exercise and disputations, especially of divinity, there should be no ambitious pertinacity to overcome his fellow in defending his own opinions, nor no ambition to show what they can do in common places,[49] he is wrongfully accused as though he did condemn utterly all school learning.

Nor Saint Augustine,[50] when he giveth warning to the logicians that they should beware of lust° to brawl and chide, doth not condemn logic, but showeth the pestilence thereof, that it might be eschewed. Also he doth not dispraise virtue, nor praise vice, who showeth the preposterous° and wrong judgement of the common people, who among virtues esteem those to be of most great value and chiefest which be of the lowest sort, and among vices most sore hate and abhor those most small faults and trifles; and so contrariwise. Anon he is accused, as though he should favour those vices which he showeth to be [less][51] grievous than others, and as though he should condemn those good deeds and benefits to which he preferreth others more holy and better. As, if a man did admonish and give us warning that it is more sure [c1ᵛ] to trust unto good deeds than to trust to the Pope's pardon, yet he doth not forsooth condemn the Pope's pardons, but preferreth that which by Christ's learning and doctrine is of more certainty. Also, if a man do teach those for to do better who tarry at home and provide for their wife and children than those who go to see Rome, Jerusalem, or Santiago;[52] and that money which they should spend in that long and perilous journey to be better and more devoutly spent upon poor folks: yet condemneth not he their good intent, but preferreth that which is more near to very godliness.

[48] Ebionites] Like the Marcionites (465), an ascetic group of early Christians.
[49] common places] L. 'theatrica ambitio' ('theatrical ambition'), so probably 'public displays' rather than 'set themes' ('commonplaces'): but in either case with showy virtuosity.
[50] Augustine] e.g. *On Christian Teaching* II. 117–20.
[51] less] *1533* and *1534* 'more', but logic and L. require 'less'.
[52] Santiago] The shrine of St James the Great at Compostela; see also 4635.

And this is a thing not only used now in our time, but also in times heretofore past: to abhor some vices as though there were none other, fawning upon the rest as° they were no vices at all; when in very deed they be more detestable than those which we so hate and abhor. Saint Augustine doth complain in his epistles that lasciviousness of the flesh is only° imputed unto the priests of Africa as a vice, and that the vice of covetousness and drunkenness be taken well nigh for a praise. This especially we speak most against and cry out upon, and exaggerate° for an [c2ʳ] exceeding abominable fact: if one touch the body of Christ with the same hands wherewith he hath touched the body of a harlot. And there be some over-raging bold that be not afraid openly to affirm that it is less sin for a woman to commit carnal act with a brute beast than to lie with a priest. Now he that something rebuketh their unshamefastness[53] doth not therefore favour the naughtiness of priests, but showeth that they regard not those offences which be a great deal more to be cried° out upon. But if a priest be a dicer, a fighter, a brawler, all unlearned, drowned and wrapped in temporal business, all given to the evil service of evil princes: yet against him they cry nothing at all, who altogether worldly and polluted doth handle and intermeddle with holy mysteries. When a priest is a flatterer or a pick-quarrel, who with his bitter tongue and false lies doth hurt the names of those who never offended him, but rather have done him pleasures, why do we not now cry out, 'Oh, what a horrible sin is this, to receive thy Lord God — who suffered his Passion for sinners — with that tongue which is full of poison of hell, and with that mouth wherewith [c2ᵛ] thou killest and slayest an innocent'? But this evil and ungraciousness we set° so little by that, in a manner, those men are even praised for it who profess themselves to be the most religious amongst religious men. There is no man that denieth but they be to be reprehended and sore rebuked who nourish and keep at home concubines, to the evil example of all the common people: but yet these other evil vices be more hateful to God. Nor he doth therefore say that 'butter is nought' who sayeth that 'honey is better and more to be preferred'; nor yet doth not approve the fever that counselleth the frenzy more to be avoided.

And it is hard to tell and express how great infection of manners and disposition doth spring of these perverse and wrong judgements. There be divers things nowadays received into the order of virtues which rather have the visor° and appearance of godliness than the nature and strength of it, insomuch that — unless we look well unto them, and take good heed of them — they do quench and utterly destroy virtue. If it had been but a little pestilence of religion which in ceremonies do lie covert,° Paul would never so sharply have spoken against them in all his Epistles. And yet do not we [c3ʳ] condemn in any place ceremonies that be moderately observed — but that all holiness be ascribed unto them we cannot suffer. Saint Augustine did prohibit those of the clergy who were in house with

---

[53] their unshamefastness] i.e. the immodesty (L. 'impudentiam') of the 'over-raging bold'.

him to use any notable vesture, but (if they would be commended of the people) that they should rather bring that to pass by their manners and virtuous living than by any sundry fashion of raiment. But nowadays it is a world° for to see what new and wonderful fashions of apparel and vesture there be. But yet I speak not against that, but this I marvel of — that those things are so overmuch regarded and set by which peradventure might by right be reprehended; and again that those things be so little regarded which we should only° behold and regard. I do not rail against the Grey friars and Black monks that they make much of their own rule, but because certain of them regard more their own rules than they do the Gospel: which thing would to God were not found in the most part of them! I do not speak against that, that some eat fish, some live with herbs, others with eggs, but I admonish those to err, and to be far out of the way, who will of those things justify themselves [c3ᵛ] after the manner of the Jews, thinking themselves better, and preferring themselves to others for such trifles of men's invention, and take it for no fault at all to hurt another man's good name with false lies.

Of the diversity° of meat° and drink Christ never commanded anything, nor the Apostles: but Paul oftentimes did dissuade us from it.[54] Christ curseth bitter slandering,[55] which also all the Apostles do detest and abhor.[56] And yet, that notwithstanding, we will appear religious in such using of meats — and in hurting men's fame we be bold and hardy! I pray you, think you that he who doth admonish these (both in general, not touching any man, and also lovingly) doth hurt religion? Who is so mad that he would be accounted eloquent for showing and bringing to light the vices that belong to monks?

But these peradventure fear lest their convents and brethren would be less obedient, and lest also there do not so many desire to be shaven[57] into their order. Yet verily no man is more obedient to his Head than he who, inspired with the Holy Ghost, is free and at liberty. True and very charity taketh all things well in worth° and suffereth all things, [c4ʳ] refuseth nothing, is obedient unto rulers, not only to those that be sober and gentle, but also to those that be sharp and rough. But yet rulers must be wise° of this, that they do not turn the obedience of other men into their own tyranny, and that they had lever° therefore to have them superstitious than holy and virtuous; whereby they might be more obedient at every beck.° They have pleasure to be called 'fathers': but what carnal father is there that would have his children ever infants and young, because° he might use his power upon them at his own pleasure? And, of the other part, all those that purpose to profit in the liberty of Christ, this they must beware of: lest (as Saint

---

[54] e.g. Rom. 14. 13–23.
[55] Matt. 5. 22.
[56] *ASD* v-8, p. 83, lists Rom. 1. 29–30, II Corinth. 12. 20, Ephes. 4. 31, I Tim. 3. 11, Titus 3. 2, I Peter 2. 1, James 1. 26, 3. 2–11.
[57] shaven] L. 'cooptari' ('enrolled').

Paul doth admonish) they make their liberty a cloak or covert° to their carnal living;[58] or (as Saint Peter teacheth) with their liberty they make a cover and a cloak to maliciousness.[59] And if that one or two do abuse this liberty, yet it is not right forthwith that all others therefore be ever kept in superstitiousness and bondage of ceremonies, like unto the Jews. And whosoever will mark it shall perceive that, amongst these religious men, no man causeth the ceremonies to be more straitly° observed than they who, under the precepts thereof, do bear rule [c4^v] and serve their bellies rather than Christ.[60]

Moreover, they need not be afraid lest such kind of Essenes[61] be not enough spread abroad in so great diversity of men's natures, whereby it is caused that nothing is so unreasonable but divers and many will love and desire it: although themselves ought more to desire that they had true professors of religion rather than many. But would to God that it were provided and ordained by a law that no man should be taken in such snares afore he were thirty years of age, before he something knew himself, or knew what the nature and virtue of true religion is. But these, who (like unto the Pharisees, doing their own business and providing for their own profit) wander about to make novices both by sea and land,[62] shall never fail of young men lacking experience whom they may allure into their veils° and nets and also deceive. There be a great number of fools and simple souls in every place.

But I desire even with all my heart, and I doubt not but so do all that be very° good men, that the religion of the Gospel should be so pleasant to every man that they (being contented therewith) should not desire the religion of Black monks or Grey friars. And I doubt not [c5^r] but so would Saint Benedict and Francis[63] themselves. Moses did rejoice that his own honour was defaced° and dimmed with the glory of Christ:[64] and so should those others be glad if, for the love of Christ's law, we set nothing by man's constitutions. I would that all Christian men should so live that these who now be called only 'religious' should appear little religious; which thing even at this day is of truth, and that in many. (For why should I dissemble that thing that is so manifest?)

And yet in the old time the beginning of the monastical life was nothing else but a going aside into a secret place from the cruelness of idolaters; and, anon after, the manner of living of religious men who followed them was nothing else but a reformation and calling again to Christ. For the courts of princes in the old

---

[58] e.g. Galat. 5. 13–18.
[59] 1 Peter 2. 16.
[60] Rom. 16. 18, Philipp. 3. 19.
[61] Essenes] A Jewish community associated with the Dead Sea around the time of Christ.
[62] Matt. 23. 15.
[63] Benedict and Francis] Reformers of monastic life: respectively c. 480–c. 550 and 1181–1226.
[64] At the Transfiguration, e.g. Matt. 17. 3–5.

time showed them christened in their titles rather than in their living. The bishops anon after were corrupted with ambition and covetousness, and the common people also fainted and waxed cold from that charity which was in the primitive Church; and for this purpose did Saint Benedict seek a solitary life, and then after him Bernard,⁶⁵ and after that divers others did associate themselves [c5ᵛ] together for this intent only: that they might use° the pure and simple life of Christian men. Then after in process of time, when their riches and ceremonies did increase, their true godliness and simpleness did abate and decrease. And now, although we see men of religion to be overmuch out of good order, and to use manners like unto Gentiles, yet is the world filled with new institutions° and kinds of religion — as though they should not fall to the same point hereafter that others have done afore them. In times past (as I said) a religious life was nothing but a solitary life: and now these be called 'religious' who be altogether drowned in worldly business, using plainly certain tyranny in worldly matters. And yet these for their apparel and title (I cannot tell what) do challenge° such holiness to themselves that they do account all others in comparison of themselves no Christian men at all. Why do we make so strait and narrow Christ's religion, which he would have so large?

If we be moved with magnifical° and high terms,⁶⁶ I pray you what thing else is a city but a great monastery? Monks be obedient to their abbot and governors: the citizens obey the [c6ʳ] bishops and curates, whom Christ himself made rulers and not the authority of man. The monks live in idleness and be fed of other men's liberality, possessing that amongst them in common which they never laboured or sweated for (yet speak I nothing of them that be vicious): the citizens bestow that which they have got with their labour and great travail to them that have need, every man as he is of ability and power. Now as concerning the vow of chastity, I dare not be bold to express what difference is betwixt the religious man unmarried and the chaste matrimony of the other.

And (to be short) he shall not very greatly lack those three vows of man's invention, that doth keep and observe purely and sincerely that first only vow which we all solemnly make unto Christ, and not unto man, when we receive our baptism. And if we compare those that be evil of one kind with those that be evil of the other, without doubt the temporal men be much better. But if we compare those who be good of the one sort with those that be good of the other, there is little difference (if there be any at all), [c6ᵛ] saving that those appear to be more religious that keep their religion and duty with less coaction.° The rest is therefore that no man foolishly stand in his own conceit,° neither for his diversity of living from other men, nor despise or condemn the rule or order of other men's living; but in every kind of living let this be our common study: that every man according

---

⁶⁵ Bernard] Early twelfth-century abbot of Clairvaux.
⁶⁶ high terms] The three monastic vows — obedience, poverty, chastity — have parallels for lay citizens.

to his power endeavour himself to attain unto the mark of Christ, which is set open to all men, and that every man do exhort others to it and also help others, neither envying them that overrun° us in this course, nor disdaining them that be weak and cannot yet overtake us.

In conclusion: when every man hath done that he can, let him not be like unto the Pharisee whom the Gospel maketh mention of, who doth boast his good deeds unto God, saying, 'I fast twice in the week, I pay all my tithes', and such forth;[67] but after Christ's counsel let him speak from the heart, and to himself and not to others, saying, 'I am an unprofitable servant, for I have done no more than I ought to do'.[68] There is no man that better trusteth than he that so distrusteth. There is no man further from true religion than he that thinketh himself to [c7r] be very religious. Nor Christ's godliness is never at worse point than when that thing which is worldly is writhed° unto Christ, and the authority of man is preferred unto the authority of God. We must all hang° of that Head if we will be true Christian men. Moreover, whosoever is obedient to a man who doth persuade and call him unto Christ, he is obedient unto Christ and not unto man. And whosoever doth tolerate and suffer those men who be subtle, cruel, and imperious, teaching that thing which maketh not for religion but for their tyranny, he useth the patience meet for a Christian man — so° that these things which they command be not utterly wicked and contrary to Christ's doctrine; for then it shall be convenient to have that answer of the Apostles at hand, 'We must rather be obedient unto God than to any man'.[69]

But we have long ago passed the measure and quantity of an epistle, so greatly the time deceiveth us while we commune and talk most pleasantly with our well-beloved friend. This book is sent unto you in Froben's print,[70] as though it were new-born again, much more ornate and better corrected than it was before. I have put unto it certain fragments[71] of my old study in times past. [c7v] Methought it most convenient to dedicate this edition (such as it is) unto you, that whosoever shall take any precepts to live well of Erasmus should have an example ready at hand of our father Volz.

Our Lord preserve you, good father, the honour and worship of all religion. I pray you, counsel Sapidus that he be wise,[72] that is, that he go forth as he hath begun; and to Wimpfeling ye shall speak also, that he prepare all his armour to

---

[67] Luke 18. 12.
[68] Luke 17. 10.
[69] Acts 5. 29.
[70] in Froben's print] E. first became acquainted with the humanist printer John Froben (1460–1527) at Basel in 1514. Their collaboration was to be wide-rangingly fruitful, and the Froben *Enchiridion* gave the work a fresh popularity throughout Europe.
[71] certain fragments] A few shorter pieces were bound in the same volume.
[72] wise] 'Sapidus' (his other name was Witz) means 'wise'. Like Wimpfeling, Ruser, and Volz, he was a friend and correspondent of E.

fight shortly with the Turks, forasmuch as he hath kept war long enough with keepers of concubines. And I have great hope and trust to see him once a bishop, and to ride upon a mule, and to be set high in honour with a mitre and cross.° But in earnest I pray you commend me heartily both unto them and unto Ruser, and the rest of my friends; and in your devout prayers made to God I pray you remember Erasmus and pray for his soul's health.

At Basel, the Eve of the Assumption of our Lady, in the year of our Lord God 1518.

INTRODUCTION

[1523 MS 1ʳ]¹ A compendious° treatise of the soldier of Christ, called *Enchiridion*, which Erasmus Rotterdam wrote unto a certain courtier, a friend of his.²

Thou hast desired of me with fervent study,° singular beloved brother in Christ, that I should describe for thee compendiously a certain craft of virtuous living,
5 by whose help thou mightest attain knowledge meet° for a true Christian man. Thou sayest that thou art weary of the pastime of court, and to compass in thy mind by what means thou mightest escape Egypt,³ with all her both vices and pleasures, and to be prepared happily with the captain Moses unto the journey of virtue. The more I love thee, the joyouser I am of this thy so holy a purpose; which
10 I trust (yea, without our help) he that did vouchsafe to give it thee shall make prosperous and bring to good effect. Notwithstanding yet have I obeyed thee, partly because thou art so great a friend of mine, partly also because thou requirest so charitable things.

Now therefore awake, pluck up thy heart, set to thy shoulders, lest either thou
15 shouldst seem to have desired my service and duty in vain, or else [I] to have satisfied thy mind without any fruit. Yea, let us both indifferently° beseech the benign spirit of Jesus that he both put wholesome things in the mind of me who write, and make the same to [1ᵛ] thee of strength and efficacy.

CHAPTER ONE

We must watch and look about us evermore
20 ### while we be in this life

The first point is, we must needs have in mind continually that the life of mortal men is nothing but a certain perpetual exercise of war — as Job⁴ witnesses, a warrior proved° to the uttermost, and never overcome — and that the most part of men be overmuch deceived; whose minds the world (as a juggler)⁵ holdeth
25 occupied with delicious and flattering pleasures; who also, as° they had conquered

---

¹ *1523 MS 1ʳ*] References (recto and verso) are to the folio numbers of British Library (online) Additional MS 89149.
² friend of his] The courtier's name was John. For different possible identifications, see O'Donnell, *An English Version*, p. xvi.
³ **Marg.** 'Egypt betokeneth bondage, affliction, vice, and blindness.'
⁴ Job 7. 1 (*Vulg.*): 'militia'.
⁵ juggler] L. 'praestigiator' (magician, trickster); Tyndale uses the term repeatedly, e.g. in his *Obedience* (from the title page onwards).

all their enemies, make holy-day out of season no otherwise verily than as in a very assured peace.

It is a marvellous thing to behold how without care and circumspection we live, how idly we sleep, now upon the one side and now on the other, when without ceasing we are besieged with so great a number of armed vices, sought and hunted for with so great craft, invaded daily with so great lying in wait.° Behold over thy head wicked devils that never sleep but keep watch for our destruction, armed against us with a thousand deceits, with a thousand crafts of noyances,° which enforce° from on high to wound our minds with weapons burning and dipped in deadly poison: than the which weapons neither Hercules nor [2ʳ] Cephalus[6] had ever a surer dart, except they be received in the sure and impenetrable shield of faith.[7] Then again, on the right hand and on the left hand, afore and behind, the world striveth against us, which (after the saying of Saint John)[8] is set all on vice and mischief,° and therefore to Christ both contrary and hated. Neither is it one manner of fight, for sometimes with guns of adversity raging as with open war it shaketh the walls of the soul, somewhiles with great promises (but most vain) it provoketh to treason, and sometimes by undermining it stealeth on us unware,° to catch us among the idle and careless men; moreover, the slippery serpent — the first breaker of peace, father of unquietness, and otherwhiles° hid in the green grass, otherwhiles lurking in his caves, wrapped together in round rolls — ceaseth not to watch and lay await° beneath unto the heel of our woman, whom he once poisoned. (By the 'woman' is understood the carnal part of a man, otherwise called sensuality.° This is our Eve, by whom the most crafty serpent doth entice and draw our minds to mortal° pleasure).

Finally, as though it were but a trifle that so great company of enemies should assault us on every side, within the very secret parts of the mind we bear about us wheresoever we go an enemy nearer than of acquaintance, nearer than of household; and, as nothing is more inward, [2ᵛ] so nothing is more perilous. This is the old Adam, made of the earth, who by acquaintance and customable° familiarity is more nearer to us than a citizen, and is in all manner studies° and pastimes to us more contrary than any mortal enemy; whom thou canst exclude with no bulwark, nor is it lawful to expel out of thy pavilion. This fellow must be watched with a hundred eyes[9] lest he utter° and betray us unto the devils.

(The succour and defence that God hath put in our city.)[10] Seeing therefore we

---

[6] Hercules [...] Cephalus] Hercules, having killed the many-headed Hydra, dipped his weapons in its gall or blood so that any wounds he subsequently inflicted were incurable; Cephalus was given a spear which unerringly hit its target.
[7] Ephes. 6. 16.
[8] Cf. 1 John 5. 19.
[9] hundred eyes] like the legendary giant Argus.
[10] (The succour [...] city.)] Added by T., apparently intended for the margin.

be vexed with so fearful and cruel war, and our cause is with so great multitude of foes who have conspired and sworn our death, who be so busy, so appointed,° so false and expert, ought not we madmen, on the other side, to arm ourselves and take our weapons in our hands, to keep watch and to have all things suspect? But we — as though all were at rest and peace — sleep so fast that we rout° again and give ourselves to idleness, to pleasure, and (as the common proverb is) 'make us a white and a smooth skin',[11] none otherwise than as though our life were nothing but a pastime together at the tavern or alehouse, and not a time of war. For instead of tents and pavilions we be locked up in our closets; instead of sallets° and hard armour we be crowned with roses and fresh flowers, be also bathed in damask° and rose-water, and [3ʳ] smoke in pomanders° and with musk-balls,° changing° points of war with riot° and idleness, and our strong weapons with the weak harp: as° this 'peace' were not of all wars the most shameful.

For whosoever is at one with vices, the same hath broken truce made between him and God in time of baptism. And thou, a madman, criest 'peace, peace' when thou hast God to thine enemy, who only is peace and Lord of peace, and with open mouth crieth the contrary by his prophet David,[12] saying 'there is no peace to sinners or wicked persons who love not God'. And there is no other condition of peace with him except that we (as long as we be in the fortress of this body) with deadly hate and with all our might should fight against vices. For if we be at one with them we shall have him twice our enemy, who only being our friend may make us blessed, and if he be our foe may destroy us: both because we stand on their side who only can never agree with God — for how can light and darkness agree? — and also because we, as men most unkind,° abide not by the promise that we made to him, but unjustly have broken the appointment made between him and us with protestation and holy ceremonies.

O thou Christian man, rememberest thou not, when thou were professed and consecrated with the holy mysteries of the fountain of life, how [3ᵛ] thou boundest thyself to be a faithful soldier unto thy captain Christ? to whom thou owest thy life twice, both because he gave it thee, and also because he restored it again to thee; to whom thou owest more than thou art able to pay. Cometh it not to thy mind how, when thou wast bound with his sacraments (as with holy gifts), thou wast sworn with words for the nonce° to take the part° of so courteous an emperor, and how thou hast destined and given thyself to great vengeance if thou shouldst not abide by thy promise? For what intent was the sign of the cross printed in thy forehead except thou, as long as thou livest, should fight under his

---

[11] See *Adages*, in *CWE* 31–36, ed. and trans. by R. A. B. Mynors and M. M. Philips (Toronto: University of Toronto Press, 1982–2006), II. iv. 75 (*CWE* 33. 228).

[12] David] Name added by T. The sentiment runs through the Psalms but is explicit in Isaiah 48. 22 and 57. 21.

standard? For what intent were thou anointed with his holy oil except thou forever shouldst fight against vices?

What shame, and how great abomination, is it counted with all men if a man forsake his king or chief lord! Why settest° thou so light then by thy captain Christ, neither refrainest for fear (when he is God) nor for love (seeing for thy sake he was made man)? Yea, and (seeing thou usurpest° his name) thou oughtest to remember what thou hast promised him. Why departest thou away from him like a false forsworn man, and goest unto thy enemy, from whence he once redeemed thee with the ransom of his precious blood? Why dost thou, so oft a renegade, war and fight under the standard of his adversary? [4ʳ] With what face° presumest thou to set up contrary banners against thy king, who for thy sake bestowed his own life? Whosoever is not on his part standeth against him, and he that gathereth not with him scattereth abroad.°[13]

Thou warrest not with[14] filthy title or quarrel only, but also for a miserable reward. Wilt thou hear, O thou whosoever warrest for pleasure of this world, what shall be thy meed? Paul, the standard-bearer in the war of Christ, answereth thee: 'the reward', sayeth he, 'of sin is death'.[15] And who would take upon him to fight in a just and an honest cause if he were sure to die, but bodily only? — and thou fightest in a wrong and also a filthy quarrel to obtain for thy reward the death of thy soul! In these mad battles which man maketh against man, either for beastly fury or for miserable necessity, seest thou not — if at any time either the great hope of the prey, or comfort of the captain, or the cruelness of the enemies, if shame of cowardness cast in their teeth, or (in conclusion)° if desire of praise hath pricked and stirred up the soldiers' minds — with what courage, and with what lusty° minds, finish they whatsoever labour remaineth, what miserable life have they, how lustily run they upon their enemies? Well is him that may go foremost! And I beseech thee, what reward seek they [4ᵛ] with so great jeopardies and diligence? Verily, but to have praise of a wretched man, their captain, and that men might say of them 'there go bold men, strong and hardy', to have haply° their names written in a harper's bead-roll,° to get a garland of oaken leaves, or at the most to bring home a little more vantage or winning with them: when we on the other side, clean contrary, be set afire neither with shame nor hope of reward, and yet he beholdeth us while we fight that shall quit° our pain if we win the field.

But what reward setteth forth the chief ruler of our game for them that win the mastery? Not mules, as Achilles did in Homer, not tripods (that is to say, meat-boards° with three feet), as Aeneas did in Virgil: but 'such as the eye never [saw nor] the ear never heard, nor could sink into the heart of man'.[16] And these be

---

[13] Luke 11. 23.
[14] with] 'having'.
[15] Rom. 6. 23.
[16] Contrasting 1 Corinth. 2. 9 (cf. Isaiah 64. 4) with *Iliad* 23. 260 and *Aeneid* 5. 110.

distributed daily now in the mean time as solace and comfort of labour to them who strongly resist. And what hereafter? Certes,° blessed immortality.

But in games of sport — as in running, wrestling, leaping, in which the chiefest part of reward is praise — they who be overcome have likewise their rewards assigned unto them. But our matter is tried with great and doubtful peril, neither we fight for praise but for life. And as reward of most value is proffered to him that acquitteth himself most manfully, so pain most [5ʳ] terrible is appointed for him that giveth° back. Heaven is promised to him that fighteth lustily: and why is not the quick courage of a gentle° stomach° inflamed with the hope of so blessed a reward, namely° when he promiseth who — as he cannot die — even so he cannot deceive?

All things be done in the sight of God, who all things beholdeth; we have all the company of heaven beholders of our conflict — and how are we not moved at the least way even for very shame? He shall praise our virtue and diligence of whom to be lauded is very felicity. Why seek we not this praise, yea, with the loss of our lives? It is a cowardful mind that will be quickened with no manner of reward: the veriest heartless coward in the world, for fear of perils, oft-time taketh courage to him.

And in worldly battles, though thy adversary be never so cruel, yet rageth he but on thy goods and body only — what more than that could cruel Achilles do to Hector? But here the immortal part of thee is assaulted. Nor is thy corpse drawn about the sepulchre as was Hector's, but thy body and soul also is cast down into hell. *There* the greatest calamity or hurt is that a sword should depart° the soul from the body. *Here* is taken from the soul her life, which is God himself. It is natural for the body to die — which if no man should kill, yet can [5ᵛ] it not but die. But the soul to die is extreme misery. With how great cautel° avoid° we the wounds of the body, with how great diligence cure we them: and set we so little of the wounds of the soul? Our hearts arise and grudge° at the remembrance of the death of the body as at a terrible and a much fearful thing, and because it is seen with bodily eyes. The soul to die, because no man seeth and few believe it, therefore very few fear it. And yet is this death more cruel than the other, even as much as the soul doth pass° the body and God excelleth the soul.

Wilt thou that I show thee certain conjectures,° examples, or tokens, whereby thou mayst perceive the sickness of the soul? Thy stomach digesteth thy meat but easily,° or haply casteth it up again: thou perceivest by and by° that thy body is out of temper. And bread is not so naturally meat° to thy body as the Word of God is meat for thy soul. If that seem bitter, if thy mind rise against it, why doubtest thou yet but that the mouth of thy soul is out of taste° and infected with some evil disease? If thy memory, which is the stomach of thy soul, keep not the learning° of God, if by continual meditation thou digestest it not, if when it is digested thou sendest it not unto all parts of the body by outward operation, [6ʳ] thou hast an evident token that thy soul is acrased.° If thy knees for weakness bow under thee and thou hast much to draw thy limbs after thee, thou perceivest plainly that thy body is evil° at ease: and perceivest thou not the sickness of thy soul when she grudgeth and is weak and faint to all deeds of piety, when she hath no strength to suffer patiently the least rebuke in the world, but is troubled and vexed with the loss of half a halfpenny? When the sight is departed from the eyes, and the ears hear no more, and all the body hath lost her feeling, no man then doubteth but that the life is departed: when the eyes of thy heart be waxed dim, insomuch that thou canst not see the most clearest light of the verity of God, when thou hearest not with thy inward ears the voice of God, when thou lackest all thy inward feeling and perceivance of the knowledge of God, thinkest thou that thy soul is alive? Thou seest thy brother ungoodly treated and thy mind is nothing moved, so° thy matter be in good case. Why feeleth thy soul nothing here? Certainly because she is dead. Why is she dead? Because her life is away (that is to say, God — for verily God is the life of the soul, and where God is, there charity is, and compassion of thy neighbour). For if thou were a quick° member how could any part of thy body ache and thou not having compassion, no, not once feeling nor [6ᵛ] perceiving it?

Take a more evident token. Thou hast deceived thy friend, thou hast committed adultery: thy soul hath caught a deadly wound, and yet grieveth it thee not at all, insomuch also that thou rejoicest as it were a great winning, and boastest thyself of that thou shamefully hast committed. Believe surely that thy soul lieth dead. Thy body is not alive if it feel not the pricking of a pin: and is thy soul alive, which lacketh the feeling of so great a wound? Thou hearest some man use lewd° and presumptuous communication, words of backbiting, words unchaste and filthy, yea, and raging furiously against his neighbours: think not thou the soul of this man to be alive. There lieth a rotten carcase in the sepulchre of that stomach, from whence such stink ariseth and infecteth every man that cometh nigh. Christ called the Pharisees 'painted sepulchres'.[17] Why so? Because verily they bare a dead soul about with them. And King David the prophet sayeth, 'their throat is a sepulchre wide open, they spake deceitfully with their tongues'.[18] The bodies of holy people be the temples of the Holy Ghost;[19] and lewd men's bodies be the sepulchres of dead corpses, that the interpretation of the grammarians to them might well be applied, *soma quasi sēma*: that is to say, it is called a 'body' because it is the 'burial' or 'grave' of the soul.[20] The breast is the sepulchre, the mouth and the throat is [7ʳ] the gaping of the sepulchre, and the body destitute of the soul is not so dead as is the soul when she is forsaken of almighty God; nor any dead corpse stinketh

---

[17] Matt. 23. 27.
[18] Ps. 5. 9.
[19] 1 Corinth. 3. 17, 6. 19.
[20] *sōma quasi sēma*] e.g. Plato, *Cratylus* 400c.

in the nose of man so sore as the stench of a soul buried four days[21] offendeth the nose of God and of all his saints.

    Conclude therefore: whensoever dead words proceed out of the heart, it must needs be that a dead corpse lieth buried within. For when (according to the Gospel) 'the mouth speaketh of the abundance of the heart',[22] no doubt it would speak the live words of God if he who is very life were there present (that is to wit,° God). In another place of the Gospel the disciples said to Christ, 'Master, whither shall we go? Thou hast the words of life'.[23] Why so, I pray thee, 'the words of life'? Certainly because those words sprang out of the soul from whence the Godhead — who restoreth us again to life immortal — never departed, no, not one moment. The physician easeth and cureth the body sometimes when it is diseased; good men oft-times have called the body dead to life again. But a dead soul nothing saving God only, of his free and singular power, can restore to life again: yea, but yet he restoreth her never again if she, being dead in sin, have once forsaken the body. Moreover, of the bodily death is the feeling little or none at all; but of the soul [7ᵛ] is the feeling eternal. And though also the soul in that case be more than dead, yet — as touching° the feeling of eternal death — she is ever immortal. Therefore, seeing we must needs fight ever afresh with new jeopardy, what dulness, what negligence, what sluggishness, yea, what deadly slumber possesseth our minds, when fear of so great peril awaketh us not out of our dreams?

    And again, on the contrary part, there is no cause wherefore either the greatness of peril, or else the multitude, violence, or subtlety of thine adversaries, should abate the courage of thy mind. It cometh to thy mind how grievous an adversary thou hast: remember also, on the other side, how present, how ready at hand, thou hast help and succour. Against thee be innumerable: yea, but he that taketh thy part himself alone is more of power than all they. 'If God be on our side what matter is it who be against us?'[24] If he stay° thee, who shall cast thee down? But thou must be inflamed and set on fire in all thine heart and burn in fervent desire of victory. Have in mind that thy business is not with a fresh soldier and a new adversary, but [him] that was many years ago discomfited, overthrown, spoiled, and led captive in triumph of us,[25] but in Christ our Head, by whose might no doubt he shall be subdued again in us [8ʳ] also.

    Take heed that thou be a member of the Body, and thou shalt be able to do all things in the power of God. In thyself thou art very weak, no man is strong in his own strength: in him thou art valiant, and nothing [is there] that thou art not able

---

[21] John 11. 39.
[22] Matt. 12. 34.
[23] John 6. 68.
[24] Rom. 8. 31.
[25] of us] L. 'a nobis', i.e. 'by us', on our behalf by Christ.

to do. Moreover, the end of our war is not doubtful, because the victory dependeth not of fortune, but is put wholly in the hands of God, and by him in our hands. No man is that hath not overcome but he that would not. The benignity of our protector never failed man. If thou take heed to answer again and to do thy part, thou hast overcome already: he shall fight for thee, and his liberality shall be imputed to thee for merit.[26] Thou must thank him only° for the victory who (first of all, and of all men only pure and immaculate from sin) oppressed° the tyranny of sin. But this victory shall not come without thy own diligence also, for he that said 'have confidence, I have overcome the world'[27] would have thee to be of good comfort, but not careless and negligent.

Of this manner (to conclude) in his strength and by him we shall overcome, if by his example we shall fight as he fought. Wherefore of this manner thou must find out a mean way between Scylla and Charybdis, that thou neither in such wise have confidence in the grace of God that thou shouldst make all sure[28] [8ᵛ] and run at large without tasting of peril; nor yet so mistrust in thyself, feared° with the difficulty of the war, that thou shouldst cast away courage, boldness and confidence of mind together with harness° and weapons also.

CHAPTER TWO

Of the weapons to be used in the war of a Christian man

And I suppose that nothing pertaineth so much to the discipline of this war than that thou shouldst surely know, and presently° have in thy mind always, what kind of armour or weapons most chiefly thou must use, with what enemies thou must encounter and joust withal;° moreover, that thy weapons be ready at hand lest thy so subtle enemy should take thee sleeper° and unarmed. In these worldly wars a man may oftentimes be at rest, as in the deep of winter or in time of truce: but we, as long as we keep war in this body, may depart from our weapons and harness° at no season,° no, not (as the saying is) 'one finger's breadth'.[29] We must keep our standing° and ever make watch, for our adversary is never idle. When he is most calm and still, when he feigneth to flee or to make truce, then most of all he imagineth guile; and thou hast never more need to look about thee than when he maketh countenance or semblance of [9ʳ] peace. Thou hast never less need to fear than when he assaulteth thee with open war.

---

[26] for merit] A controversial issue between Reformers and Catholics. To Catholics it was possible through grace and responsiveness to cooperate with God and acquire a kind of merit 'at second hand', drawing on Christ's primary and uniquely deserved merits. Reformers believed even this dependent cooperation ignored our radical helplessness.
[27] John 16. 33.
[28] make all sure] 'feel certain that everything is bound to be all right'.
[29] See *Adages* I. v. 6 (*CWE* 31. 390).

Therefore let thy first care be that thy mind be not armed.³⁰ We arm our body because° we should have no need to fear the dagger or privy murderer° of the thief: and shall we not arm the mind likewise, that he be in safeguard also? Our enemies be armed to destroy us: doth it grieve us to take our weapons of defence to save ourselves, that we perish not? They watch to kill: shall not we watch to be out of danger?

But of the armour and weapons of a Christian man we shall make mention especially when we come to the places convenient.° In the mean time, to touch the matter briefly, whosoever will assail with battle the seven nations³¹ which are called Canaanites, Hittites, Amorites, Perizzites, Girgashites, Hivites, and Jebusites — that is to say, whosoever will take upon him to fight against the whole host of vices, of the which seven be counted as chief captains — the same man must provide him of two special weapons: prayer, and knowledge (otherwise called learning). Paul would we should be ever armed, who biddeth us pray continually without stop.³² Prayer, if it be pure and perfect, lifteth up thine affection to heaven, which is a tower beyond thy enemy's reach: learning strengtheneth the wit or understanding with wholesome precepts and honest opinions, and putteth [9ᵛ] thee ever in remembrance of virtue; so that neither [should] be lacking to the other. 'These twain cleave ever together like friends, the one ever requireth the other of help.'³³ The one maketh intercession and prayeth: the other showeth what is to be desired and how thou oughtest to pray. That thou mightest pray fervently and (as James exhorteth us) without doubting or mistrust,³⁴ faith and hope bring to pass. To pray in the name of Jesus — which is nothing else but to desire things wholesome for the soul's health — only learning or doctrine teacheth thee. Said not Christ to the sons of Zebedee, 'Ye know not what ye ask'?³⁵

But prayer verily is the more excellent, as she who communeth and talketh familiarly³⁶ with almighty God. Yet, for all that, is doctrine no less necessary. And I cannot tell whether thou (who art fled from Egypt) mightest without great jeopardy commit thyself to so long a journey, so hard and full of difficulty, without the captains Aaron and Moses. Aaron, who was charged with the sacrifices and with things dedicated to the service of God in his temple, betokeneth prayer. By Moses is figured° the knowledge of the law of God. And, as knowledge of God

---

30 armed] L. 'inermis' ('unarmed', as in 1533), but 1523 could be right if 'care' is taken to mean 'anxiety about' rather than 'precaution against'.
31 seven nations] Deut. 7. 1; enemies the Israelites were to overcome, and later symbolic of the seven deadly sins.
32 e.g. Ephes. 6. 18.
33 Horace, *Art of Poetry* 410–11.
34 James 1. 6.
35 Matt. 20. 22.
36 talketh familiarly] 1523 'taketh familiarity'.

ought not to be imperfect, so prayer should not be cold, faint, slack, without courage and quickness.° Moses with the weapon of prayer [10ʳ] fought against his enemies, lifting up his hands to heaven; which when for weariness he had let down, then the Israelites had the worse.³⁷ Thou haply° when thou prayest considerest only how much of thy psalms thou hast mumbled up, and thinkest much babbling to be the strength or virtue of prayer — which is chiefly the vice of them who (as infants) cleave to the literal sense and have not yet grown up to the ripeness of the spirit. But hear what Christ teacheth us in Matthew, saying:

When ye pray, speak not much, as the ethnics° or Gentiles° do, for they think their prayers to be accepted because of much babbling. Counterfeit ye them not therefore, for your Father knoweth whereof ye have need afore ye desire it of him.³⁸

And Paul to the Corinthians despiseth ten thousand words babbled with the mouth in comparison of five spoken in knowledge.³⁹ Moses opened not his lips, and yet God said to him, 'Why criest thou so to me?'⁴⁰ Not the noise of the lips but the fervent desire of the mind (as it were a very shrill voice) beateth the ears of God.

Moreover, let this be a customable° thing with thee, as soon as thine enemy ariseth against thee, and when the vices which thou hast forsaken trouble thee again, that thou then — without tarrying, with sure confidence [10ᵛ] and trust — lift up thy mind to heaven, from whence help shall come to thee, and thither also lift up thy hands. It is a very sure thing to be occupied in deeds of piety, that⁴¹ thy deeds be applied not to worldly business but unto Christ. Yet, lest thou shouldst despise the help of knowledge, consider one thing: at the first it was enough for the Israelites to flee from their enemies, nor durst they be so bold as to provoke the Amalekites and to try° with them hand for hand before they were refreshed⁴² with manna from heaven and with water that ran out of the hard rock. The noble warrior David, refreshed and made strong with his feast, set nought by the whole host of his adversaries, saying, 'O good Lord, thou hast set a table of meat° before me to defend me against all men that trouble me'.⁴³

Believe me, brother singularly beloved in my heart, that there is none so great violence of thy foes and adversaries — that is to say, none so great temptation — which fervent study or meditation of Holy Scripture is not able to put° back, nor any so grievous adversity which it maketh not easy. And, lest I should seem to be

---

³⁷ Exod. 17. 11.
³⁸ Matt. 6. 7–8.
³⁹ 1 Corinth. 14. 19.
⁴⁰ Exod. 14. 15.
⁴¹ that] 'in order that'.
⁴² before they were refreshed] Exod. 16 and 17.
⁴³ Ps. 23. 5.

somewhat a bold interpreter (though I could defend myself with great authority): what thing, I pray thee, could more properly have figured the knowledge of the secret law of God than did manna?

[11ʳ] First, because it came not out of the earth but descended from heaven, thou seest great diversity between the doctrine of God and the doctrine of man. For all the Holy Scripture came by divine inspiration, and from God the Author of it.

The cause of the shortness° is the humility, lowliness, or humbleness of the style, under rude° words including great mystery.

To speak of the pureness of it: no mortal science is which is not defiled with some black spot° of error. Only the doctrine of Christ is everywhere white as snow, everywhere bright, everywhere pure and clean.

That it is rough and somewhat sharp betokeneth secret mysteries hid in the literal sense. If thou handle the outer side and (as it were) the cod,° what is more hard and unsavoury? They tasted but the outer rind of manna who said to Christ, 'This is a hard saying, and who may abide the hearing of it?'[44] But get out the spiritual sense, and nothing is sweeter nor more full of pleasure and sweet juice.

Moreover 'manna' is in the Hebrew tongue as much to say as 'what is this?'. Which question agreeth well to Holy Scripture, which hath nothing in it idle or in vain, no, not one tittle° or prick° unworthy to be searched, unworthy to be pondered, unworthy of this saying 'what is this?'.

It is a common use to the Holy Ghost to signify by water the knowledge [11ᵛ] of the law of God. Thou readest of the 'water of comfort' by whose banks David rejoiceth to have been nourished up.[45] Thou readest of the water which Wisdom conveyeth into the tops of every way.[46] Thou readest of the mystical° river into the which Ezekiel entered and could not wade over.[47] Thou readest of the wells that Abraham digged, which afterwards when they were stopped of the Philistines, Isaac repaired again.[48] Thou readest of the twelve fountains[49] where the Israelites refreshed themselves and made them strong to the long journey of the desert.[50] Thou readest upon the well on which Christ sat when he was wearied on his journey.[51] Thou readest of the water of Siloam, whither Christ sent the blind to

---

[44] John 6. 60.
[45] Ps. 23. 2.
[46] Sirach 24. 30–31.
[47] Ezek. 47.1–6.
[48] Gen. 26. 18.
[49] Exod. 15. 27.
[50] strong to the long journey of the desert] T. swerves around what seems a slip in E.'s 'peragratis quadraginta mansionibus' ('having made forty halts'). It was too early in the Israelite exodus for that to be true. The 'forty halts' of the *entire* journey to the promised land are listed in Numb. 33.
[51] John 4. 6.

recover his sight.⁵² Thou readest of the water poured into the basin to wash the Apostles' feet.⁵³ And because it needeth not to rehearse° all things in this signification, mention is made in Scripture of wells, fountains, and rivers, by which is signified nothing else but that we ought to inquire and search diligently for the mysteries hid in Scripture. What signifieth water hid in the veins of the earth but mystery covered or hid in the literal sense? What meaneth the same conveyed abroad° but mystery opened and expounded? which, when it is spread and dilated° [12ʳ] both wide and broad to the edifying of hearers, what cause is why it might not be called a river?

Wherefore, if thou dedicate thyself altogether unto the study of Scripture, and shalt exercise thy mind both day and night in the laws of God, no fear shall trouble thee neither by day nor night, but thou shalt against all assaults of thine enemies be armed and exercised also.

And I disallow° it not utterly if a man for a season (to begin withal) shall exercise and sport himself in works of poets and philosophers who were Gentiles, as it were in his ABC or an introductory to a more effectual thing — so° that he taste of them measurably, as youth requireth, and even as though a man took them in his way; but not abide and tarry upon them still, and to wax old and to die in them, as he were bound to the rocks of Sirens, that is to say, that he put not his whole delectation in them and so never go forward. The holy bishop Basil to such pastime exhorteth young men whom he himself had induced and brought unto the conversation° of Christian men. And our Augustine calleth again° his friend Licentius to pass the time with the Muses. Neither yet displeaseth it Jerome that a Jew should love a wench of the Gentiles taken in war.⁵⁴ Cyprian is [12ᵛ] commended because he garnished the temple of God with the spoils of the Egyptians.

But in no case I would that thou, with the learning of the Gentiles, shouldst suck of the Gentiles' vices and conversation also. Nevertheless, thou shalt find many things there which help to honest° living; nor is to be refused whatsoever an author (yea, though he be a Gentile) yet teacheth well. For Moses verily, though he were never so familiar with God, yet despiseth he not the counsel of his father-in-law, Jethro.⁵⁵ Those sciences fashion and quicken a child's wit and make him

---

⁵² John 9. 7.
⁵³ John 13. 5.
⁵⁴ Deut. 21. 10–13. The 'wench of the Gentiles' symbolises secular learning, made acceptable by the authority of such important figures in the ancient Church as St Basil the Great (*c.* 330–379), St Augustine of Hippo, St Jerome (*c.* 345–420), responsible for the Vulgate Latin Bible, and St Cyprian of Carthage (*c.* 200–258). See particularly Augustine, *On Christian Teaching* II. 144–47, and Jerome, *Letters and Select Works*, in *The Nicene and Post-Nicene Fathers*, 2nd series, vol. VI, trans. by W. H. Fremantle (Grand Rapids: Wm B. Eerdmans, 1989), Letters 66.8 and 70.2. For Basil and Licentius see *ASD* V-8, p. 113.
⁵⁵ Exod. 18. 24.

apt beforehand marvellously to the understanding of Holy Scripture: unto which to presume suddenly and rudely with hands and [feet] unwashed is in a manner a certain kind of sacrilege. And Jerome checketh° the shameless pertness of them who straightway from secular or worldly science dare take in hand once to meddle° with Holy Scripture. But how much shamefuller do they who never tasted other science, and yet at the first chop° dare do the same thing!

But as the Scripture of God is not much fruitful if thou stand and cleave still in the letter, in like manner the poetry of Homer and Virgil shall not profit a little if thou remember that it must be understood [13^r] in the allegory sense; a thing that no man can deny who hath tasted of the learning of old antiquity never so little, yea, with the tip of his tongue or with the outmost part of his lips. I would counsel thee not once to touch those wanton poets who wrote uncleanly, or at the least way that thou look not too far in them — except thou couldst the better abhor vices when they are described to thee, and (in comparison of filthy things) the more fervently love honest. Of philosophers, my mind is that thou follow them that were of the sect of Plato, because they partly° agree with us in many things, and their style and figurate° speaking draweth very nigh to the manner or kind of speaking of prophets and of the Gospel. And (to make an end shortly) it shall be profitable for thee to taste of all manner learning of the Gentiles, if so be it be done as I showed before (both in years according,° and also measurably), moreover with cautel° and judgement, discreetly;° furthermore with speed and after the manner of a man that intendeth but to pass over the country only, and not to dwell or inhabit there: in conclusion (which thing is the first), if all things be applied and referred to Christ. For so all shall be clean to them that be clean; when, on the other side, to them that be unclean nothing is [13^v] clean.[56]

And it shall be no rebuke to thee if, after the example of Solomon, thou nourish up again at home at thy house sixty queens, and of sovereign° ladies eighty, with damsels innumerable,[57] of secular science — so° that Wisdom of God be, above all other, thy best-beloved, thy turtle-dove, thy sweetheart, who only seemeth beautiful. And an Israelite now and then loveth a stranger and a barbarous damsel, overcome with her beauty: but when her hairs be shaven off and her nails pared, then of a stranger she is made an Israelite also.[58] The prophet Hosea likewise married a harlot and of her got children, not for himself but for the Lord of Sabaoth;[59] and the holy fornication of the prophet augmented the household of God.

The Hebrews, after they had forsaken Egypt, lived with light and pure white bread for a season, but it was not sufficient to so great a journey. Therefore, that

---

[56] Titus 1. 15.
[57] Song 6. 8.
[58] Deut. 21. 10–13; see note 54 above.
[59] Hosea 1. 2–11 (for the 'Lord of Hosts').

bread loathed, at once thou must make as good speed as can be unto manna of celestial Wisdom, which shall nourish thee abundantly and strengthen thee till thou have obtained thy purpose and art perfectly come unto the victory of reward that never shall cease. But thou must ever remember in the mean season that Holy Scripture may not be touched but with clean washed hands — [14ʳ] that is to understand, with a very pure mind — lest that which of itself is a preservative, or a treacle,° in thy own fault be turned to thee into poison; and manna to thee should putrefy;[60] and lest haply it should fortune° to thee as it did to Uzzah, who feared not to set to his profane and unclean hands to the ark of God inclining on the one side, and with sudden death was punished for his lewd° service.[61]

The first point is that thou have Holy Scriptures in great reverence and think them to be (as they be indeed) the decrees and answers of God, and that they came out of the secret mind and closet of God. Moved inwardly, ravished and marvellously altered and changed unto another manner of figure or shape (if thou shalt come religiously with reverence, and meekly), thou shalt see the pleasures, the delicates° or dainties of the blessed Spouse. Thou shalt see the secret and precious jewels of rich Solomon. Thou shalt see the secret treasure of eternal Wisdom. But take heed how thou press not in malapertly° into that privy parlour: the door is low, beware thou break not thy brow against the upper post and fall back again. Think on this wise and surely believe: that nothing that thou seest with thine eyes, [14ᵛ] nothing that thou handlest with thy fingers, to be indeed the same thing which it appeareth to be so surely as those things be true which thou readest in Holy Scripture; so that — if heaven and earth should perish — yet of the words of God [neither] one jot° nor tittle° shall perish, but all shall be fulfilled.[62] Though men lie, though men err, yet the verity of God neither deceiveth nor is deceived.

Of the interpreters of Scripture choose them above all others who go furthest from the letter; who chiefly (next after Paul) be Origen, Ambrose,[63] Jerome, Augustine. For I see many new divines stuck very much in the letter, and with good will give more study to subtle and checking[64] arguments than to search out the mysteries — as though Paul had not said that our law were spiritual and ought to be understood spiritually.[65] I have known men ere this, yea, and that not a few, who stand so well in their own conceit° (with the fantastical traditions,

---

[60] putrefy] Exod. 16. 20. *1523* omits 'nisi in viscera affectus transieris' ('unless you pass it into the bowels of emotion'); recovered by *1533*.
[61] Uzzah] II Sam. 6. 6–7.
[62] Matt. 5. 18.
[63] Ambrose] Bishop of Milan (c. 339–397), an older contemporary of Augustine and credited with his conversion.
[64] subtle and checking] 'cleverly scoring points and catching others out'.
[65] Rom. 7. 14, I Corinth. 2. 14.

imaginations, and inventions of man) that they disdained the interpretation of old doctors (who were nigh to Christ and his Apostles both in time and living also), and count them as dreams. Dr Duns gave them such confidence that, notwithstanding they never once read of[66] Holy Scripture, yet [15ʳ] should they think themselves to be perfect divines. Which men, though they never speak things so craftily° and full of checks,° yet whether they speak things worthily of the Holy Ghost or no, let other men judge. But if thou hadst lever° to be somewhat lusty° and quick of spirit than to be armed to contention (that is to say, unto brawling and scolding,° unto melancholy and black dispositions), if thou seek the fatness[67] of the soul rather than to satisfy the unquietness of thy mind, study chiefly old doctors, whose religion to God is more to be pondered and looked upon, whose learning is more plenteous and sage also, whose style is neither barren nor rude, and interpretation agreeable° to holy mysteries.

And I say not this because I despise these new divines, but for because I set more by things which are more profitable and more apt and agreeable for thy purpose. And also the Spirit of God hath his certain tongue or speech appropriate° to himself: he hath his figures, similitudes or parables, comparisons, proverbs, and riddles, which thou shouldst observe and mark diligently if thou shouldst understand them. The wisdom of God stuttereth and lispeth and (as it were a diligent mother) fashioneth her words according to our infancy and feebleness. [15ᵛ] She giveth milk to them who are infants in Christ and weak meat to feeble stomachs. Thou therefore make speed that thou were a man, make haste unto perfect and strong meat and prepare a man's stomach. She stoopeth down and boweth herself to thy humility and lowness: arise thou upon the other side and ascend unto her faith and excellency. It is like a monster and an unnatural thing to be ever a child. He is too heartless° that never ceaseth to be sickly. The recording° of one verse should be more savoury in thy mouth and shall nourish thee better if thou break the cod and taste of the sweetness which is within, than if thou shouldst sing the whole Psalter and understand it but only after the literal sense.

Whereof verily I warn thee the rather a great deal because I know by experience that this error hath not infected the lay people only, but also the minds of them who profess and show outward (in the habit° and names or titles of profession) perfect religion; insomuch that they think and suppose that the very service of God is put in this one thing chiefly, that is to say, if they shall say over daily and mumble up as much as they can of the psalms, and yet for the most part understand them not, no, not so much as in the literal sense verily. [16ʳ] Neither think I that any other thing is the cause why we see the charitable living of our monks and cloisterers° to decay everywhere, and to be so cold, so slacked, so faint,

---

[66] of] 'from'.
[67] fatness] i.e. fine, well-nourished condition.

and so greatly to vanish away, but that they die and end their lives in ceremonies and in the literal sense of Scripture — that is to say, they understand the Scripture as it soundeth unto the carnal ears and never enforce° to grow up unto the spiritual sense or knowledge of Holy Scripture. Neither they hear Christ crying in the Gospel, 'the flesh' (that is to say, the letter or that° ye see outward) 'profiteth not at all — it is the spirit within that quickeneth or giveth life'.[68] And they hear not Paul affirming with his Master that 'the letter killeth, it is the spirit which giveth life';[69] and again, 'we know', sayeth he, 'that the law is spiritual and not carnal';[70] and 'spiritual things must be compared with spiritual things'.[71] In time past the Father of all spiritual gifts would be honoured [in the mountain, but now he will be honoured] in the spirit.[72]

Though I dispraise not the feebleness of them who do that they only be able to do: pronouncing the mystical psalms with pure faith, without dissimulation or hypocrisy. Yea, and — as [in] conjurations or enchantments of magic certain words, which are not understood of them who pronounce them, yet are believed to be of virtue° and strength — [16ᵛ] even so the words of God, though they be not perfectly understood, nevertheless we must trust that they be profitable to them that either say or else hear them [with sincere faith and pure affection]; and that the angels who be present and understand them be moved to help us. And Paul despiseth not them who speak with tongues that thing they understand not; but he exhorteth them to leave their infancy and to follow more perfect gifts.[73] Unto which if some one man cannot attain — not through the fault of a corrupt mind, but for lack of capacity — let not that same man bark against them who enforce to obtain better things; and (after the precept of Paul) 'let not him who eateth despise him who eateth not, nor he that eateth not judge him that eateth'.[74]

Nevertheless I will not have thee, who art endued with so happy a wit, to be slow and halt° in the barren letter, but to make speed unto more secret mysteries, and to help with continual prayer that fervent desire and lusty purpose of thy mind, until he open to thee the book clasped with seven clasps[75] who hath the key of David, who also shutteth (and no man openeth) the privities° of the Father;[76] which never man knew but the Son and he to whom his Son hath vouchsafed to disclose them.[77]

[68] John 6. 63.
[69] II Corinth. 3. 6.
[70] Rom. 7. 14.
[71] I Corinth. 2. 13.
[72] John 4. 19–24. The bracketed words, lacking in 1523, are in 1533.
[73] I Corinth. 12. 30–31, 14. 13–19.
[74] Rom. 14. 3.
[75] Rev. 5. 1.
[76] Rev. 3. 7.
[77] Cf. Matt. 11. 27, but 'which' here is impersonal (the 'privities').

But whither goeth our style° aside? My intent was to [17ʳ] describe to thee the form of living, not of learning; but I turned out of the way thus far while I enforced to show thee a meet° shop° from whence thou must fetch thee a new armour of this new kind of war. Therefore (to come to thy purpose again) if thou shalt pluck out of the books of the Gentiles of everything the best, and also if thou — by the example[78] of the bee flying round about by the gardens of old authors — shalt suck out only the wholesome and sweet juice (the poison refused and passed by), thy mind shall be the better apparelled a great deal and armed to the common living and conversation° of one with another in honest manner. For the philosophers and learned men of the Gentiles in their war used certain weapons and armour not to be despised. Nevertheless, whatsoever thing of honesty or of truth thou findest anywhere, think that to be Christ's. The divine artillery forged (as poets feign) of Vulcan, which with no weapons can be pierced, is fetched but only out of the armoury of Holy Scripture, where our noble captain David laid up in store the whole apparel of war[79] for his soldiers, with which they should fight afar and at hand against the uncircumcised Philistines. With this armour was neither [17ᵛ] armed Homer's Achilles, nor Virgil's Aeneas, though they be feigned so to be: of whom the one with ire, the other with love, was overcome shamefully. And it is not spoken without reason that those weapons be not forged in the workhouses of man, but in the workhouse or forge that is common to Vulcan and Pallas (otherwise called Minerva); for poets — feigners of gods — make Vulcan lord of fire and Minerva the lady of wit° and of faculties of science and crafts. A thing which I think to be brought to pass then (as thou mayst easily perceive) when the fire of love of God hath armed thy wits, endued with honest faculties so strongly that 'if all the world should fall on thy head, yet could not the stroke put thee in fear'.[80]

But first thou must cast away the harness of proud Saul,[81] which load a man rather than be necessary or profitable, and cumbered David to fight with Goliath and to help him not at all. Moreover, from the bank of the brook of Holy Scripture thou must gather five stones (which be peradventure the 'five words' of Paul which he 'speaketh in knowledge'),[82] then take a sling in thy right hand. With these weapons is lightly° overthrown our old Enemy, the father of pride, Satan — whom at the last with what weapons did our [18ʳ] Head Christ Jesus overcome? Did he not smite the forehead of our adversary, as it had been with stones fetched out of the brook, when he answered to him tempting with words of Scripture?[83]

---

[78] example] See Seneca, *Epistles* 84; repeated in Macrobius, *Saturnalia* I (preface).
[79] whole apparel of war] In the Psalms.
[80] 'if all [...] in fear'] For E. a quotation from Horace (*Odes* III. 3. 7–8), but (as in similar instances) not necessarily for T.
[81] I Sam. 17. 38–40 (also 'five stones').
[82] I Corinth. 14. 18–19.
[83] Cf. Matt. 4. 1–11.

Wilt thou hear the instruments or artillery of Christian men's war? 'And the zeal of him', sayeth Scripture, 'shall take harness, and shall harness his creatures to avenge his enemies. He will put on justice for his breast-plate, and take for his helmet sure and true judgement, he will take a shield of equity° impenetrable (or that cannot be pierced), yea, and he will sharpen or fashion cruel wrath into a spear.'[84] Thou readest also in Isaiah, 'He is armed with justice as with a habergeon,° and a sallet° of health° upon his head, he is clothed with the vestures of vengeance, and covered as it were with a cloak of zeal'.[85] Now if we shall go to the storehouse of Paul (no faint soldier) certainly we shall find there the armour of our war: not carnal things but 'valiant in God to destroy fortresses and counsels and every high thing that exalteth itself against the doctrine of God'.[86] Thou shalt find there 'the armour of God by which thou mayst resist in a woeful day'.[87] Thou shalt find there 'the armour of justice on the right hand and on the left'.[88] Thou shalt find there 'the defence of thy [18ᵛ] sides verity' and the 'habergeon of justice', 'the shield of faith wherewith thou mayst quench all the hot and fiery weapons of the cruel adversary'. Thou shalt find there also the 'helmet of health', and the 'sword of the Spirit, which is the Word of God'.[89]

With the which all if a man shall be diligently armed and decked° or instructed,° he may boldly without fear bring forth the bold saying of Paul, 'Who shall separate us from the love of God? Shall tribulation, straitness° or difficulty? shall hunger, nakedness, peril, persecution? shall a sword?'[90] Behold how mighty enemies, and how feared of all men, he setteth at nought. But hear also a certain greater thing, for it followeth: 'But in all these things we have overcome by his help who loved us. And I am assured', sayeth he, 'that neither death, nor life, nor angels, nor powers, nor miracles, nor present things, nor things to come, nor strength, nor high, nor low, nor no other creature, shall separate us from the love of God which is in Christ Jesus.'[91] Oh, happy trust and confidence which the weapons or armour of light[92] give to Paul (that is, by interpretation, a 'little man').[93]

Of such armour therefore abundantly shall Holy Scripture minister to thee, if thou [19ʳ] wilt occupy thy time in it with all thy might, so that thou shalt [not]

---

[84] Wisd. 5. 17–20.
[85] Isaiah 59. 17.
[86] II Corinth. 10. 4–5.
[87] Ephes. 6. 13.
[88] II Corinth. 6. 7.
[89] Ephes. 6. 14–17; 'health' (L. 'salus') is 'salvation'.
[90] Rom. 8. 35.
[91] Rom. 8. 37–39.
[92] Rom. 13. 12.
[93] 'little man'] In L. 'paulus'. 1523 omits L. 'qui se etiam proiectamentum huius mundi appellat' (1533 'which calleth himself the refuse or outcast of the world'); see I Corinth. 4. 13.

need our counsel. Nevertheless, seeing it is thy mind lest I should seem not to have obeyed thy request, I have forged° for thee this little treatise called *Enchiridion* (that is to say, a certain 'little dagger'),[94] which never lay out of thy hand, no, not when thou art at meat or in thy chamber; insomuch that — if at any time thou shalt be compelled to go a pilgrimage° in worldly occupations, and shalt be encumbered to bear about with thee the very right and meet armour — yet commit° not that the subtle Lier-in-wait° and Tempter of men at any season should come upon thee and find thee utterly unarmed, but at the least let it not grieve thee to have with thee this little sword, which shall not be heavy to bear, nor yet unprofitable for defence. For it is very little, yet if thou use it wisely, and couple with it the buckler° of faith, thou shalt be able to withstand the fierce and raging assault of thy Enemy, so that thou shalt have no deadly wound.

But now it is time that I begin to give thee a certain rule of the use of these weapons, which if thou shalt put in execution or practice I trust it will come to pass that our captain Jesus Christ shall translate° [19ᵛ] thee, a conqueror, out of this little castle or garrison into his great city Jerusalem with triumph; where is no rage at all of any battle, but eternal quietness, perfect peace, and assured tranquillity. But yet, in the mean time, trust, hope, and confidence to be in safeguard, is for a great part in armour and weapon.

CHAPTER THREE

The first point of wisdom is that thou shouldst know thyself, and of two manner of wisdoms: of the true wisdom and of the apparent wisdom

That excellent good thing, then, which all men seek is peace or quietness: unto which the lovers of this world also refer all their studies.° But they seek a false peace and shoot at a wrong mark. This peace likewise the philosophers promised unto the followers of their sects — but deceivably, for Christ only giveth it, the world giveth not it.[95] To come to this quietness the only way or means is if we shall make war against ourselves, if we shall fight strongly against our own vices. For with these enemies God is at bate° with [20ʳ] deadly hate, who is our peace, who naturally° is Virtue itself and Father and Lord of all virtue. And a filthy puddle, a gout,° or a sink° gathered together of all kind of vices, of° Stoics (the most fervent defenders of virtue) is called 'foolishness'; in our Scripture it is called 'malice'. And in like manner honesty,° perfect in all points, of both parties is called 'wisdom'.

But (after the saying of the wise man) doth not wisdom overcome malice?[96]

---

[94] 'little dagger'] In Gk *lit.* 'something held in the hand'.
[95] John 14. 27.
[96] Wisd. 7. 29–30.

The father and head of malice is that ruler of darkness, Belial,° whose steps whosoever followeth, the same man walketh in the night. On the other side the ground of wisdom, and indeed Wisdom itself, is Christ Jesus; who is very° Light, and the brightness of the glory of the Father, and only° expelleth the night of the worldly wisdom; who (by the testimony of Paul), as he was made redemption and justification to us that be born again in him, even so likewise was he made our wisdom.[97] 'We', sayeth Paul, 'preach Christ crucified, which to the Jews is an occasion of ruin and to the Gentiles foolishness. But to the elect, both of the Jews and also of the Gentiles, we preach Christ, the virtue or strength of God, and the wisdom of God';[98] by whose wisdom, through his example, [20^v] we may bear away the victory of[99] our enemy, malice, if we shall be wise in him, in whom also we shall be conquerors.

Make much of this Wisdom and take her in thine arms. Worldly wisdom set at nought, which with a false title and under a feigned colour° of honesty boasteth and showeth herself gay to fools, when (after the mind of Paul) there is no greater foolishness with God than worldly wisdom — a thing that must be forgotten again of him that will be wise indeed. 'If any man', sayeth Paul, 'among you seem to be wise in this world, let him be a fool that he may be wise, for the wisdom of this world is foolishness with God.'[100] And a little afore Paul sayeth:

> It is written, 'I will destroy the wisdom of wise men, and the prudence of prudent men I will reprove'. Where is the wise man? Where is the subtle lawyer? Where is the searcher of this world? Hath not God made the wisdom of this world foolishness?[101]

And I doubt not but even now with great hate these foolish wise men bark against thee, and these blind captains or guides of blind men cry out and roar against thee, saying that thou art deceived, that thou dotest and art as mad as a Bedlam° man, because thou intendest to [21^r] depart from the world unto Christward. These be in name only Christian men, but in deed they are partly mockers of Christ's doctrine, and partly they withstand it. See that the barking of these men move thee not; whose miserable blindness ought rather to be wept, sorrowed, and mourned at than to be counterfeited.°

Oh, Lord God, what meaneth this unnatural and monstrous kind of learning, that a man in trifles and things of no value, yea, unto filthiness, only should be clear-witted, ware,° and expert — but in those things which only make for our safeguard and health,° and for the everlasting life of our souls, not to have much more understanding than a brute beast! Paul would we should be wise, but in

---

[97] 1 Corinth. 1. 30.
[98] 1 Corinth. 1. 23–24.
[99] of] 'from'.
[100] 1 Corinth. 3. 18–19.
[101] 1 Corinth. 1. 19–20 (quoting Isaiah 29. 14).

goodness — and children in evil.¹⁰² These men be wise unto all manner of iniquity, but they have no learning to do good. And forasmuch as the facundious° and eloquent Greek poet Hesiod¹⁰³ counteth him good for nothing who neither perceiveth by himself, nor giveth audience° to him that teacheth well, of what degree then shall they be counted who, when they themselves be most shamefully deceived, yet never cease to trouble, to laugh to scorn, and put in fear, them who already be come to their [21ᵛ] wits again?

But shall not the mocker be mocked? 'He that dwelleth in heaven shall mock them again,° and our Lord shall laugh them to scorn.'¹⁰⁴ Thou readest in the Book of Wisdom, 'They shall see verily and shall despise him, but God shall mock them'.¹⁰⁵ To be mocked of lewd° men is as it were a praise, but no doubt it is a blessed thing to follow our Head Christ and his Apostles, and a fearful thing truly to be mocked of God. 'I also', sayeth Wisdom, 'will laugh when ye perish, and mock you when that thing hath happened to you which you feared';¹⁰⁶ that is to say, when they — awaked out of their dream and come again to themselves, when it is too late — shall say:

> These be they whom we have had in derision, in disdain, and reproof, casting in their teeth their virtuous living and whatsoever evil thing hath been done to them who in such manner have lived beforetime: we for lack of understanding have counted their lives to be in madness and their end to be without honour.¹⁰⁷

This wisdom is beastly and (as James sayeth) diabolic and of the Devil,¹⁰⁸ and is an enemy to God; and the end of it is misery; which certainly followeth, as a footman, poison° arrogancy (otherwise called presumption); after presumption [22ʳ] followeth blindness of mind; after blindness of mind followeth fervent rage and tyranny of the affections° and appetites; after the tyranny of affections followeth the universal weeds of all vices, and liberty without grudge° of conscience to do what the lust° desireth; then followeth custom; after custom dulness or grossness° of the mind and a dazing of the wits for lack of capacity, whereby it cometh to pass that evil men perceive not their own sin and abominable living. Then death of the body oppresseth° them (astonied° and as it were a trance) and the second death¹⁰⁹ receiveth them into eternal damnation.

Thou seest how the mother of extreme mischief is worldly wisdom. But of

---

¹⁰² Rom. 16. 19.
¹⁰³ Hesiod] *Works and Days* 296–97; see also *Adages* II. v. 52 (*CWE* 33. 264).
¹⁰⁴ Ps. 2. 4.
¹⁰⁵ Wisd. 4. 18.
¹⁰⁶ Prov. 1. 26.
¹⁰⁷ Wisd. 5. 4, expanded by T.
¹⁰⁸ James 3. 15.
¹⁰⁹ second death] i.e. of the soul; cf. Rev. 2. 11 and 20. 6.

Christ's wisdom, which the world thinketh foolishness, thiswise thou readest: 'All good things came to me on heaps with her, and inestimable honesty came by the hands of her. And I rejoiced and prospered in all things because this Wisdom went before me, and I was not aware that she was mother of all goodness.'[110]

This wisdom bringeth with her as companions soberness and meekness. Meekness disposeth and maketh us apt to receive the Spirit of God, for in a person who is lowly, humble, and meek [22ᵛ] the Spirit of God rejoiceth to rest; and when the Spirit hath replenished our minds with his sevenfold grace,[111] then forthwith spring the happy herbs of all virtues, with those blessed fruits,[112] of which the chief is inward joy, joy enclosed or locked up in a secret coffer; joy known of them only who have tasted of it; joy that never vanisheth away nor fadeth with the joys of this world, but increaseth and groweth unto eternal joy. This wisdom, my brother, (after the counsel of James) must thou require of God with fervent and burning desire,[113] and (after the counsel of the wise man) thou must dig her out of the veins of Holy Scripture, as it were treasure hid in the earth.[114]

The chief part of this wisdom is that thou shouldst 'know thyself': which word to have descended from heaven believed antiquity,[115] and so much that saying pleased great authors that they judged the ground of all wisdom utterly to be contained in that point only, that is to wit,° if a man should know himself. But let the weight or authority of this decree or principle be of no value with us except it agree with our learning.° The mystical° lover in the Song of Solomon threateneth his spouse and biddeth her to get herself out [23ʳ] of the doors, except° she should know herself, saying, 'O thou beautiful among all women, if thou know not thyself, go out of doors and depart after the steps of thy flocks and feed the kids or goats'.[116]

Moreover, lest any man would presumptuously take upon him that he knoweth himself well enough, I am not sure whether any man know his body unto the utmost: and then how can a man know the state of his mind surely enough? Paul was so beloved of God that he saw the mysteries of the third heaven,[117] yet durst he not judge himself.[118] He would have judged himself no doubt if he had known himself surely enough. If so spiritual a man, who 'discerneth all things',[119] whom

---

[110] Wisd. 7. 11–12.
[111] sevenfold grace] The seven gifts of the Spirit outlined in Isaiah 11. 2–3.
[112] Galat. 5. 22–23.
[113] James 1. 5–8.
[114] Prov. 2. 4.
[115] believed antiquity] Socrates explains its origin in *Protagoras* 343b. For its heavenly origin see Juvenal, *Satires* 11. 27. See also *Adages* I. vi. 95 (*CWE* 32. 62); Tav. 61 (Taverner's selection, ed. by Neil Rhodes, is later in this volume).
[116] Song 1. 8.
[117] II Corinth. 12. 2–4.
[118] I Corinth. 4. 3–4.
[119] I Corinth. 2. 15

no man had cunning° to judge, was not surely enough known to himself, how should we carnal men presume?

In conclusion, he should seem a soldier too much unprofitable who should surely enough know the number and virtue neither of his own company nor of his enemy's host. Thou must remember also that one Christian man hath not war with another, but with himself. And verily a great host of adversaries spring out of our own self, out [23ᵛ] of the very bowels and inward parts of us — as poets feign of certain brethren, sons to the earth. And there is so little difference between our enemy and our friend that it is hard to know the one from the other: so greatly that it shall be great jeopardy lest we (through recklessness or negligence) should take our enemy's part against our friend, or hurt our friend instead of our enemy. The noble captain Joshua was in doubt of an angel of light, saying, 'Art thou on our side, or of our enemies' part?'[120]

Seeing, then, that thou hast taken upon thee to war against thyself, forasmuch also as the chief hope both of comfort and of victory also resteth in this thing only, that thou know thyself to the utmost, I will paint therefore unto thee a certain image of thyself (as it were in a table)° and set it before thine eyes, that thou mayst perfectly know what thou art inward and (as the saying is) 'within thy skin'.[121]

CHAPTER FOUR

Of the outward and inward man

A man is, then, a certain monstrous° beast compacted together of parts two or three of great diversity: of a soul, as of a certain godly thing; and of a body, as it were [24ʳ] a brute or a dumb beast. For certainly we so greatly excel not all other kind of brute beasts in perfectness of body but that we in all its natural gifts are found to them inferiors. In our minds verily we be so celestial and of godly capacity that we may surmount above the nature of angels, and be united, knit, and made one with God. If thy body had not been added to thee, thou hadst been a celestial or godly thing. If this mind had not been grafted in thee, plainly thou hadst been a brute beast. These two natures — between themselves so diverse — he that is the very Craftsman had coupled together with blessed concord, but the serpent, the enemy of peace, put them asunder again with unhappy discord, so that now they can neither be separate without very great torment and pain, nor live joined together without continual war. And plainly (after the common saying) each in other 'holdeth the wolf by the ears',[122] and may now also agree with both

---

[120] Josh. 5. 13.
[121] See *Adages* I. ix. 89 (*CWE* 32. 226).
[122] See *Adages* I. v. 25 (*CWE* 31. 404), also for the quotation which follows. Holding on and letting go are equally unwelcome.

the pleasant verse[123] of Catullus,[124] who said to his wife, 'I can neither live with thee nor without thee' — such ruffling,° wrangling, and trouble they make between themselves with cumbrous debate,° as things diverse which indeed are but one.

The body verily, as he himself is visible, so delighteth he in things [24ᵛ] visible; as he is mortal, so followeth he things temporal; as he is heavy, so sinketh he downward. On the other part the soul, mindful of her celestial nature, enforceth° upward with great violence, and with the terrestrial hest° striveth and wrestleth. She despiseth those things that are seen, for she knoweth that they are but transitory; she seeketh true things and things of substance, which be permanent and ever abiding; and, because she is immortal and also celestial, she loveth things immortal and celestial, and she rejoiceth with things of like nature — except° that she be drowned utterly in the filth of the body, and so by contagiousness of it hath gone out of kind° from her native gentleness.°

And verily neither Prometheus,[125] so much spoken of among the poets, sowed this discord in us, a portion of every beast mixed to our mind; nor our primitive condition gave it to us, that is to say, it sprang not in us naturally° nor was of nature given to us in our first creation or nativity: but sin hath evil° corrupted and decayed that which was well created, sowing the poison of dissension between them that were honestly agreed. For before that time both the mind ruled the body without business,° and the body obeyed without grudging. [25ʳ] Now it is clean contrary: the order between them is so troubled, the affections° or appetites of the body strive to go before reason, and reason is in a manner compelled to incline and to follow the judgement of the body. Thou mayst compare a man properly to a commonalty° where is debate and part-taking° among themselves, which (because it is gathered together of sundry kinds of men) for the diversity of minds, studies,° or appetites must needs be all-to-shivered° and shaken asunder with the beating together of contrary parts, except that the whole rule be in the hands of one, and he also be such a fellow that will command nothing but that which shall be wholesome and profitable to the common weal.° And for that cause it must needs be that he who is most wise should most bear rule, and he needs must obey that least perceiveth or understandeth.

Nothing is more heartless,° more gross° of imagination, or that less perceiveth what is comely than doth the common and unlearned people; and therefore ought they to obey the officers or rulers, and bear no rule nor office themselves. They that be nobles or senators must have audience° verily in common counsels, but

---

[123] may now also [...] pleasant verse] 'the pleasant verse could be applied to either party'.
[124] Catullus] T.'s addition. The precise words are in Martial's *Epigrams* (12. 46) but the sentiment is expressed e.g. in Ovid's *Amores* (III. 11. 39) and more loosely in Catullus's *Poems* (85).
[125] Prometheus] According to Horace, *Odes* I. 16. 13–15, Prometheus was forced to mix with the primeval clay of human beings a portion from every other creature on earth.

in such manner wise that the arbitrament° of free liberty to command [25ᵛ] and determine remain with the king only; whom it is meet° to be advertised,° to be put in remembrance, or counselled now and then — but it is not meet that he should be compelled, or that any man should set a foot before him. And finally, the king obeyeth no man, but the law only. The law must be correspondent and agreeable° to the original decree of nature or the example of honesty.° Wherefore if (out of order) the unruly commons and that wrangling dregs of the city shall strive to go before the seigniors,° or if the chief lords shall despise the commandment or rule of the king, then ariseth perilous sedition or division in our commonwealth, yea, and — except the provision, the decree, or authority of God succour — all the matter weigheth° and inclineth to clean extreme mischief and to utter confusion.

In a man, reason beareth the room° of a king. Thou mayst count for the 'chief lords' certain affections, and them of the body (but yet not all things so beastly): of which kind be natural reverence towards thy father and mother, special love to thy brethren, a benevolent mind towards thy friends and lovers, compassion upon them that be vexed with adversity or cumbered with sickness, fear of infamy, of slander, or loss of thy good [26ʳ] name, desire of honest reputation, and such other like. In conclusion,° there be certain motions of the body and also of the mind which utterly rebel against the decrees of reason, and be of the lowest sort abject after the manner of beastly villainy. Take them for the 'vile commonalty' and think that they be the uttermost and last grounds and very dregs of all together — as be bodily lust, riot,° envy, and suchlike diseases of the mind; which all without exception must be kept under in prison and with punishment as vile and bond servants, that they render to their master their task and work appointed to them, if they can; but, if not, stop at the least way them of their liberty, that they do no harm.

Which thing Plato perceiving by inspiration of God, wrote in his book called *Timaeus*[126] how the sons of gods had forged° in man unto their own similitude or likeness two kinds of souls: the one kind spiritual and immortal, the other (as it were) mortal and in danger to diverse perturbations or motions of unquietness — 'of which the first is voluptuousness,° the mother of all mischief; the next is sorrow, which is a fleeing and a let° or impediment unto good things; after that follow fear and presumptuous boldness, [26ᵛ] which are two mad counsellors; whom accompanieth indurate° wrath, which is nothing else but the desire of vengeance; moreover in that mortal soul is grafted flattering hope, with beastly imagination, and knowledge not governed of reason, and worldly love which layeth hands violently on all things'. These be almost the words of Plato,[127] and it

---

[126] *Timaeus*] Particularly 69c–d.
[127] words of Plato] E. follows closely Ficino's translation, originally published in Venice in 1481 (the edition available to E.); the passage is on f. 297 of the 1518 Ascensius printing (Paris): *Platonis Opera a Marsilio Ficino traducta.*

was not unknown to him that the felicity of this life should be put in refraining of such perturbations: for he writeth in the same work that they only live justly and blessedly who should have overcome those appetites, and that they only live unjustly and miserably who should be overcome of these same.[128]

And[129] unto that godly soul, that is to say unto reason, as unto a king, he appointed a place in the brain, as in the chief tower of our city, and (as thou mayst see) the highest part of our body and next to heaven, and most far from the nature of a beast, as a thing verily which is both of very thin bone and neither laden with gross sinews nor flesh, but is surely furnished and appointed° (within and also without) with powers of knowledge; that through the showing of them no debate should rise in our commonwealth which our king, reason, should not immediately perceive. But as touching° the parts of the mortal soul [27ʳ] (that is to wit,° the affections or appetites), as every one of them is either obedient or else grudgeth° against reason, so he removeth them from him.[130] For between the neck and the midriff he set that part of the soul wherein is contained boldness, wrath, or anger — a seditious affection verily, and full of debate, and therefore needs must be refrained: but it is not yet so greatly disobedient to reason, and therefore he separated it in a mean° space between the highest and lowest, lest (if it were too nigh unto the king) it should trouble the king's quietness, and again on the other side (if it were too nigh them of the lowest sort) it might lightly° be corrupted with the contagiousness of them and with them conspire and rebel against the king. Last of all, that power which desireth the voluptuous° pleasure of meat° and drink, and that power also whereby we be moved to bodily lust, he banished utterly away far from the palace, down below beneath the midriff into the liver and the paunch, that (as and° it were a certain wild beast untamed) there it might stable and dwell at the rack;° for because that power is accustomed to raise up motions most violent, and never to be obedient to the rule of the king. What beastliness, yea, and what rebellion, is in the lowest portion of the mortal [27ᵛ] soul, at the least way the privy° parts of the body may teach thee: wherein most of all rageth tyranny — which also of all members only ever among° maketh rebellion with uncleanly motions, the king crying the contrary, yea, in vain.

Thou seest then evidently how that this noble beast, man — who is so godly a thing in his upper parts and in his high powers — plainly and without any exception endeth in an unreasonable or brute beast. But the noble king, reason, ruling on high in his castle and considering his excellent majesty, imagineth no lewd,° no vile nor filthy thing. And he hath in his hand a noble sceptre of ivory, because he should command nothing but that were right; in whose top (as writeth

---

[128] *Timaeus* 42b.
[129] And] Plato's account continues into 69e–71a and 75c.
[130] him] 'reason'.

Homer)¹³¹ sitteth an eagle, because that reason, mounting up to celestial things, beholdeth from above those things that be on the ground disdainfully, as it were with eagle's eyes. In conclusion, he is crowned with a crown of gold, for gold (in letters of mystery)¹³² betokeneth wisdom; and the circle betokeneth that the wisdom of the king should be perfect and pure in every part.

These be the properties or gifts, then, of kings: first, that they should be very wise and provident,° lest they offend by ignorance; moreover, that they desire nothing but that which is honest and rightful, lest they [28ʳ] should do anything against the decree or judgement of reason, inordinately, frowardly, and corruptly. And whosoever lacketh any of these two points, count him to be not a king (that is to say, a ruler) but count him a robber.

CHAPTER FIVE

Of the diversity of affections°

Our king, reason, may be oppressed° verily, yet because of the eternal law which God hath graven in him he cannot be corrupted so greatly but that he shall grudge° and call back; to whom if all the remnant will obey, he shall never commit° anything at all either to be repented, or of any jeopardy, but all things shall be administered with great moderation and discreetly,° with much quietness and tranquillity.

But as touching the affections, verily Stoics and Peripatetics° vary somewhat, though both agree in this: that we ought to live after° reason and not after the affections. Stoics will that we use for a season° those affections which immediately are stirred up of the sensual° powers (as it were a schoolmaster to teach us our first principles), but afterwards, when we be come to judgement and do begin to examine discreetly what is to be ensued° or chosen, and what in everything is to be eschewed or forsaken, [28ᵛ] then bid they that we utterly damn° and forsake them. For then (say they) not only they be not profitable to very° wisdom, but also hurtful and noisome.° And therefore they will that a perfect wise man should lack all such motions, as diseases or sickness of the mind, yea, and scarcely they grant to a wise man those first motions (more gentle)° preventing° reason, which they call 'fantasies'° or 'imaginations'.¹³³

Peripatetics teach the affections not to be destroyed utterly but to be refrained,

---

¹³¹ as writeth Homer] A composite image perhaps alluding to (e.g.) *Iliad* 8. 247 and 24. 292–93; the distinctive sceptre was an item in Roman triumphal processions: see Juvenal, *Satires* 10. 43.
¹³² letters of mystery] 'spiritual writings'.
¹³³ 'fantasies' or 'imaginations'] Technical terms in medieval philosophy for the intermediate mental stages between experiencing a particular sense-image and transmuting it into a concept, but with alternative connotations which emphasised insubstantiality and delusoriness. E. believes in a fertile and rigorous imagination, neither desiccated nor gullible.

and that the use of them is not utterly to be refused, for because they think them to be given of nature as a prick° or a spur to stir a man to virtue: as wrath maketh a man bold or hardy and is a matter° of fortitude; envy is a great cause of policy;° and in like wise it is of the others.

Socrates, in a certain book that Plato made called *Phaedo*, seemeth to agree with Stoics, where he thinketh philosophy to be nothing else but a remembrance of death:[134] that is to say, that a mind withdraw herself as much as she can from corporeal things and from whatsoever is sensible,° and convey herself to those things which be perceived with reason only, and not of° the sensible powers.

First of all, therefore, thou must behold and consider diligently all the motions, [29ʳ] movings, or stirrings of the mind, and have them surely known. Furthermore, thou must understand that no motions be so violent but that they may be either refrained of reason or else turned to virtue. Notwithstanding, I hear everywhere this contagious opinion, that some should say 'they be constrained to vices'. And on the other side many, for lack of knowledge of themselves, follow such motions as° they were the sayings or decrees of reason, insomuch that whatsoever wrath or envy doth counsel or move them to do, that they call 'the zeal of God'. And as thou seest one commonwealth to be more unquiet than another, so is one man more inclined or prone to virtue than another — which difference cometh not of the diversity of minds, but either of the influence of celestial bodies, or of our progenitors, or else of the bringing up in youth, or of the complexions of the body. The fable that Socrates[135] wrote of carters and horses (good and evil) is no old wives' tale, for thou mayst see that some be born of so moderate, so soft, so quiet, and of so gentle a disposition, and are so easy to be handled, to be turned and wound, that without business° they may be induced to virtue, yea, and they run forward by their own [29ᵛ] courage without any spurring. So clean contrary unto some other persons thou mayst perceive that there hath happened a body rebellious as a wild untamed kicking horse, insomuch that he who tameth him shall have enough ado, and sweat apace,° and yet scarce with a very rough bit, scarce with a waster° and with sharp spurs, can subdue his fierceness.

If any such one hath happened to thee, let never the rather thy heart fail thee, but so much the more fervently set upon it, thinking on this wise: not that the way unto virtue is stopped or shut up from thee, but that a larger matter of virtue is offered unto thee. But and if it be so that nature hath endued thee with gentle conditions, thou art not therefore at once better than another man, but happier — and again on this manner wise° art thou more happy, so that thou art more bound[136] also. Howbeit, what is he that is so endued with so happy gifts of nature

---

[134] remembrance of death] *Phaedo* 64a.
[135] Socrates] *Phaedrus* 246a, 253c–254e.
[136] on this manner [...] more bound] Good fortune entails extra responsibilities.

who hath not so abundantly things enough to wrestle withal°? Therefore, in whatsoever part shall be perceived most rage or rebellion to be, in that part reason, our king, must watch most diligently.

There be certain vices appropriate° unto the countries: as breaking of promise [30ʳ] is a familiar vice to men of some country; to some riot° or prodigality; to some bodily lust or pleasure of the flesh; and this happeneth to them by the disposition of their countries. Some vices accompany the complexion of the body: as woman-loves and the desire of pleasure and wanton sports accompany the sanguine man; wrath, fierceness, cursed speaking, follow the choleric man; grossness° of mind, lack of activity, sluggishness of body, and to be given to much sleep, follow the phlegmatic man; envy, inward heaviness, to be solitary, to be self-minded, soaken,[137] and churlish, follow the melancholy person. Some vices abate and increase after the age of man: as in youth lust of the body, wasteful expenses, and inconstancy; in old age niggishness° or too much saving, waywardness, and avarice. Some vices there be which should seem appropriate to the kind:[138] as fierceness to the man, vanity to the woman and desire of wreak° or to be avenged.

It fortuneth° now and then that nature (as it were to make amends) recompenseth one disease or sickness of the mind with another certain contrary good gift or property. One man is somewhat prone to sports and is set altogether on pleasure and jocund pastimes — [30ᵛ] but the same is nothing angry, nothing envious at all. Another is chaste — but somewhat high-minded,° somewhat hasty, somewhat too greedy on the world. And there be some persons also who be vexed with certain wonderful and fatal vices — as with theft, sacrilege, and homicide — which truly thou must withstand with all thy might, against whose assault also must be cast a certain brazen wall of sure purpose.

On the other side some affections be so nigh neighbours to virtue that it is jeopardous lest we should be deceived, the diversity is so dangerous and doubtful. These affections shall be corrected and amended, and they may be turned very well to that virtue which they most nighest resemble. There is some man (because of example) who is soon set on fire, is hot at once and provoked to anger with the least thing in the world: let him refrain and sober his mind and he shall be bold and courageous, nothing faint-hearted or fearful, he shall be free of speech without dissimulation. There is another man somewhat holding,° or too much saving: let the same also add a mean° and he shall be called trusty[139] and a good husband.°
He that is somewhat flattering shall be with a little moderation [31ʳ] courteous and pleasant. He that is obstinate and stiff in his opinions may be constant. Solemness may be turned to gravity. And he that hath too much of foolish toys°

---

[137] soaken] *1533* has 'sullen', but 'soaken' may be an early variant of 'soaked' (dull, characteristic of the melancholy temperament).
[138] kind] Here 'sex'.
[139] trusty] *1533* 'thrifty'; L. 'frugalis'.

may be a good companion. And after the same manner mayst thou judge of other somewhat easier° diseases of the mind. We must beware of one thing especially, which is that we cloak not the vice of nature with the name of 'virtue', calling heaviness of mind 'gravity', cruelty 'justice', envy 'zeal', filthy niggishness 'thrift', flattering 'good fellowship', knavery or ribaldry 'urbanity' or 'merry speaking'.

The only way therefore to felicity is first that thou know thyself; moreover, that thou do nothing after the affections, but in all things after the judgement of reason. Let reason be sound and pure and without corruption. Let not his mouth be out of taste:° that is to say, let him behold honest things only. But thou wilt say, 'It is a hard thing that thou commandest'. Who sayeth nay? And verily the saying of Plato is true: 'Whatsoever things be pleasant and beautiful, the same be hard to obtain'.[140] Nothing is more hard than that a man should overcome himself: and again there is no greater reward than is felicity. Jerome spake that thing excellently, as he [31^v] doth all others:

> Nothing (he sayeth) is more happy than a Christian man, to whom is promised the kingdom of heaven. Nothing is a greater peril than he who every hour is in jeopardy of his life. Nothing is more strong than he that overcometh the Devil. Nothing is more weak than he that is overcome of the flesh.[141]

If thou ponder thy own strength only, nothing is harder than to subdue thy flesh unto the spirit. If thou shalt look on God thy helper, nothing is more easy. Thou therefore now conceive, with all thy might and with fervent mind, the purpose and profession of the perfect life; and when thou hast grounded thyself upon a sure purpose, set upon it and go to it lustily. Man's mind never purposed anything fervently that he was not able to bring to pass. It is a great part of a Christian man to desire with a full purpose and with all his heart to be a Christian man. That thing which at the first sight or meeting, at the first acquaintance or coming together, shall seem impossible to be conquered or won, in process of time shall be gentle enough and, with use, easy. In conclusion with custom it shall be very pleasant. It is a very proper saying of Hesiod: 'The way of virtue is hard at the beginning, but after thou hast crept up to the top there remaineth for thee very sure quietness'.[142]

[32^r] No beast is so wild which waxeth not tame by the craft of man: and is there no craft to tame the mind of him that tameth all things? That thou might be whole in thy body thou canst refrain and subdue thyself of° certain years to keep diet or abstinence, and to withdraw thyself from the pleasures of Venus — things which the physician (being but a man) prescribed to thee: and to live quietly all thy life canst thou not rule thine affections, no, not a few months — a thing that

---

[140] Plato] See *Adages* II. i. 12 (*CWE* 33. 22); Tav. 92.
[141] Jerome, *Letters* 125. 1.
[142] Hesiod, *Works and Days* 289-92.

God commanded thee do? To save thy body from sickness there is nothing which thou durst° not: to deliver thy body and thy soul also from eternal death thou doest not those things which infidels, ethnics,° heathen men, or Gentiles have done.

CHAPTER SIX

Of the inward and also of the outward man, and of two parts of a man, proved by Holy Scripture

Certainly I am ashamed of a great number named 'Christian' men, who for the most part (as° they were brute beasts) follow the affections° and sensual° appetites, and be in this kind of war so rude° and unexercised that they perceive not the diversity° of [32ᵛ] reason and sensuality. They suppose that thing only to be 'the man' which they see and feel, yea, and they think there is nothing else in the whole world besides the things which offer themselves to the sensible wits:° when those things which are perceived with the bodily wits are most vile, yea, are nothing in comparison of those which are not seen. Whatsoever they greatly covet, that they think is 'high justice'. They call that 'peace' which is extreme bondage, that is while reason (oppressed and blinded) followeth without resistance wheresoever the appetite or affection call. This is that miserable 'peace' which Christ, the author of very° peace, who knit two in one,[143] came to break, stirring up a wholesome war between the father and the son, between the husband and the wife,[144] between those things which filthy concord had evil° coupled together and made acquainted.

Now then, let the authority of philosophers be of little weight, except° those things all be taught in Holy Scripture (though not with the same words). That° the philosophers call 'reason' Paul calleth sometimes 'the spirit', sometimes 'the inner man', otherwhiles he calleth it 'the law of the mind'. That they call 'affection', he calleth sometimes 'the flesh', sometimes 'the body', another time he calleth it 'the outer man' and 'the law of the members'. 'Walk', sayeth Paul, [33ʳ] 'in the spirit, and accomplish ye not the desires or lusts of the flesh: for the flesh desireth contrary to the spirit, and the spirit contrary to the flesh, so that ye cannot do whatsoever things ye would.'[145] And in another place, 'If ye shall live after the flesh ye shall die: if ye shall walk in the spirit and mortify the deeds of the flesh ye shall live'.[146]

Certain this is a new change of things — that peace should be sought in war

---

[143] Ephes. 2. 14.
[144] Matt. 10. 34–36.
[145] Galat. 5. 16–17.
[146] Rom. 8. 13.

and war in peace; in death life and in life death; in bondage liberty and in liberty bondage. Paul writeth in another place, 'I chastise my body and bring him into servitude'.[147] Wilt thou hear what is liberty? 'If ye be led of the Spirit,[148] ye be not subject to the law';[149] and 'we have not', sayeth he, 'received again the spirit of bondage in fear, but the Spirit who hath elected us to be the children of God'.[150] He sayeth in another place, 'I see another law in my members, repugning° against the law of my mind, subduing me to the law of sin, which law is in my members'.[151] Thou readest also with him of the 'outer man' which is corrupt, and of the 'inner man' which is renewed day by day.[152] Plato put two souls in one man: Paul in one man maketh two men so coupled together that neither without other can be, either in heaven or hell; [33ᵛ] and again so separate that the death of the one should be the life of the other. To the same (as I suppose) pertain those things which he writeth to the Corinthians:

> The first man (sayeth Paul) was made with a soul having life, the last Adam was made with a spirit giving life. But that (sayeth he) was not first which is spiritual, but that which is beastly, and then followeth that which is spiritual. The first man came of the earth, himself being terrestrial; the second came from heaven, and he himself celestial.[153]

And because it should more evidently appear that these things pertain not only to Christ and Adam but to us all, he added saying:

> As was the man made of earth, such are the terrestrial and earthly persons; and as is the celestial man, such are the celestial persons. Therefore, as we have borne the image of the earthly man, even so let us now bear the image of the celestial man. For this I say, brethren, that flesh and blood shall not possess the kingdom of heaven, nor corruption shall possess incorruption.[154]

Thou perceivest evidently how in one place he calleth that thing 'Adam made of earth' which in another place he calleth 'the flesh' and 'the outer man' which is corrupt. And this same thing certainly is also that 'body of death' wherewith Paul aggrieved [34ʳ] cried out saying, 'Oh, wretch that I am, who shall deliver me from this body of death?'[155] In conclusion: Paul, declaring the most diverse fruits of the flesh and of the spirit, writeth in another place saying, 'He that soweth in his flesh

---

[147] I Corinth. 9. 27.
[148] Spirit] or (lower-case) 'spirit'? Both forms are really needed to convey E.'s dual connotation though deploying them consistently is virtually impossible. *1523* tries also.
[149] Galat. 5. 18.
[150] Rom. 8. 15.
[151] Rom. 7. 23.
[152] II Corinth. 4. 16.
[153] I Corinth. 15. 45–47.
[154] I Corinth. 15. 48–50.
[155] Rom. 7. 24.

shall mow of his flesh corruption, but he that soweth in the spirit shall mow of the spirit life eternal'.[156]

This is the old debate° of two twins, Jacob and Esau,[157] who before they were brought forth into light wrestled within the cloisters° of the mother's belly.[158] And Esau verily caught from Jacob the pre-eminence of birth and was first born; but Jacob prevented° him again° of his father's blessing. That which is carnal cometh first: but the spiritual thing is ever best. The one was red, high-coloured, and rough with hair: and the other smooth. The one was unquiet and a hunter: the other rejoiced with domestical quietness. And the one also for hunger sold his right which pertained to him by inheritance[159] (in that he was the elder brother) and through the motions of the voluptuous° pleasure, the cause of vile bondage, he fell from his native liberty into the bondage of sin and vices: the other procured by craft of grace that which belonged not to him by right of law. Between these two brethren, though both born were of one [34ᵛ] belly and at one time, yet was there never joined perfect concord.[160] For Esau hated Jacob, and Jacob for his part — though he quitteth° not hate for hate — yet he fleeth and hath ever Esau suspected, nor dare trust him.

So to thee, likewise, let be suspected whatsoever thing the affection counselleth or persuadeth thee to do, for the doubtful credence of [the counsellor]. Jacob only° saw our Lord:[161] Esau, as cruel and without mercy, yea, and a murderer, liveth by the sword. To conclude: our Lord, when the mother asked counsel of him, answered, saying, 'The elder shall be servant to the younger';[162] but the father, Isaac, added, 'Thou, O Esau, shall do service to thy brother; but the time shall come when thou shalt shake off and loose his yoke from thy neck'.[163] Our Lord prophesied of good and obedient persons, but the father prophesied of evil and disobedient persons. The one declareth what ought to be done of all men, the other told aforehand what the most part would do.

Paul willeth that the wife be obedient to her husband,[164] for better is, sayeth Scripture, the iniquity or churlishness of the man than the kindness or courtesy of the woman. Our Eve is carnal affection, whose eyes the subtle and crafty serpent daily troubleth and vexeth with temptation, and when she is once corrupted he

---

[156] Galat. 6. 8.
[157] Jacob and Esau] See Gen. 25 and 27; also Origen, *Homilies on Genesis and Exodus*, pp. 176f.
[158] mother's belly] Gen. 25. 22–28.
[159] Gen. 25. 29–34.
[160] Gen. 27. 41–45
[161] Gen. 28. 10–22, 32. 24–30, 35. 9–15.
[162] Gen. 25. 23.
[163] Gen. 27. 40.
[164] e.g. Ephes. 5. 22. The rest of the sentence echoes Sirach 42. 14. The underlying reference is to the conflict between reason and feelings in *all* human beings. (Imagine inverted commas around 'man' and 'woman', 'wife' and 'husband', and take them allegorically.)

goeth forth and ceaseth not [35ʳ] to provoke and entice the man also, that he through consent might be partaker of the iniquity or mischievous deed. But what readest thou of the new woman (of her, I mean, that is obedient to her husband)? 'I will', sayeth Scripture, 'put hatred between thee' (that is to say, between the serpent and the woman) 'and between her generation and thine. She shall tread down thy head, and thou shalt lay await° to her heel.'¹⁶⁵ The serpent was cast down on his breast, and the death of Christ weakened his violence — he now only layeth await to the woman's heel privily. Moreover, the woman, through the grace of faith, is now changed (as it were) into a man, and boldly treadeth down his venomous head. Grace is increased, and the tyranny of the flesh is diminished.

When Sarah was decayed, through the hands of God¹⁶⁶ Abraham grew and increased; and now she calleth him not her 'husband' but her 'lord'. Neither yet could she obtain to have a child before she was dried up and barren. What, I pray thee, brought she forth at the last to her lord Abraham, now in her old days, yea, and when she was past child-bearing? Verily she brought forth Isaac: that is to say, 'joy'. For as soon as the affections have waxed old and are weakened in [35ᵛ] a man, then at the last springeth out that blessed tranquillity of an innocent mind, with sure quietness of the mind and spirit, as it were a continual feast. And as the father let not his wife have her pleasure without advisement,°¹⁶⁷ even so hath he the sporting of the children together suspect (I mean, of Isaac with Ishmael): Sarah would not that the child of a bondwoman and the child of a free woman should have conversation° together at that age, but that Ishmael (while as yet youth was fervent) should be banished afar out of presence, lest under a colour° of pastime he might entice and draw after his own manners Isaac (yet young and tender of age). Now was Abraham full of years, and now was Sarah an old wife, and had brought forth Isaac: yet Abraham mistrusteth until the answer of God had approved his wife's counsel. He is not sure of the woman until he heareth of God, 'In all things that Sarah hath said to thee, hear her voice and obey her'.¹⁶⁸

Oh, happy old age of the man in whom so mortified is that carnal man, made of the earth, that he in nothing diseaseth° the spirit! Which consent or agreement between the flesh and the spirit, whether in all things perfect enough, might happen to any man [36ʳ] in this life or no, I durst not affirm verily. Peradventure it were not expedient, for even unto Paul was given unquietness and trouble of the flesh — 'the messenger of Satan to vex him withal' — and now when he prayed

---

¹⁶⁵ Gen. 3. 15.
¹⁶⁶ through the hands of God] In *1533* this is clearly attached to 'Abraham' but in L. it might apply to 'Sarah' (alluding to her barrenness, Gen. 16. 2).
¹⁶⁷ without advisement] Gen. 21. 9–14. Sarah does not want the two children to play together, but Abraham would not let her get rid of 'the child of the bondwoman' until God (verse 12) told him to. Allegorically, 'Abraham' (reason) follows the prompting of 'Sarah' (the senses) only when reinforced by divine instruction.
¹⁶⁸ Gen. 21. 12.

our Lord the third time that it might be taken away from him, heard he this answer only of God: 'Paul, my grace is sufficient for thee; for virtue with infirmity is tried, purged, and made perfect'.¹⁶⁹ Indeed this is a new kind of remedy: Paul, lest he should be proud, is tempted with pride; and that he might be strong in Christ, he is compelled to be weak in himself. He bare the treasure of the celestial revelations in a vessel of earth, that the excellency should depend of the might of God and not of himself.¹⁷⁰

Which one example of the Apostle putteth us in remembrance and warneth us of many things. First of all: if we are assaulted with vices, then immediately we should give ourselves to prayer afresh, and desire help of God. Moreover, that temptations to perfect men not only are not perilous, but also are very expedient to the continuance and preserving of virtue. Last of all, it is a remembrance, when all other [36ᵛ] things are full tamed, that then the vice of vainglory (even in the chief time of virtues) lieth in wait° for us; and that this vice is as it were Hydra, whom Hercules fought withal, and a quick° monster, long of life, and fruitful by reason of her own wounds; which at the last end, when all labours be overcome, can scarce be destroyed. Nevertheless, 'cruel° labour overcometh all things'.¹⁷¹ In the mean time, while the mind rageth and is vexed with vehement perturbations, by all manner means thrust together, hold down, draw near and bind this thy Proteus with tough bonds, while 'he goeth about to change himself into all manner monsters and fashions of things: into fire, into the shape of some terrible wild beast, and into a running river',¹⁷² until he come unto his own natural likeness and shape again.

What is so like Proteus as the affections and appetites of fools, which draw them sometimes into beastly lust of the body, sometimes into mad ire and wrath, otherwhiles into poison envy, now and then to diverse and strange monstrous fashions of vices? Agreeth it not well, that° the excellent cunning° poet Virgil said: 'Then shall [37ʳ] diverse similitudes and fashions of wild beasts mock thee, for suddenly he will be a fearful swine, and a foul tiger, and a dragon full of scales, and a lioness with a red mane, or shall counterfeit the quick sound of the flame of fire'?¹⁷³ But here have in remembrance what followeth: 'The more he changeth himself into all manner similitudes, the more, my son', sayeth Virgil, 'strain thy tough bands.'¹⁷⁴

And also, because° we shall not need to return again to fables of poets, thou shalt by the example of the holy patriarch Jacob learn to endure and to wrestle

---

¹⁶⁹ II Corinth. 12. 7–9.
¹⁷⁰ II Corinth. 4. 7.
¹⁷¹ Virgil, *Georgics* 1. 145–46.
¹⁷² *Georgics* 4. 440–42.
¹⁷³ *Georgics* 4. 406–09.
¹⁷⁴ *Georgics* 4. 411–12.

lustily all the night, until the morning of the help of God begin to give light, and thou shalt say, 'I will not let thee depart except thou shalt give to me thy blessing first'.¹⁷⁵ And certainly it shall be profitable to hear what reward of his victory and great virtue obtained that mighty and excellent strong wrestler. First of all, God blessed him in that same place. For evermore after that the temptation is overcome, a certain singular increase of divine grace is added unto a man, whereby he should be another time much more surely armed than he was before against the assault of his enemy. Furthermore, [37ᵛ] through touching of the thigh the sinew of the conqueror waxed faint and wasted away, and he began to halt° on the one foot.¹⁷⁶ God curseth them by the mouth of his prophet who halt on both their feet,¹⁷⁷ that is to say, them who both will live carnally and please God also, and while they frowardly° study to do both they halt in both. But happy are they in whom carnal affections are so mortified that they most of all lean to the right foot, that is to say, to the spirit. Finally his name was changed: of 'Jacob' he was made 'Israel', and of a busy wrestler he was made quiet and peaceable.

After that thou hast chastised thy flesh or thy body, and hast crucified it with its vices and concupiscence, then shall tranquillity and quietness come unto thee, and nothing shall trouble thee, so that thou mayst be at leisure to behold our Lord, that thou mayst also taste and feel that our Lord is pleasant and sweet (for that thing is signified by this word 'Israel'). God is not seen in fire, nor in the whirlwind and in the troublous rage of temptation; but after the tempest of the Devil (if so be that thou shalt endure perseverantly) [38ʳ] followeth the hissing of a thin air or wind of the spiritual consolation.¹⁷⁸ After that air hath breathed quietly upon thee, then apply thine inward eyes and thou shalt be 'Israel' and shalt say with him, 'I have seen my Lord God, and my soul is made whole'.¹⁷⁹ Thou shalt see him that said, 'No flesh shall see me'.¹⁸⁰ Consider thyself diligently: if thou be flesh, thou shalt [not] see God; if thou see him not, thy soul shall not be made whole. Take heed therefore that thou be the spirit.

CHAPTER SEVEN

Of the three parts of man: the spirit, the soul, and the flesh

Those things afore written had been, yea, a great deal more than sufficient. Nevertheless, that thou mayst be somewhat the more sensibly° known to thyself, I will rehearse° compendiously° the division of a man after the description of

---

¹⁷⁵ Gen. 32. 26.
¹⁷⁶ Gen. 32. 25.
¹⁷⁷ 1 Kings 18. 21.
¹⁷⁸ 1 Kings 19. 11–12, another reference to Elijah.
¹⁷⁹ Gen. 32. 30.
¹⁸⁰ Exod. 33. 20.

Origen,¹⁸¹ for he (following Paul) maketh mention of three parts — that is to say, of the spirit, the soul, and of the flesh; which three parts Paul joined together, writing to the Thessalonians: 'that your spirit,' sayeth he, 'your soul, and your body may be [38ᵛ] kept clean and incorrupt, that ye be not blamed or accused at the coming of our Lord Jesus Christ'.¹⁸² And Isaiah (the third part left out) maketh mention of two parts, saying, 'My soul shall desire or long for thee in the night, yea, and in my spirit and in my heart-strings I will wake in the mornings to please thee'.¹⁸³ Also Daniel sayeth, 'Let the spirits and souls of good men laud God'.¹⁸⁴

Out of the which places of Scripture Origen gathereth, and not against reason, the three portions of man. That is to wit,° the body (otherwise called 'the flesh'), which is the most vile° part of us, wherein the malicious serpent through original trespass hath written the law of sin, wherewith we be provoked to filthiness; and wherewith also if we be overcome, we be coupled and made one with the Devil. Next is the spirit, wherein we represent the similitude of the nature of God; in which also our most blessed Maker, after the original pattern or example of his own mind, hath graven the eternal law of honesty° with his finger that is so sweet — with his Spirit, the Holy Ghost: by this part we be knit to God and made one with him. In the third place, and in the middle between these two, he putteth the soul, [39ʳ] which is partaker of the sensible wits and natural motions: she, as in a seditious or wrangling commonwealth, cannot but follow the one part or the other; she is troubled of both parts, both of the flesh and also of the spirit; she is at liberty to whether° part she will incline. If she forsake the flesh and convey herself to the parts of the spirit, she herself shall be spiritual also. But and° if she cast herself down to the appetites of the body, she shall grow out of kind° into nature and vileness of the body. This is it that Paul meant, writing to the Corinthians: 'Remember ye not that he who joineth himself to a harlot is made one body with her? But he that cleaveth to our Lord is one spirit with him.'¹⁸⁵ Paul calleth the 'harlot' the frail and weak part of man. This is that pleasant and flattering woman of whom thou readest in the second chapter of the Proverbs in this wise:

> That thou mayst be delivered from a strange woman and from a woman of another country, who maketh her words sweet and pleasant, and forsaketh her husband, to whom she was married in her youth, and hath forgotten the promise she made to her Lord God. Her house boweth down to death and her paths to hell. As many as enter into her [39ᵛ] shall never return again, nor shall attain the paths of life.¹⁸⁶

---

¹⁸¹ Origen] **Marg.** 'Origen in his first book upon the Epistle of Paul to the Romans maketh this division.'
¹⁸² 1 Thessal. 5. 23.
¹⁸³ Isaiah 26. 9.
¹⁸⁴ Song of the Three Jews (the liturgical 'Benedicite', an Apocryphal addition to Daniel) 64.
¹⁸⁵ 1 Corinth. 6. 16–17.
¹⁸⁶ Prov. 2. 16–19.

The Manual of the Christian Soldier 93

And in the sixth chapter:

> That thou mayst keep thee from the flattering tongue of a strange woman, let not thy heart melt on her beauty, be not thou deceived with her becks:° for the price of a harlot is scarce worth a piece of bread, but the woman taketh away the precious soul of the man.[187]

Did he not, when he made mention of the 'harlot', the 'heart', and of the 'soul', express by name the three parts of the man? Again in the ninth chapter:

> A foolish woman, ever babbling and full of words, swimming in pleasures, having no learning at all, sitteth in the doors of her house upon a stool in a high place of the city, to call them that pass by the way and them that be going in their journey, saying, 'Whosoever is a child, let him turn in to me'; and she said unto a fool or a heartless° person, 'Water that is stolen is pleasanter, and bread that is hid privily is sweeter'. And he was not aware that there were giants and that her guests be in the bottom of hell.[188]

For whosoever shall be coupled with her shall descend into hell, and whosoever shall depart from her shall be saved. I beseech thee, with what colours could more [40ʳ] workmanly have been painted either the flattering of the poison flesh then provoking and stirring the soul of filthiness, or else the importunity of the spirit calling back, or the unhappy end of the soul if she were overcome?

To conclude therefore: the spirit maketh us gods; the flesh maketh us beasts; the soul maketh us men. The spirit maketh us religious and obedient to God, maketh us kind and merciful; the flesh maketh us despisers of God, disobedient to God, maketh us unkind and cruel; the soul maketh us indifferent,° that is to say, neither good nor bad. The spirit desireth celestial things; the flesh desireth delicate and pleasant things; the soul desireth necessary things. The spirit carrieth us up to heaven; the flesh thrusteth us down to hell; unto the soul nothing is to be imputed, that is to say, she doeth neither good nor harm. Whatsoever is carnal or springeth of the flesh, that same is filthy; whatsoever is spiritual, proceeding of the spirit, that same is pure and goodly; whatsoever proceedeth of the soul is a mean° and an indifferent thing, and is neither good nor bad.

Wilt thou more plainly have the diversity° of these three parts showed unto thee, as it were with a man's finger? Certainly I will [40ᵛ] assay.° Thou givest reverence to thy father and mother, thou lovest thy brother, thy children, and thy friend. It is not of so great virtue to do these things as it is abominable *not* to do them: for why shouldst not thou, being a Christian man, do that thing which the Gentiles do likewise naturally, yea, why shouldst not thou do that thing which the brute beast doth as well as thou? That thing that is natural shall not be imputed unto merit. But thou art come into such a strait° place that either the reverence towards thy father must be despised, the inward love towards thy children must

---

[187] Prov. 6. 24–26.
[188] Prov. 9. 13–18.

be subdued, and benevolence to thy friend set at nought — or God must be offended. What wilt thou now do? The soul standeth in the midst, as it were between two ways: the flesh crieth on her on the one side, and the spirit on the other side. The spirit sayeth, 'God is above thy father, thou art bound to thy father but for thy body only: to God thou art bound for all things that thou hast'. The flesh putteth thee in remembrance, saying, 'Except thou obey thy father, he will disinherit thee, thou shalt be called of every man lewd° and had in abomination: [41ʳ] take heed to the matter, have respect° to thy good name and fame. God either seeth it not, or is contented, or at the utmost he will be soon pleased again.' Now the soul doubteth, now wandereth she hither and thither: to whichsoever part she turn herself, such shall she be as is the thing which she goeth unto. If she obey the 'harlot', that is to say if she obey the flesh (the spirit despised), she shall be one body with the flesh: but and if she lift up herself and ascend to the spirit (the flesh set at nought), she shall be transposed and changed to the nature of the spirit. After this manner accustom to examine thyself prudently.

Great is the error of many men who oftentimes think that to be the perfect living of a Christian man, yea, and an acceptable sacrifice to God, which is but natural, and not of virtue. Certain affections,° somewhat honest in appearance, and as° they were disguised with visors° of virtue, deceive negligent persons. The judge is hasty and cruel against the felon or him that hath trespassed the law: he seemeth to himself constant, incorrupt, and a man of good conscience. Wilt thou have this man discussed°? If he favour his own mind [41ᵛ] too much, and follow a certain natural rigorousness without any grief of mind, yea, peradventure with some pleasure or delectation — but yet not inclining from the office and duty of a judge — let him not forthwithal stand too much in his own conceit:° it is an indifferent thing that he doth. But if he abuse the law from private hate or lucre: now it is carnal that he doth, and he committeth murder. But and if he feel great sorrow in his mind because he is compelled to destroy and kill him whom he had lever° to be amended and saved, also if he enjoin punishment according to the trespass with such a mind and with such a sorrow of heart as the father commandeth his singular beloved son to be cut, lanced or seared: of this manner shall it be spiritual that he doth.

The most part of men, by proneness of nature and special property,° either rejoice or abhor certain things. Some there be whom bodily lust tickleth not at all. Let them not by and by° ascribe that unto virtue which is an indifferent thing: for not to *lack* bodily lust, but to *overcome* bodily lust, is the office° of virtue. Another man hath a pleasure to fast, hath a pleasure to be at mass, hath pleasure to be much at church, hath a pleasure [42ʳ] to say a great deal of psalms. Examine after the same rule and example afore rehearsed that thing which he doth. If he regard the common fame or any advantage, it smelleth of the flesh and not of the spirit. If he do but follow his own inclination (doing that thing only which pleaseth his own mind), then hath he not whereof he ought so greatly to rejoice, but hath rather a thing which he ought to fear. Behold a jeopardous thing unto thyself: thou prayest, and judgest him that prayeth not; thou fastest, and condemnest him that fasteth not. Whosoever doth not that° thou doest, in that thou thinkest thyself better than he. Beware lest thy fast pertain to thy flesh. Thy brother hath need of thyself, and thou in the mean space° mumblest unto God and wilt not be known° of thy brother's necessity. God shall abhor this prayer: for how shall God hear thee while thou prayest, when thou — who art a man — canst not find in thine heart to hear another man?

Perceive also another thing. Thou lovest thy wife for this cause only, that she is thy wife: thou doest no great thing, for this thing is common as well to infidels as to thee. Or else thou [42ᵛ] lovest her for no other thing but because she is to thee pleasant and delectable: thy love now draweth to the fleshward. But thou lovest her for this thing chiefly, because thou hast perceived in her the image of Christ, that is to say good living, the love of God, discreetness, humility, soberness, chastity: now thou lovest her, not in herself but in Christ; yea, rather, thou lovest Christ in her. And after this manner at the last thou shalt love spiritually. We shall say more of these things, but in their places.

CHAPTER EIGHT

Certain general rules of true Christian faith

Now, for because (as meseemeth) we have opened the way (howsoever we have done it) and have prepared (as it were) certain store of stuff or matter unto the thing which was purposed, we must haste to that which remaineth, lest it should not be 'enchiridion' — that is to say, a little treatise handsome° to be carried in a man's hand — but rather a great volume. We will enforce° to give certain rules, as they were certain points of wrestling, by whose guiding or conveyance — as though we were the [43ʳ] children of Daedalus — we may easily plunge° up ourselves out of the blind errors of this world, as out of the labyrinth (that is to understand, out of a certain cumbrous maze under the ground), and come unto the pure and clear light of spiritual living. No other science is which hath not rules: and shall the craft of blessed living only be helped with no manner precepts?

There is without fail a certain craft of virtuous living and a discipline, in which whosoever exercise themselves manfully, them shall favour that Holy Spirit who is the bringer forth of all holy enforcements and goodly purposes. But whosoever sayeth, 'Depart from us, we will not have the knowledge of thy ways',[189] those men the mercy of God refuseth, because they first have refused knowledge. These rules be taken partly of the person of God, of the person of the Devil, and of our person; partly of the virtues and vices and of things to them annexed; partly of

---

[189] Job 21. 14.

the matters of virtues and vices.¹⁹⁰ These rules shall profit singularly¹⁹¹ against three evil things remaining of original sin (for, though baptism have wiped away the spot,° yet there cleaveth still in us a certain [43ᵛ] thing of the old disease left behind, partly for the custody of humility, partly for the matter and herb¹⁹² of virtue). They be named blindness, the flesh, and infirmity or weakness.

Blindness with the mist of ignorance dimmeth the judgement of reason. For the sin of our first progenitors hath not a little dusked° that so pure a light of the countenance, resemblance, and similitude of God which our Creator hath shed upon us; moreover, corrupt bringing up, froward° affections, vices, and custom of sin, hath so cankered° the law graven in us of God that scarce any signs or tokens of it appear. Then (as I began) blindness causeth that we, in the election° of things, be as good as half blind and deceived with error, so that instead of the best we follow the worst, and prefer things of less value before things of greater price.

The flesh troubleth the affections insomuch that, though we knew which were best, yet love we the contrary.

Infirmity or weakness maketh that we forsake virtue again after that we take upon us good living, so that we be overcome either with tediousness or with temptation.

Blindness hurteth the judgement; [44ʳ] the flesh corrupteth free will; infirmity weakeneth constancy.

The first point therefore is that thou can discern things to be refused from things to be accepted and allowed — and therefore blindness must be taken away, lest we stumble or stagger in the election of things. The next is that thou hate evil as soon as it is once known, and love that which is honest and good — and in this thing the flesh must be overcome, lest contrary the judgement of the mind we should love sweet and delectable things instead of things wholesome. The third is that we continue in those things which we began so well — and therefore weakness must be underset° and stowed,°¹⁹³ lest we forsake the way of virtue with greater shame than if we had been never about to walk therein.

Ignorance must be remedied, that thou mayst see which way thou oughtest to go. The flesh must be tamed, lest she lead thee aside out of the highway once known into bypaths. Weakness must be comforted,° lest when thou hast entered into the strait° way thou shouldst faint, stop, or turn back again, or lest after thou

---

¹⁹⁰ matters of virtues and vices] i.e. their outworking in practice (how they materialise), distinguished from their intrinsic form or definition (what they are in themselves). See note on 4223.
¹⁹¹ singularly] 'eminently'.
¹⁹² matter and herb] i.e. object-matter and nourishment: supplying opportunities to practise goodness.
¹⁹³ underset and stowed] 'supported and kept safe'; L. 'fulcienda'.

hast once set thy hand at the plough thou shouldst look behind thee:[194] but that [44ᵛ] thou mightest rejoice as a strong giant to haste the way, ever stretching forth thyself to those things which be afore thee, without remembrance of those things which be behind thee,[195] until thou mayst lay hand on thy reward appointed and crown promised to them that continue.

Unto these three things therefore (that is to wit, blindness, the flesh, and infirmity) we shall apply certain rules, for[196] our little power.

CHAPTER NINE

Against the evil of ignorance: the first rule
[Be confidently grounded in the Holy Scriptures]

But for because that faith is the only gate unto Christ, the first rule must be that thou judge very well both of Christ and also of Scripture given by his Spirit, and that thou believe not with mouth only, not faintly, not negligently, not as° thou were in doubt, as doth the common rascal° of Christian men: but let it set fast and immovable throughout all thy breast that there is not one jot° contained in them which should not pertain greatly unto thy health.°

Let it move thee nothing at all that thou seest a great part of men [45ʳ] so live as though heaven and hell were but some manner of tales of old wives, to fear° or flatter young children withal:° but believe thou surely and make no haste.[197] Though the whole world should be mad at once,° though the elements should be changed, though the angels should rebel: yet Verity cannot lie, it cannot but come which God told should come. If thou believe he is God, thou must believe needs° that he is true also. And on this wise think without wavering: that nothing is so true, that nothing is so doubtless, of those things which thou hearest with thy ears, which thou presently° beholdest with thine eyes, which thou handlest with thy hand, as those things be true which thou readest in the Scriptures, and as the things be true which God of heaven (that is to say, which Verity) gave by inspiration, which the holy prophets brought forth, and the blood of so many martyrs hath approved,° unto which now so many hundred years the consent of all good men have agreed and set their seals, which Christ here in his body taught with his own mouth and doctrine, and expressly presented or counterfeited° in his manners and living, [which] miracles bear witness, [which] devils also confess and so much believe that they quake [45ᵛ] and tremble for fear;[198] last of all, which

---

[194] Luke 9. 62.
[195] Philipp. 3. 13–14.
[196] for] 'in proportion to'.
[197] make no haste] 'stay calm, don't panic'.
[198] James 2. 19.

be so agreeable° unto the law of nature, which so agree between themselves and be everywhere like themselves, which so ravish the minds of them that attend, so move and change them.

If these so great tokens agree unto them,[199] what the Devil's madness is it to doubt in the faith? Moreover, of things past thou mayst easily conject° what shall follow. How many and how great things, how incredible to be spoken also, did the prophets tell before of Christ — and which of all these things came not to pass? Shall he in other things deceive, who in them deceived not? In conclusion: the prophets lied not, and shall Christ, the Lord of prophets, lie?

If with this and such other like cogitations thou shalt stir up the flame of faith, moreover if thou shalt fervently desire of God to increase thy faith, I will marvel if thou canst be long time an evil man. For who is altogether so unhappy° and full of mischief° that he would not depart from vices if so be that he utterly believed with these momentary pleasures (besides the unhappy vexation of conscience and of mind) should be purchased also eternal punishments — on the other side if he surely believed that, for [46ʳ] the temporal and little vexation of this world, shall be rewarded or recompensed to good men a hundredfold joy of pure conscience presently,° and at the last life immortal?

CHAPTER TEN

The second rule

[Be prompt and firm in resolving to fight for Christ]

Let the first point be therefore that thou doubt in no wise of the promise of God. And the next, that thou go unto the way of life not slothfully, not fearfully, but with sure purpose, with all thy heart, with a confident mind, and (if a man might give an example) with such mind as hath he who fighteth hand for hand with his enemy, so that thou be ready at all hours for Christ's sake to lose both life and goods. A slothful man will, and will not. The kingdom of heaven cometh not with gaping° but plainly rejoiceth 'to suffer violence, and violent persons violently obtain it'.[200]

Suffer not the affection of them whom thou lovest singularly to hold thee back hasting thitherward. Let not the [46ᵛ] pleasures of this world call thee back again. Let not the care of thy household be any hindrance to thee. The chain of worldly business must be cut asunder, for surely it cannot otherwise be loosed. Egypt must be forsaken in such manner that thou turn not again in thy mind at any time unto the pots of flesh.[201] Sodom must be forsaken utterly, yea, and at once. It is not

---

[199] them] the Scriptures.
[200] Matt. 11. 12.
[201] Exod. 16. 3.

lawful to look back: the woman looked back, and she was turned into the image of a stone; the man had no leisure anywhere to abide in any region thereabouts, but was commanded to haste into the mountain, except° that he had lever° to have perished.²⁰² The prophet²⁰³ crieth out that we should flee out of the midst of Babylon. The departing of the Israelites from Egypt is called 'flight' or 'running away'.²⁰⁴ We be commanded to flee out of Babylon hastily, and not to remove a little and a little, slowly.

Thou mayst see the most part of men prolonging the time, and with very slow purpose about° to flee from vices: 'when I have once rid myself out of such and such matters,' say they, 'yea, when I have brought that and that business to pass'. Oh, fool, what and if God this [47ʳ] same day take again thy soul from thee? Perceivest not thou one business to rise of another, and one vice to call in to another? Why rather doest thou not today that thing which, the sooner thou doest, the easier shall it be to be done? Be diligent some otherwhere: in this matter to do negligently, rashly, suddenly and without advisement,° is chiefly of all and most profitable.

Regard not, nor yet ponder, how much thou forsakest, but be sure Christ only shall be sufficient for all things. Mistrust not to commit thyself to him with all thy heart. Be bold to mistrust thy own self, and be bold also to put him in trust with the whole governance of thy life. Trust to thyself no more, but with full confidence cast thyself from thyself unto him, and he shall receive thee. Commit thy care and thought to our Lord and he shall nourish thee up, that thou mayst sing the song of the prophet David:

> Our Lord is my governor, I shall lack nothing. In a place of pasture he hath set me, by the water-side of comfort he nourished up me. He hath converted my soul.²⁰⁵

Be not minded to divide thyself unto two — to the world, and to Christ. Thou canst not serve two masters.²⁰⁶ There is no fellowship [47ᵛ] between God and Belial.°²⁰⁷ God loveth them not who halt° on both legs.²⁰⁸ His stomach° abhorreth them who be neither hot nor cold but (as it were) lukewarm.²⁰⁹ God loveth his souls zealously, he is jealous over them, he will possess only and altogether that

---

²⁰² Gen. 19. 15–17, 26.
²⁰³ the prophet] Jeremiah, e.g. 50. 8, 51. 6. See also Rev. 18. 4, giving rise to the application of 'Babylon' to Rome; e.g. Luther's *The Babylonian Captivity of the Church*, in *Three Treatises* [1520], pp. 113–260.
²⁰⁴ e.g. Exod. 14. 5.
²⁰⁵ David] Ps. 23. 1–3. *Vulg.* begins 'Dominus regit me' ('the Lord rules me').
²⁰⁶ Matt. 6. 24.
²⁰⁷ II Corinth. 6. 15.
²⁰⁸ I Kings 18. 21.
²⁰⁹ lukewarm] Rev. 3. 15–16.

thing which he redeemed[210] with his blood, he cannot suffer the fellowship of the Devil, whom he overcame once with [his] death. There be but two ways only: the one which by obedience of the affections° leadeth to perdition, the other which through mortifying of the flesh leadeth to life. Why doubtest thou? In thy life there is no third way. Into one of these two thou must needs enter, wilt thou or wilt thou not. Whatsoever thou art or whatsoever degree thou art, if thou wilt be saved thou must enter into the strait° way, by which few mortal men walk.[211]

But this way Christ himself hath trod, and have trodden ever since the world began whosoever have pleased God. This is doubtless a necessity not to be avoided (as it were of the goddess Adrasta,[212] otherwise called Nemesis or Rhamnusia), that is to say, it cannot be chosen but that thou be crucified with Christ as touching° the world, if thou purpose to live with Christ. [48ʳ] Why like fools flatter we ourselves, why in so weighty a matter deceive we ourselves? One sayeth, 'I am not of the clergy or a spiritual man, I am of the world: I cannot but use the world'. Another thinketh, 'Though I be a priest, yet am I no monk': let him be wise yet that so sayeth,[213] I advise him. And the monk also hath found a thing to flatter himself withal:° 'Though I be a monk', sayeth he, 'yet am I not of so strait an order as such and such'. Another sayeth, 'I am young', 'I am a gentleman', 'I am rich', 'I am a courtier', and (in conclusion) 'I am a great lord': 'those things pertain nothing to me which were spoken to the Apostles'. Oh, wretch! then it pertaineth nothing to thee that thou shouldst live in Christ? If thou be in the world, in Christ thou art not. If thou call 'the world' heaven, the earth, the sea, and this common air, no man is who is *not* in the world. But and° thou call 'the world' ambition (that is to say desire of honour, promotion, or of authority), if thou call 'the world' pleasures, covetousness, bodily lust: certainly, if thou be worldly, thou art not a Christian man.

Christ spake indifferently° to all men, saying: 'Whosoever will not take his cross and follow me, the same can [48ᵛ] be no meet° man for me or be my disciple'.[214] To die with Christ[215] as touching the flesh is nothing to thee if to live by his Spirit be nothing to thee. To be crucified as touching the world pertaineth nothing to thee if to live godly or in God pertain nothing to thee. To be buried together with Christ belongeth nothing to thee [if to arise again to eternal glory belong nothing

---

[210] redeemed] 1523 'remedied'.

[211] Matt. 7. 13–14.

[212] Adrasta] Goddess of inevitable retribution. **Marg.** 'If any be too full of insolency we say "Take heed, Rhamnusia seeth thee well enough".'

[213] that so sayeth] In E. the sense is 'I am no monk: let him who is see to this'. T. has turned it into a comment by E. on the self-excusing of the worldly man.

[214] Matt. 10. 38.

[215] To die with Christ] The fourfold argument by 'reverse implication' which follows echoes Rom. 6. 3–14 on baptism. 'If you are not interested in suffering, you have effectively ruled yourself out of any interest in Christ's glory as well.'

to thee].²¹⁶ The humility, the poverty, the tribulation, the vile° reputation, the labours, the agonies and sorrows of Christ pertain nothing at all unto thee if the kingdom of heaven pertain nothing to thee. What can be more lewd° than to think the reward to be common as well to thee as to others, and yet nevertheless to put the labours (whereby the reward is obtained) from thee to a few certain persons? What can be a more wanton thing than to desire to reign with the Head or Christ, and yet wilt thou take no pain with him?

Therefore, my brother, look not so greatly what other men do, and in comparison of them flatter thyself. To die as touching sin, to die as touching carnal desires, to die as touching the world, is a certain hard thing, and known to very few, yea, though they be monks. And yet is this the common or general profession of all Christian men. This thing a great [49ʳ] while ago thou hast sworn and holily promised in the time of baptism: than which vow, what can be added that should be more holy or religious? Either we must perish, or else without exception we must go this way to health,° whether we be kings or ploughmen. Notwithstanding though it fortune° not to all men to attain the perfect counterfeiting° or following of our Head Christ, yet all must enforce° with feet and hands to come thereto. He hath obtained a great part of a Christian man's living who with all his heart, and with a sure and steadfast purpose, hath determined to be a Christian man.

CHAPTER ELEVEN

The third rule

[Remember: hardships are inevitable but rewarding]

But lest peradventure it should fear° thee from the way of virtue, because it seemeth sharp and destitute of pleasures — partly because thou must forsake worldly commodities,° partly because thou must fight continually against three exceeding cruel° enemies (the flesh, the [49ᵛ] Devil, and the world) — set this third rule before thee always: bear thyself in hand° that all the fearful things and fantasies which appear unto thee anon,° as it were in the first entering of hell, ought to be counted for things of nought, by the example of Virgil's Aeneas.²¹⁷ For certainly, if thou shalt consider the very thing somewhat groundly° and steadfastly (these apparent things which beguiled thine eyes set at nought), thou shalt soon perceive that no other way is more commodious° than is the way of Christ, besides that this way only° leadeth to eternal life — yea, and though thou shouldst have no respect° to the reward that shall be given in the life to come.

For I beseech thee, what kind of living after the common course of the world shalt thou choose, in which thou shalt *not* suffer things enough abundantly, both

---

²¹⁶ if to arise [...] to thee] Missing from 1523 but restored in 1533.
²¹⁷ Aeneid 6. 282–94.

careful° and grievous? Who is he that knoweth not the life of courtiers, how full of grievous labours and wretched misery it is, except it be either he that never proved° it, or certainly a very° fool? Oh, immortal God, what bondage — how long, yea, and how ungoodly — must there be suffered, even unto the life's end? What a cumbrous business is there in seeking and [50ʳ] labouring to purchase the prince's love and grace, in flattering to obtain the favour of them who may either hinder or further thee! The countenances must now and then be favoured,[218] feigned, or fashioned anew. The injuries of greater men must be whispered or muttered at with silence secretly. Consequently,[219] what kind of evil can be imagined whereof the life of warriors is not full? Of either other life thou mayst be a very good witness, who hast learned both, to thy great pain and not without some jeopardy. And as touching the merchantman,[220] what is that he either doeth not or suffereth not, fleeing poverty by sea, by land, through fire and water? In matrimony, what a mountain of household cares is there; what misery feel they not there who prove and have experience of it? In bearing of offices, how much vexation, how much labour, how much peril is there?

Which way soever thou turn thyself, a huge company of incommodities° meeteth thee. The very life of mortal men, of itself, without addition of any other thing, is encumbered and tangled with a thousand miseries which are common and indifferent° as well to good as to bad. They all shall grow into a great heap of merits [50ᵛ] unto thee if they shall find thee in the way of Christ. If not, they shall be the more grievous; moreover they shall be fruitless and it must be suffered nevertheless. Whosoever war for worldly pleasure: first, how many years do they pant and blow, sweat, and canvass° the world, tormenting themselves with thought and care? moreover, for how transitory and things of nothing? last of all, with how doubtful hope? Add to this that there is no rest or easement of miseries, insomuch that, the more they have laboured, the more grievous is the pain. In conclusion, what end at the last shall there be of so tedious and laborious a life? Certainly, eternal punishment.

Go now, and with this life compare the way of virtue, which at once ceaseth to be tedious, is made in process easier, is made pleasant and delectable; by which way also we go with very sure hope to eternal felicity. Were it not the uttermost madness to have lever° with equal labour to purchase eternal death rather than life immortal? Yet these worldly men do so, yea, and for this cause the madlier, that they choose with extreme labours to go to labours everlasting, rather than

---

[218] favoured] Dropped in 1533 and possibly a scribal error, repeating 'favour' in the previous sentence. T.'s alliterative trio represents L. 'fingendi' (fashioning), so 'favoured' (if intended) would mean 'given a particular appearance'.

[219] Consequently] Here 'next', moving on to another category, soldiers.

[220] the merchantman] See Horace, *Epistles* I. 1. 46. The line was widely travelled: Aquinas quotes it via a quotation in Augustine; *ST* II (ii), q. 23, art. 7.

with mean° labours to go to immortal [51ʳ] quietness. Moreover, if the way of virtue and obedience to God were never so much more laborious than the way of the world, yet here (I mean, in the way of good living) the grievousness of the labour is assuaged with hope of reward, neither the comfort of God is lacking, which turneth the bitterness of the gall into the sweetness of honey. There (I mean, in the way of the world) one care calleth in another, of one sorrow springeth another, no quietness is there at all. Withoutforth is labour and affliction, withinforth grievous care and thought. Those little and few pleasures that be in that way make the way more grievous.

These things to be so was not unknown to the poets of the Gentiles,° who — by the punishment of Tityus, Ixion, Tantalus, Sisyphus, and of Pentheus — painted and described the miserable and grievous life of lewd° and wretched persons. Of whom is also that late confession in the Book of Wisdom: 'We be wearied in the way of iniquity and perdition, we have walked hard ways, but the way of God we knew not'.[221] What could be either filthier or more laborious than the servitude of Egypt? What could be more grievous than the captivity of [51ᵛ] Babylon? what more intolerable than the yoke of Pharaoh and Nebuchadnezzar? But what sayeth Christ? 'Take my yoke upon your neck and ye shall find rest unto your souls. My yoke', sayeth he, 'is pleasant, and my burden light'.[222]

To speak briefly: no pleasure is lacking where is not lacking a quiet conscience; no misery, on the other side, is there lacking where an unhappy conscience crucifieth the mind. These things must be more than surely known but, and° if thou doubtest yet, know the minds of them who in time past have been converted° out of the midst of Babylon unto our Lord, and by experience of them at the least way believe that nothing is more troublous and grievous than vices, and that nothing is more easy, more at liberty, more out of bondage or less drowned in business,° that nothing is so cheerful, more comfortable, than is virtue.

Nevertheless, put the case that the wages were and that the labours were like also — yet, for all that, how greatly ought a man to desire to war under the standards of Christ rather than under the banners of the Devil. Yea, how much lever were it to be vexed or suffer affliction with Christ than to swim [52ʳ] in pleasures with the Devil.

Moreover, ought not a man with wind and weather, with ship sail, and swiftness of oars,[223] to flee from a lord not very filthy only, but very cruel also and deceitful? who requireth so faithful service and so strait° a trust, who promiseth again things so uncertain, so caduke,° so transitory, and things which soon fade and vanish away; of which very same things yet deceiveth he wretches — yea, and not seldom. Or, though he perform his promise once, yet another time, when it pleaseth him,

---

[221] Wisd. 5. 7.
[222] Matt. 11. 29–30.
[223] oars] 1523 'ores'; 1533 'horses' (L. 'equis'), but the image-change might be deliberate.

he taketh them away again; so that the sorrow and thought taken for the loss of things once possessed is much more than the grievous labour in purchasing of them. After that the merchantman hath mingled together both right and wrong for the intent of increasing his goods, after he hath put his honest reputation of good report that is sprung in him, after that he hath put his life and his soul also, in a thousand jeopardies: if it so be then that the chance of fortune hap° aright at the last end, with all his travail what other thing hath he prepared for himself more than the matter° of miserable care if he keep his goods, and if he lose them [52ᵛ] a perpetual torment? If fortune chance amiss, what remaineth but that he be made twice a wretch, wrapped in double misery — partly because he is disappointed of the things whereon his hope hung, besides that because he cannot remember so great labour spent in waste without much sorrow of heart, grief of mind, and too late repentance?

No man enforceth° with sure purpose to come to good living and godly conversation° who hath not attained it. Christ, as he is not mocked, so neither mocketh he any man.

Remember another thing: when thou fleest out of the world unto Christ, if the world have any commodities or pleasures, that thou forsakest them not, but changest° trifles with things of more value. Who would not be very glad to change silver for gold and flint for precious stones? Thy friends are displeased. What then? Thou shalt find more pleasant and better companions with Christ. Thou shalt lack outward pleasures of the body: but thou shalt enjoy the inward pleasures of the mind, which be sweeter, purer, and more certain a thousandfold. Thy goods must be diminished: nevertheless, those riches increase which neither moths destroy [53ʳ] nor thieves take away.[224] Thou ceasest to be of price° in the world: but thou for all that art beloved of Christ. Thou pleasest the fewer: but yet thou pleasest the better sort. Thy body waxeth lean: but thy mind waxeth fat. The beauty of the skin vanisheth away: but the beauty of the mind appeareth bright. And in like manner if thou shalt reckon all other things, thou shalt perceive that nothing — no, not so much as these apparent things — is forsaken in this world that is not recompensed largely° with greater advantage, and more excellently a great way. But if there be any things which, though they cannot be desired without vice, [without vice] may be possessed (of which kind for the most part be the opinion of the people, favour of the commonalty,° love or to be in conceit,° authority, friends, honour due to virtue): how [oft] be all these things given without searching to them who above all things seek the kingdom of heaven.[225] A thing that Christ promised should be, and God performed to Solomon.[226]

Fortune for the most part followeth them that flee from her, and fleeth from

---

[224] Matt. 6. 20.
[225] Matt. 6. 33.
[226] 1 Kings 3. 11–14.

them that follow her. Certainly whatsoever shall happen yet to them that love God, nothing can be but prosperous unto whom loss is turned into advantage; [53ᵛ] torment, vexation, and adversity to solace; rebukes to lauds;° punishment to pleasure; bitter things to sweetness, evil things to good. Doubtest thou then to enter into this way and to forsake that other way, seeing there is so unequal comparison — yea, none at all — of God unto the Devil, of hope to hope, of reward to reward, of labour to labour, of solace to solace?

CHAPTER TWELVE

The fourth rule

[Judge everything by whether it helps or hinders progress to Christ]

But that thou mayst haste and make speed unto felicity with a more sure course, let this be unto thee the fourth rule: that thou have Christ always in thy sight as the only mark° of all thy living and conversation;° unto whom only thou shouldst direct all thine enforcements,° all thy pastimes and purposes, all thy solace° and business. And think that 'Christ' is not a voice° or sound without signification, but think him to be nothing else saving charity, simplicity, innocency, patience, cleanness: shortly, think that Christ is whatsoever Christ taught. Understand well that the Devil is no other thing but whatsoever calleth [54ʳ] away from such things as Christ taught. He directeth his journey to Christ who is carried only to virtue: and he becometh bond to the Devil who giveth himself to vices.

Let thine eye therefore be pure, and all thy body shall be bright and full of light.[227] Let thine eye look unto Christ only, as unto only and very° felicity, so that thou love nothing, marvel at nothing, nothing desire, but either Christ or for Christ: also, that thou hate nothing, abhor nothing, flee nothing, avoid nothing, but only filthiness or else for filthiness' sake. By this means it will come to pass that whatsoever thou shalt do — whether thou sleep, whether thou wake, whether thou eat, whether thou drink, moreover the very sports and pastimes, (I will speak more boldly) the certain easier° vices which we fall upon now and then as we haste to virtue — in conclusion, that all things shall grow unto a great heap of rewards. But and if thine eye shall not be pure, but shall look some otherward than unto Christ, then, if thou do any manner of things which are good or honest of themselves, yet shall they be unfruitful or peradventure very perilous and hurtful. For it is a great vice to do a good thing and not well (I mean, to do a thing and [54ᵛ] not with due circumstance and for an honest purpose).

Moreover, to a man that hasteth the straight way unto the mark of very felicity, whatsoever things shall come against him and meet him by the way, so far forth be they to be refused or received as they either further or hinder his journey. Of

---

[227] Matt. 6. 22–23.

those things be three orders or three degrees. Certain things verily be of such manner filthy that they cannot be honest:° as, to avenge wrongs done unto thee, or to wish another man harm. These things and suchlike ought always to be had in hate, yea, though thou shouldst have never so great advantage to commit them, or punishment if thou didst them not. For nothing can hurt a good man but filthiness only. Certain things, on the other side, be in such manner honest that they cannot be filthy: of which kind be to will or wish all men good, to help thy friend with honest means, to hate vices, to rejoice with virtuous communication.° Certain things verily be indifferent° or between both, of their own nature neither good nor bad, neither honest nor filthy: as health, beauty, strength, facundiousness,° cunning,° and such others. Of this last kind of things, therefore, nothing ought to be desired for itself, nor ought [55^r] to be usurped° more or less but as far forth as they shall be necessary unto the chief mark: I mean, to the following or counterfeiting° of Christ's living.

The philosophers[228] have certain marks also, imperfect° and indifferent, in which a man ought not to stand still nor tarry — which also it were meet° that a man did *use* (referring them to better purpose) and not to *enjoy* them (to tarry upon them, putting his whole felicity in them). Furthermore, these mean° or indifferent things do not all after one manner and equally either further or hinder them that be going unto Christ. Therefore they must be received or refused after° as each of them is more or less of value unto the purpose. Knowledge helpeth more unto good living than beauty, or strength of body, or riches. And though all learning may be applied to Christ, yet some helpeth more compendiously° than some. By this rule (or final end of this purpose and intent) measure the profitableness or unprofitableness of all mean things. Thou lovest [letters]:° it is very well if thou do it for Christ's sake; but and if thou love them therefore only because thou wouldst know them, then ceasest thou there whereof thou oughtest [55^v] to have made a step to climb further. But and° thou desire sciences for that intent that by the help of them thou mightest the more purer behold Christ hid in the secrets of Scripture and, when thou knowest him, for to love him; when thou knowest and lovest him, to teach, to declare, to open him to other men, and in thyself to enjoy him: then prepare thyself to the study of sciences — but not further than thou shouldst think them profitable to good living. If thou have confidence in thyself, and trustest thereby to have the greater advantage in Christ, go forth boldly as an adventurous merchant and fear not, walk as a stranger somewhat further, yea, in the sciences of the Gentiles,° and apply the riches or treasure of the Egyptians unto the honesting° of the temple of God. But if thou fear more loss than hopest of advantage, then return again to our first rule: 'know thyself', and pass not thy

---

[228] philosophers] See Augustine, *On Christian Teaching* I. 7 for the distinction between 'using' (provisional) and 'enjoying' (ultimate) goods.

bounds, keep thee within thy lists.° It is better to have less knowledge and more of love than to have more of knowledge and not to love.

Knowledge therefore hath the mastery or chief room° among mean things. After it be health, the gifts of nature, eloquence, beauty, strength, dignity, favour,° [56ʳ] authority, prosperity, good reputation, kin, friends, stuff of household. Every one of these things, as it helpeth the most nighest way to virtue, so shall it most chiefly be applied — but verily if they be offered to us as we haste in our way. If not, yet may we not turn aside from our journey supposed.²²⁹ Money is proffered to thee without asking, or meeteth thee by the way: if it let° nothing unto good living, minister it, make thee friends with the devil of iniquity.²³⁰ But and if thou fear the loss of thy good disposition or conversation, despise the advantage which is so full of damage and loss, and at the least way counterfeit that jolly° fellow Crates,²³¹ sometime of the city of Thebes: fling the grievous pack into the sea rather than it should hold thee back from Christ. That thing mayst thou do the easier if (as I have said) thou shalt accustom thyself to marvel at none of those things which be without° thee (that is to say, which pertain not to the inner man). For by that means it will come to pass that thou shouldst neither wax wild or forget thyself if these things fortune° unto thee, nor thou shalt be vexed in thy mind if they should be either denied to thee or taken away from thee, as a man who putteth the whole felicity in Christ only. But and if they [56ᵛ] chance to come unto thee beside° thy own provision, be more diligent and circumspect, having no less care than thou hadst before. Have in mind that the matter to exercise thyself virtuously on is given to thee of God, and remember the jeopardy also. But if thou have the benignity of fortune suspected, counterfeit Prometheus: do thou not receive a doubtful box,²³² but go light and naked unto that which is only very felicity.

Certainly, whosoever with great thought and care desire money as a precious thing, and think that the chief succour of life should be²³³ therein, who also think themselves happy as long as it is safe and call themselves wretches when it is lost: these men no doubt have made or feigned° to themselves many gods. Thou hast made thy money as good or equal unto Christ, if money can make thee happy or unhappy. That° I have spoken of money, understand the same likewise of honours, of voluptuousness,° of health, yea, and of the very life of the body. We must enforce to come to Christ himself, who is our mark and example of living, so fervently that we should have no leisure to care for any of those things, either

---

²²⁹ supposed] 'intended' rather than 'envisaged'; L. *proposito* (proposed).
²³⁰ Luke 16. 9.
²³¹ Crates] A wealthy man wishing to study philosophy; see Diogenes Laertius, *Lives* VI. 87. T. adds 'jolly fellow'.
²³² doubtful box] Pandora's box, a direful and delusive present arranged by Jupiter for Prometheus, who was far-sighted enough to decline it. See *Adages* I. iii. 334 (*CWE* 31. 263).
²³³ should be] i.e. 'is'.

when they were given us or else when they are taken away. For 'the time is short', as sayeth Paul: 'henceforward [57ʳ] therefore', sayeth he, 'they that use the world must be as they used it not'.²³⁴ This mind (I know well) the world laugheth to scorn as foolish and mad: nevertheless 'it pleased God by this foolishness to save them that believe' and 'the foolishness of God is wiser than men'.²³⁵

After this rule which followeth thou shalt examine whatsoever thou list.° Thou exercisest or occupiest° a craft: it is very well done if thou do it without fraud. But whereunto lookest thou? To find° thy household haply.° But for what intent to find thy household? To win thy household for Christ? Then runnest thou well. Thou fastest: verily thou doest a good work, as it appeareth outward. But unto what referrest thou thy fast? To spare thy victuals, or that thou mightest be counted the more holy? Thine eye is wanton, corrupt, and nothing pure. Peradventure thou fastest lest thou shouldst fall into some disease or sickness. Why fearest thou sickness? Lest it would take from thee the use of voluptuous pleasures? Thine eye is corrupt. But thou desirest health because thou mightiest be strong to study. To what purpose, I beseech thee, referrest thou thy study? To get thee a benefice withal°? With what mind desirest thou a benefice? Verily, to live at thy own pleasure, and not at Christ's? Thou [57ᵛ] hast missed the mark which a Christian man ought to have verily prefixed before his eyes. Thou takest meat° that thou mayst be strong in thy body, and therefore wouldst thou be strong that thou mightest be sufficient unto holy exercise and watch:° thou hast hit the mark. But thou providest for health lest thou shouldst not be strong enough unto bodily lust: thou hast fallen from Christ, making unto thee another god.

There be who honour certain saints with certain ceremonies.²³⁶ One saluteth Christopher every day, but not except° he behold his image. Whither looketh he? Verily to this point, because he hath borne himself in hand° that he shall be all that day sure from evil death. Another worshippeth one Roch. But why? Because he believeth that Roch will keep away the pestilence from his body. Another mumbleth certain prayers to Barbara or George lest he should fall into his enemies' hands. This man fasteth to Saint Apollonia lest his teeth should ache. That man visiteth the image of holy Job because° he should be without scabs. Some assign a certain portion of winnings to poor men lest their merchandise

---

²³⁴ 1 Corinth. 7. 29, 31.
²³⁵ 1 Corinth. 1. 21, 25.
²³⁶ certain saints] Saints (some more legendary than others) were often favoured as helpers because of their life experiences. See David Farmer, *Oxford Dictionary of Saints*, 4th edn (Oxford: Oxford University Press, 1997). Roch was a fourteenth-century French hermit miraculously cured of the plague; Barbara (popular in France in the later Middle Ages) and George (the patron saint of England) resisted persecution and overcame their enemies; the third-century virgin-martyr Apollonia was tortured by blows to her jaws and teeth; 'Job' is the *OT* character, canonised.

should perish by peril of sea or shipwreck. A taper is lit before Saint Sitha[237] to the intent that that thing [58ʳ] which is lost may be recovered again. In conclusion, after the same manner look how many things which either we fear or else love: so many saints have we made governors of the same things — which same saints be diverse among diverse nations, so that Paul doth the same thing among the Frenchmen that Sitha doth in England, and neither James nor John can do that thing everywhere which they do in this or that place.

Which honouring of saints, truly, except it be referred from the respect° of corporeal commodities° or incommodities unto Christ, it is not of a Christian man, insomuch that it is not very far from the superstitions of them who in time past vowed the tenth part of their goods to Hercules to the intent they might wax rich; or a cock to Aesculapius[238] that they might recover of their diseases; or who sacrificed an ox to Neptune that they might have good passage by sea or prosperous sailing. The names be changed, but verily the end or intent is indifferent to both. Thou prayest God that thou mayst not die too soon or while thou art young, and prayest not rather that he would give thee a better mind, that in whatsoever place death should come on thee it[239] should not find thee unprepared. Thou thinkest not of [58ᵛ] changing thy life, and prayest God thou mightest not die. What prayest thou for, I pray thee? Certainly that thou mightest sin as long as were possible. Thou desirest riches and cannot use riches: dost not thou then desire thy own confusion°? Thou desirest health and canst not use health: is not now thy honouring of God dishonouring of God?

In this place I am sure some of our holy men will cry out against me with open mouth, who (as sayeth Paul) 'think that lucre° is the honouring of God' and (as the same sayeth) 'with fair speaking and certain sweet benedictions deceive the minds of innocent persons, while they obey their belly and not Jesus Christ'.[240] 'Then', will they say, 'forbiddest thou the worshipping of God and saints, in whom God is honoured?' I verily dispraise not them who do these things with simple and childish superstition, for lack of instruction or capacity of wit,° so greatly as I do them who, seeking their own advantage, preach these things (which might be suffered° peradventure) instead of chief and most perfect and absolute honouring of God, and for their own lucre nourish the gross ignorance of the common people. I speak not this because I should utterly despise the ignorance of them [59ʳ] who know no better, but because I would be loath to suffer that they should have mean things (which of themselves are neither good nor bad) instead of the

---

[237] Saint Sitha] The English form of Zita (1218–1272), a lifelong domestic servant in Lucca. E. has 'Hieron', a Netherlands saint adept at finding lost objects, but T. substitutes an English saint popular for that and other everyday purposes.
[238] Aesculapius] An ancient god of medicine.
[239] it] 1523 'he'.
[240] 1 Tim. 6. 5, Rom. 16. 18.

chiefest, and trifles instead of the best. I will praise it and be content they desire health of° Roch, whom they so greatly honour, if they consecrate it unto Christ. But I will praise it more if they would pray for nothing else but that, with the hate of vices, the love of virtue might be increased.

And, as touching° to live or to die, let them put it into the hands of God and let them say with Paul 'whether we live or die, to God (or at God's pleasure) we live or die'.[241] It shall be a perfect thing if they desire to be dissolved from the body and to be with Christ;[242] if also they put their glory and joy in diseases or sickness, in loss and other damages of fortune, that they might be counted worthy who[243] even in this world should be like and conformable unto their Head, Christ. To have committed therefore such manner things (I mean, to have honoured God and the saints superstitiously) is not so greatly to be rebuked as it is perilous to abide and cleave to them. I suffer infirmity, but with Paul 'I show a more excellent way'.[244] If thou shalt examine thy studies° and all thy acts by this rule, and shalt not stand still anywhere [59ᵛ] in mean things till thou come unto Christ, thou shalt neither go out of the way at any time, nor shall do or suffer anything in all thy life which shall not turn thee unto a matter° of good living and be a cause to honour God.

CHAPTER THIRTEEN

The fifth rule

[Raise your mind from the visible to the invisible world]

Let us add also the fifth rule as an aider unto this aforesaid fourth rule: that thou put good living and the perfect honouring of God in this thing only, if thou shalt forsake things visible (which almost every one are imperfect or else indifferent)° and shalt enforce° with all thy might to ascend up unto things invisible, after° the division of man above rehearsed.° This precept is appertaining to the matter so necessary that, whether it be through negligence or for lack of the knowledge of it, the most part of Christian men, instead of true honourers of God, are but plain superstitious; and in all other things, save in the name of a Christian man only, vary not so [60ʳ] greatly from the superstition of the Gentiles.°

Let us imagine therefore two worlds, the one intelligible, the other visible: the intelligible, which also we may call the angelical world, wherein God is with the blessed minds; the visible world we may call the circles of heaven (the sun, the

---

[241] Rom. 14. 8.
[242] Philipp. 1. 23.
[243] counted worthy who] 'deemed worthy to be'.
[244] 1 Corinth. 12. 31, there referring to love.

planets, the stars) and all that included is in them (as,° the four elements). Then let us imagine man as a certain third world, partaker of these two worlds: of the visible world if thou behold his body, and of the invisible world if thou consider his soul.

In the visible world we be but strangers, we may never rest, but whatsoever offereth itself to the sensible° powers — that is to say, to the five wits° — that (with a certain apt comparison or similitude) we must apply unto the spiritual or angelical world, or else (which is a thing more profitable) let us apply it unto manners, and to that part of man which is correspondent to the angelic world (that is to say, it must be applied to the soul of man). What this visible sun is in the visible world, that is the divine mind (that is to say, God) in the intelligible world, and likewise in that part of thee which is of that same nature (that [60^v] is to say, in the spirit). Look, what the moon is in the visible world is the congregation of angels and of blessed souls, called the triumphant Church; and that in thee is thy spirit. Whatsoever the heavens above work in the earth under them, that doth God work in thy soul. The sun goeth down, ariseth, rageth in heat, is temperate, quickeneth,° bringeth forth, maketh ripe, draweth to him, maketh subtle and thin, purgeth, mollifieth, illuminateth, cheereth, and comforteth.° In conclusion then, whatsoever thou beholdest in the sun, yea, whatsoever thou seest in the grosser part of this world made of the elements (which many have separated from the heavens above and circles of the firmament), furthermore whatsoever thou considerest in the grosser part of thyself — accustom to apply the same to God and to the invisible portion of thyself (I mean, to thy soul).

So shall it come to pass that whatsoever thing shall anywhere meet any of the sensible wits, the same thing shall be to thee an occasion to honour God. When it delighteth thy corporeal eyes as oft as this visible sun spread himself on the earth with new light, by and by° call to remembrance how great is [61^r] the pleasure of the inhabiters of heaven, unto whom the eternal Sun ever springeth and ariseth but never goeth down; and think also how great is the joy of all pure minds illuminated with the light of God; and thus, by occasion of the visible creature,° pray with the words of Paul that 'he, who commanded light to shine of° the darkness, may shine in thy heart, to give light and knowledge of the glory of God in the face of Jesus Christ'.[245] Repeat and call to remembrance suchlike places of Holy Scripture in which here and there the grace of the Spirit of God is compared to the light. The night seemeth tedious to thee and dark: think on a soul destitute of the light, and dark with vices; yea, and if thou canst perceive any darkness of night in thy life, pray that the Sun of justice may arise unto thee.[246] Thiswise think and surely believe: that things invisible (which thou seest not) are

---

[245] II Corinth. 4. 6
[246] Mal. 4. 2.

so excellent, so pure, and so perfect, that things which be seen in the comparison of them are scarce shadows,° representing to the eyes a small and thin similitude of them.

Moreover, in this outward corporeal thing, whatsoever the sensible wits either desire or abhor, it shall be meet° that the spirit a great deal more should love or hate the same in the inward [61ᵛ] things. The goodly beauty of the body pleaseth the eyes: think then how honest° a thing is the beauty of the soul. It seemeth a great displeasure to behold a deformed visage: remember how odious a thing is a mind defiled with vices. And of all other things do likewise. For as the soul hath her certain beauty wherewith one while she pleaseth God, and hath also her deformity wherewith another time she pleaseth the Devil (as like is every pleasure unto like):[247] so hath she her youth, her age, sickness, health, death, life, poverty, riches, joy, sorrow, war, peace, cold, heat, thirst, drink, hunger, meat.° To conclude shortly: whatsoever is felt in the body, that same is to be understood in the soul.

Therefore in this thing resteth the journey to spiritual and pure life, if a little and a little we shall accustom to withdraw ourselves from those things which indeed are but vanities and plain shadows of things — yea, be nothing, but partly appear to be that° they be not (as voluptuous° pleasure and honour of this world), partly also vanish away and haste to return to nothing — and then shall apply and give ourselves to those things which indeed are eternal, immutable, and pure. A thing which Socrates perceived, a philosopher no perfecter in his words than in [62ʳ] his deeds.[248] For he sayeth that on this wise shall the soul depart happily from her body at the last end, if aforehand through philosophy (that is to say, through learning) she shall have death in continual remembrance, and a great while before, through despising of corporeal things and through love and contemplation of spiritual things, shall have accustomed (as it were in a manner) to be absent from her body. Neither by that cross,[249] unto which Christ calleth and exhorteth us,[250] nor by that death in which Paul willeth that we should die with our Head (as also the prophet sayeth, 'for thy sake we be slain all the day long, we be counted as sheep appointed to be killed'),[251] nor by that which the Apostle writeth in other terms, saying, 'Seek those things which be above, not which be on the earth, taste and have perceivance of things above',[252] is meant any other thing but that we at things corporeal should be astonied° and made as though we were insensible and utterly without capacity; that, the more unlearned

---

[247] like [...] unto like] See *Adages* I. ii. 21 (*CWE* 31. 167); Tav. 20.
[248] no perfecter [...] deeds] 'no less perfect in his deeds than in his words': a real philosopher. See *Phaedo* 64–68.
[249] by that cross] The sense is resumed with 'is meant' (line 1971).
[250] Matt. 10. 38.
[251] Rom. 8. 36 (quoting Ps. 44. 22).
[252] Coloss. 3. 2.

we should wax in things of the body, so much the more sweetness we might find in things pertaining to the spirit; and that so much the trulier should we live within, in the spirit, the less we should live without, in the body — in conclusion, to speak more plainly, so [62ᵛ] much the less should move us things caduke° and transitory, the more acquainted we were with things eternal, and also so much less should we regard the shadow of things, the more we should have begun to look up upon the very° true things.

This rule therefore must be had ready at hand, lest we should stand still anywhere in temporal things. But therehence (a certain apt comparison applied) let us ascend and climb up unto the love of spiritual things, and in comparison of things which be invisible let us begin to despise that which is visible. The disease of the body will be the easier if thou shouldst think that it were the remedy of thy soul. Thou shouldst take the less thought for the health of thy body if thou wouldst turn all thy care to defend and maintain the health of thy mind. The death of the body putteth thee in fear: but the death of the soul is much more to be feared. Thou abhorrest that poison which thou seest with thine eyes, because it bringeth death to thy body: yet much more is that poison to be abhorred which slayeth thy soul. Cicuta²⁵³ is poison of the body: but voluptuousness is much more presenter° poison of the soul. Thou shrinkest together and tremblest for fear, thy hair standeth [63ʳ] upright, thou art speechless, thy spirits forsake thee, and thou waxest pale, fearing lest the lightning which appeareth out of the clouds should smite thee: but how much more is it to be doubted° lest should come on thee the invisible lightning of the ire of God, which sayeth,²⁵⁴ 'Go, ye cursed persons, into the eternal fire'?²⁵⁵ The beauty of the body ravisheth thee: why rather lovest not thou fervently that fairness which is not seen? Translate° thy love unto that beauty which is perpetual, which is celestial and without corruption, and much discreetlier° shalt thou then love the caduke and transitory shape of the body. Thou prayest that thy field may be watered with rain, lest drought should hurt it: pray rather that God would vouchsafe to water thy mind, lest she wax barren from the fruit of virtue. With great care thou restorest and increasest again the waste of thy money: but with greater diligence ought the loss of thy mind to be restored again. Thou hast a respect° long beforehand of age, lest anything should be lacking to thy body: and shouldst not thou provide rather that nothing were lacking unto thy mind? And this verily ought to be done in those things which daily meet our sensible wits and for their diverse natures move us diversely with hope, fear, [63ᵛ] love, hate, sorrow, and joy.

The same thing must be observed in all manner learning,²⁵⁶ which include in

---

²⁵³ Cicuta] The hemlock with which Socrates was killed.
²⁵⁴ which sayeth] Impersonal: in E. the lightning-bolt speaks.
²⁵⁵ Matt. 25. 41.
²⁵⁶ learning] L. 'litteris' ('letters'), hence 'themselves'.

themselves a plain sense and a mystery (as° they were made of a body and of a soul), that — the literal sense little regarded — thou shouldst look chiefly to the mystery. Of which manner are the letters° of poets and of those philosophers who followed Plato; but most of all Holy Scriptures, which — as they were some Sileni[257] of Alcibiades — under a rude° and foolish covering include things pure, divine and altogether godly. For otherwise, if thou shouldst [read] without the allegory the image of Adam[258] formed of moist clay, and the soul breathed into him, and Eve plucked out of the rib, and how they were forbidden the tree of knowledge of good and ill, and the serpent enticing to eat, and God walking at the air, and how when they knew they had sinned they hid themselves, and how the angel was set at the door of Paradise with a turning sword lest after they were ejected the way to them should have been open to come in again: shortly, if thou shouldst read the whole story of the making of the world, if thou read it superficially, seeking no further than that which appeareth outward, [64ʳ] I cannot perceive what great thing thou shalt do much more than though thou shouldst read the image of clay made of° Prometheus, and how Prometheus stole fire from heaven by craft and subtlety and put it into the image and so gave life to the clay.

Yea, peradventure a poet's fable in the allegory shall be read with somewhat more fruit than a narration of holy books, if thou shouldst rest in the rind or outer part only. If, when thou readest it, the fable of the giants[259] warneth and putteth thee in remembrance that thou strive not with God or with things more mighty than thou; or that thou oughtest to abstain from such studies° as thy nature abhorreth, and that thou shouldst set thy mind chiefly unto those things (so° be they be honest) whereunto thou art most apt naturally; or thou tangle not thyself with matrimony if chastity be more agreeable° to thy manners; again that thou bind not thyself to chastity if thou seem more apt to marriage (for most commonly those things come evil to pass which thou provest° against nature); if the cups of Circe teach thee that men with voluptuousness, as with witchcraft, fall out of their minds and be changed utterly from men unto beasts; if thirsty Tantalus teacheth thee that it is a very miserable thing that [64ᵛ] a man should sit abroad° upon his riches heaped together, and durst not use them; if the stone of Sisyphus declare that ambition is laborious and miserable; if the labours of Hercules put thee in remembrance that heaven must be obtained with honest pastime° and mighty

---

[257] *Sileni*] The 1523 scribe guessed 'psalms' and added 'made'. Silenus was an unprepossessing associate of Bacchus. **Marg.** 'Sileni be images made with joints so that they may be opened; which contain outwards the similitude of a fool or of an ape or some suchlike trifle, and when they are opened suddenly there appeareth some excellent and marvellous thing. Alcibiades, a nobleman of Athens, compared the philosopher Socrates to such things, for Socrates was so simple outwards and so excellent inwards.' See *Adages* III. iii. 1 (*CWE* 34. 262).
[258] Adam] The details that follow are from Gen. 2 and 3.
[259] fable of the giants] They rebelled unsuccessfully against Jupiter.

enforcements: learnest thou not that in the fable which philosophers and also divines, the masters of good manners, teach and warn thee of?

But if thou shalt read without allegory the infants wrestling in their mother's belly, the inheritance of the elder brother sold for a mess° of gruel, the blessing of the father prevented° and taken away by fraud;[260] Goliath smitten with the sling of David;[261] and the hair of Samson shaven off:[262] it is not of much greater value than if thou shouldst read the feigning° of some poet. What difference is there whether thou read the Book of Kings and the Book of the Judges in the Old Testament, or else the history of Titus Livy, so thou have respect to the allegory in never neither°? For in the one (that is to say, in Titus Livy) be many things which would mend the common manners: and in the other be some things ungoodly no doubt as they appear at the first looking on, which also (if they be understood superficially) should hurt good manners — as the theft of David [65ʳ] and adultery bought with homicide,[263] the miserable love of Samson,[264] and how the daughters of Lot lay with their father by stealth and conceived;[265] and a thousand others of like manner. Therefore — the flesh of the Scripture despised, namely° in the Old Testament — it shall be meet and convenient° to search out the mystery of the spirit everywhere. Manna to thee shall have such a taste as thou shalt bring with thee in thy mouth.[266]

But in opening of mysteries thou mayst not follow the conjectures of thy own mind, but the reason° must be known and a certain craft which one Dionysius[267] teacheth in a book entitled *De divinis nominibus* (that is to say, 'Of the Names of God'), and Saint Augustine teacheth the same in a certain book or work called *De doctrina christiana* (that is to say, 'The Doctrine of Christian Men'). The Apostle Paul after Christ opened certain fountains and veins of allegory; whom Origen followed, and in that part of divinity easy obtained the chief room° and mastery. But our divines either set nought by the allegory, or handle it very dreamingly and unfruitfully.[268] Yet are they in subtlety of disputation equal, or

---

[260] Gen. 25 and 27: Jacob and Esau.
[261] 1 Sam. 17. 49.
[262] Judg. 16. 19.
[263] David's early thievery (e.g. 1 Sam. 27. 8–11) and his adultery with Bathsheba and murder of her husband (11 Sam. 11).
[264] Judg. 16. 4–21.
[265] Gen. 19. 30–36.
[266] in thy mouth] See Origen, *Homilies*, p. 313: God's word satisfies whatever need the faithful reader brings to it.
[267] See in Pseudo-Dionysius, *The Complete Works*, Classics of Western Spirituality, trans. by Colm Luibheid (Mahwah: Paulist Press, 1987); Augustine, *On Christian Teaching*. 'Dionysius' was traditionally identified with Paul's disciple at Athens (Acts 17. 34).
[268] dreamingly and unfruitfully] See pp. 68f., also Introduction, p. 29 for Tyndale's attitude to allegory.

rather superiors, to the old divines; but in treating of this craft (that is to say, in pure, apt, and fruitful handling the allegory) not once to be compared with them; [65ᵛ] — and that especially, as I guess, for two causes. The one cause is that the mystery can be but weak and barren which is not fortified with strength of eloquence and tempered with sweetness of oratory, in which thing our elders were passing° excellent, and we not once taste of it. Another cause is that our new divines, content with Aristotle only, expel from the schools the sect of Plato and of Pythagoras — and yet Saint Augustine preferreth these latter (I mean, Plato and Pythagoras), not only because they have very many sentences° much agreeable to our religion, but also for because the manner of their writing and the very kind of oration° (figurate, as I have said before, and full of allegories) draweth more near to the style of Holy Scripture.

No marvel therefore though the old divines commodiouslier° have handled the allegories of Holy Scripture; who with plenteous oration were able to increase and dilate,° to colour and garnish, any manner thing, were it never so barren, simple, or homely; which men also, being most cunning° of all antiquity, had studied long before in poets and books of Plato, and there had seen that thing which they should do afterwards in the divine mysteries. I had lever° therefore that [66ʳ] thou shouldst read the commentaries and writings of the old doctors, for my intent is to instruct and induce° thee, not unto striving and contention of arguments, but rather unto a pure mind. But and if thou cannot obtain the mystery when thou readest Scripture, remember yet that there is some mystery hid — which verily, though it be not yet known, yet to have trust to obtain the knowledge of it in time to come shall be much better than to rest in the literal sense which killeth.²⁶⁹

And this must be done not in the Old Testament only, but in the New also. The Gospel hath her flesh, she hath also her spirit. For though the veil be pulled from the face of Moses,²⁷⁰ nevertheless yet unto this day Paul seeth *per speculum in aenigmate*, not the thing itself and clearly but the image or similitude of the very thing, as it were 'in a glass imperfectly and obscurely'.²⁷¹ And, as Christ himself said in the Gospel of John, 'the flesh profiteth not at all, it is the spirit that giveth life'.²⁷² I verily would have been afraid to have said 'it profiteth not at all': it should have been enough to say 'the flesh profiteth somewhat, but much more the spirit'. But now Verity himself hath pronounced that 'the flesh profiteth not at all'. And so greatly it [66ᵛ] profiteth not that (after the mind of Paul) it is but death except it be referred to the spirit. Yet at the least way in this thing is the flesh profitable, that she leadeth our infirmity as it were with certain greces° or steps up to the

---

²⁶⁹ II Corinth. 3. 6.
²⁷⁰ Moses] *1523* 'Samson', underlined as if ear-marked for correction. See II Corinth. 3. 12–16 and Exod. 34. 33–35.
²⁷¹ I Corinth. 13. 12.
²⁷² John 6. 63.

spirit. The body without the spirit can have no being: the spirit of the body hath no need. Wherefore if (after the doctrine of Christ) the spirit be so great and so excellent a thing that it only giveth life, hither and to this point must our journey be directed: that in all manner letters, and in all our deeds or acts also, we have a respect to the spirit and not to flesh.

And if a man would take heed, he shall soon perceive that this is the thing only whereunto exhorteth us among the prophets especially Isaiah; and among the Apostles Paul, who almost in every epistle playeth this part and crieth that we should have no confidence in the flesh, and that in the Spirit is life, liberty, light, adoption, and those noble fruits[273] so greatly to be desired, which he there numbereth. The flesh everywhere he despiseth, condemneth, and counselleth from° her. Take heed and thou shalt perceive that our master[274] Christ doth the same thing here and there[275] — as in pulling the ass out of the pit, in restoring of blind [67ʳ] to sight, in rubbing the ears of corn, in unwashed hands, in feasting among sinners, in the parable of the Pharisee and the Publican, in fastings, in the carnal brethren, in the rejoicing of the Jews that they were the children of Abraham, in offering gifts in the temple, in praying, in dilating of their phylacteries,° and in many like places, Christ despiseth the flesh of the law, and the superstition of them who had lever be Jews openly and in sight of a man than privily in the sight of God. And then he said to the woman of Samaria:

> Woman, believe me, that hour shall come when ye shall honour the Father neither in this mountain nor at Jerusalem; but the hour shall be, and now is, when the very, true worshippers shall worship the Father in spirit and in verity. For surely the Father requireth such to honour him. The Father is a Spirit and they who honour him must honour in the spirit and verity.[276]

He signified the same thing in deed when at the marriage[277] he turned the water of the cold and unsavoury letter into wine of the spirit, making drunk the spiritual souls even unto contempt and despising of the life.

And, lest thou shouldst think it a great thing that Christ despised these things which now I have [67ᵛ] rehearsed: yea, hardily° he despised the eating of his own flesh and the drinking of his own blood, except it were done spiritually. To whom, thinkest thou, spake he these words, 'the flesh profiteth not at all, it is the spirit that quickeneth and giveth life'? Verily not to them who, with Saint John's Gospel or with a cross or *Agnus Dei*[278] hanging about their necks, think themselves safe

---

[273] Galat. 5. 22–24.
[274] master] 1523 'maker'; L. 'praeceptorem'.
[275] here and there] Luke 14. 5, John 9 ('blind' is singular in L.), Matt. 12. 1–8, 15. 1–20, 9. 10–13, Luke 18. 9–14, Matt. 9. 14–17, John 7. 1–9 (also Matt. 12. 46–50), John 8. 33–59, Matt. 5. 23–24, 6. 5–8, and 23. 5.
[276] John 4. 21, 23–24.
[277] John 2. 1–11. E. adds the interpretation.
[278] *Agnus Dei*] An image of Christ as a sacrificial lamb.

from all manner harm, yea, and suppose that thing to be very perfect religion of Christian men: but he spake it to them unto whom he opened the high mystery of eating his own body (I mean, unto the very Apostles). If so great a thing be of no value, yea, if it be of jeopardy and perilous, what cause is there wherefore we should have confidence in any other carnal things, except° the Spirit were present? Thou peradventure sayest mass daily, and livest all to thy own pleasure, and the hurts and incommodities° of thy neighbour pertain nothing to thee: yet° art thou in the flesh of the sacrament. But and if, when thou sayest mass, thou intendest to be the very same thing which is signified by receiving of the sacrament — that is to say, to be one spirit with the Spirit of Christ, to be one body with the Body of Christ and to be a quick° member of the [68ʳ] Church — if thou love nothing but in Christ, if thou think that all thy goods be common to all men, if the incommodities of all men grieve thee even as much as do thy own: then no doubt thou sayest mass with great fruit, and that because thou doest it spiritually. If thou perceive that thou art in a manner transfigured and changed into Christ, and that thou livest now less and less in thy own life, give thanks to the Spirit who only quickeneth and giveth life.

Many are wont to number how many masses they have been at every day and put their whole confidence in this thing, as in a thing most of value (even as though now they were no more bound to Christ), but as soon as they are departed out of the church they return to their old manners again. That they embrace the flesh and the outward sign of good living I dispraise not. That they there stop, I praise not. Let that be performed in thee which there is represented: the death of thy Head. Discuss° thyself withinforth and (as the saying is) 'even in thy bosom',[279] and search how nigh thou art dead to the world. For if thou be yet possessed altogether of wrath, of ambition, of covetousness, of voluptuousness, and of envy, yea, though thou touch the altar, yet art thou far from the mass. Christ was slain for thy sake: slay thou therefore again [68ᵛ] these beasts for his sake, sacrifice thyself for his sake who for thy sake sacrificed himself to his Father. If thou once° think not on these things, and yet hast confidence in the other, God hateth thy carnal and gross religion.

Thou art baptised. What then? Think not therefore that thou art ever the more a Christian man while thy mind altogether savoureth° nothing but the world. In the sight of the world and afore the face of the people thou art a Christian man, but secret and afore God thou art more heathen than any heathen man. Why so? For thou hast the body of the sacrament and art without the Spirit, which only profiteth. Thy body is washed: what matter is that, while thy mind remaineth still defiled and inquinated°? Thy body is touched with salt: what then, while thy mind is yet unsavoury? Thy body is anointed: but thy mind is unanointed. But and if

---

[279] 'even in thy bosom'] See *Adages* I. iii. 13 (*CWE* 31. 245).

thou be buried with Christ withinforth, and studiest to walk with him in the new life, I then know thee for a Christian man.

Thou art sprinkled with holy water: what good doth that if so be thou wipe not away the inward filth from thy mind?

2185 Thou honourest the saints and art glad to touch their relics: but thou despisest the chief relics which they left behind them — that is to say, the examples of pure living. There [69ʳ] is no honour more pleasant to Mary than if thou shouldst counterfeit° her humility. No religion is more acceptable to saints, or more appropriate, than if thou wouldst labour to represent° their virtues. Wilt thou
2190 deserve the love or favour of Peter or of Paul? Counterfeit the one's faith and the other's charity, and thou shalt do a greater thing than if thou shouldst run to Rome ten times. Wilt thou worship Saint Francis singularly?²⁸⁰ Thou art high-minded,° thy mind is ravished when thou beholdest money, thou art stubborn and self-minded, full of contention and wise in thy own opinion. Give this to the Saint:
2195 assuage thy mind and by the example of Saint Francis be somewhat more sober; despise filthy lucre and look sadly° on the riches of the mind; put away all striving and debates° with thy neighbours, and with goodness overcome ill. The Saint setteth more by this honour than if thou shouldst set before him a thousand burning tapers. Thou thinkest that it is a special thing to be carried to burying
2200 wrapped in the cowl or habit of Saint Francis. Trust me, like vesture shall profit thee nothing at all when thou art dead, if thy living and manners be found unlike when thou art alive.

And though that the sure example of true virtue, and how thou [69ᵛ] shouldst honour God in everything, is fetched of Christ most commodiously in such
2205 manner that in no wise thou canst be deceived: nevertheless, if that the worshipping of Christ in his saints delight thee so greatly, see thou counterfeit Christ in his saints, and for the honour of every saint (saint by saint) look thou change and put away all thy vices (vice by vice singularly),²⁸¹ or else study to embrace and counterfeit some one virtue singularly in every saint, such as thou
2210 perceivest to have reigned most chiefly in every saint singularly of them whom thou worshippest so specially. If this shall come to pass, then will I not reprove those things which be done outwardly.

Thou hast in great reverence the ashes of Paul. I damn° it not if thy religion be perfect in every point. If thou have in reverence the dead ashes or powder° of his
2215 body, and settest no store by the quick image of his mind (yet speaking and as it were breathing) which remaineth in his doctrine, is not thy religion preposterous° and out of order? Honourest thou the bones of Paul hid in the shrine, and honourest thou not the mind of Paul hid in his writings? Magnifiest thou a piece of his carcase shining through a glass, and regardest thou not the whole mind of

---

²⁸⁰ singularly] L. 'summo honore' ('with greatest honour').
²⁸¹ singularly] Here 'particularly'.

2220 Paul [70ʳ] shining through his letters? Thou worshippest the ashes, in whose presence now and then the deformities and diseases of bodies be taken away: why honourest not thou rather his doctrine, wherewith the deformities and diseases of souls are cured and remedied? Let infidels marvel at the signs and miracles, to whom they be given: but thou, who art of Christ's faith, embrace his books, that
2225 — as thou doubtest not but that God can do all things — even so thou mightest learn to love him above all things.

Thou honourest the image of the bodily countenance of Christ, formed in stone or tree° or else portrayed with colours: with much greater reverence ought to be honoured the image of his mind, which by workmanship of the Holy Ghost is
2230 figured° and expressed in the gospels. Never any painter so expressly fashioned with pencil° the proportion° and figure of the body as in the oration and doctrine of every man appeareth the image of the mind; namely° in Christ, who was very simplicity and pure verity, and therefore no discord or unlike thing at all could be between the first and chief pattern of his divine breast and the image of his
2235 doctrine and learning° (from thence deduct° and derivate). As nothing is more like the Father of heaven than his Son — who is the Word, the wisdom, the knowledge of the Father, [70ᵛ] springing forth of his most secret heart — so is nothing more like unto Christ than the word, the doctrine, and teaching of Christ, given forth of the privy° parts of his most holy breast. And ponderest thou not
2240 this image? honourest it not? lookest not thou substantially with devout eyes upon it? embracest it not in thy heart? Hast thou at home, at thy own house, relics so holy,[282] so full of virtue and strength, and (them set at nought) seekest thou things more alienate,° strange, and further off? Beholdest thou a coat or a sudary° that is said to have been Christ's, astonied as though thy wits were rapt: and art thou
2245 in a dream or a slumber when thou readest the divine answers or doctrine of Christ? Thou believest that it is a thing greater than the greatest that thou possessest, a little piece of the holy cross at home: but that is nothing to be compared to this, if thou shouldst bear shrined in thy heart the mystery of the Cross.

2250 Or else, if such things make a man religious and devout, what can be more religious than the Jews, of whom very many (though they were never so wicked) yet with their eyes saw they Christ living bodily, heard him with their ears, and with their hands touched him? What is more happy than Judas, who with his mouth kissed the divine mouth of Christ?[283] The flesh without the spirit profiteth
2255 nothing, insomuch [71ʳ] that it should not have profited the holy Virgin his mother that she of her own flesh begat him, except in her spirit she had conceived his spirit also. This is a very great thing, but hear a greater thing. As long as the very Apostles enjoyed the corporeal presence and fellowship of Christ, readest thou

---

[282] relics so holy] i.e. the teachings of Christ in Scripture.
[283] Luke 22. 48.

not how weak and how childish they were, how gross° and without capacity? Who would have desired any other thing unto the most perfect health of his soul than so long familiarity and conversation together with him that was both God and man? Yet, after so many miracles showed, after the doctrine of his own mouth taught and declared to them so many years, after sure and evident tokens that he was risen again, did he not at the last hour, when he should be received up into heaven, cast in their teeth their instability in the faith? What was the cause, then? Verily the humanity of Christ did let;° and thence it came that he said, 'Except I go away, the Holy Ghost will not come: it is expedient for you that I depart'.[284] The corporeal presence of Christ is unprofitable unto health:° and dare we in any other thing corporeal besides that put good living and the perfect honouring of God? Paul saw Christ in his humanity. What supposest thou to be a greater thing than that? Yet setteth° he [71ᵛ] nought by that, saying, 'Though we have known Christ carnally, now we do not so'.[285] Why 'knew he him not carnally'? For° he had profited and ascended up into more perfect gifts of the Spirit.

I use peradventure more words in disputing these things than should be meet for him who giveth rules. Nevertheless I do it the more diligently, and not without great cause, for in very deed I do perceive that this error is the common pestilence of all Christendom, whereof at the last in this ariseth the greater mischief inasmuch as, in a resemblance, it is very like unto holiness. For verily no vices are more perilous than they which counterfeit virtue, partly because that good men may lightly° fall into them — moreover no vices are with more difficulty cured, for because the common and unlearned people think that our religion is violated when such things are rebuked.

Let all the world cry out against me, and let certain preachers that are wont to cry out in their pulpits bark, who with right good will praise such things, looking not unto the honour of Christ (as thou mayst well perceive) but to their own advantage. For whose either indiscreet° superstition or feigned holiness I the ofter take God to record° that I neither rebuke or check° the corporeal ceremonies of Christian men and the devout minds [72ʳ] of simple persons — namely in such things as are approved by the authority of the Church — for they are now and then partly signs of piety and partly help thereunto. And because they are somewhat necessary to young infants in Christ till they wax older and grow up unto a perfect man, therefore it is not meet they should be loathed of them who are perfect; lest by their example the weak persons should catch harm. That thou doest I approve, so° the end or intent be not amiss, moreover if thou stop not there whence thou oughtest to ascend unto things more near to health. But to worship Christ with visible things instead of invisible things, and in them to put the highest point of religion, and hereof to stand in thy own conceit,° and to

---

[284] John 16. 7.
[285] II Corinth. 5. 16.

condemn other men, to set thy whole mind upon them, and also to die in them, and (to speak shortly) that thou shouldst be withdrawn from Christ by the means of the very same things which be ordained for that intent only, that they should help unto Christ: this is verily nothing else but to depart from the law of the Gospel, which is spiritual, and to fall into a certain superstition of ceremonies like unto the Jews; a thing peradventure of no less jeopardy than if, without such superstition, thou shouldst be infected with great and manifest vices of the mind — which [72ᵛ] haply° were, as thou thinkest, a more deadly disease. Be it: but the other is worse to be cured.

How much everywhere sweateth the chief defender of the spirit, Paul, to call away the Jews from the confidence of deeds and ceremonies, and to promote them unto those things which are spiritual: and yet now I see that the commonalty° of Christian men are returned hither again. But why said I 'the commonalty'? That might be suffered,° except this error had caught also a great part of priests and doctors; moreover except it had caught and infected the whole schools and flocks of them who profess a spiritual life in title and name of their religion and in their habit[286] also. If they who should be the very salt be unsavoury, wherewithal shall be others seasoned?[287] I am ashamed to rehearse with what superstition the most part of our clergy observe ceremonies of men's inventions (and yet not instituted for such purpose) and how odiously they require them of other men, what trust and how sure confidence they have in them; to tell also how indiscreetly they judge other men, and how earnestly they defend them.[288] To these their deeds they think heaven to be due, in which if they be once rooted, at once they think themselves Pauls and Antonys.[289]

They begin — Oh, good Lord! — with what gravity [73ʳ] and with how great authority to correct other men's livings° after the rule of fools and indiscreet persons (as sayeth Terence),[290] so that they think nothing well done but that they do themselves. But for all that, after they have waxed even crooked with long countenance in their own imaginations or inventions, thou shalt see that yet they perceive nothing at all what Christ meaneth, but are altogether beastly, swimming in certain churlish° vices, in their living and pastime are they so froward° that scarce they can suffer and forbear their own selves: in charity cold, in wrath fervent, in hate as tough as whiteleather,°[291] in their tongues venomous and full of

---

[286] habit] L. 'cultu' can be either 'dress' or 'conduct'; at 2465 and 4750 T. renders it 'raiment'.
[287] Matt. 5. 13.
[288] them] 'themselves'.
[289] Pauls and Antonys] Holiness is the issue here, so these are probably the two famous desert monks, Paul the Hermit (died *c.* 345) and Antony of Egypt (251–356), not the Apostle and the charismatic preacher of Padua; see Farmer, *Dictionary of Saints*.
[290] Terence] *Brothers* 1. 98–99.
[291] whiteleather] L. simply 'pertinaces' ('tough'); T.'s example is leather cured with salt to make it flexible and strong.

poison, in cloaking of privy envy conquerors, ready to strive for every little trifle, and so far are they off from the perfection of Christ that they be not once endued with those common virtues which the very ethnics° or heathen men have learned either by reason given to them of nature, or by use° of living, or by the precepts of philosophers. Thou shalt also see them in spiritual things clean without capacity, so fierce that no man shall know how to treat or handle them, full of strife and contention, greedy upon voluptuous pleasure, at the Word of God ready to spew, kind to no man, misdeeming° other men, flattering even their own selves. It is come to this [73ᵛ] point finally, with the labours of so many years, that thou shouldst be of all men the worst, and yet thinkest thyself the best; and that also instead of a Christian man thou shouldst be but a plain Jew, observing only unfruitful traditions and ceremonies of the inventions of man; and that thou shouldst have thy glory and joy, yea, and seek thy reward not in secret afore God, but openly afore the world.

But and if thou hast 'walked in the Spirit and not in the flesh',²⁹² where be the fruits of the Spirit?²⁹³ Where is charity? Where is cheerfulness or joyous mirth of a pure mind? Where is tranquillity and peace towards all men? Where is patience? Where is continuance or perseverance of a soft mind, wherewith thou lookest day by day continually for the amendment even of thy enemies? Where is courtesy or gentleness? Where is freeness of heart? Where is meekness, fidelity, and discretion (that men call measure° or soberness in taking upon him)? Where is temperance? Where is chastity? Where is the image of Christ in thy manners and conversation°? Thou sayest, 'I am no keeper of whores, no thief, no violator of holy things or robber of churches: I keep my profession'. But what other thing is this to say more than, 'I am not like other men, no extortioner, no adulterer, yea, and I fast twice in the week'?²⁹⁴ I had lever a [74ʳ] great deal have a publican, humble, lowly and asking mercy, than this kind of Pharisees ever rehearsing their own good deeds. But what was thy profession? Whether thou shouldst [not]²⁹⁵ perform that thing which thou promised long ago when thou were baptised: even that thou should be a Christian man, that is to say spiritual, and not a Jew who for the traditions of man shouldst transgress the commandments of God?

Is not the life of a spiritual man a spiritual life? Hear Paul speaking to the Romans:

> No damnation then is to them that are grafted in Christ, who walk not carnally or after the flesh: for the law of the Spirit who giveth life by the help of Christ hath delivered me from the law of sin and death. For that which the law,

---

²⁹² Rom. 8. 4.
²⁹³ fruits of the Spirit] Galat. 5. 22–23 *Vulg.*, which lists twelve, unlike the now accepted text (and E.'s own *NT*) which has nine.
²⁹⁴ Luke 18. 11–12.
²⁹⁵ not] *1523* omits but *1533* includes this. L. ('ne') is ironical.

weakened by reason of the flesh, could not perform or make good,° [God made good,] sending his Son in the similitude of flesh prone to sin, and out of sin²⁹⁶ expelled sin by flesh, that the justifying of the law might be fulfilled in us, who walk not after the flesh but after the Spirit. For they that be in the flesh savour those things which pertain to the flesh, but they who be in the spirit savour those things that pertain to the Spirit; for wisdom of the flesh is death, and the wisdom of the Spirit is life and peace, for the wisdom of [74ᵛ] the flesh is an enemy to God because she is not obedient to the law of God, nor yet can be. They that be in the flesh, then, cannot please God.²⁹⁷

What could be spoken more largely° or more plainly? Nevertheless many men, subtle and crafty to flatter or favour their own vices, but prone and ready without advisement° to check other men's, think that these things pertain nothing to themselves at all; and that Paul spake of 'walking carnally' or 'after the flesh', that same they refer unto adulterers only and keepers of queans;° that Paul spake of 'the wisdom of the flesh' which is an 'enemy to God', that they turn° to them who have learned humanity,° or that they call 'secular science'. In either other they set up their crests and clap their hands for joy, both that they neither be adulterers, and be also in all sciences stark fools. Moreover, to 'live in the Spirit' they dream to be no other thing than to do even as they themselves do, and to live as they live.

But and if they would as diligently observe the tongue of Paul as they maliciously despise the tongue of Cicero, then should they soon perceive that the Apostle calleth the 'flesh' that thing which is visible, and the 'spirit' that thing which is invisible. For he teacheth everywhere that things visible ought to serve to things invisible, and not contrariwise [75ʳ] that invisible things should be subject and serve unto things which are visible. Thou, clean out of order, appliest Christ unto those things which were meeter to be applied unto Christ. Requirest thou of me record that this word 'flesh' pertaineth not only to the filthy lust of the body? Hear what the said Apostle (doing that same which he all places doth) writeth to the Colossians:

> Let no man (sayeth he) supplant° you for the nonce° by the humility and religion of angels, which things he never saw, walking in vain, high-minded or inflated with the imagination of the flesh and not holding the Head, that is to say Christ, of whom all the Body, by couples and joints administered° up and compact, groweth into the increase of God.²⁹⁸

---

²⁹⁶ out of sin] L. 'de peccato' (from, or concerning, sin). As in E.'s *Paraphrases*, the idea is that Christ, though personally sinless, took human nature (which for everyone else entails being sinful) and (leading a genuinely human life) tackled and defeated sin from within. (*1523*, but not *1533*, repeats 'flesh prone to' before 'sin'.)
²⁹⁷ Rom. 8. 1–8.
²⁹⁸ Coloss. 2. 18–19.

And lest thou shouldst doubt that he spake of them who, having confidence in certain corporeal ceremonies, bark against the spiritual purposes of other men, take heed what followeth:

> If ye be dead with Christ *ab elementis huius mundi*,[299] from traditions, ceremonies, and inventions of men, why (as men living worldly) have ye yet such decrees among you?[300]

— putting confidence more in one thing than in another. And anon° after he, exhorting us from the same things, sayeth:

> If ye be risen up again with Christ, seek those things which are above, where Christ [75ᵛ] sitteth on the right hand of God. Savour ye those things which be above and not those things which be on the earth.[301]

Moreover, giving precepts of the spiritual life, what exhorteth he us to do at the last? Whether not[302] that we should use such or such ceremonies, whether not that we should be this or that wise° arrayed, or that we should live with such or such manner of meats, or that we should say customably° every day any certain number of psalms? He made mention of no such things. Whereof then?

> Mortify (sayeth he) your members which be on the earth: fornication, uncleanliness, bodily lust, evil concupiscence, and avarice, which is the service of idols;[303]

and a little after that he sayeth:

> Now put from you all such things: wrath, indignation, malice; (and it followeth) spoiling° yourself of the old man with all his acts, and putting on you the new man which is renewed in knowledge of God after the image of him that made him.[304]

But who is the 'old man'? Verily Adam, he that was made of earth, whose conversation is in the earth, not in heaven. By the 'earth' understand whatsoever thing is visible and whatsoever is temporal or transitory. Who is that 'new man'? Verily that celestial Man that descended from heaven, Christ. And by [76ʳ] 'heaven' understand whatsoever thing is invisible and whatsoever is eternal and everlasting. At the last, lest we should be minded to deserve God after the manner of the Jews with certain observances, as ceremonies magical, he teacheth that our deeds be pleasant and allowed of God so long as they are referred unto charity, and if also they sprang therehence, saying:

---

[299] *ab elementis huius mundi*] 'from the elements of this world'; a similar phrase lies behind the reference to 'traditions and ceremonies' in lines 2342 above and 2507 below.
[300] Coloss. 2. 20.
[301] Coloss. 3. 1–2.
[302] Whether not] 'Surely not'; L. 'num'.
[303] Coloss. 3. 5.
[304] Coloss. 3. 8–10.

> Above all these things keep charity, which is the bond of perfection: and the peace of God rejoice[305] as a victor in your hearts; in which also ye be called in one Body.[306]

I will give thee a more plain token and a more evident probation° that the word of the 'flesh' signifieth not the lust of the body only. Paul nameth often the 'flesh' and often the 'spirit' writing to a certain nation of men called Galatians, which men he called not [only] from lust of the body unto chaste living, but enforceth to withdraw them from the sect of the Jews and confidence of work,[307] into which they were induced by false apostles. In this place, therefore, when he numbereth the deeds of the flesh, mark what vices he rehearseth:

> The deeds of the flesh (sayeth he) be manifest, which are fornication, uncleanliness, wantonness or unchaste behaviour, lechery by worshipping of idols, witchcraft, [76ᵛ] hatred or enmity, debate or strife, emulation (that may be called indignation or disdain), ire (otherwise called wrath), scolding,° dissension (that is to say, diversity in maintaining of opinions), sects (or maintaining of diverse learnings), envy, homicide, drunkenness, excess in eating, and suchlike.[308]

And not long after he sayeth, 'If we live in the Spirit, let us walk in the spirit'. After that, as declaring and uttering a pestilence contrary to the spirit, he addeth saying, 'Let us not be made desirous of vainglory, provoking one the other and envying one another'.[309]

The tree is known by the fruit.[310] That thou omittest not watch,° fasting, silence, orisons,° and such other like observances, I stick° not at it; yet will not I believe that these things be done in the spirit except I may see the fruits of the Spirit. Why may I not affirm that they be done carnally when, after almost a hundred years' exercise of these things, I find in thee deeds of the flesh: impotency or weakness unto envy more than is in any woman; continual wrath and fierceness, as it were of a man of war; in scolding, lust and pleasure insatiate; malicious cursing; backbiting with tongue more venomous than the poison of a serpent; a high mind; stubbornness; lightness of promise; vanity; feigning, and flattering? Thou judgest thy brother in his [77ʳ] meat and in his drink, or in his raiment: but Paul judgeth thee of thy deeds. Doth that separate thee from worldly and carnal things that thou, in lighter matters and for less trifles verily, but are infected yet with like vices? Is he more filthy, who for his inheritance taken from him ere it came to his hands, who for his daughter defiled, for hurt done to his father, who for some

---

[305] rejoice] 'may it rejoice'.
[306] Coloss. 3. 14-15.
[307] confidence of work] 'trusting in their good works'; cf. 'confidence of deeds', line 2308.
[308] Galat. 5. 19-21 (expanded by T.).
[309] Galat. 5. 25-26.
[310] Matt. 12. 33.

office or for his prince's favour, conceiveth wrath, hatred, indignation, or disdain: is such a person, I say, more [filthy] if — for how little a trifle, yea, for nothing — thou dost all these same things much more maliciously? The smaller occasion to sin lighteth [not] but aggravateth the sin. Neither it maketh any matter in how little or how great a thing thou shouldst sin, so thou sin with like affection. Yet is there difference verily: for so much the grievouslier doth every man trespass, the lesser the occasion is wherewith he is pulled away from honesty.°

I speak not now of these monks or religious persons whose manners even the whole world abhorreth, but of them whom the common people look upon not as upon men, but as upon angels: which same ought not to be displeased with these sayings (for he that toucheth° vices nothing noteth the persons) but and if they be good men let them also be glad to be warned° of [77ᵛ] whatsoever manner it be namely° in those things which pertain to health.° Neither it is unknown to me that very many be among religious men who, with the help both of learning and of wit, have tasted of the mysteries of the Spirit. But (as Livy[311] sayeth) it fortuneth° almost everywhere that the greater part overcometh the better. Notwithstanding (if it be lawful to confess the truth), see we not that every most strait° kind of monks putteth the chief point of religion either in ceremonies, or in a certain manner and form of saying that they call their 'divine service', or in labour of the body? — which same persons if a man should examine and appose° them of spiritual things, he should scarce find any of them at all who walk not in the flesh, that is to say, carnally.

And hereof cometh this so great infirmity of mind 'trembling for fear where is no fear',[312] and therein surety° and carelessness where is most peril of all. Hereof cometh that perpetual infancy in Christ (to speak no grievouslier), that we froward esteemers of things make most of those things which only° are of no value, those things set at nought which only are sufficient, ever living after tutors or schoolmasters, ever in bondage, never [78ʳ] advancing ourselves up to the liberty of the Spirit, never growing up to the large stature of charity: when Paul crieth to certain people called Galatians, 'Stand fast, cumber ye not yourselves any more with the yoke of bondage'.[313] And in another place he sayeth:

> The law was our tutor or schoolmaster in Christ, that of° faith we should be justified; but sith° that faith is come, now are we no more under a tutor or schoolmaster, for every one of you (sayeth he) is the very son of God by faith which he hath in Christ Jesus.[314]

And not much after he sayeth:

---

[311] Livy] *The History of Rome*, XXI 4. 1.
[312] Ps. 53. 5.
[313] Galat. 5. 1.
[314] Galat. 3. 24–26.

> And we also, when we were little, were in servage° and bondage under the ceremonies and law of this world; but when the time was full expired God sent his Son, made of a woman, made under the law, to redeem them who were under the law, that we by adoption should be his sons. And for because ye be the sons of God, God hath sent the Spirit of his Son into your hearts, crying 'Abba, pater' (as a man would say, 'Daddy, father'), and therefore now no man is a servant, but a son to God.[315]

And again in another place he sayeth:

> Brethren, ye be called into liberty. Let not your liberty be unto you an occasion to live in the flesh, but in the [78ᵛ] Spirit serve one another. For all the law is fulfilled in one saying, 'Love thy neighbour as thyself". But and if ye bite and eat one the other, take heed lest you be consumed one of another.[316]

And again to the Romans:

> Ye have not received the spirit of bondage again in fear, but the Spirit that maketh you the sons of God by adoption, in whom we cry 'Abba, pater' ('Dad, father').[317]

Unto this same pertaineth also that° he writeth to Timothy, saying:

> Exercise thyself unto the deeds of piety: for bodily exercise is good but for a small thing, piety is good unto all manner thing.[318]

And to the Corinthians:

> God is a Spirit, and where the Spirit is there is liberty.[319]

But why rehearse I one or two places, when Paul is altogether at this point, that the flesh (which is full of strife and contention) should be despised, and that he might settle us in the Spirit (that is the author of charity and of liberty)? For these companions be ever inseparable: on the one side the flesh, bondage, unquietness, contention or strife; and on the other side the Spirit is peace, love, liberty. These things everywhere Paul maketh mention of among all other sayings. And seek we a better master of our religion, namely when all divine Scripture agreeth with him also? [79ʳ] This (I mean, to love) was the greatest commandment in the law of Moses, this Christ repeateth again and finisheth° in the Gospel, and for this cause chiefly was he born, for this cause died he also: to teach us not for to counterfeit the ceremonies of the Jews, but for to teach us to love. After the Last Supper, had the even[320] before his Passion, how diligently, how tenderly, how affectuously,°

---

[315] Galat. 4. 3–7.
[316] Galat. 5. 13–15.
[317] Rom. 8. 15.
[318] I Tim. 4. 7–8.
[319] II Corinth. 3. 17.
[320] had the even] i.e. 'held on the evening'.

gave he charge to his disciples, not of meat nor of drink, but of charity to be kept
of one towards another.³²¹ What other thing teacheth he, yea, what other thing
desired his disciple John, but that we should live and love one another?³²² Paul
partly° everywhere (as I have said) commendeth charity; moreover, writing unto
the Corinthians he preferreth charity both before miracles and prophecy, and also
before the tongues of angels.³²³

And say not thou by and by° that charity is to be oft at church, to crouch down
before the images of saints, to light tapers or wax candles, to iterate, to repeat thy
devotions and prayers appointed, which thou customably sayest day by day. God
hath no need of this thing. Paul calleth 'charity' to edify° thy neighbour;³²⁴ to
count that we be all members³²⁵ of one Body; to think that we all be but one in
Christ; to rejoice [79ᵛ] in God of thy brother's wealth even as thou dost of thy
own; to remedy his incommodities or losses as thou wouldst thy own; if any
brother err or go out of the right way, to warn him, to admonish him, to tell him
his fault meekly, soberly, and courteously; to teach the ignorant; to lift up him that
is fallen; to comfort and encourage him that is put aback; to help him that
laboureth; to succour the needy; in conclusion, to refer all thy riches and substance
of goods, to refer all thy study and all thy care unto this point only: that thou in
Christ shouldst help as many as thy power will extend unto; that — as he was
neither born for himself, nor lived to his own pleasure, nor died for himself, but
dedicated himself wholly unto our profits° — even so again° should we apply
ourselves and wait° upon the commodities of our brethren, and not on our own.

Which thing if it were used among our cloisterers,° nothing should be more
pleasant or easier than the life of religious persons — which we see now (clean
contrary) grievous almost everywhere and laborious, and also full of superstition
like to the Jews, nor yet pure from any vices of the lay people: yea, and in many
things [80ʳ] much more contaminated than the lay people. Which kind of men
Saint Augustine,³²⁶ if he were now alive, would not once know (in whom, being
the author and institutor of their life and conversation, many of them so greatly
rejoice), but he would cry out, saying that he could approve nothing less than this
kind of living, and that he had ordained the craft and manner of living, not after
the superstition of the Jews, but after the rule of the Apostles.

But I hear even now what certain men (who are somewhat better advised) will
answer unto me: 'A man must take heed in little small things lest, a little and a
little, he should fall into great vices'. Nevertheless, thou oughtest to take heed a

---

³²¹ e.g. John 15. 12–13.
³²² e.g. 1 John 4. 7.
³²³ 1 Corinth. 13. 1–2.
³²⁴ 1 Corinth. 8. 1.
³²⁵ members] Rom. 12. 4–5. 1523 'neighbours'.
³²⁶ Augustine] His Rule was the basis of many monastic communities.

great deal more that thou so cleave not to these 'little small things' that thou through superstition of them should fall clean from the most chief and greatest things of all. In the one is jeopardy somewhat plain and evident, but in the other is peril much grievouser. So Scylla flee that thou fall not into Charybdis. To observe these little things is wholesome verily, but to cleave utterly to them is very jeopardous. Paul forbiddeth not thee to use the law and ceremonies, but he would not that ye, who be free in Christ, should be bound either to the [80ᵛ] law or ceremonies. He condemneth not the law of deeds if a man use it lawfully.[327] Without these things peradventure thou shalt not be a Christian man, but they make thee not a Christian man. They will help unto good living even so yet, if thou use them for that purpose. But and if thou shalt begin to enjoy them, and to put thy trust and confidence in them, at once they utterly quench all the living of a Christian man. The Apostle setteth nought by the deeds of Abraham,[328] yet were they very perfect — no man doubteth — and how hast thou confidence in them?

God disdaineth a certain sacrifice called 'victims',° and the sabbaths, and certain holy days called 'new moons', of his people the Jews; of which things he himself was author and doer — and darest thou compare thy own observances to the precepts of the law of God? Yet hear God ready to spew at them and aggrieved with them:

> For what intent (sayeth he) offer ye to me the multitude of those sacrifices which ye call 'victims'? I am full, I have not had pleasure in holocausts° of wethers,° nor in tallow or inward fat of the fat beasts, nor in the blood of calves, of lambs, and of goats. When ye have come before my presence, who hath required these things of you or [81ʳ] that ye should walk in my houses? Offer no more sacrifice in vain, your incense is abomination to me. I will not suffer any more the feast called 'new moons' nor the sabbath-day with other festival days. The companies or congregation of you is infected with iniquity, the very soul of me hath hated *calendas vestras*[329] (the feasts which ye hallow the first day in every month), your customable holy days. These things be grievous unto me, I was even sick to abide them. And when ye shall extend forth your hands I will turn my eyes from you. And when ye shall multiply your prayers I will not hear them.[330]

When he rehearseth the observances and manners of the holy feasts and sacrifices, moreover when he rehearseth the multiplying of prayers, noted he not (as much as though he pointed with his fingers) the persons who measure their religion with a certain number of psalms and prayers, called 'daily service'? And mark another thing also, how marvellously the eloquent prophet expresseth the discretion° of heaping together disdain or indignation of God, so that he now

---

[327] 1 Tim. 1. 8.
[328] Rom. 4.
[329] *calendas vestras*] 'these calends° of yours'. The explanation in brackets is T.'s.
[330] Isaiah 1. 11–15.

could suffer neither with 'ears', nor 'eyes'. What things, I pray you, could he not suffer? Verily, those things which he himself had ordained to be kept so religiously, [81ᵛ] which also were observed so reverently so many years of holy kings and prophets! And these things he abhorreth (yet° in the carnal law) — and trustest thou in ceremonies made at home in thy own house (now in the law of the Spirit)?

God in another place biddeth the same prophet cry incessantly, and to put out his breast° after the manner of a trumpet³³¹ — as in a matter of earnest, and worthy of a great rebuke, and such a matter as almost could not be obtained of these men (I mean, of them who maintain ceremonies so fervently) but with great difficulty:

> Me (sayeth he) they seek from day to day, and know they will³³² my ways, as people who should do justice nor should forsake *judicium Dei sui*, the judgement or law of their Lord God. They demand of me the judgements of justice, and desire to draw nigh to God: 'Why have we fasted', say they, 'and thou hast not looked on us; and why have we meeked° our souls, and thou wouldst not know it?' Lo, in the day of your fast (answereth the prophet again) your own will is found with you, and you seek out all your debtors; lo, unto law and contention ye fast, and ye smite with your fist cruelly. Fast ye not as ye have fasted unto [82ʳ] this day, that your cry should be heard on high. Is this the fast that I have chosen, that a man should trouble himself all the day, or that a man should crook down his head as a hoop or a circle, and strew underneath him sackcloth and ashes? Wilt thou call this a fast, or a day acceptable to God?³³³

But what shall we say unto this? Doth God condemn that thing which he himself did command to be observed? Nay forsooth. What then? But to cleave and stick fast in the flesh of the law, and that we should have confidence in a thing of nothing: *that* is it verily which he hateth deadly. Therefore he showed what should be added to our fasting, praying, pilgrimage-going, and to suchlike observances. 'Be ye washed', said he, 'and made clean; take away your ill cogitations out of my sight'.³³⁴ When thou hearest 'evil thoughts', toucheth he not plainly the spirit and the inward man? The eyes of God see not outward but in secret, 'neither he judgeth after the sight of the eyes, nor rebuketh [after] the hearing of the ears'.³³⁵ God knoweth not the foolish virgins: smooth and gay outward, but empty of good works inward.³³⁶ He knoweth not them who say with lips only, '*Domine, Domine*' (that is to say, 'Master, Master').³³⁷ Moreover, he putteth us in remembrance that [82ᵛ] the spiritual life standeth not so greatly in ceremonies as in the love of thy

---

³³¹ Isaiah 58. 1.
³³² know they will] 'they want to know'.
³³³ Isaiah 58. 2–5.
³³⁴ Isaiah 1. 16.
³³⁵ Isaiah 11. 3.
³³⁶ Matt. 25. 1–13, with E.'s interpretation.
³³⁷ Matt. 7. 21.

neighbour. 'Seek', sayeth he, 'judgement or justice, succour him that is oppressed, give true judgement and right to him that is fatherless and motherless, defend the widow.'[338] Suchlike things he added when he spake of fasting:

> Is not this rather (sayeth he) that fast that I have chosen? Loose or break asunder cruel obligations, unbind the burdens that for haste[339] make them stoop to the ground who bear them. Let them who be bruised go free, and break asunder all burdens. Break thy bread to the hungry. The needy and them who have no place of habitation lead into thy house. When thou seest a naked man clothe him, and despise not thy own flesh.[340]

What shall a Christian man do, then? Shall he despise the commandments of the Church? Shall he set at nought the holy traditions of our forefathers? Shall he condemn honest customs? Nay, if he be weak and as a beginner, he shall observe them as things necessary. But and if he be strong and perfect, so much the rather shall he observe them, lest with his knowledge he should hurt his brother who is yet weak, lest also he should kill him for whom Christ died.[341] We may not omit these outward things, but of necessity [83ʳ] we must observe those other things which pertain to the spirit. Corporeal deeds be not condemned, but spiritual things are preferred. This visible honouring of God is not condemned, but God is not pleased save with invisible service and honour. God is a Spirit and is moved and stirred to mercy with spiritual sacrifice.

It is a great shame that Christian men should not know that thing which a certain poet,[342] being a Gentile, knew right well; who, giving a precept how we should serve God, sayeth, 'If God be a mind, as Scripture showeth unto us, see that thou honour him chiefly with a pure mind'. Let us not despise the author, no, though he be but a heathen man. The sentence° verily becometh a Christian man, yea, and though he were a divine; and (as I verily well have perceived) even as no man is who readeth it not, so are there very few who understand it. The intellection° of the sentence verily is this: 'like rejoiceth with like' — as who should say, 'If God be a Spirit, honour him in the spirit and not in ceremonies'. Thou thinkest that God is moved with an ox killed and sacrificed, or with the vapour or smoke of frankincense, as though he were a body or a bodily thing. God is a mind, and verily a pure mind and most subtle and perfect — therefore ought he to be honoured most chiefly with a pure [83ᵛ] mind. Thou thinkest that a taper lighted is a sacrifice: but a 'sacrifice to God', sayeth David, 'is a woeful or sorrowful

---

[338] Isaiah 1. 17.
[339] for haste] Not in L. or *1533*; perhaps 'suddenly' or 'precipitately' — or a scribal error.
[340] Isaiah 58. 6–7.
[341] 1 Corinth. 8. 11.
[342] certain poet] Dionysius Cato, a post-classical writer famous for a collection of improving couplets. See *Disticha* I. 1; 'scripture' renders L. 'carmina' (verses, songs).

spirit'.³⁴³ And though he hath despised the blood of goats or calves, yet will not he despise a heart contrite and humbled.

If thou do that thing which is applied to satisfy the eye of man, much rather add to it also that thing which the eyes of God require. Thy body is covered with a religious cowl or habit: what is that to the purpose if thy mind wear a secular vesture? If thy outer man be cloaked in a cloak as white as snow, also according to the same [let the vestments of the inner man be white as snow also]. Thou keepest silence outward: much more procure that thy mind be quiet and at rest inward. In the visible temple thou crouchest and bowest the knees of thy body: that is nothing worth if in the temple of thy breast thou stand upright against God. Thou honourest the tree of the cross: [much more follow the mystery of the Cross]. Thou keepest the fasting-day and abstainest from those things which defile not a man: and why abstainest thou not from filthy talking, which polluteth thy own conscience and other men's also? Meat is withdrawn from thy body: but why glutteth thy soul herself with cods° of beans, pease, and suchlike, which are meat meeter for swine? Thou makest the church gay of stone with goodly [84ʳ] ornaments, and honourest holy places: what is that to the purpose if the church of thy heart, whose walls the prophet Ezekiel bored through, be polluted with the abominations of Egypt?³⁴⁴ Thou keepest holy-day outward: and within all things are unquiet with the rage and striving of vices together. Thy body committeth no adultery, but thou art covetous: now is thy mind a fornicator. Thou singest or prayest with thy bodily tongue: but take heed within what thy mind sayeth. With thy mouth thou blessest: and with thy heart thou cursest.³⁴⁵ In thy body thou art closed with a strait or narrow cell: and in thy cogitation or thoughts thou wanderest throughout all the whole world. Thou hearest the word of God with thy corporeal ears: rather hear it within thy mind. What sayeth the prophet? 'Except ye hear within, your souls shall weep.'³⁴⁶ Yea, and what readest thou in the Gospel? that 'when they see they should not see, and when they hear they should not hear'.³⁴⁷ Again the prophet sayeth, 'With your ear you shall hear and shall not perceive'.³⁴⁸ Blessed be they therefore who hear the word of God within. Happy are they to whom God speaketh within, and their souls shall be saved. This 'ear to incline' is commanded by David that 'noble daughter of the king, [84ᵛ] whose beauty and goodliness is altogether within in golden hems'.³⁴⁹

Finally, what availeth it if thou do not those ill things outward, which with

---

³⁴³ Ps. 51. 17.
³⁴⁴ Ezek. 8. 7–13; often allegorised.
³⁴⁵ James 3. 8–10.
³⁴⁶ Jerem. 13. 17 (*Vulg.*).
³⁴⁷ Luke 8. 10.
³⁴⁸ Isaiah 6. 9.
³⁴⁹ Ps. 45. 10, 13.

affection thou desirest and covetest inward? What availeth it to do good deeds outward, unto which within are committed things contrary? Is it so great a thing if thou go to Jerusalem in thy body, when within thine own self is both Sodom, Egypt, and Babylon? It is no great thing to have trodden the steps of Christ with thy bodily heels, but it is a very great thing to follow the steps of Christ in thine affection. If it be a very great thing to have touched the sepulchre of Christ, shall it not be also a very great thing to have represented the mystery of his burying? Thou accusest and utterest thy sins to a priest, who is a man as thou art: take heed how thou accusest and utterest them before God, for to accuse them before God is nothing else but to hate them inwardly. Thou believest that all thy sins and offences should be washed away at once with a little paper or parchment sealed with wax, or for a little money, or with a little pilgrimage-going: thou art utterly deceived and clean out of the way. The wound is received within: the medicine therefore must needs be laid within. [85ʳ] Thine affection is corrupt, thou hast loved that which was worthy of hate, and hated that which was worthy to be loved. Sweet was to thee sour, and bitter was sweet.

I regard not what ceremonies thou usest outward, but and if (clean contrary) thou shalt begin to hate, to flee, and to abhor that which thou lately lovedst, if that wax sweet to thy appetite which lately had the taste of gall — on this wise at the last I perceive the signs and tokens of health. Mary Magdalen loved much, and many sins were forgiven her.[350] The more thou lovest Christ, the more thou shalt hate vices, for the hate of sin followeth the love of good living, even as the shadow followeth the body. I had lever that thou shouldst once hate all thy vicious living within and indeed, than to defy° them afore a priest ten times in word.

To conclude therefore: as I have rehearsed certain things because of example, even so — in all the spectacle and compass of this visible world, in the old law, in the new law, in all the commandments of the Church, finally in thyself, in all business between man and man — without is there a certain flesh, and within is a spirit. In which things if we shall not make a perverse order, nor shall put so great confidence in visible things [85ᵛ] which are seen with bodily eyes, but even as they be of value to better things: then shall we always have a respect to the spirit and to things of charity, and shall also wax not heavy as men in sorrow and pain (as these men be), not feeble, [not] ever children (as it is in the proverb), not beastly and 'dry bones' without life (as sayeth the prophet),[351] not as men in a trance (as snails in winter) and amazed, ever chiding and scolding, full of envy, malice, and backbiting; but we shall wax excellent in Christ, large in charity, strong and stable against all manner chances of fortune, not displeased with the smaller things, and yet enforcing up to things most perfect. We shall wax full of mirth,

---

[350] Luke 7. 47.
[351] Ezek. 37. 1–3.

and full also of knowledge — which whosoever doth refuse, them the noble Lord of all knowledge shall refuse.

For verily ignorance or lack of experience — which for the most part accompanieth lack of capacity and that gentlewoman whom the Greeks call Philautia[352] (that is to say, love of thyself) — only° bringeth to pass that (as Isaiah sayeth) 'we should have confidence in things of nothing and should speak vanities, should conceive labour and bring forth iniquity',[353] and should ever serve trembling and in subjection and bondage to the ceremonies of the Jews. [86ʳ] Of which manner of persons Paul speaketh, saying, 'I bear them record that the zeal of God they have, but not after knowledge'.[354] What is that they know not? Verily that 'the [end of the] law of God is Christ'[355] and that Christ is also a Spirit, yea, and is also charity.

But Isaiah more plainly describeth the miserable and unprofitable bondage of these men in the flesh. 'Therefore', sayeth he, 'my people is led in captivity because they had no knowledge, and the nobles of them perished for hunger, and the multitude of them dried away for thirst.'[356] It is no marvel that the common people be servants to the law and ceremonies of this world, as they who are unlearned, nor have wisdom more than they borrow of other men's heads. It is more to be marvelled that they who are as chief of Christ's religion in the same captivity perish for hunger and wither away for thirst. Why perish they for hunger? Because they have not learned of Christ to break barley-loaves:[357] they only lick round about the rough and sharp cod or husk, they suck out no marrow or sweet liquor. And why wither they so away for thirst? Because they have [not] learned of Moses to fetch out water out of the spiritual rock or stone,[358] nor have drunk of 'the rivers of the water of life which flow, issue, or spring out of the belly of Christ'.[359] [86ᵛ] and that was spoken verily of the Spirit, not of the flesh.

Thou therefore, my brother, lest with sorrowful labours thou shouldst not much prevail, but that with mean° exercise thou mightest shortly wax a man in Christ and lusty: diligently embrace this rule, and creep not always on the ground with unclean beasts, but — always leaning to those wings which, stirred up with the heat of the love in the minds of men, Plato[360] thinketh ever to spring afresh —

---

[352] Philautia] *Folly*'s close companion. **Marg.** 'Ignorance and love of thyself is the ground and matter of all mischief.' In *Obedience*, pp. 20 and 22, Tyndale takes it as virtually synonymous with 'philosophy'.
[353] Isaiah 59. 4.
[354] Rom. 10. 2.
[355] Rom. 10. 4; 'of God' is a *1523* addition, removed in *1533*.
[356] Isaiah 5. 13.
[357] John 6. 9–14.
[358] Exod. 17. 6.
[359] John 7. 38–39.
[360] Plato] *Phaedrus* 251.

lift up thyself, as it were with certain steps of the ladder of Jacob,[361] from the body to the spirit, from the visible world to the invisible, from the letter to the mystery, from things sensible to things intelligible, from things gross and compound unto things single and pure. On this wise, God on his side shall draw again nigh to whosoever shall draw nigh him.[362] And if thou for thy part shall endeavour to arise out of the darkness and troublous noise of the sensible powers, he will come against thee pleasantly and for thy profit out of his light inaccessible, and out of that noble silence incogitable;° where not only all rage of sensual powers, but also similitudes or imaginations of intelligible powers, cease and keep silence.

CHAPTER FOURTEEN

The sixth rule

[Remember the great difference between the way of Christ and the way of the world]

[87ʳ] And forasmuch as suddenly, to a man that writeth, one thing calleth another to remembrance, I will subscribe° the sixth rule, somewhat a neighbour to them which go before, a rule to all men as necessary unto health° as she is regarded of few. That rule is this: that the mind of him who enforceth° and laboureth to Christward should vary as much as were possible both from the deeds, and opinions also, of the common or lay people, and that the example of good living be fetched of no man's self save of Christ only. For he is the only pattern, the only and chief example and form of living, from whom whosoever wrieth° aside one inch goeth beside° the right path and runneth out of the way.

Wherefore Plato, with gravity verily (as he doth many other things), in his book *Republic* denieth that any man is able to defend virtue constantly who should not have his mind instructed with sure and undoubted opinions as touching° filthiness and honesty. But how much more perilous is it if false opinions of those things which pertain to health should sink utterly unto the deep bottom of the mind? For that consideration, therefore, thinketh Plato that this thing ought to be cared for and looked upon chiefly: that the governors themselves, whom it behoveth to lack all manner of uncleanness, should engrave in their own minds very wholesome and good opinions, [87ᵛ] both of things to be ensued° and also of things to be eschewed — that is to say, of good and ill, of vices and of virtues — and that they have them very assured, all doubts laid apart, as certain laws very goodly and ghostly.° For whatsoever thing cleaveth in the mind surely rooted with steadfast belief, that every man declareth and uttereth in his manners and conversation.°

---

[361] Gen. 28. 12.
[362] James 4. 8.

Therefore the chief care of Christian men ought to be applied to this point, that their children straightway from their cradle, amongst the very flattering of the nurses, and kissing of the father and mother, even under the hands of them who are learned, should suck in persuasion meet° and worthy of Christ; because that nothing either sinketh deeper or cleaveth faster in the mind of man than that which (as Quintilian[363] sayeth) in the young and tender years is poured in. Let be afar from the ears of little babes wanton songs of love such as Christian men sing at home and wheresoever they ride or go — much more filthy than the common people of the heathen men would suffer° to be had in use with them. Let them not hear their mother wail and wring her hands for a little loss of worldly goods, nor let them hear her cry out 'alas! that ever she was born', saying she is but a wretch, a woman lost or cast away, left alone or destitute, [88ʳ] peradventure for the loss of her sister or for some other friend. Let not them hear their father or mother[364] rebuking and upbraiding of cowardness him who hath not recompensed injury or wrong with double; nor let them hear him lauding them who have gathered together great abundance of riches, by whatsoever manner it were. The disposition of man is frail and prone to vices, he catcheth mischievous° example at once, [none] otherwise verily than tow° catch fire if it be put to. And the selfsame thing is to be done in every age,[365] that all the errors of the lay people should be plucked out again from the mind by the hard roots, and in their places should be planted wholesome opinions; and that they be so roborate° and knit together that with no violence they might be plucked asunder. Which thing whosoever hath done, the same shall easily and without business° by his own accord follow virtue, and shall count them who do otherwise worthy whom men should pity and not counterfeit.°

Unto this thing pertaineth that not indiscreet° saying of Socrates[366] (though it were rebuked of Aristotle), that virtue was nothing else but knowledge of things to be ensued and followed, and of things to be eschewed or fled. Not but that Socrates saw difference between the knowledge of honesty° and the love of the [88ᵛ] same; but — as Demosthenes[367] answered that pronunciation or utterance should be the first, the second, and also the third point of eloquence, signifying that to be the most excellent part insomuch that he thought eloquence to rest chiefly in utterance only — in like wise Socrates, disputing with Protagoras, proveth by arguments that knowledge in all virtue is of such value that vices should[368] no otherwhence proceed than lack of knowledge and of false opinions.

---

[363] Quintilian] *Institutio* I. 8. 4–5.
[364] or mother] Added by T. (but note 'him' at 2833).
[365] in every age] 'however old they are'.
[366] Socrates] e.g. *Protagoras* 352c; Aristotle, *Ethics* VII. 2. **Marg.** 'Virtue is the knowledge, or rather the love, of things to be hated and of things to be desired and loved.'
[367] Demosthenes] Reported by several classical authors, e.g. Cicero, *Orator* xvii. 56.
[368] should] 'do'.

For certainly both he that loveth Christ and he also that loveth voluptuousness,° money, false honour, no doubt both of them follow° a sweet, a good, and a beautiful thing. But the one slideth through ignorance: instead of a sweet thing embracing a thing out of measure sour, fleeing as a sour thing that which is sweetest of all; likewise following as a thing of great advantage that which is utterly to the loss, fearing that as damage which is only° lucre;° judging that beautiful which is too much filthy, and that shameful which only is honourable and glorious. In conclusion, if a man were surely and inwardly brought in belief, and if also it were translated° into the substance of his mind (as meat° into the substance of the body) that only virtue were best, were most sweet, most fair, [89ʳ] most honest, and of all things most acceptable; and on the other side if he believed that filthiness only were an evil thing, were a punishment, were filthy, and a thing to be ashamed of, and a thing full of damage or loss; and should measure this thing, not by the opinion of the common people, but by the very nature of the things: it could not be (if such persuasion or belief endured) that he should stick fast and cleave long time in evil things.

For now long ago the common people is found to be the most mischievous author or captain both of living men[369] [and also of judgement, nor was the world ever in so good state and condition but that the worst[370] have pleased the most part. Beware lest thou thiswise think, 'No man is there that doth not this, mine elders before me have walked in these steps, of this opinion is such a man, so great a philosopher, so great a divine, this is the custom and manner of living of kings, thiswise live great men, this do both bishops and popes: these verily be no common people'. Let not these great names move thee one inch. I measure or judge not the common or rascal° sort by the room,° estate, or degree, but by the mind and stomach.° Whosoever in the famous cave of Plato, bound with the bonds of their own affections,° wonder at the vain images and shadows° of things, instead of very° true things: they be 'the common people'. Should he not do preposterously° or out of order, if a man would go about to try,° not the stone by the ruler or square,° but the ruler by the stone? And were it not much more unreasonable, if a man would go about to bow and turn, not the manners of men to Christ, but Christ to the living of men?] Think it not therefore well or aright whatsoever commonly is done, if it agree not to the rule of Christ.

Yea, and therefore ought a thing to be suspected *because* it pleaseth the most part. It is, and ever shall be, a small flock[371] to whom is pleasant the simplicity or plainness, the poverty or verity of Christ. It is a small flock verily, but a blessed, as unto whom doubtless is due only the kingdom of heaven. 'Strait° is the way of

---

[369] living men] The bracketed passage is missing from *1523* (the near-repeated 'living men' suggests a cause) and supplied here from *1533*.
[370] worst] 'worst things'.
[371] small flock] Matt. 7. 14, Luke 12. 32.

virtue, and of very few trodden on, but no other way leadeth to life.' To conclude: whether³⁷² doth a wise builder fetch his example of the most common and used work? Painters set afore them none but the best tables° or patterns of imagery. Our example is Christ, in whom [89ᵛ] only be all rules of blessed living. Him may we counterfeit without exception. If thou go further in proved° men, it shall be meet that thou counterfeit and take for an example everything so far forth as they shall agree with the first example or pattern which Christ gave.

But as touching the common people of Christian men, thiswise think: none other to have been [more] corrupt (no, not among the Gentiles) inasmuch as pertaineth to the opinions of good manners. Moreover,° as touching their faith,³⁷³ advise them. This surely is doubtless, and to be abided by: faith without manners worthy of faith prevaileth nothing, insomuch also that it groweth to a heap of damnation. Search the stories of antiquity, and to them compare the manners that be nowadays. When was very honesty more despised? When was so had in price° riches, got [not] regarded whence? In what world at any time was truer that saying of the poet Horace, 'Lady Money giveth a wife with a dowry, both credence and friendship, nobleness and also beauty'?³⁷⁴ And again sayeth he, 'Nobleness and virtue, except a man have goods withal,° is viler than a rush° of straw'.³⁷⁵ Who readeth not in good earnest that biting mock of the same poet, 'O citizens, citizens, first seek money, and after [90ʳ] money virtue'?³⁷⁶ When was riot° or excess more immoderate than now? When was adultery, and all other kinds of unchaste living, either more apert° in the sight of every man, or more unpunished, or else less had in shame, rebuke, or abomination — while the captains and great men favour their own vices, in other men suffering them unpunished; and every man counteth most comely and beautiful to be done, whatsoever is used and taken up among courtiers? To whom seemeth not poverty extreme ill and utmost shame and rebuke?

In time past against keepers of queans,° against glorious and gorgeous persons, against the wonderers° of money, scoffing or jestings were cast, yea, and that with authority.³⁷⁷ In comedies, tragedies, in interludes or common plays of the Gentiles, a great clapping of hands and a shout was made for joy of the lay people at vices craftily° rebuked and checked.° At which same vices nowadays (evil° praised) is

---

³⁷² whether] 'surely a wise builder doesn't take his example from … ?'; but L. and 1533 add the alternative 'or of the best work': 'does he take it from this … or from that?'.
³⁷³ faith] i.e. their opinions. 'Moreover' is 'nevertheless'; L. 'caeterum' ('but setting that aside'): 'it's what they do, not what they believe, that is my concern'.
³⁷⁴ *Epistles* I. 6. 36–37.
³⁷⁵ *Satires* II. 5. 8.
³⁷⁶ *Epistles* I. 1. 53–54.
³⁷⁷ with authority] L. 'from wagons', a reference to travelling players permitted to deliver abuse at public festivals. See Horace, *Art of Poetry* 276, and *Adages* I. vii. 73 (*CWE* 32. 110).

made a shout and clapping of hands for joy — even of[378] the nobles and states°
of Christian men. The Athenians, in their common house appointed for disguisings° and interludes, could not forbear nor suffer a jester (playing a certain tragedy of Euripides) to sing the words of a certain covetous man, who preferred [90ᵛ] money only afore all other commodities and pleasures of man's life; and plainly it should have come to pass that they had clapped out of the play, yea, and violently cast out of the house, the player with all the fable — except° the poet (by and by° arising up) had desired them to tarry a little and behold to what point or conclusion that so great a wonderer at money should come to.

How many stories be in the histories of the Gentiles [of them] who, of the commonwealth well governed and ministered, brought nothing into their poor household but an honest opinion or reputation; who also set more by their fidelity than money, by chastity than their life; who neither in prosperity could wax wild and wanton, nor in adversity be weakened; who, content only with the conscience° of good living, desired neither honours, nor riches, nor any other commodities of fortune. It should not need to rehearse° the holiness of Phocion, the poverty of Fabricius (more excellent than any riches), the strong and courageous mind of Camillus, the strait and indifferent° justice of Brutus, the chastity of Pythagoras, the temperance of Socrates that never was subdued, the sound and constant virtue of Cato, and a thousand most goodly examples of all virtues which are read everywhere in the [91ʳ] stories of the Lacedaemonians, of the Persians, of the Athenians, and of the Romans, to our great shame verily. Holy Aurelius Augustine (as he of himself witnesseth in the commentaries of his own *Confessions*),[379] long time before he put Christ on him, despised money, counted honours for things of nought, was not moved with glory, praise, or fame, and unto voluptuous pleasures kept the bridle so strait that he (then a young man) was content with one little wench, to whom he kept also promise and faith of marriage.

Such minds, such examples among courtiers, among men of the Church — I will speak more at large: among monks also — a man shall not find. Or else, if any such shall be, by and by he shall be pointed with the finger, he shall be wondered or mocked, as it were an ass among apes;[380] he shall be called a doting fool, a grosshead,° a hypocrite, in nothing expert,° melancholy and mad; yea, and that with the common voice of all men. So we Christian men honour the doctrine of Christ, so counterfeit we it everywhere nowadays, that nothing is counted more foolish, more vile, more to be ashamed of, than to be a Christian man indeed and with all the heart: as though that either Christ in vain had been conversant° in earth, or that Christendom were some other thing [91ᵛ] now than in times past, or as° it indifferently pertaineth not to all men! I will therefore that thou from

---

[378] of] 'by'.
[379] *Confessions*] e.g. IV. 2 and VI. 15.
[380] ass among apes] See *Adages* I. v. 41 (*CWE* 31. 421).

these men vary with all thy mind, and that thou esteem the value of everything by the acquaintance or fellowship that it hath with Christ only; and as everything draweth near to the living and learning° of Christ, so esteem the value of it.

Who thinketh it not everywhere to be an excellent thing, and to be numbered among the chiefest of all good things, if a man descend of a worshipful stock and of honourable ancestors; a thing which only they call 'nobleness'? Let it not move thee one whit when thou hearest the wise men of this world — men, I mean, of sadness,° endued with great authority — so earnestly dispute of their degrees° and of their genealogies or lineage, and with gravity draw the forehead and upper brows together, as it were with a matter of a marvellous difficulty; yea, and with great enforcement they bring forth plain trifles. Nor let it move thee when thou seest another sort of men so high-minded° for the noble acts of their grandfathers or great-grandfathers that they think all others in comparison of themselves scarce worthy to be called men. But thou shalt laugh at the error of these men after the manner of Democritus, and shalt count (that which [92^r] is true indeed) that the only and most perfect nobleness is to be regenerate in Christ, to be grafted and planted in the Body of him, to be one body and one spirit with God. Let other men be kings' sons, but be thou content and to thee let it be the greatest honour that can be that thou art called, and art indeed, the son of God. Let them stand in their own conceits° because they are daily conversant in great princes' courts, but choose thou rather to be, with David, vile or abject in the house of God.[381] Take heed what manner fellows Christ chose: feeble persons, fools, vile as touching this world. In Adam we all are born of low degree. In Christ we are all one thing: neither high nor low in degree one more than another, but the very° nobleness is to despise this 'nobleness' and to become the servant of Christ. Think them to be thy ancestors whose virtues thou both lovest and counterfeitest.

Also hark what the true Esteemer of nobleness said in the Gospel against the Jews who boasted themselves to be of the generation of Abraham — who was a man verily not excellent only, not rich only, not the conqueror of kings[382] only, but also for his divine virtues was lauded of God himself. Who would not think this to be a noble thing, and worthy whereof a man might rejoice? Yet hear what was [92^v] answered unto them. 'Ye are', said Christ, 'of your father the Devil, and the deeds of your father ye do.'[383] And hear also Paul, how he esteemeth gentle blood. 'Not all they', sayeth he, 'who be of the circumcision of Israel be Israelites, nor all they that be of the seed of Abraham be the sons of Abraham.'[384]

It is a low degree and to be ashamed of that a man should serve filthiness and should have no kindred with Christ at all; who alloweth° for his kinsman none

---

[381] Ps. 84. 10.
[382] Gen. 13. 2, 14. 14–20.
[383] John 8. 44.
[384] Rom. 9. 6–7.

but such as fulfil the will of his Father that is in heaven.³⁸⁵ He is shamefully a bastard who hath the Devil to his father — and verily whosoever doeth the deeds of the Devil, the same man hath the Devil to his father, except Christ lied. But Verity cannot lie. The highest degree that can be is to be the son and heir of God, the brother and coheir with Christ.³⁸⁶ What their badges and conceits° mean, let them take heed. The badges of Christ be common to all men, and they be most honourable: which be the cross, the crown of thorn, the nails, the spear, the signs or tokens which Paul rejoiceth to bear in his body.³⁸⁷ Of nobleness now thou seest how much otherwise I would have thee perceive than the lay people imagine.

Who calleth him not 'blessed', 'rich', and 'happy' among the common people who hath heaped together at home a [93ʳ] great heap of gold? But judge thou him to be blessed enough — yea, and that he only is blessed — who possesseth Christ, the very felicity and of all things the best. Judge him happy who hath bought that noble and precious margarite° of a pure mind, either with the loss of all his goods or of his body also; and judge him happy likewise who hath found the treasure of wisdom, preciouser than all riches; and whosoever to be rich withal [who] hath bought of most rich Christ gold purified and proved with fire.³⁸⁸

What things then be these which the common people wonder at, as gold, precious stones, livelihood°? which with a wrong name are called 'riches', when in the true name they be very thorns which choke the seed of the Word of God, according to the parable of the Gospel.³⁸⁹ They be packs or fardels,° with which whosoever be laden neither can follow poor Christ by the strait way, nor enter by the low door into the kingdom of heaven. Think not thyself better by one hair if thou shouldst pass° in riches either Midas or Croesus, but think thyself more bound, more tangled, and more laden. He hath abundantly enough who can utterly despise such things. He is provided for sufficiently to whom Christ promised nothing [should be lacking]. He shall not be a-hungered to whose mouth manna of the Word of God seemeth pleasant. He shall not [93ᵛ] be naked who hath put Christ upon him. Think this only to be a loss: as oft as anything of good living³⁹⁰ is departed, and anything of vices is increased. Think it a great lucre or advantage when thy mind through increase of virtue is waxed better. Think thou lackest nothing as long as thou possessest him in whom is all things.

But what is this which wretches call 'pleasure'? Surely it is whatsoever thou canst imagine rather than that which it is called. What is it then? It is pure madness

---

³⁸⁵ Matt. 7. 21.
³⁸⁶ Rom. 8. 16–17.
³⁸⁷ Galat. 6. 14, 17.
³⁸⁸ Rev. 3. 18.
³⁸⁹ Mark 4. 7, 18–19.
³⁹⁰ good living] i.e. virtue.

and plainly (as Greeks be wont to say) it is 'the laughter of Ajax',[391] pleasant poison and a merry mischief. True and only pleasure is the inward joy of a pure conscience. The most noble and daintiest feast that can be is the study of Holy Scripture, and [the] most delectable songs be the psalms. The most pleasant fellowship is the fellowship of the Holy Ghost and the company of the saints. The most° dainties of all is the fruition° of God and to enjoy the truth. Purge now thine eyes, purge thy ears, purge thy mouth, and Christ shall begin to wax sweet and pleasant to thee; whom once tasted of savoury — yea, if Milesians, Sybarites, if all incontinent° rioters and Epicureans, yea, if the imaginers and devisers of pleasure every one should heap together all their flattering subtleties and dainty dishes — in comparison yet of Christ they [94ʳ] all shall seem to provoke thee to spew and to cast thy gorge.° That is not by and by° sweet which is savoury to a whole man. If water have the taste of wine to him who burneth in a hot fever, no man will call this 'pleasure', but a disease. Thou art utterly deceived if thou believe not that the very tears be much more pleasant to devout and holy men than be to wicked men their laughings, mockings, jestings, or scoffings; and also if thou believe not that fastings are sweeter to the one than are to the others plovers, quails, partridges, pheasants, pike, trout, porpoise, or the fresh sturgeon — thou art, I say, deceived if thou believe not that the moderate boards° of the one, appointed° with herbs and fruits, be much more delicious than the costly and loathsome feasts of the other. Finally, very pleasure is: for the love of Christ not to be once moved with false and apparent pleasures.

Moreover, behold how the world abuseth the names of 'love' and 'hate'. When a foolish young man is clean out of his wit and mad for a wench's sake, *that* the common people call 'love': and yet is there no verier hate in the world. Very love, even with its own loss, desireth to provide for another man's profit. Whereunto looketh *he* save unto his own [94ᵛ] pleasure? Therefore he loveth not her, but himself — yet loveth he not himself verily, for no man can love another except he love himself first, yea, and except he love himself aright. No man can hate any man at all except he hate himself first. Nevertheless, to love well is now and then good 'hate', and to 'hate' aright is good love. Whosoever therefore for a little lucre or pleasure to himself (as he supposeth) layeth await° to a maiden with flattering, with gifts, and with fair promises, to pluck from her the best thing she hath — that is to wit,° her perfectness, her chastity or simplicity or innocency, her good mind, and her good name — whether seemeth this man to hate or to love? Certainly there is no hate more cruel than is this hate. When the foolish father and mother favour the vices of their children, they say commonly 'how tenderly love they their children' — but rather how cruelly hate they their children who (while they follow their affections) regard not at all the wealth° of their children.

What other thing wisheth to us our most hateful enemy the Devil, than that

---

[391] laughter of Ajax] i.e. madness ending in remorse; see *Adages* I. vii. 46 (*CWE* 32. 95).

we (here sinning unpunished) should fall into eternal punishment? They call him an 'easy master' and a 'merciful prince' who at certain grievous offences either winketh° [95ʳ] or else favoureth them, that — the more unpunished men sin — the more lawfully° they might sin. But what other thing threateneth God by his prophet to them whom he judgeth unworthy of his mercy? 'I will not', sayeth he, 'visit your daughters when they commit fornication, nor your daughters-in-law when they commit adultery.'³⁹² Unto David what promised he? 'I will', sayeth he, 'with a rod visit their iniquities, and with whips their sins, but I will not cast³⁹³ my mercy from them.'³⁹⁴

Thou seest how all things are renewed in Christ, and how the names of things are changed. Whosoever love himself amiss hateth himself deadly. Whosoever is ill° merciful towards himself, the same is a tyrant most cruel. To govern well is if thou regard not.³⁹⁵ To hurt well is doing good. To destroy well is saving. Thou shalt regard and cure° thyself well if thou shalt despise the desires of the flesh. If in good manner thou shalt rage against vices of the man, thou shalt do the man a good turn. If thou shalt kill the sinner, thou shalt save the man. If thou shalt destroy that which man hath made, thou shalt restore that which God hath made.

Come off now and let us go further. What thinketh the error of the people that power, weakness, manhood, cowardness be? Call they not him 'mighty' who can lightly° hurt whom he list°? [95ᵛ] (though it be a very odious power to be able to hurt, for in that are they compared to noisome° worms and to scorpions, yea, and to the Devil himself; whose³⁹⁶ properties° be only to do harm). Only God is mighty indeed, who neither can hurt if he would, nor yet would if he could; whose nature is only to do good. But how at the last shall this 'mighty' fellow hurt another man? Shall he take away thy money? Shall he beat thy body? Shall he rob thee of thy life? If he do it to him that is a good man and serveth God, he hath done him a good cure instead of an evil: but and if he hath done it unto an ill man, the one hath ministered an occasion verily, but the other hath hurt himself; for no man is hurt but of his own self.³⁹⁷ No man goeth about to hurt another except the same man have much grievouslier hurt himself aforehand. Thou enforcest to hurt me in my money or goods: now hast thou through loss of charity hurt thyself most grievously. Thou canst not fasten a wound in me but that thou before shouldst have received a wound much more grievous. Thou canst not take from me the life of my body unless thou shouldst have slain thy own soul before. But Paul — who was a man to do wrong [96ʳ] weak and feeble, but to suffer wrong most valiant and strong — rejoiceth that he could 'do all things in Christ'.³⁹⁸

---

³⁹² Hosea 4. 14.
³⁹³ cast] *1533* 'take', but L. is 'dispergam' ('scatter').
³⁹⁴ Ps. 89. 32–33.
³⁹⁵ if thou regard not] 'if you show no favours'.
³⁹⁶ whose] i.e. 'their'.
³⁹⁷ no man […] own self] Socratic; see *Adages* III. vi. 34 (*CWE* 35. 141).
³⁹⁸ Philipp. 4. 13.

They call him 'manly' and 'bold' who, of a fierce and an impotent or impatient mind, for the least displeasure that can be rageth and seetheth and boileth in wrath, and acquitteth° a shrewd° word with a shrewd word, a check with a check, an evil turn with another. On the other side, whosoever when he hath received wrong maketh nothing ado, but dissembleth as° no such thing were done him, they call a 'coward', a 'dastard',° 'heartless',° 'meet for nothing'. Yea, but what is more contrary to the greatness of the mind than with a little word to be put aside from the quiet state and constancy of the spirit, and so greatly not to be able to set at nought another man's foolishness that thou shouldst think thou were not a man except thou shouldst overcome one shrewd turn with another? But how much more manful is it, with an excellent and a large mind, to be able to despise all manner injuries, moreover also for an ill deed to recompense° a good? I would not call him a bold man who durst jeopard on[399] his enemy, who should scale castle- or town-walls, who (his life not regarded) should put himself in all manner jeopardies — which thing is common almost to all warriors — but whoso [96ᵛ] could overcome his own mind, whosoever could will them good who do him harm, pray for them who curse him:[400] to this man is due the proper name of a bold and a strong man, and this fellow only is endued with a hardy and an excellent mind.

Let us also discuss° another thing: what the world calleth 'praise', 'rebuke', and 'shame'. Thou art praised: for what cause, and of° whom? If for filthy things and of filthy persons, this verily is a false praise and a true rebuke. Thou art dispraised, thou art mocked and laughed at: for what cause, and of whom? For honour of God, for innocency, and of ill men? This is not a rebuke, neither is no truer praise. Be it that all the world reprove, refuse, and disallow° it: yet can it not be but glorious and of great praise that° Christ himself approveth. And though all that is in the world agree, consent and allow, crying with a noble shout, 'that is a noble deed', yet can it not [but] be shameful whatsoever displeaseth God.

They call 'wisdom' everywhere: to get goods stoutly, when it is got to maintain it lustily, and utterly to look aforehand unto the time that is to come. For thus we hear them say everywhere (and that in good earnest) of them who in short time have got substance somewhat abundantly, 'he is a thrifty man, [97ʳ] ware° and wise, circumspect and provident'.° Such is the world, which is both a liar himself, and the father of lying.[401] But what sayeth Verity? 'Fool!' sayeth he, 'I will fetch again this same night thy soul from thee'.[402] He had filled his barns with corn, he had stuffed his storehouses with provision of all things necessary, he had laid up at home money abundantly enough, he thought nothing was to be done more — not because he intended (as a needy keeper) to sit abroad° on his riches heaped together, as the poets say the dragon to have kept the Golden Fleece (which thing

---

[399] jeopard on] 'risk himself against'.
[400] Luke 6. 28.
[401] John 8. 44.
[402] Luke 12. 20.

men do almost everywhere), but he intended to have spent them joyously. And yet doth the Gospel call this man a 'fool', for what is more foolish, what is of a more gross imagination and of less capacity, than to gape at the shadows and to lose the very things? which jest we be wont to laugh at in the famous dog of Aesop.⁴⁰³ And in the manners of a Christian man is it not more to be laughed, or rather to be wept, at? He should be counted a rude° and an inexpert° merchant, who should not know the saying of Terence, 'To refuse money at a season° is sometimes a great advantage'⁴⁰⁴ (or whosoever would receive a little advantage in hand when he knew great loss should follow?) How much more without advisement° or circumspection is it to make provision with so great care for this present life (which is but [97ᵛ] a shadow, every hour ready to fail) — namely° when God (if we believe the Gospel) will minister all things necessary for the same life if we have confidence in him — and for the life to come to make no provision at all (which we must needs always lead, yea, and altogether full of misery and wretchedness, if provision be not made now aforehand with great diligence)?

Hear another error. They call him 'peerless', 'politic', and 'in all things expert' who hearkeneth for all manner tidings, and knoweth what is done throughout all the world, what is the chance° of merchandise, what the king of England intendeth, what new thing is done at Rome, what is chanced in France, how the Danes⁴⁰⁵ and the Scythians live, what matter great princes have in council — to make an end shortly: whosoever can babble with all kinds of men of all manner business, him they call a 'wise man'. But what can be a more negligent thing, what less according,° than to search for those things which be done afar off and pertain to thee nothing at all, but not once to think on those things which are done at home in thy own breast and pertain even to thyself only? Thou tellest me of the trouble and business of England: tell me rather what trouble is made in thy breast by wrath, envy, bodily lust, ambition; and how nigh these be [98ʳ] brought into subjection, what hope thou hast of victory, how much of this host is put to flight, how reason is endued or appointed. In these things if thou shalt have a quick ear and also a clear eye, if thou shalt smell° and shalt be circumspect, then will I call thee 'politic' and 'peerless'; and that thing which the world is wont to cast against us, I will hurl at it again.⁴⁰⁶ He is not wise that all seeth the world, who is not wise for his own profit.

---

⁴⁰³ Aesop] A dog carrying a piece of meat sees its reflection in water and opens its mouth to get what it thinks will be better: Perry 133; and see *Adages* I. ix. 86 (*CWE* 32. 225) and III. ii. 98 (34. 261).
⁴⁰⁴ *Brothers* 216.
⁴⁰⁵ Danes] A mistake, repeated in 1533, for L. 'Daci' (Dacians).
⁴⁰⁶ hurl at it again] 'They tell us we're impractical, but we're the ones who understand *real* self-interest.'

After this manner if thou shalt examine all the cares of mortal men, their joys, their hope, fear, studies,° their minds or judgement, thou shalt find all things full of errors, while they call good evil and evil good, while they make sweet sour and sour sweet, while they make light darkness and darkness light. And this sort of men verily is most by a great deal. Notwithstanding, thou must even at once both despise them and set no store by them, lest thou shouldst be minded to be like them; and also thou must pity them, so that thou wouldst fain have them like unto thee — I mean, in Christ. And (to use the words of Saint Augustine)[407] then 'it is meet to weep at them who are worthy to be laughed at, and to laugh at them who are worthy to be wept at'. Be not in evil things 'conformable to this world', but 'be reformed in the new wit,° that thou mayst approve'° not those [98ᵛ] things which men wonder at, but 'what is the will of God, which is good, well-pleasing, and perfect'.[408] Thou art very nigh jeopardy, and no doubt fallest suddenly from the true way, if thou shalt begin to look about thee what the most part of men do, and to hearken what they think or imagine.

But suffer thou, who art the child of life and of light also, that dead men bury their dead bodies,[409] and let the blind captains of blind men to go away together into the ditch.[410] See thou once move not aside the eyes of thy heart from the first pattern and chief example, Christ. Thou shalt not go out of the way if thou follow the guiding [of] Verity. Thou shalt not stumble in darkness if thou walk after Christ while (the light shining before thee) thou shalt separate coloured° good things from good things indeed, [and evil things indeed] from apparent [evil] things. Thou shalt abhor and [not] counterfeit the blindness of the common people, raging and chafing themselves after the manner of the ebbing and flowing of the sea at the most vain illusions of worldly things, with certain courses of affections — of wrath, envy, love, hate, hope, fear, joy, sorrow — more unquiet than any Euripus.[411] Brahmins, Cynics, Stoics be wont to defend their principles churlishly° and — even the whole world repugning,° [99ʳ] and all men crying and barking against them — yet hold they stiffly that thing whereunto they once have given sure credence. Be thou bold likewise to fasten surely in thy mind the decrees of thy sect. Be bold, without mistrust and altogether, to follow the mind of thy Author, Christ, departing from all contrary opinions.[412]

---

[407] Augustine] Reshaping Rom. 12. 15 in a sermon on another topic; see *ASD* v-8, p. 235.
[408] Rom. 12. 2.
[409] Matt. 8. 22.
[410] Matt. 15. 14.
[411] Euripus] The unsettled strait between Euboea and the Greek mainland.
[412] contrary opinions] In 1523 (unlike L. and 1533) there is no break between this and the following chapter.

CHAPTER FIFTEEN

[Here follow opinions meet° for a Christian man]^413

Let this excellent learning of the true Christian faith be sure and steadfast with thee: that no Christian man should think that he were born for himself, nor that he should be minded to live at his own pleasure; but whatsoever he hath or whatsoever he is able to do, that altogether let him ascribe not to himself but unto God, the Author of it, and of whom it came; and let him suppose that his goods all be common to all men. The charity of a Christian man knoweth not improperation° or singularity.° Let him love good men in Christ, and ill° men for Christ's sake; who so loved us first when we were yet his enemies that he bestowed himself on us altogether for our redemption. Let him embrace the one because they be good, the others to make them good. He shall hate no man at all, no more verily than a faithful physician hateth the sick man. Let him be an enemy only unto vices: the greater the disease is, the greater cure° will pure charity put thereto. He is an adulterer, [99^v] he hath committed sacrilege, he is a Turk: let a Christian man defy° the adulterer, not the man; [let him despise the committer of sacrilege, not the man;] let him kill the Turk, not the man. Let him find the means that the ill man perish such as he hath made him^414 to be, but let the man be saved whom God made. Let a Christian man will well, wish well, and do well to all men unfeignedly: nor shall he hurt them who have deserved it, but shall do good to them who have not deserved it. Let him be glad of all men's commodities° as well as of his own, and also be sorry for all men's harms no otherwise than for his own. For verily this is that which the Apostle commandeth: 'to weep', sayeth he, 'with them that weep, and to rejoice with them that joy'.^415 Yea, let him take another man's harm grievouser than his own, and of his brother's wealth° be gladder than of his own.

It is not a Christian man's part to think on this wise: 'What have I to do with this fellow? I know not whether he be black or white, he is unknown to me, he is a stranger to me, he never did aught for me, he hath hurt me sometimes, but did me never good.' Think none of these things. Remember only for what deserving came those things which Christ hath done for thee — who would his kindness (done to thee) should be recompensed not on himself, but on thy neighbour. Only see of what [100^r] things he hath need of, and what thou art able to do for him. Think this thing only: 'he is my brother in our Lord, coheir in Christ, a member of the same Body, redeemed with one blood, a fellow in the common faith, called unto the very same grace and felicity of the life to come'; even as the Apostle said, 'one Body and one Spirit, as ye be called in one hope of your calling, one Lord

---

^413 Heading supplied from 1533.
^414 him] 'himself'.
^415 Rom. 12. 15.

and one faith, one baptism, one God and the Father of all, who is above all and everywhere and in us all'.⁴¹⁶ How can he be a stranger, to whom thou art coupled with so manifold bonds of unity? Among the Gentiles° those 'circumstances' of rhetoricians⁴¹⁷ were of no little value and weight, either to benevolence or malevolence: 'he is a citizen of the same city, he is of alliance, he is my kinsman', or else to say, 'he is of acquaintance, he is my father's friend, he hath well deserved, he is kind, born of an honest° stock, rich', or otherwise. In Christ all these things [either be nothing], or (after° the mind of Paul) be one and the very selfsame thing.

Let this be ever present before thine eyes, and it shall be enough: 'he is my self or my own flesh, he is my brother in Christ'. Whatsoever is bestowed on any member, reboundeth it not unto all the body, and from thence into the head? We all be members each one depending of another; members cleaving together make a body; [100ᵛ] the head of the Body is Jesus Christ; the head of Christ is God. It is done to thee, it is done to every man, it is done to Christ, it is done to God, whatsoever is done to anyone (what member soever it be), whether it be done well or evil. All these things are one: God, Christ, the Body, and the members. Such sayings have no place conveniently° among Christian men: 'like with like', and that other thing, 'diversity is mother of hate';⁴¹⁸ for unto what purpose pertain words of dissension there where so great unity is?

It savoureth not of Christian faith that commonly a courtier to a town dweller, one of the country to an inhabiter of a city, a man of high degree to another of low degree, an officer° to him that is officeless, the rich to the poor, a man of honour to a vile° person, the mighty to the weak, the Italian to the German, the Frenchman to the English, the English to the Scot, the grammarian to the divine, the logicianer to the divine, the physician to the man of law, the learned to the unlearned, the eloquent to him that is not facund° and lacketh utterance, the single to the married, the young to the old, the clerk to the layman, the priest to the monk, the Carmelites to the Jacobites — and (that I rehearse° not all diversities) in very trifles and things of nought, unlike to unlike is somewhat partial⁴¹⁹ and unkind. Where is charity (which loveth even his [101ʳ] enemy) when the surname changed, when the colour of the vesture a little altered, when the girdle, or the shoe, and suchlike fantasies of men, make me hated unto thee? Why rather leave we not these childish trifles and accustom we not to have before our eyes that which pertaineth to the very thing whereof Paul warneth° us in many places: that all we in Christ our Head be members of one Body, endued with life

---

⁴¹⁶ Ephes. 4. 4–6.
⁴¹⁷ 'circumstances' of rhetoricians] Commonly seven: who, what, when, where, why, how, and wherewith. See *ST* II (i), q. 7.
⁴¹⁸ diversity [...] hate] Cf. *Adages* I. ii. 20–22 (*CWE* 31. 165–69); Tav. 19–21.
⁴¹⁹ partial] Here 'biased against'.

by one Spirit if so be we live that we envy [not] the happier members, but should gladly succour and aid the weaker members; that we might perceive that we ourselves have received a good turn when we have done any benefit to our neighbour, and that we ourselves be hurt when hurt is done to our brother; and that we might understand how no man ought to study° privately for himself, but every man for his own part should bestow in common that thing which he hath received of God, that all things might redound or rebound thither again from whence they sprang — I mean, to Christ our Head.

This verily is the thing which Paul writeth to the Corinthians, saying:

> As the body is one and hath many members, and all the members of the body (though they be many) yet be they but one body: even so likewise is Christ. For in one Spirit we all are baptised to make one Body, whether we be Jews or [101ᵛ] Gentiles, whether we be bond or free, and we all have drunk of one Spirit; for the body (sayeth Paul) is not one member, but many. If the foot shall say, 'because I am not the hand, I am not of the body', is he therefore not of the body? [If the ear should say, 'I am not the eye, I am not of the body', is he therefore not of the body?] If all the body should be the eye, where is then the hearing? If all the body were the hearing, where then should be the smelling? But now God hath put members, every one of them, in the body as it hath pleased him. For if all were but one member, where were the body? But now verily are there many members, yet but one body. The eye cannot say to the hands, 'I have no need of thy help', and again the head cannot say to the feet, 'Ye be not to me necessary'; but those members of the body which seem to be the weaker are much more necessary, and to those which we think to be the viler members of the body we give more abundant honour; and those which be our unhonest° members have more abundant honesty, for our honest members have need of nothing. But God hath tempered and ordered the body, giving more plenteous honour to that part which lacked, because° there should be no division, debate,° or strife in the body, but that the members should care one for another indifferently.° But it is ye who are the Body of Christ, and members one depending of another.⁴²⁰

He writeth like things [102ʳ] to the Romans, saying:

> In one body we have many members and all members have not one office. Even so we, being many, are one Body in Christ, but singularly we be members each one the members of another, having gifts diverse after° the grace which is given to us.⁴²¹

And again to the Ephesians:

> Doing verity (sayeth he) in charity, let us in all manner things grow in him who is our Head, whose name is Christ, in whom all the Body compact is knit by every joint, whereby one part ministereth to another and (after the

---

⁴²⁰ 1 Corinth. 12. 12–25, 27.
⁴²¹ Rom. 12. 4–6.

operation of virtue° which springeth of the Head, and capacity of every member in receiving) maketh the increase of the Body for the edifying° of itself in charity.[422]

And in another place he biddeth every man one to bear another's burden because we be members one depending on another.[423]

Look then whether they pertain unto this Body whom thou hearest speaking everywhere after this manner: 'It is my goods, it came to me by inheritance, I possess it by right and not by fraud — why shall I not use it and abuse it after my own mind, why should I give them of it any deal at all to whom I owe nothing? I spill,° I waste, I destroy — that which perisheth is mine own, it maketh no matter to other men.' Thy members complain and grin° with their teeth for hunger, [102ᵛ] and thou spewest up partridges. Thy brother naked trembleth for cold, and with thee so great abundance of raiment is corrupted° with moths and long lying. The chance of one night hath lost thee a thousand pieces of gold, while in the mean season° some wretched wench (need compelling her) hath offered her chastity to be defiled, and thus perisheth the soul for whom Christ hath bestowed his life. Thou sayest again, 'What is that to me? I treat that which is my own after my own fashion'. And after all this, with this so corrupt mind, thinkest thou thyself to be a Christian man — who art not once° a man verily?

Thou hearest in the presence of a great multitude the good name or fame of this or that man to be hurt. Thou holdest thy peace, or peradventure rejoicest and art well content with the backbiter. Thou sayest, 'I would have reproved him if those things which were spoken had pertained to me, but I have nothing to do with him who was there slandered'. Then (to conclude)° thou hast nothing to do with the Body if thou have nothing to do with the members; thou hast nothing to do with the Head verily, if the Body pertain not to thee.

'A man', say they nowadays, 'with violence may defend and put back° violence.' I care not what the Emperor's laws [103ʳ] permit and suffer:° this I marvel at, how these voices° came into the manners of Christian men, 'I hurt him, but first I was provoked; I had lever° hurt than be hurt'. Be it that man's laws punish not that which they have permitted. But what will the Emperor Christ do if thou beguile his law, which is written in Matthew?

I command you (sayeth Christ there) not once to withstand harm but, if any man shall give thee a blow on the right cheek, offer to him also the other. And whosoever will strive with thee in the law, and take from thee thy coat, yield up also to him thy cloak or mantle. And whosoever shall compel thee to go a mile, go with him two more. Also, love your enemies (sayeth he) and do good to them who hate you, and pray for them who persecute you, who deceive or beguile you by craft of the law, that you may be the sons of your Father who

---

[422] Ephes. 4. 15–16.
[423] Galat. 6. 2, Ephes. 4. 25.

is in heaven; who maketh his sun arise upon good and ill, and sendeth rain upon just and unjust.⁴²⁴

Thou answerest, saying, 'He spake not this to me, he spake it to his Apostles, he spake it to perfect persons'. Heardest thou not how he said, 'that ye may be the sons of your Father'? If thou care not to be the son of God, the law pertaineth not to thee. Nevertheless, he is not good verily [103ᵛ,⁴²⁵ 104ʳ] who would not be perfect.

Hark also another thing. If thou desire no reward, the commandment belongeth not to thee: for it followeth, 'If ye love them who love you, what reward shall ye have?'⁴²⁶ — as who should say 'none'; for verily to do this thing (that is to say, to love them who love thee) is not virtue, but *not* to do it is an evil or a mischievous° thing. To never neither° is due anything at all where is recompensed as much for as much, or like for like. Hear Paul, both a great wise man and cunning,° and an interpreter also of Christ's laws:

> Bless (sayeth he) them that persecute you, bless them and curse them in no wise, rendering to no man ill for ill; if it could be brought to pass, yet at the least way, as much as in you is, and touching your part, having rest and peace with all men, not defending yourselves, my well-beloved brethren, but give place° and withstand you not wrath. For it is written, 'Vengeance shall be reserved to me, and I will quit° them', sayeth our Lord. But if thy enemy shall be a-hungered, give to him meat;° if he be athirst, give him drink: for if thou do this thou shalt heap coals of fire upon his head (that is to say, thou shalt make him love fervently).⁴²⁷ Moreover (sayeth he), be not overcome of evil, but overcome evil in goodness.⁴²⁸

[104ᵛ] 'What shall follow then', sayest thou, 'if I shall with my softness nourish up the knavishness or malice and the froward° or presumptuous audacity of another man, and (suffering an old injury) shall provoke a new?' If thou can without thy own ill either devoid° or put by° evil, no man forbiddeth thee to do it: if not, look thou say not 'it is better to do than to suffer'. Amend thy enemy if thou can, either loading him with benefits or overcoming him with meekness. If that help not, it is better that the one perish than both; it is better that thou shouldst wax rich with the lucre° and advantage of patience than that both twain (while either to other acquitting evil) should be made evil.

Let this therefore be a decree among Christian men: to compare with all men

---

⁴²⁴ Matt. 5. 39–41, 44–45.
⁴²⁵ 103ᵛ] Blank, without loss of text.
⁴²⁶ Matt. 5. 46.
⁴²⁷ (that is to say, thou shalt make him love fervently)] Added in *1523*. Various explanations were current. Tyndale, *Obedience*, p. 54, gives a similar one, 'that is thou shalt kindle love in him', and E.'s *Paraphrases* has 'as if conquered by your love he will be kindled [*inflammabitur*] to love you in return'.
⁴²⁸ Rom. 12. 14, 17–21.

in love, in meekness, and in benefits or doing good; but in striving, hate and backbiting, in rebukes and injury, to give place even to them that be of lowest degree — and that with good will. 'But he is unworthy', thou wilt say, 'to whom a good turn should be done and an evil forgiven.' Yet it is meet for thee to do it, and Christ is worthy for whose sake it is done. 'I will', say they, 'neither hurt any man, nor suffer myself to be hurt': yet thou, when thou art hurt, forgive the trespass with all thy heart, [105ʳ] providing always that nothing be which any man should remit or forgive unto thee. Be as ware° and diligent in avoiding that no offence or trespass proceed of thee, as thou art easy° and ready to remit another man's.

The greater man thou art, so much more submit thyself that thou in charity apply thyself to all men. If thou come of a noble stock, manners worthy of Christ shall not dishonour, but honour, the nobleness of thy birth. If thou be cunning and well learned, so much the soberlier suffer and also amend the ignorance of the unlearned. The more is committed and lent to thee, the more art thou bound to thy brother. Thou art rich: remember thou art the dispenser, not the lord — take heed circumspectly how thou treatest the common goods. Didst thou believe that property or impropration was prohibited, and voluntary poverty enjoined, to monks only? Thou art deceived: both pertain indifferently to all Christian men. The law punisheth thee if thou take anything away of another man's; it punisheth thee not if thou withdraw thy own when thy brother hath need. But Christ will punish both. If thou be an officer, let not the honour make thee more fierce, but let the charge make thee more diligent and full of care. 'I bear not', sayest thou, 'no office of the Church: I am not [100ᵛ] a shepherd or a bishop.' Let us grant you that: but art thou also not a Christian man? Consider thou of whence thou art, if thou art not of the Church.

So greatly Christ is come to contempt to the world that they think it a goodly and excellent thing to have nothing to do with him at all; and that so much the more every man should be despised, the more coupled he were to him. Hearest thou not daily, of° the lay persons in their fury, the names of a 'clerk', of a 'priest', and of a 'monk', to be cast in your teeth instead of a sharp and cruel rebuke, saying 'thou clerk', 'thou priest', 'thou monk that thou art'? And that is done utterly with [no] other mind, with [no] other voice or pronouncing, than if they should cast in your teeth 'incest' or 'sacrilege'.[429] I verily marvel why they also cast not in your teeth 'baptism', why also object they not against us with the Saracens the name of 'Christ' as an opprobrious thing. If they should say an 'ill clerk' or an 'irreligious monk': in that they might be suffered verily, as men who should note the manners

---

[429] 'incest' or 'sacrilege'] Both were hot topics — marriage of priests with nuns? marriage of Henry with Catherine? destroying religious pictures and images? — and T. carefully defines: **Marg.** 'Incest is to deal with a man's own kin. Sacrilege is to violate persons sacred to God, or to rob churches.'

of the persons, and not despise the profession of virtue. But whosoever think the deflowering of virgins to be a great praise for themselves, and also goods taken away in war [and] money either won or lost at dice or at chance, [106ʳ] when the same have nothing to lay against another man more to be despised or opprobrious, or more to be ashamed of, than the names of a 'monk' or of a 'priest': certainly it is easy to conjecture what these, in name only Christian men, judge of Christ.

There is not one Lord of the bishops and another of the temporal officers: both bear the room° of one, and to the same both must give accounts. If thou look anywhither° save unto God only either when thou receivest the office, or when thou minister it, it maketh no matter though the world call thee [not a simoniac,° he surely will punish thee as] a simoniac. If thou labour and make means to obtain a common office, not to profit in common but to provide for thy own wealth privately, and to avenge thyself on him to whom thou owest a grudge, thy office is bribery or robbery afore God. Thou huntest after thieves, [not] that he should receive his own who is robbed, but lest it should not be with thee which is with the thieves: how much difference, I pray thee, is between the thieves and thee, except peradventure that they be robbers of merchants and thou the robber of robbers? In conclusion, except thou bear thy office with this mind, that thou art ready — I will not say of thy goods only, but also with loss of life — to defend that which is right, Christ will not approve thy administration.

I will add also another thing, of the mind [106ᵛ] or judgement of Plato: no man is worthy of an office, sayeth Plato,⁴³⁰ who is gladly an officer. If thou be a prince, beware lest those perilous witches, the voices of flatterers, do enchant or bewitch thee: 'Thou art a lord, thou art free above the laws, all things be justice with thee, all things be honest with thee, to thee is lawful whatsoever thou lust,° those things pertain not to thee which are preached daily of priests'. Yea, but think thou rather (that which is true) that there is one Master over all men⁴³¹ and he is Christ Jesus, to whom thou oughtest to be as like as is possible, to whom thou oughtest to conform thyself in all things, as unto him certainly whose authority or room thou bearest. No man ought to follow his doctrine more than thou, of whom he will ask account more straitly° than of others. Think not straightway that to be right which thou desirest, but that only covet which is right. Whatsoever should be filthy to any man in the world, see that thou think not the same to be an honest thing unto thee, but see rather that thou in nowise permit unto thyself many things which are pardoned and permitted unto the common people everywhere. That which in other men is but a small [107ʳ] trespass think in thyself to be a great and a heinous outrage.

Let not thy riches, because they are greater than the common people's, bring unto thee honour, reverence and dignity, favour° and authority: but let thy

---

⁴³⁰ Plato] *Republic* e.g. VII. 520d–e.
⁴³¹ over all men] **Marg.** 'Christ is lord both of women and spiritual men.'

manners, because that they are better than the common people's, utterly deserve them. Suffer not the common people to wonder at those things wherewithal° are provoked and enticed those very same mischievous deeds which thou punishest daily. Take away this wondering at riches, [and] where be thieves, where be oppressors of the common wealth, where be the committers of sacrilege, where be errant° thieves and robbers or reavers°? Take away wondering at voluptuousness,° and where be raveners° and extortioners, where be adulterers? As oft as thou wilt appear somewhat according after thy degree among thy friends and subjects, or in the sight of them over whom thou bearest office, room, or authority, set not open thy riches or treasure to the eyes of foolish persons. When thou wilt seem somewhat wealthy, show not thyself in boast the riotous° example of expense and voluptuousness. First of all let them learn of thee to despise such things, let them learn to look upon virtue, to have measure° in price,° to rejoice in temperance, to give honour [107^v] to soberness and to sad° discretion. Let none of those things be seen in thy manners and conversation° which thine authority punisheth in the manners and conversation of the common people. Thou shalt banish evil deeds in the best wise° if men shall not see riches and voluptuousness — the matter and ground of evil deeds — to be magnified in thee. Thou shalt not despise in comparison of thyself any man, no, not the vilest of lowest degree: for common and indifferent is the price wherewith both he and thou were redeemed. Let not the noise of ambition, nor fierceness, nor weapons, nor men of thy guard defend thee from contempt: but pureness of living, gravity, manners incorrupt and sound from all manner vices of the common people shall make that no man shall despise thee.

Nothing forbiddeth in bearing rule to keep the chief room — and yet in charity to discern no room. Think bearing of rule to be of this manner: not to excel and go before other men in abundance of riches, but to profit all men as much as is possible. Turn not to thy own profit things which are common, but bestow those things which be thy own, and thy own self also together, upon the common wealth. The common people owe very many things to thee, but [108^r] thou owest all things to them. Though thy ears be compelled to suffer names of ambition (as, 'most mighty', 'most Christian', 'most holy'), yet let thy mind not be known° of them, [but refer all these things unto Christ], to whom only they agree. Let the crime 'majesty hurt or violate',[432] which other men ponder and aggravate with voice worthy of a tragedy, with thee be a very trifle. He violateth the majesty of a prince indeed who in the prince's name doth anything cruelly, violently, mischievously, and contrary to right. Let no man's injury move thee less than that which pertaineth to thy own self privately. Remember, thou art a public or a common [person], and that thou oughtest not to think but of common matters. If thou have any courage with thee, and readiness of wit, consider with thyself not

---

[432] 'majesty hurt or violate'] 'lese-majesty', treason.

how great a man thou art, but how great a charge thou bearest on thy back; and the more in jeopardy thou art besides, so much the less favour thyself — fetching example of ministering thy office not of thy predecessors, or else of flatterers, but of Christ.

For what is more unreasonable than that a Christian prince should set before him for an example Hannibal, great Alexander, [Caesar] or Pompey? in which same persons, when he cannot attain some certain virtues, yet shall he counterfeit° those things most chiefly which only are more to be refused and avoided. Let it not forthwithal be taken [108ᵛ] for an example if Caesar have done any thing lauded of them who write the histories, but if he have done anything which varieth not from the doctrine of our Lord Jesus Christ; or if it be such a thing that, though it be not to be counterfeited, yet may it be applied to the study or exercise of virtue.

Let not a whole empire be of so great value with thee that thou wouldst wittingly once bow aside from the right. Put off that, rather than thou shouldst put off Christ. Doubt not Christ hath, to make thee amends for the empire refused, things far better than the empire. Nothing is so comely, so excellent, so glorious unto kings as is to draw as nigh as is possible unto the similitude of our king, Jesus; who, as he was the greatest, even so was he also the best. But that he should be the *greatest*, that dissembled he and hid secret here in the earth. That he should be the *best*, that had he lever we should perceive and feel, because he had lever we should counterfeit that. He denied his kingdom to be of this world,[433] when he was Lord of heaven and earth also. But 'the princes of the Gentiles use dominion upon them':[434] a Christian man exerciseth not power over them who are under his rule, but charity; and whosoever is the chiefest, let the same think himself to be a minister unto all men, [109ʳ] and not the master or lord of any man.

Wherefore I marvel the more a great deal how these ambitious names of power and dominion were brought in, even unto the very popes and bishops, and that our divines be not ashamed no less indiscreetly° than ambitiously to be called everywhere 'master', 'doctor' — when Christ forbade unto his disciples that they should suffer themselves either to be called 'lords' or 'masters', for we must remember that one is in heaven our both Lord and Master, Christ Jesus, who is also the Head unto us all.[435] An 'apostle', a 'shepherd', a 'bishop' be names of office or service, not of dominion and bearing rule. A 'pope', an 'abbot' be names of charity, not of power.

But why enter I into the great sea of errors? Unto whatsoever kind of men he shall turn himself, a very° spiritual man shall see many things which he might laugh at, and more which he ought to weep at. He shall see very many opinions too much corrupted and varying from the doctrine of Christ both afar and wide;

---

[433] John 18. 36.
[434] Matt. 20. 25-27.
[435] Matt. 23. 8-10.

of which a great part springeth therehence, that we have brought in even unto the profession of Christ a certain 'world' — and that which is read of the 'world' among the old divines, men of small learning nowadays refer to 'them who [109ᵛ] be not monks'. The 'world' in the Gospel (and with the Apostles, with Saint Augustine, Ambrose, and Jerome) is called[436] nothing else but the infidels who are strangers from the faith, the enemies of the Cross of Christ and blasphemers of God. They that are such care° for tomorrow and for the time to come: for no doubt whosoever mistrust Christ, nor believe on him, the same be they who fight and strive for riches, for rule, and for worldly pleasure — as men blinded with delusions of sensible° things set their minds and whole affections upon apparent good things, instead of very good things. This world hath not known Christ, who is the very true light. This world is all set on mischief. This world loveth itself, liveth to itself, studieth to itself and for its own pleasure, for it hath not put Christ on its back, who is very charity. From this world separated Christ not his Apostles only, but all men whosoever and as many as he judged worthy of himself. By what means, then, at the last mingle we with Christendom this world condemned ever in Holy Scripture, and with the vain name of 'the world' favour, flatter, and maintain our own vices?

Many doctors be who augment this [110ʳ] pestilence, 'corrupting the Word of God' (as Paul sayeth)[437] and fashioning Holy Scripture after the manners of their time — when it is more convenient that the manners should be corrected and amended by the rule of Scripture, and not Scripture to be corrupted for the defence of evil manners. No mischievouser kind of flattering is verily than when, with the words of the Gospel and of the prophets, we flatter the diseases of minds and cure them not.

A prince heareth that 'all power is of God':[438] at once the crests arise. But why doth Scripture make thee high-minded° and fierce, rather than circumspect, full of care, and afraid? Thou considerest how God hath delivered to thee an empire to be administered and governed, but thou rememberest not that the same will ask of thee a strait reckoning of the empire, how it is ministered and ruled.

The covetous man heareth that it is forbid unto Christian men that they should have two coats at once.[439] The divine[440] interpreteth the 'second coat' to be whatsoever should be superfluous and more than enough to the necessary man and forasmuch as pertaineth to the disease of covetousness. 'That is very well', sayeth the gross° fellow, 'for I yet lack many things.'

---

[436] is called] i.e. 'is the term applied to'.
[437] II Corinth. 4. 2.
[438] Rom. 13. 1.
[439] Matt. 10. 10.
[440] The divine] Indeterminately 'some theologian', but see *ST* II (ii), q. 32, art. 6, for a discussion of what constitutes legitimate 'need' and 'surplus'.

The beastly man, and cold from charity, heareth this to be the order of charity,⁴⁴¹ that thou shouldst regard and set° more of [110ᵛ] thy own money than of another man's, and of thy own life than of another man's, of thy own fame more than of another man's. 'I will therefore', sayeth he, 'give nothing, lest peradventure I should lack myself. I will not defend another man's good name or fame, lest my own be spotted° thereby. I will forsake my brother in jeopardy, lest I myself should fall in peril also. To speak shortly, I will live altogether to myself and at my own pleasure, that no incommodity come to me for any man's cause.'

We have learned also of holy men, if they have done anything *not* to be counterfeited, that only to bring forth for an example of living. Adulterers and murderers flatter and claw° themselves by the back with the example of David. Gapers upon money lay against us rich Abraham. Princes to whom is but a sport everywhere to vitiate and corrupt virgins number to us queens and concubines of Solomon. They 'whose god is their belly'⁴⁴² lay for an excuse the drunkenness of Noah.⁴⁴³ Incests who pollute their own kin cloak their own filthiness with the lying of Lot with his own daughters.⁴⁴⁴ Why turn we our eyes from Christ to these men? I dare be bold to say that it ought not to be counterfeited, no, not in the prophets verily, nor yet in the Apostles, [111ʳ] if anything vary or wry° from the doctrine of Christ.

But if it have delighted men so greatly to counterfeit holy sinners, I say not against that which is past — so° they counterfeit them altogether. Thou hast followed David in adultery: follow him rather doing penance.⁴⁴⁵ Thou hast counterfeited Mary Magdalen a sinner: counterfeit her also loving much, counterfeit her in weeping, counterfeit her in casting herself down at the foot of Jesus.⁴⁴⁶ Thou hast persecuted the Church of God with Paul,⁴⁴⁷ thou hast forsworn thyself with Peter:⁴⁴⁸ see likewise that thou stretch forth thy neck for good living and for virtue's sake with Paul, and that thou fear not the cross with Peter. Therefore God suffereth the great captains to fall into certain vices, lest we when we have fallen should despair. But on this wise yet shall we obtain pardon with them: if, as we have been the followers and counterfeiters of them when they erred out of the way, even so now shall be their companions and fellows, accompanying them amending⁴⁴⁹ their error and walking in the right way. But now we increase and wade further in the things which were not to be

---

⁴⁴¹ order of charity] On right self-love see *ST* II (ii), q. 26, art. 4; and cf. 3055f. above.
⁴⁴² Philipp. 3. 19.
⁴⁴³ Gen. 9. 21.
⁴⁴⁴ Gen. 19. 30–38
⁴⁴⁵ Ps. 51.
⁴⁴⁶ Luke 7. 36–50.
⁴⁴⁷ Acts 9.1.
⁴⁴⁸ Matt. 26. 69–75.
⁴⁴⁹ amending] i.e. 'when they amend'.

counterfeited in them, and we deprave or corrupt with perverse interpretations many things. We turn good things to evil things (which were well done of them)⁴⁵⁰ after the manner of spiders [111ᵛ] sucking out only if there be any poison, or else turning the wholesome juice unto poison to ourselves.

What hast thou to do with rich Abraham, who makest thy money thy god? Because he was dilated° with increase of cattle, God making his substance prosperous and wealthy — and that in the law carnal⁴⁵¹ — should it therefore be lawful for thee, a Christian man, by right or wrong, whencesoever it were, to heap together the riches of Croesus, which thou shouldst evil° spend and waste, or (more sinfully) dig them into the ground at home? How greatly Abraham set not his mind upon his riches, which came to him by their own accord without seeking for, let this be a sign or token at the least way: that, without delay at the voice of God commanding him, he brought forth his only son to be slain.⁴⁵² How much, thinkest thou, would he have despised a drove of oxen, who despised his own son? And thinkest thou — who dreamest nothing else but of lucre, wonderest at nothing but at money, art ready (as soon as the hope of a little money should chance) either to deceive thy brother, or to forsake God — that there is any similitude or like thing between thee and Abraham?

The simple and innocent wenches, daughters of Lot, when they beheld all the regions on every side to rage and flame in fire so impetuously, supposing the whole [112ʳ] world to be no more than that° they saw presently with their eyes, and that no man had been preserved from so large and wasteful° burning besides themselves, lay with their father privily and by stealth: not with filthy lust but with a virtuous and holy purpose, that is to wit° lest peradventure no issue of mankind should have remained after them — and namely° when as yet that precept 'grow and multiply'⁴⁵³ was in its full vigour and strength. And darest thou compare thy filthy and prodigious uncleanness with the deed of these wenches? No, I would not doubt to set less of thy matrimony than of their incest, if verily in matrimony thou study not for children, but to satisfy thy own appetite.

David, after so many noble examples of virtue showed, fell once into adultery, opportunity offered him and not sought. Shall it be lawful therefore unto thee straightway to roll and tumble from house to house in other men's beds all the days of thy life?

Peter once for fear of death denied Christ, for whose sake afterwards he died with good will. Shall it be lawful, thinkest thou, to thee for that cause to forswear thyself for every trifle?

---

⁴⁵⁰ (which were well done of them)] Refers to the 'good things' just mentioned.
⁴⁵¹ in the law carnal] i.e. when matters were as a rule judged outwardly.
⁴⁵² Gen. 22. 1–8.
⁴⁵³ Gen. 9.7.

3655 Paul sinned, not for the nonce,° but fell through ignorance;⁴⁵⁴ but as soon as he was warned, he turned straight away and came to himself again. Thou, both ware and wise, yea, and seeing what thou doest, diest in mischief° [112ᵛ] and yet by the example of Paul strokest thou thy own head?

Matthew, commanded with a word only, without any tarrying or delay at once 3660 utterly forsook his office (which was the receiving of custom or tribute):⁴⁵⁵ and yet thou, who art sworn bond and professed to thy money, art plucked away or withdrawn neither with so many thousand examples of holy men, nor with the gospels so often heard, nor with so many preachings.

Bishops say unto me that it is read that Saint Augustine had two sovereign° 3665 ladies or concubines. But he then was a heathen man, and we be nourished up in Christ's faith; he was young, and our heads be hoar for age. It is a worshipful° thing,⁴⁵⁶ for because that he when he was young and also a heathen man, lest he should be tangled with the snares of matrimony, had a little wench instead of a wife — and yet to her who was not his wife kept he promise of wedlock. 3670 Should it be therefore less shame for us Christian men, being old, being priests, yea, being bishops, to be altogether spotted and defiled in every puddle one by one of bodily lusts? Commend me⁴⁵⁷ to good manners, when we have given to vices the names of virtues, and have begun to be more wily and subtle in defending our vices than diligenter to mend them, namely when we have learned to nourish, 3675 to underset,° and to strengthen our froward [113ʳ] opinions with help and aid of Holy Scripture!

Thou therefore, my most dearest brother, (the common people altogether set at nought with their both opinions and deeds) purely and wholly take unto thee Christ's sect. Whatsoever in this life appeareth to thy sensible powers either to be 3680 hated or loved: that every whit for the love of virtue indifferently despised, let Christ only to thee be sufficient, who is only the Author both of true judgement and of blessed living. But this thing verily the world thinketh to be pure foolishness and madness! Nevertheless, by this foolishness it pleased God to save them who on him believe: he is happily a fool that is wise in Christ, and he is 3685 wretchedly wise who is not wise in Christ.

But hear thou: as I would thou shouldst vary strongly from the common people, so I will not that thou, representing° a certain Diogenes, shouldst everywhere bark⁴⁵⁸ against the opinions and deeds of other men, and with authority condemn them, or shouldst prattle odiously against all men, or shouldst furiously preach 3690 against the living of every person; lest thou acquaint thyself with two evils — the

---

⁴⁵⁴ I Tim. 1. 13.
⁴⁵⁵ Matt. 9. 9.
⁴⁵⁶ a worshipful thing] L. 'egregia collatio' ('fine comparison'): their example supports E.'s point.
⁴⁵⁷ Commend me] 'Farewell'.
⁴⁵⁸ bark] An allusion to the popular Gk etymology of 'Cynic': 'dog-like'.

one, that thou shouldst fall into hate of[459] all men, the other, that thou when thou art hated shouldst do good to no man. But be thou all things to all men, to win all men to Christ as much as may be[460] (the commandments of God not [113ᵛ] offended). So shape and fashion thyself to all men outwardly that (within) thy purpose remain sure, steadfast and immovable. Outwards let gentleness, courteous language, softness, profitableness° provoke thy brother, whom it is meet with fair means to be induced° to Christ, and not to be driven[461] with fears and cruelness. In conclusion: that which is in the breast is not so greatly to be roared forth with cruel words as it is to be declared and uttered with honest manners. And again: thou oughtest not so to favour the infirmity of the common people that thou durst not at a time° strongly defend the Spirit then, that which is truth. With humanity men must be mended, but not deceived.

CHAPTER SIXTEEN

The seventh rule

[Aim high and avoid serious sins]

Moreover, if through infancy and feebleness of mind we cannot yet attain to these spiritual things, we ought yet to study° not the sluggisher one deal that at the least way we draw as nigh as is possible. Nevertheless, the very° compendious° way to felicity is if at once we shall turn our whole mind to the contemplation and beholding of celestial things so fervently that, as the body bringeth with it the shadow, even so should the [114ʳ] love of Christ, the love of eternal things, and the love of honest° things, bring with them the loathsomeness of caduke° and transitory things, and the hate of filthy things. For either other necessarily followeth other, and the one with the other augmenteth or diminisheth. As much verily as thou shalt profit° in the love of Christ, so much shalt thou hate the world. The more thou shalt consider things invisible, the more vile shall wax things vain and momentary. We must therefore do even that thing in the discipline of virtue which Quintilian counselleth to be done in sciences or faculties of learning: which is that we at once press up to the best.[462]

Which thing yet if through our own fault or corrupt nature will not come to pass, the next of all is that we at the least way by certain natural prudence abstain from the great vices, and that we save ourselves (as much as may be) whole and sound unto the beneficence of God. For as that body is near unto health which (though it be wasted) is free yet, and out of bondage of noisome° humours, even

---

[459] fall into hate of] 'become hated by'.
[460] I Corinth. 9. 22.
[461] driven] 1523 'drawn'; L. 'deterreri' ('frightened away').
[462] *Institutio* XII. 11. 30.

so is that mind more *capax* of⁴⁶³ the benefit of God which is not yet inquinated°
or defiled with grievous offences, though it lack yet true and perfect virtue. If we
be too weak to follow the Apostles, to follow the martyrs, to follow the virgins, at
the least way let us not commit° that⁴⁶⁴ the ethnics° or [114ᵛ] heathen men should
seem to outrun us in this plain, in this furlong or lists:⁴⁶⁵ of whom very many,
when they neither knew God whom they should reverence and worship, nor
believed any hell which they should fear or dread, yet determined they by natural
reason that a man ought by all crafts° to avoid and eschew filthiness — from the
thing itself — insomuch that many of them chose to suffer the loss of fame, the
loss of goods, and (in conclusion)° to suffer the loss of the life, rather than they
would depart from honesty. If sin of itself be such a manner thing that for no
commodities° or incommodities proffered to a man it ought to be committed,
certainly — if neither the justice of God fear° us, nor his beneficence discourage
us and move us to the contrary, if neither hope of immortality or fear of eternal
pain call us back, if neither the very natural filthiness of sin withdraw, which could
withdraw the minds of the very Gentiles — at the least way let a thousand
incommodities which accompany the sinner (and that in this life) put a Christian
man in fear: as, infamy, loss or waste of goods, poverty, the contempt and hate of
good men, grief of mind, unquietness, and torment of conscience (most miserable
of all, which though many feel not now presently, either because they be blinded
with dullness of youth or drunk with the [115ʳ] voluptuousness° of the sin, yet
shall they feel hereafter; and plainly the later it happeneth, so much the more
unhappily shall they feel it). Wherefore young men most especially should be
warned and exhorted, that they would rather believe so many authors that the
very nature and property° of sin were such indeed, than with miserable experience
to learn it in themselves; and that they would not contaminate their living before
they should know what life meant.

    If Christ be to thee so vile (to whom thou art so costly), at the least way for thy
own sake refrain thyself from filthy things. And though it be very perilous to tarry
any while in this state — as 'between two ways'⁴⁶⁶ (as it is in the proverb) —
nevertheless, unto them who cannot as yet climb up to the pure, to the perfect
and excellent virtue, it shall not be a little profitable to be in the civil or moral
virtues, rather than to run ahead into all kind of uncleanliness. Here (I mean, in
civil and moral virtue) is not the resting-place or quiet haven of felicity: but from
thence is a shorter journey and an easier stair up to true felicity. In the mean
season,° for all that, we must pray God that he will vouchsafe to pluck or draw us
up to better things.

---

⁴⁶³ *capax* of] 'suited to receive'.
⁴⁶⁴ commit that] 'behave wrongly, so that'.
⁴⁶⁵ furlong or lists] L. 'stadio' (race-course, arena).
⁴⁶⁶ 'between two ways'] L. 'trivio' ('three ways'); see *Adages* I. ii. 48 (*CWE* 31. 190).

CHAPTER SEVENTEEN

The eighth rule
[Do not be discouraged by temptations]

[115ᵛ] If the storm of temptations shall arise against thee somewhat thick and grievously, begin not forthwithal to be discontented with thyself, as though for that cause God either cared not for thee or favoured thee not, or that thou shouldst be[467] but an easy° Christian man, or else the less perfect. But rather give thanks to God because he instructeth thee as one who shall be his heir in time to come; because also he beateth or scourgeth thee as his most singularly beloved son;[468] and proveth° thee as his assured friend.

It is a very great token that a man should be rejected from the mercy of God, when he is vexed with no temptations. Let come to thy mind the Apostle Paul, who obtained to be admitted or let in even unto the mysteries of the third heaven — yet was he beaten of° the angel of Satan.[469] Let come to thy remembrance the friend of God, Job. Remember Jerome, Benedict, Francis, and with them many innumerable other holy fathers who were vexed and tempted of very great vices. If that which thou sufferest be common to so great men, be common to so many men as well as to thee: what cause is wherefore thou shouldst be smitten out of countenance, shouldst be abashed, amazed, or fall into despair? Enforce° rather and strive with thyself that thou mayst overcome as they did. God shall not forsake thee, but with temptation shall make increase,° that thou mayst be able to endure.[470]

CHAPTER EIGHTEEN

[116ʳ] The ninth rule
[Never relax your vigilance]

As expert captains are wont to do, when all things are quiet, at rest and peace, yet shall they keep watch: look thou also likewise thou have always thy mind ready and thou be circumspect unto the sudden assaults of the Enemy (who ever compasseth round about, seeking whom he might devour),[471] that thou might be the more ready at once, as soon as he assaulteth thee, to put him back° manfully, to confound him, and forthwith to tread under foot the head of the pestiferous and poison serpent.[472] For he is never overcome either more easily, more surely,

---

[467] shouldst be] i.e. 'are'; likewise 'is' in line 3770.
[468] Hebr. 12. 5–6.
[469] II Corinth. 12. 7.
[470] I Corinth. 10. 13.
[471] I Peter 5. 8.
[472] Gen. 3. 15.

or more perfectly than by that means. Moreover, it is a very wise point to dash the very young children of Babylon,⁴⁷³ even as soon as they be born, against the stone which is called Christ,⁴⁷⁴ before they should wax strong and great.

CHAPTER NINETEEN

The tenth rule

3795 [Defy Satan immediately he attacks you]

But the Tempter is put back° most of all by this means: if thou shouldst disdain and abhor him, and that mightily and straightly,° when he is first about to invade° thee (even as though thou wouldst spit at him); or else if thou shouldst pray fervently; or get thyself to some holy occupation with all thy might; or if thou 3800 shouldst answer the [116ᵛ] Tempter with words fetched out of Holy Scripture, as I have warned° thee before.⁴⁷⁵ In which thing verily it shall not profit meanly° against all kind of temptation to have certain sure sentences° of Holy Scripture prepared and ready, and especially those wherewith thou hast felt thy mind to be moved and stirred vehemently.

CHAPTER TWENTY

The eleventh rule

3805 [Beware discouragement and complacency]

Two perils especially follow good men: one, lest in temptation they should give up their hold; another, lest after victory, in their consolation and spiritual joy, they should wax wanton and stand in their own conceit° and please themselves. Therefore, that thou mayst be sure not only from night fear, but also from the 3810 Devil at midday,⁴⁷⁶ look when thy Enemy stirreth thee to filthy things that thou behold not thy own feebleness or weakness, but remember only that thou canst do all things [in Christ], who said, and not to his Apostles only but to thee also and to all his members, even unto the very lowest, 'Have confidence, it is I have overcome the world'.⁴⁷⁷

---

⁴⁷³ children of Babylon] Ps. 137. 8–9. **Marg.** is incomplete: 'The children of Babylon signifieth …'. Origen, Augustine, and Pico della Mirandola (1463–1494) in his 'Tenth Rule', identify them with temptations (see *ASD* v-8, p. 36).
⁴⁷⁴ e.g. 1 Peter 2. 6–8 (quoting Isaiah 28. 16 and Ps. 118. 22).
⁴⁷⁵ before] e.g. 384f.
⁴⁷⁶ night fear […] midday] Ps. 91. 5–6. Variously allegorised. **Marg.** 'The night fear is fear lest we should be overcome with temptation. The devil of midday is vainglory, which arises of good works.'
⁴⁷⁷ John 16. 33.

Again, when thou shalt perceive thy mind to be comforted and refreshed with certain inward and goodly delectations — whether it be after that [117ʳ] thou hast overcome thy Enemy or in some other holy work or meditation — there beware diligently lest thou shouldst ascribe anything thereof unto thy own merits, but thank only the free beneficence of God for all together, and hold down and refrain thyself with the words of Paul, saying, 'What hast thou that thou hast not received? If thou have received it, why rejoicest thou as though thou hadst not received it?'[478]

And thiswise against a double mischief° shall there be a double remedy: if thou in the conflict, mistrusting thy own strength, shouldst flee for succour unto thy Head, Christ, and put thy whole trust of conquering in the benevolence of him only; and if also in the spiritual comfort and consolation thou shouldst immediately give thanks to him for his benefit, humbly knowing° and confessing thy unworthiness.

CHAPTER TWENTY-ONE

The twelfth rule

[Use temptations to grow stronger]

When thou fightest with thy Enemy, it is not enough for thee to avoid his stroke or put it aside, except° thou pluck his weapon out of his hands and thou shouldst mightily fling it again even at its own master, [117ᵛ] and shouldst kill him with his own weapon. That shall come to pass on this wise:° if, when thou art provoked unto ill, not only thou shouldst not sin, but hereof shouldst take to thee an occasion of virtue, and — as poets elegantly feign° Hercules, when perils were put° unto him of° Juno, to have grown and hardened also in courage — thou also likewise give attendance° that by the instigation of thy Enemy not only thou be not the worse, but also thou wax better.

Thou art tempted to bodily lust: know thy weakness, and also lay apart somewhat more of lawful pleasures, and add somewhat of increase unto chaste and holy occupations. Thou art stirred unto covetousness and niggish° keeping: increase alms-deeds. Thou art moved unto vainglory: so much the more humble thyself in all things. And thus shall it be brought about that every temptation should be a certain[479] renewing of the purpose and increase of good living. There is no other craft or means verily at all of so great virtue° to weaken and overthrow our Enemy as that is: for then shall he be afraid to provoke thee afresh, lest he (who rejoiceth to be the beginner and chief captain of wickedness) should minister an occasion of more perfect living.

---

[478] 1 Corinth. 4. 7.
[479] certain] 'a particular kind of'.

CHAPTER TWENTY-TWO

[118ʳ] The thirteenth rule

[Treat every temptation as if it may be decisive]

But always take heed that thou fight with this mind and with this hope: even as though that should be the last fight that ever thou shouldst have.[480] It may be verily that the benignity and goodness of God should grant this reward unto thy virtue and noble act, that thy Enemy, once overcome shamefully, should never afterwards come upon thee again — a thing which we read to have happened to divers° holy men. Neither Origen[481] believed against reason that unto Christian men, when they overcome, the power of their enemies should be[482] diminished, while that the Adversary, once put back manfully, is never suffered to return again for to tempt the same person any more. Be bold therefore in the conflict to hope for perpetual peace.

But again, after thou hast overcome, so behave thyself even as though thou shouldst go again straight away to fight afresh: for after one temptation is overcome we must look ever for another, we may never depart from our weapons, we may never forsake our *Sto*,[483] we may never leave watch as long as we war in the garrison of this body. Every man must have always that saying of the prophet in his heart: 'I will keep my standing'.°[484]

CHAPTER TWENTY-THREE

The fourteenth rule

[Take no sin lightly]

[118ᵛ] We must take very good heed that we despise not any vice as light, for no enemy overcometh oftener than he who is not set° of. In which thing I perceive that not a few men be greatly deceived, for they deceive themselves while they favour themselves in one or two vices — which every man after his own vicious appetite thinketh to be venial[485] — and all others they grievously abhor. A great part of them whom the common people call 'perfect' and 'incorrupt' greatly defy° theft, extortion, homicide, adultery, incest: but single fornication and moderate

---

[480] thou shouldst have] L. adds 'si victor discesseris' ('if you depart as a victor').

[481] Origen] For E. this Father was as masterly in rational common sense as in spiritual allegorising (cf. 1239 and 2069); the ref. is to *Against Celsus* VIII. 44.

[482] should be] i.e. 'is'.

[483] *Sto*] lit. 'I stand', a formal commitment; L. 'statio' ('military post').

[484] Habak. 2. 1.

[485] venial] The distinction between 'mortal' and 'venial' sins (depending on whether there is explicit defiance of God and divine principles) found support in 1 John 5. 16–17. See *ST* II (i), q. 72, art. 5.

use of voluptuous° pleasures, as a small trespass they refuse not at all. Some one man, in all other vices incorrupt enough, is somewhat yet a good drinker, is in riot° and expense somewhat wasteful. Another man is somewhat liberal of his tongue. Another is cumbered with vanity, with vainglory, and with boasting. At the last, what vice shall we lack if every man favour his own vice?

It is an evident token that those men who favour any vice at all should not truly possess the other virtues, but are endued rather with certain images of virtues, which either nature, or bringing up, or finally very custom, hath grafted in the minds of the Gentiles. But he who with hate worthy of a Christian man abhorreth any one vice must needs [119ʳ] abhor all: for he whose mind true charity hath once possessed hateth indifferently° the whole host of evil things, and flattereth not himself so much as in venial things, lest he might fall a little and a little from the smallest to the greatest and, while he is negligent in lighter things, might fall from the chiefest things of all. And though thou as yet canst not pluck up by the roots the whole generation° of vices, nevertheless somewhat of our evil properties must be plucked away day by day, and something of increase must be added to good manners. After that manner shall be diminished or augmented the 'great heap' of Hesiod.[486]

CHAPTER TWENTY-FOUR

The fifteenth rule

[In the struggle, look beyond present pleasure and pain]

If the labour which thou must take in the conflict of temptation shall fear° thee, this shall be a remedy: see thou compare not grief of the fight with the pleasure of the sin, but set the present bitterness of fight against the bitterness which groweth of the sin and accompanieth him that is overcome; moreover, compare the present sweetness of the sin which enticeth thee with the pleasure of the victory hereafter, and with the tranquillity of mind which followeth him that fighteth lustily — and anon° thou shalt [119ᵛ] perceive how unequal a comparison there shall be.

But in this thing they who be but little circumspect are deceived, because they compare the displeasure of the fight with the pleasure of the sin, and consider not what followeth the one and the other. For there followeth him who is overcome grief more painful a great deal, and also of longer continuance, than he should have had in time of fight if he should have overcome; and likewise followeth the conqueror pleasure more by a great deal, and of longer durance,° than was the pleasure which drew him that was overcome to sin — a thing that he easy may judge who hath proved° both the things. Nevertheless, no Christian man ought

---

[486] Hesiod] *Works and Days* 306–07, 361–62; see *Adages* I. iii. 31 (*CWE* 31. 260).

to be altogether so lewd,° though he were daily subdued of temptation, that he would not at the least way sometimes desire to prove what thing it should be to overcome temptation — which thing the oftener a man shall do, the pleasanter shall be the victory.

CHAPTER TWENTY-FIVE

The sixteenth rule

[Never give up, even after seriously sinning]

But and° if it shall fortune° thee to have received a deadly wound, beware thou cast not away thy [120^r] shield[487] by and by° and forsake thy weapon, and so shouldst yield thyself into thy Enemy's hand. Which thing I have perceived to have happened unto many whose minds are somewhat feeble and soft, without resistance: that, after they were once overthrown, they should cease to wrestle any more, but should permit°[488] themselves altogether unto affections, nor should think of recovering their liberty again. Too much perilous is this weakness of spirit, which (now and then though it be coupled with wits which be not the worst of all) yet is it wont to bring them to that which is worst of all, yea, even into desperation verily.[489]

Against this weakness therefore the mind must be armed with this rule, that after we have fallen into sin not only we should [not] despair, but should counterfeit° bold men of war, whom not seldom shame of rebuke, and grief of the wound received, not only putteth not to flight, but sharpeneth and refresheth again to fight more fiercely than they did before. In like case also, after we have been brought unto deadly sin, let us haste anon to come again to ourselves, and take a good heart to us, and to repair again the rebuke and shame of the fall with new courage and lustiness of strength. Thou shalt heal one [120^v] wound sooner than many; thou shalt easier cure a fresh wound than an old and that which is putrefied and festered already.

Comfort thyself with that famous verse which Demosthenes is said to have used: 'A man, if he flee, will fight again'.[490] Call to remembrance David the prophet, Solomon the king, Peter a captain of the Church, Paul the Apostle, who were so great lights and examples of holiness: and yet into what great sins fell they; whom every one peradventure, yea, even for this cause God suffered° to fall, lest

---

[487] shield] 1523 'self'; L. 'clipeo' ('shield').
[488] permit] L. 'permittant' (resign, hand over).
[489] desperation verily] This is 'worst of all' because incurable. Breaching the theological virtues of faith or love is intrinsically more serious than breaching hope, but in its effects on us loss of hope is worse. See *ST* II (ii), q. 20, art. 3.
[490] See *Adages* I. x. 40 (*CWE* 32. 252); Tav. 86.

thou when thou hadst fallen should despair. Lift up thyself therefore upon thy feet, and that at once with a lusty courage, and return again to fight both fiercer and also more circumspect. It happeneth sometimes that deadly offences grow to good men into a heap of good living, while they love more fervently who were blinded and went out of their right way most shamefully.

CHAPTER TWENTY-SIX

The seventeenth rule

[Draw inspiration from Christ's crucifixion]

But against the diversity of assaults of the Enemy, diverse remedies must be applied, for unto whatsoever vice thou art stirred some [121ʳ] one remedy is better than another. Nevertheless, the only remedy, and that of all remedies far away most of virtue° against all kinds whether of adversity or else of temptation, is the cross of Christ. Which same cross is both an example to them who go out of the way, and a refreshing to them who labour, and also armour or harness° to them who fight. This is a thing to be cast against all manner weapons and darts of our most wicked Enemy.

Furthermore, it is necessary that a man be exercised diligently in this cross — not verily after the common manner, as some men repeat daily the story of the Passion of Christ, or honour the image of the cross, or with a thousand signs of it arm all their body round about on every side, or keep laid up at home some piece of that holy tree, or at certain seasons call to remembrance the Passion of Christ, for to weep upon him with humble and natural affections,° as upon a man who was very just and had suffered very great wrong and things undeserved. This is not the very° fruit of that tree. Nevertheless, let this in the mean season° be the milk of infant souls. But prepare thou thyself unto the victory, that thou mayst attain the very fruits of it. And these be those fruits which are most special: if we who be members [121ᵛ] shall endeavour ourselves to be semblable° unto our Head, Christ, in 'mortifying our affections, which be our members upon the earth'[491] — a thing which unto us not only ought [not] to be grievous, but rather pleasant and a thing greatly to be desired, if so be the spirit of Christ dwell in us. For who is he who without feigning loveth him to whom he should rejoice[492] to be as unlike as were possible, and both in living and conversation° clean contrary?

Furthermore, that with the more fruit thou mightest in thy mind record° the mystery of the Cross, every man ought to prepare unto himself a certain manner and holy craft of fighting, and therein to be diligently exercised, that, as soon as the thing is required, it should be ready at hand. That craft may be of this manner:

---

[491] Coloss. 3. 5.
[492] should rejoice] 'rejoices'.

if in crucifying of every° of thine affections thou shouldst apply that part of the cross which most especially thereto agreeth; for there is not at all any either temptation or adversity which hath not its proper remedy in that cross. As, when thou art tickled with ambition of this world, when thou art ashamed to be had in derision and to be set at nought, consider thou, O thou most lowest member, how great Christ thy Head is, and unto what vileness[493] he humbled himself for thy sake. When the evil of envy vexeth thy [122ʳ] mind, remember how kindly, how lovingly, he bestowed himself every whit unto our use and profit, how good he was even unto the worst. When thou art moved with gule,° have in mind how he drank gall with eisell.° When thou art tempted with filthy pleasure, call to mind how far off from all manner of pleasure the whole life of thy Head was, and how full of incommodities, vexation, and grief his life was. When ire provoketh thee, let come immediately to remembrance him who 'as a lamb before the shearer held his peace and opened not his mouth'.[494] If poverty wring thee ill,° or desire of having torment thee, anon° let be rolled in thy mind how the Lord of all lords was for thy sake made poor and needy, insomuch that he had not whereon to rest his head.[495]

And after the same manner if thou shalt do in all other temptations also, not only it shall not be grievous to have oppressed° thine affections, but verily pleasant and delectable; because thou shalt perceive that thou by this means art conformed and shaped like unto thy Head, and that thou shouldst (as it were) recompense him for his infinite sorrows, which for thy sake he suffered unto the utmost.

CHAPTER TWENTY-SEVEN

The eighteenth rule

[Contrast human dignity with sin]

[122ᵛ] And though this[496] remedy verily of all remedies be one the most present° and ready, most sure and quick in operation, to them who be meetly° entered into the way of living: nevertheless yet to them who are somewhat weak it shall also profit somewhat if, when affection° moveth unto iniquity, they then at once call before the eyes of the mind how filthy, how abominable, how mischievous° a thing sin should be — and, on the other side, if they ponder how great is the dignity of man. In trifles, and matters such as it skilleth° not if all the world knew, we take some deliberation and advisement° with ourselves. In this matter, of all matters most weighty, most to be pondered, before that we consent and before (as with

---

[493] vileness] i.e. lowliness. 1523 'violence'; L. merely 'quo' ('to what').
[494] Isaiah 53. 7.
[495] Matt. 8. 20.
[496] this] i.e. the previous.

our handwriting)⁴⁹⁷ we bind ourselves to the Fiend, shall we not reckon and count with our own mind and consider of how noble a Craftsman we were made, in how excellent estate° we are set, with how mighty a price we are bought, and unto how great felicity we are called; and how that man is that gentle° and noble beast for whose sake only God hath forged° the marvellous building of this world; and that he is the companion of angels, the son of God, the heir of immortality, a member of Christ, a member [123ʳ] of the Church; and that also our bodies be the temples of the Holy Ghost,⁴⁹⁸ and our minds the images and the secret habitations of the Deity? and, on the other side, that sin is the most filthy pestilence and consumption, both of the mind and of the body also? For both of them⁴⁹⁹ through innocency spring anew into their own natural kind, and through contagion of sin both putrefy and rot in this world. Sin is that deadly poison of the most filthy serpent, an obligation of the Devil and of bondage not most filthy only but most miserable also.

After thou hast considered this and suchlike with thyself, ponder groundly° and take sure advisement and deliberation whether it should be wisely done or no, for apparent momentary and poisoned little short pleasure and delectation of sin, to fall from so great dignity into so piteous and wretched estate, from whence thou couldst not rid and deliver thyself by thy own power and help.

CHAPTER TWENTY-EIGHT

The nineteenth rule

[Consider the contrast between God and the Devil]

Furthermore, compare together those two captains between themselves most contrary and unlike (I mean of⁵⁰⁰ God and the Devil). The one thou makest thy enemy when thou [123ᵛ] sinnest, and the other thy lord or master. Through innocency and grace thou art called into the number of the friends of God,⁵⁰¹ art elected into the right title and inheritance of the sons of God.⁵⁰² Through sin verily thou art made both the bondservant and son also of the Devil. The one of them is that eternal fountain and original pattern and true example of verity and sure beauty, of very true pleasure, of most perfect goodness, ministering himself to all

---

⁴⁹⁷ as with our handwriting] i.e. giving it the force of a signed bond which fatally incriminates; L. 'chirographum' is the word used in Coloss. 2. 14 (variously interpreted by commentators), where Christ is said by his death to have cancelled on our behalf a hostile bond or record.
⁴⁹⁸ 1 Corinth. 6. 15, 19.
⁴⁹⁹ both of them] i.e. mind and body.
⁵⁰⁰ I mean of] Possibly a scribal redundancy but see *OED* s.v. 1e for the verb's construction with 'at', 'to', 'of' (no early example given), and 'by'.
⁵⁰¹ John 15. 14.
⁵⁰² Galat. 4. 7.

things. The other is father of all mischief, of extreme filthiness, of utmost infelicity. Remember the benefits and goodness of the one done to thee, and the ill deeds of the other. With what goodness hath the one made thee? with what mercy redeemed thee? with what liberty and freedom endued thee? [With] what tenderness daily suffereth and sustaineth he so wretched a sinner, patiently abiding and looking for thy amendment? With what joy and gladness doth he receive thee when thou art amended and come to thyself? Contrary to all these things, with how natural° hate and envy long ago did the Devil lay await° to thy health°? Into what grievous and cumbrous vexation hath he cast thee? And also what other thing imagineth he daily but to draw⁵⁰³ [all mankind with him into eternal mischief°?

All these things on this side and that side well and substantially weighed and pondered, thus think with thyself: 'Shall I, unmindful of my original beginning from whence I came, unmindful of so great and manifold benefits, for so small a morsel of feigned and false pleasure unkindly° depart from so noble, from so loving, from so beneficial a father, and shall mancipate° and make myself bond willingly unto a most filthy and a most cruel master? Shall I not at the least way make good° to the one that thing which I would perform to a vile° man who had showed kindness, or done me any good? Shall I not fly from the other, who⁵⁰⁴ would fly from a man that coveted or were about to do me hurt?']

CHAPTER TWENTY-NINE

The twentieth rule

[Compare what God and the Devil offer you]

[124ʳ] Neither verily the rewards are less unequal than the authors of them be contrary and unlike. For what is more unequal than eternal death and life immortal? than without end to enjoy infinite felicity in the fellowship of the inhabiters of heaven, and without end to be tormented and punished with extreme vengeance in the most unhappy and wretched company of damned devils? And he that doubteth of this verily is not only not a man — he is [not] a Christian man.⁵⁰⁵ Whosoever think not on this is even madder than madness herself.

But now, besides all this, in the mean season° even in *this* life good living and wickedness have their fruits very much unlike. For of the one is gathered assured

---

⁵⁰³ draw] The scribe stopped mid-line at the foot of a page and resumed work at a new chapter. The bracketed portion here is supplied from *1533*.
⁵⁰⁴ who] 'I who'.
⁵⁰⁵ not a man [...] Christian man] *1523* is confused: 'verily is not a man not only he is a Christian man'. E. is fairly clear: 'he is not even a man, never mind (still less) a Christian man'. *1533* has 'he is not so much as a man verily, and therefore he is no Christian man'. See 3342.

tranquillity and quietness of heart, and that blessed joy of pure mind whereof whosoever hath tasted, to that man this world hath nothing so precious, nothing so full of pleasure wherewith he would be glad and desirous to change. But of that other, that is to say of wickedness, clean contrary followeth partly° a thousand other evils, partly that most miserable torment and grudge° of conscience and vexation of mind through remembrance of mischievous° deeds committed.

That other[506] is that hundredfold spiritual joy which [124ᵛ] Christ promised in the Gospel as a certain earnest° or taste of eternal felicity. These be those marvellous 'rewards' of the Apostle which 'the eye never saw, nor ear hath heard, nor hath sunk into the heart of any man, which God hath prepared for them that love him',[507] and that verily in *this* life — when in the mean season the worm of wicked men dieth not,[508] and they suffer even now with us above the pains of hell beneath. Neither any other thing is that flame in which is tormented the rich glutton of whom is made mention in the Gospel,[509] nor any other things be those punishments of them in hell, of whom the poets write so many things, save a perpetual grief or groaning of the mind, which accompanieth the custom° of sin.

Let whosoever will therefore lay apart so diverse rewards of the life to come: yet° now in this life virtue hath annexed unto her wherefore she abundantly ought to have been desired, and vice hath coupled unto it things enough for whose sake it ought to be abhorred.

CHAPTER THIRTY

The twenty-first rule

[Remember how fleeting this life is]

Moreover, consider how full of grief and misery, how short and transitory, is this present life; how on every [125ʳ] side death lieth in wait° against us; how everywhere he catcheth us suddenly and unware;° and (when no man is sure, no, not of one moment of life) how great peril is it then to prolong and continue that kind of living in which it often fortuneth,° if sudden death should take thee, thou were but lost and undone for ever.

---

[506] That other] i.e. the first of the alternatives in the previous paragraph, 'blessed joy' even in this life.
[507] 1 Corinth. 2. 9, quoting Isaiah 64. 4.
[508] Mark 9. 48.
[509] Luke 16. 19–24.

CHAPTER THIRTY-ONE

The twenty-second rule
[Beware that sin may become irreversible]

Besides all this is to be feared impenitency or obduration° of mind, of all mischiefs the extreme and worst, namely° if a man would ponder this one thing: of so great multitude how few there be who truly and with all their hearts come to themselves again, and be clean converted from sin, and with due repentance reconciled to God again, namely of them who have drawn along the lines of iniquity[510] even to the last end of their life. Slippery, verily, and easy is the fall or descent into filthiness; but 'to return back again therehence and to escape unto spiritual light: that is a work, and a great labour'.[511] Therefore at the least way — admonished and warned by the fable of Aesop[512] — before thou descend into the pit of sin, remember that it is not so easy a thing to return back again.

CHAPTER THIRTY-TWO

Remedies against certain sins,
and especially against bodily lust

[125ᵛ] Hitherto have we verily opened and declared (howsoever we have done it) common remedies generally against all kind of vices. Now we shall assay° to give also certain things in especial, by every vice separately, how thou ought to encounter and run against every sin; and first against the lust of body, than which evil no other sooner invadeth° us, nor sharplier assaileth or vexeth us, nor extendeth further, nor draweth more to their utter undoing. If at any time therefore filthy lust shall stir thy mind, with these weapons look thou shortly° check° him.

First, remember how uncleanly, how filthy, how unworthy of any man, whatsoever he were, should that pleasure be which assimileth° and maketh us (who be a divine work) equal not to beasts only, but also even unto filthy swine, to goats, to dogs, and of all brute beasts unto the most brutish; yea, which casteth us down afar beneath the condition and state of beasts — when we be appointed unto the company of angels and to the communion and fellowship of Deity.

Let come to thy mind also how momentary the same pleasure is, how impure, how ever having more of aloes than [126ʳ] of honey: and, on the contrary side, ponder how noble a thing the soul is, and how holy a thing the body of the man

---

[510] lines of iniquity] Like oxen drawing their cartload (cf. Isaiah 5. 18); 1523 'lives'.
[511] *Aeneid* 6. 128–29.
[512] Aesop] **Marg.** explains that, a goat and a fox being trapped in a pit, the fox escaped by climbing on the goat's back, falsely promising to rescue him in turn: Perry 9.

is, as I have rehearsed° in the rules above. What the Devil's peevishness° is it then, for so little, so uncleanly, tickling of momentary pleasures, which defile at one time both soul and body with ungodly demeanours, to profane or pollute the temple which Christ hath consecrated to himself with his blood?

Consider that also, what a heap of mischievous° incommodities° that flattering and pleasant pestilence bringeth with it. First of all, it pulleth from thee thy good fame, a possession most precious far away, for the rumour of no vice stinketh more carrionly° than of bodily lust. It consumeth thy patrimony. It killeth at once both the strength and also the beauty of the body. It decayeth° and greatly hurteth health. It engendereth diseases innumerable, and them most filthy. It disfigureth the flower of youth long before the day. It hasteth or accelerateth rivelled° and ill-favoured° age. It taketh away the quickness and strength of the wit.° It dulleth the sight of the mind, and grafteth in a man as it were beastly imagination. It withdraweth a man at once from all honest studies° and pastimes, and plungeth and souseth° a man every whit in the puddle and mire, be he never so excellent, that [126ᵛ] now he hath lust° to think on nothing but on that which is sluttish, vile, and filthy. And it taketh away the use of reason, which is the native property of man. It maketh youth peevish and slanderous,° and age odious, filthy, and wretched. Be wise therefore, and on this wise reckon with thyself, name by name: 'This and that pleasure came so evil to pass,⁵¹³ brought with her so much of loss, so much of disworship,° dishonour, and dishonesty,° so much of tediousness, of labour, of diseases — and shall I now again, a fool most natural,° devour the hook wittingly? Should I again commit that thing which I should repent afresh?'

Likewise also refrain thyself by the examples of other men whom thou hast known to have followed voluptuous° pleasure both filthily and also unfortunately. On the other side, encourage and embolden thyself unto chastity by the examples of so many young men, of so many young virgins nourished up delicately and in pleasantness; and (the circumstances compared together) lay against thyself thy own lewdness.° Why shouldst thou at the least way not be able to do that which such were able to do, and yet were of that kind,° of that age, so born and brought up? Love God as much as they did, and thou shalt be able to do no less than they [127ʳ] did.

Think how honest, how pleasant, how lusty and flourishing a thing is pureness both of body and mind. Also she most of all maketh us acquainted and familiar with angels and apt to receive the Holy Ghost: for verily that noble Spirit, the lover of pureness, so greatly fleeth back from no vice at all as from uncleanliness; he resteth and sporteth° himself nowhere so much as in pure and undefiled minds.

Set before thine eyes how ungodly, yea, and how altogether a mad thing it is to love, to wax pale, to be made lean, to weep, to flatter, and shamefully to submit thyself unto a stinking harlot most filthy and rotten, to gape and sing all night at

---

⁵¹³ so evil to pass] 'turned out so badly'.

her chamber window, to be made to the lure,° to be obedient at a beck,° nor dare do anything except she nod and wag her head, to suffer a foolish woman to reign over thee, to chide, to lay unkindness one on another, to fall out, to be made at one again, to give thyself willingly unto a quean° that she might mock, knock, mangle, and spoil° thee. Where is, I beseech thee, among all these things the name of a 'man'? Where is that noble mind created unto most beautiful things?

Consider also another thing with thyself: how great a flock of mischievous things voluptuousness, if she be let in, is wont to bring [127ᵛ] with her. There peradventure to other vices is some acquaintance with certain virtues: unto filthy lust is none at all, but she is annexed and coupled with the great sins always, and with very many also. Let it be a trifle or a light matter to follow queans: yet is it a grievous thing not to regard thy father and mother, to set at nought thy friends, to consume thy father's goods in waste, to pluck away another man's, to forswear thyself, to drink all night, to rob, to use witchcraft, to fight, to commit homicide, to blaspheme; yea, and unto grievouser things than these Lady Pleasure will draw thee headlong after thou once hast ceased to be of thy own power, and hast put forth thy wretched snout unto her halter.

Ponder, moreover, how that this life vanisheth away faster than smoke, is less of substance than a shadow, and how many snares death pitcheth for us,[514] lying in wait° in every place and at all seasons.° Here at this point it shall profit singularly to call to remembrance (and that name by name) if sudden death hath taken away any who sometime were of thy acquaintance, of thy familiar friends, of thy companions, or else of them who were younger than you; [128ʳ] and most especially if death have taken away any of them who in time past thou hast had [fellows of][515] filthy pastime; and learn of another man's peril to be more ware° and circumspect. Remember how deliciously° they lived, but how bitterly they departed from this life; how late they waxed wise, how late (or haply° how too late) they began to hate their mortiferous° and deadly pleasures. Let come to remembrance the straitness° of the extreme judgement and the terrible lightning of that fearful sentence never to be treated of more,[516] sending wicked men into eternal fire; and remember how that this pleasure of an hour, which is both short and little, must be punished with eternal torments. In this place ponder diligently, in a pair of balances, how cruel° and wicked a change° it should be, for the most filthy and very short itch of filthy lust, both to lose in this life the joy of the mind (much sweeter and better) and in the life to come to be spoiled of joys everlasting: moreover, with so little pleasure or delectation to purchase sorrows never to be ended.

---

[514] Ps. 18. 4–5.
[515] fellows of] Supplied from 1533 for L. 'participes' ('sharers in').
[516] never to be treated of more] L. 'non retractandae' (not to be withdrawn, inexorable): no more negotiating.

Finally, if it seem a hard thing to despise so little delectation for Christ's sake, remember what pains he took upon him for the love of thee, yea, and (besides the common injuries [128ᵛ] which he suffered in that he was a man) remember also how much of his holy blood he shed: yea, for thee how shameful and how bitter a death he suffered. And thou, of all these things unmindful, crucifiest again the Son of God,[517] iterating afresh those mad pleasures which drew and compelled thy Head and thy Lord unto so cruel torments! Furthermore, after the Rule above rehearsed,[518] call to mind how much of benefits he heaped to thee when as yet thou hadst deserved nothing at all: for which (every one) when no sufficient or like thank can be given again,° yet desireth he again no other reward but thou, after the example of him, shouldst refrain thyself from deadly and mortal pleasures, and shouldst turn thy mind unto the love of infinite goodness, infinite pleasure and beauty.

Compare together those two Venuses[519] and two Cupids of Plato: that is to say, honest love and filthy love, holy pleasure and uncleanly pastime. Compare together the unlike matter of either other, compare the natures, compare the rewards.[520] And in all temptations, but namely° when thou art stirred to filthy lust, set unto thee before thine eyes thy good angel (the keeper [129ʳ] of thee and the continual beholder of all things which thou doest or thinkest) and God (a witness ever looking on thee, unto whose eyes all things are open, who sitteth above and beholdeth the secret places of the earth): and shalt not thou be afraid before the angel present even hard by thee, afore God and before all the company of heaven looking on thee and also abhorring thee, to commit a sin so filthy that it would shame thee to do it before a vile° man being present and bearing witness? But consider a thing which is true indeed: and° if it were so that thou hadst eyes much sharper than hath a beast called lynx, or sharper than an eagle, yet with their eyes (in the clearest light that could be) could thou not behold more surely that thing which a man doth before thy face than all the privy and secret places of thy mind be open to the sight of God and of his angels.

Moreover also ponder in thy mind another thing when thou art overcome of bodily lust: of two things the one must needs follow. Either that voluptuousness, once tasted of, so should enchant and darken thy mind that thou shouldst go from filthiness to filthiness, until thou were clean blinded, [129ᵛ] and shouldst come *in sensum reprobum* (that is to say, unto a lewd and vile imagination, bond to all affections,° unto contagions and unnatural judgements),[521] and until also that

---

[517] Hebr. 6. 6.
[518] above rehearsed] Chapter 20 or 28.
[519] two Venuses] Plato, *Symposium* 180f. — a popular Neoplatonist theme.
[520] matter [...] nature [...] rewards] Their actual embodiment in particular situations, their essential and specific form ('as such'), and their consequences. See 1383 and note.
[521] Rom. 1. 28f.

thou were obstinately rooted and hardened in evil, nor could then at the latter end yield up filthy pleasure when she should have forsaken thee — a thing which we see to have happened to very many, insomuch that when the body is wasted, when beauty is withered away, when the blood is cold, when strength faileth, and the eyes wax dim, yet still continually they itch without ceasing, and with greater mischief be now filthy speakers than beforetime they have been unchaste and unclean livers: than which thing what can be more abominable and monstrous?

The other is (if peradventure it shall happen thee through special favour of God to come again to thyself) that then must that short and fugitive° pleasure be purged with very great sorrow of mind, with mighty and strong labours, with continual streams of tears. How much more wisdom therefore is it not to let enter at all the poison of carnal pleasure than either [130ʳ] to be brought into so incurable blindness, or else to recompense so little (and that also false) pleasure with so great grievance and dolorous pain?

Moreover, thou mayst take° many things of the circumstances of thy own person which might call thee back from voluptuous pleasure. Thou art a priest: remember that thou altogether art consecrated to things pertaining to God; and what a mischievous deed then, how ungoodly, how unmeet,° and how unworthy, should it be to touch the rotten and stinking flesh of a whore with that mouth wherewith thou receivest that precious Body so greatly to be honoured; and to handle loathsome and abominable filth with the same hands wherewithal (even the angels ministering to thee and assisting thee) thou executest that ineffable and incomprehensible mystery. Think greatly how they agree not: to be made one body, one spirit with God, and to be made one body with a whore.[522]

If thou be learned, so much the nobler and liker unto God is thy mind, and so much the more unworthy of this shame and rebuke.

If thou be a gentleman, if thou be a prince, the more apert° and open the abomination is, the [130ᵛ] grievouser occasion giveth it unto others, inferiors, to follow the same.

If thou be married, remember what an honest thing is a bed undefiled,[523] and give diligence (as much as infirmity shall suffer)° that thy wedlock should counterfeit° the most holy marriage of Christ and the Church, whose image it beareth, or whose similitude it includeth:[524] that is to be understood, that thy marriage have very little of uncleanness but very much of plenteous procreation. For in no kind of living can it be but very filthy to serve and to be bound to filthy lust.

If thou be young, consider busily° that thou pollute not unadvisedly the flower of thy youth (never to return again) and that thou lose not for a thing most filthy

---

[522] 1 Corinth. 6. 15–16.
[523] Hebr. 13. 4.
[524] Ephes. 5. 22–33.

thy golden years, and indeed most goodly, which both flee most swiftly and return again never. And beware also lest now, through ignorance, through lack of experience, and through negligence (the companions of youth), thou shouldst commit that thing which should grudge° thee hereafter by° all thy life, the conscience of thy misdeeds ever persecuting thee with those most bitter, most grievous and sharp stings which pleasure, when she departeth, [131ʳ] leaveth behind her.

If thou be a woman, remember that nothing more becometh thee than chastity, than shamefastness,° and fear of dishonesty.

If thou be a man, so much more art thou meet° and worthy of greater things, and unmeet and unworthy of these so lewd things.

If thou be old, wish that thou hadst some other man's eyes to behold thyself withal, that thou mightest see how evil° voluptuousness should become thee — which in youth no doubt is miserable and to be rebuked, but in an old fool verily is both wonderful° and monstrous, and also (even unto the very followers of the pleasure) a jesting or mocking-stock.° Among all monsters none is more wonderful than filthy lust in age. Oh, doddypoll,° oh, too much forgetful of thyself, at the least way behold at the glass° the hoar hairs and white snow of thy head, thy forehead full of wrinkles and eared° with sorrows, and thy carrion face most like to a dead corpse; and now at the last end, seeing thou art come even unto the pit's brink, care for other things more agreeable° unto thy years — and at the least way that which became thee to do aforetime do now, thy years putting thee in remembrance, or rather compelling thee. Even now Pleasure [131ᵛ] herself casteth thee off, saying, 'Neither I am now cleanly unto thee, nor yet thou apt or meet unto me. Thou hast played enough, thou hast eaten enough, thou drinkest enough. It is time for thee to depart.'⁵²⁵ Why holdest thou yet so fast, and art so greedy on, the pleasures of this life, when very life herself forsaketh thee? Now it is time at the last that the mystical° concubine Abishag should rest in thy bosom.⁵²⁶ Let her with holy rage of love heat thy mind, and with the embracings of her nourish thy cold members.

CHAPTER THIRTY-THREE

A short recapitulation of the remedies against the flame of lust

Finally, to make a short and compendious° conclusion, these be the most special things which will make thee sure from pleasures and enticings of the flesh.

First of all, the circumspect and diligent avoiding of all occasions: which

---

⁵²⁵ 'Thou hast played [...] depart'] Horace, *Epistles* II. 2. 214–15.
⁵²⁶ mystical concubine] 'the concubine interpreted allegorically'; 1 Kings 1. 1–4, an innocent arrangement for the old king David (who 'knew her not'). 1533 explains, 'By her is signified wisdom, a thing most meet for age, all filthiness and uncleanness laid apart'.

precept, though it were meet° to be observed in other things also — because that he who loveth perils is worthy to perish therein — but yet bodily lust most chiefly may be called those [132ʳ] Sirens which almost never man at all hath escaped save he who hath fled away far off.

Moreover, moderation of eating and drinking and of sleep, temperance and abstinence from voluptuous° pleasures, yea, from such as be lawful and permitted.

The respect° of thy own death and the contemplation of the death of Christ.

And these things also will help: if thou shalt live with such as be chaste and incorrupt; if thou shalt eschew as a certain[527] pestilence the communication of corrupt and wanton persons; if thou shalt flee idle solitariness and sluggish idleness; if thou shalt exercise thy mind strongly on the meditation of celestial things and in honest studies,° but especially if thou shalt consecrate thyself with all thy might unto the investigation or searching of mysteries in Holy Scripture; if thou shalt pray both oft and purely, and most of all when temptation invadeth° and assaulteth thee.

CHAPTER THIRTY-FOUR

Against the enticings and provokings unto avarice

If thou shalt perceive that thou art either by nature anything inclined to the vice of avarice, or stirred by the Devil, call to remembrance (after the rules above rehearsed)° the dignity of thy condition or estate; who for this thing only wast created, and also for this cause redeemed, [132ᵛ] that thou ever shouldst enjoy that infinite good thing God — for God verily hath forged° all the whole building of this world that all things should obey unto thy use and necessity. How filthy, then, and of how strait° or narrow a mind is it, not to use, but so greatly to wonder at, things dumb and most vile. Take away the error of men, and what shall gold and silver be but red earth and white? Shalt thou, the disciple of poor Christ, and called unto a better possession,° wonder at that (as at a certain great or excellent thing) which no philosopher of the Gentiles° did not set at nought? Not to possess riches, but to despise riches, is a noble thing.

But the commonalty° of them who are Christian men, in name only, cry against me and be glad to deceive themselves most craftily.° 'Very necessity', say they, 'compelleth us to gather goods together, which if there should be none at all, then could we not once live verily. If it should be thin and poor, then should we live in much displeasure;° but if it be somewhat elegant or honest,° and somewhat plenteous withal, it bringeth very much of commodities° to a man. Provision is made for health, a respect° is made to our children, we lend and profit our friends,

---

[527] certain] 'a particular kind of'.

we are the more set° by. In conclusion, a man's fame or name is better when his [133ʳ] good is some wealth.'

Of a great many thousands of Christian men thou canst scarce find one or two who say not, and also think not, these things. Nevertheless — to answer these men to both the parts[528] — first of all, because they cloak their covetousness with the name of 'necessity', I will lay against them the parable[529] rehearsed in the Gospel of the lilies and of the birds which live for a day[530] without further provision, whose example Christ exhorteth us to counterfeit.° I will lay against them how Christ would not once suffer so much as a scrip° to be carried about [of] his disciples.[531] I will lay against them that he commanded us (all other things laid apart) before all things to seek the kingdom of heaven, and promiseth that all these things shall be cast° and added to us.[532] When at any time had not they things necessary to maintain life withal sufficiently, whosoever with all their hearts have given themselves to the true life of a Christian man? And how small a thing is that which nature requireth of us? But thou countest or measurest necessity not by the use of nature or with that which is sufficient, but with the large capacity of greedy covetousness — but unto good men that hath ever been enough which was very scarce unto nature.[533] (Though verily I do not so greatly set° of these men who forsake at once their own substance every [133ᵛ] whit, that they the more shamefully might beg other men's.)

It is none of offence to possess money, but to love and set store of money is sin and annexed to vice. If thou have abundance, use the office of a good servant or minister. But and if it be plucked away, be not consumed with thought,° as though thou were robbed of a great thing, but rather rejoice that thou art delivered of a perilous fardel.° Notwithstanding, whosoever consumeth the chief study and pastime° of his life in heaping up of riches together, who gapeth at them as at a certain excellent or noble thing, and especially to be desired, and layeth them up in store privily for long time and even sufficient for the age of Nestor: the same man may peradventure be called right well a 'good merchant', but certainly I would not lightly° call him well a 'Christian man' who should depend altogether of himself and should mistrust the promise of God — whose goodness will deceive, thinkest thou, a good man who putteth his trust in him, when he so benignly both cloaketh and feedeth the poor sparrows?

But now let us consider the commodities which riches are believed to bring. First of all, by the common assent, yea, of all philosophers who were Gentiles,

---

[528] both the parts] 'necessity' and 'commodities'.
[529] Matt. 6. 26–32.
[530] for a day] 'for one day at a time'; L. 'in diem'.
[531] Matt. 10. 10.
[532] Cf. Matt. 6. 33–34.
[533] scarce unto nature] 'less than nature required'.

among profitable° good things riches hath the lowest place. And when (after° the divisions of Epictetus),[534] except virtue of the [134ʳ] mind only, all other things be without° the man, yet nothing is so much without as money, nothing bringeth so little commodity. For whatsoever is anywhere of precious stones, if thou thyself possessedst all that alone, were thy mind better to God by the value of one hair? Were thou any deal the wiser, the cunninger°? Were the health of thy body anything the more prosperous? Would it make thee lustier, goodlier, or younger?

'But it purchaseth pleasures', sayest thou: yea, but mortal° pleasures. 'It getteth a man honour': which those men give only that marvel at nothing but at plain foolishness, of whom to be praised is almost to be dispraised. Very honour is to be lauded of those who are lauded themselves. The highest honour that can be is to please Christ. True honour is the reward not of riches but of virtue. The foolish people give thee room° and place, and gaze at thee. Oh, fool, they wonder at thy apparel, not at thee! But why descendest thou not down into thyself and considerest the miserable poverty of thy mind? which if the common people saw, they would judge thee as miserable and wretched as they now call thee happy and blessed.

'But yet goods getteth friends', thou wilt say. I grant, but them feigned — and she getteth them not for thee, but for herself. And verily a rich man is in this [134ᵛ] point of all men most unfortunate, because he cannot once discern his friends from his foes. One man hateth thee privily as a hard niggard. Another envieth thee as one who art too rich. Another, looking unto himself and to his own advantage, holdeth° thee up with 'yea' and 'nay', and flattereth thee and mocketh thee even to thy face and smileth on thee — for to scrape something from thee. He who before thy face is most loving and kind prayeth God yet that thou mayst shortly die.[535] No man is so familiar of whom he heareth the truth. But if there be one special friend among a thousand who loveth a rich man without feigning, yet cannot the rich man but have all men suspect. He thinketh all men to be raveners° or gripers° gaping for carrion or dead bodies. He thinketh that all men be flies flying about for to seek their own prey.

Whatsoever therefore of commodity riches seemeth to bring, the more part or altogether is but coloured,° is but a very shadow and full of delusion: but they bring very much of ill things indeed and take away very much of good things indeed. Therefore, if thou wilt lay a just account of that which is won and of that which is lost, of that which is got and of that which is spent, no doubt thou shalt find that they never bring so much of commodities [135ʳ] but that they bring with

---

[534] divisions of Epictetus] The first-century Stoic underlined the distinction between what lies within our control and is therefore uniquely of moral importance (namely, our free reasoning faculty) and everything else. L. 'partitionem' is singular, so 'divisions' is 'categories'.

[535] shortly die] L. has a further clause, 'There is none that loveth him so heartily and entirely but that he had lever° have him dead than alive' [1533].

them and give a great deal more of displeasures — with how miserable labours are they got, with how great perils; yea, and with how much care° be they kept, with how much thought and sorrow are they lost. For which causes also Christ calleth them 'thorns',[536] because they tear and pluck asunder all the tranquillity or quietness of mind (which unto man is of all things most sweet and pleasant); and they never quench the thirst of themselves, but more and more increase and kindle it. They drive a man headlong into all mischief.°

Neither flatter thyself in vain, saying 'nothing forbiddeth but that a man indifferently° might be both rich and good'. Remember what Verity said. 'It is more easy', sayeth Christ, 'for a camel to creep through the eye of a needle than for a rich man to enter into the kingdom of heaven.'[537] And plainly without exception true is that saying of Saint Jerome, that 'a rich man is either unjust himself, or the heir of an unjust man'.[538] For great riches can never be either got or else kept without sin. Remember of how great riches they rob thee: for he hateth the sight or smell of virtue, he hateth all honest crafts, whosoever setteth his heart on gold. Moreover, the vice of avarice only is called 'idolatry' of° Paul;[539] nor with any vice of all Christ hath less acquaintance, nor the selfsame man can please both God and mammon also.[540]

CHAPTER THIRTY-FIVE

[135ᵛ] The recapitulation of the remedies
against the vice of avarice

Thou shalt lightly° cease to wonder at money if thou shalt ponder and weigh diligently very° good things with false and apparent good things; if also thou shalt examine disguised° and painted° advantage with true profit; if thou shalt learn with thy inner eyes to behold and love that noble good thing which is infinite, which only when it is present — yea, though all other things should be lacking — abundantly doth satisfy the man's mind (which is wider and of larger capacity than that it can be sufficed with all the good things of this world); if thou shalt often call again before thine eyes in what a plight the earth received thee when thou were first born, likewise in what estate° it shall receive thee when thou diest; if ever shall be present in thy memory that famous fool of whom is made mention in the Gospel, and to whom it is said, 'This night I will fetch again thy soul from thee: and then whose shall these things be which thou hast gathered together?';[541]

---

[536] Matt. 13. 22.
[537] Matt. 19. 24.
[538] *Letters* 120. 1; see *Adages* I. ix. 47 (*CWE* 32. 206); Tav. 81.
[539] Ephes. 5. 5.
[540] Matt. 6. 24.
[541] Luke 12. 20.

if thou shalt turn thy mind from the corrupt manners of the common sort unto the poverty of Mary, Christ's mother, unto the poverty of the Apostles, of the martyrs, and most of all unto the poverty of Christ thy Head; and shouldst set before thee also that fearful word of damnation *Vae* (that is, by interpretation, 'woe')[542] which he [136ʳ] so menaceth and threateneth unto rich men of this world. Then shouldst thou lightly leave wondering at riches.

CHAPTER THIRTY-SIX

Against ambition, the desire of honour and authority

If at any time ambition shall cumber and vex thy mind through her enchantments, with these remedies thou shalt arm thyself aforehand. At once (according to the rules which I gave before) hold and defend this stiffly: *that* to be honour only which springeth of true virtue; which very same yet at a time° a man must refuse, even as taught us, both with doctrine and example, our Master Jesus Christ; and believe it to be an honour only, and that greatly to be wished for unto a Christian man, if thou shouldst be lauded not of° men but of God. For whom *he* commendeth (as sayeth the Apostle), that man is perfect and worthy of honour indeed.[543] But if honour be given to a man for an [un]honest° or an [un]goodly thing, or of° unhonest persons, this is not honour verily but great dishonesty,° shame, or rebuke. If honour be given for mean° or indifferent° things — as for beauty, strength, riches, kin — yet verily shall it not be called true honour, for no man deserveth honour with that thing whereof he deserveth not to be praised. If honour be given for an honest thing indeed (I mean, for virtue), then shall [136ᵛ] it be honour verily: yet he who deserve it shall not desire it, but shall be content even with the virtue and the conscience° of his good deed.

Behold therefore how foolish, and utterly to be set at nought, be these honours for whose desire the common people so greatly rage. First of all, of whom are they given? Truly, of them with whom is no difference between honest and dishonest. Wherefore are they given? Certes,° very oft for mean things, and now and then for filthy things. To whom are they given? To him who is unworthy. Whosoever therefore giveth honour, either he doth it for fear (and then is he to be feared again);° or because thou shouldst do him a good turn, [and then he mocketh thee; or because he is astonied° at things of nought and worthy of no honour][544] (and then is he worthy to be pitied); or because he supposeth that thou art endued with such things whereunto honour is given of duty. If he judge amiss, give diligence that thou mayst be that thing which he supposeth thee to be: but and if he hit

---

[542] Luke 6. 24.
[543] II Corinth. 10. 18.
[544] Missing words supplied from 1533.

aright, then refer all the honour that is offered to thee to him to whom thou art bound for all those things whereunto the honour is given — so much is it unmeet° that thou shouldst claim the honour, as thou oughtest not ascribe to thy own self the virtue. Besides this, what is more madder than to esteem the value of thyself by the opinion of foolish men, in whose [137ʳ] hands it is to take away again whensoever they list° that very same honour which they give, and to dishonest° thee again who was so lately honested° and honoured?

Therefore nothing can be more foolish than either to rejoice for such honours when they happen, or to be sorry or mourn for them when they be taken away. Which not to be true honours thou shalt perceive at the least way by this probation:° that they be common to the worst and most lewd° persons as well as unto the best — yea, they chance to none almost more plenteously than to them who of true honours be most unworthy. Remember how blessed is the quietness of a mean life, both private (that is to say, charged with no common business) and also separated and removed out of the way from all noise, haunt,° or press.° On the other side, consider how full of pricks,° how full of cares, of perils, and of sorrows, is the life of great men. And besides all these remember how great difficulty it is not to forget thyself in prosperity; how hard it is for a man standing in a slippery place not to fall; how grievous the fall is from on high; and remember that all honour is coupled with great charge.° And forget not how strait° the judgement of the high Judge shall be against them who here in usurping° of honour prefer themselves afore other men. For surely whosoever shall [137ᵛ] humble and submit himself, him as an innocent or harmless person [mercy] shall succour: but whosoever exalteth himself as a perfect man, the same person excludeth from himself the help of grace.

Let ever the example of Christ thy Head stick fast in thy mind. What thing, as touching° the world, was more vile, more despised, less honoured, than he? How forsook he honours (yea, and that when they were proffered him)⁵⁴⁵ who was greater than any honour that could be given? How set he no store of honours when he rode on an ass?⁵⁴⁶ How condemned he them when he was clothed in a pall° and crowned with thorn?⁵⁴⁷ How inglorious or vile a death chose he?⁵⁴⁸ But whom the whole world despised, him the Father glorified. Let thy glory be in the cross of Christ, in whom also is thy health,° wealth,° saving defence, and protection. What good shall worldly honours do to thee if God cast thee away and despise thee, and the angels both abhor and defy° thee?

---

⁵⁴⁵ Matt. 4. 8 (by the Devil), John 6. 15 (by the people).
⁵⁴⁶ Mark 11. 7.
⁵⁴⁷ Matt. 27. 28–29.
⁵⁴⁸ Philipp. 2. 5–8.

CHAPTER THIRTY-SEVEN

Against elation, otherwise called pride and swelling of the mind

Thou shalt not swell in thy mind if (according to the common proverb used of° every man) thou shouldst 'know thyself': that is to say, if [138ʳ] whatsoever great thing, whatsoever good thing or beautiful, whatsoever excellent thing is in thee, *that* thou shouldst count to be the gift of God, and not of thy good — on the other side, if whatsoever is low or vile, whatsoever is foul or filthy, whatsoever is shrewd° or evil, thou ascribe that altogether to thy own self; if thou remember in how much filth thou were conceived, in how much uncleanliness born, how naked, how needy, how brutish, how wretched and how miserable thou creptest forth into this light; if thou remember unto how many diseases or sicknesses on every side, unto how many chances, unto how many encumbrances, griefs, troubles this wretched body of thine is in danger; and again how little a thing were able shortly to consume and bring to nought this cruel and unruly giant, swelling with so mighty a spirit.

Ponder also another thing: what manner thing that should be whereof thou so much rejoicest. If it be a mean° or any indifferent° thing, it[549] is a foolishness; if it be a filthy thing, it is a madness; if it be an honest° thing, it is unkindness against God, to whom only the honour is due. Remember also that no other thing can be a more sure document° or proof of stark foolishness and lack of understanding than if a man stand greatly in his own conceit;° and again remember that no kind of folly is more [138ᵛ] incurable. If thy mind begin to arise and wax great because a vile° man submit himself to thee, think how much greater, how much mightier, God leaneth over thy head; who presseth down every neck erected straight up, and bringeth every hill unto a plain; who spared not verily, no, not so much as the angel[550] when he was fallen into pride.

These things also shall be good, though they seem somewhat as they were trifles: if thou shouldst compare thyself always with excellenter[551] persons. Thou marvellest at thyself because of a little beauty of thy body — compare thyself to them who in beauty be far afore thee. A little cunning° maketh thee set up thy feathers — turn thine eyes [to them] in comparison of whom thou shouldst seem to have learned nothing at all. Moreover: if thou shouldst count not how much of good things thou hast, but how much thou lackest; and with Paul shouldst be forgetful of those things which be behind thee, and shouldst stretch forth thyself to those things which remain afore thee.[552]

Furthermore, it also shall not be an unwise thing if, when the wind of pride

---

[549] it] i.e. your rejoicing.
[550] angel] Isaiah 14. 12f., II Peter 2. 4.
[551] excellenter] 1523 'excellent'.
[552] Philipp. 3. 13.

doth blow, by and by° we should turn our very evil thing unto a remedy, as it were expelling one poison with another. That thing shall thiswise come to pass, when either fortune or folly bringeth unto us any great vice [139ʳ] or deformity of body, or any notable damage which should gnaw our mind cruelly, if then we should set that before our eyes, and by the example of the peacock⁵⁵³ we should behold ourselves chiefly in that part of us in which we be most deformed. So, I say, it will come to pass that at once our feathers will fall.

Beyond all this (besides that no other vice is more hated unto God) remember also that arrogancy, boasting, pertness, or presumption is notably hated, had in disdain, and mocked everywhere among men; when, on the other side, humility, meekness, and soberness in taking upon thee, both purchase and obtain the favour of God, and knit also unto thee the benevolence of man.

Therefore (to speak compendiously)° two things chiefly shall refrain thee from pride. The one is if thou shouldst consider what thou art in thyself — how thou art filthy in thy birth, how thou art a bubble such as riseth in water throughout all thy life, and worms' meat in thy death. And the other is if thou shalt have in continual meditation what Christ was made for thee, and how much he suffered for thy sake.

CHAPTER THIRTY-EIGHT

Against wrath [and] the desire of wreak° and vengeance

When fervent sorrow of the mind stirreth thee up [139ᵛ] unto vengeance, remember that wrath is further from nothing than from that which it falsely counterfeiteth,° that is to wit,° fortitude or manliness. For nothing is so childish, so weak, nothing so feeble and of so vile° a mind, as to rejoice in vengeance.

Thou seemest manly and therefore thou sufferest not injury to be unavenged: but (in conclusion)° by this means thou utterest° thy own childishness, in that thou canst not rule thy own mind, which is the very property° and office° of a man. How much manlier, yea, and how much excellenter were it, to set another man's folly at nought rather than to counterfeit it? 'But he hurt me,' thou wilt say, 'he was hasty and fierce, he raged against me, provoked me and gave me occasion.' The filthier he is, so much the more beware lest thou shouldst be like him. What the Devil's madness is it that thou, avenging another man's lewdness,° shouldst be made more lewd thyself? If thou shouldst despise the rebuke,° all men shall perceive that it was done undeserved: but and° if thou be moved, thou shalt make his quarrel (which did he wrong) much [better].

Furthermore, consider the very thing. If any wrong be received, that same is not eased at all with vengeance, but is augmented. For (in conclusion) what end

---

⁵⁵³ peacock] According to legend, the peacock was ashamed of its feet.

shall be there of injuries on both sides everywhere if every man goeth forth and proceed to revenge his grief? [140ʳ] Enemies increase on both the parties,° the sorrow waxeth fresh and raw again, and the longer it endureth, the more incurable it is. But with softness and with sufferance is healed now and then, yea, even he who did the wrong, and afterwards, when he is come to himself again, of an enemy is made a very trusty and faithful friend. But that very same which by vengeance thou studiest° to put from thee reboundeth back again upon thy own head, and that not without great increase of harm.

And that also shall be a sovereign° remedy against wrath, if (after the division of things above rehearsed, in the Fourth Rule)[554] thou shouldst consider that one man cannot hurt another except he will himself, save in those things only which be outward goods — which so greatly pertain not unto man, for the very° good things of the mind God only is able to take away (which he is not wont to do, but to unkind° persons) and only he can give them (which he hath not used to do unto cruel and furious persons). No Christian man therefore is hurt but of himself: injury hurteth no man but its own master.

These things also, though they be not so weighty, yet shall they help thee, that thou follow not the sorrow of thy mind — I mean, if when, the circumstances[555] of rhetoricians gathered together aptly, thou then shouldst both make light of thy own harms and also diminish the wrong done of° another man; commonly after this manner: 'He hurt me, but it will be soon amended — moreover, he is a child — he is of things inexpert° — he is a young man — it is a [140ᵛ] woman — he did it through another man's motion or counsel — he did it unware,° or when he had well drunk: it is meet° that I forgive it him.' And on the other side: 'He hurt me grievously, certain, but he is my father — my brother — my master — my friend — my wife: it is according° that this grief should be forgiven, either unto the love or else unto the authority of the person'. Or else thou shalt set one thing against another and recompense° the injury either of[556] good benefits done of him unto thee, or with thy offences done to him aforeseason;° and so shalt thou count it or make it even or quit:° 'This man hath hurt me verily, but other times how oft hath he done me good — it cometh of an unliberal mind to forget the good benefits, and only to remember a little wrong or displeasure' — 'now he hath offended me, but how often hath he been offended of me' — 'I will forgive him, that he in like wise by my example may pardon me if another time I should trespass against him'.

Finally, it shall be a remedy of much greater virtue° and of stronger operation if, in the misdoing of another man, thou shouldst think in thyself what things, how grievous things, yea, and how oft, thou hast sinned against God, and how

---

[554] Fourth Rule] i.e. Chapter 12; added by T.
[555] circumstances] See note on 3251.
[556] of] i.e. 'from, taking into consideration'.

many manner ways thou shouldst be in debt and danger to him. As much as thou shalt remit unto thy brother who is in thy debt, so much shall God forgive unto thee. This craft of paying our debt taught the common lender who lendeth to all men: he will not refuse [141ʳ] the law which he himself made. Thou, to be absolved or loosed of thy sins, runnest to Rome, sailest to Santiago, buyest pardons and indulgences most large. I dispraise not verily that thing which thou doest: but though thou shouldst do all things, yet is there no readier way nor any surer means whereby, if thou have offended, thou mightest come to favour again and be reconciled again to God than if thou, when thou art offended, shouldst be reconciled again unto thy brother. Forgive a little trespass unto thy neighbour (for it is but a small thing, whatsoever one man trespasseth against another), that Christ may forgive thee so many thousand offences.

'But it is hard', sayest thou, 'to subdue the mind when it beginneth to wax hot.' Rememberest thou not how much harder things Christ suffered for thee? What were thou when he for thy sake bestowed his precious life? Were thou not his enemy? With what tenderness suffereth he thee, daily repeating thy old sins? Last of all, how meekly suffered he rebukes, bonds, beatings, stripes,° finally death most shameful? Why boastest thou thyself of the Head, if thou care not to be in the Body? Thou shalt not be a member of Christ except thou follow the steps of Christ. 'But he is unworthy that he should be forgiven.' Even so, were not thou unworthy to whom God should have forgiven? In thy own self wouldst thou feel mercy, and against thy brother use extreme and cruel justice? Is it so great a [141ᵛ] thing if thou, being a sinner thyself, shouldst forgive another sinner, when Christ prayed his Father even for them who crucified him? Is it so hard a thing not to strike thy brother again, whom thou art also commanded to love? Is it a hard thing not to pay again° an evil thing, for which (except thou shouldst recompense[557] a good) thou shalt not be that towards thy fellow that Christ was towards [thee]? Finally, if this man be unworthy to whom for an ill turn a good should be recompensed, yet art thou worthy who should do it, and Christ is worthy for whose sake it should be done.

'But', sayest thou, 'in suffering an old displeasure I call in a new, and he will renew his injury if he should escape unpunished for this.' If without offence thou canst avoid it[, avoid it]; if thou canst ease or remedy it, ease it; if thou canst amend it, do even so. If thou canst heal a madman, heal him: if not, let him perish himself alone rather than thou wouldst perish with him. Think this man (who weeneth° that he hath done harm) worthy to be pitied and not to be punished. Wilt thou be angry with laud°? Be angry with the vice, not with the man.

But the more thou art inclined by nature to this kind of vice, so much the more

---

[557] recompense] 1523 gives this word a variety of senses: (i) the normal 'requite' or 'repay' *x* with *y*; (ii) 'weigh' or 'balance' *x* against *y* (4620); and (iii) 'give' *y* in return for *x* (as here, and cf. Rom. 12. 17 in *KJB* and Tyndale's *NT*).

diligently arm thyself long beforehand, and once for altogether print surely in thy mind this decree and purpose: which is, that thou neither say nor do anything at one time when thou art angry; believe not thyself when thou art moved; have suspected [142ʳ] whatsoever that sudden motion or rage of the mind defineth° or judgeth, yea, though it be honest. Remember that there is no other difference between a frantic person and him who rageth in ire than is between a short madness that endureth but for a season, and continual or perseverant madness. Call to thy mind how many things in anger thou hast either said or done, to be repented, which now in vain thou wouldst were changed or undone. Moreover, when wrath waxeth hot and fretteth, if thou cannot straightway save and deliver thyself altogether from anger, yet at the least way come to thyself and sober thy mind thus far forth that thou remember how thou art not well-advised° nor in thy right mind. To remember that were a great part of health. On this wise reason with thyself: 'Now verily I am thus minded, but anon° hereafter I shall be of another mind much contrary — why should I in the mean season° say against my friend (while I am moved) that thing which hereafter (when I am peaced,° and my malice ceased) I could not change? Why should I now do in my anger or malice that thing which (when I am sobered and come to myself again) I should greatly sorrow for and sore repent? Why rather should not reason, why should not piety, at the last why should not Christ, obtain that of me now which a little pause of time shall shortly hereafter obtain?'

To no man, I suppose, hath nature given so much of black choler° but at the least way he might so [142ᵛ] far forth rule himself. But it shall be a very good thing by thee, thus instructed, so to harden thy mind with reason, with continuance and custom, that thou shouldst not be moved at all. It shall be a perfect thing if thou, having indignation at the vice only, shouldst for a rebuke do again the office of charity. To conclude, even natural temperance, which ought to be in every man, requireth that thou shouldst not lose thyself altogether to affections.° Not to be wroth at all is a thing most like unto God, and therefore is it most comely and beautiful. To overcome ill with goodness, and malice with kindness, is the counterfeiting of the perfect charity of Christ Jesus. To refrain wrath and to constrain it with a bridle is the property or office of a man if he have any heart or courage with him. To follow the appetite of wrath is not of a man verily, but plainly of beasts — and that of wild beasts.

But if thou wouldst know how much uncomely it were to a man to be overcome with wrath, look (when thou art sober thyself) that thou mark the countenance of an angry person; or else (when thou thyself art angry) go unto a glass.° When thine eyes be so burning in fire, when thy cheeks be pale, when thy mouth standeth awry, thy lips foam, and all thy members° tremble and quake, when thy voice grateth and soundeth so maliciously, nor thy gestures be of one fashion — who would then judge that thou were a man?

Thou perceivest now, my most sweetest friend, how dark a matter, yea, how large a shore⁵⁵⁸ is open all abroad° to dispute of other vices after the [143ʳ] same manner. But we, in the midst of our course, will strike sail and leave the rest to thy discretion.° Neither, certain, was it my mind or purpose (for that no doubt should be an infinite work) for to proceed as I began, to withdraw thy mind from every vice — vice by vice, as it were — with sundry declamations, and to embolden and encourage the contrary virtues. I desired only that thing which I thought sufficient for thee: to show thee a certain manner or craft of a new kind of war, how thou mightest arm thyself against the evils of thy old life burgeoning forth again and springing afresh. Therefore, as we have done in one or two things (because of example), so must thou thyself do: partly° in everything separately, and most of all in those things whereunto thou shalt perceive thyself to be stirred or instigated peculiarly, whether it be through vice of nature, through custom, or of ill bringing up. Against these things some certain decrees must be written in the pure°⁵⁵⁹ of thy mind, and they must be renewed now and then, lest they should fail or be forgotten with disuse — as against the vice of backbiting, filthy speaking, envy, gule,° and other like. These chiefly be the enemies of Christ's soldiers, against whose assault the mind must be armed long aforehand with prayers, with noble sayings of wise men, with the doctrine of Holy Scripture, with examples of devout and holy men, and especially with the examples of Christ.

Though I doubt not but that reading of Holy Scripture should minister all [143ᵛ] these things to thee abundantly, nevertheless yet charity, which one brother oweth to another, exhorted me that at the least way with these sudden° and hasty writings I should further and help thy holy purpose as much as lieth in me to do: a thing which I have done somewhat the rather because I feared somewhat lest thou shouldst fall° into that superstitious kind° of religious men who, partly waiting° on their own advantage, partly with great zeal (but not 'after knowledge, or learning'),⁵⁶⁰ compass about both sea and land,⁵⁶¹ and if anywhere they have caught a man recovering from vices unto virtue, him straightway with most importune and lewd exhortations, with threatenings and flatterings, they enforce° to thrust into the order of monks — even as though without a cowl° there were no Christendom at all. Furthermore, when they have filled his breast with pure scrupulosity and doubts insoluble, then they bind him to certain traditions found° by man, and plainly thrust the wretched person headlong into a certain bondage of ceremonies, like unto the manner of the Jews, and teach him to tremble and fear, but not to love.

---

⁵⁵⁸ large a shore] 1523 'large a sore'; 1533 'large a sea'; L. 'immensum aequor' ('large sea'). The preceding phrase 'dark a matter' (conjectured here for 'lurke a matter') is T.'s addition.
⁵⁵⁹ in the pure] L. 'in albo' ('on its clear surface'); cf. Prov. 3. 3 ('table of thine heart') and see *Adages* I. vii. 34 (CWE 32. 87).
⁵⁶⁰ Rom. 10. 2.
⁵⁶¹ Matt. 23. 15.

The order of monks is not a thing that God commanded us to do, but a kind of living, to every man (after the disposition of his body and of his mind also) either profitable or unprofitable; whereunto verily, as I encourage thee not, so I discourage thee not. This thing only I warn thee of — that thou put good living neither in meat nor in raiment or habit, nor in any [144ʳ] visible things, but in those things which we have declared or showed thee before. And in whatsoever persons thou shalt find or perceive the true image of Christ, with them couple thyself. Moreover, when such men be lacking whose conversation° should make thee better, withdraw thyself as much as thou canst from company of man, and call the holy prophets, call Christ and the Apostles unto communication.° But especially make Paul of familiar acquaintance with thee. This fellow must be had ever in thy bosom, to be read and studied both night and day: finally he must be learned without the book, word by word.

Upon whom we now a good while[562] enforce with great diligence to make a comment° or enarration° — which is a bold deed truly! But notwithstanding we, trusting in the help of God, will endeavour ourself busily, lest — after Origen, Ambrose, and Augustine, lest after so many new interpreters — we should seem to have taken this labour upon us utterly either without a cause or without fruit; and also that certain busy and unquiet wranglers° (who think it perfect religion to know no good learning at all) may understand that — touching° as we in youth have embraced and made much of pure learning of old authors, as touching also that we have got us (and not without great sweat and watch)° meetly° understanding of both the tongues (both of Greek and Latin) — that we have not looked to vain and foolish fame, or unto the childish pastime or pleasure of our mind: but that we imagined [144ᵛ] long before that our Lord's temple (which some had dishonested° with ignorance and barbarousness) should of us be garnished, unto our power, with the riches of Egypt, wherewith all excellent wits might be inflamed unto the love of the Holy Scripture.

But (this so great a thing for a few days laid apart) we have taken upon us this labour for thy sake, that we should show unto thee (as it were with the finger) the way which leadeth unto Christ compendiously.° And I beseech God, the father of this holy purpose (as I hope), that he would vouchsafe benignly to favour thy wholesome enforcements, yea, that he would in changing of thee increase his grace and make thee perfect, that thou mightest wax big and strong in him, and spring up to a perfect man. In whom also fare thou well, both brother and friend, always truly singularly beloved to my mind, but now much more than before both dear and pleasant.

---

[562] a good while] An early work on Romans is mentioned in a letter to Colet (see O'Donnell, *An English Version*, p. xx), but E. may have meant 'I've been thinking about it for a long time' — the eventual result being his *Paraphrases* (1517 onwards).

At the town of St Omer,[563] the year after Christ's birth 1501, and translated out of Latin into English in the year of our Lord God 1523.

Amen quod[564]

---

[563] St Omer] A town in north-eastern France. L. is more specific: 'At the monastery of St Bertin', where Erasmus stayed while finishing the *Enchiridion*. Sts Omer and Bertin evangelised and built in the region during the seventh century.

[564] Amen quod] A signing-off formula ('So be it, according to …'), but here without a name, translator's or scribe's.

A Treatise Upon the Pater Noster

Translated by Margaret Roper (1524)

Edited by Gordon Kendal

Introduction

Erasmus's version of the Lord's Prayer (1523) complements his *Manual*.[1] It encourages the inner fusion of (human) 'spirit' and (divine) 'Spirit' which for Erasmus lies at the heart of Christian morality, while at the same time presupposing the moral seriousness which the *Manual* outlined in detail. Both are essential to his 'philosophy of Christ'. He called it later a 'paraphrase' but the book itself is simply 'the Lord's Prayer', expanded to help the user to catch not merely the meaning of the words but their weight.[2] The Gospel prayer can be a tool for catechesis (presenting theological ideas) and a vehicle for colloquy with God, but it is also a resource in becoming internally reintegrated and growing in Christlikeness.[3] At its core is an attitude of wonder, gratitude, inadequacy, and resolve, set against workaday situations where powerful but friendly Infinite engages with vulnerable and uncooperative finite. Erasmus spells this out in a manner indebted particularly to Cyprian and Augustine among the Church Fathers.[4]

An English translation by a young wife and mother, daughter to a future Lord Chancellor and with a husband suspected of Lutheran leanings,[5] inevitably arouses different kinds of interest.[6] But it is also simply the exercise of a particular translator's technique and craft — and a good one. Richard Hyrde (a tutor in the More household), in a prefatory letter mainly discussing the matter of women's learning, says of the translator:

> she hath showed herself not only erudite and elegant in either tongue, but hath also used such wisdom, such discreet and substantial judgement in expressing

---

[1] For the modern English translation by John N. Grant see *CWE* 69, pp. 55–77.
[2] Letter 1341A, in *Correspondence 1522–1523*, trans. by R. A. B. Mynors, *CWE* 9, annotated by James M. Estes, p. 324, line 780.
[3] See Hilmar M. Pabel, *Conversing with God: Prayer in Erasmus' Pastoral Writing* (Toronto: University of Toronto Press, 1997), especially pp. 109f.
[4] *St. Cyprian on the Lord's Prayer*, trans. by T. Herbert Bindley (London: SPCK, 1914); *Tertullian, Cyprian and Origen on the Lord's Prayer*, trans. and ed. by Alistair Stewart-Sykes (New York: St Vladimir's Seminary Press, 2004); Augustine, *Our Lord's Sermon on the Mount*, in *Nicene and Post-Nicene Fathers*, 1st series, vol. VI, trans. by Wm Findlay and D. S. Schaff (Grand Rapids: Wm Eerdmans, 1980), Bk II, chs 4–9.
[5] E. E. Reynolds, *Margaret Roper, Eldest Daughter of St. Thomas More* (London: Burns and Oates, 1960), p. 157. Born in 1505, in 1521 she married William Roper, a lawyer; there were five children. Her father was imprisoned in the Tower of London and executed in 1535.
[6] See *Silent But for the Word: Tudor Women as Patrons, Translators, and Writers of Religious Works*, ed. by Margaret Patterson Hannay (Kent, OH: Kent State University Press, 1985), particularly its introduction and Rita M. Verbrugge, 'Margaret More Roper's Personal Expression in the *Devout Treatise Upon the Pater Noster*', pp. 30–42.

lively the Latin, as a man may peradventure miss in many things translated and turned by them that bear the name of righteous and very well learned men.[7]

The date of first publication is unclear.[8] The preface is dated 1 October 1524 but the earliest known copy (printed by Thomas Berthelet in London and undated) is probably 1526. Hyrde mentions 'the labour that I have had with it about the printing',[9] so it seems likely that Margaret Roper's version was completed in 1524, i.e. within a year of the publication at Basel in 1523 of the Latin original. She was therefore (we might suppose) at work upon it in London while Sir John and Lady Walsh in Gloucestershire were poring over the English version of the *Manual* newly produced by their sons' tutor, William Tyndale.[10]

Some of its divergences from the source text are simply mishaps: an overlooked word or phrase, a mistranscribing, a clumsy expression accidentally giving the wrong sense; occasionally a real misunderstanding.[11] Some differences are decorative (doubling epithets in deference to a fashion), some more deliberate — omitting words which a reader might think indelicate, or inserting an epithet or a phrase to bring out the implications of what Erasmus is saying. She underlines his concern for spirituality and learning: we are not merely God's children but his 'spiritual children', Christ's prayer to the Father was not just 'for us' but 'for our learning and instruction', and (even more clearly than in Erasmus) the 'daily bread' for which we pray is the guidance and inspiration of the Spirit and Word. She emphasises the positive value in good works: we hope not merely that people who witness our 'good works' will glorify God, but that they will glorify him 'in them' (an addition not merely to Erasmus but to the Gospel text quoted). Her handling of tenses is significant, where she renders a Latin past (perfect) tense as an English present: occasionally in error, or perhaps for euphony (intending it as a smoother-sounding past tense), but sometimes evidently to accentuate the abiding influence of the definitive past event: Christ and the Spirit not merely came and did things *then*, they do them *now*.

Suchlike accidents and modifications attest to her confidence and freedom from supervision, and the survival of minor mistakes and mishaps — presumably

---

[7] For a modernised version of the letter see in *Broadview Anthology of Sixteenth-Century Poetry and Prose*, ed. by Marie Loughlin, Sandra Bell, and Patricia Brace (Ontario: Broadview Press, 2012), pp. 79–84; the words quoted are on p. 84, lines 287–93.

[8] See John Arthur Gee, 'Margaret Roper's English Version of Erasmus' *Precatio Dominica* and the Apprenticeship behind Early Tudor Translation', *RES*, 13 (1937), 257–71.

[9] In *Broadview Anthology*, p. 84, line 294.

[10] See David Daniell, *William Tyndale: A Biography* (New Haven: Yale University Press, 1994), pp. 62–63.

[11] Among recent analyses see Patricia Demers, 'Margaret Roper and Erasmus: The Relationship of Translator and Source', *wwr magazine* (women writing and reading), 1.1 (2005), 3–8.

predating the version available to Hyrde (and left untouched also in the printing of 1531) — makes it unlikely that 1526 differs materially from a putative '1524'. The translation is sympathetic and in general painstaking. She handles the familiar themes honestly and unselfconsciously, bringing to the task a rugged humility which may be a more convincing rebuttal of the low esteem frequently attaching to the craft of translation than surreptitiously inserting original ideas. The English says what the Latin says and (if handled aright) can do what Erasmus wanted it to do: deepen and authenticate Christian praying alongside moral endeavour.

The Latin text of *Precatio Dominica* I have primarily used is the transcription by Germain Marc'hadour in *Moreana* (1965) of the Yale copy of 1523 (Basel, first edition): for details see Further Reading. The most recent critical edition available is still *Opera Omnia*, ed. in ten vols by J. Clericus, vol. V (Leiden: Vander, 1704), pp. 1217–28. For details of the two English editions, virtually identical, see the separate Textual Note.

Further Reading

ERASMUS, *The Lord's Prayer*, trans. by John N. Grant, in *Collected Works of Erasmus*, vol. LXIX, ed. by John W. O'Malley and Louis A. Perraud (Toronto: University of Toronto Press, 1999), pp. 55–77

DEMERS, PATRICIA, 'Margaret Roper and Erasmus: The Relationship of Translator and Source', *wwr magazine* (women writing and reading), 1.1 (2005), 3–8

GEE, JOHN ARTHUR, 'Margaret Roper's English Version of Erasmus' *Precatio Dominica* and the Apprenticeship behind Early Tudor Translation', *RES*, 13 (1937), 257–71

HANNAY, MARGARET PATTERSON, ed., *Silent But for the Word: Tudor Women as Patrons, Translators, and Writers of Religious Works* (Kent, OH: Kent State University Press, 1985)

MARC'HADOUR, GERMAIN, 'Erasmus' Paraphrase of the *Pater Noster* (1523) with its English Translation by Margaret Roper (1524)', *Moreana*, 7 (1965), 9–63

PABEL, HILMAR M., *Conversing with God: Prayer in Erasmus' Pastoral Writing* (Toronto: University of Toronto Press, 1997)

REYNOLDS, E. E., *Margaret Roper, Eldest Daughter of St. Thomas More* (London: Burns and Oates, 1960)

STEWART-SYKES, ALISTAIR, trans. and ed., *Tertullian, Cyprian and Origen on the Lord's Prayer* (New York: St Vladimir's Seminary Press, 2004)

A TREATISE UPON THE PATER NOSTER

[a1ʳ]¹ A devout treatise upon the *Pater Noster*,² made first in Latin by the most famous doctor Master Erasmus of Rotterdam, and turned into English by a young, virtuous, and well learned gentlewoman of nineteen years of age.

[b4ʳ] Hereafter follow the seven petitions of the *Pater Noster*, translated out of Latin into English.³

The first petition:

'Our Father, who art in heaven, hallowed be thy name'

Hear, O Father in heaven, the petitions of thy children, who (though they be as yet bodily in earth) notwithstanding in mind ever they desire and long to come to the country celestial and Father's house, where they well know and understand that the treasure of everlasting wealth° and felicity (that is to say, the inheritance of life immortal) is ordained for them.

We acknowledge thine excellency, O Maker, Saviour, and Governor of all things contained in heaven and in earth. And again° we acknowledge and confess our own vileness,° and in no wise we durst be so bold to call thee 'father' (who are far unworthy to be thy bondmen), nor take upon us the most honourable name of thy 'children' (which uneath° thou vouchsafest thine angels), except° thy mere° goodness had by adoption received us into the great honour of this name. The time was when we were servants to wickedness and sin by the miserable generation of Adam. We were also children of the Fiend,° by whose instinction° and spirit we were driven and compelled to every kind of mischief° and offence. But then⁴ thou of thine infinite [b4ᵛ] mercy, by thine only-begotten Son Jesus, made us free from the thraldom of sin and deliveredest us from the Devil our father, and by violence riddest⁵ us from the inheritance of eternal fire, and at the last thou vouchsafest to adopt us by faith and baptism as members in the most holy Body of thy Son, not only into the fellowship of thy name, but also of thine inheritance.

---

¹ References are to the folio numbers in the British Library copy via EEBO; f3ᵛ and f4ʳ are lacking there and have been supplied here from Germain Marc'hadour, 'Erasmus' Paraphrase of the *Pater Noster* (1523) with its English Translation by Margaret Roper (1524)', *Moreana*, 7 (1965), 9–63.
² *Pater Noster*] 'Our Father'; E. 'Precatio Dominica' (Lord's Prayer).
³ into English] But R. leaves the actual Gospel headings in L.
⁴ then] 1526 'that'.
⁵ riddest] In E. past tense (also the following 'vouchsafest' and 'sendest'). See Introduction, p. 198.

And because° we should nothing mistrust in thy love towards us, as a sure token thereof thou sendest[6] from heaven down into our hearts the most holy Spirit of thy Son, who (all servantly° fears shaken off) boldly crieth out in our hearts without ceasing, 'Abba, pater' (which in English[7] is as much to say as 'O father, father'). And this thy Son taught us (by whom as minister thou givest us all things): that when we were (as it were) born again by thy Spirit, and at the font-stone° in baptism renounced and [had] forsaken our father the Devil, and had begun to have no father in earth,[8] then we should acknowledge only our Father celestial, by whose marvellous power we were made somewhat° of right nought, by whose goodness we were restored when we were lost, by whose wisdom incomparable evermore we are governed and kept, that we fall not again into destruction. This thy Son gave us full trust to call upon thee; he assigned us also a way of praying to thee. Acknowledge therefore the desire and prayer of thy Son, acknowledge the Spirit of thy Son, who prayeth to thy majesty for us by us. Do [c1ʳ] thou not disdain to be called 'Father' of[9] those whom thy Son — most likest thy image — vouchsafe[10] to call his 'brethren'.

And yet we ought not hereupon to take liking in ourselves, but to give glory to thee and thy Son for that great gentleness: sith° no man can here of himself aught deserve, but that thing (whatsoever good it be) cometh of thy only and free liberality. Thou delightest rather in names loving and charitable than terrible and fearful. Thou desirest rather to be called a 'father' than a 'lord' or 'master'. Thou wouldst we should rather love thee as thy children than fear thee as thy servants and bondmen. Thou first lovedst us, and of thy goodness also it cometh, and thy reward,° that we do love thee again. Give ear, O Father of spirits, to thy children spiritual who in spirit pray to thee. For thy Son told us that in those that so prayed thy delight was, whom therefore thou sendest[11] into the world that he should teach us all[12] verity and truth.

Hear now the desires of unity and concord, for it is not sitting° nor agreeable° that brethren whom thy goodness hath put in equal honour should disagree or vary among themselves by ambitious desire of worldly promotion, by contentious debate, hatred, or envy: all we hang° of one Father, we all one thing pray for and desire. No man asketh aught for himself specially or apart, but as members of one Body, quickened° and relieved° with one soul. We require° and pray in common for that which indifferently° shall be expedient and [c1ᵛ] necessary for us all. And

---

[6] sendest] L. 'immisisti' ('you sent').
[7] which in English] Parenthesis added; see Rom. 8. 15–16.
[8] no father in earth] Matt. 23. 9.
[9] of] 'by'.
[10] vouchsafe] L. 'dignatus est' ('did deign'). See Matt. 12. 46–50.
[11] sendest] L. 'missus' ('sent').
[12] us all] 'us the whole of'; John 16. 13.

indeed we dare none other thing desire of thee than what thy Son commanded us, nor otherwise ask than as he appointed us. For in so asking his goodness promised we should obtain whatsoever we prayed for in his name.[13]

And forasmuch as when thy Son was here in earth he nothing more fervently desired than that thy most holy name should appear and shine, not only in Judaea but also through all the world besides, we also, both by his encouraging and example, this one thing above all desire: that the glory of thy most holy name may replenish and fulfil° both heaven and earth, so that no creature be who dreadeth not thy high power and majesty, who do not worship and reverence also thy wisdom eternal, and marvellous goodness. For[14] thy glory, as it is great, so (neither having beginning nor ending, but ever in itself flourishing) can neither increase nor decrease — but it skilleth° yet mankind not a little that every man it know and magnify; for to know and confess thee only very God, and Jesus Christ whom thou sendest[15] into the world, is as much to us as life eternal. Let the clear shining of thy name shadow and quench in us all worldly glory. Suffer° no man to presume to take upon himself any part of glory, for glory out of thee is none, but very° slander° and rebuke.°

The course of nature also in carnal° children this thing causeth, that they greatly desire the good fame and honest reputation of their father. For we may see how glad they be and [c2ʳ] how they rejoice, how happy also they think themselves if happen their fathers any great honour (as, goodly triumph, or their image and picture to be brought into the court or common place with an honourable preface,° or any other goodly royalty,° whatsoever it be). And again we see how they wail, and how aghast and astonied° they be if chance their fathers slander or infamy. So deeply hath this thing natural affection rooted in man's heart,[16] that the fathers rejoice in their children's glory and their children in the glory of their fathers. But forasmuch as the ghostly° love and affection of[17] God far passeth° and exceedeth the carnal affection of man, therefore we thy spiritual children much more fervently thirst and desire the glory and honour of thy most holy name, and greatly are vexed and troubled in heart if he to whom alone all glory is due chance rebuked or slandered to be.

Not that any slander or rebuke can diminish or defoul the clearness° of thy glory, but that we, as much as lieth in us, in a manner do wrong and injury to thy name whensoever the Gentiles° (either not knowing or else despising the Maker and Original° of all) do worship and homage to creatures most vile: as made of

---

[13] in his name] See John 14. 13–14.
[14] For] L. 'quidem' is concessive (admittedly, certainly).
[15] sendest] E. 'misisti' ('sent').
[16] hath this thing natural affection rooted in man's heart] i.e. 'hath natural affection rooted this thing (family pride) in man's heart'.
[17] of] 'for'.

timber or stone, or other painted images, some also to oxen, some to bulls, and such other like[18] — and moreover, in all these, foul and wicked devils. In honour of them they sing hymns, to these they do sacrifice, before these they burn incense and other sweet savours. Then we thy spiritual children, [c2ᵛ] seeing all this, doubly are aggrieved: both that thou hast not that honour which is due to thee, and that these wretches perish by their own madness and folly. The Jews also never cease in their synagogues and resort° of people from despiteful° and abominable backbiting of thy only Son, whereby in the mean time they slander thee: sith it cannot be chosen, when thy Son is misfamed° (who is the very clearness of thy glory), but that infamy also must redound in thee. They cast eke° in our teeth, as a thing of great dishonesty,° the most glorious name of 'thy children', saying that it were better to be called 'thieves' or 'manquellers'° than Christian men and followers of Christ. They lay against us also that thy Son was crucified — which is to us great glory and renown.

We may thank thy mercy, Father, of[19] all this thing: that we have and acknowledge thee as Original and Causer of all our health,° that we worship also thy Son in equal authority with thee, and that we have received into our hearts the Spirit of you both. But yet, good Father in heaven, we pray thee to show thy mercy to those also: that both the Gentiles, leaving and forsaking the worshipping and homage of counterfeit images, may do all honour and reverence to thy majesty alone; and the Jews, relieved with thy Spirit, renouncing their superstitious using of the Law, may confess God from whom all things so abundantly come, may confess the Son of God by whom we receive all, may confess[20] the Holy Ghost partaker and fellow [c3ʳ] of the divine nature. Let them worship in three Persons one and equal Majesty, and acknowledge three Persons as one proper° person,[21] so that every nation, every tongue, every sex,° every age as well old as young, may with one assent advance° and praise thy most holy name.

And I would to God that we also, who bear the name of thy children, were not dishonesty to thy glory amongst those that know thee not. For, like as a good and wise son is the glory and honour of his father, so a foolish and unthrifty° child getteth his father dishonesty and shame; and he is not a natural and proper child,

---

[18] such other like] E. specifies: 'apes, leeks, onions'.
[19] of] 'for, concerning'. 1526's spacing tempts us into the sense 'Father of all this thing that we have' but 'this thing' is prospective, spelled out in three 'that'-clauses. (L. 'hoc' followed by three 'quod's.) Strictly, God is 'Father' of *us*, not of his benefits.
[20] may confess] E.'s point is that they already believe, like us, that everything comes from God, but not that God is Trinity.
[21] as one proper person] In charity to R. and fairness to E. we could imagine a distributive 'each' before 'one', the 'unconfounded' plurality of Persons ('triplicem personarum proprietatem') being as crucial to the Trinity as its unity of Substance. More likely, R. has misunderstood E.'s 'in simplici essentia' (which must refer here to the single divine Substance) — or she has unhappily inverted the meaning of 'person' mid-sentence.

whosoever do not labour all that he can to follow and be like his father in wit°
and conditions.° But thy Son Jesus is a very kind²² and natural child, for he is a
very full and perfect image and similitude of thee, whom wholly he is like and
representeth.° We who are become thy children by adoption and not by nature,
conforming ourselves after° his example, endeavour as much as lieth in us to come
to some manner likeness of thee, that likewise as thou wast most perfectly exalted
and glorified in thy Son Jesus, so (as far-forth as our weakness will suffer) thou
mayst be glorified also in us. But the ways how thou mayst be glorified in us is if
the world perceive that we live after the teaching and doctrine of thy Son — that
is to say, if they see that we love thee above all things, and our neighbour and
brother no less than our own selves; and that we ever bear good mind and love to
our enemy and adversary, also well [c3ᵛ] doing and profiting those who do us
injury and wrong. For these things thy Son bade us we should do, when he
provoked° us to the following and likeness of our Father in heaven, who
commandeth his sun to shine upon good and evil.²³

And how great a shame and dishonesty are they to thy glory who, when they
have professed and taken upon them thy name, notwithstanding do robbery and
theft, commit adultery, chide and brawl,° study° to revenge, go about to deceive,
forswear themselves by thy most holy name, among° also slander and backbite,
have their belly as their god,²⁴ despise thee, and do service and homage to worldly
riches. And truly the common sort of people for the most part esteem God after
the living and conditions of his servants. For if they may perceive that they who
have professed thy name live viciously, then they cry out and say, 'What a god is
he that hath such manner of worshippers? Fie° on such a master that hath so
unruly servants! Out upon such a father whose children be so lewd!° Banished
be such a king that hath such manner of people and subjects!' Thy Son therefore,
considering this, taught us that — likewise as he, both living and dying, ever
glorified thy name — so we also, all that we might, should endeavour by chaste
and blameless conditions to advance and praise the clearness of thy glory, saying
unto us, 'Let your light shine in the sight of men, that they may see your good
works and in those glorify your Father [c4ʳ] in heaven'.²⁵

But in us, O good Father, there is no light at all, except it will please thee to
send us any, who art the continual and everlasting spring of all light; nor we of
ourselves can bring forth no good works. Therefore, good Lord, we pray thee let
thy goodness work in us, and thy clear light shine in us, as²⁶ in all things that
thou hast created doth shine thy eternal and endless power, thy wisdom unable

---

[22] kind] Cf. 404. Probably 'genuine' (R.'s doublets are almost always synonyms), but see Verbrugge in *Silent but for the Word*, p. 42.
[23] upon good and evil] Matt. 5. 45.
[24] belly as their god] Philipp. 3. 19.
[25] Matt. 5. 16.
[26] as] 'in the same manner that'.

to be expressed, and thy wonderful goodness (which most specially yet thou vouchsafest[27] to show to mankind). Now, then, whithersoever we look, all things glorify thy name. The earthly[28] spirits both day and night never lin° praying their Lord and King. The wonderful also and heavenly engine° that we behold, the disagreeing concord moreover of the elements, the flowing and ebbing of the sea, the bubblishing° of rivers, the enduring courses of waters, so many diverse kinds of things, so many kinds of trees and of herbs, so many of creatures, and to everything the proper appointed and set nature (as in the adamant° stone to draw iron, the herbs to cure and heal diseases and sickness).

All these things, I say, what other thing do they show to us than the glory of thy name, and that thou art only very God, only immortal, only of all power and might, only wise, only good, only merciful, only just, only true, only marvellous, only to be loved and had in reverence? Then, Father, we may well see that he doth wrong to thy glorious name, whosoever take upon [c4ᵛ] himself to be called by any of these names. For though there be in us any of these rehearsed° virtues, yet all that cometh to us from thy liberal goodness.

Grant now therefore, Father, that thy name on every side be glorified, and that the light and glory of thy name may no less appear and shine in our manners and living than it shineth in thy angels and in all things that thou hast created and made; that — in like wise as they who behold and look upon this world, of[29] the wonderful and marvellous workmanship do guess the excellency of the Maker thereof — so they that know thee not, moved and stirred by our example, may both confess their own misery and wretchedness and marvel thy liberal goodness, and — by these means turned and converted — may together with us glorify the most holy name of thee, of thy Son, and of the Holy Ghost, to whom indifferently all honour and glory is due for ever. Amen.

The second petition:

'Thy kingdom come'

O Father in heaven, who art the only Causer, Maker, Saviour, Restorer, and Governor of all, both in heaven and in earth, out of whom cometh and proceedeth all authority, power, kingdom, and rule, as well to things uncreated as created, as well to things invisible as visible; whose throne and seat of majesty is the heaven, and the earth as footstool; whose kingly sceptre and mace is thine eternal and most [d1ʳ] established will, whom no power is able to withstand: once thou promise[d]st thy people by the mouths of thy prophets, for the health° of

---

[27] vouchsafest] L. 'voluisti' ('wished').
[28] earthly] L. 'aetherei' (heavenly, ethereal). Explicable by fleeting dyslexia in transcription; cf. 'hugeness' for 'lodging' (311).
[29] of] 'from'.

mankind, a certain spiritual realm which should bring into liberty those that were thine and born anew in thee, and should deliver them out of the tyrannous handling of the Fiend,° who in time past reigned as prince in the world sore entangled and cumbered with sin; and to the getting and obtaining of this realm thou vouchsafe[d]st to send from heaven down into the earth thy only Son, who (with the loss of his own life redeeming us), where we were afore servants of the Devil, should make us the children of God.

And verily thy Son, while he lived here in earth, was wont to call his Gospel the 'heavenly kingdom' and the 'realm of God', whose knowledge yet he said to be hid and kept secret[30] from us. But notwithstanding, thy children humbly require° and with fervent desire beseech thee that this realm, which our Lord Jesus challenged° for thee, might daily more and more be disclosed and opened here in earth, until that time come in which that same thy Son shall restore and render it up to thee full and whole, when all those have subdued themselves whom thy goodness ere the beginning of the world hath appointed to dwell in this realm, and when all obstinate and rebellious spirits, and all malicious and evil desires, be fully quenched and wiped away (which hitherto and at this day make war and insurrection against thy majesty, [d1ᵛ] which vex and unquiet thy commonalty):° what time thy realm shall be in sure peace and tranquillity.

For verily as yet the world, by all the means and subtleties it can, oppresseth thy children wandering here bodily in earth. As yet also corrupt and unclean affections,° and old original sin, rebel and strive against the spirit. As yet noyous° and wicked spirits, which thou banishedst and put out of the heavenly city, do assault with firely° darts from above those whom thou of thy mere° goodness hast divided from this world and, as chosen folk and partakers of thy Son, hast appointed to thy realm. Grant, Father of all might, that they whom thy goodness once°[31] hath delivered from the tyranny of sin and assigned to dwell in thy realm may, by the benefit of the same benign goodness, continue and steadfastly abide in their liberty and freedom; and that none (leaving and failing from thee and thy Son) return again in the tyrannous service of the Devil. And so both we by thy Son shall reign in thee to our wealth,° and thou in us to thy glory: for thou art glorified in our bliss, and our bliss is of[32] thy goodness.

Thy Son Jesus taught us we should despise the realm of this world, which standeth° all by riches and is held up by garrisons of men, by hosts and armour; which also, whatsoever it doth, doth by pride and violence, and is both gotten, kept, and defended by fierce cruelness. And he with the Holy Ghost overcame the wicked spirit that ruled as chief and head in the world afore he by [d2ʳ] innocency and pureness of living had the victory of sin, by meekness vanquished cruelness,

---

[30] hid and kept secret] e.g. Matt. 13. 10f.
[31] once] 'once for all' (L. 'semel').
[32] of] 'from, due to'.

by sufferance of many despiteful° rebukes° recovered everlasting glory, by his own death restored life, and by his cross had triumph upon the wicked spirits. Thus wonderfully hast thou, Father, warred and overcome. After this manner thou both triumphest and reignest in thy Son Jesus, by whom it hath pleased thee of thy goodness to take us into the congregation of the dwellers in thy realm.

Thus also thou triumphest and reignest in thy holy martyrs, in thy chaste virgins and pure confessors° — who yet neither by their own strength nor power did overcome the fierceness and displeasure of tyrants, nor the raging or the wantonness of the flesh, nor the maliciousness of this world: but it was thy Spirit, Father, whom[33] it pleased thee to give them, to the glory of thy name and the health of mankind, that was both the beginner and ender of all this in them. And we, Father, heartily desire thee that thy realm may flourish also in us who — although we do no miracles (forasmuch as neither time nor matter requireth), albeit we be not imprisoned nor tormented, though we be not wounded nor burnt, although we be not crucified nor drowned, though we be not beheaded — yet notwithstanding, the strength and clearness° of thy realm may shine and be noble in us if the world perceive that we, by the help of thy Spirit, stand steadfast and sure against all assaults of the Devil, and against the flesh ([d2ᵛ]) which always stirreth and provoketh us to those things that be contrary to the spirit), and against the world (which by all the ways it can moveth us to forsake and leave the trust that we have once put in thee).

As often soever as, for thy love,[34] we despise and set nought by the realm of this world, and with full trust hang° upon the heavenly kingdom that thou hast promised us; as often also as we forsake and leave honouring of earthly riches, and only worship and embrace the precious and ghostly° learning[35] of the Gospel; as often as we refuse those things that for the season° seem sweet and pleasant to the fleshly and carnal° appetite, and in hope and trust of eternal felicity we suffer patiently and valiantly all things, be it never so hard; as often also as we can be content to forsake our natural affections and that which we have most dear (as, our fathers and mothers, wives, children, and kinsfolk) for the love of thee; likewise, as often as we oppress° and refrain the furious and fiercely braids° of anger, and give mild and meek words to those that chide° and brawl° with us, and do good to them who do us injury and wrong; and all for thy sake: so often, Father, thou warrest in us and overcomest the realm of the Devil, and openest the might and power of thy realm. Thus it hath pleased and liked° thy wisdom, Father, by continual and grievous battle to exercise, confirm, and make steadfast the virtue and strength of thy people. Increase such strength in thy children, that they [d3ʳ]

---

[33] whom] 1526 'which'.
[34] for thy love] 'for love of thee'.
[35] precious and ghostly learning] L. 'margaritum' ('pearl'); see Matt. 13. 46.

may ever return stronger from their battle, and that, when by little and little their enemies' and adversaries' might is diminished and broken, thou mayst every day more and more reign in us.

But the time is not yet come, good Father, in which all the world have subdued themselves to thy yoke; for as yet that tyrannous Fiend hath ado with many and diverse nations. There is not yet one herd and one herd-master:°[36] which we hope shall be when the Jews also shall bring and submit themselves to the spiritual and ghostly learning[37] of the Gospel. For yet many know not how great a liberty it is, and what a dignity, and how great a felicity, to be subjects to the heavenly realm; and that is the cause why they had rather be the servants of the Devil than thy children, inheritors with Jesus, and partakers of the kingdom of heaven.

And amongst those too, Father, that walk within the cloister° of thy Church, and seem as chief in thy realm, there are not a few (alas) who hold on their Adversary's side and, as much as lieth in them, abate,° shame, and dishonest° the glory of thy realm. Wherefore we specially desire and wish for that time — which thou wouldst none to know but thyself alone[38] — in which, according° to the promise of thy Son,[39] thy angels shall come and make clean the floor of thy Church, and gather together into thy barn the pure corn, divided and severed from the cockle,° and pluck out of thy realm all manner occasion of slander: what time there shall neither be [d3ᵛ] hunger nor poverty, no necessity of clothing, no disease, no death, no pursuer,° no hurt or evil at all, nor any fear or suspicion of hurt; but then all the Body of thy dear Son, heaped° together in their Head, shall take fruition° and pleasure of thy blessed company of heaven. And they who in the mean time had rather serve the tyrannous Fiend shall together with their master be banished and sent away to everlasting punishment.

And truly this is the 'realm of Israel' which, when Jesus Christ forsook the earth and returned again to [thee], his disciples desired might shortly be restored. *Then* thou madest heaven free and rid from all rebellion, what time Lucifer° with his company was cast out: so *once*° in the day of doom° and judgement, when the bodies shall arise, thou shalt depart° the sheep from the goats;[40] and then whosoever hath here with all diligence embraced the spiritual and ghostly[41] realm of the Gospel shall be desired° and brought to thee, to the inheritance of the everlasting kingdom, to the which thy goodness had appointed them ere the world was made.

---

[36] one herd-master] John 10. 16.
[37] spiritual and ghostly learning] L. 'regnum' ('kingdom'); cf. lines 261 and 305.
[38] thyself alone] Matt. 24. 36.
[39] promise of thy Son] Matt. 13. 24–30, 37–41.
[40] sheep from the goats] Matt. 25. 33–34.
[41] spiritual and ghostly] R.'s addition.

This fortunate and happy day, which thy Son Jesus promised should come, we thy children, good Father, greatly desire — who dwell here in earth as outlaws in exile, sore laden with the hugeness[42] of the earthly body, suffering in the mean time many grievous displeasures, and sorrowing that we be withdrawn from thy company, whereof then we shall have perfect pleasure and fruition when face to face we shall [d4ʳ] see and behold our King and Father reigning in his great glory.

And yet we have not this hope and trust of[43] our own merits and deserts (which we know verily as none), but only of thy liberal goodness, whereby it liked thee to bestow thine own Son wholly[44] for us and to send us the Holy Ghost as pledge and token of this inheritance. And if it will please thee also to grant that we may steadfastly and without any wavering continue in thy Son Jesus, then thou canst not depart us from the company of thy realm. To whom, with that same thy Son and the Holy Ghost, all renown, honour, and glory is due, world without end. Amen.

The third petition:

'Thy will be done in earth as it is in heaven'

O Father, who art the Nourisher and Orderer of all whom it pleaseth thy Son to acknowledge as his brethren (and he so acknowledgeth all those that in pure faith profess his name in baptism): thy children here in earth call and cry to thee dwelling in heaven (a place far out of all changeable mutability of things created), desiring indeed to come to thy heavenly and celestial company (which is defouled with no manner spot° of evil) — saving° they know well that none can be taken and received into so great a tranquillity and quietness but only they who, with busy study° while they live here, labour to be such as [they] there must be.

[d4ᵛ] Therefore[45] it is all one realm both of heaven and earth, saving this difference: that here we have sore and grievous conflict with the flesh, the world, and the Devil; and there (although there is nothing that might diminish or defoul the wealth° of blessed souls), yet (as touching the full perfection of felicity) there is some manner miss° — which is that all the members and parts of thy Son be[46] gathered together, and that the whole Body of thy Son, safe and sound, be joined to its Head; whereby neither Christ shall lack any of his parts and members, nor good men's souls their bodies (which, likewise as they were ever here in earth

---

[42] hugeness] L. 'domicilio' ('dwelling') — meant for 'lodging'? R.'s 'h' and 'l' were very similar; see photograph of handwriting facing p. 54 in Reynolds, *Margaret Roper*.
[43] of] 'from, in virtue of'.
[44] wholly] 'unsparingly' rather than 'exclusively'.
[45] Therefore] The sense in E. ('enim') is 'Because' (explaining what has just been said, not deducing something from it).
[46] be] i.e. as they are not yet.

partakers of their punishments and afflictions, so their desire is to have them companions of their joy in heaven).[47]

And they finally[48] in this world go about to follow the unity and concord of the heavenly kingdom who — all the time they live bodily in earth — as it becometh natural and obedient children study with all diligence to fulfil° those things which they know shall content thy mind and pleasure, and not what their own sensual° appetite giveth them; not judging or disputing why thou wouldst this or that to be done, but thinking it sufficient that thus thou wouldst it — whom they know surely to will nothing but that that is best. And what thy will is we learned sufficiently of thy only-begotten and most dear Son. He was obedient to thy will, even to his own death, and thus he said for our learning and instruction, 'Father, if it may [e1^r] conveniently° be, suffer° this drink of my passion to be withdrawn from me. Howbeit yet, thy will be fulfilled and not mine'.[49] So that, then, needs must man be ashamed to prefer and set° forth his own will, if Christ our master was content to cast his own will away and subdue it to thine.

The flesh hath its proper° will and delight, which man naturally desireth to keep and follow; the world also hath a will by itself; and the Devil his will far contrary to thine. For the flesh coveteth° against the spirit which we have received of thee; and the world enticeth us to set our love on frail and vanishing things; and the Devil laboureth about that that might bring man to everlasting destruction.

Nor it is not enough that in baptism we have professed that we will be obedient to thy precepts, and there to have renounced the Devil's service, except we labour all our life to perform steadfastly that which we have professed. But that we cannot perform but° if thou give us strength to help forth our purpose: so that our will have[50] no place in us but let thy will, Father, work in us that which thy wisdom judgeth and thinketh best for us. Whosoever liveth after° the fleshly and carnal° appetite, they are dead to thee and then not as thy children. Yea, and we thy children also, as long as we are here bodily in earth, have among° not a little business° and ado in vanquishing the fleshly delight which laboureth to prevent° thy will. But grant, good Father, that thine ever overcome and have the [e1^v] better: whether it like° thee we live or die, or to be punished for our correction, or be in prosperity to the intent we should give thee thanks for thy liberal goodness. And they follow and obey the will of the Devil who do sacrifice and homage to idols, who slanderously backbite thy most honourable Son, and for envy and evil will go about to bring their neighbour into peril and destruction, and (so° they may

---

[47] likewise [...] joy in heaven] While they were on earth human souls had bodies which shared in their sufferings, hence in heaven they (the souls) will naturally want to have their bodies to share in their happiness. In Catholic teaching a human being without a body is incomplete.
[48] finally] L. 'porro' ('furthermore').
[49] Matt. 26. 39.
[50] have] i.e. 'should have'.

shortly wax rich) care not whether they do right or wrong, and are all fulfilled° with corrupt and unclean thoughts.

But this is thy will, Father, that we should keep both our body and mind chaste and pure from all uncleanness of the world; and that we should prefer and set° more by thine honour and thy Son's than all other things besides; and that we should be angry with no man, nor envy or revenge any man, but always be ready to do good for° evil — yea, and to be content rather with torments, hunger, imprisonment, banishment, and death than in anything to be contrary to thy pleasure. And that we may be able every day more and more to perform all this, help us, O Father in heaven, that the flesh may ever more and more be subject to the spirit, and our spirit of one assent and one mind with thy Spirit.

And likewise as now, in diverse places, thy children who are obedient to the Gospel obey and do after thy will: so grant they may do in all the world besides, that every man may know and understand that thou alone art the only Head and Ruler of all things, and that — [e2ʳ] in like wise as there are none in heaven who mutter and rebel against thy will — so let every man here in earth with good mind and glad cheer obey thy will and godly precepts.

Nor we cannot effectually and fully mind° what thou, good Lord, willest, except it will please thee to pluck and draw us thereto. Thou commandest us to be obedient to thy will and pleasure — and indeed they are not worthy to be called 'children' but if in all points they follow and obey their father's bidding. But sith° it hath liked thy goodness to take us (although far unworthy) into so great an honour of thy name, let it please thee also of thy gentleness to give us a ready and steadfast will, that in nothing we overhip° or be against that which thy godly and divine will hath appointed us, but that we kill and mortify our fleshly and carnal lusts, and by thy Spirit be led to the doing of all good works and all things that are pleasant under thy sight.

Whereby thou, Father, mayst acknowledge us as thy children natural, and not out of kind;° and thy Son as kind[51] and good brethren. That is to say, that both twain° may acknowledge in us his own proper benefit;[52] to whom with the Holy Ghost equal and indifferent° glory is due for ever. Amen.

---

[51] kind] Probably 'genuine'; see footnote 22 above on 'kind'.
[52] own proper benefit] i.e. our being respectively children of the Father and brothers of Christ.

The fourth petition:

'Give us this day our daily bread'[52]

O Father in heaven, who of thy exceeding goodness most plenteously feedest all things that thou [e2ᵛ] hast so wondrously created: provide for us thy children (who are chosen to dwell in thy celestial and heavenly house, and that hang° wholly and only of thy Son) some spiritual and ghostly° food; that we, obeying thy will and precepts, may daily increase and wax bigger in virtue, until after° the course of nature we have obtained and gathered a full and perfect strength in our Lord Jesus Christ.

The children of this world, so long as they are not banished nor out of their friends' favour, all that time they take little care of their meat° and drink, sith° their fathers, of their tender love towards them, make sufficient provision for them. Then much less ought we to be careful or studious,° whom thy Son Jesus taught[53] should cast away all care of the morrow-meal,° persuading and assuring us that so rich a Father, so gentle, so loving, and that had so great mind° of us, and who sent meat to the little birds, and so nobly clotheth the lilies in the meadow, would not suffer his children (whom he hath endued with so honourable a name) to lack meat and bodily apparel: but, all things set aside that belong to the body, we should specially and above all seek and labour about those things which pertain and belong to thy realm and the justice thereof.

For, as touching the justice of the Pharisees that savoureth all carnally,° thou utterly despisest and settest° nought by: for the spiritual justice of thy realm standeth° by pure faith and unfeigned charity. And it were no great matter, or show of [e3ʳ] thy plenty, to feed with bread made of corn the body (which, although it perished not for hunger, yet it must needs die and perish within short space,° either by sickness, age, or other chance), but we thy spiritual and ghostly children desire and crave of our spiritual Father that spiritual and celestial bread, whereby we are verily relieved° who be verily and truly called thy children.

That bread is thy Word full of all power, both the giver and nourisher of life: which bread thou vouchsafe[d]st to send us down from heaven what time we were like° to have perished for hunger. For verily the bread and teaching of the proud philosophers and Pharisees could not suffice and content° our mind. But that bread of thine which thou sendest[54] us restored dead men to life; of which whosoever doth eat shall never die. This bread relieved us; by this bread we are

---

[53] daily bread] Two Latin words were used for the enigmatic Gk 'epiousios': 'supersubstantialem' (in *Vulg.* Matt. 6. 11) and 'quotidianum' (*Vulg.* Luke 11. 3, and E.'s *NT* at both Matt. and Luke). R. opts for 'quotidianum' here, but 'supersubstantialem' ('more than ordinary', spiritual, sacramental) looms large, and is even underlined by R.

[54] Jesus taught] Matt. 6. 25–34.

[55] sendest] E. 'misisti' ('sent').

nourished and fattened; and by this we come up to the perfect and full strength of the Spirit.

This bread, though day by day it be eaten and distributed to every bowel of the soul, yet but° if thou, Father, dost give it, it is not wholesome nor anything availeth. The blessed body of thy dear Son is the bread whereof we be all partakers that dwell within thy large house of the Church. It is one bread that indifferently° belongeth to us all, likewise as we are but one Body, made of sundry and diverse members but yet quickened° with one Spirit. And though all take of this bread,[55] yet to many it hath been death and destruction, for it cannot be relief but to [e3ᵛ] such as thou reachest it unto, mingling it with thy heavenly grace; by the reason whereof it may be wholesome to the receivers.

Thy Son is verity and truth: truth also is the bread and teaching of the Gospel which he left behind him for our spiritual food. And this bread likewise[56] to many hath been unsavoury, who have had the mouth of their soul out of taste[57] by the fever of corrupt affections.° But and° it will please thee, good Father, to give forth this bread, then it must of necessity be sweet and pleasant to the eaters. Then it shall comfort those that be in tribulation, and pluck up those that be slidden and fallen down, and make strong those that be sick and weak, and finally bring us to everlasting life.

And forasmuch as the imbecility° and weakness of man's nature is ever ready and apt to decline into the worse, and the soul of man so continually assaulted and laid at with so many subtle engines,° it is expedient and necessary that thou daily make strong and hearten thy children with thy bread; who else are far unable to resist so many and so strong enemies, so many assaults, and so many fearful and terrible darts.° For who, Father, might abide to be had in derision of the world, to be outlawed and banished, to be put in prison, to be fettered and manacled, to be spoiled° of all his goods, and by strong hand be deprived of the company of his most dear wife and well-beloved children, but if now and then he were heartened with thy heavenly and ghostly bread?

He that teacheth the learning of the Gospel,[58] he is [e4ʳ] he that giveth us forth this bread: which yet he giveth all in vain except it be also given by thee. Many there are who receive the body of thy Son, and[59] that hear the word and doctrine of the Gospel: but they depart from thence no stronger than they came, because

---

[56] bread] Here sacramental ('blessed body of thy dear Son'); 1 Corinth. 11. 27-30. E. is comparing the two kinds of spiritual food.
[57] likewise] i.e. as in the case of receiving the sacrament.
[58] out of taste] i.e. 'unable to taste properly'.
[59] He [...] Gospel] i.e. the preacher.
[60] and] E. makes a clearer distinction between those who 'receive (L. *sumunt*, consume) the body' and those who 'hear (*audiunt*) the word'.

they have not deserved that thou, good Father, shouldst privily and invisibly reach it forth unto them.

This bread, O most benign Father, give thy children every day, until that time come in which they shall eat of it at thy heavenly and celestial table; whereby the children of thy realm shall be fulfilled° with the plenteous abundancy of everlasting truth. And to take fruition thereof it were a marvellous felicity and pleasure, which hath need of none other thing at all, neither in heaven nor earth. For in thee, O Father, alone are all things, out of whom is right nought to be desired: who together with thy Son and the Holy Ghost reignest for ever. Amen.

The fifth petition:

'And forgive us our debts, as we forgive our debtors'[60]

This is thy will and mind, O Father in heaven, who art the Maker of peace and Favourer of concord: that thy children — whom it hath pleased thy goodness to couple and join in the bonds of one assent,° and whom thou quickenest° with one Spirit, and with one baptism purgest and makest clean, and in one house [e4ᵛ] of[61] the Church accompaniest,[62] and with the common sacraments of the Church dost nourish, and whom thou hast indifferently° called to the inheritance of the kingdom of heaven, because° they should be of more strength — should[63] live together in thy house of one mind, and that there should be no strife or contention amongst the parts and members of one Body, but each to live in charity with other.

Yet insomuch as they are fain° to keep still their mortal body, it cannot be chosen but, by reason of the weakness and frailty of nature, among° displeasure and offences shall chance, whereby — though the clearness° of brotherly love and concord be not utterly extinguished and quenched — yet it is made all faint and cold, and like° in conclusion to be quenched, except° thou, Father, of thy great gentleness and mercy shouldst daily forgive those that every day offended thee. For as often as we offend our brother, so often also we offend and displease thee, Father, who commandedst we should love our brother as our own self. But thy Son, knowing well enough the imbecility and weakness of his members,[64] showed us a remedy therefore, giving us sure hope that thy goodness would remit and forgive us all our offences if we on the other side with all our heart would forgive our brother whatsoever he trespasseth against us.

And this is a very equal° and indifferent way to obtain pardon and forgiveness

---

[61] debts [...] debtors] L. 'debita' and 'debitoribus', followed also in *KJB*. Tyndale and *BCP* (1549 onwards) preferred 'trespass' (cf. line 506).
[62] of] 'which is'.
[63] accompaniest] i.e. 'bring them together'.
[64] should] 1526 'and should', which leaves the sentence without a main verb.
[65] his members] 1526 'this member'; L. is pl.

which thy Son Jesus hath assigned. For how can any man be so bold to desire his father to withdraw his [fi^r] revenging hand from him, if he himself go about to revenge a little offence in his brother? or who is of so shameless boldness that would not be afraid to say to thee, 'Slake thy anger', when he continueth in rancour and malice still towards his brother? and how can he surely boast and advance° himself as a member of thy Son — who, being free from all sin himself, prayed thee to forgive the thieves[65] on the cross — if he, all entangled with sin, and a sinner, could not find in his heart to forgive his brother, against whom now and then he offendeth? So that amongst us it may be called rather as 'mutual change° of pardon' than very° 'forgiveness'.

That sacrifice is implesant° in thy sight which is offered in remembrance of displeasure,[66] or negligence of reconciling his brother's good will. Therefore thy Son gave us this in commandment: that we should leave our offering[67] even at the altar, and hie° us apace° to our brother, and labour to be in peace with him, and then return again and offer up our reward.° Lo now, we follow that thy Son hath taught us, we endeavour° to perform that he hath done. If thou acknowledge the covenant and bargain[68] made of[69] thy Son (as we doubt not but thou doest), grant us, we beseech thee, that thing whereof we had full hope and trust by thy Son. Thus he bade us pray when he answered not a few times that we should obtain whatsoever we desired of thee in his name. He made us bold to pray to thee: vouchsafe thou by him to forgive those that call upon thee.

We [fi^v] acknowledge our own imbecility and feebleness, whereby we well perceive into how shameful and abominable offences we were like to fall into, except we were preserved by thy goodness from greater sins. And the same meekness thou leftest in us, as a remedy against the pride which we should have been in jeopardy to have fallen in daily: we offend and fall to the intent that every

---

[66] thieves] Luke 23. 34: 'Father, forgive them; for they do not know what they are doing'. Who are 'they'? A clumsy juxtaposition of details in Luke (32–34) might nudge a reader into referring Jesus's words to the two criminals crucified with him — but they are not *doing* anything, and E.'s 'parricidis' means specifically 'those killing one of their own kith or kin', i.e. the crucifiers. (E.'s *Paraphrase* also unequivocally follows the standard interpretation.) If 'thieves' is being used in the broader (*OED* 2) sense of 'evil-doer' it is curiously loose and misleading, and R. may have written 'the Jews' ('the iewes'): a common *NT* phrase expressing the tragic irony that Jesus was killed by his own people, and here a quite passable, non-technical, rendering of 'parricidis'.

[67] in remembrance of displeasure] i.e. 'still harbouring resentment'.

[68] offering] Matt. 5. 23–24.

[69] covenant and bargain] E.'s 'praescriptam conditionem' means the formula of the Lord's Prayer, the 'formam [...] praescriptam' ('form and order appointed') of line 646. For R. it is a 'covenant' because Jesus (next sentence) promises that prayers offered 'in his name' will be answered.

[70] of] 'by'.

day we might glorify thy gentleness. Grant, Father, that we may heartily forgive our brethren, that when we be in peace and unity amongst ourselves we may have thee always merciful unto us; and, if in anything we offend thee, amend us with thy fatherly correction — so° that thou utterly forsake us not, nor disinherit us, nor cast us into hell.

Once in baptism thou hast remitted us all our sins: but that was not enough for thy tender love towards us, but thou hast also showed a sure and ready remedy for the daily offences of thy children. For the which we thank thy great gentleness, who vouchsafest by thy Son and the Holy Ghost to endue us with so great benefits, to the everlasting glory of thy most holy name. Amen.

The sixth petition:

'And lead us not into temptation'

O good Father in heaven, albeit there is nothing that we greatly fear, having thee merciful unto us; and while mutual love and charity each with other maketh us thy children of more strength [f2^r] against every evil assault: yet — when we consider how weak and frail the nature of man is, and how ignorant also we be whom[70] thy goodness will judge and think worthy the continuance in thy love to the end of this life (in which as long as we are, a thousand manner of ways we be stirred to fall and ruin) — therefore we cannot be utterly sicker° and careless.°

All this life is round about beset with the Devil's snares.[71] He never ceaseth tempting us (who was not afraid with crafty subtleties to set upon thy Son Jesus). We call to mind how grievously the Fiend° assaulted thy servant Job. We remember how Saul was first thy elect and chosen servant, and within a while after cast out of thy sight. We cannot forget how David, whom thou calledst 'a man even after thine own appetite',° was drawn to that great villainy of sin that he mingled adultery with manslaughter. We consider how Solomon, whom in the beginning of his rule thou gavest wisdom above all men, was brought to that madness and folly that he did sacrifice to strange and utter° gods. We remember also what befell the chief and head of thine Apostles who, after that he had so valiantly professed that he would die with his Master, notwithstanding thrice forswore his Master.

These and such many others when we consider, we cannot but fear and abhor the jeopardy of temptation. And thy fatherly love would us always to be in this fear, because° we should not sluggishly and slothfully [f2^v] begin to trust in our own help, but defend and arm ourselves against every fault of temptation with sober temperance, watch,° and prayer — whereby we should neither provoke our

---

[71] whom] i.e. 'concerning whom'.
[72] Devil's snares] See Matt. 4. 1–11; Job 1. 12–22, 2. 1–9; I Sam. 10. 1, 15. 10–35 (Saul); I Sam. 13. 14, II Sam. 11 (David); I Kings 11. 4–8 (Solomon); Matt. 26. 33–35, 69–75 (Peter).

Enemy (remembering our own feebleness) nor be overthrown in the storm of temptation (trusting to thy aid, without which we are able to do right° nought). Thou sufferest° among° temptation to fall, either to prove° and make steadfast the sufferance and patience of thy children (as Job and Abraham[72] were tempted) or else by such scourges to correct and chasten our offences. But how often soever thou sufferest this, we pray thee thou wilt bring that same temptation to good and lucky° end, and give us strength equal to the mountenance° and weight of the evils that come upon us.

It is no little jeopardy whensoever we be threatened with loss of our goods, with banishment, rebukes,° imprisonment, with bands and bodily tormenting, and horrible and fearful death: but we are in no less peril at all° when prosperity too much laugheth on us than when we be overmuch feared° with trouble and adversity. They are an innumerable sort which fall on every side.[73] Some for fear of punishment do sacrifice to wicked devils; some, overthrown and astonied° with evils and vexations, do blaspheme thy most holy name: and again some, drowned with overmuch worldly wealth, set at nought and despise thy gifts of grace, and return again into their old and former filthiness (as the son[74] that the Scripture speaketh of who, after time he had [f3ʳ] spent and revelled° out all his father's substance by unthrifty° and ungracious rule,[75] was brought to that misery and wretchedness that he envied the swine their chaff).

We know well, good Father, that our Adversary hath no power over us at all but by thy sufferance;° wherefore we be content to be put to whatsoever jeopardy it pleaseth thee, so° it will like° thy gentleness to measure° our Enemy's assault and our strength. For so — though we be sometimes in the first meeting too weak — yet thy wisdom in the conclusion will turn it to our wealth.° So thy most dear and honourable Son was ever wont to overcome the Devil, thus the flesh, and thus the world: that when he seemed most to be oppressed he then most specially triumphed, and he fought for us, he overcame for us, and triumphed for us. Let us also overcome by his example, with thy help and by the Holy Ghost proceeding from both for ever. Amen.

---

[73] Abraham] Gen. 22. 1–12.
[74] every side] E. means 'either' — to the right and left, in good or bad fortune — but R. may mean 'on all sides'.
[75] the son] The 'prodigal' of Luke 15. 11–32, especially 15–16.
[76] unthrifty and ungracious rule] R.'s euphemism for E.'s 'scortis' ('prostitutes').

600 *The seventh petition*:

'But deliver us from the evil one'[76]

O almighty Father, it hath pleased thy mere° and liberal goodness (once when we were rid from sin) to deliver us by thy Son Jesus Christ out of the hands of our most foul and unclean father the Devil, and to elect and take us into the honour 605 both of thy name and thine inheritance: but yet of this condition, that all the while we live here in earth we should be in continual battle with our Enemy, [f3ᵛ] who leaveth no ways unassayed whereby he might draw and pluck us again into his power and authority.

We quake and tremble in heart as oftentimes as we remember how shameful a 610 father we had when we were thrall° and bond° to sin, and to how wretched and unhappy inheritance we were appointed, and how currish° and ungentle a master we served. And we know well enough his obstinate and froward° malice and evil will, who always layeth wait° and lieth ready bent to our destruction — not only with violence and strong hand, but also with trains° and subtle wiles. He never 615 sleepeth nor resteth, but always runneth up and down hither and thither like a ravenous lion,[77] lying in wait, seeking and hunting about whom he may devour.

Verily 'father' he is far unlike thee, for thou art naturally good and gentle, thou carriest home again to the flock the wandering and straying sheep,[78] thou curest and makest whole the sick and scabby[79] sheep, and relievest° the dead:[80] yea, and 620 thine enemies also and blasphemers of thy holy name thou preventest° with thy love and callest most graciously to everlasting health.° But he, of an unreasonable and insatiable hatred towards us (who never did him displeasure), laboureth and goeth about nothing else than to bring with him as many as he can into destruction. It is a sign and token of an exceeding malice, one (for nought and 625 without any commodity° of his own) to endeavour to destroy him of whom he was never [f4ʳ] wronged: but this,[81] even with his own hurt, waiteth° those hurt and damage[82] whom thou hast taken aside under thy protection.

Thou madest him not such, but he fell into this great malice after time he began to stand in his own conceit[83] and refused to be subject and obedient to thy majesty.

---

[77] the evil one] L. 'a malo', like the underlying Gk, can be read as either neuter or masculine. In his notes on the *NT* (and in what follows here) E. reads it personally.
[78] ravenous lion] See 1 Peter 5. 8.
[79] sheep] L. singular. See Matt. 18. 12.
[80] scabby] 1526 'scabbe', perhaps meant for 'scabbed' (*1531*).
[81] dead] sc. (singular) 'sheep'.
[82] this] i.e. the Devil.
[83] waiteth those hurt and damage] i.e. 'threatens hurt and damage to them'; L. 'imminet in malum eorum': 'those' is probably dative, though conceivably a condensed genitive (those's). For this obsolete sense of 'wait' see *OED* [verb] 2.
[84] stand in his own conceit] i.e. 'think highly of himself'.

630 Wherefore he, being pricked° all with envy, by crafty besieging enticed to destruction our first progenitors, envying them the joys of paradise, forasmuch as he had deprived himself of the gladness and mirth of heaven. But now he is of far greater envy because thou carriest them out of paradise into heaven[84] and (whereas they were afore appointed to death and damnation) thou (by reason of
635 the faithful trust which they have put in thy Son Jesus) callest them to everlasting bliss — and also that thou turnest his own malice into the increase of thy glory and our health.

Wherefore, though not without a cause he is of many to be feared, yet thy goodness doth comfort us, which is able to do more to our health and salvation
640 than all his malice to our destruction. We acknowledge our own imbecility° and feebleness, but yet we fear not our Enemy's assault, whether we live or die, all the while[85] we deserve to have thee our protector and defender. We fear no destruction of[86] that evil and wicked Devil all the while it is our chance to stick to him that is so good.

645 These desires and petitions of thy children, O immortal Father, if they be good and after° the form and order appointed of thy Son Jesus, then we [f4^v] nothing mistrust but that thou wilt perform that which we desire of thee. Amen.

Thus endeth the exposition of the *Pater Noster*.

---

[85] out of paradise into heaven] R. appears to suppress the interval, as if putting aside purgatory (but not predestination).
[86] all the while] i.e. 'provided that'.
[87] of] 'from'.

An Exhortation to the Diligent Study of Scripture

[Preface to the New Testament]

Translated by William Roy (1529)

Edited by Alex Davis

Introduction

The text translated here is the *Paraclesis*, the preface to Erasmus's 1516 edition of the New Testament. The title is Greek, meaning a summons or exhortation, and the work to which the *Paraclesis* summons its readers is that of reading the Bible. That may sound simple enough, but the *Paraclesis* is an account of simple things left undone. Erasmus derides an ecclesiastical establishment which he characterises as essentially perverse. For the devotees of medieval philosophers such as Aquinas and Duns Scotus, academic prestige resides not in biblical study but in the mastery of logical categories, which Erasmus disparages as a 'tedious perplexity of words, of relations, quiddities, and formalities' (272–73). Sixteenth-century Christendom has abandoned Christian Scripture for quibbling, and Erasmus argues that scholastically-trained readers cannot but secretly look down on the 'humble and rude learning' (186) of a text that is accessible to all.

The *Paraclesis* is a manifesto for a return to origins. 'Why', it asks, 'had we liefer [rather] learn the wisdom of Christ's doctrine out of men's books than of Christ himself?' (291–92) The New Testament offers immediate access to Christ's thinking.[1] It is simple, direct, compelling. Anybody can read the Bible. Everybody should. Erasmus's most audacious claim, and the one that underpins his sense of the immediacy of Scripture, is that the gospels offer not just a record of Christ's thought but his real presence, which is more efficacious even than his physical presence.[2] 'In this his testament', we read, 'he speaketh, breatheth, and liveth among us in a manner more effectually than when his body was presently conversant in this world' (295–97).

Learned Christians principally value 'the witty traditions of Aristotle and Averroes' (189–90). Meanwhile, the unlearned have little access to Scripture at all. Hence the *Paraclesis*'s famous argument for translation of the Bible, which stands at the heart of its reception in early sixteenth-century England:

> I would to God the ploughman would sing a text of the Scripture at his ploughbeam; and that the weaver at his loom with this would drive away the tediousness of time; I would the wayfaring man with this pastime would expel the weariness of his journey; and to be short I would that all the communication of the Christian should be of the Scripture, for in a manner such are we ourselves as our daily tales are. (133–38)

---

[1] Readers may be disconcerted by Erasmus's tendency to present Christ as an author, effacing the intermediary activity of the gospel writers.

[2] On this claim, see Brian Cummings, *The Literary Culture of the Reformation: Grammar and Grace* (Oxford: Oxford University Press, 2002), p. 106, and James Kearney, *The Incarnate Text: Imagining the Book in Renaissance England* (Philadelphia: University of Pennsylvania Press, 2009), p. 56.

Erasmus offers an eloquent plea for everyday life transfigured by the reading of Scripture made available in the vernacular.[3] There is an irony here, since he does so in Latin, the language of the learned European elites.[4] Nonetheless, the impact of this short passage cannot be underestimated. John Foxe records an anecdote from William Tyndale's early years, when he was serving as tutor in a Gloucestershire household. In disputation with a 'learned man' Tyndale exclaimed: 'I defy the Pope and all his laws […] if God spare my life ere many years, I will cause a boy that driveth the plough, shall know more of the scripture than thou dost.'[5] The echo of Erasmus's description of the ploughman singing is unmistakeable, and in 1528 Tyndale's *Obedience of a Christian Man* would make the debt explicit by invoking '*Paraclesis* Erasmi' as an authority on why laypeople should read Scripture.[6]

Erasmus writes: 'I would to God the ploughman would sing a text of the Scripture at his ploughbeam.' Tyndale says: 'I will cause a boy that driveth the plough, shall know more of the scripture then thou doest.' That shift, from 'I would' (*utinam*) to 'I will',[7] combined with Tyndale's implacable hostility to the ecclesiastical establishment of his day, marks the passage of Erasmus's message beyond the bounds of what he himself found acceptable.[8] The *Paraclesis* certainly aims at reform. The criticisms it offers of the Catholic Church find their echo in overtly satirical texts such as *The Praise of Folly*. Still: although it would be an unkind judgement, it would not be a completely unfair one to say that while Erasmus was willing to argue in the *Paraclesis* that a godly commoner is as true a divine as any priest, he had not fully anticipated all the implications of that thought and did not welcome them when they became clear to him. Elsewhere he would qualify his enthusiasm for lay knowledge of the Bible.[9] Nonetheless, real change of the sort he produced in Tyndale is fundamental to Erasmus's argument. The *Paraclesis* imagines Europe rejuvenated through a return to Scripture: war fading away, avarice quashed, unanimity restored through 'the pure conversation

---

[3] The striking phrase 'daily tales' translates 'cotidianae … confabulationes' (*ASD* v-7, line 97), using 'tale' in the sense of 'discourse, conversation, talk' (*OED* 1a).

[4] See the discussion of Bible translation in Neil Rhodes, *Common: The Development of Literary Culture in Sixteenth-Century England* (Oxford: Oxford University Press, 2018), pp. 29–36.

[5] Quoted in David Daniell, *William Tyndale: A Biography* (New Haven and London: Yale University Press, 1994), p. 79.

[6] *The Obedience of a Christian Man*, ed. by David Daniell (London: Penguin, 2000), p. 25.

[7] For Erasmus's Latin text, see *ASD* v-7, line 94.

[8] The two phrases are contrasted in Stephen Greenblatt, *Renaissance Self-Fashioning From More to Shakespeare* (Chicago and London: University of Chicago Press, 1980), p. 106.

[9] The address 'To The Pious Reader' attached to the *Paraphrase* of Matthew, composed in 1522, is obliged to concede that 'among the books of the Old Testament perhaps there are some you would with good reason keep out of the hands of the uneducated' — although it doesn't propose to ban them (*CWE* 45. 10–11).

of our life' (197). Reading, for Erasmus, is communication, and communication is a spur to effective action. It is characteristic that he should claim that in the gospels Christ should be seen to have 'both taught *and also done*' (262, my italics). Through the Bible, Christ 'doth chiefly perform that thing which he promised unto us when he said that he would continue with us unto the end of the world' (294–95). Scripture is the vehicle that realises the promises made in Scripture. It is the original self-fulfilling prophecy. More generally, eloquent language is marked by what the English *Paraclesis* calls 'efficacity'; it seeks its realisation or 'fulfilment'. As a discussion of the potentialities of biblical rhetoric, the *Paraclesis* is arguing for Scripture's (and for its own) appropriability. But who sets a limit to legitimate appropriation? Erasmus's celebration of persuasive speech cannot be kept completely distinct from his account of the volatile, Protean capacities of language offered in educational treatises such as the *De copia*.

The English *Paraclesis* is a case study in this textual unpredictability. It was printed anonymously in 1529 with the title *An Exhortation to the Diligent Study of Scripture*. This volume identified itself as having being been produced in Marburg by Hans Luft, a real Lutheran printer. In fact, it was printed in Antwerp, probably by Johannes Hoochstraten.[10] The translation is usually ascribed to William Roy, following a suggestion by Thomas More in his polemic *The Confutation of Tyndale's Answer*.[11] Roy was an apostate friar who had acted as William Tyndale's assistant in preparing the first English New Testament. Tyndale subsequently described Roy as an untrustworthy character, 'somewhat crafty when he cometh unto new acquaintance and before he be thoroughly known [...] able not only to make fools stark mad, but also deceive the wisest'.[12] So this was a contraband publication with a dubious author. It was also one that positioned the Erasmian account of scriptural reading as the precursor to a programme of radical reform. The *Exhortation* deploys the *Paraclesis* as a preface not to a Greek New Testament but to a translation, entitled *An Exposition*, of Martin Luther's commentary on 1 Corinthians 7 — a blistering attack on the practice of clerical celibacy. In 1529, this combination was deliberately provocative. Erasmus had been in a state of open breach with Luther since the publication of the former's *De libero arbitrio* in 1524. In England, meanwhile, the sale and possession of Lutheran materials were banned, copies of Tyndale's New Testament had been burned, and Erasmus

---

[10] See Anthea Hume, 'English Protestant Books Printed Abroad, 1525–1535: An Annotated Bibliography', in Thomas More, *The Confutation of Tyndale's Answer*, CWM 8. 1066, 1072–73. John N. King and Mark Rankin identify the printer as Merten de Kayser. See 'Print, Patronage, and the Reception of Continental Reform: 1521–1603', *The Yearbook of English Studies*, 38 (2008), 49–67 (p. 54).

[11] In the *Confutation*, More says the volume 'hath no name of the maker, but some wene it were friar Roy'. See *CWM* 8. 8.

[12] See Daniell, *William Tyndale*, p. 109.

had been enlisted as a key figure in the official campaign against evangelical thought since as early as 1523.[13] In 1528, Erasmus's friend Thomas More was commissioned by Cuthbert Tunstall, Bishop of London, to read heretical texts circulating in the vernacular and prepare a response to them.[14] More's *Confutation* was a part of this counter-offensive. It mentions Roy and the *Exhortation*, but is silent about the Erasmian contribution to the same volume. *Erasmus posuit oua; Luther exclusit pullos*: true to Tyndale's sense of his talent for mischief, William Roy had realised Erasmus's thoughts about the transformative potentialities of Scripture in the dismaying form of a fully Lutheran *Paraclesis*, egg and hatchling, proudly set side by side.[15]

Roy's translation is substantially faithful to Erasmus's Latin, although it often expands the original through epithets, doublets, and synonyms. 'Ornate' (*picturatum*) rhetoric becomes 'painted and coloured' (10); the gentiles (*Ethnicos*) acquire the description 'crafty and unfaithful' (3).[16] At several points its phrasing echoes that of Tyndale's Bible. Stylistically, it mixes exclamations (the repeated 'yea'); arrays of rhetorical questions; expansive, amplificatory lists; and numerous parenthetical constructions. It can be quite hard to follow, and there is also its peculiar, abrupt ending. But it is capable of marshalling its energies to produce moments of real concision and force, as with the attack on those who act 'as though the pith and substance of the Christian religion consisted chiefly in this: that it be not known' (124). Even at several centuries' distance from the historical moment it sought to transform, the eloquence of Erasmus's *Paraclesis* is not completely extinguished.

---

[13] See Richard Rex, 'The English Campaign against Luther in the 1520s', *Transactions of the Royal Historical Society*, 39 (1989), 85–106. I am following Alex Ryrie in his preference for 'evangelical' as a designator of early English Protestant thought. See 'The Strange Death of Lutheran England', *Journal of Ecclesiastical History*, 53 (2002), 64–92.

[14] See *CWM* 8. 1137–1206.

[15] For the proverbial claim that 'Erasmus laid the egg that Luther hatched', see the Introduction to this volume, p. 5. Subsequent editions of the *Exhortation* demonstrate a counter-movement, confirming the text's migratory tendencies. We find it paired with a translation of the more cautious address 'To the Pious Reader', or deployed as part of the prefatory materials of some early English New Testaments. The 1548 edition possibly complements the English *Paraphrases*, published under royal licence in the same year. What had once been illicit was now a semi-official publication.

[16] See *William Roye's An exhortation to the diligent studye of scripture and An exposition in to the seventh chaptre of the pistle to the Corinthians*, ed. by Douglas H. Parker (Toronto: University of Toronto Press, 2000), pp. 28–36.

Further Reading

CUMMINGS, BRIAN, *The Literary Culture of the Reformation: Grammar and Grace* (Oxford: Oxford University Press, 2002)
KEARNEY, JAMES, T*he Incarnate Text: Imagining the Book in Renaissance England* (Philadelphia: University of Pennsylvania Press, 2009)
RHODES, NEIL, *Common: The Development of Literary Culture in Sixteenth-Century England* (Oxford: Oxford University Press, 2018)

AN EXHORTATION TO THE DILIGENT STUDY OF SCRIPTURE, MADE BY ERASMUS ROTERODAMUS AND TRANSLATED INTO ENGLISH[1]

[*2ʳ] Lactantius Firmianus,[2] Christian reader — whose eloquence Saint Jerome doth greatly advance — endeavouring himself to defend and maintain the Christian faith and religion against the crafty and unfaithful gentiles, did wish and desire with fervent affection to attain the eloquence next unto Tully's,[3] counting it a high presumption (as I think) if he should have desired equal. Howbeit,° I truly — if that wishes could anything avail, at the least while I exhort and entice all mortal men unto the most holy and wholesome study of Christian wisdom and pure philosophy — would heartily desire another manner of eloquence to be given unto me than ever Cicero had;[4] although not so gloriously painted and coloured as his was, yet truly of more power and efficacity. Yea, such a vehement persuasion and strength of eloquence would I desire as the fables of old poets have noted in Mercurius, whom they feigned (as it had been with a rod of enchantment and a melodious harp) to cast men into a sudden and oblivious sleep and again to raise them at his own pleasure,[5] depressing some that are affected with his heavenly harmony into the depth of Pluto's impery,° and bringing them again out of all vexations; [*2ᵛ] other° such as they ascribed to Amphion and Orpheus, for they imagine that the one with his harmonious harp did move the stiff stones and that the other made to follow him the insensible trees;[6] other° such as the Frenchmen apply to Hercules Ogmius,[7] feigning that he

---

[1] An Exhortation ... English] Erasmus's preface to his New Testament was called the *Paraclesis*, meaning a summons or exhortation. 'Roterodamus' identifies Erasmus as the product 'of Rotterdam', his birthplace.

[2] Lactantius Firmianus] Lucius Caelius Firmianus Lactantius (c. 250–c. 325), author of the *Institutiones Divinae*, a defence of Christian theology against its pagan critics. Saint Jerome (c. 347–420) said that his writing was 'like a stream of Ciceronian eloquence'. See Lactantius, *Divine Institutes*, p. 4.

[3] Tully] Marcus Tullius Cicero (106–43 BC), Roman statesman and orator.

[4] Howbeit, I truly ... Cicero had] Erasmus wishes for a different ('another') style of eloquence from the Ciceronian as he attempts his own defence of Scripture.

[5] Mercurius] Mercury created the lyre using a tortoiseshell, and charmed Argus to sleep using his wand.

[6] Amphion and Orpheus] Legendary musicians. Amphion raised the walls of Thebes with his lyre, while Orpheus charmed the trees.

[7] Hercules Ogmius] Lucian's *Heracles*, which Erasmus translated into Latin, says that the Celts depict the god drawing behind him a crowd of men tethered at the ears by chains threaded through Hercules's tongue. It is explained that the god represents eloquence. See Lucian, *Heracles* 1.

leadeth about all men with his godly[8] eloquence as it were with certain small chains which are tied unto his tongue and run through every man's ears; other° such as the doting old age did attribute unto Marsyas;[9] or else truly (because we will not be long in repeating fables) such as Alcibiades hath granted unto Socrates, and the old comedy unto Pericles,[10] which may not only entice and delight the ears with a short and corruptible delectation or pleasure but also may leave perpetual pricks and instigations in the minds of the hearers which may ravish and transform them and leave them in another mind than they were before. The noble musician Timotheus (as we read) with his proportioned harmony was wont to inflame Alexander the great conqueror with a fervent desire to war,[11] and there have been in times past that have counted nothing of more power and efficacy than the enchantments which the Greeks call epodes.[12] Now if there be any such kind of enchantment or charm; if there be any strength [*3ʳ] in music and harmony; if there be any pleasant persuasion which hath power to allect° man's mind in to hear sentence, the same at this season would I gladly obtain to the intent that I might persuade unto all men that thing which is most wholesome and most profitable unto them, although it were better, yea and more convenient, to desire that Christ himself (whose cause I entreat) would so temper the strings of our instrument that this song may prosperously entice and move the minds of all men. For this purpose we need but little the painted arguments and coloured conclusions of the rhetoricians, for nothing so surely can garnish and perform that that we desire as the truth itself, which when it is most plain and simple is of most vehement efficacy in persuading. Neither do I count it best at this time to revocate° and call to memory the sorrowful complaint (although it be not new, yet alas it is too true and I think it could never be more justly verified then at this present time) that sith° with such great diligence all men's inventions are studied and commended yet only this immortal fountain of Christ's pure philosophy is despised and mocked of so many, yea and chiefly of them which profess to be the heads and examples of the Christian. Few there are that seek these wholesome [*3ᵛ] springs of health, and yet they that seek them do so unfruitfully look upon

---

[8] godly] The variant, present in many early editions of the *Exhortation*, is 'goodly'.

[9] Marsyas] The satyr Marsyas challenged Apollo to a musical contest, lost, and was punished by being flayed alive.

[10] Alcibiades ... Pericles] In Plato's *Symposium* 215, Alcibiades says Socrates resembles Marsyas; Cicero's *Brutus* 38 reports the comic dramatist Eupolis saying that the goddess Persuasion sat on the lips of Pericles.

[11] Timotheus] Timotheus was a famous player of the aulos, an ancient wind instrument, who performed at the courts of Philip of Macedon and Alexander the Great. His musical manipulation of the latter is the subject of Handel's choral work *Alexander's Feast*.

[12] epodes] The epode was the third and final section of a traditional choral ode. In his *Adages*, Erasmus associates epodic form with the figure of Stesichorus, the early Greek lyric poet, and with choral composition (II. ix. 94, *CWE* 34. 126).

them, adding their own glosses and opinions, that they seem rather to trouble and defile these springs of life than to drink of them sweetly that they might have in themself floods of living water running into everlasting life, which both should be to the glory of God and profit of the Christian.[13]

We see that in all other sciences which by man's policy have been invented there is no mystery so dark and secret but that the quickness of our wit hath attained it. There is nothing so hard but that diligent labour hath subdued it unto him. How chanceth it then that we embrace not with faithful hearts (as it is convenient) this pure philosophy, sith° we profess the holy name of Christ? Plato's adherents, Pythagoras's scholars, the Academics, Stoics, Epicures, the fautors° of Aristotle and disciples of Diogenes, know groundly° yea and by heart the traditions of their own sect and fight most fiercely for them, ready rather to die than to forsake their patron and author.[14] And why do not we much more give our minds and studies unto our master and prince Christ? Who would not count it a foul thing, yea and a great rebuke to him that professeth Aristotle's philosophy, if he be ignorant what his master [*4ʳ] judgeth concerning the causes of the thunder, of the rainbow, of the earthquakes and of such other natural causes, which though they were known or unknown make not them that labour to know them happy nor unhappy? And should we which are so many ways consecrated and with so many sacraments bound unto Christ think it no shame a whit° to be ignorant in his Scripture and doctrine which give us most sure comfort and felicity, and which are the anchor of the soul both sure and stable, preserving us from perishing in all tempests of temptation? Howbeit:° for what intent use we this comparison, sith it is extreme madness to compare Christ with Zeno and Aristotle, and his heavenly doctrine with their trifling traditions?[15]

Let them feign and imagine unto the captains of their sect as much as they may, yea as much as they will. Yet truly only this master and teacher came from heaven; which alone could teach sure things, being the everlasting wisdom of the father; which alone hath taught wholesome things, being the foundation of all men's health; which alone hath fulfilled to the uttermost point all that he hath taught; and which alone may perform whatsoever he hath promised. If anything had been

---

[13] fountain ... springs] Fluvial imagery appears throughout the English text in a series of metaphors that reference Jesus's encounter with the Samaritan woman described in John 4. 4–42. These images are often an addition to Erasmus's original. See *An exhortation*, ed. by Parker, pp. 32–33.

[14] Plato (*c.* 429–347 BC); Pythagoras (b. mid-sixth century BC); Aristotle (384–322 BC); and Diogenes (*c.* 412/403–*c.* 324/321 BC) were ancient thinkers. Stoicism and Epicureanism are schools of ancient philosophy. Plato's academy in Athens was established as a space for philosophical disputation.

[15] Zeno] Zeno of Elea, Greek philosopher active in the early fifth century BC, famous for his paradoxes of motion.

brought [*4ᵛ] from the Chaldees¹⁶ or the Egyptians we would the more greedily desire to know it because it came far and from a strange country (yea it is the more dear and precious that cometh from afar);¹⁷ and we are oftentimes so grievously vexed about the dream and fantasy of a foolish fellow (not only with small profit but also with great loss of time) that it is shame to rehearse it. I wonder that this desire doth not likewise tickle and entice the Christian hearts which know well enough (as the thing is indeed) that this wholesome doctrine came not from Egypt or Syria but from the very heaven and seat of God. Why do we not think with ourselves on this manner: it must needs be a new and marvellous kind of learning, sith that God himself which was immortal became a natural man and mortal, descending from the right hand of his father into this wretched world to teach it unto us? It must needs be a high and excellent thing and no trifle which that heavenly and marvellous master came to teach openly. Why do we not go about to know, search and try out with a godly curiosity this fruitful philosophy? — sith° that this kind of wisdom, being so profound and inscrutable that utterly it damneth and confoundeth as foolish all the wisdom of this world,¹⁸ may be gathered out of so small books as [*5ʳ] out of most pure springs, and that with much less labour than the doctrine of Aristotle out of so many brawling and contentious books, or of such infinite commentaries which do so much dissent, besides the incomparable fruit which needeth not here to be spoken of.¹⁹ Neither is it needful that thou be clogged with so many irksome and babbling sciences. The means to this philosophy are easy and at hand. Do only thy diligence to bring a godly and ready mind, chiefly endued with plain and pure faith. Be only desirous to be instruct° and confirmable° to this meek doctrine and thou hast much profited. Thy master and instructor (that is the spirit of God) will not from thee be absent, which is never more gladly present with any than with simple and plain hearts. Men's doctrines and traditions (besides the promising of false felicity) do confound many men's wits and make them clean to despair because they are so dark, crafty and contentious. But this delectable° doctrine doth apply herself equally of all men, submitting herself unto us while we are children, tempering her tune after our capacity, feeding us with milk,²⁰

---

¹⁶ Chaldees] The Chaldeans were a people occupying south-eastern Mesopotamia from the tenth to the sixth centuries BC.
¹⁷ yea it is the more dear … afar] Compare Aristotle's *Rhetoric*, 1404b: 'men admire what is remote'.
¹⁸ the wisdom of this world] Compare 1 Corinth. 1. 20: 'Has God not made foolish the wisdom of the world?'
¹⁹ Why do we not … spoken of] 'Why do we not sample this philosophy, since its profound wisdom may be acquired from small books as if from pure springs, and with much less labour than the doctrines of Aristotle from books or commentaries — and that is to say nothing of the incomparable benefits it brings [i.e. as well as ease of access].'
²⁰ while we are children … milk] Compare 1 Corinth. 3. 1–2, which addresses Paul's audience as 'infants in Christ': 'I fed you with milk, not solid food, for you were not ready for solid food.'

forbearing, nourishing, suffering and doing all things until we may increase and wax greater in Christ; and contrariwise it is not so low and depressed unto the weak [*5ᵛ] but it is as high and marvellous to the perfect. Yea, the more thou wadest in the treasures of this science, the farther thou art from attaining her majesty. To the children she is low and plain, and to greater she seemeth above all capacity. She refuseth no age, no kind, no fortune, no state and condition.

In so much that the sun is not more common and indifferent to all men then this doctrine of Christ, she forbiddeth no man at all except he abstain willingly, envying his own profit. And truly I do greatly dissent from those men which would not that the Scripture of Christ should be translated into all tongues that it might be read diligently of the private and secular men and women, other° as though Christ had taught such dark and insensible things that they could scant be understood of a few divines, or else as though the pith and substance of the Christian religion consisted chiefly in this: that it be not known. Peradventure° it were most expedient that the councils of kings should be kept secret, but Christ would that his councils and mysteries should be spread abroad as much as is possible.²¹ I would desire that all women should read the Gospel and Paul's epistles, and I would to God they were translated into the [*6ʳ] tongues of all men so that they might not only be read and known of the Scots and Irishmen but also of the Turks and Saracens.²² Truly it is one degree to good living, yea the first (I had almost said the chief) to have a little sight in the Scripture, though it be but a gross knowledge and not yet consummate. Be it in case° that some would laugh at it, yea and that some should err and be deceived, I would to God the ploughman would sing a text of the Scripture at his ploughbeam; and that the weaver at his loom with this would drive away the tediousness of time; I would the wayfaring man with this pastime would expel the weariness of his journey; and to be short I would that all the communication of the Christian should be of the Scripture, for in a manner such are we ourselves as our daily tales are. Let every man prosper and attain that he may and declare effectuously° his mind unto his neighbour. Let not him that cometh behind envy the foremost. Let also the foremost allect° him that followeth, ever exhorting him not despair. Why do we apply only to certain the profession which is indifferent° and common to all men? Neither truly is it meet° (sith that baptism is equally common unto all Christian men, wherein [*6ᵛ] consisteth the first profession of the Christian religion; sith other sacraments are not private; and to conclude sith the reward of immortality pertaineth indifferently unto all men) that only the doctrine should be banished from the secular and possessed only of a few whom the commonalty° call divines or

---

²¹ Christ would ... possible] See for example Luke 24. 47: 'repentance and forgiveness of sin is to be proclaimed in his name to all nations'; and Matt. 28. 19: 'Go therefore and make disciples of all nations'.
²² Turks and Saracens] Conflict with the Ottoman empire forms a backdrop to much of Erasmus's writing, with Muslims figuring both as the ultimate outsiders and (as here) as potential converts. See *Bellum*, Introduction, n. 15.

religious persons. And yet I would that these (although they be but a small company in comparison to the whole number which bear the name of Christ and are called Christian) I would, I say, desire with all my heart that they were indeed such as they are called, for I am afraid that a man may find some among the divines which are far unworthy their name and title, that is to say, which speak worldly things and not godly. Yea, and among the religious which profess the poverty of Christ and to despise the world thou shalt find more worldly pleasure and vanity than in all the world besides. Him do I count a true divine which not with crafty and subtle reasons but that in heart, countenance, eyes, and life doth teach to despise riches; and that a Christian ought not to put confidence in the succour and help of this world, but only whole to hang on heaven; not to avenge injury; to pray for them that say evil by us; to do good against evil; that all good men [*7ʳ] should be loved and nourished indifferently as the members of one body;²³ that evil men if they cannot be reformed and brought into a good order ought to be suffered; that they which are despoiled of their goods and put from their possessions and mourn in this world are very blessed and not to be lamented; that death is to be desired of the Christian sith it is nothing else but a going to immortality. If any man being inspired with the holy ghost do preach and teach these and such other things; if any man exhort, entice, and bolden his neighbour unto these things, he is a very and true divine though he be a weaver, yea though he dig and delve. But he that accomplisheth and fulfilleth these things in his life and manners, he verily is a great doctor. Peradventure° another which is not Christian shall more subtly dispute by what manner the angels understand. Howbeit,° to persuade and exhort that we may here live pure and immaculate from all vices and iniquities, and to lead an angel's life: that is the office and duty of a Christian and divine. If any man would object and say that these are gross and unsavoury things, to him would I none otherwise answer but that Christ chiefly hath taught these things and that the apostles to these have us exhorted. [*7ᵛ] This learning and doctrine be it never so unsavoury hath brought us forth so many good Christians and so thick swarms of faithful martyrs. This unlearned (as they call it) philosophy hath subdued under her laws the most noble princes, so many kingdoms, so many nations — which thing no king's power nother° learning of the philosophers was ever able to bring to pass. Neither will I resist them but that they may dispute their profound and subtle questions (if it please them) among the more perfect, howbeit the rude multitude of the Christian may be comforted, because truly the apostles did never teach such things.²⁴ Whether they knew them or no I would other men should judge.

²³ one body] See 1 Cor 12. 12: 'For just as the body is one and has many members, and the members of the body, though many, are one body, so it is with Christ.'
²⁴ Neither will I ... such things] Neither do I object to the philosophers' disputations; however, the unlearned mass of Christians should take comfort from the fact that the apostles never discussed them. The reference to the wisdom of the 'more perfect' is to 1 Corinth. 2. 6.

But truly if that the princes for their part would remember themselves and go about to fulfil with pureness of living this humble and rude learning (as they call it); if the preachers in their sermons would advance this doctrine, exhorting all men unto it and not to their own fantasies and imaginations; if schoolmasters would instruct their children rather with this simple science than with the witty° traditions of Aristotle and Averroes,[25] then should the Christianity[26] be more at quietness and not be disturbed with such perpetual storms of dissention and war. Then should this [*8ʳ] unreasonable desire of avarice, which appeteth° riches insatiably whether it be right or wrong, be some deal° assuaged and cease of his rage. Then should these contentious pleatings° which now in all things admix themselves have an end, for no man would resist° evil,[27] and to be short then should we not differ only in title and certain ceremonies from the heathen and unfaithful, but rather in the pure conversation of our life. And no doubt in these three degrees of men — that is to say, in princes and officers which are in their stead; in bishops and other priests which are their vicars; and in them that bring up the tender youth which are formed and reformed even as their master enticeth them — doth chiefly consist the whole power either to increase the Christian religion or else to restore it again which hath long been in decay. Now if these would a while seclude their own private business and lift up their hearts with a pure intent unto Christ, seeking only his glory and the profit of their neighbour, we should see verily within few years a true and godly kind of Christian spring up in every place, which would not only in ceremonies, disputations,[28] and titles profess the name of Christ, but in their very heart and true conversation of living. By this armour[29] should we [*8ᵛ] much sooner prevail against the unfaithful and enemies of Christ than with strength, violence, and threatenings. Let us join together all armies, powers, and might of sword; yet is there nothing stronger than the truth. We cannot call any man a Platonist unless he have read the works of Plato, yet call we them Christian, yea and divines, which never have read the Scripture of Christ. Christ sayeth: he that loveth me doth keep my sayings.[30] This is the knowledge and mark which he hath prescribed. Therefore if we be true Christian men in our hearts; if we believe unfeignedly that he was sent down from

---

[25] Averroes] Averroes (1126-1198), the Latinised name of the philosopher Ibn Rushd.
[26] the Christianity] Christendom.
[27] no man would resist evil] No man would retaliate against injuries. Compare Matt. 5. 39: 'But I say to you, Do not resist an evildoer. But if anyone strikes you on the right cheek, turn the other also.'
[28] disputations] dispitions 1529 (see *OED* s.v. 'disputisoun' (n)).
[29] this armour] See Ephes. 6. 11: 'Put on the whole armour of God, so that you may be able to stand against the wiles of the devil.'
[30] Christ sayeth … sayings] Compare Tyndale's rendering of John 14. 23-4: 'if a man love me and will keep my sayings, my father also will love him […] He that loveth me not, keepeth not my sayings.'

heaven to teach us such things as the wisdom of the philosophers could never attain; if faithfully we trust or look for such things of him as no worldly prince (be he never so rich) can give unto us, why have we anything in more reverence and authority than his Scripture, word, and promise, which he left here among us to be our consolation? Why recount° we anything of gravity or wisdom which dissenteth from his doctrine? Why in this heavenly and mystical learning do we counter and descant,[31] running more at riot than the common and profane interpreters in the civil law or books of physic? Winding° ourselves in it as in a trifling game or matter of small substance, commenting, [A1ʳ] tossing, and wresting it even as it cometh to our tongue's end?[32] We apply and draw this heavenly and unspotted doctrine unto our life, and measure it after our vain conversation according unto the manner of the Lesbes, which bend their rule to the fashion of their stone or timber and cut not their stone and timber to the rule.[33] And because we will not be seen ignorant in anything, but rather that we have read and know much, we do — I dare not say corrupt these fruitful springs — but that no man can deny we appropriate unto a few men that thing which Christ would have most common.[34] And this kind of philosophy doth rather consist in the affects of the mind than in subtle reasons. It is a life rather than a disputation. It is an inspiration rather than a science, and rather a new transformation than a reasoning. It is a seldom thing to be a well-learned man, but it is lawful for every man to be a true Christian. It is lawful for every man to live a godly life. Yea, and I dare be bold to say it is lawful for every man to be a pure divine. Now doth every man's mind incline unto that which is wholesome and expedient for his nature — and what other thing is this doctrine of Christ which he calleth the new regeneration but a restoring or repairing of our nature which in his first creation was good?[35] A man [A1ᵛ] may find very many things in

---

[31] counter and descant] Counterpoint and descant describe musical structures in which one melody supplements another. We pointlessly 'counter and descant' on what should need no elaboration. Compare the accusation made in Tyndale's *Obedience of a Christian Man* (p. 160): 'twenty doctors expound one text twenty ways, as children make descant upon plain song'.

[32] to our tongue's end] Words at the tongue's end are readily spoken. Erasmus's Folly in Thomas Chaloner's translation says that 'it hath ever best liked me to speak straight whatsoever lay on my tongue's end' (*Folly*, line 161).

[33] the manner of the Lesbes] The architects of Lesbos used a flexible lead ruler. Erasmus's *Adages* glosses the phrase 'by the Lesbian rule' as follows: 'This is said when things are done the wrong way round, when theory is accommodated to fact and not fact to theory, when law is suited to conduct, not conduct corrected by law' (I. v. 93, *CWE* 31. 465).

[34] And because ... most common] Because we wish to be thought learned and not ignorant, Christ's teaching is if not corrupted then at least appropriated for the use of the few, when it should be common to all.

[35] the new regeneration] Compare Tyndale's rendering of John 3. 3: 'Verily verily I say unto thee: except a man be born anew, he cannot see the kingdom of God.'

the gentiles' books which are agreeable unto this doctrine, although no man hath showed it so absolutely neither yet with such efficacity as Christ himself. For there was never such a rude and gross sect of philosophy which did teach that man's felicity rested on money; there was none so shameless to affirm that the chief point and ground of goodness consisted in this worldly honour and pleasures. The Stoics did knowledge° that no man might worthily be called wise except he were a good and virtuous liver, neither that anything was verily good and honest but only virtue, and that nothing was evil and to be abhorred but only vice and sin. Socrates (as Plato maketh mention) did teach by many reasons that injury ought not to be avenged with injury. He taught also that sith° the soul is immortal they are not to be mourned for which depart hence if they have lived well, because they are gone in to a more prosperous life. Finally he taught and exhorted all men to subdue the affections of their bodies and to apply their souls to the contemplation of those things which truly are immortal, although they be not seen with these bodily eyes.[36] Aristotle writeth in his *Politics* that there can nothing be so sweet and delicious to man but that at some time it doth displease him, only [A2ʳ] virtue except.[37] The Epicure granteth that there can be nothing delectable and pleasant in this life except the mind and conscience from whence all pleasure spring be clear and without grutch° of sin.[38] Besides that there have been some that have fulfilled a great part of this doctrine, and chiefly of all Socrates, Diogenes, and Epictetus.[39] Howbeit° sith Christ himself hath both taught and also done these things more consummately than any other, is it not a marvellous thing that these things are not only unknown of them which profess the name of Christ, but also to be despised of them, yea and to be made a laughing stock?[40] If there be anything that goeth more near to Christianity let us then disannul° these things and follow them. But sith there is no nother° thing that can make a true Christian man, why

---

[36] He taught also … eyes] Socrates is the central figure in Plato's philosophical dialogues. In the *Crito* he declares that 'we ought neither to requite wrong with wrong nor to do evil to anyone, no matter what they have done it us' (49d). The *Phaedo*, praised by Erasmus in his *Enchiridion* (1960–66), relates the exemplary death of Socrates, disparages corporeal existence, and argues for the immortality of the soul.

[37] Aristotle writeth] Ann Dalzell comments that this is 'an elusive reference not satisfactorily identified' (*CWE* 41. 416). Inexact analogues to the thought abound, however. See for example Aristotle, *Politics*, 1323a: 'For external goods have a limit […] so an excessive amount of them must necessarily do harm, or do no good, to its possessor: whereas with any of the goods of the soul, the more abundant it is, the more useful it must be.'

[38] The Epicure] Luther's *De servo arbitrio* had accused Erasmus of being an Epicurean in the sense of being an atheist, a charge he rejected (see the letter to Luther, 11 April 1526, Letter 1688, *CWE* 12. 136).

[39] Epictetus] Stoic philosopher, mid-first to second century AD. For Socrates and Diogenes, see notes 14 and 36, above.

[40] a laughing stock] Douglas Parker's edition of the *Exhortation* records this as a neologism, but the *OED* now supplies an instance of 'laughing stock' dating from 1518.

AN EXHORTATION TO THE DILIGENT STUDY OF SCRIPTURE   237

then do we recount° this immortal doctrine more abrogate° and out of use than the books of Moses?⁴¹ The first point of Christianity is to know what Christ hath taught. The next is to do thereafter and to fulfil it as nigh as God giveth us grace.

Neither think I that any man will count himself a faithful Christian because he can dispute with a crafty [A2ᵛ] and tedious perplexity of words, of relations, quiddities,° and formalities,⁴² but in that he knowledgeth° and expresseth in deeds those things which Christ both taught and accomplished. Neither speak I this to discommend their study and labour which have exercised their wits in these subtle inventions (for I would offend no man) but rather because I believe (as the matter is indeed) that the very pure and natural philosophy of Christ can be gathered out so fruitfully of no place as out of the gospels and epistles of the apostles, in which if a man will study devoutly, attending more to prayer than arguing, designing rather to be made a new man than to be armed with Scriptures unto contention,⁴³ he without doubt shall find that there is nothing pertaining unto man's felicity other else unto any operation expedient unto this present life, but it is declared, discussed, and absolutely touched. If we go about to learn anything, wherefore shall another master and instructor more please us than Christ himself? If we require a rule and form to live after, why do we rather embrace another example than the very first copy and patron, which is Christ himself? If we desire a wholesome medicine against the grievous and noisome lusts or appetites of our minds, why seek we not here the [A3ʳ] most fruitful remedy? If we appete° to quicken and refresh with reading our dull and fainting mind, I pray thee where shall we find such quick and fiery sparkles? If we covet to withdraw our minds from the tedious cares of this life, why seek we any other delectable pastimes? Why had we liefer° learn the wisdom of Christ's doctrine out of men's books than of Christ himself? Which in this Scripture doth chiefly perform that thing which he promised unto us when he said that he would continue with us unto the end of the world.⁴⁴ For in this his testament he speaketh, breatheth, and liveth among us in a manner more effectually than when his body was presently conversant in this world.⁴⁵ The Jews neither saw nor heard so much as thou mayst daily both

---

⁴¹ more abrogate ... Moses] Christ's teaching is said to have superseded that contained in the Old Testament, of which the Pentateuch or 'books of Moses' form the first part. Compare Tyndale's translation of Hebr. 8. 13: 'In that he saith a new testament he hath abrogated the old.'
⁴² relations, quiddities, and formalities] Technical terms in medieval philosophy.
⁴³ a new man] See Tyndale's version of Coloss. 3. 9-10: 'Lie not one to another that the old man with his works be put off, and the new put on, which is renewed in knowledge after the image of him that made him.'
⁴⁴ the end of the world] Compare Tyndale's rendering of Matt. 28. 20: 'And lo I am with you always, even until the end of the world.'
⁴⁵ in this his testament ... world] The Epistle to the Hebrews makes extended play with the idea that the testament of Scripture — meant in the sense of a covenant — might also function like a last will and testament. Tyndale translates Hebr. 9. 15-16 thus: 'And for this cause [Christ]

hear and see in the Scripture of Christ. There wanteth nothing but that thou bring the ears and eyes of faith wherewith he may be heard and perceived.[46] What a marvellous world is this? We keep the letters which are written from our friend. We kiss them and bear them about with us. We read them over twice or thrice. And how many thousands are there among the Christian which are esteemed of great literature, and yet have not once in their lives read over the gospels and epistles of the apostles? [A3ᵛ] Mahumet's adherents are all well instruct° in their own sect,[47] and the Jews unto this day even from their tender age study diligently their Moses. Why do not we such honour unto Christ, embracing his precepts which bring eternal life? They that profess Saint Benedict's institution (which is a rule both made of a man that was but of small learning and also written unto the secular, rude, and unlearned) observe their example, learn it by heart, and drink it into their hearts. Saint Austin's adherents are not ignorant in their rule. Saint Francis's friars do know, observe, and advance their patron's precepts, yea and carry them about with them whether soever they go.[48] Insomuch that they think not themselves in safety except their book be with them, why set they more by their rule which was written of a man than the whole Christianity by the Holy Scripture, which Christ did equally preach unto all men, which we have all professed in baptism? And to conclude, which is most holy among all other doctrines and none to be compared with it, although thou heap six hundred together, and I would to God that as Paul did write that the law of Moses had no glory in comparison to the glory of [A4ʳ] the Gospel that succeeded after it,[49] that even so the evangelies° and epistles were esteemed of the Christian so holy or had in such reverence that the doctrines of men in respect of them might seem nothing holy. I am content that every man advance his doctor at his own pleasure. Let them extol Albert, Alexander, Saint Thomas, Aegidius, Richard, and Occam.[50]

is the mediator of the new testament [...] For wheresoever is a testament, there must also be the death of him that maketh the testament.'

[46] the ears and eyes of faith] Compare Matt. 13. 16: 'But blessed are your eyes, for they see, and your ears, for they hear.'

[47] Mahumet's adherents] Muslims. Mahumet or Mahomet is a derogatory garbling of the name of Muhammad.

[48] Saint Benedict's ... Saint Francis's] Erasmus names a trio of monastic orders, each distinguished by its rule or institutional code: the Benedictines, who follow the order established by Saint Benedict (480–543); the Augustinians, named for Augustine ('Austin') of Hippo (354–430); and the Franciscan order founded by Saint Francis (1181/2–1226).

[49] the law of Moses ... after it] See for example the Epistle to the Hebrews, which is structured around an allegorical comparison between the old and new laws. (In the sixteenth century this text was attributed to Paul, although modern scholarship has queried the attribution.) Tyndale's rendering of Hebr. 3. 3 reads: 'And this man [Christ] was counted worthy of more glory than Moses: Inasmuch as he which prepared the house has most honour in the house.'

[50] Albert ... Occam] Erasmus offers a roll-call of eminent medieval scholars: Albertus Magnus (1200–1280); Alexander of Hales (c. 1185–1245); Thomas Aquinas (1225–1274), canonised in 1323;

I will diminish no man's fame nor glory, neither yet resist and reprove the old
manner of study. Let them be witty, subtle, and in a manner above capacity or
angelical,⁵¹ yet truly must they needs knowledge° that these are most true,
undoubted, and fruitful. Paul and Saint John will that we judge the spirits of
prophets, whether they are of God or not,⁵² and Saint Augustine reading all other
men's books with judgement requireth none other authority to his books. Only
in the Scripture when he cannot attain a thing he submitteth himself unto it.⁵³
And our doctor (which is Christ) was not allowed by the schools of divines but
of the heavenly father his own and godly⁵⁴ voice bearing witness, and that twice:
first at Jordan as he was baptised and after in his transfiguration [A4ᵛ] on the
mount Tabor, saying: 'This is my well-beloved son in whom I am pleased, hear

Aegidius Romanus or Giles of Rome (c. 1243–1316); Richard of Middleton (c. 1249–c. 1308);
and William of Ockham (1287–1347).
⁵¹ subtle ... angelical] Erasmus makes play with the epithets of two more medieval
philosophers, Duns Scotus (1266–1308) and St Bonaventure (1221–1274), known as *doctor subtilis*
and *doctor seraphicus*, respectively. The names that feature in Erasmus's complaints about the
medieval philosophical tradition vary, but those given in this section of the *Paraclesis* are
representative. So too are the themes. Here and elsewhere, Erasmus condemns the 'quibbling
sophistries' of its theology; its 'labyrinthine' complexities; its 'artificial style'; and its ignorance
of good authors (Letter to Maarten van Doorp, May 1515, *CWE* 3. 124–25). These attacks can be
understood in relation to a broader encounter between humanism and scholasticism. The term
scholasticism refers to an intellectual tradition shaped in the Middle Ages that looked towards
Aristotle as a key philosophical authority. Humanists such as Erasmus, by contrast, advocated
education centred on the *studia humanitatis* or liberal arts (grammar, rhetoric, poetry, history,
and moral philosophy), and prioritised pragmatic communicative effect over technical precision
in argumentation — or, very roughly, rhetoric over logic. For a discussion, see Lisa Jardine,
'Logic and Language: Humanistic Logic', in *The Cambridge History of Renaissance Philosophy*,
ed. by C. B. Schmitt, Quentin Skinner, Eckhard Kessler, and Jill Kraye (Cambridge: Cambridge
University Press, 1988), pp. 173-98. Erasmus's criticisms should not be taken at face value; in
reality the scholastic tradition remained vigorous in this period. Furthermore, Erasmus himself
is appreciative of Aquinas and others when it suits him (see for example *Manual* 76). Thus,
while advocacy of a return to plain Scripture and a disgust with over-elaborated logical analysis
are central to Erasmus's theology, at the same time they do not always mark out areas of
substantive disagreement with medieval theology.
⁵² we judge ... not] See 1 Corinth. 14. 29 and 1 John 4. 1. Tyndale's version of the latter offers a
parallel to the wording in the *Exhortation*: 'Ye beloved, believe not every spirit: but prove the
spirits whether they are of God or no.'
⁵³ Saint Augustine ... unto it] 'Augustine asks no more for his books than the judicious
attention he gives to others. With Scripture, however, what he does not understand he
nonetheless accepts.' The *Exhortation* here accurately reflects Augustine's views in his *Answer
to Faustus, a Manichean*, 11. 5. Erasmus's original, however, offers the second sentence in the
first rather than the third person: 'In the Gospels and epistles alone I venerate even what I do
not understand' (*CWE* 41. 419–20).
⁵⁴ godly] goodly 1529, modified in many subsequent editions.

you him.'⁵⁵ O this sure authority, which (as they say) hath no contradiction! What signifieth this 'hear you him'? Truly that he is only the true teacher and instructor and that we ought only to be his disciples. Now let every man with their whole affection praise their authors as much as they will. Yet was this voice without nay only spoken of Christ our saviour, upon whom descended the holy ghost in likeness of a dove which did confirm the testimony of the heavenly father.⁵⁶ With this spirit was Peter endued, unto whom the high shepherd Christ committed his sheep once, twice, yea thrice to be fed and nourished, meaning truly no other thing but that he should instruct them with the heavenly food of Christian doctrine.⁵⁷ In Paul Christ seemed in a manner new born again, whom he himself called a chosen vessel⁵⁸ and a pure preacher of his name and glory.⁵⁹ Saint John expressed in his learning that thing which he had sucked or drunk out of the holy fountain of Christ's bosom.⁶⁰ What like thing is there in Duns⁶¹ (I would not you should think that I speak it of envy)? What like thing is there in Saint Thomas? Howbeit° I commend this man's holiness and marvel at the subtle wit and [A5ʳ] judgement of the other. Why do we not all apply our diligent study in these great authors, I mean Christ, Peter, Paul, and John? Why bear we not about these in our bosoms? Why have we them not ever in our hands? Why do we not hunt, seek, and search out these things with a curious diligence? Why give we a greater portion of our life to the study of Averroes than to the evangely° of Christ? Why do we (in a manner) consume all our age in the decrees of men and vain opinions which are so contrary and dissenting among themselves? Be it in case° they be great divines that made such constitutions, yet notwithstanding only in Christ's word consisteth the exercise and inurance° of him which before God is reputed for a great divine. It is meet that we all which have professed the name of Christ (at the least if we have promised with mind and heart) that we be instruct° with the doctrine of Christ being yet tender infants in our parents' arms and wanton children at our nurse's teat. For it is imprinted most deep and cleaveth most surely

---

⁵⁵ first at Jordan … Tabor] There are descriptions of Jesus's baptism and his transfiguration in all three synoptic gospels. See for example Matt. 3. 17 and 17. 5. Tyndale offers the following translation of the divine command in the latter episode: 'this is my dear son, in whom I delight, hear him.'
⁵⁶ Yet was this voice … father] See Matt. 3. 16.
⁵⁷ Christ committed … doctrine] See John 21. 15–17.
⁵⁸ vessel] wessel 1529; corrected in subsequent editions.
⁵⁹ a chosen vessel] In Tyndale's translation of Acts 9. 15, God's voice declares of Paul: 'he is a chosen vessel unto me, to bear my name before the gentiles and kings, and the children of Israel'.
⁶⁰ Saint John expressed … bosom] Tyndale's translation of John 4. 14 reads: 'whosoever shall drink of the water that I shall give him, shall never more be athirst: but the water that I shall give him, shall be in him a well of water, springing up into eternal life.'
⁶¹ Duns] Duns Scotus (1266–1308), medieval philosopher.

which the rude and unformed shell of our soul do the first receive and learn. I would our first and unformed speech should sound of Christ. I would our ignorant childhood should be informed with Christ's evangely, and to them I would Christ should be so [A5ᵛ] sweetly taught that they might be inflamed to love him, and that after they should proceed by a little and a little, creeping by the ground, until that by insensible increments they spring up to be strong in Christ. Other men's traditions are such that many repent themselves because they have spent so much study and labour upon them. And often it chanceth that they which have most manfully fought through all their life even unto the death to defend men's doctrines and decrees, yet in the point of death have cast away their shield and have clean dissented from their author's sect. But blessed is he whom death assaileth if his heart be whole occupied in this wholesome doctrine. Let us therefore all with fervent desire thirst after these spiritual springs. Let us embrace them. Let us be studiously conversant with them. Let us kiss these sweet words of Christ with a pure affection. Let us be new transformed into them, for such are our manners as our studies be. Yea (and to be short) let us die in them. He that cannot attain them (but who is he that cannot if he will himself?) yet at the least let him submit himself unto them, recounting° them very holy and as the storehouse or treasury of God's own mind from whence cometh forth all goodness. If a man would show us a step of Christ's foot, good lord how would we [A6ʳ] kneel and worship it? And why do we not rather honour his quick and lively image which is most expressly contained in these books? If a man would bring unto us Christ's coat, whither would we not run headlong that we might once kiss it? Howbeit if thou bring out his coat, shirt, shoes, and all his household stuff, yet is there nothing that doth more truly and expressly represent Christ than the gospels and epistles. We garnish or adorn an image of wood or stone with gold and precious stones for the love of Christ. But why are not these things rather garnished with gold and gems, yea and more preciously — if so anything can be more precious than they — sith they represent much more presently Christ unto us than any image can do? As for images: what thing can they express but the figure of his body? If they express that. But the evangely doth represent and express the quick and living image of his most holy mind, yea and Christ himself speaking, healing, dying, rising again, and to conclude all parts of him, insomuch that thou couldst not so plain and fruitfully see him although he were present before thy bodily eyes.

Amen.

The Dialogue Between Julius the Second, Genius, and Saint Peter

(1534)

Edited by Alex Davis

Introduction

The subject of this *Dialogue*, Pope Julius II (1443–1513), has a good claim to be *the* Renaissance Pope. Giuliano della Rovere was elected to the papacy in 1503, at a time when its influence was weak and Italian politics was under the sway of foreign powers. Julius changed that. He reasserted control over papal territories in central Italy, expelling the Bentivoglio family from Bologna, confronting the Estense in Ferrara, and defeating the Venetians in 1509 as part of the League of Cambrai, a military coalition that also included France, Spain, and the Empire. He then turned on one of his former allies, forming the so-called Holy League against France in 1511. In 1512 the French armies were driven back over the Alps. During these conflicts, Julius led his armies in battle in person against Bologna and Perugia, and at the siege of Mirandola in 1510. At the same time, he initiated an ambitious programme of renovations in Rome, centred on the rebuilding of St Peter's Basilica by Bramante. He commissioned some of the most important and instantly recognisable works of art of the Italian Renaissance, including Raphael's *School of Athens*, Michelangelo's Sistine Chapel frescos, and his *Moses*. Julius's contemporaries found themselves caught between admiration and horror as they contemplated this amalgam of worldly ambition and crushing cultural power. For Machiavelli, Julius II was endowed with an impetuosity and force of will that matched the spirit of the age. 'Julius', he wrote, 'achieved more than any other pope with all the good sense in the world would ever have achieved.'[1] Francesco Guicciardini judged him to be 'of inestimable spirit and resolution […] worthy undoubtedly of the highest glory had he been a secular prince'.[2] Some four centuries later, he seemed to the historian Emmanuel Rodocanachi to have dominated early sixteenth-century Europe. Set alongside Julius II, monarchs were mediocrities.[3]

Julius died in 1513. In 1517, in Mainz, there appeared a satirical dialogue in Latin, anonymously printed and attributed to 'F. A. F.', entitled *De obitu Julij Pontificis Maximi* ('On the Death of the Supreme Pontiff Julius'). The text now best known as the *Julius exclusus* imagines Julius newly deceased, arriving at the gates of heaven. St Peter denies him entrance and quizzes the would-be gate-crasher on his life and character. The impiety of this scenario — a pope barred from heaven — made the text wildly popular. Within a year editions had appeared in

---

[1] Niccolò Machiavelli, *The Prince*, trans. by Tim Parks (London: Penguin, 2011), p. 100.
[2] Francesco Guicciardini, *The History of Italy*, trans. by Sidney Alexander (Princeton: Princeton University Press, 1969), p. 273.
[3] Emmanuel Rodocanachi, *Histoire de Rome: The Pontificat de Jules II, 1503–1513* ([S. I.]: Libraire Hachette, 1928), p. 1.

Strasbourg, Antwerp, Paris, Louvain, Basel, and Vienna; further printings and translations continued to appear into the seventeenth century and beyond.[4] But who was the pseudonymous 'F. A. F.'? Very quickly, Erasmus emerged as a possible author. He denied the attribution, offering up various conjectures to assist in the hunt for the culprit. Surely the author was French; or a Spaniard living in Paris; or maybe he was Ulrich von Hutten. At any rate, the dialogue wasn't stylistically like anything *he* would have written.[5] The text was never issued as Erasmus's during his lifetime. Nonetheless, the *Julius* was printed in England in 1534 as part of a programme of Erasmian translations, and by the seventeenth century it was being openly identified as his work.[6] Modern scholarship — although not unanimous — tends to believe that Erasmus wrote the *Julius exclusus*.[7] It appears in this volume on this basis and on that of its affiliations with the name of Erasmus during the period of its first translation into English.

Certainly Julius II played a key role in Erasmus's personal mythology; he is the subject of numerous references throughout his letters and other writings from this period. For Erasmus, Julius was a warmonger, and a warrior pope was a contradiction in terms. Erasmus had been an appalled spectator at Julius's triumphal entry into Bologna in 1506. It offered him the opportunity to make one of his favourite comparisons, between the pope and his classical namesake Julius Caesar. 'Pope Julius', he wrote, 'is playing war, conquering, leading triumphal processions; in fact, playing Julius to the life.'[8] Elsewhere he attacked him as 'a campaigning and conquering soldier'.[9] In the judgement of Margaret Mann Phillips, 'it was Julius II who turned Erasmus into a pacifist'.[10]

The *Julius exclusus* takes these charges and adds to them. St Peter's challenge to Julius obliges him to recount his life and achievements, and so we get an account of Julius II's campaigns, his diplomacy, his diplomatic betrayals, his pride,

---

[4] The most complete description of the *Julius exclusus*'s publication history and of the debate over its authorship is to be found in S. Seidel Menchi's introduction to the *Opera Omnia* edition of the text, *ASD* I-8.

[5] See *ASD* I-8. 10–16.

[6] See *The Pope Shut Out of Heaven Gates* (London: Roger Vaughan, 1673), which advertises itself on the title page as being translated 'from the Original of the Famous and Learned *Erasmus Roterodamus*'.

[7] There are other candidates. Diarmaid MacCulloch states that the *Julius* was 'in fact' written by Richard Pace. See *Reformation: Europe's House Divided 1490–1700* (London: Allen Lane, 2003), p. 103. The arguments for Pace's authorship are set out in Catherine Mary Curtis, 'Richard Pace on Pedagogy, Counsel and Satire' (doctoral dissertation, University of Cambridge, 1996). Menchi discusses Curtis's claims in *ASD* I-8. 25–26.

[8] Letter to Jérôme de Busleyden, 17 November 1506, *CWE* 2. 128.

[9] Letter to Andrea Ammonio, 28 November 1518, *CWE* 2. 266.

[10] Margaret Mann Phillips, *The 'Adages' of Erasmus: A Study With Translations* (Cambridge: Cambridge University Press, 1964), p. 105.

his greed, his rage, his habit of excommunicating his enemies, his drinking, his sodomy, his blasphemies, his gross excesses, and his horrible diseases.[11] Brazen, unrepentant — apparently quite unconcerned by the fact of his death — the Julius of the *Julius exclusus* is a Marlovian over-reacher. The real-life Giuliano della Rovere was the nephew of Pope Sixtus IV, who first appointed him as cardinal. The *Julius* doesn't ignore this fact, but so far as Julius himself is concerned he is a self-made man. Without any advantages of kin, or beauty, or learning, he wins his way to the top. 'For to that I came,' he brags, 'wrestling through many cares, no man supposing any likeliness in me' (161–62). It is one of the dialogue's best jokes that its third participant, Julius's Genius, turns out to be no evil angel but the helpless spectator to a career that required no supernatural assistance in plumbing the depths of depravity. 'Was it thou that moved this man to so many horrible deeds?' Peter asks Genius. Not at all, Genius responds: 'he ran so hastily of his own courage that I could scarce overtake him with any wings' (1241–43).

Yet Julius is also a figure of substance. He scores some palpable hits in the course of the dialogue, as when he makes reference to Malchus, the servant whose ear is cut off by Peter in John 18. 10–11. (Several of Peter's responses to this precedent for religious violence look anxiously legalistic.) He also manages to goad Peter into competitively boasting about his own achievements as head of the church. 'How darest thou,' Peter exclaims, 'most shameless wretch, compare and liken thy glory with mine, which is yet not mine but rather Christ's?' (1071–72 — the final, qualifying clause can't quite rescue the apostle's dignity at this moment). Towards the end of the text, a horrified St Peter is moved to comment that 'it may chance that wars thus kindled by thee, may destroy all the world'. To which, Julius's chilling response is: 'Let them burn on hardily, so the dignity and possessions of the see of Rome may be kept safe.' (937–38) The apocalyptic note isn't consistently sustained. Nonetheless, if he very often seems a variant on the comic trope of the blustering *miles gloriosus* or braggart soldier, at his most impressive Julius possesses the ability to assert the self through a rhetoric that is imbued with real eloquence and imaginative force, as with his evocation of his military triumphs (1039–57).

In these passages — which represent a reworking of the scenes that had so revolted Erasmus in Bologna in 1506, transforming them into something worthy of the artists who enjoyed the patronage of the real-life Julius II — Julius choreographs men, animals, and instruments in a triumphal spectacle that celebrates his desire for absolute dominion. This power of fantasy to reshape the world is at stake in some of the *Julius exclusus*'s most despondent moments, in which the text's ambitions for institutional reform collapse into pessimism. At the start of the dialogue, Julius's continued attachment to the things of this world

---

[11] This portrait is an intensification of historical reality; several of its details, such as an accusation of bastardy, are invented or inaccurate.

suggests an inability to face up to the fact of his death. 'How he dreameth of his dreaming life!' (119) exclaims Genius. Towards its end, however, it is Peter who is the fantasist, as Julius not-implausibly accuses him of being an anachronism. Simplicity, humility, virtue: 'thou dreamest yet', Julius scoffs, 'of the state of the church as it was in thy time' (1016). Julius ruthlessly fashions the world into the mirror of his dreaming self, while Peter's dreams just render him ineffectual. And so we get passages in which the latter's ideals are subjected to painful mockery:

> Ha, ha, ha. Then I see well, the more wretched life that a man doth live in the world, the more delicately he liveth in Christ. The more beggarly a man is here, the richer he is in Christ. The more abject that a man is here, the higher and more honourable he is in Christ. The less he liveth in this world, the more he liveth in Christ. (1153–57)

This chain of antitheses, in which worldly values exist in a contradictory relationship to those of true Christian religion, places the *Julius exclusus*'s thinking close to that of the final section of Erasmus's *Praise of Folly*. It condemns Julius as the worst sort of worldling, plainly enough. It also seems to spell the end for any project of ecclesiastical reform, as the text's interest in a revival of the church fades into the background to be replaced by a sense that the true church can never be a part of the world. (The suggestion of an inversion or collapse of values is accentuated when we realise that these sentences are actually assigned to Peter in the Latin editions of the *Julius exclusus*.)[12] And there is little in the dialogue to suggest that Julius's assessment of the situation is in any way incorrect. Sixteenth-century Europe, so appallingly responsive to Julius's narcissistic drive 'to enchain all the world', is quite unmoved by Peter's desire for a return to a time of apostolic simplicity.

Can such a potent enemy ever be defeated? A later, seventeenth-century English translation of the *Julius exclusus* invents a Marlovian end for its villain, with Julius being dragged to hell by devils, like another Faustus.[13] The version presented here sticks to its original and provides a more uncertain conclusion. Julius exits in a rage to gather his forces to storm heaven, leaving an incredulous Peter to ask Genius, 'Be all the bishops such?' (1239). We have no reason to imagine that Julius will successfully force his way through the celestial gates. Neither, though, is he decisively put in his place. The text leaves Julius in a state of narrative suspension that is a tribute to his awful, irrepressible nature.

Questions regarding projects of reform resonate through the English reception of the *Julius exclusus*. The translation presented here is entitled the *Dialogue Between Julius the Second, Genius, and Saint Peter*. It was printed twice, in 1534 and 1535. The publisher was John Byddell, who issued a number of religious texts

---

[12] The change doesn't appear in any of the editions surveyed in the *Opera omnia*. Menchi does note an earlier reassignment of lines from Peter to Julius. See *ASD* I-8, p. 210.

[13] *The Pope Shut Out of Heaven Gates*, p. 48.

throughout the 1530s, including Richard Taverner's English Bible, in 1539. The Taverner Bible was produced under the aegis of his patron, Thomas Cromwell, and Byddell too was a part of a Cromwellian project that aimed to advance an evangelical agenda alongside more strictly monarchical concerns.[14] During the period in which Byddell was most active, Henry VIII was very much interested in the assertion of his royal supremacy over the church; his appetite for theological innovation was far less certain. The attacks on papal authority favoured by Byddell aim to bridge the gap between the celebration of sovereign royal power and the interests of evangelical religion, and it is in this context that the translation of Erasmian texts became a key part of Byddell's project. Throughout the 1530s he issued a series of publications in which pious, anticlerical but reformist writing by Erasmus was made available to speak, tacitly, to more radical ends. Amongst other texts, Byddell issued the first printing of Erasmus's *Enchiridion*, Erasmus's paraphrase on Titus, and his satirical colloquy *Funus*.

The translator is anonymous, but the *Dialogue* is notable for its success in translating the encounter between pope and apostle into a colloquial English style. Some passages of historical narration are relatively bland, and the *Dialogue* retains a number of Latin jokes that read bafflingly in their new context.[15] But whenever Julius and Peter come to grips the translation comes alive. Peter insults Julius as a 'caitiff' (442). Julius declares that he should have cursed Peter 'as black as a coal' (266). Peter identifies Julius's papal paraphernalia as the 'tokens of some knavish tapster and false juggler' (36), and addresses him as a 'mad Bedlam' (959). Julius accuses Peter of 'play[ing] Jack overthwart' (985). And so on, back and forth. The *Dialogue* marks what seems to be the first appearance in English of the word 'buggerer', and it is so pleased with the coinage that it uses it three times in quick succession (380-497). If Julius anticipates Marlowe's heroes, he also recalls some of the shameless, gloriously self-incriminating narrators of Chaucer's *Canterbury Tales*, and the *Dialogue* also recalls Chaucer in its deliberate stylistic collision between high theology and vivid popular idioms.[16] At its most effective, it takes scenes of papal intrigue and European power politics, and plays them out through the language of the tavern and marketplace.

So it is easy to see why the *Julius exclusus* must have looked like a suitably subversive addition to Byddell's list. Julius offers a wonderful, monstrous exemplar of papal ambition, while his encounter with St Peter sets up a series of opportunities to attack the papacy's claim to be the legitimate inheritor of

---

[14] See Diarmaid MacCulloch, *Thomas Cromwell: A Life* (London: Penguin Books, 2018), pp. 72, 542-43. On Byddell, see John Archer Gee, 'John Byddell and the First Publication of Erasmus' *Enchiridion* in English', *ELH*, 4.1 (1937), 43-59.

[15] See for example 40-44 on the initials 'P. M.' as 'pontifex maximus' or 'pestis maxima'.

[16] In addition, the phrase 'cipher in augrim', used to mean a nobody, has Chaucerian resonances. See line 153, note.

apostolic authority. The translator's afterword draws out the point. Julius's life, we read, 'causeth me often to marvel at them that say, the pope of Rome (as they call him) cannot err' (1254–55). The fit between the translation and its Tudor contexts is not perfect.[17] The decision to translate the *Julius exclusus* must have been in some measure an opportunistic one, and we shouldn't expect complete topical relevance from the *Dialogue*. Scandalous papal misbehaviour feels on the money for England in 1534; an intricate account of Italian politics from two decades earlier, less so. In particular, the account of warring church councils that dominates the middle sections of the *Julius* — while making sense in relation to much of Erasmus's thinking on matters of ecclesiastical authority, and offering an account of events that held their relevance in the mid-1530s — may pall.[18] Brilliant in conception, in execution the *Julius exclusus* is arguably overlong, repetitious, excessively concerned with church and peninsular politics. One suspects that aspects of it might have baffled or frustrated its Tudor readers. Nonetheless, the *Dialogue* was successful enough to be quickly reprinted, and even an evangelical reader — one for whom a bad pope was little different from any other pope — might have struggled to resist its iconoclastic thrill.

Julius exclusus represents one of Erasmus's most interesting experiments in the redirection of epideictic rhetoric to satirical ends. Like Erasmus's Folly, Julius is a self-praiser, and it is possible that the *Dialogue* had many careful early modern readers. Julius's voice is often evoked in the drama of the Elizabethan period. We have already compared Julius to the protagonists of Marlowe's plays, and, like Julius, Marlowe's Tamburlaine threatens war on heaven. 'Come,' he exhorts, 'let us march against the powers of heaven.'[19] There is also a seventeenth-century ballad in which Chaucer's Wife of Bath dies and is denied entrance at heaven's

---

[17] The translator mostly preserves Erasmus's text, but a small number of passages dealing with English affairs are cut. These include a description of Henry VII as 'strait-laced' and a series of references that paint Henry VIII as a young and (by implication) slightly gullible novice monarch. See the notes to lines 140 and 146.

[18] See note 88 to the text, on Henry VIII's initial advocacy of and then opposition to a council of the Church in the 1530s. On Erasmus's thinking, see James McConica, 'Erasmus and the "Julius": A Humanist Reflects on the Church', in *The Pursuit of Holiness in Late Medieval and Renaissance Religion*, ed. by Charles Trinkaus and Heiko A. Oberman (Leiden: E. J. Brill, 1974), pp. 444–71.

[19] See *Tamburlaine the Great Part II*, in *Doctor Faustus and Other Plays*, ed by David Bevington and Eric Rasmussen (Oxford: Oxford University Press, 1995), v. 3. 48. Julius's sycophants praise him as one 'which caused all the world to quake and fear', while in the first *Tamburlaine* play Marlowe's Bajazeth has 'lately made all Europe quake for fear' (III. 3. 135). Julius hopes 'to enchain the world'; Tamburlaine 'hold[s] the Fates fast bound with iron chains' (III. 2. 173). Tamburlaine imagines he is the scourge of God (III. 3. 44); the *Dialogue* identifies Julius as the 'sore scourge wherewith God punished us so many years'. Both texts share an interest in the triumph as a cultural form.

gate.[20] But the *Julius exclusus*'s most brilliant literary inheritor appeared three centuries later. Byron's 1821 poem 'The Vision of Judgment' deals with George III's attempt to gain entry to heaven. Its opening stanzas imagine St Peter's servants overwhelmed by the numbers of the dead:

> Each day too slew its thousands six or seven
>   Till at the crowning carnage, Waterloo,
> They threw their pens down in divine disgust —
> The page was so besmear'd with blood and dust.[21]

What Byron's poem takes most from Erasmus is its satirical scenario, but the disgust at a world devastated by warfare is very much a part of the *Julius exclusus* too. It speaks, as the *Julius* as a whole spoke, to dreams of remaking the world, and to a revulsion from the various horrifying ways in which our rulers shape the way the world actually works.

Further Reading

ADAMS, ROBERT P., *The Better Part of Valor: More, Erasmus, Cole, and Vives, on Humanism, War, and Peace, 1496-1535* (Seattle: University of Washington Press, 1962)

MCCONICA, JAMES, 'Erasmus and the "Julius": A Humanist Reflects on the Church', in *The Pursuit of Holiness in Late Medieval and Renaissance Religion*, ed. by Charles Trinkaus and Heiko A. Oberman (Leiden: E. J. Brill, 1974), pp. 444–71

THOMPSON, SISTER GERALDINE, *Under Pretext of Praise: Satiric Mode in Erasmus' Fiction* (Toronto and Buffalo: University of Toronto Press, 1973)

---

[20] *The Wanton Wife of Bath, to the tune of, Flying Fame* (London: F. Coles, n.d.).
[21] 'The Vision of Judgment', in Lord Byron, *Selected Poems*, ed. by Susan J. Wolfson and Peter J. Manning (London: Penguin, 2005), lines 37–40.

THE DIALOGUE BETWEEN JULIUS THE SECOND, GENIUS, AND SAINT PETER.¹

[A2ʳ] Julius. Genius. Petrus.

JULIUS
What a mischief is this? Be not the gates open? I trow either the lock is changed, or else doubtless it is troubled.°

GENIUS²
Marry, look betime,° lest peradventure° ye hast not brought the right key. For this door is not opened with the same key wherewith thou dost open thy treasury.
5 And therefore, why hast thou not brought hither both twain? For surely this is a key of power, not of cunning.°

JULIUS
Forsooth I had never other but this. Neither I see not what needeth the other key, when this is present.³

GENIUS
Neither I of truth, but for because we be shut out in the meantime.

---

¹ The title page of the 1534 *Dialogue* features a woodcut of Giuliano della Rovere's family coat of arms of an oak tree, backed by the crossed keys of heaven and surmounted by the papal triple crown. The title is followed by a recommendation: 'Reader, refrain from laughing.' Overleaf, we find the following summary: 'A dialogue made by a certain famous learned man, pleasant and fruitful, showing how Julius the second and great bishop of Rome, knocking after his death at the gates of heaven, could not be suffered to come in, Saint Peter being the porter, albeit that in his lifetime he was called most holy, yea and by the name of holiness itself, and thereto a great conqueror in many battles, whereby he supposed himself also to be the lord of heaven. Speakers in this dialogue been these: Julius, Genius, and Petrus.'

² Genius] Julius's Genius describes himself as 'the great spirit or angel of Julius' (see below line 92), and he initially looks like a supernatural entity tasked with luring his victim to perdition. It turns out that Genius is nothing of the sort: Pope Julius sins instinctively, incessantly, and without external prompting.

³ what needeth the other key … present] Crossed gold and silver keys are part of the papal insignia. Each key is understood to represent a separate jurisdiction within which the pope exercises authority: earth and heaven. This symbolism is based on Christ's promise to Peter in Matt. 16. 19: 'I will give you the keys of the kingdom of heaven, and whatever you bind on earth will be bound in heaven, and whatever you loose on earth will be loosed in heaven.' In addition, the reference to a 'key of knowledge' in Luke 11. 52 lies behind the *Dialogue*'s allusion to keys of 'power' and of 'cunning'. Julius possesses one but not the other.

THE DIALOGUE BETWEEN JULIUS THE SECOND, GENIUS, AND ST PETER 253

JULIUS

10 This fretteth° me not a little. I will break down the gates. Hey, hey, some of you, quickly come open the gate! What a reckoning is this? Will no man come forth? What causeth this porter to tarry so long? I think he is [A2ᵛ] fallen into some drunken sleep.

GENIUS

[*Aside*] See ye not how this man esteemeth all other men of his own conditions?

PETRUS

15 [*To himself*] It is happy that we have so strong a gate, or else he would have broken it. He must needs be some giant, or some great ruffler,° or beater down of walled towns. But, O, immortal God, what a sink° I smell here! I will not be hasty in opening the door, but I shall spy here out at this grate what monster it is. [*Addressing Julius*] What art thou or what aileth thee?

JULIUS

20 Wherefore dost thou not open the gates, as fast as thou canst, which shouldest have met me, if thou had done thy duty, and all the pomp of heaven too?

PETRUS

Lordly spoken. But I pray thee tell me first of all who thou art.

JULIUS

As though thou mayst not see what I am!

PETRUS

'Mayst not see', quod he? Of truth I see a new sight, and such one as I never saw
25 before. To speak plainly: a very monster.

JULIUS

But and if thou be stark blind,⁴ I trow thou knowest of old this key? [A3ʳ] Albeit that thou knowest not this golden oak, and thou seest here too this triple crown, and also this cope° shining on every side with gold and precious stones.⁵

PETRUS

As for the silver key, indeed I know of old, after a manner and though ye have
30 brought it alone, being yet much unlike to those which Christ the true pastor or shepherd of the church did once deliver me. But how were it possible for me to know this crown so glorious, as never any strange tyrant durst wear, much more no such (certainly) as would be let in here? As for this goodly vestment, I pass

---

⁴ But and if] unless.
⁵ Albeit ... stones] Julius refers here to a combination of personal and official insignia. The oak tree featured in the arms of the della Rovere family, whilst the triple tiara or *triregnum* was worn by popes from the eighth century.

little upon,[6] which despised and was wont to tread under my feet both gold and precious stones like as I did tile stones. But what thing is here? I see both in the key, crown and garment tokens of some knavish tapster and false juggler, having my forename, that is to say Simon,[7] but nothing following my profession, which name [A3ᵛ] I confounded once by the assistance of Christ.

JULIUS
Leave these brabbling° words, if thou be wise: for I (if you know me not) am Julius the Lombard, born in Liguria, and I think thou knowest these two letters, 'P' and 'M', unless thou didst never know thy crossrow.[8]

PETRUS
I ween° they signify the greatest pestilence.[9]

GENIUS
[*Aside*] Ha, ha, ha! How right, he hitteth the nail on the head.

JULIUS
No, not so. The greatest bishop.

PETRUS
How great soever thou be, and though thou were greater than Trismegistus the nephew of great Mercurius,[10] thou shalt not be received into this place, unless thou be also optimus, that is to say holy.

JULIUS
If it make anything to the matter to be called holy,[11] thou art past all shame which doubteth to open me the gates, seeing thou was called many years ago only holy, for truly no man called me but most holy.[12] There remaineth at this day six thousand bulls ...

---

[6] I pass little upon] I am unimpressed by it.
[7] Simon] Simon Magus, who confronts Peter in Acts 8. 18–24. The *Dialogue* accuses Julius of simony, the selling of church offices.
[8] crossrow] A child's alphabet.
[9] the greatest pestilence] Julius wants 'P. M.' to stand for 'pontifex maximus' (the greatest bishop); Peter takes the initials to mean 'pestis maxima' (the greatest pestilence), and below refuses Julius entry unless he is 'optimus' (the best, line 47).
[10] Trismegistus] Hermes Trismegistus or 'Thrice-greatest Hermes', the legendary author of the 'hermetic' texts, a body of early gnostic writings that fascinated Renaissance thinkers such as Marsilio Ficino.
[11] if it make anything to the matter] if it matters at all.
[12] most holy] L. *sanctus* can mean both 'saint' and 'holy'. 'Sanctus Petrus' is only a saint; on Julius's account, the 'sanctissimus' ('most holy') pope therefore outranks him.

GENIUS
[*Aside*] Bulls indeed!¹³

JULIUS
... in which I am called, and that not once, most holy lord. Beside this I was entitled° under the [A4ʳ] name of holiness itself, and not of a holy man. Whatsoever was my pleasure ...

GENIUS
[*Aside*] Yea, though thou were stark drunk ...

JULIUS
... that, men would say, the holiness of most holy lord Julius had done.

PETRUS
Then go ask heaven of such flatterers that was wont to make thee most holy, and let those give thee felicity which gave thee holiness. But supposest thou all one,¹⁴ to be called holy or to be holy in deed?

JULIUS
Thou angerest me to the heart! If I might live again, I would neither desire this holiness nor felicity.

PETRUS
O voice, the declarer of a very holy mind! Nevertheless when I do but only look on thee I perceive much ungodliness, but no token of holiness in thee. What meaneth this new guard, so unmeet° for a bishop? For thou bringest almost twenty thousand with thee, and I see not one among them all that looketh like a good Christian man. I see a filthy sort of men, savouring nothing but of bawdry, drunkenness, and gunpowder. They seem to be hired to rob, or rather [A4ᵛ] a sort of spirits come out of hell to make battle against heaven. Now the more I behold thyself, so much less I see any step of an apostolic man.¹⁵ First of all, what a monster is here, which wearest above the garment of a priest and underneath thou lookest all fiercely and clinkest within with bloody harness? Beside all these, what a cruel look, how stubborn a face, how threatening a forehead, how haut° and disdainous° a countenance! I am truly ashamed, and very weary for to see it, that

---

¹³ Bulls indeed] 'Bubbles indeed!' Julius is referring to papal bulls or decrees, named after the lead seal or 'bulla' that authenticated them. A 'bulla' is literally a bubble. Genius's interjection 'bubbles indeed!' ('vere bullarum!' *ASD* I-8, line 48) puns on this sense: the bulls are empty and insubstantial. The translation 'Bulls indeed' may anticipate the later meaning of a 'bull' as a nonsensical jest, but 'bulls' might also be bubbles in early modern English. Compare Heinrich Bullinger, *Sermons*, sig. Hh5ᵛ: 'thei maye well be called bulles, sins thei be more vaine than bulles or blabbers in the water'. See also *Adage* II. iii. 48, *Homo bulla*, 'Man is a bubble' (Tav. 109).
¹⁴ But supposest thou all one ...] 'Do you think it's the same?'
¹⁵ any step of] any trace of.

75 there is no part of thy body but it is defiled and vitiate° with tokens of prodigious and abominable lust. And furthermore, it need not to speak how thou dost rift° and smellest altogether of excess and drunkenness, and me thinketh thou lookest as thou had of late vomited. To be short, such is the shape of all thy body that thou appearest not so broken, rotten, and overcome so much with age, as with surfeits.

[A5ʳ]GENIUS
80 [*Aside*] How right he hath painted him in his colours.

PETRUS
Yet although that I see thee but even now threatening me as it were with thy countenance, yet for all that I cannot but utter my thought. I do suspect that the most pestilent heathen Julius is come again disguised from hell to laugh me to scorn, thou art so like to him in all points.[16]

JULIUS
85 *Madisi.*[17]

PETRUS
What said he?

GENIUS
His holiness is now an angered.[18] At this word there is never one of the cardinals that would tarry in his sight, for if he did he should have felt his most holy fist, and namely after dinner.

PETRUS
90 Methink° thou perceivest very well the man's appetite. Therefore tell me who thou art.

GENIUS
I am the great spirit or angel of Julius.[19]

---

[16] heathen Julius] Julius's eulogists frequently compared him to his pagan namesake Julius Caesar. So did his critics, disparagingly. Compare Erasmus's *Invective in iambics*: 'He filled | the whole world with slaughter, war, and | bloodshed; in this too you are a second Julius' (*CWE* 85. 339).

[17] *Madisi*] S. Seidel Menchi identifies this as 'an interjection commonly used by Italian writers of the late fifteenth and early sixteenth centuries to emphasize an energetic affirmation' (*ASD* I-8, note to line 78). Michael J. Heath suggests a derivation from Italian 'ma di si' ('but say yes'). See *CWE* 28. 495.

[18] an angered] angry (compare 'an hungered' below, line 257).

[19] the great spirit or angel of Julius] Erasmus's *Adage* I. i. 72, *Genius malum*, 'An evil genius', explores 'the view of the ancients that each person had two attendant spirits whom they call *daemones* [...] and one of these plots our destruction while the other tries to come to our aid'. As in the *Dialogue*, in the *Adage* Erasmus refuses to externalise the responsibility for our actions. 'This', he writes of the evil genius, 'is the name we give to those whom we blame for our misfortunes' (*CWE* 31. 116–17).

PETRUS
But I think the evil angel?

GENIUS
What kin one soever I am, I belong to Julius.

JULIUS
95 But I say, leave these trifling tales, and open the gates, except thou had liefer° have them [A5ᵛ] broken open. What needeth many words? Seest thou what a sort of companions I bring with me?

PETRUS
Truly I see a sort of errant thieves. But to put thee shortly out of doubt, these gates must be won with other° manner of artillery.

JULIUS
100 I say here is words plenty![20] If thou wilt not speedily obey, I will bend against thee the thunderbolt of excommunication wherewith I have feared sometime the highest kings of the earth, and also many great kingdoms.[21] I trow thou seest here a bull provided for the same purpose?

PETRUS
But I pray thee what thunder or thunderbolts, what bulls, calves, and craking°
105 words dost thou speak of to me? For I never heard any such of Christ.

JULIUS
But thou shalt feel, unless thou wilt obey.

PETRUS
If thou hast in time past feared any with such cards of ten that is nothing to this place,[22] for here thou must occupy° true wares. This hold° is vanquished with good works, not with evil words. [A6ʳ] But I pray thee, threatenest thou me with
110 the thunderbolt of excommunication? Tell me by what authority.

JULIUS
By very good authority. For thou art now but a private person, neither any better than every laic° priest, yea scarcely so good, seeing thou canst not now consecrate.

PETRUS
Because I trow that I am now departed from that life.

---

[20] I say here is words plenty!] 'Enough talk!'
[21] I will ... kingdoms] Julius excommunicated several of his enemies, including the Duke of Ferrara, the Doge of Venice, and the King of France. He excommunicated the last three times, annually from 1511 to 1513.
[22] cards of ten] bluffing threats. Compare John Bale, *Yet a Course at the Romyshe Fox*, sig. H3ʳ: 'Now face out your matter with a carde of tenne.'

JULIUS
115 Even therefore.

PETRUS
But thou which art more than so dead art nothing better than I by this reason.

JULIUS
Nay, not so sir. For as long as the cardinals strive for the choosing of a new pope, so long is the office mine own.

GENIUS
[*Aside*] How he dreameth of his dreaming life!

JULIUS
120 But yet once again, open the door I say.

PETRUS
I say thou labourest all in vain, unless thou can show thy deserving merits.

JULIUS
What merits?

PETRUS
I will tell thee. Hast thou passed° all other in holy doctrine?

JULIUS
I knew never a deal,[23] nor I had leisure thereto, having so many battles. But I have
125 friars enough, if this pertain [A6ᵛ] to our matter.

PETRUS
Therefore it is like enough thou hast won many to Christ with thy good living …

GENIUS
[*Aside*] Yea, rather to hell, and that great plenty.

PETRUS
… Wast thou clear and shining with miracles?

JULIUS
Thou speakest of such matters as were clean out of use with me.

PETRUS
130 Hast thou been accustomed to pray purely and busily?

JULIUS
What trifles he prateth!

---

[23] I knew never a deal] 'I never knew much.'

PETRUS
Or was thou wont to macerate° or subdue thy body with fastings and watches°?

GENIUS
No more of these matters, I pray thee. To this man lose not thy labour.

PETRUS
I never knew other ornaments of a right bishop. If this man hath other more like
to the apostles',[24] let him show them forth.

JULIUS
Truly it is far unfitting that the great conqueror Julius (which was never yet overcome) should now give place to Peter — to speak no further, a poor fisher and in manner a very beggar. Nevertheless because thou shalt know what a great prince thou settest nought by, hear me [A7ʳ] three or four words. First of all I am born in Liguria, neither I am no Jew as thou art,[25] with whom I am sorry that I have had so much likeness to as that I was once a pilot of a ship.[26]

GENIUS
[*Aside*] That is nothing to be sorrowed for. For herein is much difference between you. For he fished to get a poor living; thou were wont at a little wage offered thee to pluck down the sails.[27]

JULIUS
Moreover of Sixtus which was doubtless the greatest pope ...[28]

GENIUS
[*Aside*] He meaneth his greatness in mischiefs.

JULIUS
... I was his nephew by his sister,[29] and first promoted by his special favour and mine own policy to spiritual dignities, then after climbed up, as it were by stairs, to the heighth of a cardinal's hat. After exercised with many sharp storms of fortune, being thereto tossed up and down with most cruel chances, and beside

---

[24] other ... apostles'] other characteristics, resembling those of the apostles.
[25] I am no Jew as thou art] Julius is anti-Semitic throughout the *Dialogue*; see the reference to his Jewish physician, below, line 211.
[26] pilot of a ship] Erasmus's *Adage* III. iv. 86, *A remo ad tribunal*, 'From the oar to the bench', records the tradition that as a youth Julius 'used to row a boat to earn a penny' (*CWE* 35. 53).
[27] For he fished ... sails] Genius's comment makes a distinction between fishing for food ('living') and working on a boat for a wage.
[28] Sixtus] Francesco della Rovere, Pope Sixtus VI (1414–1484).
[29] nephew by his sister] Giuliano della Rovere was in fact the son of Pope Sixtus IV's brother. However, he was undoubtedly the object of his uncle's patronage, which secured him entry to the college of cardinals in 1471.

many other diseases I had also the king's evil,[30] to be short, I swarmed all full [A7ᵛ] of the French pox,[31] beside all this I was a banished man,[32] odious, condemned, abject of all men, and almost past all together,[33] yet I never mistrusted to be the greatest bishop, such a courage had I ever. But as for thou wast afraid at the voice of a maiden and was glad to deny thy master.[34] A woman took clean away thy stomach! It fortuned contrariwise to me, for there was a wise woman, or sortilege,° that put me in all this trust, which in the time I was drowned in all my misfortunes whispered me privily in the ear, saying: 'Stand stiffly, and be of good courage Julian. Be not aggrieved. Whatsoever thou do or suffer, thou shalt once be crowned with three crowns, thou shalt be king of kings and lord of lords.'[35] Neither my hope than her prophecy deceived me.[36] For to that I came, wrestling through many cares, no man supposing any likeliness° in me, partly by aid of the Frenchmen succouring me in my [A8ʳ] exile, and partly with an inestimable power of money, made by usury.[37] Neither it came to pass without great policy.

PETRUS

What policy was it?

JULIUS

That is to say, not without many promised benefices, and that by sure covenant with great craft for to find sureties for the same purpose. For truly it had been too much for rich Crassus to have paid so great a sum of money at once.[38] But I speak these things to thee in vain, which every auditor doth not well perceive. I have now rehearsed thee how I crept up to mine office. Now in mine office I handled myself in such wise that there is never one among all the old bishops which in respect of me appeareth worthy the name of bishops, neither there is any of the

---

[30] the king's evil] scrofula. The *Julius exclusus* has Julius suffering from 'morbos comitiali' (epilepsy). See *ASD* I-8, line 135.
[31] French pox] syphilis. In 1497 della Rovere was reported to be ill with the pox.
[32] a banished man] In April 1494 Cardinal della Rovere left Italy for France following conflict with Pope Alexander VI (1431–1503). There he allied himself with King Charles VIII (1470–1498), assisting in a French invasion of Italy. Charles entered Naples the following year before being forced to withdraw his armies; della Rovere returned to France with him. This period of 'exile' from Rome lasted until 1503, upon Alexander's death.
[33] all together] everything. The *Dialogue*'s 'all together' is often best left as two separate words.
[34] deny thy master] All the gospels narrate the episode in which Peter denies Christ. See Matt. 26. 69–75; Mark 14. 66–72; Luke 22. 55–62; John 18. 15–18.
[35] king of kings and lord of lords] The prophecy blasphemously reassigns epithets applied to God. Compare Rev. 16. 19.
[36] Neither ... than] neither ... nor.
[37] For to that ... usury] Giuliano della Rovere was elected pope on 1 November 1503. The French monarchy in fact supported an alternative candidate, but the bribery and promises that underpinned his success were noted by all observers.
[38] Crassus] The Roman statesman Marcus Licinius Crassus (115/12–53 BC) was notoriously rich.

new bishops to whom the church, yea Christ himself, is so much bound as to me.

GENIUS
[*Aside*] How straight this beast playeth Thraso's part.[39]

PETRUS
I marvel what end thou wilt make.

JULIUS
For truly [A8ᵛ] I (with many new-found offices, as they call them) have highly increased and enlarged the pope's treasury. I found (then after) means how bishoprics might be bought without simony. For it was decreed by my predecessors, that he which chanced to have a bishopric, should depose or lay down his office, which words I did interpret in this wise: Thou art commanded to give up thine office; but that is not given up which thou hast not. Thou must buy therefore that office which thou mayest give up.[40] By this policy every bishopric was worth to me six or seven thousand ducats, beside all such exactions as be asked customably for bulls. Moreover, I got great vantage° of the new money wherewith I filled all Italy.[41] Neither I ceased at any time from gathering riches, perceiving right well (without that) that neither holy nor profane [B1ʳ] dominion could have been rightly done without that. But and to speak of greater points of my practice, I restored and delivered up Bonony then inhabited with the Bentivoles to the see of Rome.[42] I overthrew in battle the Venetians, never vanquished before.[43] I had almost take in a snare the Duke Ferrara, long vexed with battle.[44] The schismatic council I deluded in good time, feigning another

---

[39] playeth Thraso's part] boasts. Thraso is the braggart soldier in Terence's play *Eunuchus*.

[40] Thou must buy ... give up] Menchi comments that 'this malicious interpretation of the curial machinations to extort money through the system of offices and benefices is not supported by any contemporary observer' (*ASD* 1-8, note to line 161).

[41] the new money] Julius II's financial policy involved attempts to maximise revenues generated by the distribution of offices, and monetary reform involving the circulation of new silver coins to replace debased currency. These were named 'giulii' after him.

[42] Bonony ... Bentivoles] Much of Julius's papacy was devoted to reasserting control over papal territories in central Italy. In 1506 he led in person a campaign that culminated in the expulsion of the Bentivoglio family from Bologna (Latin 'Bononia').

[43] the Venetians] Formed in 1508, the League of Cambrai joined together the papacy, the emperor, and the French and Spanish monarchies in an attempt to curb Venetian influence in northern Italy. The Venetians were defeated at the battle of Agnadello in 1509.

[44] Duke Ferrara] Alfonso d'Este, Duke of Ferrara (1476–1534), was another excessively independent regional power whom Julius sought to depose. In 1510 Julius's armies marched on Ferrara's lands, with the Pope again leading them in person. On 4 July 1512 d'Este arrived in Rome for negotiations under a safe conduct, only to leave in haste two weeks later, fearing for his life.

council,⁴⁵ and so put away one mischief (as the common saying is) with another.⁴⁶ Last of all I drove the Frenchmen (then sore adread of all Christendom) clean forth of Italy,⁴⁷ and was purposed likewise to do the Spaniards (for I did wholly so intend) if the fatal sentence of God had not taken me out of this life.⁴⁸ But see here how courageous a stomach I showed. I began to view diligently the borders of high France. I let then grow my white beard,⁴⁹ when all thing was in desperation. But full suddenly cometh a golden [B1ᵛ] messenger showing that at Ravenna a certain thousands of Frenchmen were slain.⁵⁰ At such tidings Julius revived again. Moreover I lay three days for dead.⁵¹ Also I felt no life at all myself, but here (both above all other men's hope, and mine also) I revived again. So great is my authority and power with my other policy, that there is at this day never a Christian prince, but I can cause him to make war, notwithstanding they be never so sure enleagued.° For an example, I brake the last band and league which the Camerics made between my holiness⁵² and other princes (that is to say the French king and the king of Romans) so craftily, as though there had never been mention of it. Beside all this I kept so great an host, garnished so many glorious and shining triumphs, so many jolly masqueries,° so diverse buildings, and yet I left five million ducats at the time of my death, [B2ʳ] intending to prove higher masteries, if that Jew my physician (that by his sorcery did prorogue° my life) could have prolonged me anymore.⁵³ But would God now some magic could restore me to

---

⁴⁵ The schismatic council ... another council] Julius II had undertaken to summon a general council of the church within two years of his election as pope in 1503. This was delayed by the wars in Italy. When a rival council, sponsored by Julius's erstwhile allies the French king Louis XII of France (1462–1515) and the Emperor Maximilian I (1459–1519) was held at Pisa in 1511, Julius responded by convening the Fifth Lateran Council at Rome in May 1512. This episode dominates the middle section of the *Dialogue*.

⁴⁶ put away one mischief ... with another] Compare *Adage* I. ii. 4, *Clavum clavo pellere*, 'To drive out one nail by another': 'you expelled one evil by another' (*CWE* 31. 148).

⁴⁷ I drove the Frenchmen ... Italy] France was initially the papacy's ally against Venice in the Italian wars. Subsequently, Julius assembled the Holy League, bringing together Italian states, the empire, and Spanish and English forces against the French, whose armies withdrew from Italy in 1512.

⁴⁸ the fatal sentence] Julius II died on 21 February 1513.

⁴⁹ my white beard] From 1510, Julius allowed his beard to grow, and it was rumoured that he had vowed not to trim it until the French were driven from Italy. The beard can be seen in Raphael's portrait of Julius II.

⁵⁰ Ravenna] The battle of Ravenna on 11 April 1512 was in fact a victory for the French and Ferrarese forces against those of the papacy and Spain, although it involved huge casualties on all sides.

⁵¹ I lay three days for dead] Julius fell seriously ill in August 1511, and reports of his death were widespread.

⁵² Camerics] Citizens of Cambrai ('Cameracum'), in France. When the League of Cambrai collapsed in 1510, Julius allied himself with Venice against France, his former ally.

⁵³ prorogue my life] The *Dialogue* later accuses Julius of 'proroguing' the sitting of the Fifth Lateran Council.

life, that I might yet finish such things as I did gorgeously begin, albeit at the point of death I was most busy to provide that battles which I had graciously begun in all parts should not cease by my death, and I laboured that the treasure which I left might be saved for the same purpose.⁵⁴ This was my last words at my departing. Now disdainest thou to open Christ's gates to a bishop deserving so much, both of Christ and his church? He shall more marvel at these things that perpendeth° and considereth by what wisdom and policy I brought all these matters to pass, having no other help at all, as other be commonly wont, nor of my kin (for I knew never my father, which thing I say to my praise);⁵⁵ nor by beauty (for [B2v] every man abhorred my ugly face); neither by any learning (which I never tasted); nor by bodily strength (which chanced me in like manner, as I have described before); neither by favour of age (for I did all these things being an old man); not by the common friendship (for every man hated me); nor with any clemency or gentleness (which being so hard-hearted that I would often be so cruel against some to whom all other were wont to be entreated by) …⁵⁶

PETRUS
Good lord, what a tale is this?

GENIUS
[*Aside*] Although this appear to another man hard to bring to pass, yet it is but a trifle to him.

JULIUS
… but notwithstanding that fortune, age, personage of body — to make few words, both goods and men — were against me, I (having no other aid but mine own wit and money) have done these great and valiant feats in few years, leaving also so much aid to my posterity that they may have enough to [B3ʳ] do withal° for the space of ten years. I have spoken these things of myself, and that very truly, but nothing to that I could say.⁵⁷ But if one of my rhetoricians handled the matter, thou shouldst say thou heardst a god, and no man.

PETRUS
Most valiant warrior: for so much as all these matters which you show me be to me very strange,⁵⁸ and such as I never heard of before, I pray you to pardon mine

---

⁵⁴ I laboured … purpose] Julius ordered that the funds in the papal treasury pass directly to his successor, and wanted them used in a war against the Turks.
⁵⁵ I knew never my father] Little is known of Julius's father Raffaele, but the accusation of illegitimacy is inaccurate.
⁵⁶ to whom all other were wont to be entreated by] i.e. Julius is cruel to those whom others indulge.
⁵⁷ but nothing to that I could say] 'But I have said nothing compared to what I could have said.'
⁵⁸ for so much as] seeing that.

240   ignorance and rudeness, and that it be not grievous to your highness to make an answer plainly to me, in such things as I will ask of you, what be these goodly minions that follow you?

JULIUS
I keep them for my pleasure.[59]

PETRUS
What be these black company all full of scars?

JULIUS
245   They be soldiers and their captains, which have been manfully slain in battle for love of me and the church, some in the siege of Boleyn le Grace,[60] and many also at the battle against the Venetians. A great sort at the siege of Ravenna, [B3^v] to whom heaven is due by covenant. For I promised them long ago, by my great bulls, that all they should fly straight to heaven, that fought for the maintenance of
250   Julius's power, howsoever they lived before.[61]

PETRUS
Therefore to my imagination they were of this good fraternity that hath been very often grievous to me, or° thou came hither, showing forth their foolish bulls, howbeit° they made no such facing as to enter in by force.[62]

JULIUS
Therefore as far as I can see, thou wouldst not suffer them come in.

PETRUS
255   Aye, trowest thou? No, never one of the lineage. For truly, so hath not Christ taught me, to admit any that bringeth such instruments. But to them that hath clothed the naked, and feedeth them that be an hungered, given drink to the thirsty, and visiteth the sick, and help poor prisoners, and harbour the harbourless. For seeing he would they should be excluded that hath prophesied in his name,
260   that hath cast forth devils, that hath wrought miracles, [B4^r] thinkest thou then that they shall be let in, that bringeth hither nothing but a bare bull in the name of Julius?

---

[59] goodly minions ... pleasure] Julius's train includes 'minions', youths kept as lovers. During Julius's lifetime satirists accused him of sodomy. Erasmus's *Carmen iambicum* repeats the charge: 'One Nicomedes is not enough for you, even in | your old age' (*CWE* 85. 339). Julius Caesar was said to have been the lover of Nicomedes, king of Bithynia.

[60] Boleyn le Grace] Bologna, against which city Julius led his army in person in 1506. Richard Grafton's *Chronicle* (sig. Pppp2^r) refers to 'Bolonia le grace'.

[61] For I promised them ... howsoever they lived before] In bulls of 1512 Julius promised plenary absolution to those who fought against the French.

[62] howbeit they made no such facing] although they were not so defiant.

JULIUS
Ah, what if I had known this before?

PETRUS
I wot well what ye would have done if any of your friends had come from hell, and showed you these things. Ye would have proclaimed open war against me.

JULIUS
And not only that, but I should have cursed thee as black as a coal.

PETRUS
But go forth.[63] Wherefore art thou all in armour?

JULIUS
As though thou knewest not that both the swords pertained to the highest bishop, except thou wilt have men fight naked.[64]

PETRUS
Truly when I occupied thy room, I knew no sword at all but the sword of the spirit, which is the word of God.[65]

JULIUS
But Malchus will tell another tale, whose ear thou cut off, I trow without a sword.[66]

PETRUS
I remember and know that right well. But then I fought for my master Christ. Not for myself: for my master's life. Not for money, or temporal dignity. And then I fought [B4ᵛ] being neither pope nor bishop, and at that time when the keys were only promised me, but not received; neither I had received yet the holy ghost. And notwithstanding at that time I was commanded to put it up again and monished° openly that such manner of fighting was not fitting for priests, neither for any Christian man. But these things shall be more meet for another place. Why dost thou so much boast thyself to be a Lombard as though it were anything material to the vicar of Christ what country man he be?

---

[63] go forth] 'Keep talking.'
[64] both the swords] The doctrine of the two swords was developed during the Middle Ages. In 1302, Boniface VIII issued the papal bull *Unan sanctam*, which refers to the two swords of spiritual and temporal authority.
[65] sword of the spirit] See Ephes. 6. 17: 'Take the helmet of salvation, and the sword of the Spirit, which is the word of God.'
[66] Malchus] The slave whose ear is cut off by Peter. See John 18. 10-11.

JULIUS

Yes surely, for I think it the highest kind of love to advance and magnify my country. Therefore I write this title in all my coins of money, pictures in all vaults and walls.[67]

PETRUS

285 Ergo he knew his country, which knew not his father? But at the first I thought thou hadst meant of the heavenly Jerusalem the country of believers, and of the only prince of the same, by whose godly [B5ʳ] power they which be there desireth to be sanctified, that is for to say, made clean. But what meaneth this addition, 'Sixtus's nephew by his sister', whom I marvel never came hither, namely when
290 he was the high bishop, and cousin to so great a duke as thou art? Wherefore tell me I pray thee, what manner of fellow was he? Was he any priest?

JULIUS

I promise thee he was a valiant warrior, and of an high religion, that is to wit of Saint Francis's order.[68]

PETRUS

Indeed I knew sometime Francis, one of the best size among the lay fee,[69] and an
295 utter despiser of riches, pleasure, and worldly ambition. But hath that poor creature gotten him now such great rulers under him?

JULIUS

As far as I perceive, thou wilt not that any man shall rise to promotion. Truth it is, that Benet was once a poor monk.[70] Nevertheless his posterity or successors be now so rich that we popes do envy them.

PETRUS

300 [B5ᵛ] Very well. But return to thy matter of Sixtus's nephew.

JULIUS

I said for the nonce,[71] to stop their mouths, which affirm liberally that I was his son, and begotten on his sister.

---

[67] Therefore I write this title ...] Many of the pope's portrait medals and coins describe him as 'IVLIVS LIGUR' ('Julius the Ligurian'). The inscription on the outer wall of the Belvedere in the Vatican identifies Julius as the sixth Ligurian pope and a native of Savona: 'IVLIVS II PONT. MAX, LIGURUM VI PATRIA SAONENSIS.'

[68] Saint Francis's order] Francesco della Rovere, latterly Sixtus VI, was elected general of the Franciscans in 1464, having joined the order in his youth.

[69] best size among the lay fee] one of the best of laymen. A lay fee is an estate held for secular as opposed to ecclesiastical services.

[70] Benet] Saint Benedict (480–550).

[71] I said for the nonce] I said on that occasion.

PETRUS
Liberally spoken indeed. But what of that: say they not truly?

JULIUS
Howsoever it be, it is not for the pope's honour, whereto specially I must have regard.

PETRUS
To speak of regarding, surely methinks that honour could not be more regarded than if they did nothing that might justly be laid to their reproach. But I require and adjure thee, and that by thy pontifical majesty, to tell me without fabling: is this way that thou tellest me now the common trade and means to come to the high papacy?

JULIUS
Well, I wot there was no other fashion in many years, unless he that succeedeth me be made otherwise.[72] For after that I had my purpose, by and by I sent a bull under lead to warn them, lest any man should enter into the honourable see, by such means, and also renewed [B6ʳ] the said bull a little before my death.[73] How much it shall prevail, let them care that need hath.

PETRUS
I suppose there could no man describe the mischievous corrupt fashion better than thou. But one thing I marvel of: how any can be found that will take the office upon him, seeing that it is so painful to keep and dangerous to come by. When I was the bishop I could scarcely enforce any to take on him the office of a poor priest or deacon.

JULIUS
It was no great marvel. For that time the state or condition of the bishops and other fathers was nothing else but labours, watchings, fastings, preaching, and oftentimes death. But now it is all whole a king's life and better. Therefore who is it, if he have any trust at all to vanquish, that would not go to hand grips for so sweet a life?[74]

---

[72] he that succeedeth me] Erasmus had high hopes for Julius's successor, Leo X. In a letter of 1514 he compared the two: 'Julius, a pope who was by no means universally approved succeeded in rousing this hurricane of wars. Cannot Leo, who is scholarly, honourable, and devout, succeed in quieting it?' (*CWE* 2. 281–82).
[73] For after … my death] Julius issued a papal bull in 1505 condemning simony and voiding any promises or engagements made in connection with a papal election. He re-issued it in 1510 and in 1513, just a few days before his death.
[74] Therefore … life] Who would not fight hand-to-hand for such a prize if he thought he could prevail?

PETRUS
But tell forth, what said thou of Bonony? Went it out of the faith, that it needed to be restored to the see of Rome?

JULIUS
Peace, that was no matter.

PETRUS
Perchance the commonalty decayed by the [B6ᵛ] misgovernance of Bentivolus?[75]

JULIUS
No indeed! For at that time the city was most in his flowers repaired,[76] and illustrate° with many goodly buildings. And therefore I was more greedy over it.

PETRUS
I perceive the matter now. Did he not then come in by a wrong title?

JULIUS
That was not the matter. For he came to it by the favour of the whole body of the town.

PETRUS
Then the Bononies would not suffer him to rule over them?

JULIUS
Yes, marry. They held stiffly with him, and were almost altogether against me.

PETRUS
What then was the cause?

JULIUS
Plainly this was all the matter. Because he governed in such wise that there came but a few thousands of the unreasonable sums of money which he gathered of the citizens to our treasure house. Beside all this it was a very necessary thing to that which I went about. And so by help of the Frenchmen and many other which I enforced thereto with [B7ʳ] the thunderbolt of my curse, I voided him and his the town. I put in their rooms cardinals and bishops to rule the same so that no part of the profits might escape the see of Rome. Another cause was that the chief title and honour of the empire of Rome appeared altogether to be theirs.[77] But now are set forth in every part of the town our images, our titles be read, our tokens and monuments of victory be worshipped, and in many sundry places standeth a

---

[75] Bentivolus] Giovanni Bentivoglio (1443–1508).
[76] the city was ... repaired] the city was flourishing. Compare *ASD* I-8, line 284: 'Imo maxime florebat ea ciuitas ...'
[77] Another cause was that the chief title and honour ... theirs] Bologna was the most important of the Papal States after Rome.

Julius of stone or brass.⁷⁸ To be short if thou had seen with what a regal pomp and triumph I entered into Bonony,⁷⁹ perchance thou wouldst the less have set by all the triumphs of Octavians or Scipions,⁸⁰ and that it was not without a cause that I enterprised so far. For you might have seen there the very church militant and triumphant, both at once.

PETRUS
Therefore when thou reigned (as I perceived) that fortuned which Christ commanded [B7ᵛ] us to pray for in the pater noster: Let thy kingdom come to us. Now I pray thee, what heinous displeasure had the poor Venetians done to thee?

JULIUS
First of all they followed altogether the Greeks,⁸¹ and made me their laughing stock, speaking ever all they could to my reproach.

PETRUS
But was it true or false that they spoke?

JULIUS
What matters that? It is plain sacrilege once to whisper of the bishop of Rome, except it be done to his praise. Moreover, they bestowed all their benefices at their own pleasure, nor they would suffer no appeals hither, nor buy any dispensations. What need many words? They vexed the see of Rome in such wise that it could not be suffered, which moreover withheld a great part of thy patrimony.

PETRUS
Of my patrimony? I pray thee, what patrimony tellest thou me of, that left all together and poorly followed poor Christ?⁸²

---

⁷⁸ a Julius of stone or brass] Among other memorials produced in the wake of the expulsion of Giovanni Bentivoglio from Bologna in 1506, Julius commissioned a statue of himself from Michelangelo. The statue was destroyed when the city was recaptured in 1511.

⁷⁹ regal pomp and triumph ... Bonony] Erasmus was an eyewitness to Julius's triumphal entry into Bologna on 11 November 1506. On 16 November he wrote from Bologna to Servatius Rogers: 'Bentivoglio has left Bologna; the French, who have been laying siege to the town, were driven back by the citizens with the loss of a few soldiers. On St Martin's Day Julius, the supreme pontiff, entered Bologna; the following Sunday he celebrated mass in the cathedral' (*CWE* 2. 125).

⁸⁰ Octavians or Scipions] Gaius Octavius, later the Emperor Augustus (63 BC–19 AD), and the renowned general Scipio Africanus (236–183 BC).

⁸¹ the Greeks] The Venetian republic followed the example of the Greek church in resisting the papacy.

⁸² all together] everything, all at once.

JULIUS
I speak of certain towns that belong to the see of Rome, [B8ʳ] for so it pleased the most holy fathers to call a particular part of their possessions.

PETRUS
Truly ye have gotten much lucre and advantage, to my great slander. And dost thou therefore call this an intolerable hurt?

JULIUS
370 What else?

PETRUS
Yea but was their manners to be suffered? Or their love toward God decayed?

JULIUS
Tush, thou speakest of trifles. The matter is this: they withheld from us yearly infinite thousands of ducats, which had been sufficient to fund an army royal.

PETRUS
By my troth, a great loss to such an usurer! But that same duke of Ferrara, what
375 had he done?[83]

JULIUS
What had he done? A churl of all churls, whom Alexander the vicar of Christ had in such favour (though he was but of base blood) that he married one of his daughters to him and gave thereto great possessions for her dowry;[84] and yet nothing at all remembering his humanity and kindness ever barked and whined
380 against me, calling [B8ᵛ] me often schismatic, buggerer, and frantic fellow. And furthermore, he claimed many tributes which, albeit they were but small, yet a diligent curate would not utterly despise them.

GENIUS
[*Aside*] Nay, a crafty merchant.

JULIUS
But to come to our matter: it was somewhat expedient to that which I went about
385 to have that goodly town coupled to our patrimony,[85] because it lay commodiously for us. Therefore I was purposed (that once brought to pass) to give it to a kinsman of ours, a fellow very active and bold enough to attempt any manner of thing for the advancement of the church, which slew (not long ago) the cardinal of Papia

---

[83] duke of Ferrara] Alfonso d'Este (1476–1534).
[84] Alexander the vicar of Christ ... one of his daughters] Julius's predecessor Alexander VI (1431–1503) married Lucrezia Borgia (1480–1519) to Alfonso d'Este in 1502.
[85] that goodly town] Ferrara.

with his own hand, for my pleasure,[86] but as for his daughter's husband is
contented well enough.[87]

PETRUS
What hear I? Hath also the high bishops wives and children?

JULIUS
They have no wives of their own, but what strange thing is it for them to have children, sith they [C1^r] be men as other be and no geldings?

PETRUS
But tell me what caused that schismatic council?

JULIUS
It were very tedious to recite all from the first beginning, therefore I shall touch the effect as briefly as I can.[88] Certain persons began to wax weary of the court of

---

[86] a kinsman of ours ... for my pleasure] In 1511 the pope's nephew Francesco Maria della Rovere (1490–1538) stabbed to death Francesco Alidosi, cardinal of Pavia, in an open street in Ravenna. There is no evidence that Julius planned to give Ferrara to Francesco Maria, or that he ordered the murder; on the contrary, Alidosi was a papal favourite.

[87] but as for ... well enough] The thought here is obscure. Some commentators take it that the *Julius* has confused Francesco Maria with Giovanni Orisini, who married Julius's ('his') daughter; alternatively, the implication is that Julius planned to place his nephew in Ferrara because his son-in-law was content with his lot.

[88] I shall touch the effect as briefly as I can] The succeeding account of conciliar politics is in fact narrated in considerable detail. The anti-papal Council of Pisa-Milan sat from 1511 to 1512; the Fifth Lateran Council, called by Julius in response to what he regarded as an illegitimate, 'schismatic' gathering, sat from 1512 to 1517. Conciliar politics had become a major part of church history a century earlier with the Council of Constance (1414–1418), which put an end to a schism involving three claimants to the papal crown by affirming that an assembly of the church had authority even over the pope. Subsequently, calls for a council became an important instrument of reform in late medieval Christendom. So far as the *Dialogue* is concerned, Pisa-Milan expressed a genuine desire to return to godly values, while Julius's retaliatory summoning of the Fifth Lateran Council was a cosmetic sop to critics that in reality aimed to further entrench Julius's power. Modern historians tend to be equally cynical about both. For an account of the two councils, see Menchi's notes, and Christine Shaw, *Julius II: The Warrior Pope* (Oxford: Wiley-Blackwell, 1993), pp. 278–315.

The *Dialogue*'s interest in conciliarism also resonates with its Tudor contexts. In 1532 a treatise arguing in support of the king's attempt to annul his marriage to Katherine of Aragon, thought to have been partly written by Henry himself, declared that 'Euery man of what so euer state or dignite that he be, ye though he be the pope: is bounde to obey the generall counsel'. A month after Anne Boleyn's coronation, in June 1533, Henry issued an appeal for a general council of the church, fearing that he might be excommunicated by the pope. By 1535, however — that is, by the time of the second edition of the *Dialogue* — the situation was reversed, with Henry worried that a council would excommunicate him. The Scottish theologian Alexander Alesius's 1538 *Treatise concernynge generall counciles* condemns councils as instruments of papal authority. Byddell's *Dialogue* is thus the product of the

Rome.⁸⁹ They reported that all together was corrupt with filthy lucre, with prodigious and abominable lechery, with privy poisonings, sacrilege, murder, simony, and other unlawful merchandise. They said also that even I myself was a simoniac,° a drunkard, a buggerer, puffed up with a worldly spirit and altogether such a one that hath unthriftily occupied the room,° and to the great confusion of all the Christianity. And so these matters out of frame° must be (in God's name) redressed by a general council. They said thereto that I was sworn to summon a general council within two years after I took my honour, and that upon this condition I was [C1ᵛ] made pope.⁹⁰

PETRUS
But was it truly said?

JULIUS
Yea, it was truth indeed. Nevertheless I loosed myself from that oath when I thought most expedient. For what is he that will doubt anything to swear amain,° to come to such a booty? Godliness may be reverenced otherwise, as one Julius, such another as I am, was wont to say most elegantly.⁹¹ But mark the boldness of these losels,° and see to what point the matter came. Nine cardinals shrunk from me at once.⁹² They showed me they would have a council, and cited me to be there, and prayed me to sit as resident or judge. When they could not bring me to that point they sent out a general commandment everywhere, by the authority of Maximillian the emperor, and also by the authority of Louis the French king, the twelfth of that name, because the historians witnesseth that in times past the council was wont to be summoned by the emperors of Rome.⁹³ [C2ʳ] I quake in

---

relatively brief moment in which it looked like conciliar politics might offer a solution first to Henry's marital problems and then to his compromised relationship with the Catholic church. See *A glasse of the truthe*, sig. D6ʳ; MacCulloch, *Thomas Cromwell*, pp. 227, 289; and Alexander Alesius, *A treatise concernynge generall councilles, the byshoppes of Rome, and the clergy*.

⁸⁹ Certain persons ... Rome] The decision to convoke a council was announced on 16 May 1510, when a group of cardinals issued a decree saying that the papacy was in need of reform and that a council was the best instrument with which to pursue its transformation.

⁹⁰ They said ... made pope] The proceedings of the Council of Pisa-Milan reproduced in full the document signed by members of the papal conclave of 1503 (including Giuliano della Rovere, subsequently elected pope), undertaking to hold a general council of the church within two years.

⁹¹ one Julius ... elegantly] Cicero's *De officiis* records Caesar quoting Euripides: 'If wrong may e'er be right, for a throne's sake | Were wrong most right' (III. 2182).

⁹² Nine cardinals] Julius is referring to the signatories of the 1511 decrees convening the Council of Pisa-Milan. In the *Dialogue*, the 'general commandment' for the council follows Julius's refusal to become involved. In reality, the invitation was part of the decree.

⁹³ When they could not ... emperors of Rome] The Council of Pisa-Milan was supported by Louis XII and Maximilian I as part of their manoeuvring in the Italian wars. The *Dialogue* takes the council at its own estimation, as an instrument for internal reform of the church.

speaking it, how greatly they endeavour them to cut asunder the coat of Christ without any seam, which his crucifiers left whole.[94]

PETRUS
But was thou such a fellow as they reported thee?

JULIUS
What matter is it, if I were? I was the high bishop. But I put case I were more tyrannous than the Cercopians, more foolish than Morichus,[95] or most ass in the world, yea more filthy than a common sink: whosoever keepeth this key of power, it is meet he be had in reverence as Christ's vicar, and to worship him as most holy father in God.

PETRUS
Yea? Though he be an open misdoer?

JULIUS
That forceth not.[96] But to be plain, it is not convenient that he which is in God's stead in earth, and representeth all wholly as it were a god among men, should be rebuked or evil spoken by of every vile fellow.

PETRUS
But the common reason crieth against this, that we should judge well of him whom we see do openly evil, or say well of such as we perceive to be nought.

JULIUS
[C2ᵛ] I am content every man think what he list, so he say well, or else hold their peace. For truly the bishop of Rome may not be rebuked, no, not of a general council.

PETRUS
This is one thing I am assured of: whosoever is in Christ's stead here in earth, ought to be as like to him in living as can be, and so likewise to lead all his life, lest any thing may be reprehended in him, or lest any person (of his deserving) might speak evil of him. It is not well with popes and bishops if they be come to

---

[94] the coat of Christ] See John 19. 23.
[95] But I ... Morichus] 'But let us assume that I was more tyrannous than the Cercopians and more foolish than Morychus ...' The Cercopes were renowned for cunning, whilst Morychus was a name for Bacchus, mocked for foolishness. See Erasmus's *Adage* II. vii. 35, *Cercopum coetus*, 'An assembly of Cercopes': 'The story goes that there were people called Cercopes in Ephesus, who were notoriously untrustworthy, and attempted by their treachery to impose on Jove himself'; and II. ix. 1, *Stultior Morycho*, 'As big a fool as Morychus': 'Bacchus is presented by poets everywhere as a figure of fun and none too intelligent, being a tipsy god' (*CWE* 34. 19, 89).
[96] That forceth not] 'That doesn't matter.'

enforce and constrain men, rather with threatening than with good deeds; to speak well of them, whom thou canst not laud without lying, whose greatest glory is, the constrained silence of such as thinketh evil of them. But answer me hereunto. I pray thee may not the Pope (if he be a pestilent caitiff and a captain of mischief) be in no wise deposed?

JULIUS
Oh, wise man? Who should depose him, which is the highest of all?

PETRUS
[C3ʳ] Marry, so much the rather ought he to be put down. For the greater man, the more mischief may he do. And to prove that, the law civil doth not only depose an emperor for his evil ruling, but also willeth him to be put to death.[97] O, what an unhappy condition and state is the church in, which must be constrained to sustain a bishop of Rome, doing what mischief soever he list, and may in no wise bless us from such a cruel tyrant![98]

JULIUS
That reason is nought worth. For if the bishop of Rome might be put down, it must be done by the authority of a general council. Yea and beside this, a council cannot be holden without the pope's consent, for else it is but a conventicle and no council.[99] But if so be it be gathered in most due manner, yet nothing at all may be ordained and decreed, but if the pope be willing thereto. Therefore the next way I know to suppress a pope is an absolute power, whereby (if it [C3ᵛ] should be tried) one bishop is able to do more than all the whole council.[100] Therefore it is evident, that he may not be deprived his patrimony for any manner offence.[101]

PETRUS
No? Not for murder?

---

[97] the law civil ... put to death] Erasmus and Thomas More translated and wrote responses to Lucian's *Tyrannicide*, which takes as its premise the reward granted to those who put tyrants to death.

[98] bless us from] keep us free from.

[99] a council cannot be holden without the pope's consent] The bull summoning the Fifth Lateran Council affirmed that 'the right to convoke a general council and those matters that concern it belong to the Supreme Pontiff'. See *ASD* I-8, note to line 387. Julius views Pisa-Milan as a conventicle, an illegitimate assembly.

[100] one bishop] i.e. one pope.

[101] he may not be deprived ... for any manner offence] This was a key issue at stake both in the Council of Pisa-Milan and the Fifth Lateran Council. Julius's supporters claimed that a pope 'cannot be judged by any mortal save in the case of heresy', specifically mentioning murder, adultery, simony, and blasphemy as crimes that could not warrant punishment. See *ASD* I-8, note to lines 390–91.

JULIUS
Not if he killed his father.

PETRUS
Nor for adultery?

JULIUS
Enough of such words! Not if he had lain with his sister.

PETRUS
Neither for wicked simony?

JULIUS
465   No, not for six hundred simonies.

PETRUS
Not for poisoning?

JULIUS
No, nor for no sacrilege neither.

PETRUS
Nor for blaspheming against God?

JULIUS
I say no.

PETRUS
470   What if he had done all these together?

JULIUS
It forceth not. For put thereto (if thou wilt) six hundred more, and worse if thou can feign them, and join them all together, yet may not the high bishop of Rome be put out of his place for them all.

PETRUS
Thou tellest me of a dignity which I never heard of before, if he only may be as
475   naughty as he list, and no man correct him. And also a more new unhappy case of the church, if it may in [C4ʳ] no wise drive out so abominable a monster but be constrained to worship and keep such a bishop as no man would suffer to keep his horses.

JULIUS
Some say that he may be put out for one thing alone.

PETRUS
480   For what goodness is that? For as for naughtiness, it can not, if these things before rehearsed can be no causes.

JULIUS

For heresy. And yet must he be openly convict. But that is but a fable and hurteth him not a point, and this is the reason. For first of all, he may at his pleasure abrogate the law, if he like it not. And again, who dare accuse his highness of heresy? Namely, being so strong in power, and having so much aid. Moreover, if it chance him to be thrust down by the council, yet hath he a good remedy, as to revoke his heresy, if that he may in no wise deny it. To make short, there be a thousand starting holes° for to escape out easily at them, without he be altogether [C4ᵛ] a stock° and no man.¹⁰²

PETRUS

But tell me by thy popish dignity, who made all these goodly laws?

JULIUS

Who else save the bishop of Rome, wellhead of all laws? And yet may he at his pleasure both abrogate and expound, writhe and wrest them howsoever he seemeth best, for his profit.

PETRUS

An unhappy pope by my troth, which may delude not only a council but also God himself. Nevertheless against such a wretch as thou hast described to me even very now — that is to say, an open maintainer of mischief, a drunkard, a manqueller,° a simoniac, a poisoner, a perjurer, an extortioner, an open buggerer — a council is not so much to be desired as all the multitude armed with stones to kill him as a common pestilence of all the world. But go forth and tell me, for what cause thou abhorrest so much a general council?

JULIUS

Nay, but first of all, ask this one thing of great princes of the world: [C5ʳ] wherefore they hate great assemblies and temporal parliaments? Sure the cause is, that at the great confluence of so many honourable prelates, the dignity of the pope is something shadowed° and suffereth some damage. And it fortuneth ever in such assemblies, that they which be of great learning and judgement, their cunning maketh them bold to speak; such as have a clear conscience speak more liberally than is expedient for us; and likewise some there be called to great office and rule, which use their authority and power to the uttermost, among whom cometh commonly many which sore disdaineth our glory, and at their coming be of this intent, that they would pare away part both of our authority and riches. The worst of all is, that there sitteth neither better nor worse but he thinketh that he may speak lawfully against the pope by reason that he is one of the council, which else durst not once say 'buff'.¹⁰³ [C5ᵛ] Therefore I knew never council that chanced so

---

¹⁰² without he be] unless he is.
¹⁰³ say 'buff'] say anything. To not know 'whether to say buff nor baff' is to be lost for words; to be 'unable to say buff to a wolf's shadow' is to be scared to speak out.

well, but the pope hath had some of his feathers plucked, whereunto thou may bear witness thyself, unless thou have clean forgotten. For although your council holden at Jerusalem were but for trifling matters, neither of whole empires and king's ransoms as ours be now, yet James was not afraid to add a great piece of his own mind, after thou hadst given sentence, as it is evident in the fifteenth chapter of the Acts.[104] For when thou hadst clean delivered the Gentiles altogether from the burden of Moses' law, James reasoning after thee, excepted fornication, choked blood,[105] and eating of things offered to idols, correcting as it were thine ordinance and power, insomuch that some there be at this day moved by this example that say James had the authority of the pope, and not thou.[106]

PETRUS
Thinkest thou then that the kingly majesty of one high bishop is [C6ʳ] rather to be preserved and maintained in high estate and wealth than the whole multitude and commonalty of the Christian people?

JULIUS
Let every man provide the most for his own singular profit and advantage. We do work for ourselves.

PETRUS
But and if so be it Christ had done in like wise the same, then should we not have had any church at all, whereof thou boastest thyself to be only the head. And surely I do not perceive by what reason he which will be esteemed as the vicar of God may embrace a manner of living clean contrary. But tell forth now, by what pretty policy and shift° thou dashedest out of countenance the foresaid schismatic council, as thou callest it.

JULIUS
Forsooth I will tell thee truly, understand it well if that thou canst. First of all Maximilian the emperor, for so they do call him, likewise as he is very treatable,° and albeit that he had summoned by his solemn [C6ᵛ] and accustomed messengers a council, yet notwithstanding I led him another way, by such means as I will not speak of.[107] Moreover I persuaded by a little policy certain cardinals

---

[104] Therefore … Acts] Acts 15. 5-29 describes a council held at Jerusalem among the early Christian community. Peter argues that gentile converts should not be subject to Jewish law; James agrees, but says they should nonetheless abstain from a number of prohibited practices.
[105] choked blood] This phrase collapses together two of James's dietary prohibitions. Christians should refrain from 'whatever has been strangled and from blood' (Acts 15. 20).
[106] some there be … not thou] The council in Acts 15 was an episode referenced in debates over the relationship between conciliar and papal power. Julius's supporter Giovanni Francesco Poggio wrote in his *De potestate papae* that 'Peter was the successor of Christ as his vicar, not James'. See *ASD* 1-8, note to lines 446-47.
[107] such means as I will not speak of] In 1512 Maximilian signed a treaty with Julius, denounced

278   THE DIALOGUE BETWEEN JULIUS THE SECOND, GENIUS, AND ST PETER

540   in such wise that they were glad to deny that thing before notaries and witnesses which they had confirmed before by their open writings.[108]

PETRUS
And might that be suffered?

JULIUS
Wherefore not, if the pope approve the same?

PETRUS
Then it recketh little of taking an oath, seeing he will dispense withal at his
545   pleasure.

JULIUS
Nay, to speak the truth plainly, that was somewhat beyond good fashion, but there was no better shift to be made. Beside this, when I espied it would come to pass that by the envy of the council I should in many places be thrust under feet,[109] namely when it was promulgate not to exclude me but they prayed me in the
550   humblest wise to sit as resident in the council, mark what a pretty wile I [C7ʳ] found here, following the trade of my predecessors. I likewise appealed to the council next to come, complaining and feigning cause that neither the time nor place which they appointed was convenient, and by and by summoned a council to be kept at Rome, where I supposed none other would come but Julius's friends,
555   or that would be intreated, for so I learned by many examples. And in all haste to this purpose I created many such cardinals, which I thought meet for to bring my matters about.[110]

GENIUS
[*Aside*] That is to say of the most unthrifts.°

JULIUS
And again this council, unless it had been summoned by me, had been no council
560   at all. And yet for all that, it was not greatly expedient for my matters that such a company of bishops and abbots should come thither, among whom it could not be thought but that some should be godly and well-disposed persons. Therefore I gave them warning to spare their [C7ᵛ] purses, and every country should send but one or two at the uttermost. Notwithstanding when I perceived this device
565   scant° sure enough, and that those few of so many sundry provinces should

schismatics, and declared his support for the Fifth Lateran Council as the sole legitimate council of the church. The Council of Pisa-Milan was eventually abandoned.
[108] Moreover ... writings] Julius persuaded a number of the 1511 signatories to dissociate themselves from the Council of Pisa-Milan.
[109] thrust under feet] subjected.
[110] I created ... about] Julius created eight new cardinals in 1511.

altogether amount to over great a number for me, I sent them word about the time that they were preparing them to take journey to defer their coming for that time, and that the council should be prorogued unto another time, feigning for the same prorogation many probable° and apparent causes, and again by such manner of policies all such things dashed. I preventing° once again the day prescribed held a council at Rome with such alone as I provided for the same intent,[111] among whom also if there was any that durst be so bold to dissent from me, yet I was sure that the proudest of them all durst not resist me, I was so far above them all in artillery and soldiers. Now I brought this schismatic conventicle of France in such [C8^r] hatred, by this manner that followeth. First I sent out letters against the council which was kept in France to every country, where I made mention of our most holy council holden at Rome, cursing their council, calling it oftentimes the conventicle of Satan, the Devil's parliament house, a conspiracy of schismatics against the holy church.[112]

PETRUS
I think those cardinals which were the authors and doers of that wicked council must needs be false traitors.

JULIUS
As for their falsehood I let pass. But the chief captain of all this business was the cardinal of Rouen,[113] who ever applied himself (by what a popish holiness I wot not) to redress the manners of the church, and likewise showed his tenderer love in diverse places, but death happily took him, to whom succeeded a Spanish cardinal,[114] a good liver, well aged, and a doctor of divinity, which people be wont to be unfriendly to the popes of Rome.

PETRUS
[C8^v] But had your man, which thou namest to be learned in divinity, no probable reasons to lay for that which he did?

JULIUS
Yes, too many. For he said that there was never so unquiet a world as it was at those days, and that the church had never more need to have her sickness cured

---

[111] I sent them word ... intent] In fact, the postponement of the opening of the council was the matter only of a couple of weeks.

[112] the conventicle ... holy church] Here the *Julius exclusus* closely tracks the language of Julius's pronouncements against the Council of Pisa-Milan, which he denounced as a schismatic conventicle, the 'synagogue of Satan', and as a plot against the church. See *ASD* I-8, note to lines 486–87.

[113] the cardinal of Rouen] George d'Amboise (1460–1510).

[114] a Spanish cardinal] Bernardino Lopez de Carvajal (1455–1523). Neither of these figures seem to have been quite the paragons of piety described here; both aspired to the papacy, and their moves against Julius serviced this ambition.

and healed. And therefore (he said) it was my duty to help it with a general council; also that I had taken mine oath at my creation, to summon it within two years after; yea, so to be bound by virtue of mine oath, that I might in no wise be dispensed therewith, no not by the consent of the whole college of cardinals; and that it had been often put in remembrance of my brethren the cardinals and instantly desired, also often instanced by great princes, and how I could in no wise hear of it. In so much they said that every man might see, as long as Julius was living there was no likelihood to have any council. Thereto they [D1^r] alleged against me the examples of the councils holden by our predecessors, to bind me thereto, and alleged moreover certain antique laws, to prove that I and mine adherents did refuse a council, and thereupon that the very authority to let call it did pertain unto them, but for so much° as other princes did also (for the pope's pleasure) wink at the matter that then the authority to summon the council did rest only in the emperor of Rome, the which was wont in time past to command it at his own will, and to the French king, which by the title of most Christian king was wont to bear a stroke in the same.[115]

PETRUS
But did this doctor and cardinal with his part takers use in their writing to thee no such fashion as did become them?

JULIUS
No, marry. They the villains were wiser in this behalf than I would they had been. They handled the thing of troth very abominably, with great [D1^v] soberness. And they did not only refrain from evil words but they did never so much as named me without an honourable preface desiring and praying me for saints and souls that I would (according as it beseemed me, and for the performance of mine oath) sit as judge over the council and help to cure the diseases reigning in the church. Nor a man cannot think in what envy I was brought by their meek and cold fashion, specially because they sauced all their writings in with Holy Scripture, whereby it seemed some well-learned men were procured for that purpose. They joined hereto the commendation of fasting, prayer, watching, with other good deeds, to the intent they might the rather thrust me down with the title of holiness.

PETRUS
Under what pretence didst thou then summon a council?

---

[115] the emperor of Rome … the same] Contrast Julius's statement above, that 'this council, unless it had been summoned by me, had been no council at all'. The early councils of the church such as the Council of Nicea (325 AD) had been convened by the authority of the Roman emperor, and French propaganda in support of the Council of Pisa-Milan referred back to this precedent.

JULIUS
Under as goodly as might be. I told them that I was minded first of all to correct the head of the church, that is to say [D2ʳ] myself;¹¹⁶ then after the Christian princes; and last of all, the whole communality.

PETRUS
625 Surely I hear of a goodly pastance.° But now I am desirous to hear the conclusion of all together. And also it should please me well to hear what the divines in Satan's parliament decreed.

JULIUS
Most miserable and abominable matters! My heart riseth to remember them.

PETRUS
But I pray thee, may they not be spoken?

JULIUS
630 Forsooth, not well. They be far worse than sacrilege or heresy, against which if I had not set to my helping hands in time, yea both with weapon and wit, the dignity of the church had been clean cast down under foot.

PETRUS
I am with child for to hear of them.¹¹⁷

JULIUS
Yea, but I quake for to speak of them. These most ungracious wretches went first
635 about to bring the holy church (most flourishing now both in dominions and inestimable riches) to her old beggary and miserable [D2ᵛ] poverty wherein she was in the apostles' time; and to bring the cardinals (which in all worldly port° at this day passen° far all kings christened) to some poor life; that bishops, abbots and other prelates should live much more scarcely° and to be content with few
640 waiting men and horses, and as some say whores; and that the cardinals should not so universally swallow up both bishoprics, abbeys, and benefices; and that no man should keep two bishoprics; and that such priests as would heap benefice upon benefice till they had six hundred at once and care not if they might be suffered should be corrected and be content with such a living as might suffice a
645 sober and honest priest. Another was, that neither pope, bishop, nor priest should be made for money, favour, or flattering service but only for his pure life, but if the contrary should chance that he should by and by be deposed. Yea that [D3ʳ] it was also lawful to thrust out the pope also, if he were known an evil liver. And that drunken and lecherous bishops should be put from administration; that

---

¹¹⁶ I was minded … myself] Some of Julius's cardinals objected to his declaration that he expected reform to begin with the papacy.
¹¹⁷ I am with child] I am agog.

650 priests which were openly known whoremongers and misdoers should lose not only their benefice, but also be gelded; with many such like (I am weary to show all) which were only to load us with holiness, taking away our riches and dominion.[118]

PETRUS
What was ordained against these in your holy council at Rome?

JULIUS
655 Methinketh thou hast an ill remembrance. I told thee before that mine intent was nothing else but under the pretence of a council (as the proverb sayeth) to drive forth one peg with another.[119] My first sitting was driven forth with certain ceremonies and antique customs, which pleased me well enough, although they were nothing at all material. There were two solemn masses, one of the holy cross,
660 [D3ᵛ] another of the holy ghost, as though that all together should be conduced and led by his holy inspiration. Then after was made a goodly oration, all to the laud of my holiness. In the next sitting I cursed as deeply as I could those schismatic cardinals, pronouncing as damnable, accursed, and heresy all those things the which they had decreed, or should decree.[120] At the third meeting I did
665 excommunicate or curse the realm of France, and changed the marts from the city of Lyon.[121] And nevertheless in the said interdiction I excepted by name certain places of the said realm. And all this was to alien° and turn the hearts of all the people from their king, and to raise some rebel and sedition among themselves. And for to confirm the same, I sent out the curse under my bulls of
670 lead to such princes and governors as I perceived propense° and bowing toward our [D4ʳ] pretenced factions and seditions.

PETRUS
But did they nothing else?

JULIUS
That thing was done which I desired, for if our devices be regarded I know I have the victory. As for those three cardinals which were so stiff against me in those

---

[118] These most ungracious wretches ... dominion] This paragraph is not representative of the actual Pisan discussions, and is best understood as Erasmus taking the opportunity to indicate his own ideals of institutional reform, albeit hyperbolically. The proposal regarding gelding is a little more neutrally or euphemistically expressed in the Latin, which refers only to the loss of 'a member' of the body. See *ASD* I-8, line 544.
[119] to drive forth one peg with another] Adage I. ii. 4, *Clavum clavo pellere*, 'To drive out one nail by another'.
[120] My first sitting ... decree] For a summary of the Council's opening two sessions, broadly agreeing with that of the *Dialogue*, see Shaw, *Julius II*, pp. 299–300.
[121] changed the marts from ... Lyon] The privilege of holding the historic market of Lyon was transferred to Geneva.

675 naughty matters, I with all solemnity belonging thereto deprived their cardinalships. I have also given all the pensions of their benefices to other being friendly to me so that they can never be restored to them again. Themselves I have given to Satan, much rather willing to burn them clean up, if I might catch them.

PETRUS
Marry, but yet for all that, if all be as thou dost say, the decrees of that schismatical
680 parliament seemeth to be much more holy than is thy holy synod, whereof I see nothing else at all but tyrannous threatenings, cursings, and great cruelness mingled with mischief and deceit. And if so be that Satan was in deed as thou sayest, [D4ᵛ] the author of the said parliament, surely me thinketh the Devil goeth more nigh unto Christ than the sorry° ghost — the holy ghost, I would say —
685 whom ye boast the moderator of your holy counsel.

JULIUS
Nay, but take good heed what thou sayest. For in all my bulls I have cursed all such which favoureth by word or deed that same false conventicle.

PETRUS
Oh, caitiff, he is yet the same old Julius! But what was the end of this business?

JULIUS
In this case I left it.¹²² Whereto it shall come, let fortune rule.

PETRUS
690 Truly the schism remaineth still.

JULIUS
Yea, marry, I warrant thee, and that most perilous.

PETRUS
And hadst thou (being God's vicar) rather have so horrible a schism than a true council?

JULIUS
One schism, quod he? By my mother's soul, a hundred such rather than I would
695 be constrained to keep their ordinances and to make them account of all my life!

PETRUS
Thou knowest thyself so guilty?

JULIUS
What [D5ʳ] matter is that to thee?

---

¹²² In this case I left it] The Fifth Lateran Council was not closed until March 1517, four years after Julius's death.

PETRUS

It is surely so, the matter might well enough have been unmoved. But who thinkest thou shall have the victory?

JULIUS

All that is as it pleaseth fortune. Nevertheless we have more money in our party. For as for France is now with long wars stark beggared; England which I suppose be my friends, hath yet hills of gold untouched. But this I may be sure of: if France have the victory as God forfend, there must needs be a great and horrible change. Then shall our holy council of Rome be called the conventicle of Satan and I an idol of a pope, and the holy ghost is altogether theirs and we have done all by the spirit of Satan. But surely I have yet great trust in my money which I have left.

PETRUS

But what chanced then at the length against the Frenchmen and their king, whom your predecessors adorned and decorate with the title of most Christian,[123] [D5ᵛ] namely when thou canst not deny, but through their aid and help thou hast not only be succoured in thy poverty, but also exalted to this dignity much above any king or emperor, by whose aid thou didst recover Bonony with other cities and vanquished the Venetians, never overcome before? But how chanced thee to forget altogether so great kindness and so lately done? Broken so many leagues?[124]

JULIUS

It were somewhat too long to tell thee this tale from the beginning. But for to make few words, I began nothing newly of my part, but that which I was so long before with child within my mind I began to attempt, which thing I had also (for lack of opportunity, and many other causes) dissembled unto that time. For truth it is, I never favoured heartily the French nation. No more doth any Italian entirely favour any foreign nation (as we call them) any otherwise, but as the wolf doth the [D6ʳ] lamb.[125] But I being not only an Italian, but also a Genovay,[126] did so long keep those rude people my friends, as I had need of their aid and succour, which hitherto was necessary for me, where in the mean time I both suffered, dissembled and imagined many matters. But as shortly as all my matters were brought to such effect as I would have them, then remained nothing but that I should show me what I was indeed and thrust out the filthy foresters° clean out of Italy.[127]

---

[123] most Christian] A title claimed by French kings since the eighth century.

[124] Broken so many leagues] 'How did you chance to break so many leagues?'

[125] favour ... as the wolf doth the lamb] See *Adages* IV. vii. 91, *Ut lupus ovem*, 'As the wolf loves the sheep', spoken 'of a person who pretends to love for his own advantage'.

[126] Genovay] A Genovese native.

[127] what I was indeed] That is: a true Julius ('vere Iulium', *ASD* I-8, line 607), like Caesar, who warred against the Gauls.

PETRUS
What manner of beasts be they which thou callest barbarians and foresters?

JULIUS
They be men as other be.

PETRUS
Be they men sayest thou, and be not also christened?

JULIUS
730 And also Christian men too. But what is that to the purpose?

PETRUS
Ergo, they be Christian men — but peradventure without laws and learning, living beastly?

JULIUS
Without learning quod he? Marry sir, they exceed us both in learning and riches, whereat we do most envy.

PETRUS
735 What meaneth this word 'barbarians'? [D6ᵛ] Why speakest thou not?

GENIUS
I will tell thee: for he is ashamed. Italians because they be begotten of the vilest castaways of all other nations, resorting among them, being the pump° of all filthiness, yet out of their gentiles' learning they conceived such a furious pride,[128] as to call other countrymen barbarians and foresters, which word is more heinous
740 to them than to be called a murderer of thy parents or sacrilegean.°

PETRUS
So it appeareth. Nevertheless, inasmuch as Christ died for all manner of men, having no more respect to one man than another;[129] furthermore insomuch as thou professest thee to be the vicar of Christ, wherefore then didst thou not favour alike all them whom Christ hath not forsaken, but redeemed with his blood?

JULIUS
745 I can be contented to favour yea even the Indians, Africans, Ethiopians, and thereto the Greeks if they would fortify me and acknowledge me their prince by some customary [D7ʳ] duties. But as for all these three countries we refused and shaked off long sith, and next after the Greeks,[130] for because the wretches were so covetous, and would but little reverence the pope's power.

---

[128] gentiles' learning] pagan, classical writing.
[129] no more respect ... another] Compare Matt. 22. 16: 'you do not regard people with partiality' or Acts 10. 34: 'God shows no partiality' (traditionally translated: 'is no respecter of persons').
[130] the Greeks] Julius refers to fifteenth-century attempts to reconcile the Greek and Latin churches, which foundered at the Council of Florence in 1439.

PETRUS

750 Then I see well that the see of Rome is as it were the common barn of all the world.

JULIUS

A great matter surely, if we reap temporal goods of all men when we be ready to sow our spiritual seed to all men.[131]

PETRUS

What spiritual seed dost thou tell me? For hitherto I hear nothing of thee but fleshly seed. Perchance thou drawest men with thy holy doctrine to Christ?

JULIUS

755 There be enough beside me to preach if they will, which I do not inhibit so long as they bark not against our power and profit.

PETRUS

What if they be enough? What thereof?

JULIUS

What? For what cause doth the commons give to their heads whatsoever they do demand, but to knowledge that they possess whatsoever they have by licence [D7ᵛ]
760 of their princes?[132] Yea though they received never of them one mite, even so whatsoever the profane sort hath anywhere pertaining unto godliness, that must be imputed unto us as our deed, yea albeit we do but slumber all our lifetime. And yet also beside all this, we do give most large indulgences and pardons, and that for a very small sum of money. And moreover we do also dispense after the same
765 wise in great weighty matters. We give our holy blessings in every place where we come, yea and that altogether gratis.

PETRUS

I do not know what so much as one of all these matters doth mean. But return again to the effect of the purpose. For what manner of cause did thy holiness so much despise these aliens and barbarians as thou callest them, so that thou
770 haddest rather set all on heaps, than for to suffer them still in Italy?

JULIUS

I will tell thee. All these barbarous sort [D8ʳ] (but in especial the Frenchmen) be very persticious.° And as for the Spaniards differs not much from us, neither in language nor manners, yet notwithstanding I would have utterly exiled them as

---

[131] if we reap ... all men] A cunning misapplication of 1 Corinth. 9. 11: 'If we have sown spiritual good among you, is it too much if we reap your material benefits?'

[132] For what cause ... princes?] 'Why do the people grant their rulers everything that is requested from them, except to acknowledge that what they have, they have by their rulers' will?'

well as the other, to the intent that we might have used altogether our own fashion, without any check.

PETRUS
Doth the barbarous curs, as thou callest them, worship any other strange gods beside Christ?

JULIUS
Nay, but they worship him but too curiously,° insomuch that I do wonder right greatly to see how grievously they be offended with a sort of old words, the which of a truth in time past hath been much accustomed amongst us but as now they be clean left out of use.

PETRUS
But perchance they were some unthrifty° words of conjuration?

JULIUS
Marry, thou mayst say that again! For their names were simony, blaspheming of almighty God, sodomity,° intoxication or poisoning, [D8ᵛ] sortilege …

PETRUS
Peace, man!

JULIUS
Nay, they abhor such matters as much as thou dost.

PETRUS
Well, as for such names I let pass, but the thing's self doth so much reign among you as I think in any country in the world.¹³³

JULIUS
Neither those barbarians are all without vice. But because they be infect with other maladies, they wink at their own and cry out upon ours; and we on the other side do favour our own deeds and abhor theirs. We esteem poverty none otherwise than a great offence, and to be eschewed of all men, though it force not how. They contrariwise think it a point of a scarce good Christian to abound in riches, though they be gotten without fraud or guile. We dare not so much as once name drunkenship, nevertheless the Almaines° thinketh it a light fault, yea rather a merry jape or pastance° than offence; albeit we will not so much differ for this, if we agreed in all other [E1ʳ] matters. They abhor greatly usury, nevertheless we think no manner of men under heaven so meet for the church of Rome. As for buggery, they reckon so detestable that if so be a man do but once name it, they think both the air and sun by and by infected and also polluted; but we Italians be not altogether of that mind. As for simony, whose name was long sith gone

¹³³ the thing's self] the thing itself.

and banished, they flee as the Devil doth holy water, against which they had made certain laws, though they be now out of use. Albeit herein our conceit is somewhat differing and many such other they be infect with, which be clean contrary to our fashion of living, insomuch then as we be so contrary to them in our manner of life, so much more necessary it is to keep them from knowledge of our secrets. The more they be ignorant of our manners, the more praise they will give us. For if they once knew the secrets of our court, they [E1^v] would surely utter them to our rebuke. For however it fortune, they be somewhat quick in reproving their neighbours' faults. They write cursed biting books against the abusing of some of their country. They preach and cry everywhere that the see of Rome is not the see of Christ, but rather the great pump of Satan. They dispute of mine authority and power, whether I came by the popedom by reason of my good living or no; also if I ought to be taken as God's vicar or not. And so first of all by this means they diminish the good opinion that the people had in us, and so consequently abateth our authority and rule. For before such brabblings,° the people heard never other thing of us but that we did bear the room of Christ and that we had the next authority to God, yea rather checkmate with him.[134] But by reason of such unprofitable opinions, the church sustaineth intolerable damage. For [E2^r] we utter now fewer dispensations, and such other wares, and be fain to sell them better cheap. Also our rent and casualties° is less levied of bishoprics, abbotships, and other benefices. Yea and the people payeth with much worse will that which is required of them. To be short, our rents on every side decayeth, our fairs and markets waxeth barren, and that is most of all to be lamented, our dreadful darts be less and less feared. But if their malapertness come to such a wilful and beastly boldness that they dare once say that the pope being cursed of God can hurt no man with his curse, and so despise cursings, then it will shortly come to pass that we shall surely die for hunger. But if they be kept farther off from reasoning of such matters, and rather be brought in fear of our curses, for then such is the nature of such stubborn louts, that they will have us in great awe and reverence. [E2^v] And so shall we with our bulls and other instruments (if they be discretely handled) order all things as we would have it.

PETRUS

It is a heavy case if the authority of the pope and bishops depend upon this hazard, only that if their naughty living were known, they were even utterly undone. For when we lived upon earth truly we coveted nothing more than that all that we did might be known, yea even that which we did in our privy chambers. For we were most regarded when our lives were most manifest and known. But one thing I pray thee: be the princes so godly nowadays, as thou reportest them, or do they

---

[134] bear the room ... checkmate] to 'bear the room' is to hold an office; to 'be checkmate' with God is to hold the upper hand over Him.

so much fear the priests as to run one upon another, even at the beck of such an holy prelate as it might be thyself? For in my time I remember well, they were the extremest enemies we had.

JULIUS
As touching their godly living, they be not (thanked be God) very superstitious. And as to our [E3ʳ] honour they regard not very much, but maketh us their laughingstocks, except some certain of spiced° conscience which so much feareth our thunderbolt and curse as though it could hurt them that deserved it not. And yet those same persons altogether ignorant in the nature of the thing be only moved of a mad spiced conscience, rooted by long custom of time. Some there be likewise which for the hope they have to come to our riches and some for fear of us, do give place to our dignity. Other there be that think verily they shall come to an ill end which in any wise doth hurt a priest, what manner a liver soever he be. And most commonly all men, the more gentilely° they be brought up, the more they regard our ceremonies, provoked thereto by such pretty feats as we have devised, but to common people they be as fables and disguisings. Nevertheless we practice more weighty matters by [E3ᵛ] means thereof. For sometime we paint and set out the great princes of the world with glorious titles, calling him defender of the church, another defender of the faith,[135] though it be nothing so, and all such as will aid us, our well-beloved sons. They on the other side call us in all their writings most holy fathers, and sometime they submit them for to kiss our holy feet, now and then in things of no estimation give place to our power, to the intent they might be called virtuous princes. We send to some hallowed roses, caps of maintenance, swords, and such other, and also long and large bulls to confirm their dignity. And they send again to us fair coursers, men of war, and money, yea sometime fair young children. And thus one of us claweth another, as mules be wont.[136]

PETRUS
If they be so spiced conscience, yet I do not well perceive how thou shouldest so soon stir them up to so great wars, seeing thou hast broken [E4ʳ] so many truces with them.

---

[135] defender of the faith] The title *fidei defensor* had been granted to Henry VIII by Pope Leo X in 1521, and was revoked by Pope Paul III in 1530. The *Dialogue* here modifies the *Julius exclusus*, which lists the titles 'catholicum', 'serenissimum', 'illustrissimum', and 'augustum' (*ASD* I-8, lines 703–04).
[136] one of us claweth another, as mules be wont] We scratch each other's backs. See Erasmus's *Adage* I. vii. 96, *Mutuum muli scabunt*, 'One mule scratches another' (Tav. 206): 'When rascals and men of no reputation admire and cry up one another.' See *CWE* 32. 125.

JULIUS
Yet if thou be able to perceive these things which I will tell thee thou shalt perceive a conveyance° far above any of the apostles.

PETRUS
Say on, I will do my best endeavour.

JULIUS
First of all my study was ever to know the natural inclination of all countries, but namely of princes and rulers, and in like wise their conditions, affections, power, and endeavourments, which of them were friends, and which not, and so to use every and singular of them to our commodity° and profit. And to begin withal,[137] I raised the Frenchmen against the Venetians, renewing the old festered malice which had be betwixt them long before, perceiving moreover the insatiable lust of the Frenchmen to amplify their dominion, and that the Venetians did unjustly withhold divers of their cities, whereupon I intermeddled my cause with theirs, and so took a part with France against the other, and so did Maximilian also, [E4ᵛ] although he favoured them but faintly, not knowing any other means to redeem such fair towns as the Venetians withheld from him. But shortly after when the Frenchmen began to be more wealthy, then my will was — for (to say as I think) they had but over good° chance at that time — I not long after found means to raise the king of Spain (a man of no great constancy) against them, whose profit it also somewhat touched that the Frenchmen's feathers should be plucked, and that for divers matters but namely lest it might be their chance to flee into his lordship of Naples and put him out.° And albeit I loved in no wise the Venetians, yet for a face I made them my friends,[138] to the end I might set them upon the French dogs, which Venetians were not long before sore vexed of the Frenchmen. And again I made the emperor and them twain, whom a little before I had made all one. This [E5ʳ] I brought to corum,[139] with certain of my letters to the emperor (wherein I feigned the king's envy against the emperor); and partly with money (which beareth ever a great stroke with such men as have need), after I had renewed again the festered wrath which Maximilian bare against the French curs,

---

[137] And to begin withal] Julius here offers a summary of his policy in relation to France following the formation of the League of Cambrai against Venice and the high watermark of French success at the battle of Agnadello in 1509. This involved turning away from France to cultivate Ferdinand of Aragon, who contested Louis XII's claim to the kingdom of Naples; influencing the Emperor Maximilian to turn against his former ally; and exploiting English hostility towards France.

[138] for a face] in pretence. Compare Sallust, *Iugurth*, trans. by Alexander Barclay (London: Richard Pynson [1525?]), sig. G2ʳ: 'all these tokens of subiection were but for a face or cloke to couer the treason & gyle of Iugurth.'

[139] brought to corum] effected: from quorum, the minimum number or essential members of an assembly necessary to take action.

wherewith the man would have marvellously fret himself, yea though he could in no wise revenge his cause. Over this I was perfect° of the deadly enmity between the Englishmen and the Frenchmen, betwixt the Scots also and the Frenchmen. Moreover I perceived the English nation very wealthy, fierce and desirous of battle, and that specially where any thing is to get, and also somewhat superstitious, for the far distance from Rome. Finally they being somewhat wanton, half at sedition among themselves, so that I thought it easy enough to incite them against the Frenchmen.[140] All these [E5ᵛ] pageants I played, for the advantage of the church. Then after I wrapped the princes in deadly wars with my crafty letters, not leaving so much as one in all Christendom unattempt° to the same, neither the king of Hungary, nor yet of Portingale, nor the Duke of Burgony,° a man nothing inferior in dominion to many kings. But because that matter pertained nothing to them, I could in no wise induce them to invade the Frenchmen. But one thing I perceived well, that if the other princes fell once by the ears together, they should not be in quietness. Now these princes which by my practised policy made war one against another received of me again for their good service glorious titles, to the end they might be brought to believe that the more Christian blood they shed, the more godly they appeared to defend the church of God. But that thou mayst the more commend my clean conveyance and happy chance, the same time it fortuned the king [E6ʳ] of Spain held wars with the Turks,[141] which turned to his great commodity and profit, yet he leaving all together came down with all his power to aid me against the Frenchmen. And although I had incitate° the emperor against them, as I said before, yet was he otherwise bound by divers compositions between him and me, albeit that he (by their manifold benefits and aid) had won again his towns in Italy.[142] And beside all this, that he had much to do of his own, as to succour his nephew the Duke of Burgony against his mortal enemy the Duke of Gelders.[143] Yet I brought to pass that he left his nephew in the briars, and took upon him (for my pleasure) to war against France. And furthermore although there be no nation that passeth less upon the authority of the pope of Rome than the English nation, as it is open to him that list to read and mark well the life of Saint Thomas [E6ᵛ] of Canterbury and the constitutions

---

[140] the English nation ...] The *Dialogue* omits here a comment about the English being 'almost uncontrollable in their new-found liberty, brought about at last by the death of the most strait-laced of kings', Henry VII; and a character sketch of his all-too pliable successor, the 'restless and warlike' but inexperienced Henry VIII, who joined the Holy League in 1511 and made war upon France. See *CWE* 27. 189.
[141] it fortuned ... Turks] Ferdinand of Aragon conquered Tripoli in 1510. Julius wanted Spanish support, and Ferdinand agreed to divert his troops into Italy.
[142] his towns in Italy] Padua, Vicenza, and Verona were imperial territories, claimed by Venice; in 1509 they were recovered by Maximilian.
[143] Duke of Gelders] Charles of Egmond, Duke of Gelderland (1467–1538).

of the old kings,¹⁴⁴ yet the same province, so impatient of all exactions and taxes, suffered for my pleasure to be shorn to the bare skin.¹⁴⁵ To speak of the spiritualty° of that realm, it is wonder to see how they were wont to withhold from the pope of Rome all they might, yet to aid me in my business were contented to pay exactions how painful so ever they were, not marking very diligently what a window they opened to their lord and king in so doing. And to speak the blunt truth the king and his nobles was not then most circumspect to suffer such exactions to be gathered in his realm.¹⁴⁶ But to show by what crafts I brought these Christian princes one against another it were very tedious, which princes no pope before me could at any time stir up against the Turk.

PETRUS
It may chance that wars thus kindled by thee, may destroy all the world.

JULIUS
[E7ʳ] Let them burn on hardily, so the dignity and possessions of the see of Rome may be kept safe. Howbeit I did all my devoir° to rid the Italians from all wars and to cast all the business on the necks of other strange nations. Therefore let them strive as long as they list, we shall give them the looking on, and laugh them loudly to scorn.

PETRUS
Be these the acts of a good shepherd, or of a most holy father, taking on him to be called the vicar of Christ?

JULIUS
Why should they then cause a schism in the church of God?

PETRUS
Sin must then be suffered, if more hurt depend upon the medicine than remedy.¹⁴⁷ But and thou hadst suffered a council to be, there could have been no schism.

---

¹⁴⁴ Thomas of Canterbury] Thomas Becket (c. 1119–1170), who opposed Henry II's attempt to subject the church to royal power.
¹⁴⁵ shorn to the bare skin] Henry VIII's war with France, which benefitted Julius, was supported by the English clergy at great expense.
¹⁴⁶ exactions … gathered in his realm] Again the *Dialogue* modifies English material. Following the discussion of the 'window' opened to royal power by the English clergy, the *Julius exclusus* reads: 'As a matter of fact, the kings didn't realize either what a precedent they had set against themselves, in that it would be possible in future for the Roman priest to depose a prince whom he disliked. Well, the young king attacked his task with more enthusiasm than I wanted or had ordered, although I preferred him to err on that side' (*CWE* 27. 190). The implication of the *Dialogue* is vaguer: that England's secular powers weren't careful about the concessions they were making in permitting Julius's exactions, any more than her clergymen were.
¹⁴⁷ if more hurt depend upon the medicine than remedy] if the cure is worse than the disease.

JULIUS
Speak no more of that. I had liefer° have six hundred battles than one council. For what, I pray you, if they had put me down as a simoniac and a merchant of spiritual wares, and not the true vicar of God? What if so [E7ᵛ] be they had uttered my life to the common people?

PETRUS
Admit thou were never so good a bishop, yet were it better thou lost thine honour wrongfully, than to keep it in such wise as it is to the great hurt of all Christendom, if it may be said a dignity which is bestowed to a very wretch. But I should not call that given which is but rather sold, yea rather stolen. But it is come even now unto my mind, that by the provision of God thou hast been his scourge to the Frenchmen, the which first of all brought thee a pest and plague into the church.

JULIUS
I swear by my triple crown and by my glorious triumphs, if thou break my patience, thou shalt feel mine omnipotent power.

PETRUS
O mad Bedlam, what crakest° thou of thy power when I hear nothing else hitherto but an unpriestly and worldly captain? Thou gloriest that thou art able to break peace between princes, to cause battles, to cause [E8ʳ] them murder one another, which power belongeth to the Devil, not to Christ's vicar, to whom it behoveth to follow as nigh as can be his example. There is in him (I grant) an high power as can be, but such a power as ought to be adjoined with most high wisdom and knowledge of God's word, and thereby at all times ruled. There ought to be in him the wisdom of serpents, but withal must be joined the simplicity of a dove. In thee surely I see the image of power coupled with great malice and foolishness, so that if the Devil would make a deputy, he could choose none more meet than one like to thee. Tell me if thou can, wherein thou did once fulfil the office of a true apostle?

JULIUS
What can be more apostolic than for to increase the church of Christ?

PETRUS
But if the church of Christ be as it is indeed, the Christian people conglutinate° and unied° in Christ's spirit, [E8ᵛ] then me think thou hast altogether subverted this congregation in moving all the world to these most cruel bloodsheddings, to the intent thou might pass thy life in all mischief without any correction at all.

JULIUS
We call the church the temple which is made with man's hand, and the priests also, but in especial the court of Rome, and me namely, which am the head of the church.

PETRUS
But Christ made us ministers, and himself the head,[148] except any other head be sprung out of late, because one is not sufficient. But wherein is the church so much amended?

JULIUS
Now thou comest to the matter. This I will tell thee: that same hungry and poor beggarly church flourisheth now with all ornaments.

PETRUS
With what ornaments? With a sure faith in Christ?

JULIUS
Yet again thou playest Jack overthwart.[149]

PETRUS
With holy preaching?

JULIUS
Thou makest me weary of thee.

PETRUS
With contempt of worldly [F1ʳ] things?

JULIUS
Tush, let me speak. I say it is garnished with such as be worthy to be called true ornaments. For these which you spake of be but words.

PETRUS
With what ornaments therefore?

JULIUS
With goodly palaces meet for kings, with many goodly horses and mules, with great bands of men following their tails, with armies well appointed …

GENIUS
[*Aside*] With fair whores and trusty bawds.

JULIUS
… with gold, purple, customs,° so that there is no king but he might be counted as a beggar if he were compared with the riches and pomp of the pope; never a man so ambitious, but he grant himself overcome in this behalf; no man so

---

[148] himself the head] See Ephes 1. 22: 'And he has put all things under his feet and has made him the head over all things for the church.'

[149] thou playest Jack overthwart] You are being contentious for the sake of it. In the Latin, 'Rursum nugaris' (*ASD* I-8, line 816).

wealthy, but he may give us over hand;¹⁵⁰ neither any so great gains, but he may grudge at our riches. These be ornaments wherewith I have endowed and amplified the church.

PETRUS
But now tell me who first infected and surcharged the church with [F1ᵛ] such ornaments which Christ would have kept clean from all worldly fashions?

JULIUS
But what is that to our matter? We keep, occupy, and enjoy our possessions, and that is the surest way of all. Howbeit some say that Constantine did give to Sylvester the pope the whole majesty of his empire,¹⁵¹ as his horse and harness, chariot, helmet, girdle, coat armour, his guard, sword, crown of gold, yea, and that of the most purest gold, his whole army with all manner of artillery belonging to war, towns, cities, countries, and kingdoms.

PETRUS
And be there any sure specialties¹⁵² of this liberal gift?

JULIUS
None but seely° glosses joined to the decrees.

PETRUS
Peradventure it is but a fable.

JULIUS
That I conjecture myself. For who is he in his wit that would give so worthy an empire to his own father? But it pleaseth the church of Rome to give credence hereunto, and put to silence all that endeavoureth them to refel° these.

PETRUS
Yet I hear nothing [F2ʳ] saving worldliness.

JULIUS
Truth it is, for thou dreamest yet of the state of the church as it was in thy time, wherein thou with certain hungry bishops didst live very needily, subject to poverty, sweat, perils, and infinite jeopardies and dangers. But now process of

---

¹⁵⁰ give us over hand] acknowledge our superiority.
¹⁵¹ Constantine did give to Sylvester ...] Julius refers here to the Donation of Constantine, the decree in which Constantine the Great supposedly transferred authority over the Roman empire to Sylvester I. In 1440 Lorenzo Valla exposed this document as a forgery through a virtuoso display of humanistic philological expertise. As will presently become clear, worldly Julius comes to the same conclusion by a different method: he finds it psychologically implausible. Nobody gives away an empire.
¹⁵² sure specialties] certain records. A speciality is a contract under seal.

time hath changed it to better. The pope of Rome is another manner man now than he was then, as for thou wast but a cipher in augrim.¹⁵³ What if thou didst see so many sumptuous temples, so many thousands of fat beneficed priests, so many bishops which may be fellows (both in their riches and power) to kings? Such a sort of fair houses belonging to priests? Specially if thou didst see at Rome so many purple cardinals waited upon with legions of servants? So many palfreys passing far any king's? So many mules trapped with velvet, gold, and pearl, and some of them shod with silver, some with gold? [F2ᵛ] Now if thou didst see the pope himself, sitting on high in a chair of clean beaten gold and carried upon men's shoulders, and how all men fall down on their knees at the wagging of his finger, the noise of the arquebuses,° the melody of the shawms° and trumps, the clapping of hands of the people, the shoutings, all the streets shining with torches, and how hardly° the great princes of the world shall be admitted to kiss his blessed feet; if thou haddest seen the same priest of Rome setting a crown of gold upon the emperor's head with his feet,¹⁵⁴ notwithstanding he is the highest of the worldly princes (if laws written for the same be of any authority, howbeit he hath not much more of that which he should have beside the shadow and title).¹⁵⁵ These things I say, if thou hadst heard and also seen, what wouldst thou then say?

PETRUS
I would say I did see a devilish tyrant, the enemy of Christ and [F3ʳ] pestilence of the church.

JULIUS
Thou wouldst say otherwise, if thou hadst but seen one of my triumphs, whether it had been that wherein I was carried into Bonony, or such one as was at Rome after I had overcome the Venetians, or at my departing from the said Bonony to Rome again, either that same which I caused to be made at Rome last of all, at the time when so many Frenchmen were slain at the siege of Ravenna, above all likelihood and in manner possibility. If thou hadst seen the goodly band of men,

---

¹⁵³ cipher in augrim] a person of no significance; literally, a zero. 'Augrim' is related to the modern 'algorithm' and signifies a mathematical operation, while a cipher is a symbol. See Tilley C391, 'He is a Cipher among numbers'. Chaucer's *Treatise of the Astrolabe* refers to 'noumbres of augrym' (1. 7. 6), while in the *Miller's Tale* the clerk Nicholas possesses 'augrym stones' (3210), used to assist in calculation. Thomas Usk's neo-Chaucerian *Testament of Love* uses the phrase 'sypher in augrim' as the translator of the *Dialogue* does here, to signify a nobody (II. 72. 71).

¹⁵⁴ if thou haddest seen ... with his feet] The *Dialogue*'s 'with his feet' may mean 'on his feet'; alternatively, it just mangles the original, either inadvertently or for surreal effect. Compare *CWE* 27. 193: 'if you could watch the selfsame Roman priest, on foot this time, placing the golden crown on the head of the Roman emperor ...'

¹⁵⁵ howbeit he hath ... the shadow and title] The present-day Emperor retains only the outward trappings of a once-substantial power.

045 all at once in array,° the good palfreys, so great an army all in complete harness, their captains so well appointed, so goodly a sight of fair and amiable boys, the torches and cressets° burning in every corner, the costly purveyance° for banquetings, the pomp of bishops, the great and lusty port of cardinals, the glorious monuments and tokens of victory, the ransoms and [F3ᵛ] spoils gotten
050 in wars, the cry and shout of the common people and of the men of war, the joy of them and noise of their speech and feats, the melody of the shawms, the thundering of drums, the bouncing and cracking of arquebuses, the plenty of money cast among the people, and if thou hadst therewith seen my holiness, the head and author of all this goodly pomp, carried upon men's shoulders in a chair
055 of gold, as though I had been God himself, thou wouldst count the triumphs of both the Scipions, Emilians, and all the emperors but very beggary in respect of my majesty.[156]

PETRUS
Oh most gracious knight, thou hast rehearsed enough of thy chimiring triumphs,[157] insomuch that I utterly despise all those heathen princes, which your
060 holiness hath vouched to me in comparison of you, which most like an holy father in Christ hast caused so many glorious triumphs. [F4ʳ] Furthermore of so many Christian men slain for your gracious pleasure, your grace being the author and causer of the slaughter of so many legions never won yet so much as one poor soul to Christ, neither with your preaching nor living. O most fatherly love! O
065 worthiest vicar of Christ, which contented to bestow thy life to save thy flock, or else carest not for the maintenance of one pestilent caitiff, to destroy the whole world!

JULIUS
Well, I see now thou speakest all this, because thou enviest my glory, and specially when thou rememberest how poor and beggarly a bishopric as thine was in
070 respect and comparison of mine.

PETRUS
How darest thou, most shameless wretch, compare and liken thy glory with mine, which is yet not mine but rather Christ's? First of all, if thou wilt grant me that Christ is the best, and the very prince and sovereign head of the church, then is all thy pompous glory [F4ᵛ] not once to be compared to mine. For he in his own

---

[156] Scipions, Emilians] The Scipios and Aemilii were two Roman families who distinguished themselves in the wars against Carthage.
[157] chimiring] Obscure. Byddell's 1534 and 1535 texts read 'chymyring' and 'chimiryng', respectively. The adjective is an addition to the Latin (*ASD* I-8, line 875). Its sole exact match is a Middle English word meaning 'shivering'. It might also with varying likelihood signify 'charming', 'chiming', 'shimmering', or represent a derivation from 'chirm' (noise, din) or even from 'chimera'.

person gave me the keys of his kingdom, that is to say, authority to preach his law and Gospel, and committed unto me his sheep to be fed.[158] He commended my faith with his own mouth.[159] But as for thou art come to dignity by means of thy money, by partial favour of men, through deceit and subtlety, if a man so promoted may have the name of bishop. I have won to Christ by preaching God's word many thousands of souls, but thou with thy abominable living hast brought innumerable to confusion. I taught Christ to the Romans, living before in all gentility,[160] but thou hast been to the same Romans a teacher of all gentility and false worshipping. I healed such as were sick with the shadow of my body.[161] I delivered men being possessed with devils, restored the dead to life, and in every place that I came I was beneficial to all men.[162] What [F5ʳ] like I pray thee were done in all thy triumphs? I could with my word deliver whom I list to Satan, the experience whereof thou mayest see in Sapphira and Ananias her husband, the fifth of the Acts.[163] Moreover what power soever I had, I spent it to the profit of every man. But thou was ever so unprofitable to all men as thou might be. Yea, what was that thou might not do to the common confusion of all the world?

JULIUS
I wonder why thou dost not recite among thy other honours thy beggary and watchings, travailings, imprisonments, fettering, thy checks and rebukes, beating and scourging, with such like promotions?

PETRUS
Thou rememberest° me in good time. For herein I have more cause to glory than in any miracles. For Christ himself hath command us to rejoice and be glad in these things, and pronounceth us all blessed, which patiently suffereth them.[164] And so likewise Paul [F5ᵛ] sometime my fellow, in the eleventh chapter of his second epistle to the Corinthians, boasting as it were to them his valiant acts, neither so much as once remembereth any towns won by force of arms, nor legions of men slain with the sword, neither how many princes he provoked and

---

[158] keys of his kingdom ... sheep to be fed] In Matt. 16. 19 Christ promises Peter 'I will give you the keys of the kingdom of heaven'; in John 21. 17 he is commanded: 'Feed my sheep.'
[159] He commended ... mouth] See Matt. 16. 17: 'Blessed are you, Simon son of Jonah! For flesh and blood has not revealed this to you, but my Father in heaven.'
[160] in all gentility] as gentiles or pagans.
[161] I healed such as were sick ...] See Acts 5. 15.
[162] I taught Christ ... beneficial to all men] Peter is said to have founded the Christian church in Rome. He heals the sick in Acts 3. 1–10, Acts 5. 15, and Acts 9. 32–5; he is given the power to expel devils in Luke 9. 1; he restores Tabitha to life in Acts 9. 36–41.
[163] Sapphira and Ananias] See Acts 5. 1–10. Ananias and his wife Sapphira seek to test God and are struck dead.
[164] For Christ ... suffereth them] Matt. 5. 11: 'Blessed are you when people revile you and persecute you and utter all kinds of evil against you falsely on my account.'

moved to war, or any tyrannous or cruel stateliness, but rather the dangers which he was in upon the sea, his imprisonments, his whippings and scourgings, the perils of false brethren.[165] These be the triumphs of a true apostle. These be those things which a captain of Christ should glory and rejoice in. He boasteth how many he hath begotten in Christ, how many he hath withdrawn from wickedness and ungodly living, and not (as thou dost) how many thousand ducats he hath heaped together. Wherefore we now make everlasting triumphs with God in heaven, honoured and praised both of good and evil. But [F6ʳ] contrariwise, as for thee, every man curseth, unless he be like to thy self, or else such as flatter thee.

JULIUS
I never heard of such reckoning before.

PETRUS
I think the same. For how shouldst thou have any time to read over the holy gospels and the epistles which my brother Paul and I did write, being always busied about so many embassades,° so many legeys,° accounts, so many armies and triumphs. The study of Scriptures requireth a mind void of all worldly cares. The discipline of Christ doth also require a breast clean purged from the spot° of all worldly business. Thou mayst be well assured that so great a doctor as Christ was came not down from heaven to teach us any vulgar or common learning. The profession of a Christian man is no idle time, nor without cares, as to despise all pleasures as things venomous and tread riches under thy feet as thou wilt do a clot of clay, to set nothing by this life in God's cause and thy neighbours. [F6ᵛ] This is the profession of a true Christian. But for because these things seem intolerable to such as be not governed with the spirit of Christ, therefore they deflect and turn them away to vain and unfruitful ceremonies, and unto such a Christ and head, feigned by themselves, they counterfeit a like body.

JULIUS
What good thing then dost thou leave me, if thou take away my money, deprive me of my kingdom, spoil me of mine honour, and bar me of pleasure?

PETRUS
By this reason thou countest Christ himself a very wretch, which although he was lord over all together, yet was made a common laughing stock, leading all his life in poverty, sweat, fasting, hunger, and thirst and finally died a most heinous death.

JULIUS
He may perchance find some that will commend his life, but surely he shall find none nowadays that would follow it.

---

[165] And so likewise Paul ...] See the narrative in II Corinth. 11. 23–33.

PETRUS

Nay, not so, for the very praise of his life, is [F7ʳ] the following of the same. Albeit truth it is that Christ doth not bereave any of his their goods, but for such things as are falsely called good.¹⁶⁶ He enricheth them with the true and eternal riches, which he doth not before he have purged and take clean away their fleshly appetites. For even like as he was altogether heavenly, so his will is to have his body, that is to say the congregation of Christian men, knit together in his spirit, to be in all things most like to him, that is to wit, clean purged from all spots of worldliness. For else how can he be all one with him which sitteth in heaven most glorious and shining, if he were drowned over the head in worldly filthiness and dregs? But when he is once purged from such pleasures, which be rather displeasures, and moreover from all worldly affections, then at the last Christ showeth forth his incomparable treasures, and giveth unto his¹⁶⁷ a most [F7ᵛ] sweet taste of his heavenly joys, for their forsaking of such voluptuous pleasures of this world, ever mingled with a sour sauce.

JULIUS

What pleasures I pray thee?

PETRUS

Esteemed thou the gifts of prophecy, interpreting the Scriptures, the gift to work miracles, but as common gifts, and no pleasure? Moreover supposest thou Christ himself but as a vile person whom whosoever hath, hath in his possession altogether?¹⁶⁸ Finally, unless thou think that we here in this place do lead a miserable life …

JULIUS

Ha, ha, ha. Then I see well, the more wretched life that a man doth live in the world, the more delicately he liveth in Christ. The more beggarly a man is here, the richer he is in Christ. The more abject that a man is here, the higher and more honourable he is in Christ. The less he liveth in this world, the more he liveth in Christ.¹⁶⁹

---

¹⁶⁶ but … called good] Christ deprives his followers only of false goods.
¹⁶⁷ unto his] to his followers.
¹⁶⁸ whosoever … altogether] He who has Christ, has him as an absolute possession. Compare II Corinth. 6. 10: 'having nothing, and yet possessing everything'.
¹⁶⁹ Ha, ha, ha … Christ] Here the *Dialogue* converts a section of Peter's speech (*ASD* I-8, lines 939–42) into one for Julius. The sentiments that are sarcastically reframed in this passage go to the very heart of Erasmus's *philosophia Christi*. Compare, for instance, the following from his *Enchiridion*: 'So greatly Christ is come to contempt to the world that they think it a goodly and excellent thing to have nothing to do with him at all; and that so much the more every man should be despised, the more coupled he were to him' (*Manual*, 3423–25).

PETRUS

It is surely so: that Christ will have all his body be pure and [F8ʳ] clean, and namely the ministers of his word, that is to wit the bishops. And among them the higher he is, the more like he ought for to be to Christ and the less overcharged° and further from all carnal pleasures. But now I see clean the contrary, that he which will be esteemed highest in dignities and next of all to Christ himself is most of all overwhelmed in all worldly filthiness, as in riches, dominion, strength of men, battles, truces. (As for all other vices, I let pass.) And although thou be never so contrary to Christ, nevertheless thou abusest the title of Christ for the maintenance of thy devilish pride and under the pretence of him which despised the kingdom of this world thou playest the worldly tyrant, and being the right enemy of Christ thou requirest the right honour due unto him. Thou dost bless other, thy own self being cursed of God. Thou takest upon [F8ᵛ] thee to open the gates of heaven to other men, from whence thou art now thyself exclude. Thou consecratest other, thy self being unconsecrate. Thou excommunicatest other, thy self having no communion or part at all with God or his holy saints. Tell me wherein thou differest from the great Turk,[170] save only because thou allegest the title of Christ? For clearly your intents and minds are both one, your beastly lives both like, saving thou art the greater murrain° of all the world.

JULIUS

Wherefore sayest thou so, seeing mine intent hath been ever to endote° the church with all kind of goods? But there be divers which sayeth that Aristotle spake of three manner goods, whereof some be called the goods of fortune, other some goods of the body and the rest goods of the soul.[171] Wherefore I, not willing in any wise to invert and transpose this division of goods, began first of all at the goods of fortune, and perchance [G1ʳ] should have come by little and little to the goods of the soul, if that death coming the sooner upon had not too rathe° have taken me out of this world.

PETRUS

Very rathe indeed, for because thou art but three score years old and ten. But what deed were it to mingle water with the fire?[172]

JULIUS

Well, but and if these commodities lack, the common people will not set a straw by us; whereas now they both fear and worship us, which if they did not, the

---

[170] the great Turk] The Ottoman sultan.
[171] three manner goods] See Aristotle, *Politics* 1323a15, which divides goods into 'external goods, goods of the soul and goods of the body'.
[172] But what deed ... fire?] Peter is sceptical about the proposed progression from worldly to spiritual goods. See *Adages* IV. iii. 94, *Aquam igni miscere*, 'Mixing fire and water': 'This proverb ought also to be included among those indicating what is impossible' (*CWE* 36. 57).

church of God should soon decay and be overrun, unless she could defend herself against the violence of her enemies.

PETRUS

It is nothing so, for if the poor Christian people could espy in thee and such other the very gifts of God, as good living, wholesome doctrine, burning charity, the true interpreting of God's word, with other virtues requisite to the true vicar of Christ, yea and they would the rather worship thee, because they perceive thee pure and clean from all worldly [G1ᵛ] and evil affections. The commonwealth of all Christendom should much the better increase if such priests might reign which — with their sincere living, their utter despising of worldly pleasures, riches, dominions, yea and death if need were — would move both the ignorant people and also them which hath not received the faith to marvel at their godly conversation. But now Christendom is not only contract° and brought into a little angle,¹⁷³ but also if thou look nearly° thou shalt find a great number of those few that be christened in names only. But tell me I pray thee, didst thou never so much as once consider in thy mind when thou was the high shepherd of the church how it began, and by what means it was augmented, and also whereby it was established? Whether with bloody battles, great treasures, palfreys, and such other? Surely it was nothing so, but rather with patience; [G2ʳ] blood of martyrs, as mine and other; with patient suffering of imprisonments and other painful beatings. But thou callest the church enriched when the ministers thereof be even laden with worldly dominion. Thou callest it garnished and adorned, when it is polluted with gifts and pleasures of the world. Then thou callest it defended when all the world lieth by the ears for the rents and annuities of priests.¹⁷⁴ Thou sayest it flourisheth, when it is drunken in voluptuous pleasures. Thou sayest it is in good quietness, when no man dare speak against it and it aboundeth in wealthiness, or rather in vice and naughtiness, but this hast thou taught the flexible princes of the world, which blinded with their naughty learning doth call their great robberies and furious battles the defence of Christ's church.

JULIUS
To this day heard I never such things before.

PETRUS
What did the preachers then teach thee?

---

¹⁷³ a little angle] a small space. The collapse of the Byzantine Empire in 1453 and the expansion of Ottoman rule led to perceptions that Western Christendom was under siege in the early sixteenth century. Erasmus's writings often give voice to this perception in order to cue up discussions of Christian decay, as the *Dialogue* does here.
¹⁷⁴ lieth by the ears] is at odds.

JULIUS

[G2ᵛ] I heard nothing at all of them but high commendations, thundering out my great virtues and praises with painted words, calling me the great Jupiter, which caused all the world to quake and fear with my thunderbolt, yea that I was a very god, the common health of all the whole world, with many more.

PETRUS

No marvel at all truly, though none of them could season thee, seeing thou was but foolish and unsavoury salt.[175] For the office of the true vicar of Christ is to preach and teach him purely to the people.

JULIUS

Wilt thou not then open the gates?

PETRUS

To any other rather than to such a pestilent wretch! For to thee in thy conceit, we be all no better than excommunicate persons. But wilt thou have a good and profitable counsel? Thou hast a company of worthy warriors, innumerable riches, thyself a wise builder: therefore go build thee a new paradise, but take heed it be well defended, that it be not beaten down [G3ʳ] of ill spirits.

JULIUS

No, sir. I shall do a thing that shall please me a little better. I will tarry a few months, till my company be better increased and stronger, and then I will return and drive you clean out of this hold with strong hand, unless you will yield you unto me. For I doubt not but within a short space here will be above sixty thousand slain in battle.

PETRUS

O most pestilent wretch! O miserable church! But come hither Genius, for I had lever° commune with thee than with this horrible monster.

GENIUS

What say ye to me?

PETRUS

Be all the bishops such?

GENIUS

Of truth a great part of them. But this was the captain of all mischief.

PETRUS

Was it thou that moved this man to so many horrible deeds?

---

[175] season … salt] Compare Mark 9. 50: 'Salt is good; but if salt has lost its saltiness, how can you season it?'

GENIUS

No, for God. It needed not, for he ran so hastily of his own courage that I could scarce overtake him with any wings.

PETRUS

Of truth I marvel nothing at all that so few cometh to this place when so [G3ᵛ] pestilent caitiffs° be governors of the church. Notwithstanding the poor blind people I conjecture hereby is not altogether incurable that they give such honour to this foul stinking withdraught,° for the bare title of bishop.[176]

GENIUS

It is matter indeed, but I must go straight away hence, for my captain hath becked upon me to follow him, yea and for my long tarrying hath shaked his staff upon me. Therefore I will bid you farewell.

The translator to the readers.

This Julius (good reader) reigned from the year of our lord 1503 to the end of nine years and more, in such wise as appeareth in this dialogue, which thing causeth me often to marvel at them that say, the pope of Rome (as they call him) cannot err. For compare his life to the living of Timothy or Paul,[177] and I suppose thou shalt find very little agreeing. But alas, in how [G4ʳ] miserable case were they which sat in the cart, when such a Phaeton[178] had it to govern at his pleasure! What likelihood° were betwixt him (whose study was to enchain all the world in deadly malice) and them which cried evermore that we should love our enemies and pray for such as do persecute us! This Julius gave his blessing to incite one to kill another where the whole body of Scripture teacheth us patience. But if we consider this sore scourge wherewith God punished us so many years, it is high time to submit and humble ourselves unto him which will give us to drink of the water, not which the venomous natrix hath infect with her poison,[179] but such whereof if we drink, it shall make in us a well of water, leaping in to eternal life, which Christ grant us all. Amen.

---

[176] Notwithstanding ... bishop] There must be hope for the people if they honour a man as bad as Julius simply because he holds an ecclesiastical office.
[177] Timothy or Paul] Timothy travelled with Paul and is the addressee of two Pauline epistles.
[178] Phaeton] Phaeton lost control of the sun god's chariot and died.
[179] natrix] a snake.

An Epistle in Praise of Matrimony

Translated by Richard Taverner (1536?)

Edited by Neil Rhodes

Introduction

Erasmus's *Encomium matrimonii* first appeared in print in March 1518 with the title *Exhortatoria ad matrimonium*, as one of a group of four declamations. It clearly aroused considerable interest, since there were two further editions from different publishers in the same year.[1] Coinciding with the arrival of Luther on the international stage, however, Erasmus's work addressed an issue that was now enormously sensitive, and almost immediately it had a charge of heresy levelled against it by the rector of the University of Louvain.

The point at issue was whether the declamation held matrimony to be a superior state to that of celibacy. Erasmus defended himself by claiming that the work was really a *jeu d'esprit* which had been written many years earlier and that he had, anyway, drafted a companion piece in dispraise of marriage, which was to appear in his *De Conscribendis epistolis* ('On the writing of letters').[2] This work was published in 1522 and did indeed include a revised and expanded version of the declamation, now presented as an example of a letter of persuasion. It continued to be printed both separately, as the *Encomium matrimonii*, and as part of *De Conscribendis epistolis*, reaching eleven Latin editions in the first form and a further twenty-eight in the second by the time of Taverner's translation.[3]

But what made the text suspect among conservative theologians also made it attractive in England where, at the time of Henry's break from Rome, the senior prelate, Archbishop Thomas Cranmer, had married in 1532 in defiance of the laws prescribing clerical celibacy.[4] (Henry would finally marry Anne Boleyn the following year.) It was in these circumstances that Richard Taverner, a young Cambridge Greek scholar, recommended himself for employment in Cromwell's circle with an English translation of Erasmus's work. Taverner's overture to Cromwell marks the beginning of a concerted programme on Cromwell's part of producing popular, vernacular editions of Erasmian texts in order to shift public

---

[1] Erasmus, *Declamationes aliquot* (Louvain: Thierry Martens, 1518). The subsequent editions were published by Nicolas Caesar in May and by Froben in August (*CWE* 26. 529).

[2] *Apologia pro declamatione matrimonii* (1519); see *Defense of his Declamation in Praise of Marriage*, trans. by David Sider, in *Daughters, Wives, and Widows: Writings by Men about Women and Marriage in England, 1500–1640*, ed. by Joan Larsen Klein (Urbana: University of Illinois Press, 1992), pp. 89–96. The original date of composition of the declamation was probably 1498–99; see Jean-Claude Margolin in *ASD* I-5. 338.

[3] Figures from the Universal Short Title Catalogue; see also *CWE* 25. lii.

[4] Cranmer married Margarete, niece of the pastor Andreas Osiander, while staying in the newly Lutheran Nuremberg in the summer of 1532. This coincided with his appointment as Archbishop of Canterbury following Warham's death in August. (This was Cranmer's second marriage.)

opinion towards reformation, with Taverner as his principal agent.[5] The *Praise of Matrimony* was printed by Robert Redman, in late 1532 or early 1533, with a dedication to Cromwell in which Taverner wishes a 'speedy reformation' (19), which he hopes will deter people from making vows of perpetual chastity. Where Erasmus sought refuge from accusations of heresy by pointing out that declamation was a rhetorical exercise, Taverner explicitly directs his translation towards political ends. In that respect it is a key text in the early English Reformation and Taverner himself the prime mover in exploiting Erasmus to serve its agenda.

Erasmus's claim that the *Encomium* was a rhetorical exercise is one that he would also use to defend the *Encomium moriae* (*Praise of Folly*); and though it may sound disingenuous, it does in fact have some force, since the work is a persuasive composition that addresses a particular set of circumstances. The fictitious addressee is a young man of high birth whose sister has entered a nunnery following the death of their mother, so that the responsibility for carrying on the family's noble line now rests with the son. But the arguments Erasmus opens with derive from Scripture and therefore have a general application. He argues that marriage is the first of the sacraments because it was ordained in paradise, adding that 'the other [sacraments] for remedy, this for solace; the other were put to in help of nature, which was fallen, only this was given to nature at the first creation' (93–94), as Taverner puts it.[6] Erasmus points out that Christ honoured marriage with the first of his miracles (101–03), and then moves to the ultimate expression of the sacramental nature of marriage as a symbol of 'the wonderful conjunction of the divine nature with the human body and soul', citing Ephesians 5. 32; '"Great", sayeth Paul, "is the mystery of matrimony in Christ and in the church"' (120). Taverner prefers the Greek term 'mystery', which Erasmus had used in the *Novum Instrumentum*, rather than *sacramentum*, which is the term he uses in the *Encomium* itself.[7]

What this makes clear is that the *Encomium* has serious theological substance, despite its framing as an exercise in *declamatio*. Erasmus had acknowledged in

---

[5] James McConica, *English Humanists and Reformation Politics under Henry VIII and Edward VI* (Oxford: Clarendon Press, 1965), pp. 149–99; E. J. Devereux, *Renaissance English Translations of Erasmus: A Bibliography to 1700* (Toronto: University of Toronto Press, 1983), pp. 7–8; Andrew Taylor, 'Richard Taverner', *ODNB* [accessed 16 October 2019].

[6] Erasmus's views on the sacrament of marriage are complex; see Philip L. Reynolds, *How Marriage Became One of the Sacraments: The Sacramental Theology of Marriage from its Medieval Origins to the Council of Trent* (Cambridge: Cambridge University Press, 2016), pp. 730–42.

[7] *ASD* I-5. 390; *LB* 6. 856A; see Hilmar M. Pabel, 'Exegesis and Marriage in Erasmus's Paraphrases on the New Testament', in *Holy Scripture Speaks: The Production and Reception of Erasmus' Paraphrases on the New Testament*, ed. by Hilmar M. Pabel and Mark Vessey (Toronto: University of Toronto Press, 2002), pp. 175–209 (p. 178).

his defence of the work that the point most likely to cause offence was the claim which Taverner renders as 'the most holy kind of life is wedlock purely and chastely kept' (293-94).[8] His rather ambivalent gloss on this was to say 'I do not now question whether it may be called an error for someone simply to prefer marriage to celibacy, it may also be called heresy'. In fact, the *Encomium* had claimed that 'who reprehendeth [marriage] is condemnable of heresy' (58-59), so it was Erasmus himself who had brought that ugly spectre into the debate, not the Rector of Louvain.

All this helps to explain why Taverner thought Erasmus's work would provide him with a suitable *entrée* to Cromwell. Like Erasmus, evangelicals were using Paul to argue against clerical celibacy, and it is clear from Diarmaid MacCulloch's magisterial biography that the 'reformation' to which Taverner refers was driven as much by Cromwell's commitment to evangelical Christianity as it was by political and economical expediency.[9] It was this that enabled Taverner to embark on his most important work of scholarship and translation, which was neither the *Praise of Matrimony*, nor the *Adages*, but the Bible itself. Printed in 1539 through Cromwell's patronage, the Taverner Bible was superseded almost immediately by the Great Bible, but it was a work with an Erasmian spirit, closely following the Greek text of the *Novum Instrumentum* in support of a reformed Christianity.[10]

If the *Praise of Matrimony* can be linked both to the Protestant agenda for a married clergy and to the attack on 'monkery', as Taverner calls it elsewhere (Tav. 221, *Proverbs*, 1467), it can also be seen as a work that confers dignity on the married state itself. Although the wider argument that Protestantism helped to create the ideal of a companionate marriage has been challenged, there seems little doubt that the reprioritisation of the purposes of marriage within the Anglican church focussed greater attention on the conduct of married life and its conditions of mutual support, and Taverner's Erasmus contributed to this development.[11] Taverner's words 'the other for remedy, this for solace' are reflected

---

[8] *Defense*, trans. by Sider, p. 94.
[9] Diarmaid MacCulloch, *Thomas Cromwell: A Life* (London: Allen Lane, 2018). On clerical celibacy see Helen L. Parish, *Clerical Marriage and the English Reformation: Precedent, Policy, and Practice* (Aldershot: Ashgate, 2000), pp. 56-65.
[10] Harold H. Hutson and Harold R. Willoughby, 'The Ignored Taverner Bible of 1539', *Crozer Quarterly*, 16 (1939), 161-76. Cromwell also authorized Taverner's translation of the Augsburg Confession, the Lutheran statement of faith written by Melancthon, which had a foundational role in the Anglican church. It was printed by Redman in 1536.
[11] See Margo Todd, *Christian Humanism and the Puritan Social Order* (Cambridge: Cambridge University Press, 1987), p. 99. For a qualified reassertion of the ideal see Anthony Fletcher, 'The Protestant Idea of Marriage in Early Modern England', in *Religion, Culture and Society: Essays in Honour of Patrick Collinson*, ed. by Anthony Fletcher and Peter Roberts (Cambridge: Cambridge University Press, 1994), pp. 161-81; Keith Thomas, *The Ends of Life: Roads to Fulfilment in Early Modern England* (Oxford: Oxford University Press, 2009), pp. 215-16.

in 'The Forme of Solemnisation of Matrimony' in the first version of the *Book of Common Prayer* (1549). This introduces the phrase 'mutual societie, helpe, and comfort' as the third of the causes of matrimony, and Brian Cummings notes that the German Martin Bucer, who was appointed to a chair at Cambridge in the same year, argued that this should be placed as the first of the causes.[12] In the Elizabethan homily on marriage written by Bishop Jewel, who was also the author of the foundational defence of the Church of England, it does in fact come first: marriage, he writes, 'is instituted of God, to the intent that man and woman should live lawfully in a perpetuall friendly felowship'.[13] In the *Praise of Matrimony* the principle of 'friendly fellowship' is underlined in a key passage in which Taverner writes that, where friendship offers solace, 'sith it is an especial sweetness to have one with whom ye may communicate the secret affections of your mind, with whom ye may speak even as it were with your own self' (374–76), the closer bond between husband and wife provides the same comforts to an even greater degree. Taverner's words suggest that we might now reformulate the concept of the companionate marriage by reference to the Anglican origins of the modern civil partnership.[14]

Reference to the classical concept of *amicitia* reminds us that both Erasmus and Taverner were humanists as well as Christians, and after discussing scriptural texts in support of matrimony, they proceed to historical examples from antiquity and then to the law of nature. Pliny is cited for examples of 'natural commixtion' such as 'wedlock in trees' (note 23), and the argument then turns to mythology, where Orpheus is represented as the tutelary genius of marriage. His music had the power to move savage people into the civil state of matrimony, and even the rocks themselves, demonstrating that anyone opposed to marriage is 'but a stone, an enemy to nature, a rebel to God' (203). And when Orpheus manages to rescue his wife Eurydice from hell, Jupiter's concession shows us that 'also in hell [wedlock] is counted holy and religious' (209–10). These are myths 'feigned by the old and wise poets', Taverner writes, but are 'nothing fabulous or vain'. This blend of classical and Christian knowledge was at the heart of Erasmus's entire career project and it is reflected, rather astonishingly, in the frontispiece to the Taverner Bible, which (uniquely in Bibles of the period) shows Venus and Adonis in the architrave. Taverner's words on mythology were echoed by the young John

---

[12] *The Book of Common Prayer: The Texts of 1549, 1559, and 1662*, ed. by Brian Cummings (Oxford: Oxford University Press, 2011), p. 64.

[13] [John Jewel], 'Of the State of Matrimony', in *The Second Tome of Homilees* (London: R. Jugge and J. Cawood, 1571), p. 476.

[14] Lorna Hutson, '"Especyall Swetnes": An Erasmian Footnote to the Civil Partnership Act', *Literature and History*, 20.1 (2011), 5–21; see also Reinier Leushuis, 'The Mimesis of Marriage: Dialogue and Intimacy in Erasmus's Matrimonial Writings', *Renaissance Quarterly*, 57 (2004), 1278–307.

Milton in *Comus*: "'tis not vain or fabulous | [...] What the sage poets taught by the heavenly Muse, | Storied of old in high immortal verse' (lines 512–15); and that poem also ends by invoking the union of Venus and Adonis as an image of the mystical union of the soul with God. Yet Milton's masque is an *encomium virginitatis* every bit as committed as Erasmus and Taverner's *encomium matrimonii*. It was not until *Paradise Lost* that Milton would give poetic form to the arguments of the *Praise of Matrimony* on behalf of conjugal love.

The law of nature is the domain in which Christian doctrine and classical *exempla* mutually reinforce each other in the *Praise of Matrimony*, and it is the fundamental opposition between marriage and virginity that is their principal focus. Taverner expresses this more simply, and effectively, when he writes: '"But virginity", ye will say, "is a divine thing, an angelical thing." Truth it is, but on the contrary side, wedlock is an human thing' (312–14). This alliance between the sphere of humanity and the law of nature underlies Erasmus's thinking in some of his best-known works, most notably *Praise of Folly*. But the law of nature itself also underlies a rather different aspect of the *Praise of Matrimony*, which is its emphasis on the generation of resources for the good of the commonwealth. The population of the country was still recovering from the ravages of the Black Death nearly two centuries earlier, and the importance of there being a sufficient supply of working men and women to sustain the economy is a central thread of the work. The law of nature is invoked in this context to underpin ideas about the common good, or what we might call commonwealth thinking, which was characteristic of the Reformation era and of the Cromwell circle in particular.[15] Marriage and procreation 'must needs be common, which the common parent of all hath imprinted [...] this they call the law of nature' (221–22, 226), and it impels us to act for the 'public weal' and 'supply new in place of the old' (232–33). The law of nature also produces the agricultural analogy in which procreation is constructed as a labour of love: the 'diligent husband' engages in 'tillage' (227, 360–01), both in the marriage bed and on his land 'because it is for the profit of the common weal that every man tendeth well his own' (356–57).[16] And the political and economic agenda behind Taverner's translation can also be linked, in true evangelical spirit, to the divine injunction 'Be fruitful and multiply'. As the older Milton would put it, 'Our maker bids increase. Who bids abstain | But our destroyer' (*Paradise Lost* IV. 748–49). The law of nature is God's law.

But Erasmus's encomium on marriage would have an impact on English poetry well before Milton. The metaphors of tillage and husbandry, expanded into broader themes of reproduction, are central to Shakespeare's sonnets addressed

---

[15] See Neil Rhodes, *Common: The Development of Literary Culture in Sixteenth-Century England* (Oxford: Oxford University Press, 2018), pp. 12–19, 118–19.
[16] On husbandry see Lorna Hutson, *The Usurer's Daughter: Male Friendship and Fictions of Women in Sixteenth-Century England* (London: Routledge, 1994), pp. 41–51, 75–76.

to the young man: 'For where is she so fair whose uneared womb | Disdains the tillage of thy husbandry', he writes in Sonnet 2. Taverner asks 'who can bear age heavily when in his son he beholdeth his own visage that he himself bare when he was young?' (444–45). Shakespeare urges his subject to reproduce himself in a child, who will be 'new made when thou art old' so that 'thou through windows of thine age shall see, | Despite of wrinkles, this thy golden time' (Sonnet 3). However, Shakespeare's source was not Taverner but Thomas Wilson, whose *Arte of Rhetorique* (1553), reissued in 1560, provided a translation of Erasmus's encomium as an example of deliberative rhetoric, i.e. strategies of persuasion to or dissuasion from a particular course of action. Taverner's translation is a more literal version of the original than Wilson's, at times so close to the Latin syntax that it can sound awkward in English. But there are places where Taverner's faithfulness is a positive: his reference to the 'natural commixtion' (187) described by Pliny is more precise than Wilson's generalised 'marriage' and his reference to the 'undiligent citizen in the public weal' (231–32), who declines to procreate, retains the emphasis on marriage as a duty to the commonwealth in the second phrase, which Wilson omits. When Taverner departs from the literal sense he does so in a purposeful way: his translation of *fulmine* (*ASD* 1-5. 394) as 'Jupiter's thunderbolt' rather than Wilson's more straightforward 'lightning', which destroyed the ancient giants opposed to marriage, reinforces the humanist practice of using classical myth to illustrate Christian doctrine. And Taverner can also be felicitous: in the key passage that presents marriage as a deeper extension of friendship, his phrase 'especial sweetness' is much more forceful than Wilson's bland 'how pleasant a thing', while the ending of that sentence with 'permixtion of bodies, with the confederate band of the sacrament, and finally with the fellowship of all chances' (381–82) is an eloquent presentation of marriage as the sharing of life's fortunes within a union sanctified by God.[17]

Taverner can be a faithful translator in the sense that Horace objected to, but he is also faithful to the spirit of Erasmus: in his regard for Greek, in his balancing of Christian and classical wisdom, and in his investment in other English projects such as the *Adages*. In the *Praise of Matrimony* he also found a way of putting Erasmus to work on Cromwell's behalf in the first phase of the English Reformation.

Further Reading

ERASMUS, *Defense of his Declamation in Praise of Marriage*, trans. by David Sider, in *Daughters, Wives, and Widows: Writings by Men about Women and Marriage in England, 1500–1640*, ed. by Joan Larsen Klein (Urbana: University of Illinois Press, 1992), pp. 89–96

---

[17] For Wilson see Thomas Wilson, *The Arte of Rhetorique*, ed. by Thomas J. Derrick (New York: Garland Publishing, 1982), pp. 95–140.

FLETCHER, ANTHONY, 'The Protestant Idea of Marriage in Early Modern England', in *Religion, Culture and Society: Essays in Honour of Patrick Collinson*, ed. by Anthony Fletcher and Peter Roberts (Cambridge: Cambridge University Press, 1994), pp. 161–81

HUTSON, LORNA, *The Usurer's Daughter: Male Friendship and Fictions of Women in Sixteenth-Century England* (London: Routledge, 1994)

—— '"Especyall Swetnes": An Erasmian Footnote to the Civil Partnership Act', *Literature and History*, 20.1 (2011), 5–21

LEUSHUIS, REINIER, 'The Mimesis of Marriage: Dialogue and Intimacy in Erasmus's Matrimonial Writings', *Renaissance Quarterly*, 57 (2004), 1278–307

PARISH, HELEN L., *Clerical Marriage and the English Reformation: Precedent, Policy, and Practice* (Aldershot: Ashgate, 2000)

REYNOLDS, PHILIP L., *How Marriage Became One of the Sacraments: The Sacramental Theology of Marriage from its Medieval Origins to the Council of Trent* (Cambridge: Cambridge University Press, 2016)

TAYLOR, ANDREW, 'Richard Taverner', *ODNB*

THE PRAISE OF MATRIMONY

[A1ʳ] A right fruitful epistle devised by the most excellent clerk° Erasmus in laud° and praise of matrimony, translated into English by Richard Taverner, which translation he hath dedicate to the right honourable Master Thomas Cromwell, most worthy counsellor to our sovereign lord king Henry the Eighth.

[A1ᵛ] To the right honourable Master Cromwell, one of the king's most honourable counsel, his humble servant Richard Taverner sendeth greeting.

Your daily orator° (most honourable sir), pondering with himself your gratuit° bounty towards him, began busily to revolve in mind how he again on his part might somewhat declare his fervent zeal of heart towards you. Which he thus revolving, lo, suddenly (as God would) a certain [A2ʳ] epistle of Doctor Erasmus, devised in commendation of wedlock, offered itself unto his sight. Which so soon as he began to read, he thought it a thing full necessary and expedient to translate it into our vulgar tongue and so under your noble protection to communicate it to the people, namely when he considered the blind superstition of men and women which cease not day by day to profess and vow perpetual chastity before or° they sufficiently know themselves and the infirmity of their nature. Which thing, in my opinion, hath been and is yet unto this day the root and very cause original of innumerable mischiefs. I pray our lord Jesu of his infinite goodness to provide some speedy reformation[1] when it shall be [A2ᵛ] his pleasure. In the mean season° please it your goodness, right honourable sir, to accept this rude and simple translation of your servant, and ye so doing shall not a little encourage him to greater things in time coming. And thus Christ have you always in his keeping.

Amen.

[A3ʳ] An Epistle in Praise of Matrimony

Although, sweet cousin, ye be wise enough of yourself, nor need not other men's counsel, yet for the old friendship continued from our childhood betwixt us, and also for your kindness towards me, and finally because of the straight alliance

---

[1] reformation] Cromwell had not yet embarked on the dissolution of the monasteries, but that programme would soon have the effect of putting Taverner's wish into practice. The term 'reformation' itself is associated with Erasmus in English: '[Henry VIII] playnly sawe that no waye there was to a reformacion, but by this onely meane, yf the autoritie and vsurped *supremitie of the See of Rome wer extirped, abolished, and clene extincte*', *The First Tome or Volume of the Paraphrase of Erasmus upon the New Testament*, ed. by Nicholas Udall (London, 1548), sig. A4ʳ.

betwixt us,² I thought it my duty (if I would be the man whom ye have always take[n] me for, that is to say your friend and lover) of such things as I judged to belong most to the preservation and dignity of you and yours gladly and freely to advertise° you. Other men's profit sometimes we espy better than our own. I have oft followed your counsel, [A3ᵛ] which I have found no less profitable than friendly. Now if ye again will follow mine, I trust it shall repent neither me of my counselling nor you of your following.³ Our friend Antony Bald supped with me the last night, one that is (as ye know well enough) your great friend and near kinsman.⁴ An heavy feast and full of tears. He showed° me, which was a great sorrow to us both, that the good gentlewoman your mother is departed; that your sister for sorrow and desire is entered into a house of barren nuns; that the hope of your stock is turned only unto you; that your friends with whole assent have offered you a wife of great substance,° of noble blood, of excellent beauty, of gentle° manners, [A4ʳ] and finally, which beareth great love towards you. That ye yet, this notwithstanding, for some immoderate sorrow, or else some superstitious holiness, have so determined to live a chaste life and never to marry, that neither for the care of your stock, nor love of issue, nor for any requests, prayers, or tears of your friends ye can be plucked away from your purpose. But ye by mine advice shall change this mind, and leaving bachelorship, a form of living both barren and unnatural, shall give yourself to most holy wedlock. In which matter I covet° that neither the love of your friends, which else ought to overcome your mind, nor mine authority, anything should aid my cause if I show [A4ᵛ] not by clear reasons that this shall be for you both most honest, most profitable, and most pleasant — yea, what will ye say if (as this time require[s]) also most necessary?

For first of all, if the regard of honesty° moveth you, which with good men is highly considered, what thing is more honest than matrimony, whereunto Christ himself did great honour and worship, which vouchsafed not only to be present with his mother at the marriages, but also consecrated the marriage feast with the first fruits of his miracles?⁵ What is more holy than that which the creator of all things hath ordained, coupled,° sanctified; which Dame Nature herself hath enacted? What is [A5ʳ] more laudable than it, which who reprehendeth is condemnable of heresy? So honourable is matrimony as is the name of heretic slanderous. What is a thing of more equity° than to render that to the posterity

---

² straight alliance] Direct family relationship. The English 'cousin' (translating Latin *affinis*) does not need to be understood literally. The editor of the Latin declamation suggests that this is an 'affabulation' typical of Erasmus and should not be read *à clef* (ASD 1-5. 337).
³ **Marg.** 'The narration.'
⁴ Antony Bald] Probably fictitious; the name is an anglicisation of the Latin 'Antonius Baldus', which does not appear to be of significance.
⁵ first … miracles] The wedding at Cana where Christ turned the water into wine. See John 2. 1–11.

which we ourselves received of our ancestry? What act on the contrary side is done with less consideration than under the zeal of holiness to flee it as unholy and ungodly, which God, the well and father of all holiness, would have counted most holy? What thing is further from all humanity than man to abhor° from the laws of man's estate? What is a more unkind act than to deny that to your youngers, which if ye took not of your elders ye could not be he that might deny? Now if we [A5ᵛ] require° the author of matrimony, it was founded and ordained not of Lycurgus, not of Moses, not of Solon,⁶ but of the high and mighty worker of all things; of him it was also praised, enhonested,° and consecrate. For at the beginning when he had made man of the slime of the earth he thought that his life should be utterly miserable and unpleasant if he joined not Eve a companion unto him.⁷ Wherefore he brought forth the wife not of the earth as he did man, but out of the ribs of Adam, whereby it is to be understood that nothing ought to be more dear to us than the wife, nothing more conjoined, nothing more fast-glued unto us. The selfsame God after the Flood, when he was at one again with mankind, [A6ʳ] enacted (as we read in the Scripture) this law first:⁸ not that we should love bachelorship, but to increase, to multiply, to replenish the earth. But how could that be, unless men would give their labour to wedlock?

And lest we should here find cavillations° alleging the old law of Moses or the necessity of that season,⁹ I pray you what meaneth that sentence repeated also in the new law of Christ ratified and confirmed by Christ's own mouth? 'For this cause', sayeth he, 'shall man leave father and mother and stick to his wife.'¹⁰ What thing is more holy than the natural love of the child to his father? And yet the faith of wedlock is preferred above it. By whose authority? — by God's. At what time? — when not only the [A6ᵛ] old law flourished, but also when the new law of Christ began to spring. The father is forsaken, the mother is forsaken, and the wife is sticked to. The son (in the civil law) emancipate, that is to say enfranchised and out of his father's bonds, beginneth to be his own man and at liberty. The son, in the same law, abdicate, that is to say forsaken and disherited of his father, ceaseth to be his son. But only death undo wedlock, if yet that death undo it. Now, sir, if the other sacraments of Christ's church be had in great veneration, who seeth not that much worship ought to be given to this, which was both ordained of God and first of all other? And the other in earth, this in paradise; the other for remedy,¹¹ this for solace; the other [A7ʳ] were put to in help of nature, which

---

⁶ Lycurgus ... Solon] Lycurgus was a legendary figure credited with instituting the laws of Sparta, and Solon (seventh/sixth century BC) those of Athens.
⁷ Marg. 'Man first created, forthwith was coupled with a wife.'
⁸ Marg. 'The law of matrimony renewed.'
⁹ necessity of that season] i.e. the necessity of repopulating the earth after the Flood.
¹⁰ Matt. 19. 5.
¹¹ remedy] i.e. as a remedy for our fallen nature and for the avoidance of fornication.

was fallen, only this was given to nature at the first creation. If we count the laws holy which be institute of men, shall not the law of wedlock be most holy which we have received of him of whom we have received life, and which began in manner even at one time with mankind?

To be short, because he would confirm this law by some example when he was a young man and bidden, as is said, to the bridal, he came thither gladly with his mother, and not contented with so doing, did also great honour to the feast with his wonderful work, making none otherwhere the prosperous commencement and beginning of his miracles.[12] 'Why then', ye will say, 'did Christ himself [A7ᵛ] abstain from wedlock?' As though there be not very many things in Christ which we ought rather to marvel at than follow. He was born without carnal father, he proceeded without pain of his mother, he arose from death to live when the sepulchre was closed — what is not in him above nature? Let such things be appropriate to him. Let us, living within the law of nature, wonder and praise the things that be above nature, but follow those works that be for our capacity. 'But he would be born of a virgin.' Truth it is, of a virgin, but yet wedded. A virgin to his mother that became him that was God;[13] but that she was wedded, she signified unto us what we ought to do. Virginity became her, which, by [A8ʳ] the divine inspiration of the Holy Ghost being pure and immaculate, brought forth him that was most pure and unspotted; but yet Joseph was her husband, which thing setteth unto us the commendation of the laws of wedlock. How could he more commend wedlock than when he, willing to declare the privy and wonderful conjunction of the divine nature with the human body and soul, and willing to declare his ineffable and eternal love toward his church (that is to say, the company of the Christian people) calleth himself the bridegroom and the church his spouse? 'Great', sayeth Paul, 'is the mystery of matrimony in Christ and in the church.'[14] If there had been any couple in earth more holy, if there had been any [A8ᵛ] bond of love and concord more religiously to be kept than wedlock, undoubtedly he had fetched his similitude from thence. What like thing do ye ever read in all scripture of bachelorship? Honourable wedlock and the immaculate bride bed is spoken of.[15] Bachelorship is not once named. Now sir, Moses' law abhorreth barren wedlock, and therefore we read that some were put out of the commonalty° for the same cause.[16] And why so? Surely because they living unprofitably to the common weal, and for their own singular avail, did not multiply the people with any issue. If then the law damneth barren matrimony, much more it damneth

---

[12] Marg. 'A confutation.'
[13] became ... God] i.e. was appropriate to his divine nature.
[14] Ephes. 5. 32. Taverner's 'mystery' follows the term Erasmus uses in the *Novum Instrumentum*, i.e. *mysterium*, rather than the term *sacramentum*, which he uses in the *Declamatio* itself.
[15] Hebr. 13. 4.
[16] Marg. 'The law of the Jews.'

bachelors. If the infirmity of nature escapeth not punishment, certes° the froward° [B1ʳ] will shall not escape. If they were punished whose nature failed to their will,[17] what have they deserved which will not so much as put to their good will that they be not barren?

The laws of the Hebrews gave this honour unto matrimony that he that married a new wife should not be compelled that year to go forth to the battle. The city is in great jeopardy if there be not men of arms to defend it, but needs it must decay if there be not wedded men by whom the youth continually failing° may be supplied. Also, the laws of the Romans punished them that were bachelors in removing them from all promotions of the city. But such as had increased with children the common weal, to them they ordained [B1ᵛ] a reward openly to be given, as it were for their well deserving. The law of the three children is a sufficient proof for this matter.[18] For I will not here rehearse all the rest.[19] Lycurgus made a law that they which married not wives should in summer season be driven from the interludes° and other sights, and in winter go about the marketplace all naked and curse themselves, saying they suffered just punishment because they would not obey the laws.[20]

Now will ye know how much matrimony was set by° in old time? Consider the punishment for the defouling° of it. The Greeks once thought it expedient to revenge the breach of matrimony by continual wars enduring the space of ten years.[21] Furthermore, [B2ʳ] by the laws not only of the Romans, but also of the Hebrews and other nations, adulterers should lose their lives. The thief was delivered by paying four times so much as he had stolen; the sin of adultery was punished with the axe. Also among the Hebrews he was stoned to death with the people's hands, which defiled that without which the people should not be. And the rigour of their laws not contented therewith, suffered also that he which was found in adultery should be put to death without judgement, without laws, giving that liberty to the grief of the wedded men which uneath° is granted to him that in jeopardy of life defendeth himself. Doubtless wedlock must needs seem a [B2ᵛ] right holy thing, which defiled cannot be repurged° without man's blood, and the revenging whereof is neither compelled to abide the laws nor the judge, the which severity and rigour of law is neither in murder nor in treason.

But what stand we all day in written laws? This is the law of nature, not graven

---

[17] will] i.e. who were unable to have children even though they wanted to.

[18] law of the three children] Under Augustus the *ius trium liberorum* rewarded parents (male and female) who had produced three or more children.

[19] For I ... the rest] Taverner omits a section here (translated by Wilson) which gives examples of laws relating to marriage under the Roman empire.

[20] **Marg.** 'The law of the Lacedaemonians.' 'Interludes' are plays, though Lycurgus's law referred to 'exercises'. See Plutarch, *Life of Lycurgus*, 15.

[21] **Marg.** 'The Battle of Troy.'

in tables of brass, but inwardly fixed in our hearts, which who will not obey he is not so much as to be esteemed a man, much less a good citizen. For if, as the Stoics — men of sharp judgements — do dispute,° to live well is nothing else but to follow the guide of nature, what thing is so agreeable to nature as matrimony? For nothing is so naturally given, neither to man nor yet to any other kind of brute beasts, as [B3ʳ] that everyone should preserve his kind from destruction and by propagation or posterity to make it as it were immortal, which without carnal copulation (as every man knoweth) cannot be brought to pass. And it seemeth a foul shame dumb beasts to obey the laws of nature, and men after the manner of giants to bid battle against nature,[22] whose work if we will behold with eyes not dazzling,° we shall perceive that her will is that there be in every kind of things a certain spice° of wedlock. For I omit to speak of trees, whom yet by the authority of Pliny wedlock is found with so manifest diversity of the male and female that if the male tree should not with his boughs lie upon the female trees that stand about [B3ᵛ] him, coveting as it were a meddling° together, they should abide° barren and fruitless.[23] I hold my peace of precious stones, in which the same author writeth (but not he alone) that there is found both male and female.[24] I pray you, hath not God so knit all things together with certain bonds that one thing doth need another's help? What think ye to the heaven which turneth about with continual moving? I pray you, while it maketh the earth lying underneath, which is mother of all, with sundry kind of things fruitful, pouring seed (as it were) upon it, doth it not the office of a husband? But to run through each thing were over-long.

Now, to what purpose have we spoken this? Surely that you may understand [B4ʳ] by such natural commixtion° everything to have his being and continuance, without which all things to be dissolved, to perish, and to fall away. It is feigned by the old and wise poets, whose study was to cover the precepts of philosophy under mystical fables, that giants, the sons of the earth, having feet like serpents, did cast mountains upon mountains that reached up to the heaven, and so standing upon them warred against the gods.[25] What signifieth this fable? Surely that certain ungodly persons, wild and of an ungentle nature, did greatly abhor from matrimonial concord and therefore they were cast down headlong with Jupiter's thunderbolt; that is to say, they utterly [B4ᵛ] decayed and came to nought,

---

[22] giants ... nature] see 190–91 below.
[23] Marg. 'A certain kind of wedlock in trees.' See Pliny, *Natural History* 13. 7.
[24] Pliny, *Natural History* 26. 25.
[25] Marg. 'A fable and the exposition thereof.' The giant brothers Otos and Ephialtes piled Mount Pelion onto Mount Ossa in order to storm Olympus. Erasmus/Taverner's comment on the use of classical mythology to represent Christian doctrine is echoed by Milton: ''tis not vain or fabulous | [...] What the sage poets taught by the heavenly Muse, | Storied of old in high immortal verse' (*Comus*, lines 512–15).

sith° they eschewed the thing whereby mankind is only preserved. But the selfsame poets have feigned that Orpheus, being a poet and a minstrel, did move with the sweet note of his musical instrument the hard rocks of stone. What meaned they hereby? Nothing else but that a wise and an eloquent man did first prohibit the stony men, and which lived after the manner of wild beasts, from lying at large,[26] and brought them to the holy laws of matrimony. Wherefore it appeareth evidently that whosoever is not touched with desire of wedlock seemeth to be no man, but a stone, an enemy to nature, a rebel to God, by his own folly seeking his decay and undoing.

But go to,° [B5ʳ] sith we be fallen into fables nothing fabulous or vain, the same Orpheus when he descended down to hell and there moved Pluto, lord of hell, and the souls there abiding, on such wise that he might easily lead away with him Eurydice his wife, what other thing suppose we that the poets thought than that they would commend unto us the love of wedlock, which also in hell is counted holy and religious. Hereunto also belongeth that the antiquity made Jupiter lord of wedlock, and named him for the same purpose *Gamelius* and made Juno the lady of women in childbed, calling her *Pronuba* and *Lucina*,[27] superstitiously erring (I grant well) in the name of the gods, but not erring [B5ᵛ] in this that they judged matrimony a thing holy and worthy to be regarded of the gods. Surely there have been diverse laws, ceremonies, and usages among diverse peoples and nations. But there was never nation so barbarous, so far from all humanity, with whom the name of wedlock hath not been recounted° holy, hath not been recounted worshipful. This the Thracian, this the Sarmate,[28] this the man of India, this the Greek, this the Italian, this the Briton furthest of all the world, or if there be any further than they, have had in high reverence.[29] And why so? For of necessity that thing must needs be common, which the common parent of all hath imprinted, and so inwardly imprinted [B6ʳ] that the sense and feeling of it hath not only pierced the turtles and the doves, but also the most cruel wild beasts.[30] For the lions be gentle and meek to their lionesses. The tigers fight for their whelps. The asses stick not to run through fires lying in their way for the safeguard and defence of their foals. And this they call the law of nature which as it is most strong, so it is most large.° Wherefore like as he is no diligent husband[31] which, contented with the things present, tendeth full curiously° the trees ready grown,

---

[26] lying at large] Living in the wild.
[27] *Gamelius ... Lucina*] Jupiter's appellation means simply 'of marriage', while the two names for Juno refer to her roles as goddess of marriage and goddess of childbirth.
[28] Sarmate] The Sarmatians were a tribe related to the Scythians (a byword for barbarism).
[29] Briton ... world] The ancients believed that the island beyond Britain known as 'ultima Thule' was the furthest point of the world, but Britain itself was far enough.
[30] turtles ... doves] i.e. turtle-doves, which were emblems of undying love, as in Shakespeare's 'The Phoenix and the Turtle'.
[31] **Marg.** 'A similitude.'

but hath little regard either of setting° or of grafting, because that of necessity within few years those orchards, be they never so well kept, must decay and become desolate. So in like wise [B6ᵛ] he is to be judged an undiligent citizen in the public weal which, contented with the company present, hath no respect nor consideration to supply new in place of the old. No man therefore have been counted a noble and worthy citizen which hath not bestowed his diligence in begetting children and bringing them virtuously up.

Among the Hebrews and Persians he was most highly commended that had most plenty of wives, as though the country were most bound to him that with most children had enriched it. Do ye study to be more holy than was Abraham? He should never have been called *Pater multarum gentium*, that is to say 'the Father of many peoples', and that of God's own mouth, if he had [B7ʳ] fled the company of his wife.[32] Do ye labour to be reputed more religious than Jacob? He sticked° not to buy his wife Rachel with so long apprenticehood and bondage.[33] Be ye wiser than Solomon? But what a flock of wives kept he at home? Be ye chaster than Socrates? Which suffered at home in his house Xanthippe,[34] that wayward woman, not only (as he was wont to jest himself) because he might learn patience at home, but because he would seem not to halt in the office of nature. For he, a man whom the divine answer of Apollo only judged wise,[35] understood full well that under this law and condition he was begotten, to this he was born, this he did owe to nature. For if it have been well [B7ᵛ] said of the old philosophers, if it have been not without cause confirmed of our divines, if it have been rightly everywhere pronounced as a proverb that God nor nature have made nothing frustrate° nor in vain,[36] why, I pray you, hath God given us these members? Why these pricks and provocations? Why hath he added the power of begetting if bachelorship be taken for a praise? If one would give you a precious gift, as a bow, a garment, or a sword, ye should seem unworthy the thing that ye have received if either ye would not or ye could not use it. Whereas all other things be ordained by nature with most high reason, it is not likely that she slumbered and slept in making only this privy member.

[B8ʳ] Nor I hear not him which will say unto me that that foul itching and pricks of carnal lust have come not of nature, but of sin.[37] What is more unlike the truth? As though matrimony, whose office cannot be executed without these pricks, was not before sin. Moreover, in other beasts, I pray you, from whence commeth those

---

[32] *Pater multarum gentium*] Gen. 12. 2–3.
[33] Gen. 29. 18–21.
[34] Xanthippe] The wife of Socrates, popularly represented as shrewish.
[35] divine … wise] Plato reports that the Delphic oracle pronounced Socrates to be the wisest of men (*Apology* 21a).
[36] nature … in vain] Aristotle, *On the Beginnings of Animals* 2.704b.
[37] **Marg.** 'A confutation.'

pricks and provocations? Of nature, or of sin? Wonder it is if not of nature. And as touching the foulness, surely we make that by our imagination to be foul, which of the self nature is fair and holy.[38] Else, if we would weigh the thing not by the opinion of the people, but by the very nature, how is it less foul (after the manner of wild beasts) to eat, to chaw,° to digest, [B8ᵛ] empty the belly, than to use the lawful and permitted pleasure of the body?

But virtue, ye say, is to be obeyed rather than nature. As though that is to be called virtue which repugneth° with nature,[39] from whence, if virtue hath not his first beginning, certes it cannot be it which may with exercise and learning be made perfect. But the Apostles' life delighteth you, for they also followed bachelorship and exhorted other to do the same. Let the apostolical men follow the Apostles, which, because their office is to teach and instruct the people, cannot both satisfy their flock and their wives, if they should have any. Howbeit° that the Apostles also had wives it is evidently clear. Let us grant bachelorship to the bishops.[40] What, [C1ʳ] do ye follow the Apostles' form of living, being so far from the office of an Apostle, sith ye be a man both temporal and also without office? It is licenced them to be without wives, to the intent they may the better attend to beget the more children to Christ. Let this be the privilege of priests and religious men, which, as it appear[s], have succeeded the Essenes' form of living, which damned holy matrimony.[41] Your estate requireth otherwise.

'But Christ himself', ye will say, 'have pronounced them blessed which have gelded themselves for the kingdom of God.'[42] I reject not the authority, but I will expound Christ's meaning. First of all, I think this saying of Christ to appertain especially to those times [C1ᵛ] when it was expedient to be most ready and loose from all worldly businesses. Then was the time that they should flee and run hither and thither through all lands; the persecutor was at hand on every side. But now such is the state of things and times that nowhere ye may find the pureness and perfection of manners less spotted and contaminate than among wedded persons. Let the swarms of monks, friars, canons, and nuns advance° their profession as much as them lust.[43] Let them boast as much as they will their ceremonies and disguised coats whereby they be chiefly known from the temporal,° surely the most holy kind of life is wedlock purely and chastely kept.[44] Furthermore, not he

---

[38] of the self nature] Of its own nature.

[39] virtue ... nature] This is consistent with the central role given to nature in *Praise of Folly*, though there Erasmus is more critical of the Stoical position.

[40] The sense of the English here is unclear. What Erasmus means is: 'let us leave aside the question of celibacy for priests (even though the Apostles themselves had wives), since that is far from being your role'.

[41] Essenes] A Jewish sect (fl. 200 BC–100 AD) whose priests observed celibacy.

[42] Matt. 19. 12.

[43] as ... lust] As much as they like.

[44] disguised coats] Strange vestments.

only geldeth himself which liveth [C2ʳ] without a wife, but he which chastely and holily doeth the office of wedlock. And would God they were truly chaste, so many as cloak their vices under the glorious title of chastity and castration, which under the shadow° of chastity do more foully rage in filthy and beastly abomination. For I am ashamed, so help me God, here to reckon up into what shameful abominations they oft times fall, which do thus repugn against nature. To be short, Christ never commanded bachelorship to none earthly person, but he openly forbiddeth divorcement.[45] Surely, me think, he should be not the worst counsellor for the common weal, considering the fashions and manners of men, which would [C2ᵛ] grant also the priests and religious persons licence to marry, namely sith there is everywhere so great a multitude of priests, of which, alas, how few live a chaste life.[46] How much better were it to turn their concubines into wives, so that those whom they have now with great infamy, and with an unquiet conscience, they might have openly with an honest fame,° and beget children whom they may love as truly legitimate, and bring them godly up, so that neither the father shall be ashamed of them, nor they of their father. And this, I trow,° the officials of bishops should have procured long ago,[47] but that greater gains arise by the concubines than should by the wives. 'But virginity', ye will [C3ʳ] say, 'is a divine thing, an angelical thing.'[48] Truth it is, but on the contrary side wedlock is an human thing. I now speak to a man, being myself a man. A commendable thing, certes, is virginity, but yet so that this praise be not transferred to over many, which commendation, if every man commonly will begin to usurp, what can be said or thought more hurtful and more pernicious than virginity? Moreover, though in other men virginity should most of all deserve praise, yet surely in you it cannot lack blame, in whom it now standeth to preserve your noble stock, worthy of an immortal continuance. Finally, he is but a very little off from the praise of virginity which keepeth purely the [C3ᵛ] law of wedlock, and which hath a wife to the intent to beget children and not to satisfy his wanton lust. If the brother, in the law of Moses, be commanded to raise the seed of his brother which died without issue, will ye suffer the hope of your whole lineage to be utterly extinct, namely sith it is returned to you only?[49]

---

[45] divorcement] Matt. 5. 31–2, 19. 6. But Erasmus was not against divorce absolutely; see the commentary on 1 Corinth. 7 in his *Annotations on the New Testament*, translated into English by Nicholas Lesse as *The censure and iudgement of the famous clark Erasmus of Roterodam: whyther dyuorsemente betwene man and wyfe stondeth with the lawe of God* (London, 1550; STC 10450).

[46] **Marg.** 'He thinketh it expedient for priests to have wives.' On the issue of clerical celibacy and the Protestant legitimisation of married clergy see Parish, *Clerical Marriage and the English Reformation*.

[47] officials of bishops] The presiding officers or judges of bishops' courts.

[48] **Marg.** 'A confutation.'

[49] Deut. 25. 5–6.

Nor I am not so ignorant but that I know well enough that the praises of virginity have been rehearsed° and celebrated with great volumes of some of our old fathers. Among whom Jerome so advanceth it that in manner he despiseth wedlock and was provoked° of the bishops that were of the true opinion to rechant and sing a new song.[50] But let this heat° be granted to those times. How [C4ʳ] I would wish those that thus everywhere without discretion do exhort the youth (not yet known to themselves) to bachelorship and virginity to bestow their labour in describing the form of chaste and pure matrimony. But yet they which are so well pleased with virginity be not displeased with the wars against the Turks, which pass us so far in number, whose judgement, if it be right, it shall chiefly be thought right and holy busily to beget children and supply youth sufficient for the use of the wars — except perchance they think to prepare guns, weapons, ships to the wars, and think little need of men. The same do allow to slay with the sword the parents of infidels, to the intent [C4ᵛ] that their children might be baptised, yea, unknowing also. If this be true, how gentler a deed were it to bring the same to effect with the office of intermarrying, each with other. No nation is so cruel that abhorreth not the murder of infants. Laws of princes in manner with like rigour punish them that cause that which is conceived in the woman to come forth dead, and them that make them barren with medicines. Why so? For there is small diversity betwixt him that murdereth that which begin to be born and him which procureth that nothing can be born. This that in your body either drieth up, or with the great danger of your health putrefieth and corrupteth, which in your sleep [C5ʳ] falleth away, had been a man if ye were a man yourself. The old law of the Jews curseth him which, when he is commanded to lie with his brother's wife that is dead,[51] casteth his seed on the earth that nothing should be engendered, and is judged unworthy life which envyeth° life to the fruit that is to be born. But how little from him differ they which have enjoined° themselves perpetual barrenness. Do they not seem to kill so many men as should have been born if they had given their labour to the begetting of children? I pray you, if a man have a piece of ground rank° of nature, which untilled he suffereth to be continually barren, is not this man punishable by the civil law, because it is for the profit [C5ᵛ] of the common weal that every man tendeth well his own?[52] If he be punished which neglecteth his ground, which (be it never so well tilled) bring forth nothing else than wheat or beans or peas, what punishment is he worthy

---

[50] rechant] A neologism; here, with a pun on 'recant'. For Jerome on virginity see Letter 22 to Eustochium and *Against Jovinian*.
[51] brother's ... dead] i.e. with the wife of his brother that is dead. See Gen. 38. 8–10 (the story of Onan).
[52] common weal ... own] For a contemporary discussion of the relation between private and public interest see Thomas Starkey, *A Dialogue between Reginald Pole and Thomas Lupset* (c. 1530).

which refuseth to till that ground which, tilled, beareth men? And in tillage of the earth is required a long and painful° labour, here the short tillage is also enticed° with a pleasure, as it were a reward, prepared therefore. Wherefore, if the sense of nature,[53] if honesty, if natural affection, if devotion, if gentleness, if virtue anything move you, why abhor ye from that which God ordaineth, nature enacteth, reason enticeth, the scriptures both of God and man praise, the laws [C6^r] command, the whole consent of all nations approve, to which the example of every good man provoketh?

That if the most part of things (yea, which be also bitter) are of a good man to be desired for none other purpose but because they be honest,[54] matrimony doubtless is chiefly to be desired, whereof a man may doubt whether it hath more honesty than pleasure. For what thing is sweeter than with her to live with whom ye may be most straightly° coupled, not only in the benevolence of the mind, but also in the conjunction of the body. If a great delectation of mind be taken of the benevolence of our other kinsmen, sith it is an especial sweetness to have one with whom ye may communicate the secret affections° of [C6^v] your mind, with whom ye may speak even as it were with your own self, whom ye may safely trust, which supposeth your chances to be his, what felicity, think ye, have the conjunction of man and wife, than which nothing in the universal world may be found either greater or firmer? For with our other friends we be conjoined only with the benevolence of minds; with our wife we be coupled with most high love, with permixtion° of bodies, with the confederate band of the sacrament,[55] and finally with the fellowship of all chances.[56]

Furthermore, in other friendships how great simulation is there? How great falsity? Yea, they whom we judge our best friends, like as the swallows flee [C7^r] away when summer is gone, so they forsake us when fortune turneth her wheel. And sometime the fresher friend cast out the old. We hear of few whose fidelity endure till their life's end. The wife's love is with no falsity corrupted, with no simulation obscured, with no chance of things minished,° finally with death only (nay, not with death neither) withdrawn. She, the love of her parents; she, the love of her sisters; she, the love of her brethren despiseth for the love of you; her only respect is to you, of you she hangeth,° with you she coveteth to die. Have ye riches? There is one that shall save it, there is one that shall increase it. Have ye none? There is one that may seek it. If ye have wealth your felicity [C7^v] is doubled; if

---

[53] Marg. 'Epilogue.'
[54] That if ...] i.e. Even if we grant that...
[55] confederate ... sacrament] The bond of being allied with another in covenant with God. 'Confederate' in this sense is a neologism.
[56] the fellowship of all chances] The Latin reads *et fortunarum omnium societate copulamur* (*ASD* I-5. 406), where *fortunarum* may refer either to life's fortunes, as Taverner translates it here, or to material property.

adversity, there is one which may comfort you, which may sit by side, which may serve you, which may covet° your grief to be hers. Do ye judge any pleasure to be compared with this so great a conjunction? If ye tarry at home there is at hand which shall drive away the tediousness of solitary being. If from home, ye have one that shall kiss you when ye depart, long for you when ye be absent, receive you joyously when ye return. A sweet companion of youth, a kind solace of age. By nature, yea, any fellowship is delectable to man, as whom nature hath created to benevolence and friendship. This fellowship, then, how shall it not be most sweet, in which everything is common to them both? And contrarily, [C8ʳ] if we see the savage beasts also abhor solitary living and related in fellowship, in my mind he is not once to be supposed a man which abhorreth from this fellowship most honest and pleasant of all. For what is more hateful than that man which, as though he were born only to himself, liveth for himself, seeketh for himself, spareth° for himself, doth cost° to himself, loveth no person, is loved of no person? Shall not such monster be adjudged worthy to be cast out of all men's company into the mid-sea with Timon the Athenian, which because he fled all men's company was called Misanthropus, that is to say 'hate-man'.⁵⁷ Neither dare I here propound unto you those pleasures, which, whereas [C8ᵛ] they be naturally most sweet to man, yet (I cannot tell how) of the great wits they be dissembled rather than despised.⁵⁸ Albeit, who can be born with so rigorous a disposition (I will not say dumpish° and dastardly) which may not be taken with such kind of pleasures, namely if he may attain them without the offence of God and man, without the loss of his good name? Certes, I would call him no man, but a plain stone. Albeit, that pleasure of bodies is the least part of the goods that wedlock hath. But imagine that ye can contemn° this as unworthy for a man, howbeit that without these we deserve not once the name of a man, let it be put (if ye will) among the most base commodities of wedlock.

[D1ʳ] Now, sir, what can be more amiable than chaste love, nay, what more holy and honest? There increaseth by the means a sweet flock of alliances;⁵⁹ there is doubled the number of parents, of brethren, of sisters, of nephews. For nature can give one only mother, one only father. By wedlock another father, another mother is gotten, which, because they have committed their own flesh unto you, cannot but love you most tenderly. Now sir, how highly will ye esteem this thing when your fair wife shall make you a father with a fair child? When some little young babe shall play in your hall, which shall resemble you and your wife? Which with

---

⁵⁷ Timon ... hate-man] 'Timon, or the Misanthrope' was one of the first dialogues translated by Erasmus for the Latin edition of Lucian which he published with More (Paris, 1506).
⁵⁸ dissembled rather than despised] i.e. learned authorities pretend not to be aware of the sexual pleasures in marriage rather than condemn them outright.
⁵⁹ alliances] Taverner's 'flock of alyesses', which is not recorded in the OED, renders Erasmus's *affinium turba* (ASD I-5. 299).

a mild lisping or amiable stammering [D1ᵛ] shall call you 'Dad'.⁶⁰ Now add unto your wife's love the bond more strong than any adamant,⁶¹ which not death himself can burst asunder.

> O how blessed, sayeth Flaccus, be they
> Whom the fast knot of wedlock doth tey,⁶²
> Whose steadfast love by no plaint can start,
> Till only death them twain do part.⁶³

Ye have them that may delight your age, that may close your eyes, that may do the office of the burials, in whom ye may seem regenerate,° whom, being alive, ye shall be thought not to have died. Your goods which ye have gotten go not to strange heirs. Thus, when ye are passing out of the world and have fully executed all together, yet not death himself can seem sharp nor bitter unto you. Age must creep upon us all, whether [D2ʳ] we will or not. By this policy nature hath provided that in our children and nephews we may be renewed and flourish fresh again. For who can bear age heavily when in his son he beholdeth his own visage that he himself bare when he was young? Death is prepared for all. But by this only way the providence of nature assayeth, as it were, a certain immortality while she thus maketh one thing to issue out of another, like as a young plant which is cut off from the tree springeth freshly up, nor he seemeth not to be utterly quenched which dieth leaving issue behind.

But I know well enough what among these ye murmur° against me.⁶⁴ 'A blessed thing is wedlock, if all prove according [D2ᵛ] to the desire. But what if a wayward wife chanceth? What if an unchaste, what if unnatural children?' There will run in your mind the examples of those whom wedlock have brought to utter destruction. Heap up as much as ye can, but yet these be the vices of men and not of wedlock. Believe me, an evil wife is not wont to chance, but to evil husbands. Put this unto it, that it lieth in you to choose out a good one. 'But what if after the marriages she be marred?'⁶⁵ Of an evil husband, I will well, a good wife may be marred, but of a good the evil is wont to be reformed and mended. We blame wives falsely. No man, if ye give any credence to me, had ever a shrew to his wife but through his own default.° And [D3ʳ] of good parents commonly be born like children. Howbeit the children also, howsoever they be born, commonly do prove

---

⁶⁰ 'Dad'] The first citation for this term in the *OED* is the 1533 edition of the translation of Erasmus's *Enchiridion*. See *Manual*, line 2520.
⁶¹ adamant] A stone of exceptional hardness, but also identified with the lodestone, which gives it the power to attract.
⁶² tey] Tie. Not recorded in the *OED* as an alternative spelling and used only for the rhyme.
⁶³ Horace, *Odes* 1. 13, lines 17–20.
⁶⁴ **Marg.** 'The refutation of the incommodities of marriage.'
⁶⁵ marriages … marred] 'Married and marred' was a proverbial expression; see Tilley M701.

such as they be formed and fashioned in their bringing up. Now sir, I see no cause why ye should fear jealousy. This is the sickness of foolish lovers. The chaste and lawful love knoweth no jealousy. What, do the tragedies come to your mind? This adulterous woman struck in sunder her husband with an axe.[66] This poisoned him. That woman with her hateful manners did drive her husband to death. Why rather do not Cornelia, wife to Tiberius Gracchus, come to your remembrance? Why do not Alcestis, so good a wife of not so good an husband? Why dost not either Julia, wife of Pompeius, [D3^v] or Portia, the wife of Cato, run in your mind? Why do not Artemisia, worthy eternal memory? Why do not Hypsicratea, wife to Mithridates, king of Pontus? Why not come into your mind the most gentle behaviour of Tertia Aemilia, the wife of Scipio Africanus? Why do not the faithfulness of Turia? Why do not Lucretia and Lentula come in mind? Why do not Aria, so highly commended of Pliny?[67] Why do not others innumerable, whose honest and chaste living and faithfulness toward their husbands could not be altered nor corrupted not by death?

'A rare bird in earth', ye say, 'is an honest woman'. And imagine ye again yourself worthy to have a rare wife. 'A good woman', sayeth the wise man, [D4^r] 'is a great felicity.'[68] Be bold to hope one worthy for your manners.°[69] And very much (as touching this matter) lieth in the fashioning of her and in the behaving of yourself towards her whom ye choose. 'But sweeter,' ye will say, 'is liberty. Whosoever taketh a wife taketh a pair of fetters which nothing, save only death, can shake off.' What can be sweet to a man alone? If liberty were sweet, it were best, by mine advice, to take a companion with whom ye may part° this so pleasant a thing. Howbeit, what is more free than this bondage, where either is so bound to other that neither would be enfranchised?[70] Is not every man bound to his friend? Yet no man complaineth that his liberty is take[n] away. But ye fear lest if [D4^v] death should take away your children ye should fall into sorrow.[71] If ye fear to be childrenless, for this very cause ye ought to marry a wife which only may be the cause that ye be not childrenless. But what search ye out so diligently — nay, so narrowly and curiously — all the incommodities° of matrimony, as who should say the single life had no incommodity at all? As who should say there were any life of man that is not subject to all the chances of fortune. He must get him out of the world which will bear no incommodity. That if ye will have respect to the life in heaven, this life of man is to be said a death and no life. But if ye keep

---

[66] This ... axe] As Clytemnestra did Agamemnon in some versions of the story.
[67] Cornelia ... Pliny] Julia, Portia, Artemisia, Hypsicratea, Tertia Aemilia, Turia, and Lucretia all appear in Boccaccio's *De mulieribus claris* (*On Famous Women*), as does Clytemnestra.
[68] Prov. 18. 22.
[69] manners] Latin *mores*, which is the word Erasmus uses, gives the best sense here.
[70] bound ... enfranchised] Liberated from bondage.
[71] **Marg.** '*Orbitas.*' ['Family bereavement']

your mind within the bounds of man's estate, nothing is neither safer, neither [D5ʳ] quieter, neither pleasanter, neither amiabler, neither happier than the wedded life. Mark the thing by the end. How many see ye which have once assayed wedlock that go not greedily to it again. Did not my friend Mauricius, whose excellent prudence is not unknown unto you, after the death of his wife whom he so singularly loved, marry the next month after a new wife.[72] Not so greatly for the impatiency of his lust, but he thought his life no life without a wife, a sweet companion of all things. Doth not Jovius, our friend, now woo his fourth wife?[73] So he loved them when they lived that he seemed comfortless. So when one died he hated to be a widower, as though he faintly had [D5ᵛ] loved them.

But what reason we of honesty and pleasantness, when not only profit enticeth, but also necessity constraineth to wedlock. Take matrimony away and within few years mankind shall be utterly gone. Xerxes, king of Persia, when he beheld out of an high tower the great multitude of men, he could not refrain weeping, because that of so many thousands of men within three score years none should be left alive.[74] Why the thing that he understood of his army do not we consider of all mankind? Wedlock taken away, who one of so many regions, provinces, realms, cities, towns within an hundred years shall be left alive? Go we now and advance bachelorship, which bringeth mankind to destruction? [D6ʳ] What pestilence, what plague, can be sent on man either from heaven or from hell more hurtful? What of any flood can be feared more dangerous? What can be looked for more heavy and grievous, though the fire of Phaeton should come again when all the world was destroyed with fire.[75] And yet for all that, in such troublous seasons many are wont to be left alive; but by bachelorship surely nothing can be left. We see what a rout° of diseases, how many casualties daily and nightly lie in wait upon the fewness of men. How many do the pestilence take away? How many do the sea swallow up? How many do battle consume? For I will not speak of these quotidian deaths. Death flyeth about [D6ᵛ] everywhere: he runneth, he carrieth, he hasteth to quench mankind; and do we yet advance bachelorship and flee wedlock? Unless perchance the life of the Essenes and Dulopolitans, which do damn wedlock, do please us, whose pestilent sects be multiplied and increased with ungracious people, never failing.[76] Do we look that God will give us the same virtue that he hath given, as they say, to the bees, so that without the company of woman we might be great with

---

[72] Mauricius] Thomas More, who married Alice Middleton a month after the death of his first wife, Jane, in September 1511.
[73] Jovius] Erasmus's pupil William Mountjoy married for the fourth time in 1523.
[74] Xerxes ... alive] See Herodotus, *Histories*, 7. 44–46.
[75] Phaeton ... fire] The son of Apollo who tried to drive the chariot of the sun, but was unable to control it and so set fire to the earth.
[76] Dulopolitans] Dulopolis was a city of slaves (from Greek *doulos* = slave). See Pliny, *Natural History* 5. 104.

child and gather with our mouths seeds of posterity out of the flowers? Do we require that, like as the poets feign that Minerva issued out of Jupiter's brains, so in like manner children should leap out of our heads? Or, to be short, [D7ʳ] that according to the old fables men should spring out of the earth, out of stones thrown forth, out of hard trunks of trees?⁷⁷ Out of the lap of the earth many things do spring without our labour. Little plants spring up oftentimes under the shadow of their mother. But unto man nature hath given one only way of deriving issue, which is that by the mutual labour of man and woman mankind should be preserved, which if men would flee as ye do, truly these things which ye so highly advance should not be. Ye advance bachelorship, ye magnify virginity; but neither bachelors neither virgins should be if ye take away the use of wedlock. Why then is virginity preferred? Why is it in so [D7ᵛ] high reputation if it be the destruction of man? It was commended but for a time, and but in few, for it pleased God to show to men a certain token and, as it were, a representation of the heavenly life 'where they neither marry nor be given in marriage'.⁷⁸ But for an example a few be sufficient; a multitude is not profitable. For like as not, all grounds, be they never so rank, be sown to the sustenance of man, but part is let alone, part dight° to the pleasure and feeding of the eyes.⁷⁹ For the very copy° and plenty of the thing in so much arable ground suffereth some part to be left barren and fruitless. But if none at all were sown, who seeth not but that we must return to the fruit of trees wherewith they lived in [D8ʳ] old time before the invention of tillage.° So bachelorship in so great a multitude of men, in a few, I grant, is commendable; in all, a thing greatly to be dispraised.

But admit that in other men virginity had the name of an high virtue, yet in you surely it should be vicious. For other men shall seem to have intended a pureness of living; ye shall be judged a traitorous murderer of your lineage, which, when ye might have maintained by honest wedlock, ye have suffered to perish by foul bachelorship. Admit it lawful out of a great number of children to offer one virgin to God. The uplandish° men that dwell in the country offer to God the first of their fruit, not their whole crop. But ye must [D8ᵛ] remember that ye only be left the last and the leavings° of your stock. And I pray you, what diversity° is there whether ye slay or refuse to save him, which may by you only be saved — and easily saved? But the example of your sister provoketh you to chastity.⁸⁰ Nay, for this very cause only, ye ought most chiefly to eschew bachelorship. For now ye understand that the hope, which before was common to you both, of preserving your stock is revolved° and cast whole upon your back. Let us pardon the frail kind of the woman; let us pardon the indiscreet age.⁸¹ The maid overcome with

---

⁷⁷ fables ... thrown forth] As in the story of Deucalion; see Ovid, *Metamorphoses* I. 381–415.
⁷⁸ Matt. 22. 30.
⁷⁹ **Marg.** 'A similitude.'
⁸⁰ **Marg.** 'A violation.'
⁸¹ indiscreet age] youthful lack of sound judgement.

sorrow did amiss. Through the enticements of foolish women and foolish friars she hath cast herself headlong. Ye being elder [E1ʳ] must needs remember that ye be a man. She would needs die with her ancestors, but your labour must be that they die not. Your sister hath withdrawn herself of her duty; remember now that ye ought to fulfil the parts of two. The daughters of Lot sticked not to lie with their father, judging it better to maintain their lineage by unlawful and abominable incest than to suffer it clean to fall away.[82] And will not ye then by matrimony, which is honest, holy, chaste, without offence, with high pleasure maintain your stock, which shall else be utterly extinct?

Wherefore let us suffer them to follow the life of Hippolytus.[83] Let them, I say, embrace bachelorship which either can [E1ᵛ] be husbands, but fathers can be none, or whose bare° living is not able to bring up children, or whose stock may be maintained by other, or surely is such that better it were for the common weal to be quenched than maintained.[84] But ye, when (witnessing the physician,[85] a man neither unlearned nor no liar) ye seem by your nature very apt to engender much posterity, when ye have great inheritance, coming also of a stock so good, so noble, that without great sin and the great hurt of the common weal it cannot be quenched. Furthermore, sith your age is lusty and flourishing, nor ye lack not the beauty of the body, and when there is offered you a wife, so lusty° a maid, so well born as may be — [E2ʳ] chaste, sober, demure, godly, having an angel's face, with fair lands — when your friends beseech you, your kindred weep, your affinity call on,[86] your native country requireth, the very dead corpses of your ancestors rising out of their graves obtest° the same of you, do ye yet tarry, do ye yet think upon bachelorship? If a thing scarce honest should be required of you, if an hard thing, yet either the requests of your friends, either the love of your stock ought to overcome your mind. How much, then, more right and convenient is it that the tears of your friends, the affection of your country, the natural love of your ancestors ought to obtain that of you whereunto God's laws and man's [E2ᵛ] exhort, nature pricketh, reason leadeth, honesty allureth,° so many commodities provoke, necessity also constraineth? But now we have brought forth arguments abundantly enough. I trust long ago, through mine advertisement,° ye have changed your purpose and applied your mind to wholesomer counsels. Fare ye well.

---

[82] Gen. 19. 30-36.
[83] Hippolytus] In some versions of the myth Hippolytus rejects Artemis/Venus in order to follow Artemis/Diana, goddess of chastity and of hunting. (This is the basis of Shakespeare's *Venus and Adonis*.)
[84] or surely ... maintained] This is garbled. The Latin reads *aut certe eiusmodi est, vt magis Reipublicae conducat intermori quam propagari* (ASD I-5. 428), i.e. 'or is of such a kind that it would surely be better for the commonwealth to be extinguished rather than increased'.
[85] witnessing the physician] on the evidence of the doctor.
[86] your affinity call on] your family urge you.

Proverbs, or Adages

Translated by Richard Taverner (1539, rev. 1545)

Edited by Neil Rhodes

Introduction

Erasmus's collection of proverbs, the *Adagia*, was a lifelong project. It first appeared as the *Adagiorum collectanea* in Paris in 1500, when it contained just over 800 proverbs, and Erasmus continued to revise and expand it until his death in 1536. By 1508 it had already reached 3260 entries and had acquired the title 'Chiliades', the Greek term for 'thousands', which Taverner also uses. What had previously been a pocket-book was now on its way to becoming a classic Renaissance 'copious text', a folio volume with commentary on the origins of individual sayings and their changes in meaning as they morph through different literary contexts.[1] In 1515 the collection expanded still further, as Erasmus added essays — reflections on moral and political issues in a tradition that stretches from Plutarch to Montaigne and beyond — such as the widely reprinted *Dulce bellum inexpertis* ['war is sweet to those with no experience of it'], which would have its own stand-alone English version.[2]

Taverner's first translations of *Adagia* appeared three years after Erasmus's death in *The Second Booke of the Garden of Wysedom* (1539), where they were presented as the 'third book' of the same work.[3] They were expanded and reprinted separately in the same year, which is why the *Proverbs* of 1539 (ostensibly the first edition of the work) is referred to as having 'newe addicions' on the title page. Nevertheless, this little volume is even more modest in size than the *Collectanea*, with only 185 entries, and though Taverner added another forty to these in 1545, the book did not dilate in the way that Erasmus's collection did. Instead, Taverner offers a somewhat freewheeling interpretation of his source text, pushing at the boundaries of what might be considered a translation at all. What he also does in the 1545 version is to supply the English equivalent of Erasmus's originals, as well as an additional tranche of proverbs, rather than offer more extended observations on the meaning of individual sayings. This domestication

---

[1] See Brian Cummings, 'Encyclopedic Erasmus', in *The Copious Text: Encyclopedic Books in Early Modern England*, ed. by Abigail Shinn and Angus Vine, special issue, *Renaissance Studies*, 28.2 (2014), 183–204.
[2] For a succinct overview of the *Adagia* see *The Adages of Erasmus*, ed. by William Barker (Toronto: University of Toronto Press, 2001), pp. ix–xlvii. The standard scholarly study remains that of Margaret Mann Phillips, *The 'Adages' of Erasmus: A Study with Translations* (Cambridge: Cambridge University Press, 1964); on the English translation see Erika Rummel, 'The Reception of Erasmus' *Adages* in Sixteenth-Century England', *Renaissance and Reformation/ Renaissance et Réforme*, 18.2 (1994), 19–30.
[3] On Taverner's *Garden of Wysedom* and the *Proverbs* see Neil Rhodes, *Common: The Development of Literary Culture in Sixteenth-Century England* (Oxford: Oxford University Press, 2018), pp. 116–17.

of the Latin for the English market was clearly successful, since the collection was reprinted in 1550, 1552 (two issues), and 1569, representing a publication range that spans thirty years and four reigns (though it was not reprinted under Mary) during a period of exceptional instability. Taverner is quite prepared to apply this timeless wisdom to current conditions ('as we now see' is a typical intervention), so it is remarkable that the substance of the text was not revised between 1545 and 1569.[4]

This perhaps says something about the adaptability of the proverb form, and of its authenticator — Erasmus himself. Luther called him, sneeringly, 'king of the amphibians', and he himself complained that in Germany he was regarded as a papist and in Rome as a Lutheran.[5] So it is appropriate that one of Taverner's longest entries should be for *Polypi mentem obtine*: 'Obtain the mind of the fish called polypus. By this we be admonished according to the time to fashion our manners and to make our semblant and countenance' (1017). Taverner is anxious to point out that this has nothing to do with the vile arts of flattery, and it is certainly in keeping with the kind of sturdy prudence that characterises many of his glosses on individual proverbs. We might think of this as many of its first readers would have done, as a compendium of advice that would enable those of the middling sort to prosper (the 'commodity' of a course of action is invoked on more than one occasion), but also, in particularly desperate times, to survive.

Taverner begins by presenting what he calls 'The Prologue of the author'. This might seem doubly inappropriate in that what follows is both a translation and a collection of material whose authority derives from its *not* being authored.[6] Proverbs represent commonly accepted truths rather than the inventive power of the individual. They can be found in many authors, as Erasmus's *Adagia* illustrates and Taverner replicates more sparingly, but their origins lie either in the oracles of the gods, at the high end of the spectrum, or in the wisdom of the people.[7] However, there are various ways in which the collection can be understood as authored. Taverner's arrangement of the proverbs does very roughly follow that of Erasmus from 1508 onwards, but not consistently so. Erasmus had placed *Amicorum communia omnia* in pole position in 1508, but Taverner buries it away

---

[4] '[O]ur incomparable Prince Henry VIII' was still being thanked for his curtailment of holidays under Elizabeth; see *Prouerbes or adagies, gathered out of the Chiliades of Erasmus by Richard Taverner* (London: William How, 1569), fol. 39ᵛ.

[5] For Luther see Roland H. Bainton, *Erasmus of Christendom* (London: Collins, 1970), p. 261; for Erasmus's self-perception see the letter to Paolo Bombace (19 January 1524), *CWE* 10. 159; cf. letters to More (November 1520), *CWE* 8. 97; and to Cardinal Trivulzio (12 April 1531) in *Erasmus*, ed. by Richard L. DeMolen (London: Edward Arnold, 1973), p. 174.

[6] On the idea of the author in the early modern period see Kevin Pask, *The Emergence of the English Author: Scripting the Life of the Poet in Early Modern England* (Cambridge: Cambridge University Press, 1996).

[7] *CWE* 31. 5.

towards the end of his collection and adds a cautious comment on its radical message about the common ownership of goods. Taking up Erasmus's reference to the *conoebium*, he points out that this is much closer to the communion used in the primitive church amongst the Apostles 'than doth either our monkery at this day, or the wicked Anabaptistical sect' (1466–67). Resituating the *conoebium* in the middle ground is the strategy of the polypus and Taverner returns to the communion in his final proverb, *Panem ne frangito*, 'Break not bread'. This is one of the 'symbols' of Pythagoras which immediately follow *Amicorum communia omnia*. By placing it at the end Taverner gives his collection an explicitly Christian stamp, but he also uses it to appeal against the 'discord' and 'contention' between factions within the Church: 'We be all partakers of one bread and of one cup' (1567–68). The proverb is adapted to schismatic times.

This is how Taverner ends. But he begins on a political note which is very different from the radical Christianity of Erasmus's 'Friends' proverb: 'no man can be a good ruler unless he hath been first ruled'. This puts monarchical government in place of Erasmus's communal ideal, and it comes without scriptural trappings. But if it marginalises the Christian, it also reinforces the humanist tenor of the collection, signalling the importance of the ruler's education and thus of the humanist's role as educator, instilling in his princely charge a respect for discipline and a sense of the importance of self-discipline.[8] Threatening reminders that 'Kings have many ears and many eyes' and that 'Kings have long hands' follow, buttressed now by St Paul, who would have rulers 'obeyed even for conscience sake' (70). Echoing Tyndale's *The Obedience of a Christian Man*, this would have gladdened the heart of Henry VIII, and one can sense Henry's baleful shadow at various points behind this collection. Between its first appearance in 1539 and the additions of 1545, Taverner's patron, Thomas Cromwell, had been executed, reminding all those in his circle that the role of counsellor to the prince was a perilous one. This is the context in which the term 'anarchy' first appears in English. It is a humanist importation (a Greek term taken from Erasmus) and Taverner uses it to make the point that this is a 'mischief surely in manner worse than any tyranny' (892). A prudent observation in 1539, the year before Cromwell's fall, and perhaps even more so in 1545.

It is fair to say that Taverner's interventions Protestantize Erasmus, but they do so with a wary eye on the monarch, who 'must be obeyed even for conscience sake'.[9] One of Taverner's longest glosses is on 'With sluggers or unhardy persons it is always holiday' (819). Most of this is translated directly from Erasmus, as Taverner explains, but he ends with a dutiful reference to Henry's wisdom in

---

[8] As Erasmus himself set out in *The Education of the Christian Prince* (1516), written for the future Charles V.

[9] See John K. Yost, 'Taverner's Use of Erasmus and the Protestantization of English Humanism', *Renaissance Quarterly*, 23.3 (1970), 266–76.

getting rid of 'superfluous holy days' alongside a dismissive comment on the pope's lack of religious authority on religious matters in England. Taverner is on safe ground here, as doctrinal rectitude chimes with economic expedience, and the reduction in the number of holidays would doubtless have won approval among the thrifty hard-working folk of the middling sort who would have constituted Taverner's principal market. Elsewhere, though, Taverner treads more cautiously, as in his gloss on 'Nothing too much', where he uses the Horatian principle of the golden mean to advocate a middle way between abolishing 'all honest ceremonies, traditions, and laws' (411–12) and retaining the same, even when they have become corrupted and abused. This middle way is in harmony with Erasmus's own position on matters of religion, but it may also reflect Henry's desire in the latter part of his reign to be seen as a proponent of the *via media*.[10] And throughout the *Proverbs* there is a fine line between principle and expedience. Writing about the proverb that warns against judging by appearances, Taverner says 'All that have the Gospel hanging at their girdles be no gospellers' (422–23). This looks initially like another illustration of the *via media*, but if we take it in conjunction with the proverb on the polypus it sends a rather different signal: that in dangerous times everyone will wear a mask.

This last point glances towards a different aspect of authorial input in proverb collections, which is to do with arrangement. In rhetorical terms this is the domain not of *inventio*, which is the part of rhetoric usually associated with rhetoric, but with *dispositio*, the second and largely neglected part of the subject. Beginnings and endings are covered by *dispositio*, and so are groupings of proverbs on similar themes. For example, from *Intempestiva benevolentia* to *Aequalem tibi uxorem quaere* Taverner filters Erasmus in assembling a sequence of proverbs on fellowship and matching, adding two that do not appear in the *Adagia*: *Leona societas*, 'The fellowship of a lion' and *Non bene cum sociis regna Venusque manent*, 'Love nor lordship will abide no fellowship'. These juxtapositions highlight the ways in which proverbial advice can be reformulated in order to reflect different sets of circumstances. This is at the heart of *Intempestiva benevolentia*, 'Unseasonable friendship differeth little from enmity', which is perhaps the most striking way in which circumstances may translate a condition or a relationship into its opposite. There is a time and place for everything. That particular observation might itself have found a place in Taverner's *Proverbs*, and though it doesn't, it is nevertheless implicit in the collection as a whole, explaining why some proverbs contradict one another. The juxtaposition of contradictory proverbs was a recognised feature of such collections and became known as the 'crossing of proverbs'.[11] But this is

---

[10] See Diarmaid MacCulloch, *Thomas Cromwell: A Life* (Oxford: Oxford University Press, 2018), p. 449.

[11] See Nicholas Breton, *Crossing of Proverbs* (London: G. Eld for J. Wright, 1616), printed in two separate parts in the same year. Breton published a companion volume, *Soothing of Proverbs*, in 1626.

not something designed to produce gridlock. There is a sequence in Taverner that runs from 'There is an alteration of all things' through 'Change of things is pleasant' to 'Know time' (Tav. 68–70). The first looks to be a matter for regret, the second contradicts it, and the third shows you how to make the most of what is a necessary condition of life. Proverbs are in one sense timeless, but in another sense they are all about 'occasion', and collections such as Taverner's provide the reader with an armoury of wisdom to apply to every set of circumstances. This is something that emerges from the way in which Taverner selects from and arranges his Erasmian sources.

Proverbs might also seem to be barren ground for the deployment of the third part of rhetoric, which is *elocutio* or 'style'. As a form of *sententia* they may be 'scattered through all parts of a speech [and] contribute no small *copia* to a speech', Erasmus wrote in *De copia*, but it is difficult to see how a form that is defined by its compression could itself exhibit *copia*.[12] Yet there is a proverb to suit every occasion, and every set of circumstances, including those of the proverb's own composition. Taverner's comment on *Grata brevitas* illustrates the point: 'Unto little things is a certain grace annexed', he writes, rather gracefully; 'The English proverb is thus pronounced: *Short and sweet*' (1423). And there are other proverbs which show how this most laconic of forms is nonetheless capable of a certain stylistic elegance. For example: *Ama tanquam osurus, oderis tanquam amaturus*, which Taverner renders as 'Love as in time to come thou shouldst hate, and hate as thou shouldst in time to come love', neatly preserving the figure of *antimetabole*. Yet again this is about timing, but there is more to it than that. This kind of stylistic formulation captures the endlessly shifting circumstances of life: changing places, the forming of new alliances and new enmities, replicated in the construction of the rhetorical figure itself.

There are a number of ways, then, in which we can understand Taverner's *Proverbs* as a literary work, but what of its impact on other literary works? Proverbial forms of thought were deeply ingrained in sixteenth-century literary culture — something that is evident in the titles of plays such as *Like will to Like* or *All's Well that Ends Well* — and the early Tudor playwright (and grandfather of John Donne) John Heywood gathered many of them in his verse compilation *A Dialogue of Proverbs*. We can see them at work in Wyatt's satire 'A spending hand', as well as in the more specific instance of Gascoigne's long poem 'Dulce Bellum Inexpertis', and we can point to many examples in Shakespeare, in the poems as well as the plays: 'Know time' is echoed in *The Rape of Lucrece* in Lucrece's diatribe against 'opportunity' (line 876f.), while 'We look not what is in the wallet behind' is adapted by Ulysses in *Troilus and Cressida* in the speech that begins 'Time hath, my lord | A wallet at his back' (III. 3. 139f.). These and some other examples are cited in the notes to this edition.

[12] Erasmus, *On Copia of Words and Ideas*, trans. by Donald B. King and H. David Rix (Milwaukee: Marquette University Press, 1999), p. 80.

We need to see this kind of 'borrowing' in the broader context of a Renaissance culture of commonplacing, in which sententious observations, whether proverbs in the conventional sense or not, were extracted and recycled to a degree that makes efforts at author attribution redundant.[13] It would, anyway, be difficult to identify Taverner as a source rather than any other proverb collection, including Erasmus's Latin. But one section of Taverner's *Proverbs* that is rather suggestive is the sequence from *Homo bulla*, 'Man is but a bubble', to *Quod factum est*, 'The thing that is done cannot be undone' (Tav. 109–12). The last of these appears prominently in *Macbeth* (III. 2. 11–12), reverberating through the play in various contexts, including Lady Macbeth's tormented recollections in the sleepwalking scene. The proverb links Lady Macbeth's utterance back to 'If it were done when 'tis done', while the previous injunction in Taverner 'to do the thing speedily' (716) prompts the second half of the sentence in Shakespeare. And these proverbs on 'doing' appear alongside the reflection on the transience of life, 'Man is a bubble'. It is the witches who are the bubbles of the earth (I. 3. 77), rather than Macbeth himself, but Taverner's addition of the English version of *Homo bulla*, 'Today a man, tomorrow none', captures the mood of Macbeth's 'Tomorrow, tomorrow, and tomorrow', with its reflection that 'Life's but a walking shadow' (V. 5. 18, 23), while harking back to his wife's accusations that he is no man (I. 7. 49–51). Furthermore, the 'adage' that Lady Macbeth scornfully references to describe her husband's hesitation over the murder, 'Letting "I dare not" wait upon "I would" | Like the poor cat i'th'adage' (I. 7. 43–44), is the only one to appear twice in Taverner's collection: 'The cat would fish eat, but she will not her feet wet' (967, 1225–26). So it does look rather as though Taverner's book provided Shakespeare with a proverbial matrix for some of the central lines of thought in *Macbeth*.

Taverner's *Proverbs* represent a further stage in the English Protestantization of Erasmus, which in his case began with the *Praise of Matrimony*. They also represent an important strand of vernacular humanism which links the Reformation era in England to the later Elizabethan literary renaissance. Unlike Erasmus's folio volumes, Taverner's *Adages* remained a pocket-sized compilation of useful wisdom, something that could act as a practical guide to dealing with all eventualities. They appeared at the very end of the period of Cromwell's control, when Erasmian texts were being co-opted in support of the government's reformist agenda, and they negotiated the more difficult period of Henry's conservative last years, and the reigns of Edward and Mary, before being reprinted for a final time under Elizabeth on the eve of the 1570s, the decade which saw the opening of the London theatres and the emergence of the new poetry of Edmund

---

[13] Taverner's *Proverbs* was, however, used in Withals's *Dictionarie*; see Richard Taverner, *Proverbs or Adages by Desiderius Erasmus*, introd. by De Witt T. Starnes (Delmar: Scholars' Facsimiles and Reprints, 1977), pp. vii, xiv.

Spenser. In the context of the times, and with the fate of Taverner's patron in mind, we might almost think of them as a survival guide.

Further Reading

CUMMINGS, BRIAN, 'Encyclopedic Erasmus', in *The Copious Text: Encyclopedic Books in Early Modern England*, ed. by Abigail Shinn and Angus Vine, special issue, *Renaissance Studies*, 28.2 (2014), 183–204

ERASMUS, *The Adages of Erasmus*, ed. by William Barker (Toronto: University of Toronto Press, 2001)

PHILLIPS, MARGARET MANN, *The 'Adages' of Erasmus: A Study with Translations* (Cambridge: Cambridge University Press, 1964)

RHODES, NEIL, *Common: The Development of Literary Culture in Sixteenth-Century England* (Oxford: Oxford University Press, 2018)

RUMMEL, ERIKA, 'The Reception of Erasmus' *Adages* in Sixteenth-Century England', *Renaissance and Reformation/Renaissance et Réforme*, 18.2 (1994), 19–30

YOST, JOHN K., 'Taverner's Use of Erasmus and the Protestantization of English Humanism', *Renaissance Quarterly*, 23.3 (1970), 266–76

PROVERBS, OR ADAGES

[A1ʳ] Proverbs or adages with new additions gathered out of the *Chiliades* of Erasmus by Richard Taverner.

[A1ᵛ] The Prologue of the author.

Forasmuch as I think it will be no less pleasant than profitable unto you, good readers, to hear some of the most neat and handsome proverbs which the incomparable learned man, Erasmus [of] Rotterdam, hath in his book of *Chiliades*[1] gathered together out of the most approved authors (although it be a matter of great importance to handle them in their kind,[2] and a province far surmounting the slender capacity of my wit), yet for your sakes and for the love I bear to the furtherance and adornment of my native country, I will not stick after my accustomed manner, which is *rudiori ac crassiori Minerva*,[3] to make here a brief collection of some of them. If ye shall like my study and industry taken in this behalf, I will be glad; if not, yet my honest heart is not blamed.

Fare ye well.

[A2ʳ] 1. *Nemo bene imperat, nisi qui paruerit imperio* [I. i. 3][4]

No man can be a good ruler unless he hath been first ruled. Certes,° nothing is truer than this proverb, both because no prince, no ruler, no master, can well do his office unless he first were a subject and under the correction either of his parents, tutors, governors, or teachers; and also because that a man must first rule his own lusts, and be himself obedient to right reason, ere he can well govern other.

2. *Qui quae vult dicit, quae non vult audiet* [I. i. 27][5]

He that speaketh what he will shall hear what he will not. Let men beware how they rail.

---

[1] *Chiliades*] From the 1508 edition onwards the collection was known as *Adagiorum chiliades* ['thousands of proverbs'].
[2] handle … kind] Treat them in relation to the proverb genre, i.e. by explaining their latent meaning. This is what Taverner calls the 'declaration' at line 1329.
[3] *rudiori … Minerva*] 'more gross and unrefined than Minerva' (terms reversed); cf. *Adagia* I. i. 37: *Crassa Minerva. Pingui Minerva. Crassiore Minerva*.
[4] Tilley S 246.
[5] Tilley S 115. **Marg.** 'Terence [*Andria*, 920].'

25   [A2ᵛ] 3. *Sero sapiunt Phryges* [1. i. 28]⁶

The Trojans are wise too late. When the siege of Troy had endured for the space of ten years, then at last the Trojans, which now had suffered innumerable mischiefs, began to take counsel whether it were best to send home again fair Helen, the occasion of all their misery. But when their country was now with
30   continual wars wasted and destroyed, it was too late to be wise. Even so it is of many at this day. They be wise, but too late.

4. *Piscator ictus sapiet* [1. i. 29]⁷

The fisher stricken will be wise. A certain fisherman, when he had drawn up his net and began now to take in his hands the fishes which he had caught, chanced
35   [A3ʳ] to take up also a scorpion, which forthwith struck him. 'Well', quoth he, 'now that I am stricken I will beware.' The English proverb is in this fashion pronounced: *The burnt child fire dreadeth.*

5. *Factum stultus cognoscit* [1. 1. 30]⁸

A thing done, the fool knoweth. But a wise man forseeth and considereth things
40   afore they come to pass.

6. *Malo accepto, stultus sapit* [1. i. 31]⁹

The fool, when he hath taken hurt, waxeth wise. The wise man seeth the danger and mischief of things aforehand. Certainly, 'had I wist'° is a fool's word. And therefore the Englishman sayeth: *Better is one forethought than two after.*

45   [A3ᵛ] 7. *Felix quem faciunt aliena pericula cautum*

He is happy, whom other men's perils maketh ware.

8. *Bos lassus fortius figit pedem* [1. i. 47]¹⁰

An old beaten ox fasteneth his foot the stronger. Jerome used this proverb writing to St Augustine¹¹ to fear him that he, a young man, should not provoke St Jerome,
50   at that time old. Forasmuch as though sage and ancient persons be not soon stirred to revenge themselves, sith° they be now, as it were, weary for age, yet if

---

⁶   Tilley T 528.
⁷   Tilley F 332.
⁸   Homer, *Iliad* 17. 31–32; 20. 197–98. Cf. Tilley F 332.
⁹   Tilley E 220.
¹⁰ Tilley O 108.
¹¹ writing to St Augustine] Jerome, *Letters* 102. 2. 2.

there be no remedy but they must needs meddle, they will give much tougher and more earnest strokes. The English proverb sayeth thus: *An old dog biteth sore.*

[A4ʳ] 9. *Malum bene conditum ne moveris* [I. i. 62][12]

Move not an evil that is well laid. An incommodity° well couched is not to be stirred.

10. *Stultus stulta loquitur* [I. i. 98][13]

A fool speaketh foolish things. And as our English proverb sayeth: *A fool's bolt is soon shot, whereas the wise man speaketh seldom and wittily.*

11. *Oculis magis habenda fides quam auribus* [I. i. 100][14]

Credit is rather to be given to the eyes than to the ears; that is, the things that be seen are more certain than that be heard.

12. *Multae regum aures, atque oculi* [I. ii. 2][15]

Kings have many ears and many [A4ᵛ] eyes, as who should say, nothing can be spoken, nothing done so secretly against kings and rulers, but by one means or other at length it will come to their knowledge. They have ears that listen an hundred miles from them; they have eyes that espy out more things than men would think. Wherefore it is wisdom for subjects not only to keep their prince's laws and ordinances in the face of the world, but also privily: namely sith Paul would have rulers obeyed even for conscience sake.[16]

13. *Longae regum manus* [I. ii. 3][17]

Kings have long hands. They can bring in men, they can pluck in things, though they be a great way off.

---

[12] Diogenianus, *Proverbs* 6. 54. Cf. Tilley L 317.
[13] Tilley F 459 and 465.
[14] Tilley C 815.
[15] Tilley K 87; S 795.
[16] **Marg.** 'Romans 15.' The reference should be to Romans 13. 5. The citation of Paul is Taverner's addition to Erasmus.
[17] Tilley K 87.

[A5ʳ] 14. *Malo nodo malus quaerendus cuneus* [I. ii. 5]¹⁸

To a crabbed knot must be sought a crabbed wedge. A strong disease requireth a strong medicine. A shrewd° wife, a shrewd husband to tame her. A boisterous horse, a boisterous snaffle.°

15. *Malum consilium consultori pessimum* [I. ii. 14]¹⁹

Evil counsel is worst to the counsellor. Counsel is a certain holy thing, and as it ought gladly to be taken when occasion requireth, so it ought advisedly, purely and without fraud to be given when one needeth it. Otherwise without doubt God's hand will appear to take punishment of him that with falsehood and guile hath foiled° a thing both holy [A5ᵛ] and divine. To this agreeth Ecclesiasticus: 'whosoever', sayeth he, 'giveth a lewd° counsel, it shall turn upon himself and he shall not know from whence it cometh'.²⁰ Here I think it not amiss to make report of a certain pleasant fable written in Greek, not much dissenting from this purpose, which is this.²¹

The lion for weakness of age being sick and keeping himself in his den, all the other beasts according to their duty and allegiance come to look how their king doth. Only Reynard the fox absenteth herself. Wherefore the wolf, now espying a good occasion,° accuseth the fox of treason unto the lion's majesty, as one that despiseth the king and governor of all beasts and [A6ʳ] which of frowardness° and traitorous heart will not with other beasts visit his majesty as their allegiance required. While the wolf was thus accusing the fox, the fox privily° cometh in and heareth the end of the wolf's complaint. Now when the lion looked up and espied Reynard, forthwith he gnasheth with his teeth against her. But she, after she had obtained a space to purge° herself, thus beginneth to make her defence. 'I beseech you, sir king,' quoth she, 'what one beast of all that be here assembled to visit your majesty is so careful and busy to do you good and to help you as I am, which have run about ever since ye sickened to seek counsel for your malady, and now at last I have searched out [A6ᵛ] a sovereign medicine of the physicians.' The lion, hearing this, straight charged her to tell the medicine. 'Truly', quoth the fox, 'if ye will flay the wolf and wrap yourself in his skin, ye shall find (say they) ease of your pain.' The lion, light of credit,²² forthwith ran upon the wolf and slew him, who thus killed, the crafty fox laughed that the slanderous and evil counsel of the wolf lighted upon his own pate.° Let all counsellors bear this example well in mind if

---

¹⁸ Tilley P 289.
¹⁹ Tilley C 691.
²⁰ **Marg.** '[Eccles.] 27. [30.]'
²¹ Perry 258.
²² light of credit] gullible, easily deceived.

they be nothing moved with fables: let them at least be admonished with the history of Aman in the book of Hester, which is in the Bible.[23]

16. *Suum cuique pulchrum* [1. ii. 15][24]

Every man thinketh his own thing fair. Man's mind is so [A7ʳ] infected with the blind love of itself that thou shalt find no man so sober, so ware, so looking about him, but in esteeming his own things doteth.

17. *Patriae fumus, igni alieno luculentior* [1. ii. 16][25]

The smoke of a man's own country is much clearer than the fire in a strange country. The country wherein we be born pleaseth naturally every man best, and he longeth continually to see it, yea, be his own country never so unkind to him. Let his own countrymen banish him, exclude him, thrust him out never so spitefully, yet he cannot so harden his heart but he must needs love it, desire to hear of it, be glad to be at one with it again. Which thing the examples of most [A7ᵛ] renowned persons have well declared.

18. *Frons occipitio prior* [1. ii. 19][26]

The forehead is afore the hinder part of the head. As who should say, the thing a man seeth done afore his face and in his own presence is for most part better done than that is done behind his back.

A certain man, as Aristotle telleth, was asked what thing best feedeth a horse; he answereth, 'the master's eye'.[27] Hitherto pertaineth also the story that Gelly telleth.[28] A certain man well fed had a very lean horse. Now when he was asked what was the cause that his horse was so lean, he answered that this ought not to seem any marvel at all if he were in better liking° than his horse, forasmuch as he himself fed himself, [A8ʳ] but his servant fed his horse. These things tend all to this end, that every man should as much as maybe execute his own business, his calling, his office by himself and not by vicars or deputies, as now we see done, well near of all degrees of men.

There be kings, there be cardinals, there be bishops, prelates, and sundry other officers and magistrates in Christendom, which do all by vicars and deputies, but themselves live in most idleness and in all kinds of pleasure, like popes. Would God these would take example of our most vigilant prince and sovereign, lord

---

[23] Esther 6–7.
[24] Tilley C 812.
[25] Tilley S 572.
[26] Pliny, *Natural History* 18. 31.
[27] Aristotle, *Oeconomica* 1. 6.
[28] Aulus Gellius, *Attic Nights* 4. 20. 11.

king Henry the Eighth, who not only setteth vigilant deputies and ministers under him, but also looketh himself right busily upon his [A8ᵛ] charge committed unto him of God.

19. *Aequalis aequalem delectat* [1. ii. 20][29]

Like delighteth the like. Likeness of manner, equality of age, similitude in all things wonderfully knitteth persons together and gendereth friendship. We see young persons keep company with young persons, aged with the aged; we see learned men resort to learned, unthrifts do gather together with unthrifts, and good fellows with such as be good fellows, and so forth.

20. *Simile gaudet simili* [1. ii. 21][30]

The like delighteth in the like, or as the Englishman sayeth: *Like will to like*. Similitude, as Aristotle sayeth, is mother of love.[31] Wherefore where a full likeness in all points is between [B1ʳ] persons, there no doubt is most vehement and ardent love.

21. *Semper similem ducit Deus ad similem* [1. ii. 22][32]

God always draweth the like to the like.

22. *Semper graculus assidet graculo* [1. ii. 23][33]

Alway[s] the jay sitteth with the jay. These proverbs be of one sense and meaning.

23. *Figulus figulo invidet, faber fabro* [1. ii. 25][34]

The potter envieth the potter, the smith the smith. The Englishman pronounceth this proverb in this sort: *One beggar biddeth° woe that another by the door should go*. Assuredly, where men exercise one science,° there commonly the likeness of the science doth rather gender heart-burning° than it doth love or benevolence.

---

[29] Cicero, *De Senectute* 3. 7.
[30] Tilley L 286.
[31] Marg. '*Similitudo mater amoris*'. The expression does not seem to be from Aristotle, but cf. *Rhetoric* 1. 11; also 'Likeness glues love' (Donne, 'Change', *Elegies* 3. 23).
[32] As above; cf. also B 393.
[33] Tilley L 283.
[34] Tilley P 514.

24. *Cretensis Cretensem* [I. ii. 26][35]

[B1ᵛ] One false merchant deceiveth another. The men of Crete were in old time much reproved for their falsehood and deceit.

25. *Cretiza cum Cretensi* [I. ii. 29][36]

165　Practise craft with the crafty. Of the vanity and dissimulation of the Cretans the apostle Paul also speaketh.[37] This proverb biddeth us otherwhiles° to dissemble with dissemblers, namely where singleness° will take no place. The English proverb sayeth: *He had need to have a long spoon that should eat with the Devil*, meaning that he which must have to do with crafty persons ought himself to know
170　craft.

26. *Principium dimidium totius* [I. ii. 39][38]

The beginning is half the whole. There be many great delayers. Long they be ere they can be persuaded to set upon an honest act, so many perils they cast. 'Tomorrow, [B2ʳ] tomorrow', they say, 'we will begin.' But this tomorrow is ever
175　coming but never present. Wherefore whoso with good courage ventureth upon his matters hath already half done.

27. *Satius initiis mederi, quam fini* [I. ii. 40][39]

Better it is to remedy the beginnings than the ends. Stop a disease, sayeth the poet Ovid, while it is in the coming.[40] Medicine is sought for too late, when by long
180　continuance of time the disease catcheth one's strength.

28. *Audaces fortuna iuvat* [I. ii. 45][41]

Fortune helpeth men of good courage. He that feareth that his matters shall not have good success shall never bring his matters to pass. A coward verily never obtained the love of a fair lady. Also, another English proverb sayeth: *Spare to*
185　*speak and spare to speed.*

---

[35] Tilley C 822; cf. also G 440.
[36] As above.
[37] **Marg.** 'Titus 1. [12.]' Paul is citing the Greek poet Epimenides (sixth century BC).
[38] Tilley B 254.
[39] Tilley E 202.
[40] **Marg.** '*Venienti occurrite morbo* [Ovid, *Remedia amoris* 91–92].'
[41] Erasmus gives this as *Fortes fortuna adiuvat*, CWE 31. 187.

29. *Fratrum inter se ire sunt acerbissime* [I. ii. 50][42]

[B2ᵛ] The discord of brethren between themselves is most bitter. This to be true we have many examples out of histories, of Cain and Abel, of Romulus and Remus, of Jacob and Esau, and of infinite other.

30. *Taurum tollet, qui vitulum sustulerit* [I. ii. 51][43]

He that hath borne a calf shall also bear a bull; he that accustometh himself to little things by little and little shall be able to go away with greater things. One named Milo was wont every day to bear a certain way on his shoulders a calf.[44] At length the calf grew to a great ox: his daily exercise made him still able to bear the ox when the ox was now of an exceeding great quantity. Ye see what masteries use worketh.

[B3ʳ] 31. *Vivorum oportet meminisse* [I. ii. 52][45]

We ought to remember the living. There be many that love to talk of dead men, yea and with dead men as much as in them lyeth. And if they go about to extend their liberality and to do any good deeds, they had liefer° lash° out their wicked Mammon on the dead than on the quick.[46] So little regard they have to the lively images of God,[47] whom God nevertheless so tendereth° that whatsoever we bestow upon them he counteth bestowed even upon himself. Also this proverb hath place against them that immoderately bewail the dead. Whereunto agreeth our English proverb saying: *We ought to live by the quick and not by the dead.*

32. *Mature fias senex, si diu velis esse senex* [I. ii. 59][48]

[B3ᵛ] Become an old man betime° if thou wilt be an old man long. By this we be monished° that while we are strong and lusty we cease from over much labours, and also from such riots, dalliance, and surfeiting as commonly youth desireth. For whoso continueth in them shall fall into age, that is to say, into weakness of nature or ever he beware.[49] Wherefore if he intend to live long and to live many winters an old man, let him forsake the fond° rages of youth betimes. This proverb in English is thus: *Begin betime for to be sage if thou will lead long old age.*

---

[42] Tilley H 211.
[43] Tilley B 711.
[44] Milo] Milo of Croton, a famous Greek strong man; see Quintilian, *Institutio oratoria* 1. 9. 5; cf. also *Adages* II. iii. 10.
[45] Tilley Q 12.
[46] they ... quick] they had rather lavish their money on the dead than on the living.
[47] lively images of God] i.e. human beings (not a reference to idolatry).
[48] Cicero, *De Senectute* 10. 32.
[49] or ever he beware] unless he is careful.

33. *Oportet remum ducere qui didicit* [I. ii. 76]⁵⁰

He ought to hold the oar that hath learned it. That is to say: every man must practise that science° and [B4ʳ] faculty° that hath been afore taught him. Let not the shoemaker meddle further than his shoes. Let the ploughman talk of his plough.

34. *Ex uno omnia specta* [I. ii. 78]⁵¹

By one consider all, that is to say, of the proof of one thing, conjecture the rest. Of a piece of men's proceedings guess the residue.

35. *Ex aspectu nascitur amor* [I. ii. 79]⁵²

Of sight is love gendered.° No man loveth the thing he knoweth not; of companioning and resorting together springeth mutual love. And namely the eyes be lures and baits of love.⁵³ Wherefore if thou will not love the thing that is unlawful for thee to love, abstain from beholding. 'He that beholdeth a woman', sayeth Christ, 'with a lust unto her hath already played an adulterer's part with her in his heart. If thine eye, therefore, [B4ᵛ] be an impediment and let° unto thee, pluck it out. Better it were for thee to enter into heaven without an eye than with both eyes to be cast into hell-fire.'⁵⁴ Now we read that certain philosophers even for this cause (and amongst them Democritus) plucked out their own eyes because they were the occasioners and provokers of all evil affections and lusts.⁵⁵ But albeit Christ meant not that we should so deform our bodies and spoil ourselves of a member of the same, which otherways is very profitable unto us, yet we Christian men be so inhibited by this commandment of Christ that we ought not to fasten our eyes where it is not lawful. For better it were to lack the operation of the eyes and never to behold things delectable° to the eye than by the same to [B5ʳ] be in danger of damnation. The Englishman hath a pretty proverb sounding much to the same purpose, which is this: *That the eye seeth not, the heart rueth not.*

---

⁵⁰ Plutarch, *Moralia* 440A.
⁵¹ Tilley L 342.
⁵² Tilley L 501.
⁵³ eyes ... love] A popular theme in English Renaissance literature; cf. Shakespeare, *Love's Labour's Lost* IV. 3. 324–28.
⁵⁴ **Marg.** 'Matthew 5. [28–29.]'
⁵⁵ **Marg.** 'Democritus.' See Aulus Gellius, *Attic Nights* 10. 17.

240 36. *Candidae musarum ianuae* [1. ii. 85]⁵⁶

The doors of the Muses be without envy. That is to say, learned persons ought freely, gently, and without envy admit others unto them that desire to be taught or informed of them.

37. *Ad consilium ne accesseris ante quam voceris* [1. ii. 90]⁵⁷

245 Come not to counsel afore thou be called.

38. *Iucundissima navigatio iuxta terram, ambulation iuxta mare* [1. ii. 91]⁵⁸

It is most pleasant rowing near the land and walking near the sea. Man is much delighted with variety.

39. *Non est eiusdem et multa et* [B5ᵛ] *oportuna dicere* [1. ii. 99]⁵⁹

250 It is not for one man to speak both many words and apt words. This proverb teacheth us to eschew much talk, forasmuch as for most part he must needs fail in his speech that loveth to have many words. To this agreeth the wise man in his proverbs where he sayeth that unto much speaking is sin annexed.⁶⁰ Also our English proverb is not to be forgotten, which sayeth: *Where many words be, the*
255 *truth goeth by.*

40. *Quot homines, tot sententiae* [1. iii. 7]⁶¹

So many men, so many wits. So many heads, so many judgements.⁶² The apostle Paul,⁶³ not forgetful hereof, advertiseth° us that for the excluding of contention we suffer° every man to abound° in [B6ʳ] his own sense,⁶⁴ whose counsel, if our
260 divines in Christendom would follow, there should not be at this day so great dissention in the Church in matters of small weight. For there be many things which, without danger of the Christian religion, may be unknown well enough.⁶⁵

---

⁵⁶ Cf. Diogenianus, *Proverbs* 3. 23.
⁵⁷ Tilley C 678.
⁵⁸ Plutarch, *Moralia* 621D and 14D.
⁵⁹ Tilley M 1293. **Marg.** 'Quintilian.' Implicit in Quintilian's definition of rhetoric in *Institutio oratoria*, 2. 14–15.
⁶⁰ Prov. 10. 19.
⁶¹ Tilley M 583.
⁶² So many ... judgements] Terence, *Phormio* 454. A topical theme, echoed by others in the Cromwell circle; cf. Thomas Starkey, who associates 'diversitie of opinion' with 'discord', *A Preface to the Kynges Hyghnes* (London, 1536), sigs A2ᵛ–A3ʳ.
⁶³ **Marg.** 'Romans 9.'
⁶⁴ abound ... sense] follow his own opinion.
⁶⁵ many things ... enough] The view that certain issues in religion are matters of indifference is known as adiaphorism.

41. *Emere malo quam rogare* [1. iii. 20][66]

I had lever° buy than beg. Or as the Englishman pronounceth: *He that goeth a-borrowing goeth a-sorrowing*. Hereby is signified that a thing obtained with much suit and prayer is indeed dearly bought. For assuredly, to an honest heart it is death to beg, unless it be of his special friend, of whom he might be as bold as upon himself, insomuch that he had rather buy the thing very dear for his money [B6ᵛ] than to get it by petition at another man's hand.

42. *Ubi amici, ibi opes* [1. iii. 24][67]

Where friends be, there be goods. Whereunto our English proverb alludeth: *A friend in court is worth a penny in purse*. By this is meant that friends be better than money and that unto the sustentation° of man's life, friends be more available without money than money without friends. And for this cause amongst the Scythians, as Lucian declareth, he was counted the richest man which had the surest and best friends.[68] But now, if a man will have respect to the manners of these days, we had need to turn the proverb and say 'where goods be, there be friends'.

[B7ʳ] 43. *Durum est contra stimulum calcitrare* [1. iii. 46][69]

It is hard kicking against the goad. It is evil striving against the stream, that is to say, it is great folly to struggle against such things as thou canst not overcome or to provoke them who, if they be stirred, may do thee displeasures; or to wrestle with God's providence and the incommodity which thou canst not avoid, by thy impatient bearing not only not to eschew it, but also to double the same.

44. *Pecuniae obedient omnia* [1. iii. 87][70]

Unto money be all things obedient. This proverb was never better verified than at this day amongst Christian men, which nevertheless by their profession ought to despise worldly goods.[71]

---

[66] Tilley B 783.
[67] Quintilian, *Institutio oratoria* 5. 11. 41.
[68] **Marg.** 'The manner of the Scythians.' See Lucian, *Toxaris*, the first of Lucian's dialogues to be translated by Erasmus.
[69] Tilley F 433. **Marg.** 'Acts 10.' The reference should be to Acts 9. 5.
[70] Tilley M 1084. **Marg.** 'Eccles. 10. [19.]'
[71] profession ... goods] i.e. profession of faith, religion. This is at the core of Erasmus's 'philosophy of Christ', illustrated by *Amicorum omnia sunt communia*; see n. 339 below.

45. *Veritas simplex oratio* [I. iii. 88][72]

[B7ᵛ] Truth's tale is simple. He that meaneth good faith goeth not about to gloze° his communication with painted words. Plain and homely men call a fig a fig, and a spade a spade. Rhetoric and colouring of speech proveth many times a man's matter to be naught.

46. *Tunica pallio propior est* [I. iii. 89][73]

My coat is nearer me than my robe or gown. The English proverb sayeth thus: *Near is my coat, but nearer is my shirt*. By this is signified that one friend is nearer unto a man than another is.

47. *Omnes sibi melius esse malunt, quam alteri* [I. iii. 91][74]

Every man loveth himself better than he loveth another. Whether this saying may stand with Christ's doctrine, which biddeth us love our neighbour as ourself, let the doctors and professors of divinity discuss. For some there be that put degrees of charity, and will that charity should begin first at a man's own self.

48. *Multa cadunt inter calicem supremaque labra* [I. v. 1][75]

[B8ʳ] Many things fall between the cup and the mouth. The occasion of this proverb was this. There was a certain person called Ancaeus, which was son to Neptune. This Ancaeus, in sowing time of vines, called sore° upon his servants for to apply their work, with which importune calling on,[76] one of his servants being even for weariness of the labour moved against his master: 'Well, master', quoth he, 'as hastily as ye now call upon us, it shall not be your chance ever to taste wine of this vine.' After, when the vine tree [B8ᵛ] did spring up happily, and the grapes were now ripe, the master triumphing and much rejoicing calleth for the servant and commandeth him to press wine into his cup. Now when he had the cup full of wine in his hand, ready to set it to his mouth, he putteth his said servant in mind of his words, upbraiding him of his false prophesying. The servant then bringeth forth this sentence to his master: *Between the cup and the lips may come many casualties*. While the servant was thus speaking, and even as the master was lifting up the cup to his mouth, behold the chance: suddenly cometh running in another servant and telleth how a great wild boar is destroying the vineyard. Which tidings, as soon as Ancaeus heareth, [C1ʳ] forthwith he setteth down his

---

[72] Tilley T 593.
[73] Tilley P 250.
[74] Tilley N57. **Marg.** 'Terence.'
[75] Tilley T 191. **Marg.** 'Terence.' However, the story is not found in Terence.
[76] with ... calling on] Importunate urging.

cup and runneth upon the wild boar, of whom, while he was chasing of him, he was grievously wounded and so died.

Let this example teach men not to trust on the slipperiness of fortune. For it commonly cometh to pass that when men think themselves most sure, they be soonest deceived.

49. *Bis pueri senes* [1. v. 36][77]

Old folk are twice children, or double children. Aristotle in his *Politics* writeth that after two and fifty years the sharpness of wit waxeth blunt and dull, wherefore commonly from that time men and women grow every day more childish and more, so that when they come once to extreme age, as to four score or thereabout, they differ in wit and fashions° [C1ᵛ] very little from children.[78] I say commonly, for all be not so, but such as exercise not their memory, and will not retain their minds occupied in the practice and continual exercise of honest and comely° businesses.

50. *Ne Hercules quidem contra duos* [1. v. 39][79]

Not Hercules against two. That is to say, though a man never so much excelleth other in strength, yet it will be hard for him to match two or more at once. And one man may lawfully give place to a multitude.

51. *Unus vir nullus vir* [1. v. 40][80]

One man no man. One man left alone and forsaken of all the rest can do little good.

52. *Ne sutor ultra crepidam* [1. vi. 16][81]

Let not the shoemaker go beyond his shoe. Pliny rehearseth this history.[82] [C2ʳ] When the most cunning° and excellent painter Apelles had made any goodly and excellent piece of work, he was wont to set it out towards the street's side that men might look upon it and talk their fancies° of it; and he himself would also lie lurking in a corner to hear men's judgements what faults were found in his work, to the intent if there were anything amiss he might amend it. Amongst other there

---

[77] Tilley M 570.
[78] Aristotle, *Politics* 7. 19; cf. also *Rhetoric* 2. 14.
[79] Tilley H 436.
[80] Tilley M 353.
[81] Tilley C 480.
[82] **Marg.** 'Apelles the cunning painter.' See Pliny, *Natural History* 35. 85; cf. also Stefano Guazzo, *Civile Conversation*, trans. by George Pettie (London, 1581), sig. B7ᵛ.

came to the stall where his work stood out to be seen, a shoemaker, which, viewing well the picture, anon espied a fault in the shoes that there lacked a latchet.° Apelles against° the next day amendeth the fault. The next day the shoemaker cometh again, and taking a little pride that he had found a fault in so cunning a man's work beginneth [C2ᵛ] to find another fault in the leg. Apelles, not suffering his sauciness, cried out unto him: 'Let the shoemaker not pass the shoe'. Certes, every man ought to meddle no further than he can skill° of. Every man, sayeth Aristotle, is a mere judge of that himself is learned in.[83] For he sayeth a blind man ought not to dispute of colours. And therefore Quintilian writeth that sciences should be happy if only artificers might judge of them.[84]

53. *Nequicquam sapit qui sibi non sapit* [I. vi. 20]

He is in vain wise that is not wise for himself. This proverb how true it is I will not dispute, but sure I am that men of our time keep this saying so jump° that he is not counted worthy to be called a man which by any means cannot seek his own advantage. Howbeit, I cannot deny but a [C3ʳ] man may very well after an honest sort look to his own profit and gains, where he is in that place as he may help himself. For as our common proverb sayeth: *He is an evil cook that cannot lick his own fingers.*

54. *Dicendo dicere discunt* [I. vi. 30]

By speaking men learn to speak; by writing men learn to write; by singing to sing. Briefly, every science is gotten by learning of the same.

55. *Nunquam ex malo patre bonus filius*

Of an evil father cometh never a good child. For as our English proverb testifieth: *The young cock learn[s] to crow of the old.*

56. *Mali corvi malum ovum* [I. ix. 25][85]

Of an evil raven an evil egg. These two proverbs be of one [C3ᵛ] meaning. Of evil is engendered evil. The child for the most part followeth the father's steps. 'An evil tree', sayeth Christ, 'can bring forth no good fruit.'[86] Our foreparents Adam and Eve were for their transgression deprived of original justice, of the true fear of God, of the true and pure love of God, of the true and perfect knowledge of

---

[83] a mere judge of] a judge only of. Aristotle, *Nicomachean Ethics* 1. 3.
[84] Quintilian] The source appears to be Jerome, *Letters* 66. 9. 2; see *CWE* 32. 288–89.
[85] Tilley B 376.
[86] **Marg.** 'Matt. 5.' The reference should be to Matt. 7. 18.

God etc. Wherefore all we that be sprung of them cannot but be likewise spotted and naturally corrupted with the same vices.

57. *Qualis vir talis oratio* [1. vi. 50][87]

As the man is, so is his talk. The talk of honest men is honesty, the talk of knaves is knavery.

58. *Facile cum valemus, recta consilia aegrotis damus* [1. vi. 68][88]

When we be hale,° we easily give good counsels to the sick. This [C4ʳ] sentence of Terence is not much unlike the wise answer of Thales the sage, who, being demanded what is the most hard thing to do, answered 'to know thyself'. Again, when the same Thales was demanded what is the easiest thing of all, he answered 'to give good counsel to other'.[89]

59. *Quae supra nos, nihil ad nos* [1. vi. 69][90]

The things that be above us belong nothing unto us. This was the saying of Socrates.[91] But we may also turn it the contrary way: the things that be underneath us pertain nothing unto us. For as we ought not curiously to ensearch° what things be done in heaven, so is it no little folly narrowly° to seek what is done under the earth. And as it becometh not Jack Straw to reason of prince's matters, so again it is [C4ᵛ] not seeming for persons of honest havour° to be ever busy in every trifling matter.[92]

60. *Optat ephippia bos piger, optat arare caballus* [1. vi. 71][93]

The slow ox wisheth for the saddle and the gelding to ear° the ground. No man is contented with his lot: the courtier would dwell in the country, the dweller in the country would be a courtier, the bachelor wisheth himself married; again, when he is married he would be unmarried.

---

[87] Tilley M 75.
[88] Tilley M 182. Terence, *Andria* 309–10.
[89] **Marg.** 'The answer of Thales.' See Diogenes Laertius, *Lives of the Philosophers* 1. 36.
[90] Tilley T 206.
[91] Socrates] Xenophon, *Memorabilia* 1. 1. 11–12.
[92] Jack Straw] Popularly regarded as one of the three leaders of the Peasants' Revolt of 1381 and the subject of an anonymous Elizabethan play, *The Life and Death of Jack Straw* (1593).
[93] **Marg.** 'Horace [*Epistles* 1. 14. 43].'

61. *Nosce teipsum* [1. vi. 95][94]

Know thyself. Plato ascribeth this divine sentence unto Apollo.[95] But whose saying soever it was, certes it is both true and godly and worthy of Christian men to be continually borne in mind.

62. *Ne quid nimis* [1. vi. 96][96]

Nothing too much. Or as we [C5ʳ] commonly say in English: *Too much of nothing is good*. There is, sayeth Horace, a measure in things and certain lists° over which and on this side which the right cannot stand.[97] Measure no doubt is an high treasure. Some cannot do but they overdo, either in the redress of the abuses of the church they will run too far and quit and clean take away all honest ceremonies, traditions, and laws, or else in the maintaining of that is honest they will without choice stiffly defend, yea, and keep still in their churches all customs, ceremonies, and traditions, be they never so detestably abused and gone from the first institution.[98] So hard it is to keep the golden mediocrity which the said poet Horace full wittily defendeth.[99]

63. *Sponde, noxa praesto est* [1. vi. 97][100]

[C5ᵛ] Be surety for another and harm is at hand. What loss, what utter undoing, cometh by suretyship, who knoweth not? Albeit, I grant, a man must bear with his friend, and in case of necessity also with the poor and needy.

64. *Non omnes qui habent citharam, sunt citharoedi* [1. vii. 7]

All that have harps be no harpers. Outward signs many times deceive men. All that have the Gospel hanging at their girdles be no gospellers.[101] Nor again, all

---

[94] Tilley K 175.
[95] Plato, *Charmides* 164d.
[96] Tilley M 793.
[97] Horace, *Satires* 1. 1. 106–07; *Epistles* 1. 18. 9.
[98] Some ... institution] Unchanged between 1539 and 1545, despite the fall of Thomas Cromwell. The observation may reflect Henry VIII's idea of himself as the keeper of a middle way in religion; see MacCulloch, *Thomas Cromwell*, p. 449.
[99] **Marg.** '*Auream quisquis mediocritate* [*diligit*] *etc.*' ['Whoever cultivates the golden mean', *Odes*, 2. 10.]
[100] Tilley S 1009.
[101] gospellers] Those who profess to follow the truth of the Gospel. A Reformation-era coinage, which the *OED* ascribes to Thomas More, who uses it pejoratively, but it was also used by evangelicals in a neutral or positive sense, as it is here. Those who wanted to advertise their devotional seriousness might have a Bible or other religious text attached to a cord around the waist; these became known as 'girdle books'.

that dispraise the lewd fashions of the papists be not forthwith heretics. We ought not to judge according to the outward appearance of things.

65. *Simia simia est, etiamsi aurea gestet insignia* [1. vii. 11]¹⁰²

An ape is an ape although she wear badges of gold. This proverb [C6ʳ] advertiseth° us that the ornaments of fortune do not change the nature of man. The occasion of this proverb, as telleth Lucian, came hereof.¹⁰³ A certain king of Egypt kept up a number of apes and caused them to be taught the form and way of dancing. For like as no beast approacheth nearer to the figure of man than the ape, so there is none other beast that either better or more willingly counterfeiteth man's acts, gestures, and fashions than this beast. Being therefore anon taught the feat° of dancing, they began to mask, clad in purple robes, with visors on their faces. Thus of long time this gorgeous sight delighted exceedingly the king and his lords and ladies, till at last a merry fellow bringing privily in his bosom a good sort of nuts [C6ᵛ] did cast them in the floor among the maskers. Here forthwith the apes so soon as they saw the nuts, forgetting their dancing, began to show what they were, and of dancers returned to apes, and tearing asunder their visors and dancing apparel scambled° and went together by the ears for the nuts, not without great laughing of the lookers on. It is to be feared lest at this day there be in Christendom many apes (that is to say counterfeiters, which by a Greek word we commonly call hypocrites) decked in purple badges and cognisances,° that is to wit,° which bear outward signs and badges of great holiness as though they were lambs, but inwardly they be ravenous wolves.

66. *Artem quaevis alit regio*

[C7ʳ] Art or cunning° every country nourisheth; that is to say, cunning men, and such as have any faculty° or science,° whether soever they go shall lack no living.¹⁰⁴ Cunning, they say, is no burden. It neither can be taken from thee by thieves, and into what part of the world soever thou go, it followeth thee. Suetonius writeth that it was showed before unto the Emperor Nero by his astronomers that the time should come when he should be put out of his empire, by reason whereof he gave himself much the more eagerly unto the study of music, insomuch that he became very excellent, and then he was wont to have oft in his mouth the said proverb; and esteemed it the foulest reproach that could be laid unto him to be called an evil harper or player upon instruments.¹⁰⁵ The same [C7ᵛ] thing also (as in another place is mentioned) did happen unto Dionysius, king of the Syracusans,

---

¹⁰² Tilley A 262, 263, 266.
¹⁰³ Lucian, *Piscator* ['The Fisherman'], 36.
¹⁰⁴ whether soever they go] wherever they go.
¹⁰⁵ Suetonius … instruments] See Suetonius, *Twelve Caesars* VI. 40; Dio Cassius, *Roman History* LXIII. 27.

which after he was thrust out of his kingdom, came to Corinth and there did set up a school and taught children letters and music. For this cause among the Greeks is art or cunning called the port or haven of necessity unto men mortal, that is to say, the only refuge in poverty.[106] Wherefore so many as be wise, though they have abundance of worldly goods for the time, yet let them not despise honest arts, neither yet be reckless° in bringing up their children and putting them to learning or some faculty, whereby if fortune fail they may yet get them a living.

68. *Omnium rerum vicissitudo est* [1. vii. 63][107]

There is an alteration of all things. [C8ʳ] This sentence of Terence signifieth that in men's things nothing is perpetual, nothing stable, but all pass and repass even like to the ebbing and flowing of the ocean sea. Whereunto the English proverb alludeth that sayeth: *After a low ebb cometh a flood.* Which hath the same sense that the Latin hath.

69. *Iucunda vicissitudo rerum* [1. vii. 64][108]

Change of things is pleasant. Where shift of things is not, man's mind anon shall wax weary and dull. For assuredly, such is the nature of things, so great loathsomeness there is of man's appetite that nothing can be so sweet but shall be abhorred if it be any long while used. Nothing is so gallant,° so excellent, that can long content the mind. And therefore the poet Juvenal writeth very handsomely: 'A seldom use of pleasures maketh [C8ᵛ] the same the more pleasant'.[109] Shift and variety hath so great force in everything that by reason of the newness otherwhiles° things that be not all of the best do please men very well.

70. *Nosce tempus* [1. vii. 70][110]

Know time. Opportunity is of such force that of honest it maketh unhonest, of damage advantage, of pleasure grievance, of a good turn a shrewd° turn; and contrariwise of unhonest honest, of advantage damage, and briefly to conclude, it clean changeth the nature of things. This opportunity or occasion (for so also ye may call it) in adventuring and finishing a business doubtless beareth the chief stroke,[111] so that not without good skill° the paynims° of old time counted it a divine thing.

And in this wise they painted her. They made her a goddess standing [D1ʳ] with

---

[106] Marg. 'Science the port of need.'
[107] Tilley C 233. **Marg.** 'Terence [*Eunuchus* 276].'
[108] Tilley C 229.
[109] Juvenal, *Satires* 11. 208.
[110] This is a version of the Greek concept of *kairos* and the Shakespearean 'Ripeness is all' (*King Lear* v. 2. 11).
[111] beareth the chief stroke] has the most influence in achieving a result.

feathered feet upon a wheel and turning about the circle thereof most swiftly, being on the former° part of her head all hairy and on the hinder part bald, so that by the fore part she may easily be caught, but by the hinder part not so.[112]

71. *Male parta male dilabuntur* [I. vii. 82][113]

Evil gotten good[s] go evil away. It is commonly seen by the high providence of God that goods unlawfully gotten vanish away: no man knoweth how.

72. *Occultae musices nullus respectus* [I. vii. 84]

Of music hid is no regard. Have a man never so excellent learning or knowledge in any feat, yet if he be not known, he is had in no price.[114] A like thing is read in Ecclesiasticus: 'Of wisdom hid and of treasure cast in a corner cometh [D1ᵛ] no profit.'[115]

73. *Una hirundo non facit ver* [I. vii. 94][116]

It is not one swallow that bringeth in summer. It is not one good quality that maketh a man good. Swallows be a token of the beginning of summer, yet one swallow is no sure token. Also ye may use this proverb when ye may signify that one day or little time is not enough for the achieving of a great matter. Which is all one with this in English: *Rome was not built in one day*.

74. *Aequalem tibi uxorem quaere*

Seek thee an equal wife, that is to wit, one that is not above thine estate.

75. *Altera manu fert lapidem, panem ostentat altera* [I. viii. 29][117]

He beareth a stone in one hand and bread in the other. Such persons be in England not a few.

76. *Bis dat, qui cito dat* [I. viii. 91][118]

He giveth twice that giveth quickly. He that doth a man a good turn speedily and without delay [D2ʳ] doth him a double benefit.

---

[112] As depicted by the figure of *Occasio* in Alciati and other Renaissance emblem books; cf. Spenser, *Faerie Queene* II. 4. 4–5.
[113] Tilley G 90.
[114] he ... price] he is not valued for it.
[115] **Marg.** 'Cap. 26.' The reference should be to Eccles. 20. 32.
[116] Tilley S 1025.
[117] **Marg.** 'Plaut[us, *Aulularia* 194–95].'
[118] Tilley G 125.

77. *Honos alit artes* [I. viii. 92][119]

Honour maintaineth cunning. Be a man never so excellent in any science or feat, if he be nothing promoted or set by,° anon he is discouraged, yea and all they that be students of the same be in like wise discouraged. On the contrary part, let cunning persons be had in honest reputation and be worthily preferred, anon ye shall see both them and other by their example strive who may excel other[s].

78. *Verecundia inutilis viro egenti* [II. vii. 2][120]

Shamefastness° is unprofitable to a needy person. This proverb admonisheth us to cast away bashfulness where need constraineth. For shamefastness is very unprofitable unto many things, but in especial when the matter requireth [D2ᵛ] to attempt all ways possible. *Spare to speak and spare to speed.*

79. *Munerum animus optimus* [II. vii. 5][121]

The mind of gifts is best, that is to say, in the gifts or presents of friends the price or value of the thing that is sent is not to be considered, but the mind rather of the sender, as the renowned king Xerxes received thankfully of an uplandish° man a handful of water.[122] And Christ also preferred the widow's two farthings afore all the rich men's offerings.[123]

80. *Multis ictibus deiicitur quercus* [I. viii. 94][124]

With many strokes is an oak overthrown. Nothing is so strong but by little and little may be brought down. Wherefore young men ought not to be discouraged by the greatness of an enterprise, so it be honest, for by continuance, seem it never so hard, it may be reclaimed [D3ʳ] and overcome.

81. *Dives aut iniquus est, aut iniqui haeres* [I. ix. 47][125]

A rich man is either wicked or a wicked man's executor or heir. This proverb St Jerome himself useth.[126] How true it is, not only experience teacheth, but our leader and captain Christ also in his doctrine declareth unto us, which because he would fray° us from the wicked Mammon, sayeth: 'a camel shall sooner pass

---

[119] Tilley H 584.
[120] Tilley B 98.
[121] Tilley G 97.
[122] Sir Thomas Elyot uses this example in his dedication of *The Governor* to Henry VIII.
[123] **Marg.** 'Luke 21. [3.]'
[124] Tilley S 941.
[125] Tilley M 364.
[126] Jerome, *Letters* 120. 1. 7; *Homilies* 16.

through a needle's eye than a rich man enter into heaven'.[127] Meaning that it is exceeding hard for such as flow in worldly goods to have a mind untangled with the same, and to bear themselves upright towards God and man. Yet I will not gainsay but a man may be rich and not put his confidence in his riches, as David, Job, Abraham, and many other patriarchs [D3ᵛ] were.

82. *Satius est recurrere quam currere male* [1. ix. 32][128]

Better it is to run back again than to run forth amiss. Many be either so shamefast, or else so stiff in their own opinion, that they had lever° run forth still in error and out of the way than to apply themselves to better and more wholesome counsels.

83. *Merx ultronea putet* [1. ix. 53][129]

Proffered ware stinketh. Service that is willingly offered is for most part to be suspected.

84. *Annosa vulpes haud capitur laqeuo* [1. x. 17][130]

An old fox is not taken in a snare. Long experience and practice of wily and subtle fellows maketh that, though indeed they be great jugglers,° dissemblers, and privy workers of falsehood, yet they [D4ʳ] cannot easily be taken in a trap.

85. *Summum ius, summa iniuria* [1. x. 25][131]

Extreme law is extreme wrong. This is to say, then most of all men swerve from right and equity when they most superstitiously stick to the letters of laws, not regarding the intent of the makers. For this is called *summum ius*, that is to say, the extremity or rigour of the law, when all the strife and contention is upon the words of the law without any respect to the meaning and purpose of the law-makers. This fondness of some superstitious lawyers doth Mark Tully copiously and pleasantly allude in his oration for Murena.[132]

---

[127] **Marg.** 'Matt. 19. [23–24.]'
[128] From Lucian, *Asinus* 18.
[129] Tilley S 252.
[130] Tilley F 647.
[131] Cf. Tilley R 122, but 'Much law but little justice' may not mean the same thing. **Marg.** 'Terence [*Heautontimoroumenos* 795–96].'
[132] Mark Tully] i.e. Marcus Tullius Cicero. **Marg.** 'Cicero [*Pro L. Murena* 11. 25f.].'

86. *Vir fugiens et denuo pugnabit* [1. x. 40]¹³³

A man that fleeth will also fight again. By this we be taught that we should not be forthwith discouraged [D4ᵛ] for a little misfortune. Neither yet cast them clean up that have run aside. For as the English proverb sayeth: *He runneth far that never cometh again.*

87. *Bonae leges ex malis moribus procreantur* [1. x. 61]¹³⁴

Good laws be gendered of evil manners. Laws, as testifieth the apostle Paul, be not made for the righteous persons, but for whoremongers, adulterers, thieves, traitors, man-slayers, and such other.¹³⁵ If all were good we should need no laws.

88. *Corrumpunt mores bonos colloquia prava* [1. x. 74]¹³⁶

Naughty communications spill° good manners. This proverb declareth that commonly we prove such as they be with whom we be conversant.

89. *Magistratus virum indicat* [1. x. 76]¹³⁷

[D5ʳ] Authority declareth a man. The meaning of this proverb is this: that in a private life, where no rule is borne, a man's disposition and manners be not espied. But let him once be put in office and authority, so that in manner he may do what him lusteth, anon he showeth himself what he is. Epaminondas properly turned the proverb the contrary way.¹³⁸ For when the Thebans even of spite had put him to a very vile office in the city, he despised it not, but with such diligence executed the room° that where before it was counted an office scarce honest, now it was had in high reputation. And to such as marvelled why he would take so vile and disworshipful° an office upon him, he answered in this wise: 'Not only a room or office declareth the man, but a man declareth [D5ᵛ] the office'.

---

¹³³ Tilley D 79.
¹³⁴ Tilley M 625.
¹³⁵ **Marg.** '1 Tim. [9–10.]'
¹³⁶ Tilley C 558. **Marg.** Menander [*Sententiae* 808]. Quoted by St Paul in 1 Corinth. 15. 33. Erasmus noted that this was a favourite observation of his English friend John Colet.
¹³⁷ Tilley A 402. Perhaps most strikingly illustrated in English by Shakespeare's *Measure for Measure* (and Whetstone's *Promos and Cassandra*, which is one of the play's sources).
¹³⁸ **Marg.** 'Epaminondas.' Greek general of the fourth century BC who liberated Thebes from Spartan rule. See Plutarch, *Moralia* 811b.

90. *Conscientia mille testes* [I. x. 91]¹³⁹

The conscience is a thousand witnesses. Nothing so much accuseth a man as his own conscience.

91. *Festina lente* [II. i. 1]¹⁴⁰

Make slow haste, or haste thee slowly. This is as much to say as 'temper thy haste with sloth'. To this agreeth our English proverb, which is: *An hasty man never getteth good.* Also, *soft fire maketh sweet malt.* If ye list to know more of this proverb most worthy continually to be borne in mind, read the *Chiliades* of Erasmus, who handleth this matter at large.¹⁴¹

92. *Difficilia quae pulchra* [II. 1. 12]¹⁴²

Hard or difficult be those things that be goodly or honest.¹⁴³ This sentence of the wise man Solon declareth unto us that the way [D6ʳ] of honesty, of virtue, of renown is uneasy, painful, jeopardous,° hard; which thing also teacheth us our guide and saviour Christ, saying that narrow is the way which leadeth to life.¹⁴⁴ Wherefore let not the difficulty or hardness of the thing withdraw us from honest enterprises.

93. *Nemini fidas, nisi cum quo prius modium salis absumpseris* [II. 1. 14]¹⁴⁵

Trust no man unless thou hast first eaten a bushel of salt with him. Without fail it is hard at this day to meet with one whom thou mayest trust in all things.

94. *Multas amicitias silentium dirimit* [II. i. 26]¹⁴⁶

Silence breaketh many friendships. This adage monisheth° us that with oft accompanying and frequent speakings unto, friendships be both gotten and maintained, and again, with absence and leaving [D6ᵛ] off they be commonly broken. Whereunto also agreeth our English proverb, which sayeth: *Out of sight, out of mind.*

---

¹³⁹ Tilley C 601. From Quintilian, *Institutio oratoria* 5. 11. 41.
¹⁴⁰ Tilley H 192.
¹⁴¹ *Chiliades* of Erasmus] This proverb is the subject of one of the longest essays in the *Adagia*.
¹⁴² Tilley T 178, 181.
¹⁴³ **Marg.** 'Solon.' See Diogenes Laertius, *Lives of the Philosophers* 1. 76.
¹⁴⁴ **Marg.** 'Matt. 7. [14.]'
¹⁴⁵ Tilley F 685.
¹⁴⁶ Tilley S 438.

95. *Quod in animo sobrii est, id est in lingua ebrii* [II. i. 55][147]

The thing that lieth in a sober man's heart is in the tongue of the drunkard. Drunken folk can keep no counsel. Wherefore it is wisdom both to keep thyself from that vice, lest thou utterest in thy drunkenness the thing that afterward shall repent thee, and also not to keep company with such, nor to disclose thy heart to them that be subject to this foul vice, lest they happen to turn thee to displeasure.

96. *Occasione dumtaxat opus improbitati* [II. i. 68][148]

Lewdness lacketh but occasion. Wicked and ungodly persons may [D7ʳ] well for a time dissemble, but when any occasion is given them, forthwith they appear in their likeness and show themselves what they be.

97. *Ama tanquam osurus, oderis tanquam amaturus* [II. i. 72][149]

Love as in time to come thou shouldst hate, and hate as thou shouldst in time to come love. There is no man, be he never so much thine enemy, but hereafter may chance to be thy friend. It is therefore the property of a prudent and wise man so to temper his affection as well in love as in hatred, as he sustain no incommodity by the same.[150] Now, though Christianity requireth of us a perfect love of our neighbour and forbiddeth all suspicion, yet we are not by the same commanded to communicate our secret counsels and the affections of our heart to all men alike. And [D7ᵛ] again, though we ought to hate no person, no, not our most bitter enemies, yet the frailty of man's nature is so great, and the occasions be so many on both parties to be given, that a man ought in this case to distrust himself. And as he ought in things not proceeding according to his desire look and hope for better, so it is wisdom in prosperity when all is as thou wouldst have it, to fear and suspect the worst.

98. *Ignis, mare, mulier, tria mala* [II. ii. 48][151]

Fire, sea, woman — three evils. What thing is more dangerous than fire? What more perilous than the sea? And what more cumbrous° than a shrewd wife?

99. *Exercitatio potest omnia* [II. ii. 53][152]

Exercise° can bring to pass all things. Nothing, sayeth Seneca, is so hard but man's mind can [D8ʳ] overcome it, and continual practising bring it into an

---

[147] Tilley H 333.
[148] Tilley O 70.
[149] Tilley T 309.
[150] temper his affection] moderate his feelings.
[151] Menander, *Sententiae* 323.
[152] Tilley U 24.

acquaintance.°¹⁵³ There be no affections so wild, so unruly, but discipline and awe may tame them. What thing soever the mind commandeth, she obtaineth. Some have accustomed themselves never to laugh. Some have forbidden themselves wine, some bodily lust etc. From this disagreeth not the common proverb which we have in English: *Use maketh masteries.*

100. *Fallacia alia aliam trudit* [II. ii. 63]¹⁵⁴

One deceit driveth out another. As we see one nail driven out with another nail, so doth many times one craft and guile expel another.

101. *Sera in fundo parsimonia* [II. ii. 64]¹⁵⁵

It is too late sparing° at the bottom. This sentence of Seneca is worthy to be written upon the doors [D8ᵛ] of all storehouses, all counting houses, upon all caskets, all vessels of wine, or suchlike things.¹⁵⁶ It monisheth us to spare betimes and not to follow the common sort of prodigal younkers,° which, when their lands and goods be once fallen into their hands, think there is no bottom of their father's bags and coffers, nor no bounds of their lands.

102. *Amicus magis necessarius, quam ignis et aqua* [II. 1. 75]¹⁵⁷

A friend is more necessary than either fire or water. Assuredly, how necessary, trusty, and faithful friends be is then at last known when a man hath need of them. There is no person, be he never so rich, never so mighty, never so much in his prince's favour — yea, though he be himself a prince, a king, a kaiser° — but needeth the aid of friends. [E1ʳ] For as without fire and water man's life cannot consist, so neither can it stand without the use, familiarity, and service of familiars,° whom the Latins even for this self° cause do call *necessaries*, and amity or friendship they call *necessitudinem*. Wherefore the proverb meaneth that two of the greatest commodities that can be are gathered of friendship, that is to wit, pleasure and profit. For there is nothing neither more delectable or cheerful than is fire, neither more profitable than is water. Yea, also our English proverb doth not much swerve from the same which sayeth: *A friend in court is worth a penny in purse.*

---

¹⁵³ **Marg.** 'Seneca [*On Anger*, Bk II].'
¹⁵⁴ Tilley D 174; Terence, *Andria* 778–79.
¹⁵⁵ Tilley B 551.
¹⁵⁶ **Marg.** 'Seneca [*Letters* 1. 5]'.
¹⁵⁷ Plutarch, *Moralia* 51B; cf. Cicero, *De Amicitia* 6. 22.

103. *Quam quisquis norit artem, in hac se exerceat* [II. ii. 82]¹⁵⁸

Let every man exercise himself [E1ᵛ] in the faculty that he knoweth. Let the cobbler meddle° with clouting° his neighbour's shoes, and not be a captain in field or meddle with matters concerning a commonwealth. Let them judge of controversies in the Christian religion that be learned in the same, and not every Jack ploughman.¹⁵⁹

104. *Iniquum petendum, ut aequum feras* [II. iii. 26]¹⁶⁰

Ask that is unreasonable that thou mayest bear away that is reasonable. If thou wilt beg an oak of thy friend, ask twenty or an hundred oaks. This craft our merchant men, and other that sell whatsoever ware it be, know well enough. For if thou cheapest° anything of them, forthwith they will not be ashamed to ask double or treble the price of it. If they do it, sayeth Erasmus, because [E2ʳ] the cheaper should be the more willing to give the reasonable and due price, it may perchance be suffered, but if they do the thing of a mind to circumvent and deceive the ignorant and simple persons, and to make them believe the thing is of much more value than indeed it is, surely the craft is devilish, intolerable, and far unmeet° for Christian persons.¹⁶¹

105. *Quot servos habemus, totidem habemus hostes* [II. iii. 31]¹⁶²

Look how many bondmen we have and so many enemies we have. Every man naturally desireth to be at liberty, and therefore he cannot but hate in his heart those that keep him in bondage. And this is the cause why also tyrants that will of their subjects make bondmen be so abhorred, so detested and cursed of them, that at the last they conspire all together to expulse them, [E2ᵛ] as infinite examples in chronicles do testify.

106. *Optimum est aliena insania frui* [II. iii. 39]¹⁶³

It is best to use another man's madness. We use, enjoy, or take the commodity of other men's madness, when the thing that other men do rashly or foolishly we apply to our profit, pleasure, and commodity.

---

¹⁵⁸ Cf. 52. *Ne sutor ultra crepidam*.
¹⁵⁹ Jack ploughman] Erasmus had called in the *Paraclesis* (*Exh.*, 133–35) for a vernacular Bible that would be accessible to the ploughman, a figure from Langland onwards associated with social and religious reform.
¹⁶⁰ Tilley M 272.
¹⁶¹ Erasmus cites Quintilian, *Institutio oratoria* 4. 5. 16, but the Christian interpretation is Taverner's addition.
¹⁶² Tilley S 242.
¹⁶³ Tilley M 462.

107. *Ingens telum necessitas* [II. iii. 40][164]

Necessity is a sore weapon. This proverb is diverse ways to be verified.

108. *Iucundi, acti labores* [II. iii. 43][165]

Labours once done be sweet. Assuredly, this is naturally engraven in the mind of every mortal person, that after painful labours and perils the remembrance of them is to him right pleasant.

109. *Homo bulla* [II. iii. 48][166]

Man is but a bubble or bladder [E3ʳ] of the water. As who should say, nothing is more frail, more fugitive, more slight than the life of man. If ye require the English proverb, it is this: *Today a man, tomorrow none.*

110. *Furem fur cognoscit, et lupum lupus* [II. iii. 63][167]

The thief knoweth the thief, and the wolf the wolf. One false harlot soonest knowest another.

111. *Antequam incipias consulto, ubi consulueris, mature facto opus est* [II. iii. 70][168]

Afore thou begin it is necessary for thee to take counsel, and when thou hast taken counsel, to do the thing speedily.

112. *Quod factum est, infectum fieri non potest* [II. iii. 72][169]

The thing that is done cannot be undone. For only this one thing, sayeth a certain poet, is denied unto God himself,[170] to make [E3ᵛ] that things should be undone which once were done. How great folly then is it for a mortal creature to call again (as they say) yesterday.[171]

---

[164] Tilley N 58.
[165] Tilley L 7.
[166] Tilley M 246.
[167] Tilley T 115.
[168] Sallust, *Catilinae conjuratio* 1. 6.
[169] Tilley T 200. A proverb with particular resonance in Shakespeare, *Macbeth*; see III. 2. 14, V. 1. 57–58, and cf. I. 7. 1–2.
[170] certain poet ... God himself] Erasmus refers to the tragedian Agathon; cf. Aristotle, *Nicomachean Ethics* 6. 2.
[171] Cf. 'O call back yesterday, bid time return', Shakespeare, *Richard II* V. 1. 65.

113. *Iustitia in se virtutem complectitur omnem* [II. iii. 73][172]

Justice compriseth in it all virtue. He that is a perfect righteous or just man without question lacketh no virtue.

114. *Mendacem memorem esse oportet* [II. iii. 74]

A liar ought not to be forgetful. It is very hard for him that lieth always to agree in one tale unless he hath a right good memory, forasmuch as the remembrance of things feigned is far more hard than the memory of true things. By reason whereof for the most part the devisers and forgers of lies are by this means taken: [E4ʳ] while forgetting what they spake afore, they speak things contrary and repugnant° to their former tale.

115. *Non omnia possumus omnes* [II. iii. 94][173]

All men cannot do all things. This is the saying of the poet Virgil.[174]

116. *Multae manus onus levius reddunt* [II. iii. 95][175]

Many hands make a light burden.

117. *Sine Cerere et Baccho friget Venus* [II. iii. 97][176]

Without meat and drink the lust of the body is cold. The best way to tame carnal lust is to keep abstinence of meats and drinks. Ceres among the paynims° was taken for the goddess of corn, Bacchus for the god of wine, and Venus for the goddess [E4ᵛ] of love. Our English proverb confirmeth the same, which sayeth: *A lickerous° mouth, a lickerous tail.*

118. *Aegroto dum anima est, spes est* [II. iv. 12][177]

The sick person while he hath life hath hope. So sweet a thing is life that he that is brought never so low yet hopeth to live.

---

[172] Tilley J 105.
[173] Tilley M 315.
[174] Virgil, *Eclogues* 8. 63.
[175] Tilley H 119.
[176] Tilley C 211. **Marg.** 'Terence [*Eunuchus* 732].'
[177] Tilley L 269.

119. *Hostimentum est opera pro pecunia* [II. iv. 14][178]

Service is a recompense for money. He that for my service or travail giveth me money is acquitted.° I owe him nothing. His money is no better than my service. And as we say in our English proverb: *Set the hare's head against the goose giblet.*

120. *Nec omnia, nec passim, nec ab omnibus* [II. iv. 16][179]

Neither all things, nor in all places, nor of all men. This proverb [E5^r] teacheth us that in taking of rewards we show ourselves not only shamefast,° but also ware° and circumspect. For there be some things which is not seeming for a man to take. There is also a place and time that it were much better for one to refuse the gift that is offered than to take it. And again there be some of whom it is no honesty to receive any gift.

121. *Tempus omnia revelat* [II. iv. 17][180]

Time discloseth all things. Nothing is covered but shall be revealed; nothing is hid that shall not be known, sayeth Christ.[181]

122. *Quo semel est imbuta recens, servabit odorem, testa diu* [II. iv. 20][182]

A vessel will keep long the savour wherewith it is first seasoned. For this cause Quintilian[183] counseleth us forthwith even from our youth to learn the best things, sith [E5^v] nothing sticketh more fastly than that that is received and taken of pure youth not yet infected with perverse and crooked manners or opinions. For verily, full true is our English proverb: *That is bred by the bone will never away.*

123. *Nemo mortalium omnibus horis sapit* [II. iv. 29][184]

No man in the world is wise at all hours. It is only belonging to God, and properly due unto him, never to commit folly. There is, I say, no man but otherwhiles doteth, but is deceived, but playeth the fool, though he seem never so wise. When I say 'man' I except not the woman.

---

[178] Tilley T 616. **Marg.** 'Plautus [*Asinaria* 172].'
[179] Tilley 167 'All things fit not all persons' is the closest English equivalent.
[180] Tilley T 333.
[181] Matt. 10. 26.
[182] Tilley L 333. Horace, *Epistles* 1. 2. 69–70.
[183] Quintilian, *Instiutio oratoria* 1. 8. 4.
[184] Tilley M 335.

124. *Sui cuique mores fingunt fortunam* [II. iv. 30][185]

A man's own manners do shape him his fortune. Men commonly, when any adversity chance, accuse [E6ʳ] fortune, or when they see other men to prosper well in their matters, they say it is their fortune. So they lay all together upon fortune, thinking there is such a thing called fortune that ruleth all. But surely they are highly deceived. It is their own manners, their own qualities, fetches,°[186] conditions, and proceedings that shape them this fortune; that is to say, that cause them either to be set forward or backward, either to prosper or not to prosper.

125. *Dies adimit aegritudinem* [II. v. 5][187]

Time taketh away grievance. There is no displeasure so great, no hatred so impotent, no sorrow so immoderate, but time assuageth it.

126. *Ne puero gladium* [II. v. 18][188]

Commit not a sword to a [E6ᵛ] child. Whosoever putteth a child or a foolish and ignorant person (which indeed differeth nothing from a child) in authority and office commiteth a sword to a child. Albeit I study in these proverbs to be short, yet it becometh not me, an Englishman and the king's servant, to pass over with silence the thing that Erasmus, being a stranger unto us, vouchsafed here to record of the most prudent and excellent prince Henry VII, father to our most dread sovereign lord that now is.[189] This excellent king, sayeth Erasmus, being a prince of a very sharp judgement, and also one that had a wonderful grace in giving of witty and quick answers, when on a time he had heard a certain doctor of divinity preach, which was one of the sect of those that were called mendicant [E7ʳ] friars,[190] and the friar had spent his whole sermon in raging out with open mouth like a mad man against the life of princes (for there be some that by this way seek to get them a name), and was asked how he liked the friar's preaching: 'Truly', quoth the king, 'methought that a naked sword was committed to the hands of a madman.'[191]

---

[185] Tilley M 630.
[186] fetches] far-reaching efforts: a neologism in this sense, but cf. also *Folly*, line 2188.
[187] Tilley T 322.
[188] Tilley S 1050.
[189] Marg. 'The saying of the most excellent prince king Henry the seventh.'
[190] mendicant friars] Monastic orders, often itinerant, committed to leading a life of poverty and evangelising the Gospel.
[191] This excellent king ... madman] Erasmus added this anecdote to the *Adagia* in 1515 (*CWE* 33. 425).

127. *Vulpes non iterum capitur laqueo* [II. v. 22]¹⁹²

The fox is not eftsoons° taken in a snare. He that wise is will not the second time stumble at the same stone.

128. *Mendici pero non impletur* [II. v. 24]¹⁹³

A beggar's scrip° is never filled. They that have a beggar's heart, the more thou givest them, the more will they crave.

129. *Simiarum pulcherrima deformis* [E7ᵛ] *est.* [II. v. 54]¹⁹⁴

The fairest of apes is foul. That that of the own kind is unhonest cannot be made honest.¹⁹⁵ To be a bawd, to be a harlot, is unhonest of the self° nature; wherefore in whatsoever person it be, or after what sort, it cannot be made honest. Semblably° it is to be judged of all other things.

130. *Exiguum malum ingens bonum* [II. v. 65]¹⁹⁶

A little evil, a great good. Of a little incommodity and labour otherwhiles is gathered most great and high commodity. To this agreeth the excellent sentence of Musonius that Aulus Gellius remembreth in his 6th book, which is this: if thou do any honest thing with labour, the labour goeth away, the honesty remaineth.¹⁹⁷ But if thou do any dishonest thing with pleasure, the pleasure goeth away, [E8ʳ] the dishonesty remaineth.

131. *Mores amici noveris, non oderis* [II. v. 96]¹⁹⁸

Know the fashions° of thy friend, but hate them not. In the manners of friends some vices ought to be dissimuled° and winked at.

132. *Ignavis semper feriae sunt* [II. vi. 12]¹⁹⁹

With sluggers or unhardy persons it is always holiday.²⁰⁰ They that flee labour wish for holidays wherein they may loiter and give themselves to good cheer and

---

¹⁹² Probably from Diogenianus, *Proverbs* 2. 15.
¹⁹³ Tilley B 242.
¹⁹⁴ Plato, *Hippias major* 289b, citing Heraclitus.
¹⁹⁵ That … unhonest] Those who are of a dishonest class of person.
¹⁹⁶ Diogenianus, *Proverbs* 6. 62.
¹⁹⁷ **Marg.** Aulus Gellius, [*Attic Nights*] 16. [1.]'
¹⁹⁸ Tilley F 710.
¹⁹⁹ Tilley D 67.
²⁰⁰ holiday] holy daye 1539, 1545. This is given as both one and two words in the essay on the proverb. I have generally standardised it as modern 'holiday', since this is more appropriate to

pleasures. For amongst the old paynims,° as full eloquently declareth Erasmus, certain holidays were therefore given to the uplandish° folk and craftsmen that in the same they might with honest disport° and play refresh them of their weariness and travail.²⁰¹ And to the intent the pastime should be the more moderate, they mingled therewith religion, that is to [E8ᵛ] wit,° service of the gods. 'But at this day', sayeth Erasmus, 'the common sort of Christians do foully abuse holidays, which in times past were instituted and ordained for a godly use, spending them upon banquetings, upon revellings, stews,° dice, cards, frays,° bickerings, and upon all naughtiness; neither is there at any time more lewdness and mischief done than on holidays, when men ought most of all to abstain from lewdness. Neither do we ever follow more the paynims than when chiefly we should play the Christians. And whereas it is evident and plain that the thing which was invented for the maintenance of religion or devotion is now grown to the utter destruction and subversion of religion, yet', sayeth this excellent clerk,° 'I cannot [F1ʳ] know for what consideration and purpose the bishops of Rome do daily multiply the holidays, and do continually increase them into an infinite number, whereas it had been much more convenient in this behalf to follow wise physicians, which according to the quality of the diseases do change their medicines and remedies, having this only as a mark afore their eyes, that they prescribe such things unto their patients as be profitable to the restoring and preservation of health. Wherefore, sith now it is apparent that the thing once well institute[d], having regard to those times, is now by the change of men's manners become a decay of devotion, I pray you, what matter were it to change the constitution,° moved of the same consideration that the [F1ᵛ] elders° did first constitute it. That I say of holidays, the same is to be judged of many other things. Not', sayeth he, 'that I condemn the Christian men's holidays, but that I would not have them increase into such innumerable a number, and that I would wish rather that those few holidays which the authority of the ancient fathers have ordained might be converted to that use whereunto they were first invented. For with true Christian folk every day, to say the truth, is the Sabbath day and is feastful. But again, to evil disposed persons and unthrifts the very feastful and holy days be less feastful than be the working days.'²⁰² Hitherto have I translated the words of that renowned clerk Erasmus. But now in England, thanked be God, through the [F2ʳ] high benefit of our incomparable prince Henry VIII, divers superfluous holy days be already abrogate.° Neither do we tarry° the bishop of Rome's redress in matters of religion, which, as it seemeth, forceth no more of

---

the Latin. However, the sense of 'holy day' is also intended throughout and where that sense is paramount I have used that form.
²⁰¹ **Marg.** 'The institution of holidays.'
²⁰² Erasmus added the attack on the proliferation and abuse of holidays in 1515.

Christ's church (over which nevertheless he pretendeth to have the charge) than the hireling passeth upon the flock of sheep, as Christ himself declareth.

133. *Vino vendibili suspensa hedera nihil opus* [II. vi. 20][203]

Wine that is saleable and good needeth no bush or garland of ivy to be hanged before.[204] Like as men will seek out good wine, though there be no sign at all to direct and appoint° them where it is to be sold, so all good things need no commendation of any outward badge or token. Good merchandise, and also pure and [F2ᵛ] substantial things of what kind so ever they be, do praise themselves. The English proverb is thus: *Good wine needeth no sign*.

134. *Timidi nunquam statuerunt tropheum* [II. vi. 25][205]

Cowards never yet won a field, or never had the victory. In old time they that had gotten the victory in battle were wont to erect and set up some great stone, pillar, or other thing for a sign of victory, which mark they called *Trophaeum*. Now such as be cowards, and which cast° many perils and doubts, shall never come to this glory, forasmuch as such exceeding renown and glory cannot happen without great perils and dangers. And as it is to be thought of the events and chances in wars, so it is of all other valiant and hardy [F3ʳ] enterprises. We have a proverb in English which is of like sense with this Latin proverb, albeit it be not so cleanly, which is this: *A false heart never laid fair lady*.

135. *Ne quaere mollia, ne tibi contingent duria* [II. vi. 48]

Seek not soft things, lest hard things happen unto thee. It is commonly seen that they which unmeasurably seek pleasures do fall, ere they be ware, into bitter and hard grievances.

136. *Pluris est oculatus testis unus, quam auriti decem* [II. vi. 54][206]

One eye witness is of more value than ten ear witnesses. That is to say, far more credit is to be given to such as report the thing they saw with their eyes than to such as speak but by hearsay.

---

[203] Tilley W 462.
[204] bush ... ivy] Used as an inn sign from the Romans onwards.
[205] Tilley H 302, which is the familiar 'Faint heart never won fair lady', not Taverner's 'false' (875), which in this context may mean something like 'unreliable'.
[206] Tilley E 274; cf. II. *Oculis magis habenda fides quam auribus* above.

137. *Multitudo imperatorum Cariam* [F3ᵛ] *perdidit* [II. vii. 7]

The multitude of rulers destroyed the country of Caria.²⁰⁷ This country was sometime a very flourishing realm, and by the discord and dissension of the citizens among themselves, while every man strove to be a lord, it was brought at last to a thing of naught. Wherefore this proverb advertiseth us that nothing is more noisome nor more pestiferous to a commonweal than the overmuch liberty of a multitude, where no man chiefly is obeyed, but every man doth as him lusteth.° This unlawful liberty or license of the multitude is called an 'anarchy', a mischief surely in manner worse than any tyranny.²⁰⁸

138. *Coeno puram aquam turbans nunquam invenies potum* [II. vi. 83]²⁰⁹

If thou trouble the pure water with the mire thou shalt never [F4ʳ] find drink. This proverb is wont to be said when the things which of themselves be very good a man marreth with the medley of things that be nought. As if a man would deprave° the most excellent faculty of divinity with heretical opinions, or with filthiness of words, or finally with any profane and strange doctrines.

139. *Sustine et abstine* [II. vii. 13]²¹⁰

Sustain and abstain. This sentence is worthy to be written on all doors, posts, walls, yea and in every corner wheresoever a man casteth his eye. The author of it is Epictetus,²¹¹ a noble philosopher; by which two words he hath comprised all that pertain to the felicity of man's life, and that that other philosophers could scarce declare in so many great volumes [F4ᵛ] hath he declared by these two words, 'sustain' and 'abstain'. By the first word we be taught strongly to bear adversity, and by the second to abstain from all unlawful pleasures and pastimes.

140. *Naturam expellas furca, tamen usque recurret* [II. vii. 14]²¹²

Thrust out nature with a crotch,°²¹³ yet will she still run back again. It is an hard thing, doubtless, to strive against nature. A crooked bough of a tree, be it never so much driven another way with a fork or crotch, yet if thou once take away the

---

²⁰⁷ Caria] The south-western corner of what is now Turkey.
²⁰⁸ anarchy] This is the first citation for the word in the *OED*. Erasmus uses the Greek term and says that this is 'an evil almost worse than tyranny' (*CWE* 34. 6).
²⁰⁹ Diogenianus, *Proverbs* 3. 95.
²¹⁰ Tilley B 135.
²¹¹ Epictetus] A Greek Stoic philosopher; but the source is in fact Aulus Gellius, *Attic Nights* 17. 19. 6, as Erasmus points out.
²¹² Marg. 'Horace [*Epistles* 1. 10. 24].'
²¹³ crotch] This is the only citation in the *OED* for 'crotch' as 'fork' in the sense of an agricultural instrument.

fork, anon it returneth to the own nature and course again. So in like wise, if man contrary to his nature and bringing up take upon him another person either for fear, or for shame, or for some other cause, let an occasion be offered and anon he returneth [F5ʳ] to his own manners and nature. 'If he hope that he shall not be espied', sayeth Terence, 'again he cometh to his own disposition and inclination';²¹⁴ as he that feareth to commit offences not for any love he hath to virtue, but for fear of the staff or sword, and forthwith ye shall see him return to his old kind. 'For assuredly, their kind and natural inclination', sayeth Pindarus, 'can neither the crafty fox, neither the wild lion change.'²¹⁵ For tame thou never so much the lion, he will still return to his native fierceness, neither will the fox by any means forget her natural wiliness, be she never so much meekened and made tame.

141. *Ovium nullus usus, si pastor absit* [II. vii. 26]²¹⁶

There is no goodness of sheep if [F5ᵛ] the shepherd be away. Servants do nothing well where the master is absent. Scholars°do no good when the teacher is gone. That commonalty°²¹⁷ is nothing worth that is not governed by the authority of a prince. *In summa*, where is an anarchy and no monarchy²¹⁸ — I mean, where one head and ruler is not, but every man as a lord doth what him lusteth — there is nothing well done.

142. *Parit puella, etiam si male adsit viro* [II. vii. 30]²¹⁹

A young woman or wench bringeth lightly forth children, although she be not half well known of man. The cause hereof is that youth is much more ready to conceive than age. Sembably, a fine wit is ready to take anything [that] is taught anon, though he hath but an evil master. And so of all other things.

[F6ʳ] 143. *Non decet principium solidam dormire noctem* [II. vii. 95]²²⁰

It is not seeming for a captain or ruler to sleep all the whole night. This proverb monisheth that vigilancy and busy revolving of mind doth most of all become

---

²¹⁴ Marg. '*Si sperat fere clam rursum ad ingenium redit* [Terence, *Adelphi* 71].'
²¹⁵ Marg. 'Pindarus [*Olympians* 11. 19–20].'
²¹⁶ Diogenianus, *Proverbs* 7. 58.
²¹⁷ commonalty] The term was used in the sixteenth century to refer both to the 'commonwealth', as here, and to the 'common people'. It was spelled in various ways and is cognate with the term 'community'.
²¹⁸ *In summa*] to sum up; in short.
²¹⁹ Diogenianus, *Proverbs* 8. 22.
²²⁰ Tilley C 69 (from Homer, *Iliad* 2. 24 and 61).

captains, princes, magistrates, and rulers, which sustain so great a burden of businesses upon their shoulders.

144. *Felix qui nihil debet* [II. vii. 98]²²¹

Happy is he that oweth nothing. This proverb he shall find true and true again, which once hath tasted what it is to be indebted. He that hath not tasted, let him read Plutarch, and how wretched a thing it is to owe he shall easily espy.²²² For what is more miserable than so oft to be ashamed; so oft to flee thy creditors' sight; to hide thyself, to lie, to dissemble; [F6ᵛ] now lamentably to submit thyself, now to fall to entreaty, now openly to be called upon in courts; to be shunned, to be gazed upon, to be marked with the finger as thou passest by; and shortly to conclude, not to be thine own man nor under thine own power. For all these and with these many other incommodities doth debt bring with it. The English proverb also testifieth that *he that goeth a-borrowing goeth a-sorrowing*.²²³

145. *In magnis et voluisse sat est* [II. viii. 55]²²⁴

In great matters it even sufficeth that a man hath willed. Will otherwhiles° namely in things that pass a man's power deserveth great praise and commendation, although his enterprise take not effect.

146. *Viri infortunati procul amici* [II. viii. 81]²²⁵

The friends of an unfortunate [F7ʳ] person be far off. When fortune once beginneth to fail thee, anon, thy friends are gone.

147. *Venter auribus caret* [II. viii. 84]²²⁶

The belly hath no ears. When the belly's matter is in hand, honest reasons be not admitted nor heard.

148. *Praesentem fortunam boni consule* [II. ix. 33]

Take in good worth thy present fortune.²²⁷

---

²²¹ Tilley N 254.
²²² **Marg.** 'Plutarch *de Vitandis Usuris* [*Moralia* 829C].'
²²³ The English proverb] Cf. Tav. 41. *Emere malo quam rogare.*
²²⁴ Propertius, *Elegies* 2. 10. 6.
²²⁵ Menander, *Sententiae* 34.
²²⁶ Tilley B 286.
²²⁷ Take in good worth] accept without complaint.

149. *Qui e nuce nucleum esse vult, frangit nucem* [II. ix. 35][228]

He that will eat the kernel out of the nut breaketh the nut. He that look[s] for profit may not flee labours. This proverb, therefore, is against idle persons which flee pains, who be very well resembled to cats by the English proverb, saying thus: *The cat would fish eat, but she will not her feet wet.*[229]

[F7ᵛ] 150. *Obsequium amicos, veritas odium parit* [II. ix. 53][230]

Flattery and following of men's minds getteth friends, where speaking of truth gendereth hatred. Such is now and ever hath been the fashion of the world, that who telleth the truth is for most part hated, and he that can flatter, and say as I say, shall be mine own white son.[231] Our English proverb agreeth with the same: *He that will in court dwell must needs curry favel.*[232] And ye shall understand that 'favel' is an old English word and signifieth as much as 'favour' doth nowadays.

151. *Omnia sapientibus facilia* [II. ix. 56]

All things be easy unto wise men. There is nothing so hard, but with prudent counsel may be brought to pass.

152. *Nota res mala, optima* [II. ix. 85][233]

[F8ʳ] An evil thing known is best. It is good keeping of a shrew that a man knoweth. For when one is once accustomed to a shrew, or any other incommodity whatsoever it be, it is no grief.

153. *Multi te oderint, sit te ipsum amas* [II. x. 26]

Many shall hate thee if thou love thyself. Undoubtedly, nothing is more hurtful to a man than self-love is; neither is it possible but that he must needs displease many that pleaseth himself and standeth best in his own conceit.

---

[228] Tilley K 19. **Marg.** 'Plautus [*Curculio* 55].'
[229] *The cat would fish eat*] Lady Macbeth cites 'the cat in the adage' as she urges her husband to kill Duncan (Shakespeare, *Macbeth* I. 7. 45).
[230] Tilley T 562.
[231] own white son] A beloved or favourite son (neologism).
[232] *curry favel*] to use insincere flattery. This is the term that Puttenham uses for the figure of *paradiastole*, 'as when we make the best of a bad thing', *The Arte of English Poesie*, Bk III, ch. 17.
[233] Tilley H 166.

154. *Qui nimium properat, serius absolvit* [III. v. 60]²³⁴

He that hasteth overfast maketh an end the later. Overmuch in nothing is commendable.

155. *Quando id fieri non potest quod vis, id velis quod possis* [III. vi. 4]²³⁵

When that thing cannot be done that thou wouldst, will that [F8ᵛ] thou canst.²³⁶

156. *Boni pastoris est tondere pecus, non deglubere* [III. vii. 12]

It is the parts° of a good shepherd or pastor to shear the sheep and not to pluck off their skins. This proverb did Tiberius Caesar, an emperor of Rome, answer to certain of his friends, which counselled him to enhance the rents and exactions of such as held of him.²³⁷ Also Alexander, king of Macedonia, surnamed the Great, when one advertised him that he might take far greater tributes of the cities he had conquered, answered again on this wise: 'I hate that gardener which cut[s] off the herbs by the hard roots' — meaning the same thing that Tiberius meaned. This proverb agreeth as well upon kings and other magistrates [G1ʳ] as upon bishops, curates, and all other ecclesiastical ministers.

157. *Aliquid mali propter vicinum malum* [I. i. 32]²³⁸

Evil betideth because of an evil neighbour. What displeasures and inconveniences come to honest men by the occasion of evil neighbours, not only histories declare, but also daily experience teacheth. Lord God, what personages, what families, what cities — yea, what realms and whole countries — have been utterly subverted and overthrown by the malice of neighbours. Again, on the other side, nothing is better, nothing more commodious nor pleasant than is a good and honest neighbour, which thing is elegantly declared by our English proverb, which speaketh in this wise: *A near neighbour is better than a far friend.*

158. *Faber compedes quas fecit ipse gestet* [I. i. 86]²³⁹

[G1ᵛ] The fetters that the smith hath made, let him wear them himself. The proverb which commonly we use in English for this purpose is this: *Such ale as he hath brewed, let him drink himself.* Verily, many there be which make a rod for their own arse.

---

²³⁴ Tilley H 198; cf. 91. *Festina lente*.
²³⁵ **Marg.** 'Terence [*Andria* 305–06].'
²³⁶ will that thou canst] i.e. desire that which you *are* able to do.
²³⁷ Suetonius, *Life of Tiberius* 32. 2.
²³⁸ Added in 1545. Tilley N 108.
²³⁹ Added in 1545.

1015   159. *Polypi mentem obtine* [1. i. 93]²⁴⁰

Obtain the mind of the fish called polypus. By this we be admonished according to the time to fashion our manners and to make our semblant° and countenance; which thing the poet Homer seemeth much to commend in Ulysses, whom he nameth a personage of sundry fashions.²⁴¹ The proverb took the original and commencement of the nature of this fish, which, as authors write, do oftentimes change colours, and namely in fear; for when the fishermen go about to take and pursue him, he cleaveth fast to the stones and rocks in the sea, and like to what [G2ʳ] stone he cleaveth unto,²⁴² he counterfeiteth and resembleth the colour of the same in his body to the end that he should not be apprehended of the fishermen. Now let no man think that by this proverb is taught foul and detestable flattery, whereby some men do by their blandishments and sugared tongue accommodate themselves in all things to all men; or that here is taught the vicious inequality of manners which the poet Horace doth wittily rebuke in his book of sermons,²⁴³ and which the writers of histories do note in Catiline and in Anedius Cassius the emperor;²⁴⁴ and to be short, holy writ noteth in every wicked person, saying that 'the fool changeth as doth the moon, whereas the wise man, according to the example of the Son, continueth always one and like to himself'.²⁴⁵ For in Alcibiades a man may doubt whether [G2ᵛ] the thing be worthy of reprehension or of praise.²⁴⁶ Certes,° the dexterity of his manners and wit was no less gracious than wonderful, which played so the Polyp that at Athens he would pleasantly jest, he would use merry taunts and scoffs, he would keep goodly horses and live minionly° and elegantly. The same man amongst the Lacedemonians²⁴⁷ was shaven, did wear a pall,° washed in cold water according to their guise.° Amongst the Thracians he warred and made good cheer. And when he came to Tissaphernes²⁴⁸ he gave himself to daintiness,° to softness of living and to haughtiness of mind, according to the manners of the country. But there is a certain ungentle, hard, and wayward simplicity of the rude and untaught people,

---

²⁴⁰ Added in 1545.
²⁴¹ *Odyssey* 1. 1.
²⁴² like to what stone] All editions read 'loke', i.e. 'looks', but 'like' makes more sense.
²⁴³ Horace ... sermons] *Satires* 2. 7. 6–20. Horace called his satires *sermones*.
²⁴⁴ Catiline ... Anedius Cassius] The first is the Roman senator who conspired to overthrow the Republic in 63 BC; the second, also known as Vulcacius Gallicanus, was one of the authors of the biographies of the Roman emperors in the *Historia Augusta*, written in late antiquity.
²⁴⁵ holy writ] Eccles. 27. 11. The Latin reads 'cum sapiens solis exemplo sui semper sit similis' (*ASD* II-1. 200), i.e. 'the example of the sun'.
²⁴⁶ Alcibiades] *c*. 450–404 BC. Greek political leader and general who changed his allegiance from Athens to Sparta, then from Sparta to Persia, and finally back to Athens. Erasmus's description is taken from Plutarch, *Moralia* 52E.
²⁴⁷ Lacedemonians] Spartans.
²⁴⁸ Tissaphernes] The king of Persia.

which would have every man live after [G3ʳ] their own fashion and condemn whatsoever like not them.

Again, there is a certain honest reason whereby good men otherwhiles follow other men's fashions, lest either they should be odious, or at the least way do no good, but rather hurt, or to the intent they might bring themselves or others out of great dangers. As did Ulysses being with Polyphemus in counterfeiting and dissimuling° many things, and amongst the wooers of his wife playing the part of a beggar.[249] Also as Brutus did by counterfeiting the fool.[250] David also by feigning himself mad.[251] Yea, and St Paul also, the apostle, by a certain holy bragging glorieth in himself that he used this godly wiliness, making himself of all sorts to all men to the intent to win all men to his master [G3ᵛ] Christ.[252] Finally, with this Latin proverb agreeth that which is commonly in every man's mouth in England: When ye art at Rome, do as they do at Rome. Albeit this English proverb is taken forth of a verse in Latin, which is: *Cum fueris Romae, Romano vivito more.*[253]

160. *Ignem igni ne addas* [1. ii. 8][254]

Put not fire to fire. Add not calamity to calamity, lest being already chauffed° thou be yet more chauffed. Plato in his second book of laws forbiddeth children the drinking of wine until they come to the age of 18 years, lest if the heat of the wine be added to the fervency of the age, they should seem to commit fire to fire.[255] This proverb is touched in English where it is said that we ought not [to] put fire to tow.°

161. *Si crebro iacias, aliud alias ieceris* [1. ii. 13]

[G4ʳ] He that often casteth shall sometime through one chance and sometime another.[256] By this is signified that we ought to assay and tempt° a thing often and not to be forthwith weary nor discouraged, though at one time the matter frame° not according to our mind and expectation.

---

[249] *Odyssey* 9 and 17. Polyphemus was the one-eyed Cyclops blinded by Ulysses.
[250] Brutus] Lucius Junius Brutus, the first consul of Rome, feigned stupidity in order to protect himself from the tyranny of Tarquin (*CWE* 31. 134).
[251] David] 1 Sam. 16. 13.
[252] St Paul] 'I have become all things to all people, that I might by all means save some' (1 Corinth. 9. 22). This is the Christian heart of adage I. iii. 86 'a man for all seasons', not included by Taverner.
[253] verse in Latin] Attributed to St Ambrose.
[254] Tilley F 785.
[255] Plato] *Laws* 2. 666a.
[256] casteth ... another] 'casteth' translates *iacere*, to throw, as in 'to throw the dice'. The sense requires 'succeed' after 'sometime'.

1070   162. *Serere ne dubites* [I. ii. 41]

Doubt not to plant. By this we be taught not to be weary nor slothful to achieve some such things whereof no loss cometh, but much profit may proceed, though not presently, yet in time coming; though not for ourselves, yet at least way for our posterity.

1075   163. *Ubi timor, ibi pudor* [I. ii. 64]

Where awe is, there is shamefastness. Unto this accordeth the saying of Terence: *Omnes deteriores sumus licentia.*[257] We be all the worse by overmuch sufferance° to do [G4ᵛ] what we lust. And again we see that the most part of men abstaineth from transgression of the law and enormities for fear of punishment.

1080   164. *Festo die si quid prodegeris, pro festo egere liceat, nisi peperceris* [I. ii. 69]

If on the holiday ye make waste, ye may on the working day go a-begging, unless ye spare the better. This is the sentence of the poet Plautus, whereby we be admonished not to use excess in fare nor yet in apparel in solemn and feastful days as the common sort of people doth.[258]

1085   165. *Ignavi vertitur color* [I. ii. 89][259]

The coward changeth colours. Whereas the wise man and hardy feareth nothing at all of such things as the common sort of men dreadeth — no, he feareth not death, but in an honest and just quarrel is most ready constantly to hazard [G5ʳ] his life and all that he hath.[260]

1090   166. *Minutula pluvia imbrem parit* [I. iii. 2][261]

A mizzling rain gendereth a great wet. And as we commonly say in English: *Many a little maketh a great.* This proverb also hath place where we declare that a thing which at the beginning is little groweth still greater and greater.

167. *Hostium munera, non munera* [I. iii. 35][262]

1095   The gifts of enemies be no gifts. The opinion of them in old time was that amongst all other things men ought to observe and mark of whom they receive gifts or

---

[257] Terence, *Heautontimoroumenos* 483.
[258] Plautus, *Aulularia* 380–81.
[259] Tilley C 773.
[260] Echoed by Shakespeare, *Merchant of Venice* II. 7. 9 ('Who chooseth me must give and hazard all he hath').
[261] Tilley D 617.
[262] Tilley G 109.

presents, forasmuch as those gifts which come from them that would us no good do oftentimes turn to our destruction and utter undoing, as by many examples my author Erasmus confirmeth.²⁶³ Nevertheless, he calleth this opinion but a superstition, willing us [G5ᵛ] notwithstanding to mark diligently what they be that would give us anything, saying that the proverbs even of Holy Scripture command us that we be not so sure and careless of our reconciled enemy.

168. *Finem vitae specta* [1. iii. 37]²⁶⁴

Mark the end of the life. The history how the wise Solon answered King Croesus, that no man could be named happy till he had happily and prosperously passed the course of his life, is very common.²⁶⁵ And they that have not heard it may read it in my book *The Garden of Wisdom* where it is at large declared.²⁶⁶ This proverb also is confirmed by our English proverb, which sayeth: *At even men should the fair day praise.* As who should say: before night be come, we cannot praise the fairness of the day because there [G6ʳ] may come in an hour that cannot all the day before. And even so it is of man's life.

169. *Suo ipsius indicio forex parit* [1. iii. 65]²⁶⁷

The rat dieth by uttering of herself. This proverb took the beginning of the property of this vermin, for the rats be wont to make a noise much more than mice do, and do more rumble about and make a noisome crying while they gnaw candles' ends or such other trifles; to which noise many men hearkening forthwith, though it be in the dark night, throw at them and so kill them. Semblably, many men and women there be which by their own noise and bewraying of themselves seek their own band° and destruction.

170. *Generosioris arboris statim planta cum fructu est* [1. iii. 74]²⁶⁸

The plant or grass of a gentle tree beareth fruit anon. By this is meant that pregnant° [G6ᵛ] and noble wits be quickly ripe and bring forth good fruit for the commonwealth.

---

²⁶³ Erasmus's principal example is the exchange of gifts between Hector and Ajax in *Iliad* Bk 7.
²⁶⁴ Tilley E 125.
²⁶⁵ Perhaps most famously in the verdict of the Chorus at *Oedipus Tyrannus* 1528-30.
²⁶⁶ See Richard Taverner, *The Second Booke of the Garden of Wysedom* (London, 1542), fols 31-32.
²⁶⁷ Cf. Terence, *Enuchus* 1024. 1545 and subsequent editions give the Latin as *Sub ipsius iudicio sorex parit*.
²⁶⁸ Quintilian, *Institutio oratoria* 8. 3. 77.

171. *Non est cuius libet Corinthum appellere* [1. iv. 1]²⁶⁹

It is not for every man to arrive at Corinth. The occasion of this proverb grew after the mind of some men after the hard and dangerous arrival at the port of Corinth. Other there be that refer the original of this proverb to the fair Lais, an harlot of great name that dwelt at the said city of Corinth.²⁷⁰ For this Lais, for the excellency of her beauty and her sweet entertainment of her lovers, gained great sums of money, and very great resort was unto her, even of the richest and most noble personages of all Greece, but none was received if he gave not the hire and price that she demanded. [G7ʳ] Now she asked an exceeding great quantity of money, and hereof, they say, arose this proverb 'It is not for every man to arrive at Corinth', forasmuch as he sailed thither to Lais in vain, which could not give her her own asking. So that this proverb is of like sense with that our English proverb, which sayeth: *Every man may not be a lord.*

172. *Sub omni lapide scorpius dormit* [1. iv. 34]²⁷¹

Under every stone sleepeth a scorpion. This proverb admonisheth us that we speak not rashly and unadvisedly amongst captious and calumnious persons. For whatsoever we touch, it is to be feared that they will bite at it. Now certain it is that the scorpions be wont in diverse countries beyond the sea to lie lurking under stones, which stones, so soon as a man unaware [G7ᵛ] take up, forthwith he receiveth a wound of the scorpion.

173. *Nihil graculo cum fidibus* [1. iv. 37]²⁷²

The jay is unmeet for a fiddle; as who should say: what make fools and unlearned persons with good letters?²⁷³ For the jay is a bird of a foolish and irksome chattering and also loveth assemblies of such as be of the like kind, by reason whereof through mutual chattering the noise is the more odious and grievous. On the other side, the fiddle, harp, or any other musical instrument requireth silence and attent° audience. Aulus Gellius applieth this proverb very featly° to these gross and rude men, haters of all humanity and good letters, which be wont to scorn all good learning and the students of the same.²⁷⁴

---

²⁶⁹ Tilley M 202. Erasmus cites this proverb at the opening of *De Copia*; cf. Horace, *Epistles* 1. 17; Aulus Gellius, *Attic Nights* 1. 8.
²⁷⁰ William Painter retells the story of Lais in *The Palace of Pleasure* (1567), Bk II, ch. 13.
²⁷¹ Tilley S 894.
²⁷² Tilley J 38.
²⁷³ good letters] fine literature: a humanist ideal that Erasmus often refers to as *bonae literae*.
²⁷⁴ *Attic Nights*, preface 19; 'humanity' refers to Greek and Latin literature and culture, as in the title of the Classics degree *Literae humaniores*, rather than 'humankind'.

[G8ʳ] 174. *Ita fugias, ne praeter casam* [I. v. 3]²⁷⁵

So flee that thou run not past thy cottage. By this we be taught that we should not so flee one vice that we run into another. For some there be which through the heat of fleeing overpass also those things where they might have commodiously rested.

175. *Flamma fumo est proxima* [I. v. 20]²⁷⁶

The flame is next to the smoke. This proverb teacheth us that peril and danger ought in time to be fled, and that he which would eschew evil must first eschew the occasion of evil; according to our English proverb: *He that will no hurt do must do nothing that long thereto.* As, for example, he that would not be corrupted, [G8ᵛ] let him abstain from the company of naughty persons; he that will not lie with whores, let him abstain from kissings and other wanton entertainments.

176. *Crambe bis posita mors est* [I. v. 38]²⁷⁷

Crambe twice sod° is death.²⁷⁸ This *crambe* is a certain kind of worts or, after the mind of Athenaeus, *crambe* in old time was all one with that which the Latin men call *raphanus*, and we call 'radish'.²⁷⁹ Now this *crambe* was in old time much used in feasts and banquets, but if it were twice sod it was so loathed and abhorred that the Greeks made a proverb on it. For as often as they would signify a thing again and again repeated, not without tediousness and grievance, they said forthwith in their language: '*crambe* twice served is death'.²⁸⁰

[H1ʳ] 177. *Saepe etiam stultus fuit opportuna locutus*

Oftentimes even the fool hitteth the nail on the head and speaketh things in place. This proverb therefore admonisheth us not to reject nor despise an wholesome and right sentence spoken otherwhiles out of a rude fellow's mouth.

---

²⁷⁵ Terence, *Phormio* 766–68.
²⁷⁶ Plautus, *Curculio* 53–54.
²⁷⁷ Tilley C 511.
²⁷⁸ twice sod] This predates the *OED*'s first citation of the expression (1601) to mean 'stale, unpalatable'.
²⁷⁹ Athenaeus] Greek rhetorician (fl. late second to early third century AD), citing Theophrastus, *Historia plantarum* 4. 16. 6.
²⁸⁰ *Crambe* may be the origin of 'Corambis', the name for Polonius in *Hamlet* Q1. See Doris V. Falk, 'Proverbs and the Polonius Destiny', *Shakespeare Quarterly*, 18.1 (1967), 23–36, on the relevance of this adage to *Hamlet*.

386   *Proverbs, or Adages*

178. *Silentii tutum praemium* [III. v. 3]²⁸¹

There is a sure reward of silence. For verily, by silence no man offendeth, but by speaking oftentimes. Our English proverb sayeth: *In little meddling lieth great ease.*

179. *Salem et mensam ne praetereas* [I. vi. 10]²⁸²

Pass not over salt at the table, as who should say: 'neglect not the company of friends' or 'break not the laws of amity'. For with these things in old time were friends reconciled, and kept mutual [H1ᵛ] feasts and banquets one with another.

180. *Dii facientes adiuvant* [I. vi. 17]²⁸³

The gods do help the doers. Hereby is meant that the heavenly power is an aid and help not to loiterers and idle persons, but to laborious and painful° folk and such as put to their own good wills.

181. *Non omnino temere est, quod vulgo dictitant* [I. vi. 25]²⁸⁴

That which is in every man's mouth is not spoken without cause. By this proverb we be taught to be very ware° and circumspect that we run not into the speech of the people through our indiscreetness, though it be without just cause and falsely.²⁸⁵ The English proverb sayeth thus: *It is like to be true that every man sayeth.*

182. *Domum cum facis ne relinquas* [H2ʳ] *impolitam* [I. vi. 26]²⁸⁶

When thou makest an house, leave it not unfinished. By this we be bidden that whatsoever matter or affairs we once begin, we bring the same to a perfect and full end.

183. *Heroum filii noxae* [I. vi. 32]

The children of most renowned and noble personages be for most part destructions to a commonwealth. Verily our elders have observed from time to time that the children of most excellent and wise men have grown much out of kind from the virtues and prowess of their progenitors. And therefore Demosthenes imputed this thing to a certain fatal destiny. Also Aelius Spartanus setteth forth this matter with many examples, declaring that commonly it cometh

---

²⁸¹ Plutarch, *Moralia* 207D.
²⁸² No clear source, but related to Taverner's final proverb, *Panem ne frangito.*
²⁸³ Tilley G 236.
²⁸⁴ Tilley M 204.
²⁸⁵ that we run not … people] that we avoid becoming the object of popular calumny.
²⁸⁶ Hesiod, *Works and Days* 746-47.

to pass that such persons as be notable and [H2ᵛ] excellent — either in virtue, in learning, or in the gifts of fortune — have either had no children at all, or else have left such behind them, as it had been better for the commonwealth they had died without children.²⁸⁷ Finally, our common English proverb sayeth that the wisest men have most fools to their children.

184. *Domesticum thesaurum calumniari turpe est* [I. vi. 49]

It is a foul thing for a man to slander the creature or things of his own house. We have a very praty° proverb in English, which we use in the same sense: *It is an evil bird that defileth her own nest.*

185. *Nostris ipsorum alis capimur* [I. vi. 52]²⁸⁸

We be taken with our own feathers. This proverb riseth of the fable that showeth how the eagle, which [H3ʳ] was stricken through with an arrow when she saw the arrow made of birds' feathers, wherewith she was wounded, said 'We be now caught not of others, but even of our own feathers'. It is applied upon them which minister the occasion of their own mischief and trouble, like to the English proverb: [He] *hath made a rod for his own arse.*

186. *Neque mel, neque apes* [I. vi. 62]²⁸⁹

I have neither honey nor bees. As who should say, 'I have no honey because I have no bees, nor will not take the pains to keep and abide the biting and stinging of them'. To this agreeth that is commonly said: *Dulcia non meruit qui non gustavit amara.* That is to say, 'he hath not deserved the sweet, which hath not tasted the sour'. Also another proverb sayeth, 'The cat would fish eat, but she will not her feet [H3ᵛ] wet'.²⁹⁰

187. *Tussis pro crepitu* [I. vi. 63]²⁹¹

A cloak for the rain.²⁹² The Latin proverb rose of them which with a loud cough or 'hem' hide and dissemble their fartings, which kind of people even this day, not without great laughter, be found out. And it may be applied upon him which covereth his fault or frailty with some other thing. As if a man being taken in the

---

²⁸⁷ *Severus* 20. 4. Aelius Spartanus was one of the authors of the *Historia Augusta*, a collection of lives of the Roman emperors which Erasmus edited for Froben in 1518.
²⁸⁸ Tilley F 166. Derived from a fragment of Aeschylus.
²⁸⁹ Tilley S 1035.
²⁹⁰ Cf. Tav. 149. *Qui e nuce nucleum esse vult, frangit nucem.*
²⁹¹ Tilley F 64.
²⁹² This does not translate the Latin, which means 'a cough for a fart'.

house of a fair woman which hath no good name feigneth that he came thither to have a shirt made of her, or for other affairs. This is a cloak for the rain.

188. *Fertilior seges est alieno semper in arvo* [1. vi. 72][293]

The corn in another man's ground seemeth ever more fertile and plentiful than doth our own. By [H4ʳ] this is noted the lightness, new-fangledness and inconstancy of mankind, which esteemeth ever strange things better than his own.

189. *Fecem bibat, qui vinum bibit* [1. vi. 73][294]

He that hath drunk the wine, let him drink the dregs. He that hath had the use and fruition of the sweet, let him be content to take some part of the sour.

190. *Tecum habita* [1. vi. 87][295]

Dwell with thyself. That is to say, measure thyself by thine own substance; and knowing as well thy vices as thy good qualities, behave thyself in everything accordingly.

191. *Tuo te pede metire* [1. vi. 89][296]

Measure yourself by your own foot. The painters and carvers of images hold opinion [H4ᵛ] that the just measure of every man consisteth in seven of his own feet. By this proverb we be therefore warned that we dilate not ourselves beyond our condition and state, neither yet esteem ourselves by the praises of flatterers, or opinion of the people, or by the favour of false fortune, but only by our proper and true qualities.

192. *Non videmus manticae quod in tergo est* [1. vi. 90][297]

We look not what is in the wallet behind. Aesop, the writer of fables, feigned that every man and woman hath a wallet, whereof the one part hangeth before us on our breast, and the other behind us on our shoulders.[298] But into the side that hangeth before our eyen° we put other men's faults, and our own faults we put in the part behind. By this he signifieth that [H5ʳ] we will easily espy faults in other men, but at our own we be wont to wink.° And according to the evangelical

---

[293] Tilley N 115.
[294] Aristophanes, *Plutus* 1084–85; cf. Tilley W 466.
[295] Cf. Tav. 225. *Choenici ne insideas*.
[296] Tilley F 567.
[297] Tilley W 20.
[298] Perry 266; cf. Shakespeare, *Troilus and Cressida* III. 3. 139–41.

proverb, we can see a mote° in other men's eyes, where in our own we cannot espy a great beam.²⁹⁹

193. *Intra tuam pelliculam te contine* [I. vi. 92]

Keep you within your own skin. The fable out of which this proverb is thought to be taken is this.³⁰⁰ A certain ass, being weary of his own state and envying the high state of the lion, had gotten — I cannot tell where — a lion's skin and got it upon his back, and so for a certain season was esteemed and taken for a lion indeed; till at last, after he was espied to be an ass and so known of the men of the country, he was not only laughed to scorn and shaken out of the strange [H5ᵛ] and unmeet° skin, but also was all-to° beaten of the peasants till he groaned again. This good got the ass because he would not keep him in his own skin. So we be admonished that forgetting our own state and powers we go not about higher things than appertaineth to our ability. Let every man observe and try himself whereunto he is naturally inclined and disposed. For surely, he that contrary to his allotment and calling will set upon great things must needs be espied and so be thrown down again to his great confusion.

194. *In vino veritas* [I. vii. 17]³⁰¹

In wine is truth. Verily, large drinking, and especially of wine, taketh away the cloak and dissimulation of man's mind, [H6ʳ] and whatsoever lieth hid in the breast it bringeth to light. Furthermore, Pliny, a great learned man, writeth that wine so much bewrayeth° the secrets of the mind that there have been men which in their large and merry drinking have uttered their own bane and destruction.³⁰² Our common proverb agreeth hereunto, which sayeth: *Children, drunkers,° and fools cannot lie.*

195. *Omnia idem pulvis* [I. vii. 27]³⁰³

All is one self, dust or ashes. To earth we came and to earth we shall. Yea, the Scripture sayeth that ashes we be and to ashes we shall revert.³⁰⁴ Now amongst ashes or dust, I pray you, what great difference is there? How will ye discern the

---

²⁹⁹ evangelical proverb] Matt. 7. 3–5.
³⁰⁰ Perry 188. Erasmus identifies the ass in this story with 'the ass at Cumae', the subject of *Adagia* I. vii. 12 (not included by Taverner).
³⁰¹ Tilley W 465.
³⁰² Pliny, *Natural History* 14. 141.
³⁰³ Lucian, *Dialogues of the Dead* 1. 3.
³⁰⁴ Genesis 3. 19.

ashes of a king, of an [H6ᵛ] emperor, of a duke, of a great bishop, from the ashes of a cobbler, yea, of a beggar?³⁰⁵

196. *Currus bovem trahit* [I. vii. 28]³⁰⁶

Ye set the cart before the horse. This proverb hath place in things done preposterously, clean contrarily, and arsy versy, as they say. As, for example, if a wife would rule her husband, if the scholar would teach his master, if the commons would tell their prince what he had to do; finally, if the affection° or sensuality would guide reason, as 'alack for pity!' in these cases, and in many other more, it is often seen.

197. *Ab equis ad asinos* [I. vii. 29]³⁰⁷

Promoted or descended out of the hall into the kitchen. This is where a man is brought from a better state, study, office, or kind of living to a worse.

198. *Bipedum nesquissimus* [I. vii. 42]³⁰⁸

[H7ʳ] The starkest knave that goeth on two legs. This is spoken of a very evil-disposed person and which in lewdness passeth the very brute beasts.

199. *Canis vindictam* [I. vii. 47]³⁰⁹

A dog hath a day. There is none so vile° nor simple a person but at one time or other may avenge himself of wrongs done unto him. Wherefore it is a wise man's part to condemn no man.

200. *Ante victoriam encomium canis* [I. vii. 55]³¹⁰

Ye triumph before the victory. Such there be not a few which glory of things too soon, before they have fully brought them to effect.

201. *Velocem tardus assequitur* [I. vii. 67]³¹¹

The slow overtaketh the swift. The poet Homer writeth how halting° Vulcan, what time he suspected his wife Venus to have used [H7ᵛ] in his absence overmuch

---

³⁰⁵ Cf. Shakespeare, *Hamlet* v. 1. 154–62.
³⁰⁶ Tilley C 103; cf. Lucian, *Dialogues of the Dead* 16. 2.
³⁰⁷ Tilley H 713.
³⁰⁸ Pliny, *Letters* 1. 5. 14.
³⁰⁹ Erasmus claims the source of the proverb to be the legendary story that Euripides, the tragedian, was torn to pieces by hounds; see *CWE* 32. 96.
³¹⁰ Tilley V 50.
³¹¹ Homer, *Odyssey* 8. 329–32.

familiarity with Mars, invented this craft and policy to take them together with the manner.³¹² He made by his craft little praty° chains, so subtle and fine that they could not be well espied, with which chains, after that he had overspread his bed, he made as though he should go forth upon some business, and so departed. Forthwith, Mars and Venus be gotten to the same bed together after their accustomed fashion. But anon, while they were even in the midst of their dalliance, and the more they ruffled° the more they wrapped themselves in bonds, lo, suddenly Vulcan her husband returneth, and taking them in the manner calleth all the gods to wonder upon them. Thus Mars, which was counted the swiftest and most hardy of all, was by [H8ʳ] Vulcan, which was halt and lame, caught through policy and craft.

202. *Intempestiva benevolentia nihil a simultate differt* [I. vii. 69]

Unseasonable friendship differeth little from enmity. Many there be, which, while they study to do a man good, do him much harm, or otherwise be molest° and grievous unto him, forasmuch as they have no respect nor consideration of the time.

203. *Leona societas*³¹³

The fellowship of a lion. For the declaration° of this proverb I must rehearse unto you a fable of Aesop, which is this. The lion, the ass, and the fox entered into a certain fellowship together, so that whatsoever they should take in hunting should be divided amongst them. When now they had got a good prey, the lion had the ass make partition between [H8ᵛ] them. The ass, being but a blunt and dull beast, divided the booty into three equal parts, whereat the lion, being sore displeased and angry that he had no better portion than the rest, runneth upon the ass and teareth him in pieces. Which done, and the fox only being left behind, he commandeth him to make partition anew. The fox assigned well near the whole prey to the lion, leaving to himself a very little portion. 'Yea, marry,' quoth the lion, 'I can thee good thank, thou hast made a wondrous good and right portion. Who taught thee this way to divide?' The fox answered. 'Verily, sir lion,' quoth the fox, 'that did the calamity of the ass.' By this we be taught not to enter into society with our betters; or if by negligence or casualty° we do, that we do, according to the example of the [I1ʳ] fox, depart with° some portion of our own right unto them, lest we lose life and all together.

---

³¹² with the manner] in the unlawful act.
³¹³ Perry 149, but not in Erasmus.

1345   204. *Non bene cum sociis regna Venusque manent*[314]

Love nor lordship will abide no fellowship. That is to say: the nature of man or woman is such that, like as he or she cannot abide any other to love the same person that he or she loveth, so also he cannot well endure in his heart another to be joined with him in impery° or governance, but coveteth as well in the one as
1350   in the other to be alone.

205. *Da mihi mutuum testimonium* [I. vii. 95][315]

Claw me, claw thee.[316] Bear witness with me and I will bear witness with thee. But against these sorts of persons, which be wont to bear record one with another, we have another proper° English proverb to cast them in the teeth with and [I1ᵛ] to
1355   elude their mutual testimony, when we answer again and say: *Ask my fellow if I be a thief.*

206. *Mutuum muli scabunt* [I. vii. 96][317]

One mule claweth another.[318] This is of like sense with that before.

207. *Ferrum ferro acuitur* [I. vii. 100][319]

1360   Iron whetteth iron. This proverb of Solomon is also of the same signification with the other before remembered.

207. *Aequalem tibi uxorem quaere* [I. viii. 1][320]

Marry thy like. What inconveniences proceed of unequal marriages, as when the old person marrieth with the young, the poor with the rich, the ignoble with the
1365   noble, who seeth not?

208. *Spartam nactus es, hanc orna* [II. v. 1][321]

Ye have gotten the country of Lacedemonia; now see ye employ your study to adorn and furnish the same. This proverb teacheth us [I2ʳ] that whatsoever

---

[314] Ovid, *Ars Amatoria* 3. 564. This had acquired proverbial status by the sixteenth century but is not in Erasmus.
[315] Cicero, *Pro Flacco* 4. 9.
[316] Cf. 'we saye, clawe me, clawe ye [...] as euery thefe myght lyghtely proue hymselfe a true man, in bearyng recorde to another as false as he, and takynge re|corde of the same again'; William Tyndale, *The Exposition of the First Epistle of Saint John* (1531), fol. lxx.
[317] Tilley M 1396.
[318] mule] All editions have 'moile', which is not recorded in this sense in the *OED*.
[319] Prov. 27. 17; Tilley I 91a.
[320] Tilley E 178; B 465.
[321] Cicero, *Letters to Atticus* 4. 6. 2.

ministration, office, house, land, or province we chance to obtain or come by, we should apply and accommodate ourselves to the same, and bear ourselves according to the dignity thereof, and go no further. Let the private person do as becometh a private person and not meddle with princes' matters. Art thou a courtier? Then play the courtier. Art a curate or parson? Exercise the office of a curate. If ye be a bishop, do as apperteineth to a bishop. If ye be a judge, show yourself neither friend nor foe, but a judge. Finally, let every man be contented with his allotment. For like as a skilful pilot or governor of a ship in every tempest playeth the good pilot, so in like manner a wise man in all states and fortunes bears himself wisely. Thou hast the world at [I2ᵛ] will, and goods and lands plentifully — administer them prudently and wisely. Thou hast it not, use the commodities of poverty. Thou hast learning, use it to live well. Thou hast it not, vex not thyself — goodness sufficeth for the obtaining of everlasting health. The old painters painted Venus in such sort that with her feet she trod upon a snail,[322] signifying that a good housewife ought to keep at home and go little abroad, forasmuch as her office consisteth within the house. Now, that a little well-furnished is better than a great deal unfurnished and neglected declareth also the English proverb by word, which sayeth in this wise:

> A little house well filled
> A little ground well tilled
> And a little wife well willed

is best.

209. *Canes timidi vehementius latrant*[323]

[I3ʳ] Fearful dogs do bark the sorer. Great braggers commonly be least fighters, and most cowards, even as the most barking dogs, be for the most part least biters.

210. *Dulce bellum inexpertis* [IV. i. 1][324]

Battle is a sweet thing to them that never assayed it. He that listeth to know more of this proverb, let him go to Erasmus, which handleth in his *Chiliades* this proverb both right copiously and also eloquently.[325]

---

[322] snail] More typically a tortoise, as in Alciati's *Emblems*. Ben Jonson adapts the figure for the sub-plot of *Volpone*.
[323] 1539 resumes at this point. *Vehementius* emends Taverner's *vehementis*.
[324] Tilley W 58.
[325] Erasmus ... *Chiliades*] The longest essay in the *Adagia* (forty pages in *CWE*) and a work in its own right. For Erasmus's pacifism see also *Bellum* and *Peace*.

211. *Donum quodcunque dat aliquis proba* [IV. i. 15]

What gift soever one giveth thee, allow it and take in worth.[326] A given horse, we say, may not be looked in the mouth.

212. *Cura esse quod audis* [IV. i. 92][327]

See thou be that thou art reported and borne in hand to be.[328] Rich men for the most part are praised [I3ᵛ] of the poor and called wise, just, honest, learned, godly, and all that good is. Now Horace biddeth them look and put their diligence that they become such persons indeed as they hear themselves bruited° and borne in hand.

213. *Mulierem ornat silentium* [IV. i. 97][329]

Silence garnisheth a woman. Assuredly there is no tire,° no apparel that better becometh a woman than silence. Which thing also the apostle Paul requireth while he forbiddeth women in the church or congregation to speak, but willeth them to ask their husbands at home if they be in doubt of anything.[330]

214. *Quod opus non est, asse carum est* [IV. iv. 99]

That needeth not is too dear of a farthing.[331] Cato, which is the author of this proverb, among [I4ʳ] his other precepts and lessons of husbandry teacheth the husbandman to be a seller and no buyer, and to buy only such things as he must needs use.[332] 'For such things', quoth he, 'as thou needest not be over-dear of a farthing'; as who should say, be a thing never so cheaply bought, yet it is dear if it be not necessary.

215. *Grata brevitas* [IV. v. 25][333]

Shortness is acceptable. Unto little things is a certain grace annexed.[334] Some things do please men by reason of the greatness and quantity. Again there be other things which even for that very cause be acceptable and had in price because they be little. The English proverb is thus pronounced: *Short and sweet*.

---

[326] take in worth] See note 227 above.
[327] Tilley S 214; **Marg.** 'Horace [*Epistles* 1. 16. 17–19].'
[328] borne in hand to be] professed to be.
[329] Tilley S 447.
[330] Paul] 1 Corinth. 14. 34–35.
[331] farthing] One quarter of one old penny and the coin of least value.
[332] Seneca, *Letters* 94. 27 (to his son Marcus), citing Cato the Elder.
[333] The source is the Greek *Anthologia Palatina* 9. 784.
[334] **Marg.** 'The grace of briefness.'

216. *Non est beatus, esse qui se nescit* [IV. v. 4]³³⁵

[I4ᵛ] He is not happy that knoweth not himself happy.

217. *Amicus certus in re incerta cernitur* [IV. v. 5]³³⁶

A friend certain is espied in a thing uncertain; that is to say, in adversity, where a man's matters are inconstant, doubtful, and full of danger. And therefore if ye will do well, do as the English proverb biddeth thee: *Prove thy friend ere thou have need.*

218. *Avarus nisi cum moritur, nil recte facit* [IV. v. 6]³³⁷

A covetous man doth no man good but when he dieth. They that give themselves only to the hoarding up of money be profitable to nobody while they live. Only their death bringeth pleasure and profit to their heirs and executors.

219. *Sapiens sua bona secum fert* [IV. v. 9]³³⁸

[I5ʳ] The wise man carrieth about with him his goods. By this is signified that those only be indeed and truly ours which be within us, as learning and virtue.

220. *Nihil ad Parmenonis suem* [I. i. 10]³³⁹

Nothing to Parmeno's sow. The occasion of this proverb was this. There was a certain man called Parmeno, who was of that sort of men which also in our times be wont so featly° to counterfeit and represent sundry voices, as well of men as of beasts, that they that heard him and saw him not would have thought them true voices and not counterfeited. In which kind of pastime there be many that delight exceedingly much. This Parmeno, then, as he was by this feat° and quality very acceptable and pleasant to the people, so his fame and bruit° for his excellency in [I5ᵛ] this behalf did not a little flourish above the rest. Wherefore, when diverse others for gain's sake studied to counterfeit the same and to represent the grunting of the sow as did Parmeno, anon the people were wont to cry: 'Well done! But nothing to Parmeno's sow.' Now a certain witty fellow, espying that the judgement of the people proceeded rather of imagination than of truth, and carrying under his clothes a very pig indeed, hid himself from the people's sight as the manner was. Forthwith, the pig cryeth. The people, thinking it to be but a counterfeit voice,

---

³³⁵ Tilley K 182.
³³⁶ **Marg.** 'Ennius.' The source is Cicero, *De amicitia* 17. 64, citing Ennius. Tilley F 694.
³³⁷ **Marg.** 'Terence.' From the aphorisms of Pubilius Syrius, which Erasmus had edited, not Terence. Tilley M 85.
³³⁸ Tilley M 207.
³³⁹ Plutarch, *Moralia* 674B–C.

began according to their manner to cry 'Tush, what is this to Parmeno's pig?' Here the fellow bringing forth out of his clothes the very pig indeed, and openly showing it to them all, dasheth their [I6ʳ] foolish judgement. Assuredly, such a fond° beast is the people that the thing that they once take into their heads, be the contrary never so apparent, they stiffly uphold.

221. *Amicorum omnia sunt communia* [I. i. 1][340]

Amongst friends all things be common. The author of this proverb is Pythagoras, an ancient philosopher.[341] Neither did he only speak it, but also brought in such a certain communion of life and goods as Christ would have used amongst all Christians. For as many as were admitted of him into the fellowship and company of his doctrine, all the money and substance they had, they laid it together, which thing not only in word but also in deed was called *coenobium*. Certes, this communion of those heathen Pythagorians [I6ᵛ] resembled much better that communion used in the primitive church amongst the Apostles than doth either our monkery at this day, or the wicked Anabaptistical sect,[342] which will have no rulers, no order, but which go about to disturb the whole world with horrible confusion.

222. *Amicitia aequalitas. Amicus alter ipse* [I. i. 2][343]

'Friendship', sayeth Pythagoras, 'is equality, and all one mind or will, and my friend is as who should say another "I".'[344] He pronounced also many *enigmata* or symbols,° of which I intend of some to make here a brief rehearsal.

---

[340] Tilley F 729. Erasmus moved this proverb to the beginning of the *Adagia* in 1508. On its importance in Erasmus's thought see Kathy Eden, *Friends Hold All Things in Common: Tradition, Intellectual Property, and the Adages of Erasmus* (New Haven: Yale University Press, 2001).

[341] **Marg.** 'Pythagoras.' Erasmus cites Cicero, Diogenes Laertius, and Aulus Gellius as authorities for ascribing this saying to Pythagoras.

[342] monkery ... Anabaptistical sect] The first is a Reformation-era term of abuse for monasticism (the first citation in the OED is 1528). The second emerged as a cohesive movement in 1527 and achieved notoriety with the communist 'kingdom of god' set up by John of Leiden in the Munster rebellion of 1534–35. Anabaptism was condemned by both Protestants and Catholics.

[343] Tilley F 761 and F 696.

[344] Pythagoras] Erasmus gives the source as Aristotle, *Magna moralia* 2. [11 and 15], while also attributing the saying to Pythagoras of Samos, Greek philosopher of the sixth century AD.

SYMBOLA ALIQUOT PYTHAGORAE[345]

223. *Ne gustaris quibus nigra est cauda*[346]

'Taste not', said Pythagoras, 'of [I7ʳ] things that have black tails.' That is to say, meddle not with naughty fellows and such as have black and defamed° manners.

224. *Stateram ne transgrediaris*[347]

Overgo not the beam or balance. That is to say, do nothing beside right and equity.

225. *Choenici ne insideas*[348]

Sit not upon the measure. Erasmus thinketh that by this dark sentence is meant we should not live upon the measure or diet given us at other men's hands, but that every man by his own industry and labour ought to seek him goods whereby he may lead a clean and honest life, and not by slothfulness to haunt idleness and other men's meat.[349] For it is the fashion of a flatterer and parasite to live off another man's trencher and to have no honest faculty whereby thou [I7ᵛ] mayest live of thine own.

226. *Ne cuivis porrigas dexteram*[350]

Hold not forth thy hand to every man. He meaneth we should not unadvisedly admit everybody into our friendship and familiarity.

227. *Arctum anulum ne gestato*[351]

Wear no strait ring. As who should say, cast not thyself into bondage or into such a kind of life from whence thou canst not afterward wind out thyself. For whosoever weareth on his finger a narrow and strait ring, in manner layeth bands on himself and imprisoneth himself.

---

[345] SYMBOLA ALIQUOT PYTHAGORAE] 'Some symbols of Pythagoras'. Taverner's use of the term 'symbol' (following Erasmus's 'Symbola') to mean a saying or sententious statement predates the first citation in *OED* (Nashe 1594) by half a century. He may have been led by *OED* sense 1a. 'A formal authoritative statement or summary of the religious belief of the Christian church', which dates from 1530. Erasmus included thirteen sayings of Pythagoras in the first edition of the *Adagia*, the *Collectanea* of 1500, taken from Jerome, *Against Rufinus* 3. 39.
[346] Tilley T 197.
[347] Diogenes Laertius, *Lives* 8. 17 (the life of Pythagoras, which is the source of several of the following proverbs).
[348] *Choenici*] Emended from *Coenici*, 1539, 1545. Cf. Tav. 191. *Tuo te pede metire*.
[349] Erasmus ... meat] Erasmus cites Homer, *Odyssey* 18. 2–4 to support his reading (*CWE* 31. 34).
[350] Tilley H 68.
[351] Tilley R 129.

228. *Ignem gladio ne fodito*[352]

Dig not fire with a sword. Here Pythagoras meaneth, as Plato expoundeth, that we should not labour in vain to go about the thing that in no wise can be brought to pass.[353]

[18ʳ] 229. *Cor ne edito*[354]

Eat not thy heart. That is to say, consume not thyself with cares and thoughts of worldly things, for that eateth and gnaweth a man's heart.

230. *A fabis abstineto*[355]

Abstain from beans. There be sundry interpretations of this symbol; but Plutarch and Cicero think beans to be forbidden of Pythagoras because they be windy and do engender impure humours, and for that cause provoke bodily lust.[356]

231. *Cibum in matellam ne immittas*[357]

Put not meat into a piss-pot. Plutarch expoundeth this saying thus: cast not good sentences into the mind of a wicked person.[358] So that it is all one in effect with that saying of Christ: 'cast not [18ᵛ] pearls afore swine'.[359] For speech is the meat of the mind, but this meat is corrupted and doth putrefy if it fall into an unsound mind. Unto this looked the poet Horace where he sayeth: 'unless the vessel be pure, whatsoever thou pourest into it, it waxeth sour'.[360]

232. *Ad finem ubi perveneris, ne velis reverti*[361]

When thou comest to the end, turn not back again. He monisheth us that when our time is come, and when we have run our course so that we must now depart this wretched world, we then draw not back again, desirous to begin our life anew.

---

[352] Diogenes Laertius, *Pythagoras*.
[353] Plato, *Laws* 6. 780c.
[354] Tilley H 330.
[355] Tilley B 119.
[356] Plutarch, 'On the Education of Children', *Moralia* 12F; 286E; Cicero, *De divinatione* 1. 30. 62.
[357] Tilley M 834.
[358] Plutarch, *Moralia* 12F.
[359] **Marg.** 'Matthew 7. [6.]'.
[360] Horace, *Epistles* 1. 2. 54.
[361] Diogenes Laertius, *Pythagoras*.

233. *Tollenti onus auxiliare, deponenti nequaquam*

Help the taker of a burden, but not the layer down. As who should [K1ʳ] say: further such as labour to attain to virtue, but such as be slothful and lay down all honest labours, help not.³⁶²

234. *Per publicam viam ne ambules*³⁶³

Walk not by the highway. That is to say, as St Jerome expoundeth it: follow not the errors of the people.³⁶⁴ For it is not possible that those things which be best can please the most part of folk. This precept of Pythagoras is not much disagreeing from the evangelical doctrine of Christ, which monisheth us to flee the broad and wide way that the most part of men walk in, and to enter into the narrow and strait way which is little beaten but leadeth to immortality and life everlasting.³⁶⁵

235. *Adversus solem ne loquitor*

Speak not against the sun.³⁶⁶ That is to say: strive not against manifest [K1ᵛ] and evident things. For the thing that is apparent and which no man denyeth we call as clear as the sun.

237. *Hirundines sub eodem tecto ne habeas*³⁶⁷

Keep no swallows under the same roof of thy house. That is, bring not up, neither keep thou company with such as in thy prosperity seek thy friendship, but in adversity, or when they have their desire, forsake thee. The swallow's property° is in the springtime of the year to repair to a man's house and under his roof to nestle, but so soon as she once hath brought up her young, when it is towards winter, anon she forsaketh his company without any thanksgiving or good turn-doing for harbouring and lodging of her. Such unkind brides, [K2ʳ] or rather beasts, there be not a few in the world, which nevertheless, till they have obtained their prey that they hunt for, pretend to bear most hearty and entire love unto thee. But the end declareth all.

---

³⁶² Taverner is more certain in his interpretation of the proverb than Erasmus is, who cites Jerome, *Against Rufinus* 3. 39, to suggest that it may mean 'add a further burden to those who carry one already; do not help them to lay it down'.
³⁶³ Diogenes Laertius, *Pythagoras*.
³⁶⁴ **Marg**. 'Jerome [*Against Rufinus* 3. 39].'
³⁶⁵ **Marg**. 'Matthew 7.' The spelling of the modern expression 'straight and narrow' obscures the point that 'straight' here means 'narrow', not 'straight ahead'.
³⁶⁶ No source has been identified, though it may, paradoxically, be itself a source for Donne's 'The Sun Rising'.
³⁶⁷ Jerome, *Against Rufinus* 3. 39.

238. *Panem ne frangito*

Break not bread. Here he admonisheth us, sayeth Erasmus, that we break not amity or friendship, which thing is signified by bread. For in old time it was the manner to join friendship by eating together of bread. And therefore also Christ, our captain and saviour, by distributing of bread did stablish and, as it were, consecrate perpetual amity between his disciples and followers. Wherefore, when Pythagoras commanded his disciples not to break bread, he meant not that they should not break the bread which they did eat, but the thing [K2ᵛ] which by breaking of bread in those days was understood, that is to wit,° a sure and perpetual amity and love between themselves. What shall I say? Christian men be indeed breakers, but no eaters of this bread that Pythagoras speaketh of. What discord, what contention, what mortal hatred is between Christians, it would make a true Christian man's heart bleed to see. And yet Christ with a far greater solemnity taught his disciples this concord than ever Pythagoras did.[368] At a solemn supper the night before his departure out of this world from us, he took bread, and thanks given, brake it and said to his disciples, 'Take, eat, this is my body, which is betrayed and broken for you. This do ye in remembrance of me' etc. Lo, with how express and lively a sacrament [K3ʳ] he hath incorporated us into himself. He maketh us all one with him, yea, and all one together within ourselves. And yet setting this most sacred symbol and sacrament at naught, by malice and discord we dissever ourselves one of us from another, yea, and consequently from him that thus in his own body hath knit us together. 'Is not the bread', sayeth St Paul, 'which we break the partaking of the Lord's body?'[369] For we being many be one bread and one body. We be all partakers of one bread and of one cup. Christ himself speaking of Judas, who ungently betrayed him, said, 'He that eateth bread with me hath lifted up his heel against me'. I pray you, do not we Christian men (at least way which will so be called) express and resemble Judas? Yearly by this [K3ᵛ] solemn sacrament we be incorporate in Christ, we be partakers of his body, we eat the mystical bread.[370] This in outward appearance is a symbol and argument of an exceeding unity and burning charity. But inwardly very Judases, yea, and outwardly too, we lift up our heels, we kick, we spurn against Christ. Wherefore to return to my purpose, we be breakers and not eaters or, to speak more truly, we be unworthy eaters of this mystical bread,

---

[368] **Marg.** 'Matt. 26; Mark 14; Luke 22; 1 Corinth. 11.' Christ speaks of 'divisions' and 'factions' among his followers in 1 Corinth. 18–19.

[369] **Marg.** '1 Corinth. 10.'

[370] Yearly ... bread] The annual feast of Corpus Christi on the Thursday after Trinity Sunday. The celebration was contentious in Protestant England, since it affirmed the real presence of Christ in the Eucharist; it was abolished in 1548, but later reintroduced.

not discerning the Lord's body. And for this cause, I mean for the profanation of this sacrament, no doubt the terrible threatenings that St Paul speaketh of be come upon us. Many of us be weak and many sleep.

FINIS

TEXTUAL NOTES

Erasmus in English presents its texts in modernised form. As a rule, if a word form appears as a headword in the *OED*, it is retained; if it appears as a variant of another headword, it is changed to that form. Punctuation is emended. These textual notes explain the editorial procedures specific to individual texts and record significant editorial interventions, as well as substantive variations between editions of a text.

The Manual of the Christian Soldier (1523)

TEXTUAL NOTE

Neither the manuscript of *1523* nor the printed edition of *1533* (with the Prefatory Epistle) exists in more than one version. The present edition is modernised but not over-polished, and obvious errors (chiefly scribal) of omission, displacement, or miswriting have been amended without comment; but where the text makes reasonable sense, in itself or in relation to the Latin, it has been left as it stands: any residual clunkiness might be the translator's. Footnotes or square brackets accompany longer or more significant changes or insertions. The translator's marginal notes have been reproduced selectively. The summarising bracketed cross-heads at the beginnings of chapters are editorial. As *1523* and *1533* are better regarded as distinctive works in their own right (though lineally related) than as witnesses to a single English text, no attempt is made here to record their numerous differences (see also the last paragraph of the Introduction).

Early modern editions surveyed:

- *1523* London, British Library Additional MS 89149 ['Alnwick']. 'A compendeus tretis of the sowdear of Crist called encheridion [...] translated oute of latten into englisshe in the yere of our lorde god [1523]'
- *1533* STC 10479. *A booke called in latyn Enchiridion militis christiani and in englysshe the manuell of the christen knyght* (London: Wynkyn de Worde, 1533). British Library copy [EEBO]

A Treatise upon the Pater Noster (1524)

TEXTUAL NOTE

There are two existing versions of the English *Pater Noster*, both published in London by Thomas Berthelet, and neither dated; '1526' and '1531' are the dates commonly given to them. Apart from some differences in spelling and punctuation, none substantive, they are virtually the same. A third and earlier version ('1524'), equally similar, is credibly supposed to have existed in print but is now lost.

Early modern editions surveyed:

- *1526*   STC 10477. *A devout treatise upon the Pater noster* (London: Thomas Berthelet, n.d. [1526]). The EEBO reproduction of the British Library copy lacks the penultimate facing pages; for these, the transcription by Germain Marc'hadour in *Moreana* 7 (1965) of the only other surviving copy (at Yale) has been followed.
- *1531*   STC 10477.5. *A devout treatise upon the Pater noster* (London: Thomas Berthelet, n.d. [1531]). A single copy survives (at the John Rylands Library, Manchester).

22   then] that *1526*; than *1531*
503   his members] this membre *1526*; his membre *1531*

An Exhortation to the Diligent Study of Scripture (1529)

TEXTUAL NOTE

The 1529 English translation of the *Paraclesis* attributed to William Roy (STC 10493) is the source for all subsequent sixteenth-century versions of the text. It was initially printed with Luther's commentary on 1 Corinthians 7; then alongside a translation of the letter 'To the Pious Reader' from Erasmus's *Paraphrase* of the Gospel of Matthew; and as part of the prefatory materials of several English New Testaments. Many of these volumes are of uncertain character as regards date or publisher. All display minor variations in spelling and punctuation. I have taken the 1529 edition as my base text, incorporating the printer's errata and modernising spelling and punctuation. The notes that follow record substantive editorial interventions to the 1529 text and substantive differences between it and later versions of the text. They do not attempt a full collation of editions or comparison between them. Douglas H. Parker's modern edition collates and compares all non-biblical versions of Roy's text, plus the versions appearing in two New Testaments from 1549 and 1550. I have looked at witnesses to all these bar one: the first 1534 edition (STC 10493.5) exists in a unique copy in the Huntington Library, and here I have relied upon Parker's edition to supply a note of significant variants. I have also added an expanded but incomplete survey of New Testaments.

Modern editions:

- William Roye, 'An exhortation to the diligent studye of scripture' and 'An exposition in to the seventh chapter of the pistle to the Corinthians', ed. by Douglas H. Parker (Toronto: University of Toronto Press, 2000)
- *The Paraclesis of Erasmus of Rotterdam to the Pious Reader*, ed. and trans. by Ann Dalzell, CWE 41. 393–422

Early modern editions surveyed:

- 1529   STC 10493. *An exhortation to the diligent studye of scripture / made by Erasmus Roterodamus. And translated in to inglissh* (Antwerp: Johannes Hoochstraten, 1529)
- 1534a STC 10493.5. *An exhortacyon to the dylygent study of scripture* (Norwich: Robert Wyer, n.d. [1534?])
- 1534b STC 10494. *An exhortacyon to the dylygent study of scripture* (Norwich: Robert Wyer, n.d. [1534?])
- 1536   STC 2835.2. *The new Testament yet once agayne corrected by Wylliam Tyndall*. (s.n., n.d., [1536?])
- 1542   STC 2848. *The Newe Testament yet once agayne corrected* (s.n., n.d. [Antwerp: M. Crom, 1542?])

- 1548 STC 10494.5. *An Exortaction to the diligent study of scripture* (London: Thomas Randalde and Wyllyam Hyll, n.d. [1548?])
- 1549 STC 2856. *The Newe Testament of our saueour* (London, s.n., 1549?)
- 1550 STC 2821. *The new testament in Englishe* (London: John Cawood, 1550)

1	Jerome] Hierome 1529
5	presumption] presumptyou 1529 (corrected in errata on sig. I7ʳ to 'presumption')
13	into] en to 1529 (corrected in errata to 'in')
17	affected] affected 1529; allected 1534b, 1536, 1542, 1548, 1549, 1550
18	and that] paragraph break 1550
20	godly] goodly 1534b, 1548, 1550; godlye 1542, 549
22	or else truly] paragraph break 1549
30	efficacity] efficacye 1534b; efficacie 1548, 1550
31	Now if] paragraph break 1549
31	Now] omitted in 1542
32	of] omitted in 1549
34	season] ceason 1529, 1536, 1542, 1549, 1550; season 1534b, 1548
36	although] And though 1542, 1549
37	strings] strynge 1550
42	efficacity] efficacy 1534b; efficacye 1548
50	them] hem 1550
50	to trouble] trouble 1549; o trouble 1550
51	that] hat 1550
52	into] nto 1550
53	profit] oofyte 1550
61	fiercely] fyersly 1548; fresly 1549; sternly 1550
64	foul] foulde 1542; fouled 1549
66	other natural] othernaturall 1529
69	a whit] awhitte 1529
72	perishing] pressynge 1542; presshinge 1549
72	How be it] paragraph break 1542, 1549
80	had been] had be 1534b, 1548, 1550
83	afar] farre 1536, 1549
110	children] chylden 1550
114	science] sciences 1536, 1549, 1550
124	understood] vnderstonde 1529, 1536, 1542, 1549; vnderstande 1534b; vnderstand 1548, 1550
124	not known] no knowne 1542, 1549
137	should be of the] shulde be the 1548
138	tales] tables 1536, 1542, 1549, 1550

142 truly] trluy 1529 (corrected in errata to 'truly')
143 equally] equall 1534b, 1548
153 worldly] wordly 1529, 1548; worldly 1534b; worldlye 1536, 1542, 1549, 1550
154 worldly] worldye 1529; worldly 1534b, 1548; worldlye 1536, 1542, 1549, 1550
190 then] paragraph break 1542, 1550
190 Christianity] Christente 1529, 1534b, 1536, 1542, 1548, 1549, 1550
193 some deal] soone all 1550
206 disputations] dispitions 1529; dysputacyons 1534b, 1548; dispicyons 1536, 1542, 1549, 1550
209 Let us] paragraph break 1550
217 no] now 1549
217 worldly] wordly 1529, 1534b; worldly 1536, 1548, 1549, 1550; worldlye 1542
218 be he never so rich] be he neuer ryche 1548
220 Why recount] paragraph break 1542, 1550
222 counter] countre 1529, 1536, 1542, 1549, 1550; counte 1534b, 1548
222–23 profane interpreters] porophane interpretors 1529
224 game] gaue 1549
224 tossing] rollynge 1550
228–29 or timber ... rule] of theyr stone, or tymbre to ye rule. 1534b; or tymbre to the rule 1548
233 a life] life a 1549
236–37 it is lawful ... life] But it is lefull for euery man to lyue be a true christen. It is lefull for euery man to a godly lyffe 1549
246 worldly] wordly 1529, 1536; worldly 1534b, 1548; worldlye 1542, 1549; wordlye 1550
248 verily] derelye 1534b, 1548
255 truly are] true are 1536, 1542, 1549; are true 1550
258 The epicure] paragraph break 1542
261 and chiefly] paragraph break 1542
264 but also] But 1536, 1542, 1549; but 1550
267 nother] nother 1529, 1536, 1542, 1548, 1549; other 1534b; no ther 1550
267 make] meke 1550
269 point] poyntes 1550
277–78 can be gathered ... place] can be gathered so frutfully out of no place 1550
278 fruitfully] fruteful 1534a, 1534b; frutful 1548
284 please] blease 1548
294–95 the end of the world] the ende of worlde 1529, 1536, 1542, 1549; the end of the worlde 1534a, 1534b, 1548, 1550
295 For in this] new paragraph 1550
302 there] he 1549
306 embracing] embrace 1550
309 rude] rule 1548

311	Francis's] Franciskes 1529
312	they go] hey go / 1549
313	safety] savete 1529; sauete 1534b, 1536, 1548, 1542, 1549; safete 1550
313	they] thy 1549
324	nor glory] no glory 1529; nor glory 1534a, 1534b, 1548, 1550
332	godly] goodly 1529, 1534a, 1534b, 1548; godly 1536, 1542, 1549, 1550
333	baptised] baptyses 1550
335	O] O 1529, 1534a, 1534b, 1536, 1542, 1548, 1550; On 1549
337	whole] holy 1550
343	the] that 1548
344	In Paul] new paragraph 1536, 1542, 1550
345	vessel] wessel 1529; corrected in subsequent editions
346	thing] thinke 1529; corrected in subsequent editions
347	Duns] Scotus 1542, 1549
348	envy] ennye 1529
352	them] then 1548
352	Why have we them not ever in our hands?] Why haue we not them not euer in oure hands 1550
363	unformed] enformed 1549
364	speech] speace 1549
368	spring] shryng 1534b; shring 1548
374	Let us] paragraph break 1536, 1542, 1550
375	thirst] thriste 1529; thryste 1534b, 1536, 1548, 1549, 1550; thirste 1542;
379	least] laste 1550
396	fruitfully] frutefulle 1548
398	Amen] omitted in 1550

The Dialogue Between Julius the Second, Genius, and Saint Peter (1534)

TEXTUAL NOTE

The English *Dialogue* was printed by Robert Copeland for John Bydell in an undated edition, most likely in 1534. A second edition appeared the following year. The translator is anonymous. I have taken the 1534 edition as my base text. Both the 1534 and 1535 editions print the text as continuous prose. I have presented it as dramatic dialogue, adding in stage directions, principally to clarify the role of Genius. The notes that follow record editorial interventions to the 1534 text and substantive differences between it and the 1535 version of the text.

Modern editions:

- *The Julius exclusus of Erasmus*, trans. by Paul Pascal, ed. by J. Kelley Sowards (Bloomington and London: Indiana University Press, 1968)
- *Julius Excluded From Heaven: A Dialogue*, ed. and trans. by Michael J. Heath, *CWE* 27. 155–97

Early modern editions surveyed:

- 1534? STC 14841.5. *The dialoge between Iulius the seconde, Genius, and saynt Peter* (London: Robert Coplande for John Byddell, n.d. [1534?])
- 1535   STC 14842. *The dyaloge bytwene Iulius the seconde, Genius, and saynt Peter* (London: John Byddell, 1535)

49	called] cal= 1535	
90	Methink] Me think 1534, 1535	
108	wares] warre 1535	
112	laic] layke 1534, 1535	
125	friars] feres 1534, 1535	
158	privily] preuyly 1534; prinyly 1535	
167	been] be 1534; ben 1535	
179	bishoprics] byshopryches 1534, 1535	
195	wholly] holy 1534; holly 1535	
210	masteries] maystryes 1534; maistries 1535	
216	left] leaued 1534; lefte 1535	
219	wisdom] wysdom 1534; wysoome 1535	
249	fly] fle 1534, 1535	
249	fought for the] fought the for 1534; fought for the 1535	
255	hath not Christ] hath not Chryste 1534; hath Chryst not 1535	
294	size] syse 1534, 1535	
301	nonce] nonst 1534; nonest 1535	
329	Bentivolus] Bentinofus 1534, 1535	
335	to rule] to be rule 1535	

340	citizens] cyrezyns 1534, 1535
340	to] so 1535
347	monuments] monnmentes 1534; monumentes 1535
358	spoke] spoke 1534; spake 1535
359	What matters that?] What maters that? 1534; What mater is that? 1535
362	in] in 1534; I 1535
388	(not long ago)] not in parentheses 1535
414	that] ᵗ 1534; the 1535
416	the] che 1535
428	wholly] holely 1534, 1535
441	thinketh] thynke 1535
441	save] saue 1534; but 1535
510	riches] rychesse 1534, 1535
520	choked] cloked 1535
593	summon] somdd 1534; sommonde 1535
595	whole] hole 1534; omitted in 1535
636	riches] rychesses 1534, 1535
667	alien] alyene 1534, 1535
714	somewhat] omitted in 1535
753	hitherto] hyderto 1534; hitherto 1535
770	for] omitted in 1535
776	other] omitted in 1535
783	names] names 1534; maners 1535
791	deeds] dedes 1534; ded 1535
798	of] omitted in 1535 ('manner men')
810	the abusing] thabusyng 1534; the abusynge 1535
836	even] omitted in 1535
885	plucked] blucked 1535
888	I might] I might 1534; I my might 1535
904	to] co 1535
914	of] af 1535
932	nobles] nobylles 1534, 1535
933	brought] bronght 1535
950	people] people people 1535
964	adjoined] adioyned 1534; ioyned 1535
983	beggarly] beggarly 1534; beggery 1535
996	riches] rychesse 1534; richesse 1535
1022	riches] rychesse 1534, 1535
1055	been] be 1534; ben 1535
1058	chimiring] chymyring 1534; chimiryng 1535
1069	as] 1535; omitted in 1534
1127	bar] bare 1534, 1535

1145 forsaking of such] omitted in 1535
1147 interpreting] entrepretynge 1534; enterpretyng 1535
1213 flexible] flexible 1534; vexyble 1535
1228 riches] rychesse 1534, 1535

An Epistle in Praise of Matrimony (1536?)

TEXTUAL NOTE

The only sixteenth-century edition of the *Praise of Matrimony* is the one printed by Robert Redman in late 1532 or early 1533 (see Devereux, p. 8) and the British Library copy of this edition is the copy text for the present edition. The date of 1536 given in the ESTC is almost certainly incorrect. Elisions have been silently expanded (e.g. thintent = the intent). Marginal comments have been included in the footnotes only where they represent a substantive addition to the text.

Modern editions:

- 'A Right Fruitful Epistle … in Laud and Praise of Matrimony' in *Daughters, Wives, and Widows: Writings by Men about Women and Marriage in England, 1500–1640*, ed. by Joan Larsen Klein (Urbana: University of Illinois Press, 1992)

Early modern editions surveyed:

- 1532–33   STC 10492. *A ryght frutefull epystle, deuysed by the moste excellent clerke Erasmns [sic] in laude and prayse of matrimony* (London: Robert Redman, [1532–33]). All citations in the textual notes are to this edition.

1	Erasmus] Erasmns
6	Taverner] Tavernour
56	fruits] fruetz
73	understood] understand
77	increase] crease
100	is said] sayd is
101	contented] contended
127	Jews] Iwes [**marg.**]
131	escape] eschape
142	proof] proue
148	defouling] defoyling
151	adulterers] aduowterers
152	adultery] aduowtre
172–73	eyes not dazzling] yees nat dasselling
184	run] renne
192	fable] fabule [**marg.**]
201	lying] leyng
206	hell] hellys
211–12	*Gamelius … Pronuba … Lucina*] Gamelium … pronubam … Lucinam [Taverner retains the accusative forms from the original Latin]
217	been] be

218	India]	Inde
225	run]	renne
225	lying]	leynge
226	foals]	fooles
230	orchards]	orcheyardes
237	country]	contre
242	buy]	bye
245	jest]	geste
255	a sword]	aswerde
287	worldly]	wordly
320	little off from]	lytle of, from
324	lineage]	lygnage
327	celebrated]	celebrate
328	Jerome]	Hierome
333	describing]	descryuynge
338	slay]	slee
344	For there]	Forther
357	common weal]	commune wele
366	example]	ensample
393	seek it. If ye]	seke it yf ye
395	grief]	greffe
409	Athenian]	Athenyense
412	how) of]	how (of
418	contemn]	contempne
422	increaseth … alliances]	accreseth … alyesses
423	sisters]	systerne
423	nephews]	neuewes
431	burst]	braste
465	adulterous]	aduouterous
465	struck]	stroke
492	single]	sengyll
492	incommodity]	incommodie
496	safer]	sauffer
518	fire. And]	fyar, And
518	troublous]	trobelous
520	wait]	wayght
525	Dulopolitans]	Dupoitans
525	damn]	dampen
566	amiss]	a mys
583	quenched, furthermore]	quenched. Further/-more
589	scarce]	scase
597	wholesomer]	holsommer

Textual Notes

Proverbs or Adages (1545)

TEXTUAL NOTE

Taverner's selection from Erasmus's *Adagia* first appeared in 1539, three years after the last edition to be printed in Erasmus's lifetime. This was expanded in 1545, when Taverner added English versions of the Latin proverbs, and I have used 1545 as my copy text, recording additions to 1539 below. There were further editions in 1550, 1552, and 1569. Taverner does not gives the corresponding numbers of Erasmus's *Adages* for each proverb and I have supplied these, with the exception of a handful which do not appear to have an Erasmian source. I have expanded and sometimes corrected Taverner's references, but I have generally avoided identifying classical sources which he does not refer to. These may be found in *CWE*, to which I am much indebted. Instead, since this edition aims to represent the reception of Erasmus in English, I have cross-referenced Taverner's proverbs in Tilley and I have given occasional illustrations of their use in English texts of the period. I have identified a classical source (following *CWE*, and in many places Erasmus himself) in the relatively few instances where there seems to be no English equivalent in Tilley. I have recorded the marginalia from 1545 where they constitute a substantive addition to the text, but not when they merely act as pointers.

Both the British Library and the EEBO facsimile (taken from the Huntington) copies of 1545 are imperfect and I have used the copy in Edinburgh University Library (shelf mark F^x 33.43) as my copy text. I most grateful to Danielle Spittle for locating this copy, which at the time of my enquiry was not listed either in the online catalogue or the printed catalogue.

I have not attempted to collate the texts of the different editions, but have occasionally recorded variants. Otherwise, all references are to 1545 and represent instances where the process of modernisation might be regarded as emendation.

There is no modern edition of Taverner's English selection from Erasmus's *Adagia*.

Early modern editions surveyed:

- 1539a STC 23711a. Richard Taverner, *The second booke of the Garden of wysdome. (The thyrde boke.)* (London: R. Bankes, 1539). Book III is derived from Erasmus's *Adagia*.
- 1539b STC 10437. [Desiderius Erasmus], *Proverbes or adagies with newe addicions gathered out of the Chiliades of Erasmus by R. Tauerner* (London: R. Bankes, 1539)
- 1545 STC 10438. *Prouerbes or adagies gathered out of the Chiliades of Erasmus by Richarde Tauerner. With newe additions as well of Latyn prouerbes as of Englysshe* (London: E. Whytchurche [sold by William Telotson], 1545)

- 1550 STC 10439. [Title as 1545] (London: W. Powell, 1550)
- 1552 STC 10440. [Title as 1545] (London: N. Hill, 1552)
- 1569 STC 10441. [Title as 1545] (London: W. How, 1569)

5   neat] nette
6   Rotterdam] Roterodam
10   country, I will] country. I will
35   struck] strake
36–37 The English … *dreadeth*] added 1545
43–44 Certainly … *after*] added 1545
48   Jerome] Hierome
53   The English … *sore.*] added 1545
53   *An old*] And old
58–59 And as … *wittily.*] added 1545
59   wise man] wyseman
62   heard] harde
90   Reynard the fox] only the fox 1539b; Raynerd the fox 1545
93   visit his majesty] vysite maiestye 1539b
96   Reynard] ye Foxe 1539b
100   since] sithence 1539b; sythens 1545
108   Aman] Aiman 1539b
126   Gelly] **Marg.** Aulus Gellius 1539b
148   or … *like*] added 1545
157–59 The Englishman … *go*] added 1545
167–70 The English … *craft*] added 1545
184–85 Also … *speed*] added 1545
203–05 Also … the *dead*] added 1545
211   beware] be ware
212   betimes] by tyines
212–13 This … *age*] added 1545
227   adulterer's] aduowterers
238–39 The Englishman … *rueth not*] added 1545
253–55 Also … *goeth by*] added 1545
256   *sententiae*] sentenciae
264–65 Or … *a-sorrowing*] added 1545
271–72 Whereunto … *purse*] added 1545
290–310 Fol. xvi (sigs B8^{r-v}) is missing from the EEBO facsimile
295–96 The English proverb … *shirt*] added 1545
330   fashions] fascyons
356   sciences] sciens
364–65 For as our common … *fingers*] added 1545
370–71 For as our English … *old*] added 1545

407–08 Or as we commonly … *good*] added 1545
454 became] bacame
463 reckless] recheless
468–70 Whereunto … *hath*] added 1545
485 business doubtless] busyness: doubtles
503–05 Also ye may use … *day*] So of al other thynges 1539b
506–07 *Aequalem* … *estate*] 1539b; omitted 1545
524 *Spare … speed*] added 1545
565 allude] illude 1539b, 1545
568–70 Neither … *cometh again*] added 1545
569 run aside] runnen aside
574 man-slayers] mansleers
585 scarce] skace
594–95 To this agreeth … *malt*] added 1545
612–13 Whereunto … *mind*] added 1545
620 *dumtaxat*] duntaxat 1539b, 1545
629 though Christianity] though christianitie 1539; through christianity 1545
647–48 From this … *masteries*] added 1545
650 deceit] disceyt 1539b, 1545
670–72 Yea … *purse*] added 1545
693–94 tyrants that will of their subjects] tyrannes that wol oftheir subgiettes
709–10 If ye require … *none*] added 1545
711 *Furem*] 1539b; *Furum* 1545
729–30 taken: while] taken while
737 is cold] 1539b; in colde 1545
740–41 our English … *tail*] added 1545
742 *Aegroto*] Egroto 1539b, 1545
748 And as we say … *giblet*] added 1545
763–64 For verily … *away*] added 1545
773 fortune] fortue
782 sword] swearde
811 his 6th book] his. vi. boke 1539b, 1545
823 might] mought 1539b, 1545
825 mingled] mengled 1539b, 1545
828 banquetings] bankettynges 1539b, 1545
828 dice] dyes 1539b, 1545
844–63 Fol. xlii (sigs F1^v–F2^r) is missing from the EEBO facsimile
854 our incomparable] oure, incomparable
855 superfluous] superflouse
865 The English … *sign*] added 1545
873–75 We have … *lady*] added 1545
882 report] reaporte

883   hearsay] heare saye
884   *imperatorum*] *imparatorum* 1539b, 1545
891   unlawful] unleful 1539b, 1545
908   Thrust] Thurst 1539b, 1545
920   fierceness] fyernes
940   *Felix*] Foelix 1539b, 1545
949–50   The English ... *a-sorrowing*] added 1545
956   unfortunate] infortunate
965–67   This proverb ... *feet wet*] added 1545
972–74   Our English ... nowadays] added 1545
989   *vis, id*] 1539b, vis id 1545
991   *pecus, non*] pecus non 1539b, 1545
1011   wear] were
1022   like] loke 1539b, looke 1545
1036   jest] geste
1040   daintiness] deyntines
1041   haughtiness] hawtnes
1056–57   *Romano vivito more*] Romano vivite more
1071   achieve] achewe
1091   wet] weat
1096   observe] obshue
1109   *praise*] preisen
1147   assemblies] assembles
1164   whores] hoores
1169   banquets] bankettes
1174   things in place] in thynges place
1178   silence] scilence
1227   wet] weate
1246   painters] payneters
1268   peasants] paisantes
1271   ability] habilitie
1310   slow] slaw
1323   *benevolentia*] benevolencia
1334   equal] egall
1339–40   portion. Who] portion, who
1358   mule] moile 1545, 1552, 1569
1373   parson? Exercise] person exercise
1378   bears] beare
1391   *vehementius*] 1539b; vehementis 1545
1417   farthing] farding
1423   The English ... *sweet*] added 1545
1427   thing uncertain] thynge in certayne

1428–30 And therefore … *need*] added 1545
1438 *Parmenonis*] parmenonis 1539b; Permenonis 1545
1439 The occasion] occasion 1539, 1545
1462 fellowship] felowship 1539b; folowshyp 1545
1479 *Choenici ne insideas*] Coenici ne insides 1539b; Coenici ne insideas 1545
1491 strait] streyght
1491 cast] caue 1539b; caste 1545
1510 mind, but] mynde. But 1539b, 1545
1530 against the sun] ayenste the son 1539b, 1545
1540 harbouring] harbroughynge 1539b; harbroghynge 1545
1552 understood] vnderstande 1539b, 1545
1561 incorporated] incorporate
1573 burning] brennyng 1539b, 1545

NEOLOGISMS

The following words and meanings appear to predate their earliest mention in *OED*, or to vary from their definitions there. References in square brackets are to *OED* sections.

administered[1]	supplied	*Manual* 2400
aforeseason[2]	before, earlier	*Manual* 4621
of fresh	*mod.* afresh	*Manual* 4153
agreeable (*absol.*)	fitting	*Pater Noster* 55
allegory (*attrib.*) [1b]	figurative	*Manual* 415
alienate (*adj.*)	foreign	*Manual* 2243
amain	with full force	*Jul.* 408
anarchy	unrestrained liberty of the people	*Proverbs* 927
anywhither	anywhere	*Manual* 3442
appoint	point to	*Proverbs* 862
appropriate [4b]	belonging particularly	*Manual* 964
assimile	make like	*Manual* 4123
bowel (*sing., fig.*)	inward part ('of soul')	*Pater Noster* 442
bringing up	upbringing	*Manual* 943
bubblish (*v.*)	gush forth	*Pater Noster* 169
buggerer	buggerer	*Jul.* 380
bulls [n. 3. 4]	bubbles, nonsense	*Jul.* 52
call [II. 11] as	name, describe	*Pater Noster* 516
cankered	rusted	*Manual* 1393
canvass	batter, assault	*Manual* 1605
carrionly	loathsome(ly)	*Manual* 4138
cast [1d]	scatter	*Manual* 3080
chimiring	shimmering [speculative]	*Jul.* 1058
chop [4b]	encounter	*Manual* 412
churlish	tenacious[3]	*Manual* 3208
clap out [5c]	drive off	*Manual* 2928
commit (*absol.*)	behave wrongly	*Manual* 3727
commodities[4]	advantages	*Manual* 1570

---

[1] 1523 'and ministered', L. 'sumministratum'.
[2] But s.v. 'season': 'afore seasons'.
[3] L. 'mordicus'.
[4] See s.v. 'commodity' [3].

companion (*v.*)	spend time together	*Proverbs* 224
confederate	to be allied with another in covenant with God	*Matrimony* 381
constitution [3b]	regulated arrangement	*Manual* PE 443
contentious	quarrelsome	*Exh.* 98
corruptious[5]	corrupting	*Manual* PE 439
covert (*sb.*)	disguise	*Manual* PE 564
crotch	fork	*Proverbs* 908
dangerful	dangerous	*Manual* PE 446
decay (*v. tr.*)	make worse	*Manual* 799
deduct	derived, drawn	*Manual* 2235
deface	outshine	*Manual* PE 588
disguised [4]	purported, specious	*Manual* 4443
dispute	maintain	*Matrimony* 165
dissemble [3] at	ignore	*Manual* PE 303
disworshipful	dishonourable	*Proverbs* 587
either [3b] other	either	*Manual* 1591
enarration	commentary	*Manual* 4759
enhonest	make honourable	*Matrimony* 69
enleagued	allied	*Jul.* 205
enforcement[6]	encouragement	*Manual* 1379
every [4a]	each	*Pater Noster* 122
exaggerate	emphasise	*Manual* PE 494
ex[s]timulate	*mod.* stimulate	*Manual* PE 402
fall [62e] into	be taken by	*Manual* 4735
fall [94d] out	disagree	*Manual* 4173
fatness (*fig.*)	healthy condition	*Manual* 486
fatted	*mod.* fattened	*Pater Noster* 440
feeder [4a]	shepherd	*Manual* PE 178
fetch (*sb.*)	far-reaching effort	*Proverbs* 775
fiercely (*adj.*)	fierce	*Pater Noster* 267
figurate	figurative, symbolic	*Manual* 423
firely (*adj.*)	fiery	*Pater Noster* 222
for [27]	in proportion to	*Manual* 1424
footstool	support for feet	*Pater Noster* 196
gallant	fine, splendid	*Proverbs* 475
gentilely	in a gentile manner	*Jul.* 851
give [55b] back	retreat	*Manual* 140

[5] 1533 'corruptuous'.
[6] See s.v. 'enforce' [2].

Neologisms

cast one's gorge [5]	vomit food	*Manual* 3044
gout	sluice, drain	*Manual* 644
gratuit	free	*Matrimony* 7
griper	extortioner	*Manual* 4413
gross [13]	dull, stupid	*Manual* 2259
grosshead	dullard	*Manual* 2954
grossness [5]	stupidity	*Manual* 713
handsome [1b]	convenient	*Manual* 1369
herd-master	shepherd	*Pater Noster* 279
illustrate	made illustrious	*Jul.* 331
imbecility	feebleness	*Pater Noster* 459
impleasant	unpleasing	*Pater Noster* 518
improperation[7]	private possession	*Manual* 3220
incitate	incited	*Jul.* 916
inquinate	pollute	*Manual* 3724
institution [6a]	regulated arrangement	*Manual* PE 607
instruct [4]	equip	*Manual* 601
jolly [*adj.* 12]	splendid	*Manual* 1778
jot	tiny mark	*Manual* 467
jump (*adv.*)	precisely	*Proverbs* 360
laic	lay	*Jul.* 112
learning [2c]	teaching	*Manual* 2963
logicianer	logician	*Manual* 3274
macerate	cause to waste away	*Jul.* 132
magnifical	glorious	*Manual* PE 615
mancipate	bind oneself	*Manual* 4056[8]
of this manner	thus	*Manual* 257
masqueries	masques	*Jul.* 209
mean [1e] of	refer to	*Manual* 4034
minionly	delicately	*Proverbs* 1037
misfame (*v.*)	insult, abuse	*Pater Noster* 105
mix [1c] to	intersperse with	*Manual* 796
mocking-stock	laughing-stock	*Manual* 4296
momentary	transitory	*Manual* 1463
monstrous	marvellous	*Manual* 767
moreover	nevertheless, setting aside[9]	*Manual* 2900
morrow-meal	next day's meal	*Pater Noster* 420
nearly	carefully	*Jul.* 1200

[7] 1523 'in properation'.
[8] From a passage supplied from 1533.
[9] L. 'caeterum'.

niggish	niggardly	*Manual* 3842
obtest	implore	*Matrimony* 588
oration [3]	language	*Manual* 2082
own white son	favourite, *n.*	*Proverbs* 972
partly	on the one hand (not only)	*Manual* 2542[10]
partaking	taking sides	*Manual* 805
pastime	occupation	*Manual* 2043
perceivance	perception	*Manual* 184
perfect [*adj.* 7]	fully aware	*Jul.* 896
permit [*v.* 4]	hand over	*Manual* 3924
persticious	superstitious	*Jul.* 772
pertness	impudence	*Manual* 409
philautia	self-love	*Manual* 2757
pleatings	pleadings, wranglings	*Exh.* 194
plunge [1b]	raise	*Manual* 1372[11]
poison	poisonous	*Manual* 708
preface	inscription[12]	*Pater Noster* 84
preposterous	topsy-turvy	*Manual* 2216
prodigious	causing wonder	*Manual* 3645
propense	well-disposed	*Jul.* 671
pure (*sb.*)	clear surface	*Manual* 4724
rechant	recant	*Matrimony* 329
recompense (*v.*)	balance against[13]	*Manual* 4620
repurge	cleanse again	*Matrimony* 159
resist	retaliate	*Exh.* 195
revel out	squander	*Pater Noster* 587
reward	gift, oblation[14]	*Pater Noster* 522
rigorousness	rigour	*Manual* 1328
bear the room [12c] of	represent	*Manual* 3441
ruffle	embrace rudely	*Proverbs* 1318
ruffler	vagabond	*Jul.* 16
sacrilegean	one guilty of sacrilege	*Jul.* 740
savour [4a] of	be characterised by	*Manual* 3269
scabby	scabbed	*Pater Noster* 619[15]
scamble	struggle with others	*Proverbs* 440

[10] Here (and at 422, 4075, and 4720) 1523 renders L. 'cum ... tum' ('not only *this* but moreover *that*': rhetorically moving to a climax, not describing distributively).
[11] L. 'emergere'.
[12] L. 'inscriptione'.
[13] L. 'compensabis'.
[14] From God or due to him; see also line 51.
[15] See note 80 in text.

Neologisms

schoolman	academic	*Manual* PE 52
sensibly [3a]	vividly	*Manual* 1229
servantly	servile	*Pater Noster* 30
set forth [144h, i]	favour, give priority to	*Pater Noster* 354
size [n. 1, 12b]	kind	*Jul.* 294
sodomity	sodomy	*Jul.* 784
sudden [A.7]	extempore	*Manual* 4732
summulary	summariser	*Manual* PE 54
symbol	brief or sententious statement	*Proverbs* 1473
out of taste [4b]	unable to discriminate	*Manual* 170
tey	tie	*Matrimony* 433
troubled	tampered with	*Jul.* 2
unattempt	unattempted	*Jul.* 904
usurp [4b]	take (not wrongly)	*Manual* 1740
utter [8a]	reveal	*Manual* 4581
veil	snare[16]	*Manual* PE 581
vileness[17]	low condition	*Manual* 3984
vileness	lowliness	*Pater Noster* 15
visor	*fig.* outward appearance	*Manual* 1324
voice [9b]	word	*Manual* 1706
war (*v.*) [2d]	serve as soldier	*Manual* 109
waster	cudgel	*Manual* 952
wise	alert, careful[18]	*Manual* PE 557
wonder [*v.* 3a]	*trans.* (without 'at')	*Manual* 2953

---

[16] L. 'nassam' for 'veils and net'.
[17] Miswritten in 1523 as 'violence'.
[18] L. 'cavendum'.

GLOSSARY

abate	*tr.* diminish, weaken
abhor	shrink (from)
abide	remain
abound	**abound in one's own sense**, follow one's own opinion (*OED* 4)
about to	engaged in, preparing for
abroad	spread out
abrogate	annulled, abolished
accompany	join together
according	*adj.* fitting, seemly; **according to**, in accordance with
acquaintance	familiarity
acquit	repay; **acquitted**, discharged (of a debt)
acrase	impair, weaken
adamant	loadstone
administer	supply
admonish	forewarn
advance	extol, praise; magnify; boast of
advertise	1. warn, notify; 2. advise; **advertisement**, advice
advise	**advisement**, caution, consideration; **well-advised**, thinking clearly
affect	*also* **affection** (*sb.*), desire, feeling, emotion, passion; **affected**, inclined, disposed; **affectuous**, ardent, eager, with feeling
affiance	trust
aforeseason	before, earlier
after	according to, in accordance with
again	1. back, in reply; 2. on the other hand; 3. in turn
against	near the beginning of (*OED* 11)
agree	**agree to**, adjust, accommodate oneself to; **agreeable**, suitable, appropriate, corresponding
alien	*v.* alienate; **alienate**, *adj.* foreign, unconnected
allect	persuade, entice, elicit
allow	approve, commend
all-to	completely
allure	win over
Almaines	Germans
amain	with full force

Glossary

among	1. all the while; 2. sometimes
an	if
and	*also* **and if**, if
anon	1. at once, straight away; 2. soon
anywhither	anywhere
apace	quickly
apert	manifest
appete	*v.* desire; **appetite**, will, preference
appoint	1. equip, supply; 2. point to
appose	challenge, examine
appropriate	belonging particularly
approve	1. prove; 2. confirm
arbitrament	right, free exercise
arquebuses	firearms
array	ranks
artificer	practitioner
as	as though, as if; 'e.g.'
assay	attempt
assent	common mind
assimile	make like
astonied	dazed, bewildered
at all	in every way
at a time	sometimes
attendance	attention
attent	attentive
audience	1. hearing; 2. attention
avoid	1. remove, banish; 2. fend off
await	**lay await**, waylay, prepare to ambush
a whit	at all
back	**give back**, retreat; **put back**, repulse
band	shackles, imprisonment
bare	poor, scanty
bargain	agreement
bate	strife, enmity
bead-roll	list of persons prayed for
bear	**bear oneself in hand**, be sure, reckon; **bear the room**, represent
because	so that
beck	gesture, command
Bedlam	mad
be it in case	it may be that

Belial	the Devil
beside	away from, without
betime	promptly, early
bewray	reveal
bid	1. threaten; 2. enjoin, command
black choler	bile
board	table; **meat-board**, dining-table
bolt	sift
bond	enslaved
bourd	jest
brabble	*v.* quarrel, clamour; **brabbling**, quarrelling
braid	outburst, commotion
brawl	quarrel
breast	voice
bruit	*sb.* reputation; **bruited**, spoken of, reputed
bubblish	gush
buckler	shield
Burgony	Burgundy
busily	earnestly; **business**, anxiety, care, trouble
but if	unless
by	1. for; 2. to; 2. during; **by and by**, immediately
caduke	transitory, perishable
caitiffs	wretches
calends	festival (new moon)
cankered	rusted
canvass	batter, assault
care	be anxious; **careful**, worried; **careless**, untroubled
carnal	worldly
carrion(ly)	loathsome, corpse-like
case	**be it in case**, it may be that
cast	1. add; 2. scatter; 3. forecast, anticipate; **cast one's gorge**, vomit food
casualty	chance; **casualties**, incidental charges
cautel	caution, care
cavillation	quibble
certes	assuredly, certainly
challenge	claim
chance	*sb.* 'ups and downs'; *v.* happen
change	exchange
charge	responsibility
chauffed	heated

Glossary

chaw	chew
cheap	*v.* offer a price for; **cheaper**, *sb.* buyer
check	*sb.* trick, clever argument; *v.* 1. rebuke, reprove; 2. counter; **checking**, *adj.* catching out
chide	give abuse
choler	**black choler**, bile
chop	encounter
churlish	coarse, tough, tenacious
claw	**claw by the back**, flatter
clearness	glory, splendour
clerk	scholar; **clerkly**, scholarly, erudite
cloister	domain; **cloisterer**, monk; **cloisters**, womb
clout	mend with a patch
coaction	compulsion
cockle	weed, thorn
cod	husk, pod
cognisance	badge or device of recognition
colour	appearance; **coloured**, 1. simulated; 2. specious
comely	decent, honest
comfort	*v.* strengthen; **comfortable**, 1. cheering; 2. refreshing
comment	commentary
commit	*absol.* behave badly
commixtion	mixing, intermarrying
commodious	of advantage; **commodity**, advantage, benefit
commonalty	1. civic community, commonwealth, state; 2. common people
communication	conversation
companion	*v.* spend time together
compendious	*adj.* 1. summary, succinct; 2. direct
composition	dispensation, discharge of liability
conceit	1. opinion; 2. fancy; design; **in conceit**, highly esteemed
conclude	**to conclude, in conclusion**, briefly
conditions	behaviour
confederate	be allied with another in covenant with God
confess	proclaim one's belief courageously
confirmable	1. compliant; 2. harmonious
confusion	ruin
conglutinate	joined together
conject	infer; **conjecture**, 1. indication; 2. proof
conjure	invoke
conscience	consciousness
consequently	next in order

constitution	1. regulated arrangement, institution; 2. ordaining
contemn	despise
content	*v.* fill
contract	shrunken
convenient	befitting
conversant	1. dwelling; 2. associating; **conversation**, 1. fellowship; 2. way of life, conduct
convert	redirect, turn
conveyance	skilful contrivance
cope	a long cloak
copy	abundance
corrupt	spoil, ruin; **corruptious**, corrupting
cost	*v.* spend money
counterfeit	1. imitate, copy (without deceit); 2. represent
couple	tie together
covert	*sb.* disguise, pretext; *adj.* hidden
covet	desire (not necessarily with envy)
cowl	monk's hooded garment
craft	artifice; **craftily**, skilfully
crake	boast; **craking**, boastful
creature	creation
cressets	vessels containing flammable material
crook	bend, curve
cross	bishop's staff, crosier
crotch	fork
cruel	hard, severe
cry upon	exclaim against, complain about
cumbrous	troublesome
cunning	*adj.* 1. skilful; 2. learned; *sb.* learning, knowledge, expertise
cure	*sb.* care, attention; *v.* care for; **curiously**, carefully
currish	base
custom	habitual practice; **customable**, habitual, regular
customs	taxes
daintiness	fastidiousness
damask	rose-water
damn	condemn
dart	missile
dastard	1. dullard; 2. coward
dazzling	confused, dimmed
debate	*sb.* contention, fight

decay	*tr.* make worse
deck	1. clothe; 2. equip
declaration	explanation
deduct	*part.* derived, drawn
deface	outshine
defamed	having a bad reputation
default	shortcomings
define	prescribe
defoul	violate
defy	1. curse; 2. reject
delectable	delightful
delicate	*sb.* delight
deliciously	pleasantly
depart	distinguish, separate; **depart with**, surrender
deprave	corrupt
desire	invite
despiteful	insulting
devoid	remove, put to flight
devoir	endeavour
dight	appointed (for)
dilate	amplify
disagree	differ
disallow	disapprove
disannul	cancel
discreet	judicious, fair; **discretion**, good judgement
discuss	investigate
disdainous	disdainful
disease	*v.* 1. unsettle; 2. harm
disguised	specious, pretended; **disguising**, masquerade
dishonest	*v.* dishonour; **dishonesty**, dishonour, disgrace
displeasure	discomfort
disport	recreation
dispute	maintain
dissemble at	ignore
dissimule	overlook
disworship	disgrace; **disworshipful**, dishonourable
divers	several (not necessarily diverse); **diversity**, distinction, difference
document	evidence
doddypoll	fool
doom	judgement, decision
doubt	fear

drunker	drunkard
dumpish	insensible
durance	continuance
durst	darest
dusk	*v.* obscure
ear	*v.* plough
earnest	pledge, foretaste
easy	1. light; 2. poor; 3. uncommitted; **easier**, venial; **easily**, poorly, ineffectively
edify	build up, strengthen
effectuous	effectual; **effectuously**, 1. effectively; 2. urgently
eftsoons	a second time
eisell	vinegar
eke	also
elders	those who lived in former times
election	choice
embassades	ambassadorial delegations
enarration	commentary
endeavour	work hard
endote	endow
enforce	strive; **enforcement**, 1. encouragement; 2. endeavour
engine	1. artifice; 2. structure
enhonest	make honourable
enjoin	prescribe (for)
enleagued	allied
ensearch	examine
ensue	*tr.* imitate, follow
entice	make attractive
entitled	addressed
envy	grudge
equal	just
equity	1. what is fair and right; 2. justice
errant	wandering
estate	condition
ethnic	pagan, non-Christian
evangely(-ies)	Gospel(s)
even	namely
every	each
evil	1. imperfect(ly); 2. bad(ly)
exaggerate	emphasise
except	unless, if … not

exercise	practice
expert	knowledgeable, experienced
eyen	eyes
face	1. bearing; 2. effrontery
fact	deed
faculty	ability
facund	*also* **facundious**, eloquent
failing	dying out
fain	obliged
fall into	be taken by
fame	reputation
familiar	close friend
fancy	supposition, arbitrary notion
fantasy	imagination
fardel	1. bundle; 2. burden
fashions	1. manners; 2. behaviour
fatness	*fig.* healthy condition
fautors	adherents
favour	*sb.* goodwill, grace; *v.* make to look well; **-favoured**, -looking
fear	frighten
feat	*sb.* skill; **featly**, 1. aptly; 2. cleverly
feeder	shepherd
feign	1. invent; 2. fashion; **feigning**, fiction
fetch	*sb.* far-reaching effort
fie!	(expression of disgust) 'so much for …!'
fiend	enemy, the Devil
figure	*v.* represent; **figurate**, illustrative
find	1. devise; 2. provide for
finish	bring to perfection
firely	*fig.* burning, ardent
foil	defile
follow	strive after
fond	foolish
font-stone	receptacle for water at baptism
for	1. in proportion to; 2. instead of; 3. because; 4. in return for
foresters	forest-dwellers
forge	make
former	front
for so much	forasmuch

forth	**set forth**, favour
fortune	happen
frame	fare; **out of frame**, disordered
fray	*sb.* brawl; *v.* scare
fretteth	angers
from	1. without; 2. away from
froward	perverse, refractory
fruition	enjoyment
frustrate	*adj.* useless
fugitive	fleeting
fulfil	1. fill; 2. do; 3. observe; 4. keep
gallant	fine, splendid
gape	long, desire
gender	*v.* create, engender
generation	family, stock
Gentile	pagan, non-Christian; **gentilely**, in a gentile or pagan manner
gentle	1. noble; 2. graceful, refined; **gently**, generously
ghostly	spiritual
give back	*also* **give place**, retreat, withdraw; **give room**, make way
glass	mirror
gloze	*v.* elaborate speciously
good	**make good**, fulfil, perform
gorge	throat; **cast one's gorge**, vomit food
go to	get away! (playful expression of impatience or disbelief)
gout	sluice, drain
gratuit	free
grece	step, stair
grin	*v.* bare teeth (unsmiling)
griper	extortioner
gross	crude, dull; **grosshead**, dullard
groundly	thorough(ly), well-groundedly
grudge	1. complain, recoil; 2. trouble, grieve
grutch	complaint
guise	manner
gule	gluttony
habergeon	coat of mail
habit	1. dress; 2. demeanour
hale	in good health
halt	*v.* limp; *adj.* (*also* **halting**), lame

hand	**bear oneself in hand**, be sure, reckon
handsome	handy, convenient
handwriting	written bond
hang	*also* **hang of**, depend upon
hap	turn out; **haply**, perchance, perhaps
hardily	firmly
hardly	with difficulty
harness	equipment
haunt	company
haut	haughty
havour	behaviour
health	1. well-being; 2. salvation
heap	*v.* gather
heart-burning	resentment
heartless	1. sluggish; 2. foolish
heat	fervour
herb	crop, pasture
herd-master	shepherd
hest	bidding, attraction
hie	hasten
high-minded	arrogant
hold	*sb.* stronghold; **hold up**, support, back up; **holding**, mean, grasping
holocaust	burnt offering
honest	*v.* honour, adorn; *adj.* honourable, good; **honesty**, goodness, honour
howbeit	1. though, although; 2. nevertheless
humanity	human learning, culture, literary learning or scholarship in the classical languages
husband	manager
if	though
ill	*sb.* evil; *adv.* wrongly; **ill-favoured**, ugly
illustrate	adorned, made illustrious
imbecility	feebleness, weakness
imperfect	not ultimate
impery	1. supreme rule, command, sovereignty; 2. empire
impleasant	unpleasing
improperation	impropriation, private ownership
incitate	incited
incogitable	inconceivable
incommodity	1. misfortune; 2. disadvantage

incontinent	intemperate
increase	provision, sustenance
indifferent	impartial, equal, neutral, impartially applicable; **indifferently**, equally
indiscreet	of poor judgement
induce	1. lead; 2. draw
indurate	obstinate, hardened
inexpert	lacking experience
inquinate	*v.* pollute
instinction	instigation
institution	regulated arrangement
instruct	1. equip; 2. instructed
intellection	meaning
interlude	play
intermeddle	concern oneself with (not necessarily unwelcomely)
inurance	exercise
invade	attack
jeopard on	run risk against; **jeopardous**, dangerous
jolly	splendid
jot	tiny mark
juggler	magician, trickster
jump	*adv.* precisely
kaiser	emperor
kind	*sb.* 1. species; 2. specific nature; 3. sex; *adj.* genuine, close; **out of kind**, degenerate, improper
know	1. make known; 2. recognise, acknowledge; **knowledge**, *v.* acknowledge
laic	of the laity
large	widespread; **largely**, 1. generously; 2. abundantly, fully
lash (out)	lavish
latchet	thong
laud	praise
lawfully	freely
lay at	assault; **lay await**, waylay, prepare to ambush
learning	doctrine, teaching
leavings	remains
legeys	leagues
let	*sb.* hindrance, obstruction; *v.* hinder
letters	1. learning; 2. writings

lever	rather, preferable
lewd	1. wicked, evil; 2. unlearned
lickerous	1. greedy; 2. lecherous
liefer	rather
light	**set light by**, despise
lightly	easily
like	*v.* please, suit; *adj.* likely; **likelihood**, likeness; **likeliness**, promise of success
lin	cease
list	1. *sb.* limit (*OED* II.8.a); **lists**, bounds; 2. *v.* desire
livelihood	revenue, sustenance; **living**, manner of life; **lively**, 1. fresh; 2. alive;
losels	worthless persons
Lucifer	day-star, the Devil
lucky	blessed, fortunate; **luckily**, successfully
lucre	advantage, good, benefit
lure	trap; **make to the lure**, (falconry) entice hawk to decoy
lust	desire, inclination; **lusty**, 1. eager, vigorous; 2. beautiful
macerate	waste through fasting
magnifical	glorious
make good	fulfil, perform; **make sure**, believe to be all right
malapert	wicked
mancipate	bind, subject oneself
manners	character, disposition
manqueller	murderer
margarite	pearl
mark	end, objective, target
masqueries	masques
masteries	**make masteries**, perform a notable deed
match with	combat
matter	1. basis, source; 2. opportunity, potential
mean	*sb.* moderation; *adj.* 1. (in the) middle; 2. moderate; **mean season**, meanwhile
mean of	*v.* allude, refer to
measure	*sb.* moderation; *v.* regulate, balance
meat	food; **meat-board**, dining-table
meddle	concern oneself with (not necessarily unwelcomely), busy oneself; **meddling**, mingling
meek	*v.* humble, lower
meet	*adj.* fitting, suitable; **meetly**, *adj.* moderate, tolerable
member	limb, organic part

mere	sheer, unmixed
mess	dish
methink	it seems to me
mind	*sb.* care; *v.* wish
minionly	delicately
minished	diminished
mischief	wickedness; **mischievous**, evil
misdeem	judge unfavourably
misfame	insult, abuse
mislike	displease
miss	*sb.* lack
mocking-stock	laughing-stock
molest	injurious
monish	warn; **monished**, warned
monstrous	marvellous, prodigious
moreover	nevertheless, 'setting that aside'
morrow-meal	next day's meal
mortal	deadly; **mortiferous**, causing death
most	greatest
mote	speck
mountenance	mass
murderer	**privy murderer**, knife
murmur	complain
murrain	plague
musk-ball	perfume receptacle
mystical	allegorical [1523]; spiritual [PE]
namely	particularly, especially
narrowly	with close attention
natural(ly)	by nature, ingrained
naughty	1. nasty; 2. unfavourable; **naughtiness**, (serious) wickedness
nearly	carefully
needs	necessarily
never neither	none at all
neverthelater	nevertheless
niggish	stingy, mean
no nother	nothing else
nominal	*sb.* (philosophical) nominalist
nonce	**for the nonce**, deliberately, expressly
note	point out
nother	neither

noy	*v.* harm; **noisome**, harmful; **noyance**, harm, trouble; **noyous**, injurious
obduration	hardening
obtest	implore
occasion	opportunity
occupy	1. carry on, practise; 2. make use of
of	1. from; 2. by; 3. for the duration of; 4. for, concerning
office	1. duty; 2. service; **officer**, place-holder, official
once	1. at all, even; 2. some time; **at once**, 3. all together; 4. definitively; 5. some (future) time
only	*adj.* alone; *adv.* exclusively
oppress	crush, overpower, subdue
or	ere, before
oration	language; **orator**, petitioner, suppliant
ordinance	provision
original	*sb.* maker
orison	prayer
other	*conj.* or; *adj.* another
otherwhiles	sometimes
out of frame	disordered
overcharged	burdened
over good	too good
overhip	neglect
overrun	overtake, outrun
own white son	*sb.* favourite
painful	1. arduous; 2. painstaking, hard-working
painted	purported, feigned
pall	robe, cloak
pardon	condone, allow
part	share; **parts**, function; **party(-ies)** side(s); **partial**, biased (for *or* against); **part-taking**, taking sides; **partly**, 'on the one hand (but also)'
pass	1. excel, surpass; 2. turn out; **passed**, surpassed; **passen**, pass
pastance	recreation
pastime	occupation
pate	head
paynim	pagan
peace	*v.* calm
peevishness	foolishness

pencil	brush
peradventure	perhaps
perfect	1. mature, finished; 2. fully aware
Peripatetic	follower of Aristotle
permit	hand over
permixtion	intermingling
perpendeth	ponders
persticious	superstitious
phylactery	small container for Scripture texts
pick-quarrel	quarrelsome person
pilgrimage	journey (not necessarily religious)
piller	thief
place	**give place**, withdraw
pleatings	pleadings, wranglings
poison	poisonous
policy	diligence
poll	rob
pomander	perfumed ball or container
port	1. bearing; 2. style of living
possession	inheritance
powder	dust
praty	1. ingenious; 2. crafty
preface	inscription
pregnant	full of ideas, sharp
preposterous	topsy-turvy, disordered
present	effective, powerful; **presently**, 1. now, directly; 2. in one's presence
press	*sb*. throng, pressure
pretend	profess
prevent	1. go before, anticipate; 2. supplant; **preventing**, delaying
price	value, esteem, worth
prick	*sb*. 1. tiny mark; 2. goad, vexation; *v*. incite
privy	inmost; **privities**, secrets, secret places; **privy murderer**, knife; **privily**, secretly
probable	plausible
probation	proof
profit	*sb*. advantage, good; *v*. advance; **profitable**, helpful, beneficial
propense	well-disposed
proper	1. one's own, distinct; 2. appropriate
property	nature, characteristic behaviour, individual quality
proportion	shape

prorogue	1. extend; 2. suspend
prove	1. try, test; 2. experience; **proved**, esteemed, attested
provident	having foresight
provoke	summon, call, urge (to action)
pump	the well of a ship where bilge water collects
pure	*sb.* clear surface
purge	exonerate
pursuer	persecutor
purveyance	provision
put back	repulse; **put by**, divert, put aside; **put out**, expel; **put unto**, impose
quean	prostitute
quick	1. alive; 2. acute, sharp-minded; **quicken**, enliven, give life to; **quickness**, liveliness
quiddities	essences
quit	*v.* repay; *adj.* clear, settled
rack	animal feeding-frame
rank	fertile
rascal	rabble
rathe	quickly
ravener	plunderer
real	*sb.* (philosophical) realist
reason	method, principle
reaver	robber
rebuke	disgrace, shame
reckless	careless
recompense	1. balance, weigh against; 2. give in return
record	*sb.* witness; *v.* meditate, ponder
recount	reckon; **recounted**, regarded (as); **recounting**, reckoning
refel	disprove
regenerate	brought back to life
rehearse	1. narrate, recite, set out; 2. mention; **rehearsed**, described
relieve	1. raise; 2. restore; 3. feed
religious	monastic
remember	remind
represent	1. imitate, reproduce; 2. manifest
repugn	oppose, fight against, contend (with); **repugnant**, contradictory
repurge	cleanse again

require	1. request; 2. wish; 3. enquire about
resist	remain
resort	coming together
respect	*sb.* attention, consideration, reference, reckoning; *v.* refer
revel out	squander
revocate	recall
revolve	turn back
reward	gift, offering
rift	belch
right	*adv.* precisely
riot	debauchery; **riotous**, debauched
rivelled	wrinkled
roborate	strengthened
room	1. office, role; 2. place, authority, rank; **bear the room**, represent; **give room**, make way
rout	*sb.* horde; *v.* snore
royalty	lordship, high rank
rude	1. uneducated; 2. common
ruffle	1. disturb, unsettle; 2. embrace rudely; **ruffling**, tumult, disorder
ruffler	vagabond, especially used of soldiers
rush	*sb.* stalk
sacrilegean	one guilty of sacrilege
sadly	seriously, steadfastly; **sadness**, gravity
sallet	helmet, headpiece
saving	though, except
savour	have the quality
scamble	struggle with others
scant	scarcely
scarcely	sparingly
scholar	student
schoolmen	academics, theologians
science	(branch of) knowledge; set of skills
scold	quarrel
scrip	bag
scripture	inscription, writing
season	time; **aforeseason**, before, earlier; **mean season**, meanwhile
seely	1. pious; 2. pitiful; 3. foolish; 4. insignificant
seignior	elder, noble
self	same

semblable	like; **semblably**, similarly; **semblant**, *sb.* appearance
sensible	connected with *or* perceived by the senses; **sensibly**, vividly; **sensual**, of the senses; **sensuality**, sense-faculties
sentence	idea, sentiment
servage	slavery; **servantly**, servile
set by	esteem, value; **set light by**, despise; **set of**, regard(ed); **set forth**, favour
setting	planting
shadow	1. image, reflection; 2. cloak, pretence; **shadowed**, cast into shade
shamefast	modest, reticent (used in both a positive and a negative sense); **shamefastness**, modesty
shawms	wind instruments, ancestors of the oboe
shift	expedient, device
shiver	break, split; **to-shivered**, broken, split
shop	workshop
short	small; **shortly**, at once
show	inform
shrewd	1. shrewish, bad-tempered; 2. malicious
sicker	assured
simoniac	one who trades in sacred matters or spiritual goods
singleness	honesty
singularity	separateness; **singularly**, individually
sink	sewer, pit, cesspool
sith	*also* **sith that**, since
sitting	suitable
skill	*sb.* cause; *v.* 1. have knowledge (of); 2. matter, make a difference; 3. concern, matter to
slander	shame, disgrace; **slanderous**, shameful
sleeper	*adj.* asleep
smell	be perceptive
snaffle	bridle-bit
so	provided, so long as
soaken	dull
sod	boiled
sodomity	sodomy
solace	recreation, leisure
some deal	somewhat
somewhat	something
sore	*adv.* intemperately
sorry	dismal
sortilege	fortune-teller

souse	immerse
sovereign	excellent; **sovereign lady**, concubine
space	time
spare	*v.* hoard; **sparing**, economising
spice (of)	kind (of); **spiced**, over-scrupulous, delicate
spill	destroy
spirituality	clergy
spoil	plunder, remove
sport	*v.* be delighted
spot	stain
square	right-angled measuring tool
stand by	depend on
standing	military station
starting holes	escape routes
state	dignitary
stay	*v.* support
stews	brothels
stick	hesitate; **stick at**, object to
stock	block, inanimate lump
stomach	'heart' (seat of thoughts and desires)
stow	store safely, protect
straight(ly)	1. directly; 2. immediately
strait	1. confined, narrow; 2. rigorous
stripe	blow, lash
study	*sb.* 1. desire, interest, aim; 2. effort, application; 3. occupation, project; *v.* 1. intend, attempt, 2. strive, aim; 3. engage in; **studious**, heedful
style	*lit.* pen; *fig.* writing
subscribe	write next
substance	wealth
sudary	napkin bearing traces of sweat
sudden	extempore
suffer	1. let, permit; 2. bear, put up with; **sufferance**, permission, allowance
summulary	(theological) summariser
supplant	bring down
suppose	intend
sure	dependable; **make sure**, believe to be all right; **surety**, confidence
sustentation	maintenance
symbol	brief or sententious statement

table	tablet, picture
take	consider
tarry	wait for
taste	**out of taste**, unable to discriminate
temporal	*sb.* the lay people
tempt	attempt
tender	*v.* hold dear
that	that which
thought	anxiety
thrall	captive
tillage	agriculture
time	**at a time**, sometimes
tire	dress, attire
tittle	tiny mark
to-shivered	broken, split
touch	mention; **touching**, concerning; **touching as**, given that, considering
tow	flaxen fibre, hemp
to wit	namely
toy	amusement
train	trap
translate	move
treacle	salve, medical compound
treatable	tractable
tree	wood
trope	obliquely used word or phrase
troubled	tampered with
trow	believe
try	measure, test; **try with**, tackle, engage
turn	apply
twain	two
unattempt	unattempted
underset	support, shore up
uneath	scarcely
unhappy	wicked
unhonest	dishonourable, unseemly
unied	united
unkind	ungrateful
unmeet	unfitting, inappropriate, unsuitable
unshamefastness	immodesty

unthrifts	dissolute or prodigal persons; **unthrifty**, 1. degenerate, base; 2. wasteful
unware	*adv.* unexpectedly; *adj.* ignorant
uplandish	rustic
use	*sb.* experience; *v.* observe, practise
usurp	take (not necessarily wrongly)
utter	*adj.* distant, foreign; *v.* reveal
vantage	advantage
veil	snare, net
very	*adj.* true, real, actual; *adv.* genuinely
victim	animal for sacrifice
vigils	watches
vile	lowly (not necessarily loathsome); **vileness**, low condition, lowliness
virtue	strength, effectiveness
visor	outward appearance, disguise
vitiate	vitiated
voice	word, saying
voluptuous	of the senses (not necessarily inordinate); **voluptuousness**, indulgence of senses
wait	*sb.* ambush; *v.* manifest, inflict; **lie in wait**, waylay, prepare to ambush; **wait on**, serve, benefit
want	lack, need
ware	1. perceptive, knowledgeable; 2. vigilant, wary, cautious
warn	advise, notify
wasteful	destructive
waster	cudgel
watch	*sb.* 1. religious vigil; 2. staying awake; 3. vigilance
weal	*also* **wealth**, well-being, happiness
ween	think
weigh	sink down
well	easily
wether	ram
whether	which
whit	**a whit**, at all
withal	with
withdraught	privy or sewer
white	**own white son**, *sb.* favourite
whitleather	strong and flexible white leather
winch	recoil, wince

winding	proceeding
wink	1. connive; 2. close the eyes (not, as in the modern sense, momentarily)
wise	*sb.* manner; *adj.* careful, alert
wist	known
wit	mind, understanding; **wits**, senses; **to wit**, namely
withal	with, also
without	outside
witty	ingenious
wonderer	admirer; **wonderful**, astounding
world	great thing
worshipful	worthy
worth	**take in worth**, value, accept
wrangle	dispute
wreak	vengeance
writhe	twist
wry	swerve
yet	still
younker	fashionable young gentleman

BIBLIOGRAPHY

ADAMS, ROBERT P., *The Better Part of Valor: More, Erasmus, Colet, and Vives, on Humanism, War, and Peace, 1496-1535* (Seattle: University of Washington Press, 1962)

AESOP, *Aesopica: A Series of Texts Relating to Aesop, or Ascribed to Him*, ed. by Ben Edwin Perry (Urbana: University of Illinois Press, 1952)

ALESIUS, ALEXANDER, *A treatise concernynge generall councilles, the byshoppes of Rome, and the clergy* (London: Thomas Berthelet, 1538)

ANON. [Henry VIII], *A glasse of the truthe* (London: Thomas Berthelet, 1532)

ANON., *The Wanton Wife of Bath, to the tune of, Flying Fame* (London: F. Coles, n.d.)

AQUINAS, THOMAS, *Summa Theologica*, trans. by Fathers of the English Dominican Province, 3 vols (London: Burnes and Oates, 1947)

ARISTOTLE, *The "Art" of Rhetoric*, trans. by John Henry Freese (London and New York: William Heinemann and G. P. Putnam's Sons, 1926)

—— *Politics*, trans. by H. Rackham (London and New York: William Heineman Ltd and G. P. Putnam's Sons, 1932)

AUGUSTIJN, CORNELIUS, *Erasmus: His Life, Works, and Influence*, trans. by J. C. Grayson (Toronto, Buffalo, and London: University of Toronto Press, 1991)

AUGUSTINE, *Our Lord's Sermon on the Mount*, in *Nicene and Post-Nicene Fathers*, 1st series, vol. VI, trans. by Wm Findlay and D. S. Schaff (Grand Rapids: Wm Eerdmans, 1980)

—— *The City of God against the Pagans*, trans. by R. W. Dyson (Cambridge: Cambridge University Press, 1998)

—— *On Christian Teaching*, trans. by R. P. H. Green (Oxford: Oxford University Press, 1999)

—— *Answer to Faustus, a Manichean (Contra Faustum Manichaeum)*, trans. by Roland Teske, S. J., ed. by Boniface Ramsey (New York: New City Press, 2007)

BAINTON, ROLAND H., *Erasmus of Christendom* (London: Collins, 1970)

BALDWIN, T. W., *William Shakspere's Small Latine & Lesse Greeke*, 2 vols (Urbana: Illinois University Press, 1944)

BALE, JOHN, *Yet a Course at the Romyshe Fox* (Zurich: Oliver Jacobson [Antwerp: A. Goinus], 1543)

Bible, *A Translation from the Latin Vulgate*, trans. by Ronald Knox (London: Burnes and Oates, 1955)

—— *New Revised Standard Version* (Oxford: Oxford University Press, 1989)

The Book of Common Prayer: The Texts of 1549, 1559, and 1662, ed. by Brian Cummings (Oxford: Oxford University Press, 2011)

BRETON, NICHOLAS, *Crossing of Proverbs* [two parts] (London: G. Eld for J. Wright, 1616)

BULLINGER, HEINRICH, *A Hundred Sermons Vpon the Apocalips* (London: John Day, 1561)

BURNS, J. H., *Lordship, Kingship, and Empire: The Idea of Monarchy, 1400-1525. The Carlyle Lectures 1988* (Oxford: The Clarendon Press, 1992)

—— and THOMAS M. IZBICKI, eds, *Conciliarism and Papalism* (Cambridge: Cambridge University Press, 1997)
BYRON, GEORGE GORDON, *Selected Poems*, ed. by Susan J. Wolfson and Peter J. Manning (London: Penguin, 2005)
CAVE, TERENCE, *The Cornucopian Text: Problems of Writing in the French Renaissance* (Oxford: The Clarendon Press, 1979)
CAVENDISH, MARGARET, *Political Writings*, ed. by Susan James (Cambridge: Cambridge University Press, 2003),
CICERO, *On Duties*, trans. by Walter Miller (London and Cambridge, MA: William Heinemann and Harvard University Press, 1913)
—— *Brutus. Orator*, trans. by G. L. Henderson and H. M. Hubbell (London and Cambridge, MA: William Heinemann and Harvard University Press, 1939)
CANON, ELIZABETH BELL, *The Use of Modal Expression Preference as a Marker of Style and Attribution: The Case of William Tyndale and the 1533 English 'Enchiridion Militis Christiani'* (New York: Peter Lang, 2010)
COTTIER, JEAN-FRANÇOIS, 'Erasmus's *Paraphrases*: A "New Kind of Commentary?"', trans. by Karen Mak and Nancy Senior, in *The Unfolding of Words: Commentary in the Age of Erasmus*, ed. by Judith Rice Henderson (Toronto, Buffalo, and London: University of Toronto Press, 2012), pp. 27–46
CUMMINGS, BRIAN, *The Literary Culture of the Reformation: Grammar and Grace* (Oxford: Oxford University Press, 2002)
—— 'Encyclopedic Erasmus', in *The Copious Text: Encyclopedic Books in Early Modern England*, ed. by Abigail Shinn and Angus Vine, special issue, *Renaissance Studies* 28.2 (2014), 183–204
—— 'William Tyndale and Erasmus on How to Read the Bible: A Newly Discovered Manuscript of the English *Enchiridion*', *Reformation*, 23.1 (2018), 29–52
CURTIS, CATHERINE MARY, 'Richard Pace on Pedagogy, Counsel and Satire' (doctoral dissertation, University of Cambridge, 1996)
CYPRIAN, *St. Cyprian on the Lord's Prayer*, trans. by T. Herbert Bindley (London: SPCK, 1914)
—— in *Tertullian, Cyprian and Origen on the Lord's Prayer*, trans. and ed. by Alistair Stewart-Sykes (New York: St Vladimir's Seminary Press, 2004)
DANIELL, DAVID, *William Tyndale: A Biography* (New Haven: Yale University Press, 1994)
DANTE, *The Divine Comedy*, trans. by C. H. Sisson (Oxford: Oxford University Press, 1993)
DAVIES, OLIVER, *God Within: The Mystical Tradition of Northern Europe* (London: Darton, Longman and Todd, 2006)
DEMERS, PATRICIA, 'Margaret Roper and Erasmus: The Relationship of Translator and Source', *wwr magazine* (women writing and reading), 1.1 (2005), 3–8
DEVEREUX, E. J., *Renaissance English Translations of Erasmus: A Bibliography to 1700* (Toronto: University of Toronto Press, 1983)
DODDS, GREGORY D., *Exploiting Erasmus: The Erasmian Legacy and Religious Change in Early Modern England* (Toronto, Buffalo, and London: University of Toronto Press, 2009)
ENENKEL, KARL A. E., ed., *The Reception of Erasmus in the Early Modern Period* (Leiden: Brill, 2013)

ERASMUS, DESIDERIUS, *Declamationes aliquot* (Louvain: Thierry Martens, 1518)
—— *A very pleasaunt and fruitful diologe called the Epicure*, trans. by Philip Gerrard (London: Richard Grafton, 1545)
—— *The first tome or volume of the Paraphrase of Erasmus vpon the Newe Testamente*, trans. by Nicholas Udall et al. (London: Edward Whitchurch, 1548)
—— *The seconde tome or volume of the Paraphrase of Erasmus vpon the Newe Testament*, trans. by various hands (London: Edward Whitchurch, 1549)
—— *The pope shut out of heaven gates*, trans. by anon. (London: Roger Vaughan, 1673)
—— *Precatio Dominica*, in *Opera Omnia*, ed. by Johannes Clericus, ten vols, vol. v (Leiden: Vander, 1704), pp. 1217–228
—— *A Book Called in Latin Enchiridion Militis Christiani and in English The Manual of the Christian Knight* [1533] (London: Methuen, 1905)
—— *Erasmi Opuscula: A Supplement to the Opera Omnia*, ed. by Wallace K. Ferguson (The Hague: Martinus Nijhoff, 1933)
—— *Ausgewählte Werke*, ed. by Hajo and Annemarie Holborn (Munich: Beck'sche Verlag, 1964)
—— *The Praise of Folie*, trans. by Sir Thomas Chaloner, Early English Text Society No. 257 (London, New York, and Toronto: Oxford University Press, 1965)
—— *Erasmus*, ed. by Richard L. DeMolen (London: Edward Arnold, 1973)
—— *Enchiridion Militis Christiani, An English Version* [1534], Early English Text Society, ed. by Anne M. O'Donnell SND (Oxford: Oxford University Press, 1981)
—— *Adages*, in *CWE*, vols 31–36, ed. and trans. by R. A. B. Mynors and M. M. Phillips (Toronto: University of Toronto Press, 1982–2006)
—— *Correspondence*, in *CWE*, vol. 6, trans. by R. A. B. Mynors and D. F. S. Thomson (Toronto: University of Toronto Press, 1982)
—— vol. 7, trans. by R. A. B. Mynors (Toronto: University of Toronto Press, 1987)
—— *The Handbook of the Christian Soldier*, trans. by Charles Fantazzi, in *CWE*, vol. 66, ed. by John. W. O'Malley (Toronto: Toronto University Press, 1988)
—— *Correspondence 1522–1523*, trans. by R. A. B. Mynors, in *CWE*, vol. 9, annotated by James M. Estes (Toronto: University of Toronto Press, 1989)
—— *The Erasmus Reader*, ed. by Erika Rummell (Toronto, Buffalo, and London: University of Toronto Press, 1990)
—— *Defense of his Declamation in Praise of Marriage*, trans. by David Sider, in *Daughters, Wives, and Widows: Writings by Men about Women and Marriage in England, 1500–1640*, ed. by Joan Larsen Klein (Urbana: University of Illinois Press, 1992), pp. 89–96
—— *On Copia of Words and Ideas*, trans. by Donald B. King and H. David Rix (Milwaukee: Marquette University Press, 1999)
—— *The Lord's Prayer*, trans. by John N. Grant, in *CWE*, vol. 69, ed. by John W. O'Malley and Louis A. Perraud (Toronto: University of Toronto Press, 1999), pp. 55–77
—— *The Adages of Erasmus*, ed. by William Barker (Toronto: University of Toronto Press, 2001)
—— *Opera Omnia Desiderii Erasmi Roterdami* [Amsterdam edition], v-8, ed. by J. Domański (Leiden: Brill, 2016)
FALK, DORIS V., 'Proverbs and the Polonius Destiny', *Shakespeare Quarterly*, 18.1 (1967), 23–36

FARMER, DAVID, *Oxford Dictionary of Saints*, 4th edn (Oxford: Oxford University Press, 1997)

FICINO, MARSILIO (trans.), *Platonis Opera a Marsilio Ficino translata* (Paris: Ascensius, 1518)

FLETCHER, ANTHONY, 'The Protestant Idea of Marriage in Early Modern England', in *Religion, Culture and Society: Essays in Honour of Patrick Collinson*, ed. by Anthony Fletcher and Peter Roberts (Cambridge: Cambridge University Press, 1994), pp. 161–81

FOUCAULT, MICHEL, *Discipline and Punish: The Birth of the Prison*, trans. by Alan Sheridan (London: Penguin, 1991)

FOXE, JOHN, *Acts and Monuments* (London: John Day, 1563)

—— *Actes and Monuments* (London: John Day, 1583)

GASCOIGNE, GEORGE, *The glasse of government* (London: [Henry Middleton] for C. Barker, 1575)

——, *A Hundredth Sundrie Flowres*, ed. by G. W. Pigman III (Oxford: Clarendon Press, 2000)

GEE, JOHN ARCHER, 'Tindale and the 1533 English *Enchiridion* of Erasmus', *Proceedings of the Modern Language Association*, 49.2 (1934), 460–71

—— 'John Byddell and the First Publication of Erasmus' *Enchiridion* in English', *English Literary History*, 4.1 (1937), 43–59

—— 'Margaret Roper's English Version of Erasmus' *Precatio Dominica* and the Apprenticeship behind Early Tudor Translation', *RES*, 13 (1937), 257–71

GONZALES, LAURA, and REBECCA ZANTJER, 'Translation as a User-Localization Practice', *Technical Communication*, 62.4 (2015), 271–84

GRAFTON, ANTHONY, and LISA JARDINE, *From Humanism to the Humanities: Education and the Liberal Arts in Fifteenth- and Sixteenth-Century Europe* (Cambridge, MA: Harvard University Press, 1986)

GRAFTON, RICHARD, *A chronicle at large* (London: Henry Denham for Richard Tottell and Humphrey Toye, 1569)

GREENBLATT, STEPHEN, *Renaissance Self-Fashioning From More to Shakespeare* (Chicago and London: University of Chicago Press, 1980)

GUICCIARDINI, FRANCESCO, *The History of Italy*, trans. by Sidney Alexander (Princeton: Princeton University Press, 1969)

HANNAY, MARGARET PATTERSON, ed., *Silent But for the Word: Tudor Women as Patrons, Translators, and Writers of Religious Works* (Kent, OH: Kent State University Press, 1985)

HARVEY, GABRIEL, *Gabriel Harvey's Marginalia*, ed. by G. C. Moore Smith (Stratford Upon Avon: Shakespeare Head Press, 1913)

HENRY SJ, PAUL, 'The Place of Plotinus in the History of Thought', in *Plotinus: The Enneads*, abridged by John Dillon (Harmondsworth: Penguin, 1991), pp. xlii–lxxxiii

HILL, CHRISTOPHER, review of Margot Todd, *Christian Humanism and the Puritan Social Order*, *Albion*, 211 (1989), 102–04

HUIZINGA, JOHAN, *The Waning of the Middle Ages* (Harmondsworth: Penguin, 1955)

—— *Erasmus and the Age of Reformation*, trans. by F. Hopman (Princeton: Princeton University Press, 1984)

HUTSON, HAROLD H., and HAROLD R. WILLOUGHBY, 'The Ignored Taverner Bible of 1539', *Crozer Quarterly*, 16 (1939), 161–76

HUTSON, LORNA, *The Usurer's Daughter: Male Friendship and Fictions of Women in Sixteenth-Century England* (London: Routledge, 1994)

—— '"Especyall Swetnes": An Erasmian Footnote to the Civil Partnership Act', *Literature and History*, 20.1 (2011), 5–21

JARDINE, LISA, 'Logic and Language: Humanistic Logic', in *The Cambridge History of Renaissance Philosophy*, ed. by C. B. Schmitt, Quentin Skinner, Eckhard Kessler, and Jill Kraye (Cambridge: Cambridge University Press, 1988), pp. 173–98

—— *Erasmus, Man of Letters: The Construction of Charisma in Print*, revised edn (Princeton: Princeton University Press, 2015)

JEROME, *Letters and Select Works*, in *The Nicene and Post-Nicene Fathers*, 2nd series, vol. VI, trans. by W. H. Fremantle (Grand Rapids: Wm B. Eerdmans, 1989)

[JEWEL, JOHN], 'Of the State of Matrimony', in *The Second Tome of Homilees* (London: R. Jugge and J. Cawood, 1571)

JONES, EMRYS, *The Origins of Shakespeare* (Oxford: The Clarendon Press, 1977)

KEARNEY, JAMES, *The Incarnate Text: Imagining the Book in Renaissance England* (Philadelphia: University of Pennsylvania Press, 2009)

KENNY, ANTHONY, *Medieval Philosophy* (Oxford: Oxford University Press, 2005)

KING, JOHN N., and MARK RANKIN, 'Print, Patronage, and the Reception of Continental Reform: 1521–1603', *The Yearbook of English Studies*, 38 (2008), 49–67

KIRK, KENNETH E., *The Vision of God* (London: Longmans, Green and Co., 1932)

LACTANTIUS, *Divine Institutes*, trans. by Anthony Bowen and Peter Garnsley (Liverpool: Liverpool University Press, 2003)

LEUSHUIS, REINIER, 'The Mimesis of Marriage: Dialogue and Intimacy in Erasmus's Matrimonial Writings', *Renaissance Quarterly*, 57 (2004), 1278–307

LIVINGSTONE, E. A., ed., *The Oxford Dictionary of the Christian Church*, 3rd edn (Oxford: Oxford University Press, 1997)

LOUGHLIN, MARIE, SANDRA BELL, and PATRICIA BRACE, eds, *Broadview Anthology of Sixteenth-Century Poetry and Prose* (Ontario: Broadview Press, 2012)

LUCIAN OF SAMOSATA, *Heracles*, in *Lucian*, trans. by A. M. Harmon (London and New York: William Heinemann, 1913)

LUTHER, MARTIN, *The Freedom of a Christian*, trans. by W. A. Lambert, rev. by Harold J. Grimm, in *Three Treatises* [1520], with *To the Christian Nobility of the German Nation* and *The Babylonian Captivity of the Church* (Philadelphia: Fortress Press, 1978), pp. 265–316

MACCULLOCH, DIARMAID, *Reformation: Europe's House Divided 1490–1700* (London: Allen Lane, 2003)

—— *Thomas Cromwell: A Life* (Oxford: Oxford University Press, 2018)

MACHIAVELLI, NICCOLÒ, *The Prince*, trans. by Tim Parks (London: Penguin, 2011)

MARC'HADOUR, GERMAIN, 'Erasmus' Paraphrase of the *Pater Noster* (1523) with its English Translation by Margaret Roper (1524)', *Moreana*, 7 (1965), 9–63

MARLOWE, CHRISTOPHER, *Doctor Faustus and Other Plays*, ed. by David Bevington and Eric Rasmussen (Oxford: Oxford University Press, 1995)

MCCONICA, JAMES, *English Humanists and Reformation Politics under Henry VIII and Edward VI* (Oxford: Clarendon Press, 1965)

—— 'Erasmus and the "Julius": A Humanist Reflects on the Church', in *The Pursuit*

of Holiness in Late Medieval and Renaissance Religion, ed. by Charles Trinkaus and Heiko A. Oberman (Leiden: E. J. Brill, 1974), pp. 444–71
—— *Erasmus* (Oxford: Oxford University Press, 1991)
McGRATH, ALISTER E., *The Intellectual Origins of the European Reformation* (Oxford: Blackwell, 2004)
MORE, THOMAS, *The Confutation of Tyndale's Answer*, ed. by Louis A. Schuster, Richard C. Marius, and Richard J. Schoeck, *The Yale Edition of the Complete Works of St. Thomas More*, vol. 8 (New Haven and London: Yale University Press, 1973)
MOZLEY, J. F., 'The English Enchiridion of Erasmus, 1533', *The Review of English Studies*, 20.78 (1944), 97–107
OAKLEY, FRANCIS, *The Conciliarist Tradition: Constitutionalism in the Catholic Church 1300–1870* (Oxford: Oxford University Press, 2003)
ORIGEN, *Homilies on Genesis and Exodus*, trans. by Ronald E. Heine (Washington: The Catholic University of America Press, 1982)
PABEL, HILMAR M., *Conversing with God: Prayer in Erasmus' Pastoral Writing* (Toronto: University of Toronto Press, 1997)
—— 'Exegesis and Marriage in Erasmus's *Paraphrases on the New Testament*', in *Holy Scripture Speaks: The Production and Reception of Erasmus' Paraphrases on the New Testament*, ed. by Hilmar M. Pabel and Mark Vessey (Toronto: University of Toronto Press, 2002), pp. 175–209
PARISH, HELEN L., *Clerical Marriage and the English Reformation: Precedent, Policy, and Practice* (Aldershot: Ashgate, 2000)
PARKER, DOUGLAS H., 'Religious Polemics and Two Sixteenth Century English Editions of Erasmus's *Enchiridion Militis Christiani*, 1546–1561', *Renaissance and Reformation*, 9.3 (1973), 94–107
—— 'The English "Enchiridion Militis Christiani" in the Seventeenth, Eighteenth, and Nineteenth Centuries', *Renaissance and Reformation*, 19.3 (1995), 5–21
PASK, KEVIN, *The Emergence of the English Author: Scripting the Life of the Poet in Early Modern England* (Cambridge: Cambridge University Press, 1996)
PHILLIPS, MARGARET MANN, *The 'Adages' of Erasmus: A Study with Translations* (Cambridge: Cambridge University Press, 1964)
PLATO, *Lysis. Symposium. Gorgias*, trans. by W. R. M. Lamb (London and Cambridge, MA: Harvard University Press, 1991)
—— *Euthyphro. Apology. Crito. Phaedo. Phaedrus*, trans. by Harold North Fowler (Cambridge, MA: Harvard University Press, 2014)
PLOTINUS, *The Enneads*, abridged by John Dillon (Harmondsworth: Penguin, 1991)
POLLNITZ, AYSHA, 'Religion and Translation at the Court of Henry VIII: Princess Mary, Katherine Parr and the *Paraphrases* of Erasmus', in *Mary Tudor: Old and New Perspectives*, ed. by Susan Doran and Thomas S. Freeman (Houndmills: Palgrave Macmillan, 2011), pp. 123–37
PSEUDO-DIONYSIUS, *The Complete Works*, Classics of Western Spirituality, trans. by Colm Luibheid (Mahwah: Paulist Press, 1987)
REX, RICHARD, 'The English Campaign against Luther in the 1520s', *Transactions of the Royal Historical Society*, 39 (1989), 85–106
REYNOLDS, E. E., *Margaret Roper, Eldest Daughter of St. Thomas More* (London: Burns and Oates, 1960)

REYNOLDS, PHILIP L., *How Marriage Became One of the Sacraments: The Sacramental Theology of Marriage from its Medieval Origins to the Council of Trent* (Cambridge: Cambridge University Press, 2016)

RHODES, NEIL, *Common: The Development of Literary Culture in Sixteenth-Century England* (Oxford: Oxford University Press, 2018)

—— with GORDON KENDAL, and LOUISE WILSON, eds, *English Renaissance Translation Theory* (London: MHRA, 2013)

RICHARDS, JENNIFER, *Voices and Books in the English Renaissance: A New History of Reading* (Oxford: Oxford University Press, 2019)

RODOCANACHI, EMMANUEL, *Histoire de Rome: The Pontificat de Jules II, 1503–1513* ([S. I.]: Libraire Hachette, 1928)

ROYE, WILLIAM, '*An exhortation to the diligent studye of scripture*' *and* '*An exposition in to the seventh chapter of the pistle to the Corinthians*', ed. by Douglas H. Parker (Toronto: University of Toronto Press, 2000)

RUMMEL, ERIKA, 'The Reception of Erasmus's *Adages* in Sixteenth-Century England', *Renaissance and Reformation/Renaissance et Réforme*, 18.2 (1994), 19–30

RYRIE, ALEX, 'The Strange Death of Lutheran England', *Journal of Ecclesiastical History*, 53 (2002), 64–92

SALLUST, *Here begynneth the famous cronycle of the warre, which the romayns had agaynst Iugurth*, trans. by Alexander Barclay (London: Richard Pynson [1525?])

SCOT, REGINALD, *The discouerie of witchcraft* (London: [Henry Denham] for William Brome, 1584)

SHAW, CHRISTINE, *Julius II: The Warrior Pope* (Oxford: Blackwell, 1993)

SHRANK, CATHY, 'Mirroring the "Long Reformation": Translating Erasmus' Colloquies in Early Modern England', *Reformation* 24.2 (2019), 59–75

SIDNEY, PHILIP, *An Apology For Poetry (Or, The Defence of Poesy)*, ed. by Geoffrey Shepherd, rev. by R. W. Maslen (Manchester and New York: Manchester University Press, 2002)

TAULER, *Spiritual Conferences*, trans. and ed. by Eric Colledge and Sister M. Jane OP (Rockford: Tan Books, 1978)

—— *Johannes Tauler: Sermons*, Classics of Western Spirituality, ed. by Maria Shrady (Mahwah: Paulist Press, 1985)

TAVERNER, RICHARD, *Proverbs or Adages by Desiderius Erasmus*, introduction by De Witt T. Starnes (Delmar: Scholars Facsimiles and Reprints, 1977)

TAYLOR, ANDREW, 'Richard Taverner', *ODNB*

THOMAS, KEITH, *The Ends of Life: Roads to Fulfilment in Early Modern England* (Oxford: Oxford University Press, 2009)

THOMPSON, CRAIG R., 'Erasmus in Tudor England', in *Actes du Congrès Erasme, Rotterdam 27–29 Octobre 1969* (Amsterdam: North Holland Publishing Company, 1971), pp. 29–68

—— 'Scripture for the Ploughboy and Some Others', in *Studies in the Continental Background of Renaissance Literature: Essays Presented to John Lievsay*, ed. by Dale B. J. Randall and George Walton Williams (Durham: Duke University Press, 1977), pp. 3–28

THOMPSON, GERALDINE, *Under Pretext of Praise: Satiric Mode in Erasmus' Fiction* (Toronto and Buffalo: University of Toronto Press, 1973)

TODD, MARGO, *Christian Humanism and the Puritan Social Order* (Cambridge: Cambridge University Press, 1987)
TYNDALE, WILLIAM, *Tyndale's New Testament* [modern spelling], ed. by David Daniell (New Haven: Yale University Press, 1989)
—— *The New Testament 1526*, ed. by W. R. Cooper (London: The British Library, 2000)
—— *The Obedience of a Christian Man* [1528], ed. by David Daniell (Harmondsworth: Penguin, 2000)
USK, THOMAS, *Testament of Love*, ed. by Gary W. Shawver (Toronto, Buffalo, and London: University of Toronto Press, 2002)
VERBRUGGE, RITA M., 'Margaret More Roper's Personal Expression in the *Devout Treatise Upon the Pater Noster*', in *Silent But for the Word: Tudor Women as Patrons, Translators, and Writers of Religious Works*, ed. by Margaret Patterson Hannay (Kent, OH: Kent State University Press, 1985), pp. 30–42
WILSON, THOMAS, *The Arte of Rhetorique*, ed. by Thomas J. Derrick (New York: Garland Publishing, 1982)
YOST, JOHN K., 'Taverner's Use of Erasmus and the Protestantization of English Humanism', *Renaissance Quarterly*, 23.3 (1970), 266–76

www.ingramcontent.com/pod-product-compliance
Lightning Source LLC
Chambersburg PA
CBHW071433300426
44114CB00013B/1419